*The publisher gratefully acknowledges the generous
contribution to this book provided by the
S. Mark Taper Foundation.*

Living Letters of the Law

Living Letters of the Law

Ideas of the Jew in
Medieval Christianity

Jeremy Cohen

UNIVERSITY OF CALIFORNIA PRESS
Berkeley • *Los Angeles* • *London*

The cost of preparing this manuscript was offset
by a grant from the Diaspora Research Institute of
Tel Aviv University.

University of California Press
Berkeley and Los Angeles, California

University of California Press, Ltd.
London, England

Library of Congress
Cataloging-in-Publication Data

Cohen, Jeremy
    Living letters of the law : ideas of the Jew in
  medieval Christianity / Jeremy Cohen.
        p.   cm. —(The S. Mark Taper
    Foundation imprint in Jewish studies)
    Includes bibliographical references and index.
    ISBN 0-520-21680-6 (alk. paper). —
ISBN 0-520-21870-1 (alk. paper)
    1. Judaism (Christian theology)—History of
  doctrines—Middle Ages, 600–1500. I. Title.
  BT93.C64   1999
  261.2'6'0902—dc21   99-20634
                                                CIP

Manufactured in the United States of America

08   07   06   05   04   03   02   01   00   99
10   9   8   7   6   5   4   3   2   1

Contents

Acknowledgments

Work on this book has extended over much of the present decade, and I gratefully acknowledge my indebtedness to the many individuals who have helped me bring the project to its conclusion. Martin Goodman, Ora Limor, Ivan Marcus, Marc Raphael, Michael Signer, David Stern, and Kenneth Stow graciously agreed to read portions of the manuscript in various stages of its evolution and provided me with invaluable constructive criticism. Many others responded graciously to my variegated calls for assistance, including Ram Ben-Shalom, Martin Bertram, Naomi Cohen, Sander Gilman, Thomas Hahn, Colum Hourihane, Aryeh Kasher, Joel Kraemer, Sara Lipton, Joseph Lynch, Robert Markus, Aharon Oppenheimer, Alexander Patschovsky, Kenneth Pennington, Judith Rosen, Shlomo Simonsohn, Michael Toch, and John Van Engen; I remain appreciatively in their debt.

Fellowships at the Shalom Hartman Institute in Jerusalem, at the Hebrew University's Institute for Advanced Studies, and from the National Endowment for the Humanities allowed me precious time for pursuing this project; and grants from the Melton Center for Jewish Studies and the College of Humanities at The Ohio State University, the State of Israel's Ministry of Absorption, and the Diaspora Research Institute at Tel Aviv University helped to offset the expenses of my research. I am similarly grateful to the directors and staffs of the Escuela de Estudios Hispano-Americanos in Seville, where I profited from several fruitful and pleasant weeks of research, and the Herzog August

Bibliothek in Wolfenbüttel, Germany, which allowed me to organize an international symposium on the subject of this book in 1993. The characteristically good nature and dedication of librarians too numerous to mention here have consistently served me well.

Finally, my wife and children have never wavered in their support for my work. In the appreciation that we share for the powerful impact of ideas and symbols on our lives, the bustle of our busy household and my historian's vocation have blended to imbue my life with meaning and with satisfaction.

Abbreviations

AHDL	*Archives d'histoire doctrinale et littéraire du Moyen Age*
AHR	*American Historical Review*
AJSR	*Association for Jewish Studies Review*
ASJD	*The Apostolic See and the Jews: Documents*
CCCM	Corpus Christianorum, Continuatio mediaevalis
CCM	*Cahiers de civilisation médiévale*
CCSL	Corpus Christianorum, Series latina
CJ	*The Church and the Jews in the XIIIth Century*
CSEL	Corpus scriptorum ecclesiasticorum latinorum
FWW	*From Witness to Witchcraft: Jews and Judaism in Medieval Christian Thought*, ed. Jeremy Cohen, Wolfenbütteler Mittelalter-Studien 11 (Wiesbaden, Germany, 1996)
GCS	Die griechischen christlichen Schriftsteller
HTR	*Harvard Theological Review*
ICM	*Islam et Chrétiens du Midi (xiie–xive s.)*, Cahiers de Fanjeaux 18 (Toulouse, France, 1983)
JIM	*Judentum im Mittelalter: Beiträge zur christlich-jüdischen*

	Gespräch, ed. Paul Wilpert, Miscellanea mediaevalia 4 (Berlin, 1966)
JJS	*Journal of Jewish Studies*
JMH	*Journal of Medieval History*
JQR	*Jewish Quarterly Review*
MGH	Monumenta Germaniae historica
MSC	*Les Mutations socio-culturelles au tournant des xie–xiie siècles*, ed. Raymonde Foreville, Études anselmiennes 4 = Spicilegium beccense 2 (Paris, 1984)
PAPV	*Pierre Abélard, Pierre le Vénérable: Les Courants philosophiques, littéraires et artistiques en Occident au milieu du xiie siècle*, Colloques internationaux du Centre National de la Recherche Scientifique 546 (Paris, 1975)
PG	Patrologia graeca
PL	Patrologia latina
RB	*Revue bénédictine*
REA	*Revue des études augustiniennes*
REJ	*Revue des études juives*
RIM	*Religionsgespräche im Mittelalter*, ed. Bernard Lewis and Friedrich Niewöhner, Wolfenbütteler Mittelalter-Studien 4 (Wiesbaden, Germany, 1992)
RMAL	*Revue du Moyen Age latin*
RT	*Revue thomiste*
RTAM	*Recherches de théologie ancienne et médiévale*
SC	Sources chrétiennes
SCH	Studies in Church History
ST	*Summa theologiae*

Introduction

Some years ago, I offered a course on the history of Judaism at a Protestant seminary in the midwestern United States. Both as a Jew and as a historian committed to studying the interdependence of Christian and Jewish civilizations, I found it gratifying that my course fulfilled a distribution requirement in church history at the seminary; the genuine interest of Christian divinity students in my Judaic subject encouraged me no less. Surprisingly, however, my interaction with the president, the dean, and some faculty colleagues at the school proved less gratifying. Although I understood my role in their community primarily as an academic one, to teach about Jewish civilization, they took but a secondary interest in my instruction. Instead, they habitually focused on the satisfaction they derived from my presence at their seminary, from having, as they put it, "a Jew in our midst." In their eyes, my Jewish identity—or what they believed that identity to be—somehow rounded out their picture of how their Christian community should properly appear. For these colleagues, who welcomed me onto their campus with genuine, memorable warmth, I functioned less as the historian I construed myself to be and more as a player on a theological stage set long before my arrival.

This book concerns that stage and its players. Throughout much of its history, in various manners and to differing extents, Christianity has accorded Jews and Judaism a singular place in a properly ordered Christian society. From the people who received God's Old Testament, to those who parented, nurtured, and, allegedly, murdered Jesus, to those whose conversion will signal the second coming of Christ, Jews have had distinctive tasks in Christian visions of salvation history. The idea that Christendom needs the Jews to fill these special roles has, in fact, contributed to the survival of the Jewish minority in a Christian world, with varying results. On one hand, the Christian idea of Jewish identity crystallized around the theological purpose the Jew served in Christendom; Christians perceived the Jews to be who they were *supposed* to be, not who they actually *were*, and related to them accordingly. As Bernard of Clairvaux, one of the most prominent Christian theologians of the Middle Ages, put it in the twelfth century, "the Jews are not to be persecuted, killed, or even put to flight. . . . Indeed, the Jews are for us the living letters (*vivi . . . apices*) of Scripture, constantly representing the Lord's passion."[1] For Bernard, as for many medieval churchmen, the Jews embodied a particular reading of Holy Scripture, one that established the truth of Christianity in its own right and illuminated the contrasting Christian exegesis of the Bible. As such, the Jews' nature, their personality, and their historical mission derived directly from essential dictates of Christian doctrine and hermeneutics. On the other hand, when Christian theologians awakened to the disparity between the Jew they had constructed and the real Jew of history, they could construe the latter's failure to serve the purposes allotted him as an abandonment of his Judaism. This, in turn, might render him less suited for the protection granted Jews who did function "properly" in Christian society.

In order to meet their particular needs, Christian theology and exegesis created a Jew of their own, and this book investigates the medieval history of such a hermeneutically and doctrinally crafted Jew, from Augustine of Hippo to Thomas Aquinas. In prior publications I have studied the contribution of Dominican and Franciscan friars to Christian perceptions of Jews and Judaism in the High Middle Ages;[2] here I examine key chapters in the earlier history of the "hermeneutical Jew"—that is, the Jew as constructed in the discourse of Christian

1. See below, chapter 6.

2. Jeremy Cohen, *The Friars and the Jews: The Evolution of Medieval Anti-Judaism* (Ithaca, N.Y., 1982), "The Jews as the Killers of Christ in the Latin Tradition, from Augustine to the Friars," *Traditio* 39 (1983), 1–27, and "Scholarship and Intolerance in the Medieval Academy: The Study and Evaluation of Judaism in European Christendom," *AHR* 91 (1986), 592–613.

theology, and above all in Christian theologians' interpretation of Scripture.[3] On what basis did a Bernard of Clairvaux come to identify the Jews as the living letters of biblical law, whose survival, not whose destruction, best served God's plan for the triumph of the Catholic Church? How did this idea take shape in the thought of Augustine, and how did early medieval churchmen adapt the Augustinian idea to the changing world of European Christendom? What happened in the twelfth century to undermine, however gradually, the presuppositions of Augustine's idea, even as theologians like Bernard did not hesitate to reaffirm it, and where, set against this background, do the thirteenth-century friars and their attack on rabbinic literature fit into our story?

In addressing these questions, this book does not survey the oft-studied policies of the Catholic Church and of secular rulers toward European Jewish communities, nor does its focus fall primarily on the interactions of medieval Jews and Christians. Beyond demonstrating the phenomenon of the hermeneutically crafted Jew in Christian theology of the Middle Ages, I have not dedicated my book to advancing any particular thesis concerning the chronology or the key figures of the Jewish-Christian dispute. Rather, I attempt a threefold contribution to an understanding of the place of the Jews in the cultural and intellectual history of medieval Christendom. First, by analyzing the developing ideas of the Jew in medieval Christian thought, I hope to add to our appreciation of the theologians responsible for these ideas; in some cases, existing scholarly treatments of their doctrine concerning the Jews remain incomplete. Second, as a whole, my book maps evolving

3. I first proposed the formulation of the "hermeneutical Jew" in papers on "Anti-Jewish Discourse and Its Function in Medieval Christian Theology," presented to the New Chaucer Society in August 1992, and on "The Muslim Connection: On the Changing Role of the Jew in High Medieval Theology," presented at the Herzog August Bibliothek in Wolfenbüttel, Germany, in October 1993 and subsequently published in *FWW*, pp. 141–62. The term has since found explicit acceptance in Paula Fredriksen, "*Excaecati occulta justitia Dei*: Augustine on Jews and Judaism," *Journal of Early Christian Studies* 3 (1995), 321 n. 61, and "Divine Justice and Human Freedom: Augustine on Jews and Judaism, 392–398," in *FWW*, p. 52 n. 52. Cf. also the usage of "theological Jew" in Gilbert Dahan, *Les Intellectuels chrétiens et les Juifs au Moyen Âge* (Paris, 1990), p. 585; the approach to seventh-century Byzantine texts proposed by David M. Olster, *Roman Defeat, Christian Response, and the Literary Construction of the Jew* (Philadelphia, 1994); and the new perspective on Gregory the Great offered by Robert A. Markus, "The Jew as a Hermeneutic Device: The Inner Life of a Gregorian *Topos*," in *Gregory the Great: A Symposium*, ed. John C. Cavadini (Notre Dame, Ind., 1995), pp. 1–15. I am grateful to Professor Markus for sharing his paper with me in advance of its publication.

attitudes toward Jews and Judaism among Christian intellectuals from late antiquity until the High Middle Ages. Although I have made no attempt to provide an all-inclusive survey, I have endeavored to highlight the most interesting and influential patterns in the theological mentality of the period. Third, I elaborate a new basis for dealing with these issues that will, I believe, allow us to advance beyond the conclusions of previous scholarship.

That Christianity accorded the Jews theological importance is hardly a recent discovery; as we shall see, medieval Jews themselves recognized that importance and occasionally pointed it out to their Christian overlords. With the growth of medieval and Jewish studies at modern universities, many investigators of the past century have identified, catalogued, edited, annotated, summarized, and described the literature of medieval religious polemic. Some have moved beyond avowedly polemical texts and authors to mine large collections of Christian sources for all of their comments on Jews and Judaism. Still others have written valuable monographic studies of particular polemical texts or of actual disputations. As this book proceeds, students of the field will readily discern my indebtedness to the efforts of numerous predecessors and colleagues. Yet I believe that much of this prior research has stopped short of a sufficiently comprehensive analysis of the Christian thought in which Jews and Judaism figure significantly, an analysis which accurately gauges the depth and complexity of that significance. Specifically, it does not suffice to comb through the works of a Christian theologian, to amass all of his comments concerning Jews and Judaism, to organize the citations according to their ostensive subjects, and then to assess these data relative to the statements of other theologians—prior, contemporary, and later. Although such a procedure may track the impact of the Christian doctrine on the Jews that one author may have bequeathed to his successors, it is incapable of elaborating the meaning of a given text or attitude within its own historical setting. For it unfairly assumes that Christian writers and readers of the past shared the concerns of the modern historian—that is, the topical categories of anti-Judaism used to classify the data amassed—and deliberately formulated their respective attitudes accordingly. This method of study typically overlooks the broader matrix of theological issues in which that of the Jews assuredly took its place, but only as one cog in a larger wheel. One ought not simply to ask how the intellectual background of a particular writer, the events of his life, and the climate of his times may have resulted in his contribution to our story. Where the data permit, one must struggle to analyze that contribution against the referential system defined by the larger corpus of the theologian's writings and by related texts that afford them an instructive cultural context.

I therefore proceed from the premise that the origins, the character, and the role of the hermeneutical Jew derive from a theological agenda encompassing much more than the Jews themselves; and I devote my energies here to pinpointing the place of the Jews within that agenda. New Testament and patristic scholars have already recognized the value of such an approach, which has also figured in Frank Manuel's recent study of Judaism in postmedieval Christian eyes. Yet the important advances made by recent historians, literary critics, and historians of art notwithstanding, a systematic study of the function of the Jew in medieval Christianity remains a desideratum. Regrettably, in his book Manuel merely devoted a brief introductory chapter to the subject—with not a single footnote!—and hastily discounted the Middle Ages as "a thousand-year estrangement" that severed any meaningful connection between Christian theological scholarship and Judaism.[4] Although the connections between medieval churchmen and the Jews (hermeneutically crafted or not) may not have struck Manuel as interesting or consequential, they deserve the historian's attention nonetheless. Even if, in his inception, in his function, and in his veritable power in the Christian mind-set, the hermeneutical Jew of late antique or medieval times had relatively little to do with the Jewish civilization of his day, his career certainly influenced the Christian treatment of the Jewish minority, the sole consistently tolerated religious minority, of medieval Christendom. Medieval Christian perceptions of this Jew's personality contributed amply to the significance of Judaism and anti-Judaism in Western intellectual and cultural history. Viewed more broadly, these perceptions shed light on the place and purpose of the "other" in the collective mentality of the medieval Christian majority.

Although my interest lies with the hermeneutically crafted Jew of the Middle Ages and his distinguishing characteristics, the medieval churchmen I discuss were clearly not the first—or the last—Christians to construct a Jew in accordance with the needs of their theology. Undeniably, our story begins *in medias res;* and, seeking an instructive

---

4. Frank E. Manuel, *The Broken Staff: Judaism through Christian Eyes* (Cambridge, Mass., 1992); pp. 15–29 concern the Middle Ages.

context for it, one might well situate it at the center of three concentric spheres of late ancient theological concern with the Jew. In two cases, considerations of time and space will allow neither for a comprehensive overview of the extant sources nor even for a hasty survey of recent scholarship. Still, these expressions of early Christianity's interest in Judaism constitute the foundation of the medieval intellectual history I relate, and they justly demand attention, however selective and limited.

First, the books of the New Testament—above all the Gospels and Acts, several of the Pauline epistles, and Hebrews—abound with representations of the Jews and Judaism, many of them hostile. Together, these characterizations in Christian Scripture attest to a process whereby first-century Christians began to assert the validity of their beliefs by negating those of "mainstream" Jews. Owing to the origins of Christianity within the Jewish community, much of this anti-Jewish discourse undoubtedly stemmed from disputes over biblical messianic prophecy between the earliest Christians—themselves Jews—and other Jews who refused to countenance their Christological convictions. Although countless passages throughout the New Testament give expression to such processes then at work, we shall here dwell briefly on the earliest and foremost of these Jewish Christians whose ideas have survived: Paul, Christianity's presumably first and self-proclaimed apostle to the Gentiles.

As Paul sought converts for the church from outside the Jewish community, he portrayed the Jews and Judaism with an ambivalence that would have far-reaching theological consequences, both in the very fact of its ambiguity and in the wide array of conflicting interpretations it invited. Whether its real opponents were Jewish Christians who required circumcision of Gentile proselytes entering the church or Jews with no Christian leanings, Paul's Epistle to the Galatians distinguishes sharply between faith in Jesus and the observance of the Torah. "We ourselves, who are Jews by birth and not Gentile sinners, yet who know that a man is not justified by works of the law but through faith in Jesus Christ, even we have believed in Christ Jesus . . . , because by works of the law shall no one be justified" (2:15–16). Indeed, "all who rely on works of the law are under a curse" (3:10), and Paul seemed to suggest that the Jews' appreciation of Scripture had resulted in their rejection by God:

> For it is written that Abraham had two sons, one by a slave and one by a free woman. But the son of the slave was born according to the flesh, the

son of the free woman through promise. Now this is an allegory: These two women are two covenants. One is from Mount Sinai, bearing children for slavery; she is Hagar. . . . She corresponds to the present Jerusalem, for she is in slavery with her children. But the Jerusalem above is free, and she is our mother. . . . Now we, brethren, like Isaac, are children of promise. But as at that time he who was born according to the flesh persecuted him who was born according to the spirit, so it is now. But what does Scripture say? "Cast out the slave and her son; for the son of the slave shall not inherit with the son of the free woman." So, brethren, we are not children of the slave but of the free woman. (4:22–31)

Galatians reaches the conclusion (5:6) that "in Christ Jesus neither circumcision nor uncircumcision is of any avail," for which Paul soon provided a more elaborate theological argument in his Epistle to the Romans. Romans echoes and develops some of Galatians' central themes: the futility of the law in the achievement of salvation, the sinfulness of the Jews, and God's covenant of grace with those who descended spiritually from Abraham by emulating his faith. Romans (9:25) refers to the Gentiles who embrace Jesus with God's words to Hosea, "Those who were not my people I will call my people," while invoking the prophecy of Isaiah to proclaim the repudiation of the Jews: "Though the number of the sons of Israel be as the sand of the sea, only a remnant of them will be saved."

Nevertheless, in an apparent about-face that has long perplexed New Testament scholars,[5] Paul proceeded immediately to endow his Jewish coreligionists with a critical role in the divine economy of salvation. For having deduced that a Gentile fares no worse than a Jew in the eyes of God, and having castigated the Jews for their rejection of Jesus, the Christological portion of Paul's epistle to the Gentile Christians of Rome concludes on a note of qualification regarding the nation of Israel:

I ask, then, has God rejected his people? By no means! . . . So I ask, have they stumbled so as to fall? By no means! But through their trespass salvation has come to the Gentiles, so as to make Israel jealous. . . . For if their rejection means the reconciliation of the world, what will their acceptance mean but life from the dead? If the dough offered as first fruits is holy, so is the whole lump; and if the root is holy, so are the branches. But if some of the branches were broken off, and you, a wild olive shoot, were grafted

5. See the judicious overview of the state of the field in Heikki Räisänen, "Paul, God, and Israel: Romans 9–11 in Recent Research," in The Social World of Formative Christianity and Judaism: Essays in Tribute to Howard Clark Lee, ed. Jacob Neusner et al. (Philadelphia, 1988), pp. 178–206.

in their place to share the richness of the olive tree, do not boast over the branches. . . .

For if you have been cut from what is by nature a wild olive tree and grafted, contrary to nature, into a cultivated olive tree, how much more will these natural branches be grafted back into their own olive tree. Lest you be wise in your own conceits, I want you to understand this mystery, brethren: A hardening has come upon part of Israel, until the full number of Gentiles come in, and so all Israel will be saved. . . . As regards the gospel they are enemies of God, for your sake; but as regards election they are beloved for the sake of their forefathers. (11:1–28)

No matter how one might ultimately choose to define Paul's intentions, our present interests would underscore several key aspects of this message. Presenting the Jews so as to facilitate his doctrinal instruction of Gentile Christians, Paul attributed momentous importance to the people of Israel. This importance bespoke a divinely ordained mission that found expression over the course of human history: before Jesus, during his lifetime, and subsequent to his death. Precisely in their identification with the sacred text of Scripture—"the Jews are entrusted with the oracles of God" (Romans 3:2); they are "the adherents of the law" (Romans 4:14)—the Jews had contributed to the salvation of the world and would continue to do so. God gave them the law "to increase the trespass," with the result that "where sin increased, grace abounded all the more" (Romans 5:20). The Jews' rejection of Jesus constituted the ultimate trespass and allowed the Gentiles to enter into God's covenant. Upon the completion of this process, the Jews will regain God's favor, and their conversion will signal the final redemption, "life from the dead" and all. The Jews have not entirely forfeited their election. They still serve a vital purpose, pedagogic and eschatological, which demands their survival until the end, when "all Israel [*pâs Israél*] will be saved."

Struggling to find consistency in Paul's attitudes regarding the Jews, modern Christian writers continue to debate the ramifications of these texts. Some have discerned a Pauline stratum at the base of Christian antisemitism; others have found his ideas virtually free of hostility toward Judaism, which they instead attribute to Paul's later interpreters.[6] For our purposes, Paul's undeniable ambivalence retains a primary im-

---

6. Cf., for example, the views of Rosemary R. Ruether, *Faith and Fratricide: The Theological Roots of Anti-Semitism* (New York, 1974), pp. 95–107, with those of John G. Gager, *The Origins of Anti-Semitism: Attitudes toward Judaism in Pagan and Christian Antiquity* (New York, 1983), esp. chaps. 11–15, and Lloyd Gaston, *Paul and the Torah* (Vancouver, B.C., 1987).

portance, as does his retention of Israel and Israel's relationship with Scripture within the divine economy of salvation. During the decades after Paul, these issues continued to exercise key voices in the formulation of primitive Christianity, including those of the evangelists, the author of Hebrews, and the apostolic fathers. Over the course of the centuries that followed, their ideas underwent further development and received more systematic expression in the *Adversus Iudaeos* polemic (arguments "against the Jews") of many church fathers—Justin Martyr, Melito of Sardis, Tertullian, Origen, Eusebius of Caesarea, Ephrem the Syrian, Aphrahat, John Chrysostom, Ambrose of Milan, and others—which gave rise to a genre of Christian literary expression unto itself. Patristic concern with the Jew and his Judaism constitutes the second contextual sphere within which our story took shape.[7]

Paul's view of the error of the Jews as the obverse of the truth of Christianity lived on, encasing all subsequent reflection on Judaism in Christian theology. Yet as the Gentile constituencies of Christian churches increased and the intensity of direct interaction between Jews and Christians subsided, the teachings of *Adversus Iudaeos* shifted their emphasis. They now served chiefly to fuel attacks by Gentile Christians, who had never converted to Judaism, against Christians who still observed Jewish law. Seeking to justify the departure of the church from the synagogue, Christian preachers tried to demonstrate not only that observance of the old law without belief in Jesus was insufficient but that it was inherently wrong. The New Testament had replaced the Old; and just as the Gentile church had replaced the Jewish people as the community of God's elect, so too had the inauguration of a new gospel rendered the old law at least counterproductive if not thoroughly sinful.

---

7. Owing to the avowedly cursory and selective nature of this overview, I have sought to keep the notes to a minimum. For instructive overviews and ample bibliography on patristic attitudes toward the Jews, see Marcel Simon, *Verus Israel: A Study of the Relations between Christians and Jews in the Roman Empire (135–425)*, trans. H. McKeating (New York, 1986), chaps. 5–6; A. Lukyn Williams, *Adversus Judaeos: A Bird's-Eye View of Christian Apologiae until the Renaissance* (Cambridge, England, 1935); Ruether, *Faith and Fratricide*, pp. 117–82; Miriam S. Taylor, *Anti-Judaism and Early Christian Identity: A Critique of the Scholarly Consensus*, Studia Post-biblica 46 (Leiden, Netherlands, 1995); Samuel Krauss, *The Jewish-Christian Controversy from the Earliest Times to 1798, Volume I: History*, ed. and rev. William Horbury, Texte und Studien zum antiken Judentum 56 (Tübingen, Germany, 1995), chap. 1; and Guy G. Stroumsa, "From Anti-Judaism to Antisemitism in Early Christianity?" in *Contra Iudaeos: Ancient and Medieval Polemics between Christians and Jews*, ed. Ora Limor and Guy G. Stroumsa, Texts and Studies in Medieval and Early Modern Judaism 10 (Tübingen, Germany, 1996), pp. 1–26.

Beyond Jews and Jewish Christians, Christian *Adversus Iudaeos* polemic soon found additional targets. Clamoring for acceptance in a
hostile Roman world, early Christian teachers proclaimed both to their
pagan detractors and to prospective pagan converts that Christianity
was not a recently contrived distortion of biblical Judaism but the genuine continuation and fulfillment thereof. Ancients placed the highest
value on antiquity, and Greco-Roman civilization typically respected
the Jews as one of the oldest peoples of all. From an ancient Mediterranean perspective, why convert to Christianity if its novelty, perhaps
the very source of its attraction, constituted prima facie evidence of its
invalidity? The discourse of *Adversus Iudaeos* supplied the answer: Despite their literal observance of biblical law, the Jews had forsaken
God's covenant of old, whereas the Christians, interpreting that law
figuratively, had maintained it. Inverting the biblical typology of Israel's redemption from Egyptian bondage, commemorated in the very
season of Passover during which Jesus was crucified, the second-
century bishop Melito of Sardis reassigned the roles of oppressor and
oppressed, damned and saved, in his *Peri Pascha* (On the Paschal Sacrifice),[8] presumably a liturgical poem for the celebration of Easter:

> You killed your Lord at the great feast.
> And you were making merry,
>   while he was starving;
> you had wine to drink and bread to eat,
>   he had vinegar and gall;
> your face was bright,
>   his was downcast;
> you were triumphant,
>   he was afflicted;
> you were making music,
>   he was being judged;
> you were giving the beat,
>   he was being nailed up;
> you were dancing,
>   he was being buried;
> you were reclining on a soft couch,
>   he in grave and coffin.
> O lawless Israel, what is this unprecedented crime you committed,
>   thrusting your Lord among unprecedented sufferings,
>   your sovereign
>   who formed you,

8. On alternative options for translating the title of this work, see Melito of Sardis,
On Pascha and Fragments, ed. and trans. Stuart George Hall (Oxford, 1979), p. 3 n. 1.

> who made you,
> who honored you,
> who called you 'Israel'?
> But you did not turn out to be 'Israel';
> you did not 'see God,'
> you did not recognize the Lord.[9]

God had therefore disowned the Jews, annulled their ritual law, and transferred their inheritance to the church, which now constituted the only true Israel, not a recently arrived impostor.

Even after pagans had undergone Christian baptism, an incentive to preach to them against the Jews remained. Especially in the large metropolitan centers of the Eastern empire, where sizable Jewish and Christian communities intermingled freely, Christians frequently emulated Paul's Galatian correspondents and looked upon Judaism and its biblical rituals as the "real thing." Christianity might be a watered-down "Gentile's Judaism" in their eyes, whereas the truly authentic biblical religion belonged to the Jews; for rituals that surely mattered—a holy day like Passover or the New Year, a familial rite of passage, an oath to cement a major business transaction—a visit to a Jewish home or synagogue could make perfect sense. Alarmed by such Judaizing tendencies, churchmen disparaged the Jews in order to bolster Christian self-confidence: Christianity and Judaism did not lie on the same continuum, such that the former naturally directed its adherents toward the latter. On the contrary, as Melito explained to his parishioners, "in the same way as the model is made void, conceding the image to the truly real . . . , the [Jewish] people was made void when the church arose."[10] The rites of the Jews, once precious, have been rendered worthless, and the hermeneutical downfall of Israel has caused its disinheritance.

Casting old and new covenants as contradictory, however, may smack of dualism. The "heretic" Marcion and others like him argued that the savior-God of the New Testament could not possibly have created—or entered—the material world of the Old Testament or authored its inferior law. There were actually two cosmic powers, one supremely good and the other inferior if not utterly evil, who ruled over two worlds, one spiritual and the other material; the struggle between these powers and their respective realms determined the fate of

9. Melito, *Peri Pascha* 79–82, ibid., pp. 42–45.
10. Melito, *Peri Pascha* 43, ibid., pp. 20–21

the cosmos at large and that of every individual. In defense of their monotheism and in opposition to the dualists, orthodox fathers of the church sought to establish the divine authorship of the Old Testament on one hand and the incontrovertible superiority of Christianity over Judaism on the other. And once again, polemic against the Jews nourished the patristic argument. The deficiencies of the old law reflected not upon its divine legislator but upon its Jewish practitioners, and the guilt of the latter should not devolve onto the former. Jew and dualist heretic, ran the argument, thereby had much in common. Each understood—in fact, misunderstood—the old law entirely in its literal sense: One accepted it wholeheartedly on that basis; the other rejected it outright. Of the heretic who denied the incarnation of God in the body of Jesus, the North African Tertullian pleaded that he "now give up borrowing poison from the Jew—the asp, as they say, from the viper."[11] As for the Jews, Justin Martyr declared to his Jewish interlocutor Trypho in his famous *Dialogos* (Dialogue) of the second century, "you are a people hard of heart, and without understanding, and blind, and lame, and sons in whom there is no faith."[12] The precepts of the old law had no salvific value, but they constituted God's resulting punishment for Jewish sin, which ranged from their idolatry to their crucifixion of Jesus and to their persistent hatred of Christians. Circumcision, argued Justin, "was given for a sign, that you should be separated from the other nations and us, and that you alone should suffer the things that you are rightly suffering now, and that your lands should be desolate and your cities burned with fire, and that foreigners should eat up the fruits before your face, and none of you go up to Jerusalem."[13] So, too, the Sabbath, the sacrifices in the temple, and other cultic rites of ancient Israel condemn the Jews for their misdeeds. And, now that Jesus had proffered an entirely different sort of legislation, "the law given at Horeb is already antiquated. . . . A law set over against a law has made the one before it to cease, and a testament [*diathēkē*] coming into existence later has limited any previous one."[14]

---

11. Tertullian, *Adversus Marcionem* 3.7–8, ed. and trans. Ernest Evans (Oxford, 1972), 1:188–91.

12. Justin Martyr, *Dialogos* 27.4, in Edgar J. Goodspeed, ed., *Die ältesten Apologeten* (Göttingen, Germany, 1914), p. 121; trans. in Justin Martyr, *The Dialogue with Trypho*, trans. A. Lukyn Williams (London, 1930), pp. 54–55.

13. Justin Martyr, *Dialogos* 16.2, in Goodspeed, *Die ältesten Apologeten*, p. 109; trans. in Justin Martyr, *Dialogue*, pp. 32–33.

14. Justin Martyr, *Dialogos* 11.2, in Goodspeed, *Die ältesten Apologeten*, p. 102; trans. in Justin Martyr, *Dialogue*, p. 23, with slight modifications.

Only a genuinely Christian hermeneutic allowed for enjoying the true value of the law without suffering from its drawbacks. Interpreted properly in its Christological sense, the law was intrinsically good; those who misunderstood it were sinful.

When churchmen addressed their anti-Jewish polemic to non-Jewish audiences—to undercut the credibility of Jewish Christians, to legitimate Christianity in the eyes of pagans (whether hostile or sympathetic), to combat reverence for Jews and Judaism among Christians, and to counter the dualist biblical exegesis of heretics—they naturally depicted Jews in a fashion that would advance their own theological agenda. As one historian of this early period has written, "at the root of the matter lies, then, not the actual condition or behavior of the Jews, but rather the image of the Jews required for the purposes of Christian theology."[15] But note well: Throughout this process of self-definition and propagation, Christianity never dispensed with this hermeneutically crafted Jew. From the first stages in its development, the Jew *served a purpose*—or a mélange of purposes—in the new religion, purposes that rendered *Adversus Iudaeos* a basic medium for Christian self-expression, whose applications far exceeded direct confrontations between Christian and Jews. Simply put, the Jew had a particular role to play in a divinely ordained historical drama. His role stemmed from his failure to embrace Christianity when Jesus, his own kinsman, came to redeem him and his people before all others. This failure, in turn, had a chiefly hermeneutical basis; it derived from a deficient reading of the biblical covenant that God had revealed to him, an inability to discern the fulfillment of the Old Testament in the New.

As the church fathers of the second, third, and fourth centuries formulated some of the vital presuppositions for medieval Christian constructions of Jews and Judaism, their work revealed a developmental trend that also set a precedent for things to come. Guy Stroumsa has recently highlighted the process whereby Christian anti-Judaism intensified, growing increasingly harsh and more intolerant, between the second and fourth centuries. In the wake of Constantine's conversion, churchmen envisioned a new Christian identity that would integrate the Roman polity and society, an identity the Jews did not share; it followed that "the Jews, together with the pagans and heretics, had to

15. David Rokeah, "The Church Fathers and the Jews in Writings Designed for Internal and External Use," in *Antisemitism through the Ages*, ed. Shmuel Almog, trans. Nathan H. Reisner (Oxford, 1988), p. 64.

be publicly vanquished and humiliated."[16] *Adversus Iudaeos* polemic grew more ad hominem, casting slurs on contemporary Jews, depicting them in demonic terms, and displaying less concern for the nexus between the Jew, his Scripture, and his literalist interpretation of it. Bewailing the attraction that contemporary Judaism still exerted upon Christians in Antioch, for example, John Chrysostom focused his *Adversus Iudaeos* sermons much less on the didactic and eschatological role of the Jew than his predecessors had, and he emphasized the radical disjunction of Judaism and Christianity much more:

> Where Christ-killers gather, the cross is ridiculed, God blasphemed, the father unacknowledged, the son insulted, the grace of the Spirit rejected. Indeed, is not the harm even greater than where demons are present? In a pagan temple the impiety is open and obvious and can hardly seduce or deceive one who has wits about him and is soberminded. But in the synagogue they say that they worship God and abhor idols. They read and admire the prophets and use their words as bait, tricking the simple and foolish to fall into their snares. The result is that their impiety is equal to that of the Greeks, but their deception is much worse. They have an altar of deception in their midst which is invisible and on which they sacrifice not sheep and calves but the souls of men. In a word, if you admire the Jewish way of life, what do you have in common with us? If the Jewish rites are holy and venerable, our way of life must be false. But if our way is true, as indeed it is, theirs is fraudulent. I am not speaking of the Scriptures. Far from it! For they lead one to Christ. I am speaking of their present impiety and madness.[17]

Chrysostom minimized the link between the Jews and their Bible; emphasizing the dissonance between the Judaism of Scripture and the Jews of his day, John constructed synagogue and church as mutually exclusive. He depicted the Jews as the bearers of evil intentions, insulting and dishonoring their biblical heritage, not misinterpreting it in ignorance. He demonized the Jews, elaborating their affinity with the devil, relegating them to the status of pagans, and at times, it would seem, even doubting their humanity. Though he called for Christians to abhor the Jews, not to attack them, he mapped out no place for Judaism in a properly ordered Christian world. Stroumsa has argued that the harsher, demonic anti-Judaism that I and other historians have deemed

---

16. Stroumsa, "From Anti-Judaism to Antisemitism," p. 23.

17. John Chrysostom, *Logoi kata Ioudaíōn* 1.6, PG 48:852; I have proposed but one modification of the translation in Wayne A. Meeks and Robert L. Wilken, *Jews and Christians in Antioch in the First Four Centuries of the Common Era*, Society for Biblical Literature, Sources for Biblical Study 13 (Missoula, Mont., 1978), p. 97.

characteristic of the later Middle Ages thus had its origins in the fourth-century attitudes exemplified by Chrysostom.[18] I would agree that the pattern of development in patristic perceptions of the Jews adumbrates that of our ensuing medieval story with strikingly suggestive similarities. I believe, however, that the medieval history related in this book constitutes more than just a repetition of a familiar tale.

No less than anything else, that which distinguished the medieval career of Christianity's hermeneutical Jew was the formative influence of Augustine of Hippo, who received Christian baptism within months after John Chrysostom began to deliver his sermons against Jews (and Judaizers) in Antioch.[19] Augustine not only adopted a more moderate stance on the Jewish question than did his contemporary patristic colleagues like Chrysostom, Ambrose of Milan, and Cyril of Alexandria; his own *Adversus Iudaeos* teaching, itself yet another explication of Paul, also endowed the Jews, their sacred texts, and their presence in Christendom with a new dimension to their purpose, one that has, in various ways, controlled the Western idea of the Jew ever since.

Augustine's teachings provide the third, most delimited sphere of contextual background to this study; but because of their formidable impact and authority among Christian theologians throughout the medieval period, the ideas of Augustine are an integral part of our story, and we must consider them at length. Part 1 of this book seeks to understand Augustine's acclaimed doctrine of Jewish witness in its Augustinian context. Part 2 considers how three prominent prelates of the early Middle Ages—Gregory the Great, Isidore of Seville, and Agobard of Lyons—construed the role of the Jew in a properly ordered Christendom: In markedly different ways, each of these men sought to adapt patristic theology and Roman legal precedent to the new Christian mentalities and environments of postclassical Europe. Each of them reacted outspokenly to the presence and proper function of the Jew in

18. Stroumsa, "From Anti-Judaism to Antisemitism," passim. Although Chrysostom aired his outrage over respect showed by Christians for Jews and for Jewish ritual in Antioch in his own day—and as Robert Wilken has shown in *John Chrysostom and the Jews: Rhetoric and Reality in the Late 4th Century* (Berkeley, Calif., 1983), one must appreciate his sermons against the additional background of Emperor Julian's plan to rebuild the Jewish temple in Jerusalem—his portrayals of the Jew and Judaism are no less theologically crafted than those of other church fathers. For, as Wilken has observed, p. 159, John's vitriolic negation of Judaism was truly "an attempt to argue for the truth of the Christian religion."

19. J. N. D. Kelly, *Golden Mouth: The Story of John Chrysostom—Ascetic, Preacher, Bishop* (Ithaca, N.Y., 1995), p. 62; Peter Brown, *Augustine of Hippo: A Biography* (London, 1967), p. 124.

their society. To what extent did they adhere to or depart from established tradition? How can we appreciate them as complying with, modifying, or resisting the ideas of Augustine? The diversity of their ideas notwithstanding, I believe that the doctrine of Jewish witness and its postulates served them all as a pivotal point of departure. Part 3 treats changes in perceptions of the Jews during the twelfth century. I argue that the broadening cultural horizons of European civilization during the age of the Crusades served gradually to modify the prevailing Christian constructions of the Jew in a variety of ways. Even as Augustinian doctrine still found ample expression, Christendom's encounter with Islam, its new commitment to rational argument in matters theological, and its initial exposure to talmudic Judaism challenged hitherto prevalent assumptions. The presence of other infidels threatened the singularity of the contemporary Jew in Christian eyes, just as dialectic questioned his rationality and the Talmud raised doubts concerning his theological identity. Nevertheless, it took time for these processes to work significant change in the Christian mind-set, and outright condemnation of contemporary Judaism as unacceptable in Augustinian terms appeared only in the thirteenth century. Part 4 first reviews the thirteenth-century papal condemnations of rabbinic literature and the mendicant mission to the Jews in light of new and recently published documentary sources. It concludes with the notably ambivalent formulations of the Dominican friar Thomas Aquinas, whose writings testify both to a growing delegitimization of contemporary, postbiblical Judaism and to the lasting legacy of Augustine at one and the same time.

The ambivalent note on which this book closes comports well with the substance of its conclusions. The voices assembled here confirm that as the Middle Ages wore on, the culpability of the Jew steadily increased in Christian eyes. Medieval Christianity eventually demonized him; by the thirteenth century, some churchmen had come to view contemporary Judaism as a willful distortion of the biblical religion that the Jews should ideally have preserved and embodied. Yet at least two reservations are in order. As gradually as constructions of Jews and Judaism developed among Christian theologians, it could take longer—centuries longer, at times—for popes and canonists to translate the new ideas into the deliberate, official policy of the Catholic Church, or for the new ideas to alter the patterns of day-to-day relationships between Christians and Jews. Furthermore, the new ideas never displaced the old ones; rather, they took their place beside them.

The teachings of Augustine, of the church fathers who preceded him, and, above all, of Paul the apostle have retained a critical influence in Christian theology. Straying far afield from the purview of this book, one notes that Christian churches today still view the Jews as a unique textual community, defined by its biblical hermeneutic, bearing directly on the meaning of the Christian covenant. In Christian theologies, "the Jew in our midst" still has an essential role to play as the drama of salvation history continues to unfold.[20]

20. Throughout this book, full bibliographical citations appear at the first reference to a work in the footnotes to each chapter and in the bibliography. As frequently happens, the transliteration of Hebrew and the rendition of names in other languages present problems that defy an entirely consistent solution, especially if one seeks to avoid being overly awkward. I have tended to Anglicize personal names when referring to them discursively (e.g., Nachmanides, Yechiel of Paris, Raymond of Penyafort), but not when these names themselves appear in foreign-language phrases and titles (e.g., *Wikkuah Rabbenu Yehiel*, "Chronologia biographica s. Raimundi"). When a Hebrew work includes a romanized title, I have cited it as such, noting the language of the text in brackets. I have generally followed the new Jewish Publication Society translation of the Hebrew Bible and the Revised Standard Version of the New Testament. Although I have regularly consulted available translations of ancient and medieval sources, all other translations are my own unless noted otherwise.

PART ONE

Augustinian Foundations

From the earliest days of the history of the church, Christian ideas of Jews and Judaism responded to the imperatives of Christian theology and to the essential characteristics of the Christian interpretation of Scripture. The course of modern civilization has shown how such ideologically and hermeneutically derived constructions have continued to bear on the interaction of Christian and Jew, at times with cataclysmic results. Inasmuch as this book concerns the medieval history of those Christian ideas in the Latin West, it begins with Augustine of Hippo. From theology and philosophy to music and literary criticism, from his sexual obsessions to a penchant for autobiography and self-understanding, Augustine of Hippo bequeathed so much to Western civilization that one need hardly wonder if this bequest included his ideas on Jews and Judaism. Indeed, modern students of Jewish-Christian relations typically attribute the theological foundations of the medieval church's Jewish policy to Augustine, referring as a matter of course to the legacies and principles of Augustinian anti-Judaism. Chief among these ranks his doctrine of toleration for the Jews of Christendom inasmuch as they, subjugated and dispersed, bear living witness to the biblical roots and verities of Christianity.[1]

---

1. For example, see Bernhard Blumenkranz, *Les Auteurs chrétiens latins du Moyen Âge sur les Juifs et le Judaisme* (Paris, 1963), and the articles collected in his *Juifs et Chrétiens: Patristique et Moyen Âge* (London, 1977); Rosemary R. Ruether, *Faith and*

Despite limitless modern interest in Augustine, scholars have still not explicated much of the complexity in his teaching on the Jews and Judaism; above all, most have neglected the place of that teaching within the broader context of Augustine's life and work. As they typically do in the *Adversus Iudaeos* traditions of the Catholic Church, inconsistency and ambivalence regarding Jews and Judaism abound in the Augustinian corpus. Notwithstanding Bernhard Blumenkranz's seminal study of Augustine's *Tractatus adversus Iudaeos* (Treatise against the Jews), in which he cites more than eleven hundred pertinent passages in Augustine's other works,[2] Augustine appears to have had relatively little concern with Jews or Judaism in his day. The overwhelming majority of his pronouncements merely echo the important themes of long-established Pauline and patristic traditions: spiritual/Christological versus literal/carnal interpretation of the Bible; contrasts and continuities between the old, Mosaic covenant and the new, Christian testament; God's rejection of the Jews and election of the Gentiles, the true descendants of Abraham; Jewish blindness and guilt in the death of Jesus and rejection of Christianity; and the inappropriateness of Jewish life in the postcrucifixion era. As Louis Ginzberg observed nearly a century ago, Augustine's pronouncements concerning the Jews "belong to the weakest and least important productions of his pen."[3]

Still, a distinctive Augustinian legacy does resonate sharply in the history of Jewish-Christian relations; and, given that the Jews per se did not figure prominently on the agenda of Augustine the bishop or Augustine the theologian, one rightly wonders, why this resonance? The Jewish question for Augustine surely deserves our attention, but chiefly insofar as it functioned within the broader framework of Augustinian thought and instruction. In the following chapter, we shall therefore review Augustine's noteworthy pronouncements concerning

Fratricide: The Theological Roots of Anti-Semitism (New York, 1974), pp. 148–49; Kenneth R. Stow, "Hatred of the Jews or Love of the Church: Papal Policy toward the Jews in the Middle Ages," in *Antisemitism through the Ages*, ed. Shmuel Almog, trans. Nathan H. Reisner (Oxford, 1988), pp. 73ff., and *Alienated Minority: The Jews of Medieval Latin Europe* (Cambridge, Mass., 1992), pp. 17–20; Gilbert Dahan, "L'Article *Iudei* de la *Summa Abel* de Pierre le Chantre," *REA* 27 (1981), 105–126; Jeremy Cohen, *The Friars and the Jews: The Evolution of Medieval Anti-Judaism* (Ithaca, N.Y., 1982), pp. 19ff.; and Shlomo Simonsohn, *The Apostolic See and the Jews: History*, Pontifical Institute of Mediaeval Studies: Studies and Texts 109 (Toronto, 1991), pp. 4–6, 290ff.

    2. Bernhard Blumenkranz, *Die Judenpredigt Augustins* (Basel, 1946); see also his "Augustin et les Juifs, Augustin et le Judaïsme," *Recherches augustiniennes* 1 (1958), 225–41.

    3. Louis Ginzberg, "Augustine," *The Jewish Encyclopedia* (New York, 1902), 2:314.

the Jews at key junctures in his career, and only then shall we turn to his sole overtly anti-Jewish treatise and its well-known call for preserving the Jews of Christendom.[4] Next, we shall analyze Augustine's distinctive doctrine of Jewish witness, its components and the chronology of its development. Finally, against the background of several preeminent concerns of Augustinian theological discourse, we shall attempt to understand the significance of the doctrine for Augustine and the logic of its appearance at a particular stage in his life.

4. Jesús Alvarez, *Teología del pueblo judío* (Madrid, 1970), p. 15, noted that Augustine dedicated four treatises to the subject of the Jews: *Sermo* 96 on the prodigal son (Luke 15:11–32); *Epistula* 196 to Bishop Asellicus (see below, chapter 1, at n. 56); the *Tractatus adversus Iudaeos*; and another sermon no longer extant.

The Doctrine of Jewish Witness

Augustine of Hippo (354–430) lived during an age of transitions. During his lifetime, the division between Eastern and Western capitals of the Roman Empire became a permanent one, as the imperial government in the city of Rome itself entered the last generations of its history. More than any later fifth-century event, like the deposition of the last Western emperor in 476, the sacking of Rome by the Germanic Visigoths in 410 signaled the decline of classical civilization in contemporary eyes. Political change, with its accompanying social ferment, induced many to question the presuppositions upon which their societies and worldviews rested, contributing roundly to the cultural anxiety that characterized this period, to experimentation with new notions of personal power and security that sought to allay such anxiety, and to the propagation of new value systems in keeping with these ideas. Where, ultimately, did personal fulfillment lie? How might one seek to achieve it?

As the Roman Empire stood on the brink of a new era, so did the Christian church. Augustine formally embraced Christianity soon after Theodosius the Great declared it the official religion of the empire.

An earlier version of this chapter, entitled "Augustine on Judaism Reconsidered," was presented to the annual meeting of the Medieval Academy of America in 1991. I subsequently reformulated my conclusions in a paper on "Anti-Jewish Discourse and Its Function in Medieval Christian Theology" delivered to the New Chaucer Society in 1992.

Although the imperial ban on the pagan cult capped the victory of the recently persecuted Christian church over its detractors, it confronted church and state alike with an array of new problems. Christianity had claimed to spurn the pleasures and powers of this world, sharply demarcating the realms of God and Caesar, looking forward to an apocalypse that would replace existing political institutions with the rule of Christ and his saints. A Christian empire might ensure the safety and supremacy of Christians and their church, but how did it bear on the Christian quest for salvation and its underlying philosophy of human history? Furthermore, if Constantine's conversion earlier in the fourth century and Theodosius's marriage of the empire to the church decades later appeared to vindicate the Christian revolution against classical pagan civilization, how did the sacking of imperial Rome by the "barbarians" figure in this equation? Did it, as the old pagan aristocracy suggested, manifest the gods' wrath over the conversion of the empire to Christianity? If not, precisely what significance attached to such events of political history in God's plan for the salvation of the world?

Like these and other issues of his day, the course of Augustine's life, itself rife with conversions, transitions, power struggles, and intense self-examination, has been studied exhaustively. Alongside the decline of Rome and the triumph of the Roman Catholic Church, it too heralded the approaching junction between classical antiquity and the ensuing Christian Middle Ages. The concerns of Augustine's career invariably informed his distinctive ideas of the Jew. To trace the history of those ideas properly, one must appreciate the chronology of their appearance during Augustine's life and their place in the Augustinian worldview.

AUGUSTINE ON THE JEWS AND JUDAISM

THE EARLY YEARS: ON THE AGES OF MAN

Between his conversion to Christianity in 386 and his arrival in the North African town of Hippo in 391, Augustine formulated his renowned sevenfold scheme for the periodization of human history. In the *De Genesi contra Manichaeos* (On Genesis against the Manicheans, 388–389), Augustine found a biblical foundation for his theory in the story of creation in six days, and in the nature of the seventh day, the Sabbath, in particular: "I think that the reason why this rest is ascribed to the seventh day should be considered more carefully. For I see

throughout the entire text of the divine scriptures that six specific ages of
work are distinguished by their palpable limits, so to speak, so that rest
is expected in the seventh age. And these six ages are similar to the six
days in which those things which Scripture records that God created
were made." On this basis Augustine proceeded through the six days of
the Genesis cosmogony, linking them to the successive eras of terrestrial
history, even linking the biblical refrain, "and there was evening and
there was morning," to specific developments within each historical period. When he reached the primordial Tuesday Augustine wrote:

> It was therefore morning from the time of Abraham, and a third age like
> adolescence came to pass; and it is aptly compared to the third day, on
> which the land was separated from the waters. . . . For through Abraham
> the people of God was separated from the deception of the nations and the
> waves of this world. . . . Worshipping the one God, this people received the
> holy scriptures and prophets, like a land irrigated so that it might bear
> useful fruits. . . . The evening of this age was in the sins of the people, in
> which they neglected the divine commandments, up to the evil of the terrible
> king Saul.
>
> Then in the morning was the kingdom of David. . . . It is aptly compared
> to the fourth day, on which the astral bodies were fashioned in the sky. For
> what more clearly signifies the glory of a kingdom than the excellence of
> the sun . . . ? The evening of this age, so to speak, was in the sins of the
> kings, for which that people deserved captivity and slavery.
>
> In the morning there was the migration to Babylonia. . . . This age ex-
> tended to the advent of our lord Jesus Christ; it is the fifth age, that is, the
> decline from youth to old age. . . . And so, for the people of the Jews that
> age was, in fact, one of decline and destruction. . . . Afterwards those people
> began to live among the nations, as if in the sea, and, like the birds that
> fly, to have an uncertain, unstable dwelling. . . . God blessed those creatures,
> saying "Be fertile and increase . . . ," inasmuch as the Jewish people, from
> the time that it was dispersed among the nations, in fact increased signifi-
> cantly. The evening of this day—that is, of this age—was, so to speak, the
> multiplication of sins among the people of the Jews, since they were blinded
> so seriously that they could not even recognize the lord Jesus Christ.[1]

Augustine's review of biblical history from Abraham to Jesus may appear to add little, if anything at all, to standard patristic doctrine concerning the Jews. Yet this early Augustinian text, whose subsequent
influence in medieval historiography surpassed its importance even for
Augustine himself,[2] already demonstrates how various other issues of

---

1. Augustine, *De Genesi contra Manichaeos* 1.23, PL 34:190–93.
2. On the sevenfold periodization of history, see, among others, Auguste Luneau,
L'Histoire du salut chez les pères de l'Église: La Doctrine des âges du monde, Théologie

pressing concern led Augustine to dwell upon the Jews and Judaism. Here the characterization of the Jews somehow exemplifies his approach to biblical exegesis—in this case allegory, and the allegorical interpretation of Genesis in particular. Moreover, inasmuch as the Jews dominate much of the divine plan for human history, they assume significance in the exposition of Augustine's scheme of salvation history, a connection to which Augustine returned soon thereafter in his *De vera religione* (On the True Religion, 389–391). Here he reviewed the six or seven proverbial ages in the life of a human being as they apply both to the "old," exterior or earthly man, and to the "new," inward or heavenly man, a contrast that similarly bears on the totality of human history. Adumbrating his later theory of the two cities, Augustine thus proposed that

> the entire human race, whose life extends from Adam to the end of this world, is—much like the life of a single person—administered under the laws of divine providence, so that it appears divided into two categories. In one of these is the mass of impious people bearing the image of the earthly man from the beginning of the world until the end; in the other is a class of people dedicated to the one God, but which from Adam until John the Baptist led the life of the earthly man while subject to a measure of righteousness [*servili quadam iustitia*]. Its history is called the Old Testament, which, while appearing to promise an earthly kingdom, is in its entirety nothing other than the image of the new people and the New Testament, promising a heavenly kingdom.[3]

Augustine's allegory of the six ages assumes both microcosmic and macrocosmic proportions, reflecting the experience of the individual and that of society at large. The Jews and their religion are again, in pre-Christian times, at center stage; here, in the *De vera religione*, they also bridge the chasm between the two species of human existence. Their Old Testament pertains to the life of earthly man, proffering the rewards of an earthly kingdom. Yet somehow this covenant of the Jews entails "a measure of righteousness," complicating the evaluation of its character. If correctly interpreted, it embodies the image of the new man and the New Testament. Such interconnections between exegesis, philosophy of history, and the Jews will prove critical to an appreciation of Augustine's place in our story.

---

historique 2 (Paris, 1964); and Paul Archambault, "Ages of Man and Ages of the World," *REA* 12 (1966), 193–228. See also below, chapter 3, on Isidore of Seville.

3. Augustine, *De vera religione* 26.49–27.50, CCSL 32:218–19.

AT THE TURN OF THE CENTURY

During the final decade of the fourth century, Augustine's ideas and career matured considerably. His polemic against the Manicheans continued to develop, with additional subtlety and with sustained vigor. His vehement opposition to the Donatists enhanced his leadership role in the African church and contributed to his notion of the coercive role of the state in a properly ordered Christian society. And his understanding of human will and divine grace in the process of an individual's salvation changed dramatically—a transformation we shall consider again below. The thirty-three books of the *Contra Faustum* (Against Faustus, 397–398) testify to much of this development and, not surprisingly, offer insight into the molding of Augustine's perspective on Jews and Judaism.

The *Contra Faustum* reiterates both the fundamental importance of the figurative interpretation of Scripture and, by way of example, the correspondence between the days of creation and the ages of world history;[4] once again, exegesis and philosophy of history emerge as interdependent. Yet the persistent attacks of the dualist Faustus upon the Old Testament demanded that Augustine clarify his evaluation of the old law and of the people of the book with greater precision. He thus affirmed the accuracy and the authority of the books of Hebrew Scripture. He posited a perfect concord between the two testaments, inasmuch as everything in the Old Testament instructs concerning the New. "All that Moses wrote is of Christ—that is, it pertains completely to Christ—whether insofar as it foretells of him in figures of objects, deeds, and speech, or insofar as it extols his grace and glory."[5] Such prefiguration by word and event lies at the heart of the biblical typology with which Augustine responded to the Manichean polemic. All of the contents of the Old Testament were historically true (in the case of narrative) and/or valid (in the case of prophecy and precepts), and this accuracy underlay the truth of their prefigurative significance. At great length did Augustine therefore defend the stories and commandments of the Old Testament, seeking to demonstrate both their intrinsic coherence and their corresponding Christological value. To be sure, Augustine hardly deviated from accepted Pauline and patristic doctrine

---

4. See below, n. 8.
5. Augustine, *Contra Faustum* 16.9, CSEL 31:447.

on the relative authority of the two covenants. Teachings of the Old Testament lost their worth as signifiers upon the inauguration of the New. The "true bride of Christ . . . understands what constitutes the difference between letter and spirit, which two terms are otherwise called law and grace; and, serving God no longer in the antiquity of the letter but in the novelty of the spirit [she] is no longer under the law but under grace."[6] Because Jesus fulfilled the law, Christians observe its precepts more thoroughly in their spiritual sense, while the Jews, over the course of time, have in fact neglected their literal observance—and still refuse to believe in Jesus and his church. Nevertheless, even in the wake of the crucifixion the Old Testament has not lost its value and function altogether. It continues to offer testimony to the truth of Christian history and theology.

What, then, of the Jews, those who continue to accept the Old Testament and persist in rejecting the New? How does their survival comport with the divine plan for human history, now that the symbolic, typological value of Judaism has outlived its necessity? Augustine's reply, bound to assert the triumph of the church over the synagogue and yet to subvert the Manichean rejection of biblical history, included strands of the Augustinian doctrine of Jewish witness so essential to the present inquiry. First, following established Christian tradition, Augustine perceived in Cain a type of the Jews and in Abel a figure of Jesus. Punished with an existence of exile and subjugation for the murder of their brother, the Cain-like Jews consequently bear a God-given mark of shame that ensures their miserable survival:

> Now behold, who cannot see, who cannot recognize how, throughout the world, wherever that people has been scattered, it wails in sorrow for its lost kingdom and trembles in fear of the innumerable Christian peoples . . . ? The nation of impious, carnal Jews will not die a bodily death. For whoever so destroys them will suffer a sevenfold punishment—that is, he will assume from them the sevenfold punishment with which they have been burdened for their guilt in the murder of Christ. . . . Every emperor or king who has found them in his domain, having discovered them with that mark [of Cain], has not killed them—that is, he has not made them cease to live as Jews, distinct from the community of other nations by this blatant and appropriate sign of their observance.[7]

6. Ibid. 15.8, p. 432.
7. Ibid. 12.12–13, pp. 341–42. On medieval traditions concerning Cain and their ancient sources, see Oliver F. Emerson, "Legends of Cain, Especially in Old and Middle English," *Publications of the Modern Language Association* 21 (1906), 831–929; Ruth Mellinkoff, *The Mark of Cain* (Berkeley, Calif., 1981), esp. pp. 92–98; and Gilbert Da-

Insofar as they are typified by Cain (Genesis 4:1–15), why need the Jews thus endure? Augustine made no mention of their scriptures in this regard but simply explained: "Throughout the present era (which proceeds to unfold in the manner of seven days), it will be readily apparent *to believing Christians* from the survival of the Jews, how those who killed the Lord when proudly empowered have merited subjection."[8] Owing to their punishment and guilt, the survival of the Jews in exile vindicates the claims of Christianity in the eyes of Christians themselves; for this reason has God ensured that none of the Gentile rulers obliterates them or the vestiges of their observance.

Second, Augustine also found in Ham, the rebellious son of Noah (Genesis 9:18–27), a figure of the Jewish people, now enslaved to the church of the apostles and to the Gentiles (prefigured in Noah's worthy sons, Shem and Jafeth, respectively):

> The middle son—that is, the people of the Jews . . . —saw the nakedness of his father, since he consented to the death of Christ and related it to his brothers outside. Through its [that is, the Jewish people's] agency, that which was hidden in prophecy was made evident and publicized; and therefore it has been made the servant of its brethren. For what else is that nation today but the desks [*scriniaria*] of the Christians, bearing the law and the prophets as testimony to the tenets of the church, so that we honor through the sacrament what it announces through the letter?[9]

In the case of their likeness to Ham, Augustine beheld in the Jews "desks of the Christians," that is, an implement for preserving, transmitting, and expounding the prophecies of Christianity inscribed in the Old Testament. The Jews authenticate these scriptures, demonstrating now to *the enemies of the church* that the biblical testimonies to its legitimacy and even to its victory over them have not been forged. By consequence, "in not comprehending the truth they offer additional testimony to the truth, since they do not understand those books by which it was foretold that they would not understand."[10]

Third, the *Contra Faustum* links the substance of Augustine's anti-Jewish polemic with that of his attack upon heretics in general, and the Manicheans in particular. Citing 1 Corinthians 11:19 ("there must be factions [*hairéseis*] among you in order that those who are genuine

---

han, "L'Exégèse de l'histoire de Caïn et Abel du xiie au xive siècle en Occident," *RTAM* 49 (1982), 21–89, 50 (1983), 5–68.

8. Augustine, *Contra Faustum*, 12.12, pp. 341–42 (emphasis mine).
9. Ibid. 12.23, p. 351.
10. Ibid. 16.21, p. 464.

among you may be recognized"), Augustine accorded both Jews and
heretics the function of defining, albeit by contrast, the essential teachings of the church: "All who receive and read any books in our canon
where it is demonstrated that Christ was born and suffered as a mortal,
even though they do not respectfully clothe that mortality made bare
in suffering with the harmonious sacrament of [Christian] unity . . . —
although they may disagree among themselves, Jews with heretics or
one sort of heretic with another—still prove useful to the church in a
particular condition of servitude [servitutis], either in bearing witness
or [otherwise] in constituting proof."[11] Like the Jews, the Manicheans
err by understanding the Old Testament solely in its carnal sense; and
they, too, although not completely excised from the cultivated olive
tree of God's elect (Romans 11), "have remained in the bitterness of
the wild olive."[12] Yet in their rejection of biblical doctrine the Manicheans approximate pagans more than do the Jews;[13] for, unlike the
Jews, they seek "to break the commandments of the law, even in whose
figures we recognize that Christ is prophesied."[14]

THE OLDER AUGUSTINE

For an instructive example of Augustine's teaching on the Jews during
the later stages of his career, we turn to his monumental De civitate
Dei (On the City of God, ca. 414–25), composed in the wake of the
sacking of Rome by the Visigoths in 410 and during years of controversy with the Pelagians. Again we encounter a work that Augustine
neither addressed to the Jews nor wrote out of particular interest in
them but that necessarily considered Jewish existence, Jewish books,
and Judaism within the context of its central concerns. As Augustine
traced the parallel histories of heavenly and earthly cities from creation
until his own era, he continued to resort to typological oppositions
between the church and the Jews that abounded in the patristic Adversus Iudaeos tradition—Sarah versus Hagar, Jacob versus Esau, and

---

11. Ibid. 12.24, pp. 352–53; cf. also 15.2. Augustine rendered the Latin of Paul's
epistle as "oportet et haereses esse, ut probati manifesti fiant inter vos." On the importance of this theme for Augustine, see Anne-Marie la Bonnardière, "Bible et polémiques,"
in Saint Augustin et la Bible, ed. Anne-Marie la Bonnardière, Bible de tous les temps 3
(Paris, 1986), pp. 329–31; and also below, n. 124.
    12. Augustine, Contra Faustum 9.2, p. 309.
    13. Ibid. 16.10.
    14. Ibid. 16.25, p. 470.

so forth. He reaffirmed the correspondence between old and new covenants—the former hidden in the latter, the latter revealed in the former—such that the teachings of the Old Testament were true both in
their proper, historical sense and in their prefigurative, typological
sense. Yet the temporal validity of the Old Testament remained limited;
with the temple in Jerusalem destroyed, continued literal observance of
Mosaic law was meaningless and, with regard to God's plan for human
salvation, essentially irrelevant.[15]

What, if anything, had changed in Augustine's teaching? Augustine
had hinted in the De vera religione that the history of the heavenly city
in pre-Christian times corresponded to that of the Jewish people. Anti-
Christian fallout from the debacle of 410 now induced Augustine to
highlight the superiority and independence of this sacred history,
against the culture of its earthly counterpart; and, alongside the motifs
of his earlier works, the De civitate Dei therefore blends several positive
elements into its otherwise negative portrayal of the Jews. Especially
during the period of the Old Testament, the Hebrews stood out as the
first monotheists: Their prophets, their wisdom, and their written language were the most ancient; the contents of their Scripture were indisputably authentic and free of contradiction; and, contrary to charges
that the Jews had falsified them, the textual traditions of the Hebrew
Bible are reliable even now.[16] Expanding upon the earlier suggestion
of the De vera religione, Augustine instructed: "The adversaries of
the City of God, belonging to Babylon," may well include "the Israelites according to the flesh, the earth-born citizens of the earthly Jerusalem";[17] but earthly Israel and Jerusalem nonetheless symbolize the
heavenly city.[18] Through the Hebrew people, "through some who were
knowledgeable and some who were ignorant, there was foretold what
would occur from the advent of Christ until the present, as it continues
to transpire."[19] Had the Jews not sinned repeatedly against God, and

---

15. For instance, Augustine, De civitate Dei 15.2, 16.26, 16.37, 17.18.

16. Ibid. 15.11ff., 18.38ff. This stance, however, did not obviate Augustine's general
preference for the readings of the Septuagint; see Bernhard Blumenkranz, Die Judenpredigt Augustins (Basel, 1946), pp. 74–84, esp. pp. 79–82, and the many citations adduced
therein. See also the more recent study of William Adler, "The Jews as Falsifiers: Charges
of Tendentious Emendation in Anti-Jewish Christian Polemic," in Translation of Scripture (Philadelphia, 1990), pp. 1–27.

17. Augustine, De civitate Dei 17.4, CCSL 48:557.

18. Ibid. 15.2; and see the important analysis of F. Edward Cranz, "De civitate Dei,
XV,2, and Augustine's Idea of the Christian Society," Speculum 25 (1950), 215–25.

19. Augustine, De civitate Dei 7.32, CCSL 47:213.

had they not, ultimately, put Jesus to death, independence, dominion, and Jerusalem would still be theirs.[20] And though the biblical Ishmael, the disinherited older son of the patriarch Abraham, typifies the synagogue in its relationship with God, Augustine did not disqualify the Jews from God's blessing of Abraham's children altogether:

> Isaac is the law and prophecy; Christ is blessed in these even through the mouth of the Jews, just as if he were blessed by one who does not know him, since they do not understand the law and prophecy. . . . The nations serve him; the princes adore him. He is lord over his brother, since his people rules the Jews. . . . He who has cursed him is accursed; and *he who has blessed him is blessed. Our Christ, I say, is blessed—that is, he is truly mentioned—even by the mouths of the Jews, who, although they err, nonetheless chant the law and the prophets.* (They think they are blessing another [messiah], whom they await in their error.)[21]

Despite their misguided intentions and their outcast state, the Jews bless Christ and, almost despite themselves, they are thus recipients of divine blessing as well. For all their iniquity and misunderstanding, Augustine allotted the Jews a distinctive function and character in God's plan for human history and salvation, a role that extended from the period of the Old Testament into that of the New. This is his acclaimed doctrine of Jewish witness to the truth of Christianity, the innovative feature of Augustinian anti-Judaism par excellence, which the De civitate Dei elaborates with clarity and emphasis:

> Yet the Jews who slew him and chose not to believe in him . . . , having been vanquished rather pathetically by the Romans, completely deprived of their kingdom (where foreigners were already ruling over them), and scattered throughout the world (so that they are not lacking anywhere), are testimony for us through their own scriptures that we have not contrived the prophecies concerning Christ. . . . Hence, when they do not believe our scriptures, their own, which they read blindly, are thus fulfilled in them. . . . For we realize that on account of this testimony, which they unwillingly provide for us by having and by preserving these books, they are scattered among all the nations, wherever the church of Christ extends itself.[22]

Within the De civitate Dei's more nuanced exposition of the early stages in the history of salvation, and not simply in support of the figurative exegesis of the Bible that dominated the Contra Faustum, Augustine here reoriented and sharpened several ideas of his earlier,

20. Ibid. 4.34.
21. Ibid. 16.37, CCSL 48:542 (emphasis mine).
22. Ibid. 18.46, p. 644.

anti-Manichean treatise: The Jews survive as living testimony to the antiquity of the Christian promise, while their enslavement and dispersion confirm that the church has displaced them. Yet here, in the *De civitate Dei,* Augustine added significantly to the substance of his earlier formulation:

> For there is a prophecy given previously in the Psalms (which they still read) concerning this, where it is written . . . : "Slay them not, lest at any time they forget your law [*legem tuam*]; scatter them in your might."[23] God thus demonstrated to the church the grace of his mercy upon his enemies the Jews, because, as the Apostle says, "Their offense is the salvation of the Gentiles." Therefore, he did not kill them—that is, he did not make them cease living as Jews, although conquered and oppressed by the Romans— lest, having forgotten the law of God, they not be able to provide testimony on our behalf in this matter of our present concern. Thus it was inadequate for him to say, "Slay them not, lest at any time they forget your law," without adding "scatter them." For if they were not everywhere, but solely in their own land with this testimony of the scriptures, the church, which is everywhere, could surely not have them among all the nations as witnesses to the prophecies given previously regarding Christ.[24]

The *De civitate Dei* does not suffice with explicating the phenomenon of Jewish survival as the fulfillment of divine prophecy. It interprets the divine prophecy of Jewish survival as a mandate for the faithful: Slay them not, that is, ensure their survival and that of their Old Testament observance; and scatter them, guaranteeing that the conditions of their survival demonstrate the gravity of their error and the reality of their punishment.

We shall soon return to a review of Augustine's pronouncements concerning the benefits of continued Jewish survival and their proper implications for Christian policymakers. It remains for us first to consider

---

23. Psalm 59:12, according to the numeration of the Masoretic Text, which I have followed throughout in direct references to the Bible. The reading of *legem tuam* follows some Greek versions (*nomoû tou*), which evidently underlay the Old Latin version of Augustine; the Masoretic Text, the received versions of the Septuagint, and the Vulgate all read "my people ['*ammi, laoû mou, populi mei*]." Jerome also encountered a Latin reading of *populi tui*; see his *Epistula* 106.33, CSEL 55:263–64: "*Ne occidas eos, ne quando obliviscantur populi tui.* Pro quo in Graeco scriptum est: *legis tuae*; sed in Septuaginta et in Hebraeo non habet *populi tui*, sed *populi mei*; et a nobis ita versum est." Cf. also Origen, *Hexapla*, ed. Fridericus Field (1875; reprint Hildesheim, Germany, 1964), 2:187; and the various Latin readings reviewed by Amnon Linder, review [in Hebrew] of Shlomo Simonsohn, *Ha-Kes ha-Qadosh veha-Yehudim*, in *Zion*, n.s. 61 (1996), 484–85.

24. Augustine, *De civitate Dei* 18.46, CCSL 48:644–45.

Augustine's sole work dedicated explicitly to anti-Jewish polemic, the brief *Tractatus adversus Iudaeos* (Treatise against the Jews), evidently composed during the final years of his life (ca. 429),[25] containing little that is new or distinctive. This sermon first discusses the Pauline doctrine of the inversion of Jews and Gentiles in the divine plan for salvation, noting that the Jews still refuse to acknowledge the Christological import of biblical testimonies. Despite the Jewish claim that Christianity has forsaken the teachings of the Old Testament, it has, in fact, fulfilled them; because Christians now obey the law in its spiritual sense, its literal observances have been rendered obsolete—"not because they have been damned but because they have been changed; not that the things, which themselves used to be signified, might perish, but in order that the signs of these things might suit their times."[26] In support of these claims, the *Tractatus* presents a Christological interpretation of the three Psalms (45, 69, 80) entitled "for the things that shall be changed"—*pro iis quae immutabuntur* or *commutabuntur*—a misreading of the Hebrew *shoshannim* (lit. lilies), perhaps for *shinnuyim*, changes.[27] Echoing earlier etymologies, Augustine concluded that the Jews are not "the true Israel, that is, that which will see the Lord face to face."[28] These changes wrought in the economy of salvation, Augustine maintained, demand that the Jews be confronted with the more evident (*apertioribus*) biblical testimonies. "Why do the Jews not realize that they have stayed put in useless antiquity [*in vetustate supervacanea*], rather than object to us, who hold the new promises, that we do not observe the old?"[29] The *Tractatus* then adduces an array of additional, oft-quoted biblical texts to present to the Jews, in the hope

25. The *Tractatus* receives no mention in Augustine's *Retractationes*, composed during the last years of his life.

26. Augustine, *Tractatus adversus Iudaeos* 3.4, PL 42:53.

27. Or perhaps, as Ivan Marcus has suggested to me, for *sheshonim*, referring to those that differ, and also from the same verbal root, *sh-n-h*. Cf. the Septuagint's *hypèr tōn alloiōthēsoménōn*.

28. Augustine, *Tractatus adversus Iudaeos* 5.6, col. 55. On Philonic, early Christian, and rabbinic use of this motif, see Gerhard Delling, "The 'One Who Sees God' in Philo," in *Nourished with Peace: Studies in Hellenistic Judaism in Memory of Samuel Sandmel*, ed. Frederick E. Greenspahn et al., Scholars Press Homage Series 9 (Chico, Calif., 1984), pp. 27–41; Jonathan Z. Smith, "The Prayer of Joseph," in *Religions in Antiquity: Essays in Memory of Erwin Ramsdell Goodenough*, ed. Jacob Neusner, Studies in the History of Religions (Supplements to *Numen*) 20 (Leiden, Netherlands, 1968), pp. 265–68 with nn.; and Elliot R. Wolfson, *Through a Speculum That Shines: Vision and Imagination in Medieval Jewish Mysticism* (Princeton, N.J., 1994), esp. chap. 1.

29. Augustine, *Tractatus adversus Iudaeos* 6.8, col. 56.

that they may see the light and convert, or that they may at least be convicted of their error.[30] Once again, Augustine instructed on the function of the Jew in a properly ordered Christian world—here in a rhetorical query addressed, as it were, to the Jews themselves: "Do you not rather belong to the enemies of him who states in the Psalm, 'My God has shown me concerning my enemies, slay them not, lest at any time they forget your law; scatter them in your might'? Wherefore, not forgetting the law of God but transporting it as testimony for the Gentiles and a disgrace for yourselves, unknowingly you furnish it to that people called from the rising of the sun to its setting."[31]

THE DOCTRINE OF WITNESS:
COMPONENTS AND CHRONOLOGY

This brief survey of Augustine's developing thought on the Jews yields several preliminary conclusions: First, Augustine deviated relatively little from previous apostolic and patristic teaching on the subject. Second, Augustine formulated that which distinguished him from his predecessors, his doctrine of Jewish witness, prior to and independently of his sole, specifically anti-Jewish work, the *Tractatus adversus Iudaeos*. And third, Augustine's distinctive interpretation of Jewish history appeared to hinge upon more basic themes of Augustinian theology.

Owing to the impact of Augustine on subsequent generations in the history of Christian-Jewish relations, this doctrine of Jewish witness warrants careful review and analysis. One can profitably distinguish between six distinct arguments which typically fortify Augustine's view that the Jews have a valuable function in Christendom and that Christians must therefore permit them to live and to practice their Judaism.

    1.   The survival of the Jews, scattered in exile from their land and oppressed into servitude, testifies to their punishment for rejecting (and crucifying) Jesus and to the reward of faithful Christians by contrast. The image of the murderous, exiled Cain can serve as the prototype of the Jewish people in this respect.

30. Ibid. 1.2, 6.8, 10.15.
31. Ibid. 7.9, col. 57.

2. Not only does the survival of the Jews thus confirm the truth of Christianity, but their blindness and disbelief also fulfill biblical predictions of their repudiation and replacement.

3. Prefigured by the biblical Ham, the Jews are enslaved within Christendom; carrying and preserving the books of the Old Testament wherever they go, they offer proof to all peoples that Christians have not forged biblical prophecies concerning Jesus. Jews accordingly serve Christians as guardians (*custodes*) of their books, librarians (*librarii*), desks (*scriniaria*), and servants who carry the books of their master's children to school (*capsarii*) but must wait outside during class.[32] Much like those who helped to build Noah's ark but perished in the flood,[33] they "appear with regard to the Holy Scripture that they carry much as the face of a blind man appears in a mirror; by others it is seen, but by himself it is not seen."[34] As history unfolds in its path toward salvation, "the Jews inform the traveler, like milestones along the route, while themselves remaining senseless and immobile."[35]

4. The Jews provide such corroborating testimony not only in their books but also in their continued compliance with biblical law. Their steadfast refusal to abandon their distinctive religious identity (*forma Iudaeorum*)[36] beneath the oppression of Gentile rulers, especially those of Rome, has proven admirable and valuable.

5. The words of Psalm 59:12, "Slay them not, lest at any time they forget your law; scatter them in your might," constitute a prophetic policy-statement on the appropriate treatment of the Jews in Christendom. Slaying the Jews, thus prohibited, refers above all to preventing their observance of Judaism, and not simply to their physical liquidation.

6. Hand in hand with Jewish survival, the refutation of Judaism contributes directly to the vindication of Christianity. Paradoxically,

---

32. For Augustine's various similes, see: "custodes librorum nostrorum," *Sermo* 5.5, CCSL 41:56; "librarii nostri," *Enarrationes in Psalmos* 56.9, CCSL 39:700; and "capsarii nostri," ibid. 40.14, 38:459. See also Augustine's explanation that "servi, quando eunt in auditorium domini ipsorum, portant post illos codices et foris sedent" (*Sermo* 5.5, CCSL 41:56).

33. Augustine, *Sermo* 373.4.4, admittedly of doubtful authorship.

34. Augustine, *Enarrationes in Psalmos* 56.9, CCSL 39:700. On the mirror and mirror images in Augustinian thought, see Karl F. Morrison, " 'From Form into Form': Mimesis and Personality in Augustine's Historical Thought," *Proceedings of the American Philosophical Society* 124 (1980), esp. p. 292.

35. Augustine, *Sermo* 199.1.2, PL 38:1027.

36. Augustine, *Enarrationes in Psalmos* 58.2.2, CCSL 39:746.

such a mandate for anti-Jewish polemic hardly bespeaks an urgency for effective Christian missionizing among the Jews. In keeping with the teachings of Paul, their conversion will come in due course; meanwhile, the worth of their service as witness and foil outweighs the disadvantage of their living as infidels among believers.

These arguments are blatantly interconnected, but not all of them appear together in every formulation of the doctrine of witness. A chronological review of the Augustinian corpus[37] reveals that, despite the importance attributed to Jewish history in Augustine's early works, like the *De Genesi contra Manichaeos* and *De vera religione*, the doctrine of witness is absent. It made its earliest partial appearances at the end of the fourth century, first in *Contra Faustum* and then in *De consensu evangelistarum* (On the Agreement of the Evangelists, ca. 400);[38] these works include the first three of the six arguments listed above—the testimonial value of Jewish survival in exile, of Jewish disbelief, and of Jewish books—and they begin to hint at the fourth—the value of Jewish persistence in the practice of Judaism. Yet, although they note the loyalty of the Jews to their law, Augustine's works of this period do not evaluate Jewish behavior in the positive terms of his later writings; nor do they understand God's protection of the Jews from extinction metaphorically, in terms of observance of the biblical commandments. Albeit with approval, Jewish survival is *described*, within the framework of biblical typology (for example, Cain or Ham), rather than *preached* as a matter of policy. Significantly, these texts make no mention of Psalm 59:12. They shy away from acknowledging postponement of the hope for the conversion of the Jews. And they include no deliberate mandate for anti-Jewish polemic.

Only in the middle of the second decade of the fifth century did developments in Augustine's teaching begin to bring his doctrine of Jewish witness to its mature formulations, those that bore most dramatically on medieval Christian attitudes toward Jews and Judaism. In

37. On the chronology of Augustine's works, in both the discussion and the table that follow, see, among others, Peter Brown, *Augustine of Hippo: A Biography* (London, 1967); Johannes Quasten et al., *Patrology* (Westminster, Md., 1986), 4:355ff.; A. Kunzelmann, "Die Chronologie der Sermones des hl. Augustinus," in *Miscellanea agostiniana* (Rome, 1930–31), 2:417–520; and Henri Rondet, "Essais sur la chronologie des 'Enarrationes in Psalmos' de Saint Augustin," *Bulletin de littérature ecclésiastique* 61 (1960), 111–27; 65 (1964), 120–36; 68 (1967), 180–202; 71 (1970), 174–200; 77 (1976), 99–118.

38. See Augustine, *Contra Faustum*, cited above, nn. 8ff., and *De consensu evangelistarum* 1.14.22, 1.26.40.

his exposition of Psalm 59 (ca. 414), Augustine included the fifth element of his doctrine on the list above, discerning in the psalm explicit instruction for the proper treatment of the Jewish people in a Christian world: "Slay them not, lest at any time they forget your law; scatter them in your might." No longer was Jewish survival simply to be explained, after the fact, with reference to the typological significance of Cain and/or Ham. Augustine's later works present the continued existence of the Jews, given the service they perform, as the object of the psalmist's outspoken prophecy in its own right.[39] Curiously, Cain and Ham no longer figure in three such late considerations of the value of Jewish survival: in *De civitate Dei* 18 (420–425),[40] *De fide rerum invisibilium* (On Faith in Things Unseen, 420–425),[41] and *Tractatus adversus Iudaeos* (ca. 429).[42] The *De civitate Dei* itself deals strictly with the historical sense of the story of Cain and Abel, not with its prophetic allegory, and it refers the reader seeking a typological exposition to the *Contra Faustum*.[43] As he explained in the *De fide rerum invisibilium*, Augustine beheld in the principle of "Slay them not," not the allegorical fulfillment of the Old Testament, but practical guidelines for the implementation of the new order:

> Therefore it was made to happen that they would not be eradicated so as to have their sect completely cease to exist. But it was dispersed throughout the world, so that, carrying the prophecies of grace bestowed upon us in order to convince the infidels more effectively, it would benefit us everywhere. And this very point which I am stating—accept [*accipite*] it, inasmuch as it had been prophesied: "Slay them not," he said, "lest at any time they forget your law; scatter them in your might." Therefore they have not been killed in this sense, namely, that they have not forgotten those things which used to be read and heard among them. For if they were to forget the holy scriptures entirely (even though they do not now understand them), they would be undone in the Jewish rite itself, be-

---

39. Augustine, *Enarrationes in Psalmos* 58, esp. 58.1.15–58.2.11, CCSL 39:740–753. 58.1.19 ends with the exhortation, "Quid hic respondebit infelix Pelagius," indicating that the commentary could not date from much before 414, when Augustine became actively involved in the Pelagian controversy. See Rondet, "Essais sur la chronologie," pp. 180–82; and Elizabeth A. Clark, *The Origenist Controversy: The Cultural Construction of an Early Christian Debate* (Princeton, N.J., 1992), p. 232 and n. 307.

40. See above, at nn. 22, 24.

41. On the dating of this work, see the comments of M. P. J. Van den Hout, CCSL 46:lx–lxi, who finds distinctive parallels between the *De fide rerum invisibilium* and *De civitate Dei* 18.

42. See above, n. 31.

43. See below, n. 94.

cause, if they would know nothing of the law and the prophets, the Jews could be of no benefit.[44]

Beyond admonishing Christians to accept the dictates of Psalm 59, Augustine here clarified in unequivocal terms the fourth element in his doctrine of Jewish witness: that precisely their practice and knowledge of biblical law and prophecy afforded the Jews a valuable function in Christendom. Consequently, Augustine's later works interpret the mandate for Jewish survival to apply above all to the Jews' observance of their commandments—not merely to their physical protection, which had concerned Augustine in the *Contra Faustum*.[45] And, owing to this value of Jewish religious observance, Augustine now cast the Jews in somewhat praiseworthy terms, despite their grave theological error. As Augustine explained the prophecy of Psalm 59:12 to Bishop Paulinus of Nola in 414,

> That same nation, even after being conquered and subjugated, would not participate in the pagan rites of the victorious people but persisted in the old law, so that within it [the Jewish people] there would be witness of the Scriptures throughout the world, wherever the church would be established. For by no clearer proof is it demonstrated to the nations what is observed most advantageously—that the name of Christ is distinguished by such great authority in the hope for eternal salvation, not as a sudden contrivance, conceived by the spirit of human presumption; rather, it had been prophesied and recorded previously. . . . Therefore "slay them not"; do not destroy the name of that nation, "lest at any time they forget your law"—which would surely happen if, having been forced to observe the rites and ceremonies of the gentiles, they would not retain their own religious identity at all.[46]

Finally, only in these later works did Augustine enunciate the sixth element in his doctrine of Jewish witness: its implications for attracting the Jews to Christianity and for what might well be termed the "polemical imperative" of the patristic *Adversus Iudaeos* tradition. Despite his call for the survival of Judaism, Augustine did not abandon the Pauline hope for the conversion of the Jews; instead, he was willing to postpone its fulfillment to the distant future. Expounding Psalm 59, he

---

44. Augustine, *De fide rerum invisibilium* 6.9, CCSL 46:16.

45. See also Augustine, *Enarrationes in Psalmos* 58.1.21, CSEL 39:744; and contrast *Contra Faustum* 12.12, CSEL 25:341: "non corporali morte interibit genus inpium carnalium Iudaeorum."

46. Augustine, *Epistula* 149.9, CSEL 44:356; cf. *De civitate Dei* 7.32, and *Enarrationes in Psalmos* 58.2.2.

thus explained that only in the wake of their salutary dispersion (verse
12, *disperge eos in virtute tua*) would the Jews convert at the proverbial
evening of time, suffering humiliation like dogs (verse 15, *convertentur
ad vesperam et famem patientur ut canes*); joining ranks with the uncircumcised (*illi de circumcisione, isti de praeputio*), they would flock
to the church—yielding exultation in God's mercy in the succeeding
morning (verse 17, *exsultabo mane misericordia tua*) of salvation.[47]
Augustine well understood the compromise that his policy entailed, and
he could evenhandedly assess the resulting benefits and liabilities, as he
did in the *De fide rerum invisibilium:* "Therefore they have not been
killed but scattered, so that, although they lack the means to be saved
through faith, they still keep in their memory that whereby we might
profit—in their words our opponents, in their books our partisans, in
their hearts our enemies, in their codices our witnesses."[48] Notwithstanding such preservation of the Jews without faith or the means to
salvation, their testimonial function mandated the citation of their own
Bible against them, in order to validate the beliefs of Christianity. In
the *Tractatus adversus Iudaeos*, Augustine called repeatedly for anti-
Jewish polemic independent of any mission to the Jews, entirely in the
interest of Christendom: "But when these [biblical testimonies] are re-
cited to the Jews, they despise the Gospel and the apostle; and they do
not hear what we say, because they do not understand what they read.
. . . Therefore [*ergo*], testimonies should be taken from the holy scriptures, whose authority is very great among them, too; if they refuse to
be restored by the benefit which they offer, they can be convicted [*convinci*] by their blatant truth."[49] Why ought Christians to cite Scripture
to the Jews, knowing that their plaints will fall on deaf ears? The logic
of Augustine's prescription may seem puzzling: The Jew does not heed
the testimony of the Bible; therefore, read it to him! Yet construed and
preserved as Augustine would have him, fixed "in useless antiquity,"
the Jew served as a foil for Augustine's apologetic and as fuel for the
discourse of his patristic theology. (See the chronology of Augustine's
arguments as outlined in Table 1).

---

47. Augustine, *Enarratio in Psalmos* 58.2.2–10, CCSL 39:746–52. See also *De civitate Dei* 20.29–30, and *Tractatus adversus Iudaeos* 5.6.

48. Augustine, *De fide rerum invisibilium* 6.9, CCSL 46:16.

49. Augustine, *Tractatus adversus Iudaeos* 1.2, PL 42:51–52; see also 6.8 (col. 56),
"sive consentient sive dissentiant," and 10.15 (cols. 63–64), "sive gratanter, sive indig-
nanter audiant Judaei."

TABLE I

ELEMENTS OF THE AUGUSTINIAN DOCTRINE OF JEWISH WITNESS: A CHRONOLOGY OF NOTEWORTHY TEXTS

1. Jewish survival in exile marks punishment for rejection of Jesus (prefigured by Cain)
2. Jewish blindness and disbelief confirm biblical prophecy
3. Jews carry their books in servitude to the church, testifying to prophecies of Christianity, refuting charges of forgery (prefigured by Ham)
4. Jews' perseverance in religious observance (despite Gentile/Roman conquest) is of testimonial value, praiseworthy
5. Psalm 59:12, "Slay them not"; Christians must let Jews live as Jews
6. Jews must be refuted in proof of Christianity, even without admission of defeat or conversion (hope for which thus postponed)

	Date	1	2	3	4	5	6
Contra Faustum	397	+	+	+	+/-ᵃ		
Sermo 200	393–405			+			
De consensu evangelistarum	400	+		+	+/-		
Enarr. in psalm. 56	395–408	+	+	+			
Sermo 202	405–11			+			
Enarr. in psalm. 40	400–410			+			
Sermo 5	410–19	+		+			
Epist. 137	411–12	+		+			
Enarr. in psalm. 136	412			+			
Enarr. in psalm. 58	413–15	+		+	+	+	+
Epist. 149	414	+		+	+	+	
De civitate Dei	414–25	+		+	+	+	+/-
Contra duas epist. Pelagianorum	420			+			
De fide rerum invisibilium	420–25	+	+	+		+	+/-
Tract. adv. Iudaeos	429–30	+	+	+		+	+

ᵃ +/- less than fully explicit

JEW, TEXT, EVENT, AND BODY

Recognizing the contributions of other investigators to an appreciation of the doctrine of Jewish witness,[50] we can now move forward to a

50. Above all, see Bernhard Blumenkranz, *Die Judenpredigt*, and "Augustin et les Juifs, Augustin et le Judaïsme," *Recherches augustiniennes* 1 (1958), 225–41; Marcel Dubois, "Jews, Judaism and Israel in the Theology of Saint Augustine: How He Links the Jewish People and the Land of Zion," *Immanuel* 22/23 (1989), 162–214; and Paula Fredriksen, "*Excaecati occulta justitia Dei:* Augustine on Jews and Judaism," *Journal of Early Christian Studies* 3 (1995), 299–324, and "Divine Justice and Human Freedom: Augustine on Jews and Judaism, 392–398," in *FWW*, pp. 29–54. I have discussed the

deeper appreciation of Augustine's constructions of Jews and Judaism. At the outset, one must refrain from attributing these Augustinian perceptions to direct, personal interaction between the bishop of Hippo and the Jews of his day. Evidence of Jewish settlement in northern Africa during the late imperial period allows only inconclusive estimations of the size and vitality of specific Jewish communities. Various studies of this question, in fact, reason circularly, relying predominantly on the limited evidence provided by Augustine himself.[51] Jewish communities clearly existed in numerous North African locations, but no good indication of their size or significance exists; one highly doubts that Augustine beheld the sort of Jewry encountered by John Chrysostom in late-fourth-century Antioch or by Cyril of Alexandria in early-fifth-century Egypt.[52] Nor can one simply stipulate a direct link between the proselytizing activity of Jews and the Judaizing tendencies of Christians. The available data may suggest that Augustine should have known and dealt with practicing Jews,[53] but his dealings with them undoubtedly lacked the intensity and dangers experienced by John and Cyril. Augustine's own writings confirm this impression. Although they reveal some actual contact with contemporary Jews, much more clearly do they document the limitations of Augustine's familiarity with the Jewish community and with Judaism. Augustine knew an occasional word of Hebrew at most. His allusions to the particulars of Jewish

---

contributions of these three scholars at greater length in Jeremy Cohen, "'Slay Them Not': Augustine and the Jews in Modern Scholarship," *Medieval Encounters* 4 (1998), 78–92.

51. See, among others, Paul Monceaux, "Les Colonies juives dans l'Afrique romaine," *REJ* 44 (1902), 1–28; Jean Juster, *Les Juifs dans l'Empire romain: Leur condition juridique, économique et sociale* (Paris, 1914), 1:207–9; H. Z. Hirschberg, *A History of the Jews in North Africa: From Antiquity to Our Time* [Hebrew] (Jerusalem, 1965), 1:51–54; and Marcel Simon, *Verus Israel: A Study of the Relations between Christians and Jews in the Roman Empire (135–425)*, trans. H. McKeating (New York, 1986), pp. 331–33.

52. See Yann le Bohec, "Inscriptions juives et judaïsantes de l'Afrique romaine," *Antiquités africaines* 17 (1981), 165–207, and "Juifs et judaïsants dans l'Afrique romaine: Remarques onomastiques," ibid., pp. 209–29. And cf. Robert L. Wilken, *Judaism and the Early Christian Mind: A Study of Cyril of Alexandria's Exegesis and Theology* (New Haven, Conn., 1971), and *John Chrysostom and the Jews: Rhetoric and Reality in the Late 4th Century* (Berkeley, Calif., 1983); and Wayne A. Meeks and Robert L. Wilken, *Jews and Christians in Antioch in the First Four Centuries of the Common Era*, Society for Biblical Literature, Sources for Biblical Study 13 (Missoula, Mont., 1978).

53. Recently, see Helmut Castritius, "*Seid weder den Juden noch den Heiden noch der Gemeinde Gottes ein Ärgernis* (1. Kor. 10,32): Zur sozialen und rechtlichen Stellen der Juden im spätrömischen Nordafrika," in *Antisemitismus und jüdischen Geschichte: Studien zu Ehren von Herbert A. Strauss*, ed. Rainer Erb et al. (Berlin, 1987), pp. 47–67; and le Bohec, "Inscriptions juives," p. 203.

religious practice are so few and so unimpressive that one cannot jus-
tifiably conclude that they derived from personal experience. Augustine
acknowledged that his estimation of the reliability of the Jewish texts
of Scripture stemmed from hearsay. If some of the unnamed individuals
who assisted Augustine in understanding the Old Testament were Jewish, he owed the overwhelming preponderance of his knowledge of
postbiblical Jewish tradition to other patristic writers, most notably
Jerome.[54] Augustine's laments over the continued refusal of the Jews
to accept Christianity—typically contrasted with the more successful
attraction of Jews to the church in apostolic times—fail to indicate that
they resulted from any personal disappointment in missionary activity.[55] Most of the strictures against Judaizing in the Augustinian corpus
appear in lists of unacceptable practices in Christian life, hardly establishing that Augustine deemed such behavior a clear and present danger
in his community.[56]

Rather, the doctrine of Jewish witness took shape against the backdrop of several major themes in Augustine's theology and writings: the
interpretation of the Old Testament, especially Genesis; the appraisal
of terrestrial history; and the assessment of human sexuality.[57] Relating
to the Jews in varying degrees, these central concerns of Augustine
clearly overshadowed his inclination to anti-Jewish polemic. They
ranked much higher on his theologian's agenda, and, to the extent that

54. See Blumenkranz, *Die Judenpredigt*, pp. 59–74, with nn. to numerous passages
in the Augustinian corpus.

55. See the passages cited ibid., pp. 110–12.

56. Even Augustine's frequently cited *Epistula* 196 to Bishop Asellicus, which contains Augustine's most extensive attack on Judaizing Christians, manifests little sense of
urgency. The letter notes at the outset that it originated at the insistence of a third bishop,
Donatian, that Augustine formulate such a position. And until its concluding paragraph
(16, CSEL 57:229), the letter makes no mention of a specific threat to the contemporary
church; only then does it refer to one Aptus (otherwise unknown to Augustine) who,
Asellicus wrote, "is teaching Christians to Judaize and thus . . . calls himself Jew and
Israelite so that he might forbid them [non-kosher] foods." Nowhere does Augustine's
letter inveigh against the Jews of his day as the root of such evil within the church.
Recent scholarly investigations minimize the extent to which Jews of the imperial period
engaged in missionary activity; see Shaye J. D. Cohen, "Was Judaism in Antiquity a
Missionary Religion?" in *Jewish Assimilation, Acculturation, and Accommodation: Past
Traditions, Current Issues, and Future Prospects*, ed. Menachem Mor, Creighton Uni-
versity Studies in Jewish Civilization 2 (Lanham, Md., 1992), pp. 14–23; and Martin
Goodman, *Mission and Conversion: Proselytizing in the Religious History of the Roman
Empire* (Oxford, 1994), chap. 6. Cf., however, the differing views of Louis H. Feldman,
Jew and Gentile in the Ancient World (Princeton, N.J., 1993), esp. chap. 11.

57. Karl F. Morrison has drawn a similar connection in *"I Am You": The Hermeneutics of Empathy in Western Literature, Theology, and Art* (Princeton, N.J., 1988),
pp. 81–97; see also his "'From Form into Form.'"

he did take an interest in the Jews and Judaism, they controlled the nature and the extent of that interest. I shall first consider these Augustinian concerns individually and then evaluate their significance for our story.

BIBLICAL EXEGESIS

Early in his career as a biblical commentator, in his *De Genesi contra Manichaeos*, Augustine distinguished between the literal or carnal meaning of the sacred text and its spiritual or allegorical sense; the literal sense understands Scripture exactly as "the letter sounds"; the allegorical, the figures or enigmas the letter contains. Significantly, Augustine did not yet equate this contrast with another one: that between history, which relates events of the past, and prophecy, which foretells those of the future. In this early Augustinian schema, one may interpret both history and prophecy either literally or allegorically. History and prophecy, in other words, denote the chronological orientation—or orientations—perceived in the narrative, whether or not, in the case of history, the narrated events actually transpired. Literal and allegorical refer to disparate levels of meaning sought by the reader in the text—as in the Jews' literal or carnal observance of the Sabbath, which contrasts with its allegorical understanding by Christians.[58] Here, in his first Genesis commentary, Augustine interpreted the opening chapters of Scripture chiefly in their figurative, allegorical sense,[59] though he considered them both as history and as prophecy and, in retrospect, he later regretted his inability adequately to expound on their literal sense.[60]

The independence of Augustine's distinctions between literal and allegorical, on one hand, and history and prophecy, on the other hand, was short-lived. Within several years of his first commentary on Genesis, Augustine returned to the interpretation of the biblical cosmogony in his *De Genesi ad litteram liber imperfectus* (An Unfinished Book on the Literal Interpretation of Genesis, ca. 393), in which he listed a

---

58. Augustine, *De Genesi contra Manichaeos* 2.2.3, PL 34:197: "Secundum litteram accipere, id est non aliter intelligere quam littera sonat." Augustine alludes to a carnal understanding of Sabbath observance in 1.22.33, col. 189; cf. G. Folliet, "La Typologie du *Sabbat* chez Saint Augustin: Son interprétation millénariste entre 389 et 400," *REA* 2 (1956), 371–90.

59. See Augustine, *Retractiones* 1.9.

60. Augustine, *De Genesi ad litteram* 8.2, CSEL 28,1:232–33, citing *De Genesi contra Manichaeos* 2.2.3.

fourfold scheme of biblical interpretation: "according to history, according to allegory, according to analogy, according to etiology. It is history when past deeds (of God or of humans) are recorded; allegory, when statements are understood figuratively; analogy, when the congruence of old and new testaments is demonstrated; etiology, when the causes of statements and deeds are related."[61] The particulars of this passage and its context—an avowedly literal commentary on Scripture—appear to signal some change in Augustine's hermeneutic. One cannot help but infer a measure of opposition between history and allegory; although the definition of history—the narration of events—remains the same as in *De Genesi contra Manichaeos*, its differentiation from allegory suggests a link between the historical and the nonallegorical—namely, the literal. No longer did Augustine allow for the possibility of nonfactual history; that is, a narrative about the past relating events that never, in fact, occurred. And Augustine's inclusion of much figurative interpretation—that is, *not* exactly the "the letter sounds"—in a commentary he entitled *On the Literal Interpretation of Genesis* hints further that he wished to reevaluate the essence of the literal sense. Nevertheless, if Augustine harbored the intention of definitively identifying the historical with the literal in the early 390s, it remained unfulfilled for quite some time. This first rendition of his literal Genesis commentary was admittedly *imperfectus*, a failed attempt abandoned prior to its conclusion.

Perhaps this failure derived directly from Augustine's inability to define and to capture the literal, nonfigurative understanding of the

---

61. Augustine, *De Genesi ad litteram liber imperfectus* 2, CSEL 28,1:461. To avoid unnecessary confusion, I have relegated an intervening development in Augustine's exegetical theory to this note. In *De utilitate credendi* (On the Utility of Believing, 391) 3.5, CSEL 25:7–8, Augustine distinguished between history, a record of things past—whether or not they have actually occurred—and allegory, a figurative, rather than literal, exegesis. To these he added two more modes of interpreting the Old Testament: etiology, that which explains the cause of an event or statement; and analogy, that which clarifies the correspondence between Old and New Testaments. At this point, however, even though history and allegory appear in the same list, they are not yet cast as opposites; for a historical passage may well relate that which never happened, "quid non gestum, sed tantummodo scriptum quasi gestum sit." See also Robert A. Markus, *Saeculum: History and Society in the Theology of St Augustine* (1970; reprint, Cambridge, England, 1988), pp. 188–89 with nn., who argues that Augustine, at this early stage in his career, differentiated both between history and prophecy as "two kinds of texts" and between historical and prophetic "kinds of exposition" (as in the *De Genesi contra Manichaeos* above). According to Markus, within two years the *De Genesi ad litteram liber imperfectus* manifested a convergence of these two distinctions.

Bible that he had hoped to convey; and, until the turn of the century, at least, his interpretation of the Old Testament remained over-whelmingly figurative.[62] The first books of the *De doctrina christiana* (On Christian Doctrine), which Augustine wrote in 397, boldly sub-ordinate the literal meaning of Scripture to its allegorical sense, inas-much as "there is no reason for us to signify, that is, to give a sign, if not to draw forth and transmit to the mind of another that which transpires in the mind which gives the sign."[63] Provided that one in-terprets Scripture so as to enhance his Catholic faith, the grounding of the interpretation in the concrete reality of the sign—that is, the de-pendence of a figurative reading upon the literal meaning of the text—matters relatively little. In fact, "a person supported by faith, hope, and charity so that he retains them resolutely does not need the scrip-tures except for teaching others,"[64] whereas "he who honors or ven-erates some signifier while ignorant of what it signifies is enslaved to the sign."[65] Not the plain meaning of the biblical text but the doc-trine—and unity—of the church serves as ultimate arbiter in the rec-onciliation of ambiguities,[66] because the Bible "asserts only the Catholic faith in matters past, future, and present."[67] Despite the attribution of value to Mosaic law in the historicizing typology of the *Contra Faus-tum*, it too belittles the value of the literal sense in its own right. Many provisions of the law—for instance, the uncleanliness of nonkosher animals—can be understood only figuratively;[68] Augustine pointed out that Philo the Jew himself recognized that much in the Old Testament,

---

62. The steadfastness of this Augustinian orientation has been instructively consid-ered by Joanne McWilliam, "Weaving the Strands Together: A Decade in Augustine's Eucharistic Theology," in *Collectanea augustiniana: Mélanges T. J. van Bavel*, ed. Ber-nard Brunig et al., Bibliotheca Ephemeridum theologiarum lovaniensium 92 (Louvain, Belgium, 1990), 2:497–506.

63. Augustine, *De doctrina christiana* 2.2.3, ed. and trans. R. P. H. Green (Oxford, 1995), pp. 56–59 (with departures from Green's translations).

64. Ibid. 1.39.43, pp. 52–53.

65. Ibid. 3.9.13, pp. 144–47. In 3.6.10, Augustine explained that the Jews were somewhat better off than pagans in this regard; though the Jews were so enslaved, their servitude was to God, and thus pleasing to him whom they could not behold.

66. Ibid. 3.2.2, p. 132: "Cum ergo adhibita intentio incertum esse perviderit quo-modo distinguendum aut quomodo pronuntiandum sit, consulat regulam fidei, quam de scripturarum planioribus locis et ecclesiae auctoritate percepit." See also the insightful analysis of Michael A. Signer, "From Theory to Practice: The *De doctrina christiana* and the Exegesis of Andrew of St. Victor," in *Reading and Wisdom: The De doctrina chris-tiana of Augustine in the Middle Ages*, ed. Edward D. English (Notre Dame, Ind., 1995), esp. pp. 85–89.

67. Augustine, *De doctrina christiana* 3.10.15, pp. 148–49.

68. Augustine, *Contra Faustum* 6.7.

when understood literally, casts "the disgrace of ridiculous fables" on books of divine authorship, and he resorted to allegory as a result.[69] Therefore,

> one should not believe that there is anything narrated in the prophetical books which does not signify something in the future—except things placed so as to explain those matters which foretell of that king [Christ] and his people, whether through literal or figurative speech and deeds. For, just as in harps and other such musical instruments, not all things which are touched resonate with sounds, only the strings; the other parts of the entire body of the harp have been fashioned in such a way that those [strings], which the musician will strike to create a pleasant sound, may be appropriately fastened and stretched. So too in these prophetic narratives, those matters of human history selected by the prophetic spirit either relate things of the past because they signify the future or, if they signify no such thing, are interspersed so as to connect those matters which do resound with such significance.[70]

The predetermined doctrinal lessons of Scripture's allegorical sense, which may not contradict Catholic belief, impose limits on the literal, although the literal sense hardly controls the use of the allegorical.

Scholars have noted instructive links and parallels between the educationally oriented hermeneutic of the *De doctrina christiana* and the introspective account of Augustine's conversion related in the *Confessiones* (Confessions, 397–400). In Peter Brown's words, "Augustine's attitude to allegory summed up a whole attitude to knowledge" in the *De doctrina christiana*; in the *Confessiones*, this attitude to allegory provided Augustine with the basis for knowledge of himself.[71] Composed in the immediate aftermath of the *De doctrina christiana* and the *Contra Faustum*, the *Confessiones* thus continues to employ the nonliteralist, figurative hermeneutic that dominates Augustine's fourth-century compositions. Contrasting well with statements of Augustine's later career, it follows the lead of the earlier Genesis commentaries in its symbolic interpretation of the creation story. As Augustine wrote in the final pages of the *Confessiones*, the opening verses of Genesis, in their instruction to man and woman to "be fertile and increase," jus-

69. Ibid. 12.39, CSEL 25:365.
70. Ibid. 22.94, p. 701.
71. Brown, *Augustine of Hippo*, pp. 253, 260ff. Among many other works, see also James J. O'Donnell, *Augustine* (Boston, 1985), pp. 81ff.; and Robert W. Bernard, "The Rhetoric of God in the Figurative Exegesis of Augustine," in *Biblical Hermeneutics in Historical Perspective: Studies in Honor of Karlfried Froelich on His Sixtieth Birthday*, ed. Mark S. Burrows and Paul Rorem (Grand Rapids, Mich., 1991), pp. 88–99.

tified the very principle of allegorical exegesis: "I perceive in this blessing the capacity and power granted us by you, both to express in numerous ways what we may have understood in a single way, and to
understand in numerous ways that which we may have read, expressed
only in one obscure fashion."[72]

Only as he approached the second decade of the fifth century,[73] with
the account of his own spiritual awakening behind him, did Augustine
finally nurture the literal dimension of his hermeneutic to its maturity—
again with regard to the opening chapters of Genesis—in his massive
De Genesi ad litteram (On the Literal Interpretation of Genesis). Early
in this commentary, Augustine explained his new exegetical approach
by rejecting an allegorical understanding of Genesis 1:5 (in its Old
Latin translation: "evening was made, and morning was made, one
day"); namely, "that in 'evening was made' is signified the sin of the
rational creature and that in 'morning was made' is signified its restoration. But this is an argument of prophetic allegory—which we have
not undertaken in this treatise. For we have now endeavored to speak
of the scriptures according to the proper sense of past events, not according to the mysteries of future ones."[74] In this programmatic statement, Augustine has overcome the distance between the two contrasts—literal versus allegorical, on one hand, and history versus
prophecy, on the other—that characterized his earlier work. The literal
interpretation of the biblical past, the goal of the *De Genesi ad litteram*,
is now equated with the historical truth of the biblical narrative and
concerns "the proper sense of past events"; allegorical or prophetic
interpretation alludes to "the mysteries of future ones." Yet if literal
and allegorical also refer to chronological orientation in the interpretation of biblical narrative, not merely to the degree that such inter-

72. Augustine, *Confessiones* 13.24, CCSL 27:263–64.

73. As Signer, "From Theory to Practice," pp. 88–89, has observed, the exegetical
orientation of books 2 and 3 of *De doctrina christiana* found additional expression in
Augustine's *Epistula* 71 of 403 to Jerome, criticizing the latter's reliance on the Hebrew
original of the Old Testament. In Signer's words, "Augustine's basis for interpreting
Scripture is ecclesiastical unity and consensus. Part of this process seems to be the exclusion of the Jews from the process of consultation. From the perspective of the *DDC*
the Jews are restricted to a single language and are ignorant of appropriate hermeneutical
rules. Within the perspective of Augustine's letter, they are perverse and sow confusion
in Christian communities"—a far cry, it would seem, from Augustine's subsequent portrayal of the Jew as valuable witness wherever Christianity might spread.

74. Augustine, *De Genesi ad litteram* 1.17, CSEL 28,1:24–25. Augustine renders the
Latin of Genesis: "et facta est vespera, et factum est mane dies unus." On the dating of
this work, see below, n. 102.

pretation focuses either on the sign (exactly as "the letter sounds") or on what it signifies ("figuratively and in enigmas"),[75] how is the "literal" sense genuinely plain or literal? Augustine responded that the literal meaning of Scripture denotes first and foremost the intention of the "writer of the sacred books";[76] accordingly, "when we read the divine books amidst so great a number of true interpretations, which are . . . fortified with the sanity of the Catholic faith, let us emphatically choose that one which clearly manifests what he (whom we are reading) intended."[77] One must immediately take note that this criterion of authorial intention hardly precludes the "literal" understanding of the Bible's language as metaphorical. For example: The first light of creation, understood literally, refers simultaneously to earthly light and spiritual light;[78] God made man, but had Scripture related that he formed him with bodily hands, "we ought sooner to believe that the writer used a metaphor";[79] even though Scripture's report that the eyes of Adam and Eve were opened (Genesis 3:7) after their sin does not mean that they were previously closed, these words "we ought not to consider an allegorical narrative."[80] Such metaphoric interpretations of past events fall well within the realm of the literal sense, because the author clearly intended them. "The narrative in these books [like Genesis] is certainly not of the genre of figurative speech like that in the Song of Songs, but of a completely historical genre, like that in the books of Kings and others of this sort."[81]

The precise change that the De Genesi ad litteram marked in Augustine's hermeneutical outlook warrants further qualification. Despite the allegorical emphasis of his earlier Old Testament exegesis, Augustine had already affirmed the reality and importance both of the literal sense and of the exposition of biblical narrative as history. Yet the unabashed identification of the literal with the historical that one en-

---

75. Cf. Augustine, De Genesi ad Manichaeos 2.2.3, cited above, n. 58.
76. Augustine, De Genesi ad litteram 1.19, CSEL 28,1:28.
77. Ibid. 1.21, p. 31.
78. Ibid. 4.28.
79. Ibid. 6.12, p. 185; cf. the similar argument of Moses Maimonides, Guide of the Perplexed 2.25.
80. Augustine, De Genesi ad litteram 11.31, p. 364.
81. Ibid. 8.1, p. 229. See Bertrand de Margerie, Introduction à l'histoire de l'exégèse, 3: Saint Augustin (Paris, 1983), chap. 2, on Augustine's allowance for multiple meanings within the literal sense itself, which, however, ought not to be confused with the coexistence of literal and figurative meanings in the same biblical passage (e.g., De Genesi ad litteram 8.4, 8.7).

counters in the *De Genesi ad litteram* underscores the priority of the "literal" sense for Augustine. Although "no Christian will dare say that events should not be interpreted figuratively,"[82] literal interpretation now takes precedence. It commandeers the lion's share of Augustine's exegetical energy, and it engages him well beyond his previously acknowledged need to establish the historical reality upon which Christological allegory and typology depend. Even in the case of the paschal lamb, so critically important a prefiguration of the crucified Jesus, Augustine acknowledged the exegete's mandate first to accept and to define Scripture's literal, historical meaning:

> He [Christ] is the sheep which is sacrificed on the Passover; yet that was prefigured not only in speech but also in action. For it is not that that sheep was not a sheep; it clearly was a sheep, and it was killed and eaten. Something else was prefigured in this actual fact, though not like that fattened calf which was slain for the banquet of the younger son when he returned [Luke 15:11–32]. In that latter case the narrative itself consists of figures, not of events with figurative significance. For the Lord himself, not the evangelist, narrated this. . . . The narrative of the Lord himself was a parable, in which it is never required that the things conveyed in speech be shown to have literally occurred.[83]

In the case of narrative *intended* by the biblical writer as history, however, the factual event must be expounded first, and, as John Hammond Taylor has observed, its exposition commands Augustine's definite preference. When considering the account of Adam and Eve in Paradise, the *De Genesi ad litteram* first contrasts the figurative discourse of Scripture (*locutio figuratarum rerum*) with its exposition in a literal sense (*ad litteram*), then such a figurative exposition (*figurate*) with a rightful or proper one (*proprie*), and finally the allegorical understanding of the text (*secundum allegoricam locutionem*) with its rightful one (*secundum propriam*). In short, figurative and allegorical contrast with

---

82. Ibid. 1.1, p. 1.
83. Ibid. 8.4, p. 236. It is instructive to compare these comments of Augustine with those of Nicholas of Lyra centuries later, who identified the Christological significance of the paschal lamb as primary within the intention of the biblical author. See Nicholas's *Postilla litteralis* ad Exodus 12:1, 13:10, in *Biblia sacra cum glossis, interlineari, et ordinaria, Nicolai Lyrani postilla, ac moralitatibus, Burgensis additionibus, et Thoringi replicis* (Venice, 1588), 1:145F–146B, 150GH. See also Jeremy Cohen, "Scholarship and Intolerance in the Medieval Academy: The Study and Evaluation of Judaism in European Christendom," *AHR* 91 (1986), 610 and n. 49; and Herman Hailperin, *Rashi and the Christian Scholars* (Pittsburgh, Pa., 1963), esp. pp. 184–91.

literal and proper.[84] Gone is the license that Augustine had previously allowed the Catholic reader of the Bible in the early books of the *De doctrina christiana*; there, as long as an interpretation accords with the doctrine of the church, anything goes.[85] Here, in the *De Genesi ad litteram*, the objectively determined historical facts take precedence, and only when the intention of the author remains indeterminable may the exegete reach a conclusion based on faith alone. A Christian must believe that Christian faith will comport with the literal meaning of Scripture:

> If those irrationally impelled by reason of a stubborn or dull mind refuse to believe these things [in Genesis], they still can find no reason to prove that they are false. . . . Clearly, if those things rendered here in a material sense could in no way be accepted in a material sense and the true faith yet preserved, what other option would remain but that we understand those things as spoken figuratively, rather than impiously to condemn Holy Scripture? Yet if these things understood in a material sense not only do not impede but defend the narrative of divine eloquence more effectively, there will be no one, I think, so unfaithfully stubborn as to see those things expounded in their proper sense according to the rule of faith and yet prefer to remain in his former opinion (if perchance they had seemed to him open to figurative interpretation alone).[86]

In direct contrast to the *De Genesi ad Manichaeos*, Augustine's literal commentary accordingly seeks to show how everything in Genesis is to be understood primarily not in the figurative but in the proper sense.[87] Owing to Christianity's axiomatic identification of Judaism with the literal interpretation of the Bible, I shall argue below, Augustine's increasingly positive inclination to a literalist hermeneutic undoubtedly nourished the development of his conception of the Jews.

84. Augustine, *De Genesi ad litteram* 8.1–8.2, pp. 231–33; Augustine, *The Literal Meaning of Genesis*, trans. John Hammond Taylor, Ancient Christian Writers 41–42 (New York, 1982), 2:253–54 n. 9.
85. I would argue that Augustine's treatment of Tyconius's rules and the subject of curriculum late in the third (30.42–37.56) and fourth books of the *De doctrina christiana*—those portions of the work composed ca. 426–427—bespeaks increased recognition of a need for systematic regimen in Christian hermeneutic and accords well with the exegetical shift I am delineating. Cf. Augustine's *Retractiones* 2.4.1, CSEL 36:136; and, for a survey of the major issues and scholarly viewpoints, Eugene Kevane, "Augustine's *De doctrina christiana*: A Treatise on Christian Education," *Recherches augustiniennes* 4 (1966), esp. 103–12.
86. Augustine, *De Genesi ad litteram* 8.1, pp. 231–32; cf. 1.21, and, again, the parallel argument of Maimonides, *Guide of the Perplexed* 2.25, 2.30.
87. Augustine, *De Genesi ad litteram* 8.2, p. 233; see also above, n. 84.

TERRESTRIAL HISTORY

The social historian Robert Nisbet has deemed the historical ideas of
the *De civitate Dei* a veritable cornerstone of the Western idea of progress: "Reality for Augustine lay in the unitary human race and its
progress toward fulfillment of all that was good in its being."[88] Like
his biblical hermeneutic, however, Augustine's valuation of thisworldly
human experience developed over time; the two concerns influenced
one another considerably.

Although commonly agreeing that Augustine's philosophy of history
changed considerably during the course of his adult life, scholars of the
last half-century have struggled to define precisely when, how, and
why. Some forty years ago, F. Edward Cranz linked a major shift in
this dimension of Augustine's doctrine to his changing ideas on divine
justice and human freedom, on grace and human will.[89] Late in the
380s, in the *De Genesi contra Manichaeos* and the *De vera religione*,
Augustine translated Platonic notions of the gradual process whereby
the human soul achieves philosophical perfection into his sevenfold
schema of humanity's spiritual development throughout earthly history. During the next decade, however, as Augustine retreated from his
belief in a human's ability to will faith in God, he replaced the seven
ages of history with a fourfold division that emphasized the radical
disjunction between epochs and the absolute dependence on divine
grace: before the law, under the law, under grace, and the perfect peace
of the final redemption (*ante legem, sub lege, sub gratia, in pace*). Especially in the wake of the *Ad Simplicianum* (To Simplicianus, 396),
Augustine's earlier sense of innate progress in human spiritual history
gave way to a quintessential contrast between the damned and the
saved, which ruled out the possibility for any secular or political experience, even the Christianization of Rome, to serve as the vehicle for
salvation. This comported well, Cranz maintained, with Tyconius's assertion of identity between Old and New Testaments, which Augustine
now adopted: There is a single principle of salvation, not a series of
grades that an individual—or the entire human race—ascends in turn.
A stark opposition between unredeemed and redeemed, which deprived
the Jewish past of the significance that it had had in Augustine's earlier

---

88. Robert Nisbet, *History of the Idea of Progress* (New York, 1980), p. 64.
89. F. Edward Cranz, "The Development of Augustine's Ideas on Society before the
Donatist Controversy," *HTR* 47 (1954), 255–316.

notion of seven ages, now facilitated his two-tiered interpretation of human history in the *De civitate Dei*.[90]

Much in Cranz's argument may prove correct, but his claim that Augustine's new understanding of the human condition devalued the historical importance of the Jews hardly comports with a careful review of the Augustinian corpus. Only at the end of the 390s did Augustine begin to elaborate the unique, testimonial function of the Jews in sacred history, and only in his later works—the *De civitate Dei*, for example— did the doctrine of Jewish witness achieve its full expression.[91] I therefore believe that an alternative appraisal of Augustine's historical thought by the historian Robert Markus proves more instructive for the present discussion.

Focusing above all on the *De civitate Dei*, Markus has singled out two key features of the older Augustine's philosophy of history: On one hand, Augustine posited a sharp, qualitative distinction between sacred and profane history, which emerged after years of contemplating

90. Cf. Johannes van Oort, *Jerusalem and Babylon: A Study into Augustine's City of God and the Sources of His Doctrine of the Two Cities*, Supplements to *Vigiliae christianae* 14 (Leiden, Netherlands, 1991), esp. pp. 108ff., 159–60, who argues—contra both Cranz and Markus, discussed below—that the opposition between the two cities pervaded Augustine's historical thought from early in his career and underwent little essential change. See also the helpful study of A. Lauras and Henri Rondet, "Le Thème des deux cités dans l'oeuvre de Saint Augustin," in *Études augustiniennes*, Théologie 28 (Paris, 1953), pp. 99–160.

91. See Cranz's "*De civitate Dei*, XV,2." Cranz's theory presents additional difficulties as well. First, Augustine did not completely discard his sevenfold periodization of history in the wake of the *Ad Simplicianum*, but he invoked it even in later works which Cranz adduced as exemplifying his new outlook on grace—from the *Contra Faustum* 12.8 and *De catechizandis rudibus* (On Catechizing the Uninstructed, 399–400) 22.39, to the *De civitate Dei* 22.30. Cf. additional citations in Luneau, *L'Histoire du salut*, pp. 289–90, Archambault, "Ages of Man," pp. 205–6, and van Oort, *Jerusalem and Babylon*, pp. 94ff. Regarding the passages cited here, I find it difficult to agree completely with Cranz, "Development of Augustine's Ideas," p. 279 (cf. also Luneau, *L'Histoire du salut*, p. 380), that "the context of gradual progress is dropped, and while Augustine continues to make use of the six ages, the Old Testament periods serve merely as convenient chronological divisions." On the idea of historical progress, see also Nisbet, *History of the Idea of Progress*, pp. 54ff. Second, the historical-philosophical ramifications of this new outlook on grace do not appear to have pointed directly toward the ideas of the *De civitate Dei*, which refuses to associate the conversion of Rome's emperors with the fulfillment of Christian history. On the contrary, the *Contra Faustum*, which Cranz deemed particularly indicative of Augustine's changed perceptions, finds vindication for the doctrine of the church in "these very kings of the earth, now gainfully subjected to the rule of Christ" (13.7, CSEL 25:385; and cf. 22.60). Indeed, according to the *Contra Faustum*, actualizing the psalmist's messianic prophecy that "'all kings of the earth shall bow to him, all nations shall serve him' (Psalm 72:11), Christian emperors, placing the complete trust of their piety in Christ, have triumphed most gloriously over his sacrilegious enemies, who placed their hope in the worship of idols and demons" (22.76, p. 676).

the human condition, from a limitation of sacred history to that recounted by the divinely inspired authors of Scripture, and in the wake
of the sacking of Rome by the Visigoths in 410. The Augustinian
theology of disjunction between the realms of sacred and profane, Markus has demonstrated, first received clear-cut expression during the second decade of the fifth century. On the other hand, although Augustine
denied Christian Rome ultimate significance in his scheme of salvation
history, he likewise rejected the apocalyptic equation of Rome with the
evil Babylon. Rather, he reconciled the contemporary alliance of church
and empire as reflecting the imperfections of the *saeculum*, the locus
of interpenetration of heavenly and earthly cities—none other than the
present, pre-eschatological world that enshrines the essential ambiguities of human experience:

> At the most fundamental level, that of their ultimate allegiance, men were
> starkly divided between the two cities. But the *saeculum*, and the societies,
> groups and institutions whose careers constitute it, embraced both poles of
> the dichotomy. . . . To speak of the *saeculum* as the region of overlap be-
> tween the heavenly and earthly cities, while true, is misleading if understood
> in terms of the logical notion of an overlap between two mutually not
> exclusive classes. For in their eschatological reality the two cities are, of
> course, mutually exclusive, while in their temporal reality they are indistinct:
> here the primary *datum* for Augustine is the integrity of the *saeculum*, or,
> more precisely, of the social structures and historical forms in which it is
> embodied. . . . All we can know is that the two cities are always present in
> any historical society; but we can never . . . identify the *locus* of either.[92]

Augustine thus refused to view even the Christian church of his age as
perfect or to identify it with the heavenly city. By the same token,
however, he could hardly dismiss the structures of society and the
events of terrestrial history as profane and worthless. Inasmuch as the
eschaton has yet to materialize, these social structures and historical
events constitute the framework for the experiences of both cities. They
are, in a word, all there is. Citizens of the heavenly city must therefore
work to uphold the institutions of the saeculum, their imperfection
notwithstanding, just as they yearn for liberation from them.

Markus's model of the saeculum as a key to the older Augustine's
understanding of history informs an appreciation of the doctrine of
Jewish witness on several grounds. Augustine elaborated both ideas

---

92. Markus, *Saeculum*, pp. 101–2. Cf. also the insightfully nuanced discussion
in John M. Rist, *Augustine: Ancient Thought Baptized* (Cambridge, England, 1994),
chap. 6.

during the last two decades of his life, and the chronology hints at further parallels between the two. Among these, the paradoxical ambiguity that characterizes the institutions of the saeculum, and the resulting responsibility of God's saints to function at once in two contradictory realms,[93] will prove helpful in understanding the distinctive historical mission that Augustine assigned to the Jews. No less important, first expressions of the ideas of the saeculum coincided with the completion of the *De Genesi ad litteram*. For as Augustine had fallen back from allegorical and typological exegesis to embrace a more literalist hermeneutic, he necessarily took increased interest in the history of this world; indeed, the proper, literal truth of biblical narrative and the historical events of biblical antiquity were one and the same. When the *De civitate Dei* portrayed Cain as the founder of the earthly city, it deliberately avoided his typological prefiguration of the Jews that had allowed the younger Augustine to explain their survival; in the midst of a lengthy historical assessment of the primordial fratricide, Augustine now wrote: "Such was the founder of the earthly city—in which manner he also prefigured the Jews, by whom Christ the shepherd of humans (whom Abel the shepherd of livestock prefigured) was killed. Yet because this concerns prophetic allegory, I refrain from expounding it now; and I remember that in this regard I argued certain things against Faustus the Manichean."[94] The contrast between the standard patristic Cain of the *Contra Faustum* and the realistic portrayal he receives in the *De civitate Dei* is striking; as Peter Brown has suggested, "it is like coming from the unearthly symbolic figures of Type and Antetype that face each other in the stained-glass windows along the walls of a Gothic cathedral, to the charged humanity of a religious painting by Rembrandt."[95] Augustine's exegesis and historical philosophy evidently developed in tandem, endowing his writing with new life and conviction. Not by happenstance did a retreat from the typology of Cain in rationalizing the doctrine of Jewish witness accompany the emergence of Augustine's unconventional exegesis of Psalm 59:12 ("Slay them not").[96]

---

93. See the more recent—and compelling—discussion in Robert A. Markus, *The End of Ancient Christianity* (Cambridge, England, 1990), chaps. 4–5.

94. Augustine, *De civitate Dei* 15.7, CCSL 48:462.

95. Brown, *Augustine of Hippo*, p. 321.

96. See also above, n. 43; and Peter Brown, "St. Augustine's Attitude to Religious Coercion." *Journal of Roman Studies* 54 (1964), 107–16, on connections in Augustinian doctrine between exegesis, historiosophy, and those outside the Catholic Church.

HUMAN SEXUALITY

Augustine's new regard for the concrete realities of human experience surfaced in yet another cluster of his favorite subjects: the human body, sex, and sinful concupiscence. It is most instructive to note the convergence of scriptural exegesis, chiefly that of Genesis, and the investigation of human history within the evolving Augustinian doctrine on the sexual nature of human beings.

In an earlier study I analyzed Augustine's maturing interpretation of God's primordial blessing to human beings (Genesis 1:28), "Be fertile and increase, fill the earth and master it," as an index of developments in his estimation of human sexuality, noting the correspondence between these developments and the changing character of his biblical hermeneutic.[97] The *De Genesi contra Manichaeos* asks of this verse, "Should it be construed in a physical sense [*carnaliter*] or in a spiritual sense [*spiritualiter*]?"; and it responds straightforwardly, "Indeed, we can rightly understand it in a spiritual sense."[98] Not only does the *Confessiones* maintain an allegorical interpretation of Genesis 1:28, but, as I noted above, it views this primordial blessing of human sexuality as scriptural support for the entire enterprise of figurative exegesis.[99] As Verna Harrison has argued in another context, ascetic renunciation—which figures so prominently in the *Confessiones*—and allegorical exegesis truly go hand in hand: "The interpretive move from letter to spiritual meaning directly parallels the ascetic's transfer of attention and desire from material to spiritual realities."[100] But when, in his final years, Augustine reflected upon the shortcomings of the *De Genesi contra Manichaeos*, he turned directly to "Be fertile and increase" to demonstrate the inadequacies of this avowedly allegorical hermeneutic. To his earlier refusal to allow that God had intended a

---

97. Jeremy Cohen, *"Be Fertile and Increase, Fill the Earth and Master It": The Ancient and Medieval Career of a Biblical Text* (Ithaca, N.Y., 1989), pp. 245–59 with nn.; cf. also Elizabeth A. Clark, "Heresy, Asceticism, Adam, and Eve: Interpretations of Genesis 1–3 in the Later Latin Fathers," in *Ascetic Piety and Women's Faith: Essays on Late Ancient Christianity,* by Elizabeth A. Clark, Studies in Women and Religion 20 (Lewiston, N.Y., 1986), pp. 363–73, David G. Hunter, "Resistance to the Virginal Ideal in Late-Fourth-Century Rome: The Case of Jovinian," *Theological Studies* 48 (1987), 45–64, Peter Brown, *The Body and Society: Men, Women and Sexual Renunciation in Early Christianity* (New York, 1988), chap. 19, and Markus, *End of Ancient Christianity,* pp. 57–62.

98. Augustine, *De Genesi contra Manichaeos* 1.19.30, PL 34:187.

99. See above, n. 72.

100. Verna F. Harrison, "Allegory and Asceticism in Gregory of Nyssa," *Semeia* 57 (1992), 113–30.

mandate for sexual reproduction in Paradise, he now replied, "I do not at all agree."[101] Corresponding to crossroads in the unfolding of his exegetical and historical ideas, this reversal in Augustine's appreciation of human sexuality began to appear in the aftermath of the *Confessiones*, and it received its first clear-cut expression in the ninth book of the *De Genesi ad litteram*. Only toward the end of his commentary, in one of the last chapters to be written, did Augustine proceed with absolute certainty, daring to label as ridiculous (*ridiculum istuc est*) the earlier patristic view that Adam and Eve were not yet ready for sexual activity and that their unauthorized sexual union amounted to theft from the symbolic fruit of the tree of knowledge.[102] Once again, the new outlook found its place in the great synthesis of *De civitate Dei*:

> We have no doubt whatsoever that, in accordance with the blessing of God, to be fertile and increase and fill the earth is the gift of marriage, which God established originally, prior to human sin, creating male and female, which sexual quality is indeed evident in the flesh. . . . Although all of these things can appropriately be given a spiritual meaning, masculine and feminine cannot be understood [as Augustine had understood them in the *De Genesi contra Manichaeos*][103] as a simile for characteristics of the same individual human being, one of whose attributes being that which rules, another that which is ruled. But inasmuch as it is most clearly evident in the different sexual characteristics of the body, it would be very absurd to deny that male and female were created for the purpose of producing offspring, that they might be fertile and increase and fill the earth.[104]

Sexual desire and reproductive activity, held Augustine, pertain to human nature not only after the fall from Paradise but also in the state of grace that preceded the fall.

If dramatic shifts in Augustine's opinions on exegesis and sexuality occurred at the same stage of his career and bore directly upon one another[105] so too must one appreciate the appropriateness of human

101. Augustine, *Retractiones* 1.9.3, CSEL 36:48–49.
102. Augustine, *De Genesi ad litteram* 11.41.57, CSEL 28,1:376. P. Agaësse and A. Solignac, in their edition of Augustine, *La Genèse au sens littéral*, Oeuvres de Saint Augustin 48–49 (Paris, 1972), 1:28–31, contend that Augustine probably wrote books 1–9 of *De Genesi ad litteram* by 410, and almost certainly by 412; that he composed books 10–12 between 412 and 415; and that he hastily wrote the final chapters of book 11 just prior to the publication of the entire work. On the dating of the *De Genesi*, see also Clark, "Heresy, Asceticism, Adam, and Eve," pp. 368ff.
103. See above, n. 98.
104. Augustine, *De civitate Dei* 14.22, CCSL 48:444.
105. The intriguing view that Augustine identified rhetoric with fornication, advanced by Marjorie O'Rourke Boyle, "Augustine in the Garden of Zeus: Lust, Love, and Language," *HTR* 83 (1990), 117–39, depends primarily on citations from his earlier

sexual relationships within the historical-theoretical framework of the saeculum. Peter Brown thus appraised these first years of the fifth century as a critical transitional period in Augustine's career:

> A man whose own conversion had been prompted, in part, by the call of the desert, Augustine had come, within only ten years, to think about the Catholic Church from a viewing point deep within the structures of the settled world. . . . If the Catholic church was to remain united, it could do so only by validating Roman society. The bonds that held subjects to emperors, slaves to masters, wives to husbands, and children to parents could not be ignored, still less could they be abruptly abandoned in order to recover an "angelic" mode of life. They must, rather, be made to serve the Catholic cause.[106]

Other scholars have similarly analyzed Augustinian ideas on sexuality against the backdrop of the status of terrestrial history and institutions. Margaret Miles advocated "the thesis that Augustine's development in these areas moves from the tendency to view the body as the ground of existential alienation to affirmation of the whole person."[107] She concluded that Augustine's later writings, "while apparently focusing on sexuality, actually use the issue as the testing ground for other issues: the power and the authority of the church and the question of whether the church will be the bastion of intellectual specialists or a layman's church."[108] More recently, Robert Markus concurred that human sexuality afforded Augustine singular insight into both the glory and the misery of the fallen human condition. Genesis commentary proved a benchmark for the progress of Augustine's thought on all of these issues; in keeping with Augustine's distinctive notion of the saeculum, "a rehabilitation of the flesh" stood at the foundation of "a defence of Christian mediocrity."[109] No doubt the best evidence for this argument remains Augustine himself, who paid tribute to the divine

---

works (i.e., *Confessiones* and prior); this comports with my earlier suggestion (above, n. 85) that the guidelines for Christian rhetoric and eloquence outlined in the fourth book of *De doctrina christiana* befit a later stage in the development of Augustinian doctrine, when human speech, history, and sexuality are valued more highly than previously. On similar issues, cf. also Eugene Vance, "Saint Augustine: Language as Temporality," in *Mimesis: From Mirror to Method, Augustine to Descartes*, ed. John D. Lyons and Stephen G. Nichols Jr. (Hanover, N.H., 1982), pp. 20–35, 251–52, and "Augustine's Confessions and the Poetics of the Law," *Modern Language Notes* 93 (1978), 618–34.

106. Brown, *Body and Society*, pp. 398–99. See also the interesting study of Hunter, "Resistance to the Virginal Ideal," esp. p. 64.

107. Margaret Ruth Miles, *Augustine on the Body*, American Academy of Religion Dissertation Series 31 (Missoula, Mont., 1979), p. 7.

108. Ibid. pp. 76–77.

109. Markus, *End of Ancient Christianity*, chap. 4, esp. pp. 45, 57–62.

blessing of human sexuality as the *De civitate Dei* neared the crescendo of its conclusion: "That blessing which he had conveyed before the sin, stating 'Be fertile and increase and fill the earth,' he did not wish to withhold even after the sin, and the fecundity thereby granted has remained in the condemned species. The guilt of sin could not remove the wonderful power of the seed—and even more wondrous, the power by which the seed is produced—instilled and somehow ingrained in human bodies."[110] The younger Augustine, the Augustine of the late 380s and the 390s could never have reached such a judgment. These words characterize the viewpoint of an older, more experienced Augustine, who formulated his doctrine of Jewish witness during the same stage of his life.

THE AUGUSTINIAN SENSE OF THE JEW

I have reviewed these preeminent themes in Augustinian thought at some length, because their intersection—the meeting of text, body, and concrete historical event—offers the most enlightening framework for appreciating Augustine's construction of Jews and Judaism. Not by coincidence did his most thorough formulation of this doctrine, earmarked by its appeal to Psalm 59:12, take shape during the same years as his resolute commitment to literalist exegesis, his enhanced appreciation of terrestrial history, and his more sympathetic attitude to human sexuality. How, then, did each of these trajectories in Augustinian thought intersect the doctrine of Jewish witness?

The link between Judaism and the literal interpretation of Scripture hardly requires additional demonstration. Augustine explained, repeatedly and pointedly: The Jews preserve the literal sense, they represent it, and they actually embody it—as book bearers, librarians, living signposts, and desks, who validate a Christological interpretation of the Old Testament. Unlike the "true bride of Christ," the Jew knows not the difference between letter and spirit. While precisely this blindness obviates his salvation, it simultaneously facilitates his role as witness.[111] From such a perspective, the more important the literal—that is, the original, historical—meaning of biblical narrative in the instruction of

---

110. Augustine, *De civitate Dei* 22.24, CCSL 48:846.

111. For further consideration of Augustine on Jewish blindness, see Jeremy Cohen, "The Jews as the Killers of Christ in the Latin Tradition, from Augustine to the Friars," *Traditio* 39 (1983), 8–10, 22.

Christianity, the more valuable the Jewish presence in a properly ordered Christian society.

Like the saeculum in the Augustinian philosophy of history, Augustine's Jew constitutes a paradox, a set of living contradictions. He survived the crucifixion, though he deserved to die in punishment for it;
he somehow belongs in Christendom, though he eschews Christianity;
he accompanies the church on its march through history and in its
expansion throughout the world, though he remains fixed "in useless
antiquity." This Jew pertains, at one and the same time, to two opposing realms. The *De vera religione*, recall, identifies the promise of
the Old Testament with an earthly kingdom, not a heavenly one, but
states that believers in the one God before Jesus "led the life of the
earthly man while subject to *a measure of righteousness*."[112] Augustine's literalist Jew exemplified the folly that the *De doctrina christiana*
terms "a miserable enslavement of the spirit: to take signs for things
[of consequence in themselves], to be unable to lift the eye of the mind
above the physical creature to see the eternal light"; but such error
among biblical Jews was different, Augustine noted, "since they were
subjugated to temporal things in such a way that the one God was
commended by them in everything."[113] Identifying the earthly Jerusalem prefigured by Sarah's handmaid Hagar (compare Galatians 4:21
and following) with the synagogue, the *De civitate Dei* likewise demonstrates what Gerard Caspary has termed the parameter of "concentric structures" in the Pauline and patristic exegesis of classic biblical
pairs: Granted that Hagar and Sarah, or the two cities they signify, are
opposites; yet, "a certain part of the earthly city has been rendered an
image of the heavenly city, by symbolizing not itself but the other city,
and therefore a servant [*serviens*]."[114]

Although the three Augustinian texts just cited refer primarily to

112. See above, n. 3 (emphasis mine). Admittedly, one may question how many
Israelites Augustine would have actually included in this description.

113. Augustine, *De doctrina christiana* 3.5.9–3.6.10, ed. Green, pp. 140–43.

114. Augustine, *De civitate Dei* 15.2, CCSL 48:455. And see Cranz, "*De civitate
Dei*, XV,2"; and Gerard E. Caspary, *Politics and Exegesis: Origen and the Two Swords*
(Berkeley, Calif., 1979), chap. 3 (esp. pp. 112ff., on the parameters of "ethical polari-
zation," "hierarchical subordination," "concentric structures," and "temporal precedence" in Christian hermeneutic—all of which function to "insure directionality and at
the same time protect the dialectical pair" on the Pauline exegetical circle). On the singularity of Hagar's dual status as *image* of the earthly Jerusalem, which, in imaging the
heavenly city, renders her the *image of an image* as well, see also Jill Robbins, *Prodigal
Son / Elder Brother: Interpretation and Alterity in Augustine, Petrarch, Kafka, and Levinas* (Chicago, 1991), pp. 8ff.

pre-Christian times, the *De civitate Dei* proceeds to extend the enigmatic status of the Jews into the present age of the church. Sugges-
tively, Augustine's account of the annals of the heavenly city on earth
breaks off with the establishment of Christianity. Inasmuch as "since
the coming of Christ, until the end of the world, all history is homo-
geneous,"[115] one may not construe contemporary political events as
the essence of God's plan for human redemption, and they command
minimal attention in the Augustinian review of sacred history. In this
vein, the passage of the *De civitate Dei* that records the life and death
of Jesus and elaborates the doctrine of Jewish witness at length makes
mere mention of Augustus Caesar, that "by him the world was paci-
fied."[116] The *pax romana* may well have endowed the saeculum of the
Christian era with its defining political character; but neither its agents
nor its institutions, before or after the conversion of Constantine,
could claim membership ex officio in the heavenly city. As a result,
Augustine's magnum opus pays less attention to Roman imperial history than to the history of the Jews in their dispersion! Although they
themselves were damned, their unique, testificatory role in the divine
economy of salvation contributes to the ultimate victory of Christianity, and their history, before and after Jesus, more closely adumbrates
the direction of the earthly history of the heavenly city. Rooted in and
defined by membership in the earthly kingdom, the Jews—in their servile and testimonial capacity—nevertheless benefit the church and retain some connection to the heavenly kingdom too. Forging a link between otherwise conflicting realms, Augustine's Jews thus share in the
functional value of the saeculum, that temporary, ambiguous domain
of intersection between earthly and heavenly cities so critical to the
Augustinian worldview. Just as the sacking of Rome in 410 moved
Augustine to define Rome's purpose in Christian salvation history,
perhaps the continued existence of the Jews in a Christian age demanded rationalization—rationalization provided by the doctrine of
witness. Like the concrete events of terrestrial experience through and
from which the Christian church yearns for its final redemption, the
Jews belong to history, and yet, as signposts along the road to salvation, they point to its culmination.[117]

115. Markus, *Saeculum*, pp. 20–21.
116. Augustine, *De civitate Dei* 18.46, CCSL 48:643. See Markus, *Saeculum*, p. 52,
and van Oort, *Jerusalem and Babylon*, pp. 158–59 and n. 711.
117. Van Oort, *Jerusalem and Babylon*, esp. pp. 274ff. and 365ff., situates Jewish-
Christian traditions at the root of Augustine's doctrine of the two cities.

The same Jew who embodied—for better or for worse—the literal sense of the Bible and the material reality of earthly experience also represented a straightforward and positive appreciation of human sexuality. Biblical and rabbinic Judaism construed the divine instruction of the first parents to "be fertile and increase" not only as an obligation but also as evidence of divine election. Along with their creation in the image of God, the sexual nature of human beings situated them on a cosmic frontier of sorts, midway between angels and beasts, blessed with unique opportunity and yet encumbered by singular responsibility. In most strains of ancient Judaism, marriage, sexual reproduction, and family life constituted norms of foundational importance; they pertained directly to the rationale for all human existence on earth and, in particular, to the place of the chosen people within the divine economy of salvation.[118]

Augustine's allegorical exegesis of "Be fertile and increase" in the *De Genesi contra Manichaeos*, throughout the *Contra Faustum*, and near the end of the *Confessiones* thus comported well with disparaging references to the carnality of the Jews. Despite their presumptions to ascetic and spiritual perfection, Augustine contended that the Manicheans emulated the "impious nation of carnal Jews" and shared in the Jewish life of "carnal disorder."[119] Yet when Augustine subsequently responded to the anti-ascetic convictions of Jovinian and the Pelagians, he encountered ideas much more akin to a Jewish understanding of human nature and sexuality. Paradoxically, against these "views of a silent majority that believed as firmly as did their Jewish neighbors that God had created humanity for marriage and childbirth,"[120] Augustine evinced a more favorable appraisal of human sexuality, and he tempered his attack upon the Jews. The stereotype of

118. Among others, see Cohen, *"Be Fertile,"* and Daniel Boyarin, *Carnal Israel: Reading Sex in Talmudic Culture* (Berkeley, Calif., 1993).

119. Augustine, *Contra Faustum* 12.12–13, CSEL 25:341–43; cf. also 9.2, 12.4, 12.24, 15.2, 16.13, 16.19. As Vance, "Augustine's Confessions," p. 627, has observed, figurative exegesis entailed for Augustine "the repression of that obscure, lust-begetting, uncanny, killing letter of the Old Law and its re-vision in the New." According to Vance, pp. 631ff., the commentary on Genesis in the *Confessiones* signified for Augustine a personal re-creation and a ritual of liberation from sin. "Since the Old Law had come to dominate Augustine through the intimately related forms of an idolatrous love of letters and a passionate attachment to creation, especially to women, who, through Eve, had wreaked so much havoc in the creation, obviously only through new experiences of language and love may Augustine be redeemed from the Letter and the Law of Sin."

120. Brown, *Body and Society*, p. 401. See also Brown's enlightening discussion in "Late Antiquity," in *A History of Private Life, 1: From Pagan Rome to Byzantium*, ed. Paul Veyne (Cambridge, Mass., 1987), esp. pp. 266–67.

the carnal Jew admittedly did not disappear,[121] but anti-Jewish polemic in general—and this stereotype in particular—figure much less prominently in Augustine's later, anti-Pelagian writings than one might otherwise expect. In their focus on original sin, on the resulting impossibility of meriting salvation through the observance of the law, on the correspondingly all-important character of divine grace, and on the essential differences between old and new covenants, these treatises forego numerous opportunities to liken Pelagian error to Jewish error; the Jews are notably absent from much of the discussion. Where Augustine did allude to them more extensively, as in the *De spiritu et littera* (On the Spirit and the Letter, 412) and the *Contra duas epistulas Pelagianorum* (Against Two Letters of the Pelagians, 420–421), he avoided an overly explicit equation of that carnal mind which Paul deemed hostile to God (Romans 8:7) with the mentality of the Jews.[122] On one occasion, Augustine openly rejected the conclusion that "the law of works was in Judaism but the law of faith in Christianity" as fallacious (*fallat ista discretio*).[123] Rather than contrast Christians with Jews and heretics, as he had done repeatedly in the anti-Manichean treatises considered above, he now consistently preferred to distinguish between varieties of precepts and, more importantly, between manners of responding to God's commandments.

Why this curious shift in Augustine's appraisal of human sexuality, when, in view of the Pelagians, one might have expected a change of heart in the opposite direction? Augustine, I believe, had previously recognized that the dualistic Manicheans' strength derived in large measure from their deprecation of worldly pursuits, especially those of marriage and procreation, and he therefore interpreted "Be fertile and increase" figuratively to defend the unity of Scripture and its deity, effectively devaluing sexual reproduction. So too, to the extent that Catholic doctrine permitted, Augustine now agreed with his Pelagian opponents concerning the primordial sanctity of marriage and un-

---

121. E.g., Augustine, *Tractatus adversus Iudaeos* 7.9, PL 42:57: "Istum autem Israel scimus esse carnalem, de quo idem dicit [Apostolus], 'Videte Israel secundum carnem.' Sed ista isti non capiunt, et eo se ipsos carnales esse convincunt." Robbins, *Prodigal Son*, provides a most interesting discussion of this motif in Augustine's works in particular (esp. pp. 37ff.) and in Western literary tradition in general.

122. For example, Augustine, *De spiritu et littera* 17.29, 19:34. Augustine's closest approximation of such an equation appears in *Contra duas epistulas Pelagianorum* 3.4.9, CSEL 60:495, where faith and love are contrasted with the Jews' "earthly cupidity and carnal fear [*terrena cupiditas metusque carnalis*]."

123. Augustine, *De spiritu et littera* 13.21, CSEL 60:173.

tainted sexual desire, reading the biblical mandate for procreation literally and thereby attempting to co-opt the appeal in the stance of his
enemies.[124] Surely, one cannot write off such development in Augustinian thought to polemical opportunism; it, too, derived from a more
literalist reading of Genesis and a more positive appreciation of thisworldly existence. It also informed the doctrine of Jewish witness. Like
sex in the aftermath of the fall, the Jew exemplifies the imperfection of
the contemporary Christian world, but somehow he retains a place
within that world. He and his observance serve as living testimony—
to God's original intentions for human life and to his future plans; to
the Jews' own error and, by contrast, to the truth of the Christian faith.

In the wake of the previous patristic *Adversus Iudaeos* polemic, Augustine's doctrine of Jewish witness marked a singular development in
the history of Christian perceptions of Jews and Judaism. Contrary to
prevailing scholarly opinion, I have endeavored to demonstrate that
one should not attribute this doctrine to actual contacts that may have
transpired between Augustine and the Jews of his day. Proof of such
an explanation simply does not exist; moreover, that line of argument
exaggerates the importance of the Jews among the diverse issues that
engaged Augustine, who evidenced no deliberate intention of departing
from the consensus of his patristic predecessors in this regard. Rather,
one must appreciate the distinctive features of Augustinian anti-
Judaism as emerging from within the heart of Augustinian thought.
Changing considerations of exegesis, philosophy of history, and anthropology gradually converged, especially during the last two decades
of Augustine's career, to yield a new construction of the Jews in his
theological discourse—one that reflected and responded to the needs
of that discourse. The injunction to "slay them not, lest at any time
they forget your law," presupposed a Jew very different from the Jews
of the Roman Empire: a Jew who had remained stationary in useless
antiquity, a Jew who, in fact, never was.

Augustinian hermeneutic fashioned such a Jew nonetheless, and this

124. I have argued this at length in *"Be Fertile,"* pp. 252ff. This conclusion militates
against that of Fredriksen, *"Excaecatio occulta justitia Dei,"* pp. 323–24, who rejected
Blumenkranz's contention ("Augustin et les Juifs," p. 237) that "la polémique antijuive
est intimement liée a la polémique antihérétique." While the connection between the two
polemics may have been other than what Blumenkranz maintained, the fact remains that
Augustine's anti-Manichean and anti-Pelagian agenda had an impact on his attitude to
the Jews and that Augustine attributed to heretics a historical function not dissimilar to
that of the Jews. See the citations above, nn. 11–12.

construction had a long and colorful career. I have suggested elsewhere[125] that Augustine made a fourfold contribution to Christian anti-
Judaism in the medieval West: the recognition of a definite need for the
Jews (appropriately dispersed and subjugated) within Christian society;
the focus of Christian anti-Jewish polemic on the interpretation of the
Old Testament; the direction of such polemic to Christian and pagan—
but not to Jewish—audiences; and a lack of concern with postbiblical
Judaism. Why polemicize and missionize among the Jews if Christendom required their presence? Why concern oneself with postbiblical Judaism if the Jews, as Augustine construed them, preserved and embodied
the law of Moses and if the development of Judaism effectively stopped
on the day of Jesus' crucifixion, when the Old Testament gave way to the
New? I would now add two qualifications to this assessment of Augustine. First, earlier Christian theologians, those mentioned in the introduction to this book along with others, may have anticipated certain aspects of this "Augustinian" outlook on the Jews. Yet the doctrine of
Jewish witness was new, and it conditioned the transmission of "standard" patristic *Adversus Iudaeos* doctrine to Augustine's medieval successors. Second, just as Augustine had reformulated the ideas of the earlier fathers, so too did churchmen who followed him develop new
applications and understandings for the doctrine of witness, which
quickly assumed an independent life of its own.

With this in mind, the time has come to study the history of the
medieval Christian perception of the Jew more thoroughly. If one tends
to remember the medieval Christian posture toward the Jews and Judaism as Augustinian, that hardly means that Augustine himself would
have concurred. His profound impact on and authority among his successors meant that few could reject his teaching, but many reinterpreted
it in keeping with changing ideas and historical circumstances. The
history of the idea of the Jew as witness has much to teach us concerning the medieval Christian thinkers who inherited it—and concerning their Christianity. Although the idea unavoidably bore on the
realia of Christian-Jewish relations, my primary interest remains with
the fate of Christianity's hermeneutical Jew himself. What happened to
him as the Augustinian mind-set and historical context that had
spawned him receded into the past?

125. Cohen, *Friars and the Jews*, pp. 20–22.

PART TWO

The Augustinian Legacy in the Early Middle Ages

Adaptation, Reinterpretation, Resistance

Though Augustine's ideas conditioned Christian conceptualizations of Jews and Judaism for centuries to come, they underwent a gradual process of adaptation and reformulation that commenced almost immediately. For three prominent churchmen of the period—the Italian Pope Gregory the Great (ca. 540–604), the Spanish Archbishop Isidore of Seville (ca. 570–636), and the Frankish Archbishop Agobard of Lyons (769–840)—the Augustinian legacy could permit considerable latitude in the formulation of an ideological posture toward the Jews, and the attitudes of these men varied widely. Some investigators have preferred to understand their divergent viewpoints as gravitating between two different patristic outlooks that medieval theologians inherited from their predecessors: the intolerance of John Chrysostom, who aimed to undermine a Jewish presence in a properly ordered Christian society, and the relative tolerance of Augustine, grounded in the spirit of Paul's Epistle to the Romans, that sanctioned and ordained such a presence. Recognizing the complex ambivalence in Augustine's constructions of Jews and Judaism, however, I present the ideas of these three early medieval churchmen as rooted in his legacy, even as they departed from it in various respects. One ought not to characterize Augustine as an advocate of Jews and Judaism. The Jews per se hardly ranked high on his theological or episcopal agenda. His memorable exegesis of Psalm 59:12 entailed considerably more than "Slay them not"; as Augustine himself explained the words of the psalmist, "It was inadequate for him to say, 'Slay them not . . . ,' without adding further, 'Scatter them.'" And for all that the doctrine of Jewish witness proved innovative, Augustine never intended to stray from the mainstream of patristic tradition. Written at the end of his life, his *Tractatus adversus Iudaeos* accordingly reiterates Pauline teaching on the futility of the law and the rejection of Israel, indicts the Jews of its day for complicity in Jesus' crucifixion ("whom you in your parents led to his death"), and berates the Jews for their blindness, deafness, and violent anger (*saeviendo*).[1] Moreover, differences among them notwithstanding, Gregory, Isidore, and Agobard all acknowledged that the Jews still had a particular role to play in the Christian economy of salvation and that their function presupposed their right to exist. Much as they had crystallized for Augustine, these prelates' constructions of the Jews continued to emerge at the juncture of biblical hermeneutic, the philosophy of history, and anthropology in their respective theologies. Pursuant to his own particular context and outlook, each of these ecclesiastical leaders preserved the metaphorical significance that the Jews had found in the Augustinian corpus: as embodiments of that which is incomplete and imperfect in the present, Christian world, and as an index of that which separates this world from its final redemption.

What, then, accounts for the distinctive developments of the early Middle Ages in our story? How did Gregory, Isidore, and Agobard adapt what they had inherited from Augustine, from other church fathers, and from Roman law to the context of a rapidly changing Christian society and culture? What allowed for the sharp differences in their Jewish policies? How, for instance, did Gregory espouse a more tolerant stance vis-à-vis the Jews without ever enunciating the Augustinian exegesis of Psalm 59:12, whereas Isidore and Agobard advocated much harsher policies and yet cited patristic precedent for maintaining the Jews within Christendom?

A helpful treatment of these issues must take note of critical developments that followed the fall of the Western empire in the cultural and intellectual history of the Latin West. Though early medieval theologians may have made few original contributions to Christian doctrine and biblical exegesis, numerous scholars have observed that their worldview was narrower, that it tended to streamline complex and ambivalent conceptions of the fathers who preceded them. Robert Mar-

---

1. Augustine, *Tractatus adversus Iudaeos*, esp. 7.10, PL 42:59.

kus has suggested that this amounted to "the eclipse of the 'secular' dimension in Christians' consciousness,"[2] the decline and disappearance of the intermediate realm of the saeculum that had distinguished Augustine's own mentality and had characterized the eschatology, the time-related rituals, the sacred space of holy places, and the monasticism of fifth-century Christendom. In the wake of the fall of the Roman Empire, and especially in the ideas of Gregory the Great, Christian conceptions of the world began to divide sharply and more simplistically between the presently opposing realms of good and evil and to strive toward the ultimate resolution of such divisiveness: in society at large, in the Catholic Church, and within each and every individual. This tendency invariably bore upon the interpretation of sacred texts, the appreciation of Christian history, and the understanding of the human being. Militating against Augustine's guardedly positive valuation of non-Christian ideas and institutions in a Christian world, the new, medieval mentality undermined the literal exegesis of Scripture, just as it justified the study of classical sciences and texts solely insofar as they enhanced the understanding of Scripture. It abandoned the Augustinian bifurcation between secular and spiritual history. And it ceased to uphold Augustine's exoneration of the human body, as distinct from the soul, from the sinfulness of sexual desire. Christian interpretation of the Hebrew Bible now focused almost exclusively on its spiritual, allegorical sense. No line of demarcation between earthly and heavenly cities dominated God's plan for human history; recent political developments—the fall of the empire and the conversion of the Roman world to Christianity—might accordingly signal the imminence of the final redemption. Despite the proper subordination of one to the other, human body and soul shared in the carnality of sin. Only in concert, through disciplined self-sacrifice and divine service, could they facilitate the return of the human being to God.

What room did the new Christian mind-set leave for the Jews and Judaism? Augustine's doctrine of Jewish witness had hinged precisely on that intermediate realm of independent, albeit limited, worth that one discerned in the Bible's literal sense, in terrestrial history, and in the sexuality of the human body. At the same time as early medieval churchmen inherited the doctrine of witness, the successes of the church

2. Robert A. Markus, *The End of Ancient Christianity* (Cambridge, England, 1990), p. 17.

in eradicating paganism and suppressing dissidence detracted from the testimonial value of Judaism; along with his literal reading of Scripture, "the Jew had become redundant, except as a reminder that there were real, literal Jews and a handful of pagans still left to be converted in remote corners" of the world.[3] The return to a monistic conception of Christian history, one that drew no distinction between the politics of this world and the road to ultimate salvation, further undermined the Augustinian evaluation of the Jews. And a retreat from Augustine's focus on the goodness of nature in matters sexual and anthropological undermined yet another basis on which his ideas had suggested a didactic, constructive purpose for Judaism within Christendom.

In the big picture, one may not conclude that early medieval theologians disavowed the Augustinian doctrine of Jewish witness; we shall be exploring trends and variations in orientation that developed gradually and altered prevailing conceptions only over the course of many generations. Yet one must also acknowledge that Christian attitudes toward Jews did not remain unchanged between the time of Augustine and the High Middle Ages. Post-imperial Christendom no longer adhered to several vital presuppositions of the doctrine of Jewish witness, and this only compounded the inconsistencies and ostensive contradictions in Christian attitudes toward Jews and Judaism. Lacking Augustine's singular perspective on the saeculum, his successors found themselves heirs to a Jewish policy that did not quite comport with their medieval conceptual framework. And sharing a view of the church as a community united in the body of Christ, Gregory, Isidore, and Agobard placed considerably less emphasis on the positive role of the Jew in their midst; instead, they aspired to a world where that Jew would no longer be necessary. One can best appreciate these early medieval prelates as struggling to reconcile their Augustinian heritage with a worldview that resisted its accommodation. Gregory made no deliberate effort to confront this tension, but his ideas expressed it nonetheless; the apparent disjunction between the relatively tolerant spirit of his papal correspondence and the unhesitating anti-Judaism of his exegetical works is therefore highly instructive. Isidore avowed the implications of "Slay them not," but, in his new scheme of Christian *Heilsgeschichte,* the historical role of the Jews would soon climax in

3. Robert A. Markus, "The Jew as a Hermeneutic Device: The Inner Life of a Gregorian *Topos,*" in *Gregory the Great: A Symposium,* ed. John C. Cavadini (Notre Dame, Ind., 1995), p. 10.

an end to their presence. Agobard, too, affirmed the traditions of Pauline, Augustinian, and Gregorian moderation; yet he intimated repeatedly that the relevance of the Augustinian outlook had been compromised, and his discomfort with it heralded more ominous developments of the High and later Middle Ages.

CHAPTER 2

Gregory the Great

Between Sicut Iudaeis *and*
Adversus Iudaeos

If Augustine stood on the precipice overlooking the end of late antiquity, Pope Gregory the Great, more than any other single individual, led the Latin West into the Middle Ages. In the history of Christianity, Gregory's literary career and pontificate (590–604) mark the end of the patristic period and the entry of Roman Catholicism and its church into a patently different phase in their development. From the perspective of most medieval Christian readers of the Bible, for example, Gregory was the first of the great master-exegetes, "le premier des maîtres."[1] In matters ecclesiological, Walter Ullmann has suggested that Gregory's ideal conception of a properly ordered Christian society, his "*societas reipublicae christianae* . . . , is the prophetic vision of medieval Europe."[2] And, in the political history of the West, the complexities of Gregory's relations with Byzantium and the Germanic kingdoms of Europe depict him as having traversed a new frontier. Conscious of change and continuity in the image of Rome, and ever sensitive to the role of the church as the primary institutional heir to the Western empire, he evidently moved beyond the perception of Latin Christendom espoused by Emperor Justin-

---

1. Henri de Lubac, *Exégèse médiévale: Les Quatre Sens de l'écriture*, Théologie 41–42, 59 (Paris, 1959–64), 1, 2:537–48 (quotation on 538). See also René Wasselynck, "L'Influence de l'exégèse de S. Grégoire le Grand sur les commentaires bibliques médiévaux (viie–xiie s.)," *RTAM* 32 (1965), 157–204.

2. Walter Ullmann, *The Growth of Papal Government in the Middle Ages*, 2d ed. (New York, 1962), p. 37.

ian several decades before him—that is, as completely subject to Byzantine imperial control—but did not yet express that of Charlemagne two centuries later—that of a rightly distinct political entity.

Gregory's role as a trailblazer extends to our story as well. As one modern historian of the papacy has confirmed, "With respect to the Jews, as with everything else Pope Gregory touched, he is a founder of papal tradition, one of those great men who work for the future as they respond to the turmoil of the present collapse."[3] In the unfolding history of Jewish-Christian relations, Gregory blended Augustinian theology and principles of Roman law into policies that figured significantly in medieval canon law for centuries to come.[4] At the same time, he reformulated traditional motifs of *Adversus Iudaeos* theology in a manner that seemed to accord entirely neither with the singular features of Augustinian doctrine nor with the norms of his own administrative policy. Students of Gregory's teaching concerning the Jews have typically differentiated between the executive rulings of his papal correspondence and the doctrinal pronouncements of his biblical commentaries, as if the pope's actions diverged from his theological principles in the Jews' regard. Although I seek to harmonize the various tendencies in Gregory's outlook as much as possible, the generic distinction between correspondence and commentary provides a convenient basis for a review of his instruction.[5]

SICUT IUDAEIS

During the thirteen and one-half years of his pontificate, Gregory addressed the subject of the Jews and their communities in more than

3. Edward A. Synan, *The Popes and the Jews in the Middle Ages* (New York, 1965), p. 35.

4. Kenneth R. Stow, *Catholic Thought and Papal Jewry Policy, 1555–1593*, Moreshet: Studies in Jewish History, Literature and Thought 5 (New York, 1976), p. xix and n. 12; Walter Pakter, *Medieval Canon Law and the Jews*, Münchener Universitätsschriften—Juristische Fakultät—Abhandlungen zur Rechtswissenschaftlichen Grundlagenforschung 68 (Ebelsbach, Germany 1988), pp. 62 n.75, 91ff.; and Gilbert Dahan, *Les Intellectuels chrétiens et les Juifs au Moyen Âge* (Paris, 1990), pp. 137ff. (esp. with n. 4). For a revisionist view of Gregory's Jewish policy, to be cited again below, see Ernst Baltrusch, "Gregor der Grosse und sein Verhältnis zum römischen Recht am Beispiel seiner Politik gegenüber den Juden," *Historische Zeitschrift* 259 (1994), 39–58.

5. Previous treatments of Gregory and the Jews include Solomon Katz, "Pope Gregory the Great and the Jews," *JQR*, n.s. 24 (1933–34), 111–36; James Parkes, *The Conflict of the Church and the Synagogue: A Study in the Origins of Antisemitism* (London, 1934), pp. 210–21; Salo Wittmayer Baron, *A Social and Religious History of the Jews*, 2d ed. (New York, 1952–83), 3:29ff., 242ff.; and Bernard S. Bachrach, *Early Medieval Jewish Policy in Western Europe* (Minneapolis, Minn., 1977), pp. 35–39.

two dozen letters, which divide readily among several chief concerns. Although many scholars have reviewed the specific circumstances and legal ramifications of Gregory's decrees, we reconsider them here for their ideological underpinnings—that is, for their perceptions of the Jewish condition and purpose in Christian society.

Responding to the complaints of Jews, Gregory intervened on at least six occasions to prevent violence against Jews, their synagogues, and their religious practices. In March 591, a Jew named Joseph complained to the pope that Bishop Peter of Terracina had repeatedly expelled the Jews of that town from their places of worship. Gregory admonished the bishop that

> if such is the case, we wish that your fraternity restrain himself from contention of this sort and that, as we have stated, the place which they acquired with your knowledge for their gatherings be allowed them for their meetings just as was the custom. For those who disagree with the Christian religion one must join to the unity of the faith by means of clemency, kindness, warning, and persuasion, so that those whom the charm of preaching and the foreseen terror of future judgment could have induced to believe might not be repelled by threats and fears. It is fitting, then, that they freely convene to hear the word of God from you rather than be terrified by excessive harshness.[6]

Gregory evinced determination to redress the injustice done the Jews, and several months later he appointed two other bishops to join with Peter in assuring the Jews a house of worship and putting their complaint to rest. "We forbid that these said Hebrews be oppressed or afflicted in unreasonable fashion; but, just as they are permitted by Roman law to live, so may they maintain their observances as they have learnt them without any hindrance, as justice would dictate."[7] Later in 591, a report from southern France elicited similar instruction to the bishops of Arles and Marseilles:

> Many of the Jews dwelling in those areas have been led to the baptismal font more through the use of force than by preaching. I grant that intention of this sort is worthy of praise, and I admit that it derives from love for our Lord. But unless sufficient support of Holy Scripture follows this same

6. Gregory, *Epistulae* 1.34, CCSL 140:42 (Shlomo Simonsohn, ed., *ASJD*, 492–1404, Pontifical Institute of Medieval Studies: Studies and Texts 94 [Toronto, 1988], p. 3). Here and throughout, I have followed the numeration of Dag Norberg, ed., *Sancti Gregorii Magni Registrum Epistularum*, CCSL 140–140A; discrepancies from the numeration of the MGH are noted in 140A:1182–83.

7. Gregory, *Epistulae* 2.45, CCSL 140:137 (Simonsohn, *ASJD*, 492–1404, p. 7); cf. *Codex theodosianus* 16.8.9, in Amnon Linder, ed., *The Jews in Roman Imperial Legislation* (Detroit, Mich., 1987), pp. 189–91.

intention, I fear that either nothing worthwhile will proceed from it or, additionally, that those souls which we wish to be saved might eventually— may it never happen—be lost. For, when anyone approaches the baptismal font not as a result of the sweetness of preaching but under duress, he returns to his earlier superstition, and then dies in a worse state inasmuch as he seemed to be reborn. Therefore, your Fraternity may arouse such men through frequent preaching, so that on account of the pleasantness of their instructor they might wish even more to change their old life. For thus is our intention correctly actualized, and the soul of the convert is not then driven to its erstwhile vomit.[8]

Later in the decade, when a Jewish convert to Christianity brought a crucifix into the synagogue of Cagliari, seeking to prevent Jewish worship, Gregory cited the Roman statute permitting Jews to maintain their old synagogues despite their inability to erect new ones. Even if Christian missionaries should claim to act out of zeal for the faith, they should deal with the Jews in moderation, "so that the wish [to convert] may be elicited from them, and not that they be led against their will."[9] In 602, similarly minded Christian zealots in Naples received more outspoken condemnation: "Those who sincerely wish to usher strangers to the Christian religion toward the proper faith should apply themselves gently, not harshly, so that antagonism might not drive far away the disposition of those whom reason, clearly presented, could attract. For whoever do otherwise, and under such a pretext seek to remove them from the accustomed practice of their rite, are proven to tend to their own concerns more than God's."[10] In 598, with words that would have critical impact on ecclesiastical policy toward the Jews centuries hence, Gregory encapsulated the rationale for these various rulings in a letter to the bishop of Palermo, against whom the Jews had also lodged a complaint with the pope. "Just as the Jews should not [*Sicut Iudaeis non . . .*] have license in their synagogues to arrogate anything beyond that permitted by law, so too in those things granted them they should experience no infringement of their rights."[11]

8. Gregory, *Epistulae* 1.45, CCSL 140:59 (Simonsohn, *ASJD, 492–1404*, pp. 4–5).

9. Ibid. 9.196, CCSL 140A:750–52 (Simonsohn, *ASJD, 492–1404*, pp. 19–20). Cf. Linder, *Jews in Roman Imperial Legislation*, pp. 287–89, 398–402; and see also Bachrach, *Early Medieval Jewish Policy*, pp. 155–56 n. 5, and Jean Juster, *Les Juifs dans l'Empire romain: Leur condition juridique, économique et sociale* (Paris, 1914), 1:353–390.

10. Gregory, *Epistulae* 13.13, CCSL 140A:1013–14 (Simonsohn, *ASJD, 492–1404*, pp. 23–24).

11. Ibid. 8.25, CCSL 140A:546–47 (Simonsohn, *ASJD, 492–1404*, pp. 15–16). On the subsequent history of the *Sicut Iudaeis* bull and formula, see Solomon Grayzel, "The Papal Bull *Sicut Judaeis*," in *Studies and Essays in Honor of Abraham A. Neuman*, ed.

Although Gregory's opposition to baptizing the Jews under duress acknowledges the rightfulness of their presence in his Christian society, one finds little evidence that he deemed that presence a necessity. On the contrary, Gregory's correspondence also alludes to an additional priority of his policy, no less important: undermining that presence through the conversion of the Jews to Christianity. In his letter quoted above, Gregory did not merely command his bishops to desist from anti-Jewish violence; he directly instructed them to preach to the Jews and thus win their souls for the church.[12] He frequently prescribed that baptized Jews receive special protection and financial rewards, because "we should, with reasonable moderation, aid those whom our Redeemer deems worthy to convert from the Jewish perdition to himself."[13] Nor did the danger of insincere conversion, which informed Gregory's insistence that Jews not be baptized against their will, militate otherwise in this case; as he wrote to a Sicilian deacon in 594, at least the souls of subsequent generations would be protected: "We do not work pointlessly, if by easing the burdens of their financial obligation we lead them to Christ's grace, because, even if they themselves come with little faith, those who shall be born of them will already be baptized with more faith. So do we gain either them or their children. And however much we remove from their financial obligations for Christ's sake is not serious."[14] Gregory's apocalyptic expectations rendered the task of converting the Jews an urgent one, and he therefore proposed to dispense with the normally required period of the catechumenate for prospective proselytes, "because, owing to the impending destruction, the nature of the time demands that [the fulfillment of] their desires not be postponed at all."[15]

If the exigencies of history motivated Gregory to bend ecclesiastical rules and expedite the conversion of Jews, how much the more so did he stand by the restrictive half of his *Sicut Iudaeis* formula and en-

Meir Ben-Horin et al. (Leiden, Netherlands, 1962), pp. 243–80; and Shlomo Simonsohn, *The Apostolic See and the Jews: History,* Pontifical Institute of Mediaeval Studies: Studies and Texts 109 (Toronto, 1991), pp. 39–94.

12. Gregory, *Epistulae* 1.34, 1.45, 13.13, cited above, in nn. 6, 8, 10. On Gregory's conversionist policy toward the Jews, see Bernhard Blumenkranz, *Juifs et Chrétiens dans le monde occidental, 430–1096* (Paris, 1960), pp. 95–99, 141–42; and Simonsohn, *The Apostolic See and the Jews: History,* pp. 240–41. Even Bachrach, *Early Medieval Jewish Policy,* p. 27, acknowledges the anti-Jewish character of this policy.

13. Gregory, *Epistulae* 4.31, CCSL 140:251 (Simonsohn, *ASJD, 492–1404,* pp. 10–11).

14. Ibid. 5.7, CCSL 140:273–74 (Simonsohn, *ASJD, 492–1404,* pp. 11–12).

15. Ibid. 8.23, CCSL 140A:543–44 (Simonsohn, *ASJD, 492–1404,* pp. 14–15).

deavor to prevent encroachments of Jews and Judaism on Christianity. He objected to the sin (*nefas*) of the sale of sacred objects to a Jew, ordering the vessels restored,[16] and he responded vehemently to reports of Judaizing among Christians; Romans who advocated refraining from work on the Jewish Sabbath Gregory labeled "preachers of Antichrist," who, at the end of days, will observe both Saturday and Sunday as days of rest. Because the Antichrist "feigns his death and resurrection from the grave, he wishes Sunday to be kept holy; and, because he compels the people to Judaize—in order to restore the exterior observance of the law and subordinate the perfidy of the Jews to himself—he wishes Saturday to be observed."[17] At least ten of Gregory's letters prohibit Jewish ownership of Christian slaves, "so that the Christian religion, might not be defiled through its subjugation to the Jews—may it never happen."[18] Once again, the pope took care that his decrees comported with the protective provisions of Roman law, and he upheld the rights of Jews to sell slaves acquired expressly for resale and to retain Christian serfs (*coloni*) on their estates.[19] Yet, as he explained to the kings and queen of the Franks, the ownership of Christian slaves by Jews subverted the very integrity of Christ and his church:

> For what are all Christians if not the members of Christ? All of us know that you faithfully revere the head of these members; but your excellency should ponder how contradictory it is to honor the head and to permit the members to be oppressed by its enemies. We therefore request that your excellency's decree remove the evil of this abuse from her/his kingdom, so that you might better prove yourself to be a worthy devotee of Almighty God, insofar as you release his faithful from his foes.[20]

16. Ibid. 1.66.

17. Ibid. 13.1, CCSL 140A:991–93 (Simonsohn, *ASJD, 492–1404*, pp. 22–23); cf. also 3.37. I am grateful to Bernard McGinn for confirming the originality of this Gregorian description of the Antichrist.

18. Ibid. 3.37, CCSL 140:182–83 (Simonsohn, *ASJD, 492–1404*, pp. 8–9); see also 2.45, 4.9, 4.21, 6.29–30, 7.21, 8.21, 9.105, 9.214, 9.216. On Gregory's slave policy, see Blumenkranz, *Juifs et Chrétiens*, pp. 202–6, 328–29; Pakter, *Medieval Canon Law*, pp. 91ff.; and Simonsohn, *The Apostolic See and the Jews: History*, pp. 160–62.

19. See the discussion of Bachrach, *Early Medieval Jewish Policy*, pp. 36–37, 156 nn. 58–60, about whether Gregory neglected the more stringent provisions of Justinian's legislation, enforcing only the more lenient statutes of the *Codex theododianus*; and cf. Juster, *Les Juifs dans l'Empire romain*, 2:71–77, and Blumenkranz, *Juifs et Chrétiens*, p. 328f. See also below, n. 46.

20. Gregory, *Epistulae* 9.214, 9.216, CCSL 140A:774–75, 779 (Simonsohn, *ASJD, 492–1404*, pp. 20–21).

Relative to the standards of his day, Gregory may indeed have "pursued a manifestly pro-Jewish policy,"[21] but tolerance did have its limits. Gregory held firm on the issue of slaves, and his commitment to proselytizing among the Jews strayed from the logic of Augustinian doctrine. His attempt to forge a balanced policy notwithstanding, Gregory harbored no love for the Jews.

ADVERSUS IUDAEOS

Gregory's exegetical works, and his *Moralia* on Job above all, also make frequent reference to the Jews and Judaism; just as his administrative policy toward the Jews claimed to maintain the precedents of imperial and ecclesiastical legislation, so too did his theological instruction offer a patchwork of traditional patristic anti-Jewish motifs. These pertained primarily to the Jews of first-century Judea, who, blinded by the clouds of ignorance, their hearts frozen in jealousy and infidelity, victimized Jesus and his followers and were consumed by the fire of their malice as a result.[22] Gregory laid particular blame on the Jewish leadership, the priests, and the Pharisees, who pressed for Jesus' execution and persecuted even those three or five thousand Jews who converted to Christianity in its aftermath.[23] Echoing Augustine, Gregory attributed the guilt of the Jews to error, rather than deliberate intention; for, as he alluded to the mystery of the incarnation in 1 Corinthians 2:8, had they known it, "they would not have crucified the Lord of glory."[24] Presented with the goods of their redemption, the promises made to their forefathers, the signs of Jesus' miracles, and the bountiful testimony of Scripture, these Jews nonetheless displayed no will to believe:

> For Judea "awaited the light but did not see," because she persisted in prophesying that the redeemer of humankind would come but did not recognize him upon his coming; and the eyes of the mind, which she opened to hope, she closed to the light's actual presence. She did not see the beginning of daybreak, inasmuch as she unreliably neglected to acknowledge the

21. Bachrach, *Early Medieval Jewish Policy*, p. 38.

22. Gregory, *Homiliae in Hiezechihelem* 1.2.10–13, 1.12.1; *Moralia in Job* 18.31.50–18.32.51, 27.27.51–27.28.52, 29.28.55.

23. Gregory, *Moralia* 9.28.44, see also 2.30.49–2.36.59, 30.9.32; cf. Simonsohn, *The Apostolic See and the Jews: History*, p. 294, who claims that Gregory blamed only the Pharisees for the crime of deicide.

24. Gregory, *Moralia* 9.28.44.

birth of the holy church, and although she believed that it was weakened by the deaths of its members, she did not know what power it was achieving.[25]

The Jews' blindness and rejection of their own salvation proceeded from their immersion in worldly affairs and pleasures, much as the Hebrew patriarch Isaac craved the meat prepared by his son Esau and unwittingly transmitted the true, spiritual blessing of God's covenant to Jacob. The Jews could respond only to the outward significance of Jesus' miracles; they lacked the ability to understand the Bible spiritually as one must, and, crippled by their own self-reliance, they worried too much over the sins of others to tend to their own.[26] Throughout their wicked designs and behavior, Gregory saw the handiwork of the devil: "Armed, the enemy of old ravished the Jewish people, because he extinguished the life of faith among them with darts of fraudulent advice, so that precisely in the conviction that they cleaved to God, they may oppose his rule."[27] God consequently deprived the Jews of the prophecies, miracles, and virtues they had enjoyed under the Old Testament before Jesus, transferring them all to the previously despised Gentiles, with whom he now inaugurated a new, superior covenant:

> While the people of the Jews remained under the rule of the Law, and the whole Gentile world knew none of God's precepts, the former appeared to rule through their faith, and the latter lay deeply suppressed because of their disbelief. But when Judea denied the mystery of the Lord's incarnation, the Gentile world believed, and the rulers sank into disfavor, and they who had been suppressed in the guilt of their perfidy were raised in the liberty of the true faith. . . . For when He removed the spoils of virtue from the Jews, He housed the splendor of his gifts in the heart of the Gentiles, wherein, on account of its faith, he considered it fitting to reside. This in fact occurred when the people of the Jews accepted the words of God only according to the letter, which kills, and the Gentile world, having been converted, penetrated them with the spirit, which gives life.[28]

Just as he did to the house of Eli and to Samuel, respectively, God disowned the Jews and adopted the Gentiles, but he also transformed

---

25. Ibid. 4.11.21, CCSL 143:178; see also 6.19.34, 14.53.62, and *Homilia in Evangelia* 2.22.3.

26. Gregory, *Homiliae in Hiezechihelem* 1.6.2–6, 1.10.16; *Moralia* 10.29.48, 11.19.30, 14.29.34, 14.39.47, 20.15.40, 27.14.26, 30.1.2–3, 33.28.49, 33.33.57. Gregory's comparison of the Jews to Isaac echoes the Augustinian motif cited above, chapter 1, n. 21.

27. Gregory, *Moralia* 6.4.5, CCSL 143:287, alluding to the *armatus* of Job 5:5; see also 1.36.51, 6.1.1, 9.28.44, 18.30.47, 27.26.49, 29.30.58, 30.25.72.

28. Ibid. 11.16.25, CCSL 143A:600–601.

the nature of his covenant: Letter gave way to spirit, law to grace, harshness to mildness, divine vengeance to salvation, and death to life. No wonder the Israelites at Sinai received their laws standing beneath the mountain, whereas Jesus preached his gospel directly from the mountain itself.[29]

"Her appearance having been altered," wrote Gregory, Judea still "is tortured by grief" over her plight,[30] and the Jews, like Eli's sons, remain in an impiety from which there is no return.[31] Turning from the Jews of first-century Palestine to those of his own day, Gregory followed Augustine and reckoned the Jews' disbelief, which construes the loss of light as advantageous, an integral part of their punishment.[32] Though contemporary Jews encounter the Christological testimonies of Scripture and receive exhortation from Christian preachers on a daily basis, they continue to insult God in their self-inflicted blindness, incurring divine wrath still further and compounding their misery.[33] And yet, as long as the Jews mingle with other peoples, their condemnation by God serves a didactic purpose; Job, Gregory explained in the *Moralia*, thus "trains the mind's eyes directly on the singular misfortune of the Israelite people, and, with the destruction of one people, he demonstrates what punishment awaits all those that are arrogant."[34] Moreover, on numerous occasions in his writings, Gregory anticipated the final conversion of Israel, which will ultimately redress the frustrations and failures now experienced by Christian missionaries in preaching to the Jews. Just as Job finally received true consolation from his brethren, so will Christ and his church take comfort in the spiritual faith of carnal Israel:

> The holy Church now is troubled by the aversion of the Hebrews and then is restored by their conversion. . . . That is, those who recover from the error of their earlier disbelief and forsake the perverse life on account of which they had resisted the teachers of righteousness console Christ and console the Church. Is it not an awful shame to preach futilely to hard hearts, to take the trouble to demonstrate the truth, but to find no com-

---

29. Gregory, *Homiliae in Hiezechihelem* 1.12.6; *Expositiones in librum primum Regum* 3.5; *Moralia* 2.2.2, 2.36.59, 7.8.8–11, 11.41.55, 18.38.59–18.39.61, 21.2.5, 22.18.44.

30. Gregory, *Moralia* 9.33.49, CCSL 143:490.

31. Gregory, *Expositiones in librum primum Regum* 3.5; *Homiliae in Hiezechihelem* 1.2.10–13, 1.12.6; *Moralia* 9.5.5, 27.14.26, 27.28.52, 33.3.7.

32. Gregory, *Expositiones in librum primum Regum* 2.49; *Moralia* 9.6.6.

33. Gregory, *Expositiones in librum primum Regum* 3.5; *Moralia* 6.21.36–6.22.37, 18.30.47.

34. Gregory, *Moralia* 9.5.5, CCSL 143:458–59; cf. praef. 5.12.

pensation for one's efforts—in the conversion of one's listeners? Nevertheless, the ensuing progress of their listeners is a great comfort for preachers.

Why, then, did Job's brethren approach him only after all of his suffering had passed? "Truly because the Hebrews at the time of his [that is, Christ's] passion, rejecting the proclamation of the faith, refused to believe that he whom they had established by his death to be a man was God. . . . But at the end of time all Israelites shall join together in the faith . . . and go back to the protection of him whom they had fled." Only then will the salvific efforts of Christ, prefigured by the suffering Job, be fully rewarded. Hence Gregory's resonant call to the Jewish people: "Thus let the believing Hebrews gather at the end of the world and redeem their pledges of offerings to the savior of humankind in the power of his divinity, as if to the healed Job."[35]

Gregory's Christian reading of Jewish history may have forecast the happy ending that Paul had envisioned, but major obstacles remained. The devil still abides among the Jews, maintained Gregory, and through the agency of Antichrist he continues to enlist their support. "The synagogue opposes its founder, not out of fear as previously, but now in outright resistance. Being transformed into the limbs of the devil and believing that the man of lies is God, the more it is raised up high against the faithful, the more it prides itself that it is the body of God."[36] As Gregory noted in his correspondence,[37] the bonds between Antichrist and Judaism continue to undermine the integrity of Christendom,[38] and he expected more blatant cooperation between the two powers in advance of the final redemption. Even as Jews will flock to the church at the end of days, some of their coreligionists will continue to persecute them for doing so.[39] In sum, the enmity of the synagogue toward Christianity endures and intensifies. "The wounds it inflicted on the believers upon the advent of the savior are clearly less than those with which it seeks, even now, to strike the Church with the advent of the Antichrist. For it makes itself ready for that time, in order to encumber the lives of the faithful with its collected strength."[40]

35. Ibid. 35.14.24–34 (quotation from §27, CCSL 143B:1791–92); see also praef. 10.20, 9.8.9, 19.12.19, 20.22.48, 27.14.26, 29.2.4, 30.9.32.
36. Ibid. 31.23.42, CCSL 143B:1578.
37. See above, n. 17.
38. Gregory, Moralia 25.16.34, 27.26.49–50, 33.33.57, 34.4.8.
39. Gregory, Homiliae in Hiezechihelem 1.12.7.
40. Gregory, Moralia 31.22.41, CCSL 143B:1578; see the lengthy description of the future works of Antichrist in books 33–34.

THE LOGIC OF GREGORIAN ANTI-JUDAISM

Although medieval historians consistently accord Gregory an important role in the evolution of public policy toward the Jews of European Christendom, the specific characterization of his attitudes has varied considerably. Some scholars have written of Gregory's "deep-seated aversion" and his "deepest horror and loathing" for the Jews;[41] others have praised his "scrupulous concern for justice and humanity," labeling him the Jews' intransigent protector.[42] Meanwhile, some investigators have highlighted the disparity between the Jewish policy of Gregory's papal bulls and the outlook expressed in his doctrinal-exegetical works, perhaps attributing greater significance to one or the other,[43] whereas others have viewed Gregory's attitude toward the Jews as essentially coherent.[44] Yet nearly all Gregorian scholars acknowledge Gregory's tremendous debt to the doctrine of Augustine, and the ensuing appraisal of Gregory proceeds from a comparison of the ideas of the two churchmen—both their specific formulations on Jews and Judaism and the more fundamental doctrinal principles in which these formulations were grounded.

On one hand, even though Gregory never cited Augustine's exegesis of Psalm 59:12, his dependence on Augustinian teaching concerning the Jews is evident. We recall that Augustine grounded the doctrine of Jewish witness, as elaborated in the De civitate Dei and elsewhere, in the historical reality of the Jews' survival and, in particular, in their subjugated status under Roman rule: "Yet the Jews who killed him [Jesus] and chose not to believe in him . . . , having been vanquished rather pathetically by the Romans, completely deprived of their kingdom . . . and scattered throughout the world . . . , are testimony for us through their own scriptures. . . . For there is a prophecy given previously in the Psalms . . . : 'Slay them not.' "[45] Given the administrative context in which Gregory had to define the status of what he unquestionably still perceived as Ro-

---

41. Katz, "Pope Gregory the Great," p. 119; Parkes, Conflict, p. 219.

42. Robert A. Markus, "Gregory the Great and a Papal Missionary Strategy," in The Mission of the Church and the Propagation of the Faith, ed. G. J. Cuming, SCH 6 (Cambridge, England, 1970), p. 30; and Dahan, Les Intellectuels chrétiens, p. 138.

43. Parkes, Conflict, pp. 219–21; Baron, Social and Religious History, 3:242 n. 33.

44. Kenneth R. Stow, "Hatred of the Jews or Love of the Church: Papal Policy toward the Jews in the Middle Ages," in Antisemitism through the Ages, ed. Shmuel Almog, trans. Nathan H. Reisner (Oxford, 1988), pp. 74–76; and Rosemary R. Ruether, Faith and Fratricide: The Theological Roots of Anti-Semitism (New York, 1974), p. 200.

45. See above, chapter 1, nn. 22, 24.

man Jewry, one can readily discern the logic of his translation of Augustinian theology into papal policy: If Augustine had deemed the status of the Jews under Roman rule to be the fulfillment of biblical prophecy, it behooved Gregory, head of the Roman Church, to maintain that aspect of imperial policy and govern his subjects accordingly. Gregory claimed justification for his Jewish policy in terms of Roman legal precedent, both in the application of the Theodosian Code to the protection of synagogues and the restriction of Jewish slaveholding and in a recurring appeal to the general import of Roman legislation. Inasmuch as the Jews "are permitted by Roman law to live, so may they maintain their observances as they have learnt them without any hindrance, as justice would dictate."[46] His principle of *Sicut Iudaeis* invokes a similar rationale, limiting Jewish rights to that which is "permitted by law [*permissum est lege*]."[47] Furthermore, the recurring emphasis on the public rituals of the Jews—their holy days, their celebrations, their communal worship and its venue—in Gregory's protective edicts bespeaks the Augustinian notion that the divine mandate of "Slay them not" entails the perpetuation of their Judaism, the *forma Iudaeorum*,[48] and not merely the preservation of their lives. As we have seen, Gregory acknowledged the didactic purpose of Jewish survival in a dispersed, subjugated state. He reaffirmed Augustinian instruction that the blindness of the Jews in Jesus' day resulted in their persecution of him and that such blindness, then and now, constitutes divine punishment for their sin. Gregory's aforecited rationale for preaching to contemporary Jews despite their intransigence reads much like the directive of Augustine's *Tractatus adversus Iudaeos*: "Testimonies should be taken from the holy scriptures, whose authority is very great among them, too; if they refuse to be restored by the benefit which they offer, they can be convicted [*convinci*] by their blatant truth."[49]

46. As quoted above, n. 7. This appears to be the only instance where Gregory qualified *leges* with the adjective *romanae*. Usually he wrote of Roman statutes simply as leges; see *Thesaurus Sancti Gregorii Magni*, Series A (formae), comp. Justin Mossay and Bernard Coulie, Corpus Christianorum—Thesaurus Patrum Latinorum, (Turnhout, Belgium, 1986), microfiche pp. 10106–7, 10114. Both Bachrach, *Early Medieval Jewish Policy*, pp. 35–38, and Baltrusch, "Gregor der Grosse," have argued persuasively that Gregory's protection of the Jews actually exceeded the limits of both the *Codex theodosianus* and Justinian's *Corpus iuris civilis*, in fact contravening their restrictive statutes. In emphasizing that the *leges* of which he wrote were in fact *romanae*, might Gregory have recognized the uncertainty of the justification for his ruling of *Sicut Iudaeis*?

47. Cf. Stow, "Hatred of the Jews," p. 74, and *Alienated Minority*, pp. 23–24.

48. See above, chapter 1, n. 36.

49. See above, chapter 1, n. 49.

On the other hand, the role and the image of the Jews in the Gregorian corpus depart from the Augustinian model in several noteworthy respects. First, Gregory's theological-exegetical works ascribe historical importance to the Jews of Jesus' day and to the Jews of the end of time, paying minimal attention to contemporary Jewry. Although his policy as pope applied the spirit of Roman law and the Augustinian doctrine of Jewish witness in practice, he did not depict the Jews of his own age as significant players in the unfolding drama of Christian salvation history. Rather, Gregory looked forward to the final days of that history, when all remaining Jews would accept Christianity, and such anticipation comports well with his justification of special allowances for Jewish proselytes. A mandate for missionary preaching to the Jews likewise accompanied the prohibition against using force to convert the Jews, in the hope that, "demonstrating what we tell them with evidence from their own books, we might be able, with the help of God, to direct them into the arms of mother Church."[50] This emphasis too one generally finds lacking in the works of Augustine, who paid lip service to the traditional apostolic longings for the conversion of the Jews but accorded little urgency or hope for success to contemporary missionary efforts.[51] Lastly, Gregory elaborated much more extensively than did Augustine on the Jews' alliance with the devil and Antichrist, who had determined the direction of Jewish history in the past and would continue to do so in the future. Gregorian doctrine conveys a pronounced sense of enmity between the Jews and the faithful, emanating directly from the ongoing, insidious opposition of Satan to the designs of God. In such subversion "the Jews now excessively persist; hence, as long as they lovingly inhabit the place of their treachery, they fight against the redeemer."[52] Gregory's protection of Jewish rights notwithstanding, one leaves his writings with an appreciation of the Jews' historical role far more negative than that of Augustine.

In his departures from Augustinian attitudes toward Jews and Judaism, Gregory manifested—and, in fact, exemplified—the new, distinctive mentality of early medieval Latin Christendom described briefly

---

50. Gregory, *Epistulae* 13.13, CCSL 140A:10.
51. See the citations adduced by Bernhard Blumenkranz, *Die Judenpredigt Augustins* (Basel, 1946), pp. 110–12.
52. Gregory, *Expositiones in librum primum Regum* 1.92, CCSL 144:107–8; cf. Richard Kenneth Emmerson, *Antichrist in the Middle Ages: A Study of Medieval Apocalypticism, Art, and Literature* (Seattle, Wash., 1981), p. 79.

at the beginning of part 2 of this book.[53] His was a mind-set that beheld all experience and reality as a continuous unity, an outlook that perceived reality essentially as one but, in its unredeemed state, as reflecting the divisiveness of sharp, fundamental oppositions. As Carole Straw has written so eloquently,

> to understand Gregory one must begin by recognizing that he has modified the paradoxes of the mature Augustine and that the fluid boundaries of late antiquity have all but vanished. The supernatural is mingled with the world of ordinary experience, and in surprising ways. Visible and invisible, natural and supernatural, human and divine, carnal and spiritual are often directly and causally connected. . . . In Gregory's world, invisible reality exists alongside the visible reality it sustains and determines. The other world is at one's very elbows, though often hidden to those of carnal minds. . . . Gregory tends to link causally flesh and spirit, present and future worlds, displaying a certainty and predictability in their interconnection. . . . As the spiritual and carnal boundaries are broken for body and soul, this world and the next, so too the boundaries between the self and others weaken, and social unity is intensified. Each individual exists only as a member of the larger, transcendent body of Christ, which is political and social as well as religious. . . . To pursue a separate course is to subvert both self and society, to imitate the devil's delusion of self-sufficiency.[54]

Paradoxically, both dualism and monism appear to characterize this Gregorian worldview, and one must distinguish carefully the different levels of reality that manifest them. Gregory's thought is rife with foundational contrasts: God and the devil, Christ and Antichrist, New Testament and Old, faithful and infidel, spiritual and carnal, heavenly and terrestrial, virtuous and sinful. Yet the dissonance endemic to these oppositions pertains to a sinful, unredeemed reality, and it functions in the divine master plan expressly to underscore the need for restoration. In other words, good and evil members of these oppositional

53. Although I quote at length in the ensuing discussion from the most recent extensive study of Gregorian theology, Carole Straw, *Gregory the Great: Perfection in Imperfection* (Berkeley, Calif., 1988), readers should also recognize my debt to the contributions of other authors. These include Claude Dagens, *Saint Grégoire le Grand: Culture et expérience chrétiennes* (Paris, 1977); Jeffrey Richards, *Consul of God: The Life and Times of Gregory the Great* (London, 1980); William D. McReady, *Signs of Sanctity: Miracles in the Thought of Gregory the Great*, Pontifical Institute of Medieval Studies—Studies and Texts 91 (Toronto, 1989); Robert A. Markus, "The Sacred and the Secular: From Augustine to Gregory the Great," *Journal of Theological Studies*, n.s. 36 (1985), 84–96, and *The End of Ancient Christianity* (Cambridge, England, 1990); and Judith Herrin, *The Formation of Christendom* (Princeton, N.J., 1987), chap. 4.
54. Straw, *Gregory*, pp. 9–11.

pairs struggle fiercely in the world of Gregory's experience, but, ultimately, their combat facilitates a salvific resolution. Though plagued by the inadequacies and evils of his age, Gregory thus awaited the eschaton more eagerly than did Augustine. For him, God's world is truly an integrated one: Visible and invisible realities exist continuously, side by side, and are essentially equivalent. Political institutions, societies, and cultures all adhere to a single, grand divine scheme of things, from which their raison d'être derives; if the Middle Ages remembered Gregory somewhat unfairly as a destroyer of classical culture, he unquestionably strove to marshal all facets of human creativity in the perfection of Christendom, attributing value to nothing that made no such contribution.[55] Even the devil works God's will in the final analysis.[56] Straw has thus perceived "a grammar of reconciliation and complementarity" at the base of Gregory's singular vision of sacramental reality:

> Gregory sees carnal and spiritual realms as interrelated, connected as endpoints of a continuum. Like faces of a coin, ends of a stick, or poles of a magnet, they are extremities of a single whole. . . . Though opposite, carnal and spiritual realms are very much united through various degrees of complementarity and reconciliation. At any one moment, only a single aspect of the relationship might appear, such as the conflict between spirit and flesh, or the sympathy of body and soul. But when opposition is overt, unity is latent.[57]

Gregory found the key to reconciliation in Christ, who alone could successfully mediate the boundary between humanity and divinity, who resolves the tension of all such cosmic oppositions, and whose covenant and church integrate the various dimensions of spiritual and temporal experience into a perfect, Christian whole.

This general pattern of Gregory's thought informed his biblical hermeneutic, his philosophy of history, and his anthropology in a manner

---

55. Tilmann Buddensieg, "Gregory the Great, the Destroyer of Pagan Idols: The History of a Medieval Legend Concerning the Decline of Ancient Art and Architecture," *Journal of the Warburg and Courtauld Institutes* 28 (1965), 44–65. Among others, see also Richards, *Consul of God*, chap. 4; Marc Reydellet, *La Royauté dans la littérature latine de Sidone Apollinaire à Isidore de Séville*, Bibliothèque des écoles françaises d'Athènes et de Rome 243 (Rome, 1981), chap. 9; Pierre Riché, *Education and Culture in the Barbarian West from the Sixth through the Eighth Century*, trans. John J. Contreni (Columbia, S.C., 1976), pp. 145–57; and Dagens, *Saint Grégoire*, esp. chaps. 1–2, 7.

56. Gregory, *Moralia* 2.29.48, 6.18.31.

57. Straw, *Gregory*, p. 18.

that may well help to account for his departure from Augustinian constructions of Jews and Judaism. Unlike the mature Augustine, Gregory displayed an "addiction to the allegorical interpretation of Scripture."[58] His exegesis categorically emphasized the allegorical and moral, and it extended but minimal attention to the literal sense of Hebrew Scripture. To be sure, Gregory acknowledged the historical sense in his well-known cover letter to Leander, which accompanied the completed *Moralia* on Job: "It should be known that some passages we run through in a historical interpretation, some passages we analyze allegorically through typological exegesis, and some we discuss solely in their allegorical, moral sense; yet some, as we probe more meticulously, we investigate simultaneously by all three methods." Nevertheless, Gregory's preference lay almost exclusively with figurative interpretation, as his voluminous *Moralia* and other exegetical works reveal, and as he admitted just several sentences later in the same letter to Leander: "Sometimes, in fact, we neglect to explain the plain words of the historical sense, so that we not arrive too slowly at the concealed meanings; and sometimes they cannot be understood in a literal sense, because, when understood according to their visible meaning only, they produce nothing edifying for their readers but only error."[59] Such hermeneutical procedure allowed Gregory considerable latitude in his commentaries and frequently resulted in multiple, even contradictory, expositions of the same biblical figure or verse. The agitation of the earth depicted in Job 38:12–13, for example, can refer either to that of the wicked by Christ or to that of the church by Antichrist![60] Past and future are often confused.[61] Asses, the raven, and the northerly direction signify both Jews and Gentiles;[62] the horse both right and wrong;[63] a hammer both the power of the devil and that of heaven;[64]

58. Paul Meyvaert, "Gregory the Great and the Theme of Authority," *Spode House Review* 3 (December 1966), 5. In addition to the works cited in notes 53–55 above, see also Sandra Zimdars-Swartz, "A Confluence of Imagery: Exegesis and Christology According to Gregory the Great," in *Grégoire le Grand*, ed. Jacques Fontaine et al., Colloques internationaux du C.N.R.S. (Paris, 1986), pp. 327–35; de Lubac, *Exégèse médiévale*, 2,1:53–98; and Beryl Smalley, *The Study of the Bible in the Middle Ages*, 3d ed. (Oxford, 1983), pp. 32–35.

59. Gregory, *Moralia*, epist. ad Leandrum 3, CCSL 143:4; cf. the helpful comments of Jean Laporte, "Une Théologie systématique chez Grégoire," in *Grégoire le Grand*, ed. Jacques Fontaine et al., Colloques internationaux du C.N.R.S. (Paris, 1986), p. 235.

60. Gregory, *Moralia* 29.2.4–29.3.5.

61. Ibid. 34.7.12, for instance.

62. Ibid. 1.16.23–24, 2.1.6, 27.43.71, 29.26.52, 30.9.28–34.

63. Ibid. 31.23.42.

64. Ibid. 34.12.23.

oxen both stubborn Jews and resolute Christian preachers;[65] the elders of Job 12:20 both the Hebrew patriarchs who foretold of Jesus and the Jews who subsequently rejected him.[66] Whether or not one attributes such ostensive self-contradiction to Gregory's "grammar of reconciliation and complementarity," such a hermeneutical method could accord little value to literal exegesis. If pressed for interpretative consistency, the pope might well have responded: "Unless we investigate the mysteries of the allegories in these words, those things which ensue—if considered solely within the historical narrative—are entirely worthy of disregard."[67] In a remark often quoted by his students and detractors alike, Gregory similarly justified to Leander his lack of concern for grammar and eloquence. "I have not seen fit to preserve that style of speech which the standards of external refinement prescribe . . . ; for I deem it entirely inappropriate to subordinate the words of the heavenly oracle to the rules of Donatus."[68]

Similar "heavenly" considerations dictated Gregory's perspective on terrestrial history. Much as he devalued the nonfigurative, historical sense of Scripture, so did he exclude the Augustinian saeculum from his own understanding of human experience and society. Gregory did retain the Augustinian notion of a "pilgrim people" in this world, the chosen "who, considering this life a sort of exile for themselves, yearn with all of their hearts for their supernal homeland," as opposed to those "who set their hearts on earthly pleasures."[69] But one fails to find in the Gregorian corpus evidence of overlap or ambiguity in the relationship between the two communities; one encounters none of the recognition of independent, albeit limited, value in worldly achievements and institutions that is so impressive in Augustinian thought.[70] Conversely, Gregory saw no reason to distinguish between the history of salvation and that of earthly politics and society. Unhesitatingly he identified the church with the body of Christ and its members with his. Gregory's "historical consciousness was shaped by a sense of the crumbling away of the secular institutions and the profane traditions rooted in Rome's ancient past."[71] For him, the divine economy of salvation

65. Ibid. 1.16.23–24, 35.16.36–39.
66. Ibid. 11.15.24.
67. Ibid. 18.40.61, CCSL 143A:927–28.
68. Ibid., epist. ad Leandrum 5, CCSL 143:7.
69. Ibid. 18.30.47–48, CCSL 143A:916–17.
70. Markus, *End of Ancient Christianity*, passim.
71. Markus, "Sacred and the Secular," p. 93.

was plainly apparent in the affairs of this world: He discarded the fundamental Augustinian distinction between *Christianitas* and *Romanitas*, and, in the words of another recent biographer, his "unending search for a reconciliation of these differing concepts constitutes the restless core of his being."[72] Retreating from the anti-apocalyptic orientation of Augustinian eschatology, Gregory had little doubt that this quest would soon reach its end. Recent events included the conversion of the Gentiles, the decline of classical culture, the downfall of pagan Rome, the victory of Catholicism, and the consolidation of papal authority in the West, on one hand, and the trials of the Germanic and Byzantine invasions, on the other. What could be more suggestive of the last days, of the final struggle between Christ and Antichrist, than such a blend of encouragement and tribulation in the affairs of this world? And what, in turn, could constitute a more pressing reason to propagate the faith? Among the chief goals of Gregory's pontificate "was purely and simply to win as many souls as possible for Christ before the end of the world."[73] Unlike Augustine's historical account of the heavenly city, which effectively stopped with the establishment of Christianity and thereby sought to defuse an apocalyptic reading of current events, the spotlight of Gregory's historical concern—as opposed to his predominantly allegorical interest in the old dispensation—fell precisely on the first and second comings of Christ and on the teleological progression from the one to the other.

Finally, Gregory's excision of the saeculum from his reading of Christian history struck a corresponding note in his anthropology. As Pierre Daubercies[74] and others have shown, Gregorian doctrine abandons the body–soul dualism of earlier patristic literature; and it also departs from the older Augustine's restoration of natural goodness to the human body—the Augustine who taught that sinful carnality assuredly afflicts the flesh but resides primarily in the soul. Signaling a new tendency in medieval Christian doctrine, Gregory recast the conflict between spiritual and carnal as that between heavenly and terrestrial. Created by God, both body and soul may be intrinsically good. Yet vice misleads them both to seek fulfillment in the perishable goods

---

72. Richards, *Consul of God*, p. 69.

73. Ibid., p. 54; and see the more thorough discussion of Dagens, *Saint Grégoire*, chaps. 7–9.

74. Pierre Daubercies, *La Condition charnelle: Recherches positives pour la théologie d'une réalité terrestre* (Paris, 1958), and "La Théologie de la condition charnelle chez les maîtres de haut Moyen Âge," *RTAM* 30 (1963), 5–54.

and pleasures of this world, regarding whose value—even when subordinated to higher, spiritual priorities—Gregory was emphatically
pessimistic. For instance, Gregory acknowledged the sacramentality of
marriage and the essential innocence of marital intercourse. "There
ought to be legitimate coupling of the flesh for the sake of progeny,
not pleasure; and bodily intercourse should be for the purpose of be-
getting children, not the satisfaction of vices." Nonetheless, as Gregory
had forewarned in the same paragraph, "even that licit intercourse of
spouses cannot transpire without the pleasure of the flesh . . . [which]
very pleasure cannot possibly be without sin."[75] Unlike Augustine,
given the continuous, all-embracing unity of his spiritual cosmology,
Gregory could not make peace with a Christian modus vivendi that
smacked of imperfection or mediocrity. In our present case,

> sexual expression betrays the fidelity one owes God in both body and soul,
> for participation in God embraces the whole human personality. The body
> of the Christian enjoys a kind of physical unity in his stability in the body
> of Christ—so much so that the Christian himself, Christ's spouse, commits
> a form of adultery and disloyalty in possessing earthly loves. . . . Sexuality
> inevitably leads one toward the self-centered individualism of the family,
> with its web of ties to the secular world, its numerous burdens and anxieties.
> In contrast, the religious community possesses the tranquillity needed to
> realize man's highest vocations: contemplation, charity, and continence.[76]

Pope Gregory accordingly called for rigorous regulation of human sexuality in particular and for the constant combat of body and soul
against the lures of all worldly passion in general. Not without cause
does Western history remember Gregory as the early medieval theologian of monasticism par excellence. In his view, monastic discipline
extends the best, perhaps the sole, possibility for subduing worldly
commitment, facilitating the truly spiritual, contemplative life, and
reaping the supernal rewards of Christianity.[77]

The foregoing discussion of doctrinal differences between Augustine

75. Gregory, *Epistulae* 11.56a.8, MGH, Epistulae 2:340–41. On the importance of
this letter in ecclesiastical tradition, see Pierre J. Payer, *Sex and the Penitentials: The
Development of a Sexual Code, 550–1150* (Toronto, 1984), pp. 35–36, 65.

76. Straw, *Gregory*, p. 134. On Augustine's defense of "Christian mediocrity," see,
above all, Markus, *End of Ancient Christianity*, passim.

77. In this regard, see also Robert Gillet, "Spiritualité et place du moine dans l'église
selon Saint Grégoire le Grand," in *Théologie de la vie monastique*, Théologie 49 (Paris,
1961), pp. 323–51; Jean Leclercq, *The Love of Learning and Desire for God: A Study
of Monastic Culture*, 3d ed., trans. Catharine Misrahi (New York, 1982), pp. 25–36;
and Matthew Baasten, *Pride According to Gregory the Great: A Study of the Moralia*,
Studies in the Bible and Early Christianity 7 (Lewiston, N.Y., 1986).

and Gregory should by no means obscure the profound influence of
the one upon the other,[78] even in the matter of the Jews, but it should
allow us to mitigate the seeming dissonance between the protection of
Jews and Judaism in Gregory's correspondence and the insistently anti-
Jewish instruction of his biblical commentaries. At the outset, one must
take issue with the specific formulation of such presumed disparity: As
ruler of Rome and head of its church, Gregory did not pursue a policy
of protecting the Jews per se; rather, he pursued a policy that balanced
privilege and restriction. If comparison with other churchmen and rulers has led historians to highlight his moderation in this regard, perhaps
even to argue that it exceeded the limits permitted in imperial legislation, such an appraisal does not fairly estimate the sense of Gregory's
ideas. His guideline of *Sicut Iudaeis* reiterated the need to restrict the
Jews even before it mandated their protection. As noted previously,
Gregory deemed the status of the Jews in Roman law to be the translation of received Christian doctrine into public policy. Having narrowed the distance—and obliterated any presumed contradiction—between imperial and ecclesiastical history, the pope sought to maintain
what he perceived to be an underlying *Christian* sense of right and
equity in Roman law. Hence his appeals to treat both Jews and Jewish
converts to Christianity "as justice would dictate [*annuente iustitia*]"
and not to oppress the Jews—like any other rightful component of
Roman society—"in unreasonable fashion [*contra rationis ordi-
nem*]."[79]

Alongside Roman law, Gregory also inherited from his predecessors
long-established theological and exegetical traditions of *Adversus
Iudaeos*, most of which he incorporated unquestioningly into his own
writings. And yet, as we have seen, the very monistic impulse that
collapsed the barriers between *Romanitas* and *Christianitas* in his
Catholic worldview—thus impelling him to enforce the statutory protection of the Jews—detracted in his thought from the doctrinal considerations that had undergirded Augustine's doctrine of Jewish witness. Augustine had accorded the Jews a distinct, constructive
testimonial function in a properly ordered Christian society, precisely

---

78. See Jaroslav Pelikan, *The Christian Tradition: A History of the Development of
Doctrine* (Chicago, 1971–89), 1:350ff.
79. See above, n. 7; for Gregory's other uses of these two phrases, cf. *Thesaurus
Sancti Gregorii Magni*, microfiche pp. 1177, 15840.

because of those intermediate categories, imperfect but valuable nonetheless, that distinguished his biblical hermeneutic, his reading of terrestrial history, and his anthropology. Gregory, however, true to his postclassical "grammar of reconciliation and complementarity," devalued the literal meaning of Holy Scripture, rejected the secular neutrality of historical events, and saw little redeeming social worth in the sexuality of the human body. From his exegetical vantage point, the Jews surely pursued and embodied the literal sense of the Bible, denying the reciprocity and continuity between Old Testament and New, thwarting the interests of the church.[80] Now that Christianity had spread as far as England, what pagans still required Jewish testimony to validate the scriptural evidence for Christianity?[81] Gregory's reading of history similarly depreciated the Jewish contribution to Christendom. Set against his allegorical interest in the old dispensation, his historical concern focused on the new, Christian order, that which mediated the distance between this world and the other, extending from Christ's first appearance on earth until the second. Whereas Augustine likened the periods in a human life to the divisions of all of terrestrial history, Gregory posited the correspondence of the ages of a human being to those of the post-crucifixion church![82] This historical perspective invariably defined the Jew as obstructing the ministry of the incarnate Christ, even to the point of violent persecution and deicide. Christians are members of Christ, Jews of Antichrist.[83] Moreover, inasmuch as the church's victory over paganism and heresy, coupled with its having outlived the empire, suggested that the end of history was near, the conversion of the Jews loomed large and urgent as a final obstacle to be surmounted in advance of the second coming.[84] Finally, from the anti-terrestrial orientation of Gregorian anthropology,

80. De Lubac's magisterial study of the *Exégèse médiéval* (2,1:53–128) proceeds almost directly, with minimal interruption, from the allegorical exegetical "'barbarie' de saint Grégoire" to the characteristically Jewish "bovinus intellectus" perceived by high medieval Christian theologians, which I discuss in part 3 of this book.

81. Cf. Gregory, *Homilia in Evangelia* 2.32.4–5: Now that Christianity is no longer persecuted and has spread throughout the world, the emphasis of Christian preaching must fall on the quality of the confession of faith, so that Christians will truly be the members of Christ. See also *Moralia* 34.4.8.

82. Ibid. 19.12.19, CCSL 143A:970–71: "Sicut uniuscuiusque hominis, sic sanctae Ecclesiae aetas describitur. Parvula quippe tunc erat. . . . Adulta vero Ecclesia dicitur. . . . Universae quippe Ecclesiae . . . adolescentulae vocantur. . . . Cum in diebus illis Ecclesia, quasi quodam senio debilitata. . . ."

83. See above, nn. 20, 36–38.

84. See the comments of Dagens, *Saint Grégoire*, pp. 352ff.

Judaism and Christianity could well appear antithetical. For the Jews, well recognized in late antiquity for their commitment to a life of marriage and sexual reproduction,[85] exemplified an ungodly dedication to the pursuits and pleasures of the material world. If Augustine in his later years proved less eager to designate the Jewish people as carnal, Gregory did so repeatedly and without reservation. In the days of Jesus, "the disbelieving people perceived the body of the Lord carnally [*infidelis populus carnem Domini carnaliter intellexit*], because they believed him to be completely human."[86] So too in his own day, Gregory identified the Jews with Antichrist, and thus with the members of the body of the beast (*membra carnium eius*) of Job 41:14: "All the wicked, who do not arise in desire to understand their spiritual homeland, are the flesh [*carnes*] of this Leviathan."[87]

Whereas the Jew had provided exegetical and historical continuity in Augustinian thought, he now signified disunity and discontinuity in Gregory's Christian scheme of things. This pope's meticulous, perhaps obsessive concern for proper order, coupled with his veneration of tradition, perpetuated and institutionalized the right of Jews to live as Jews in Christendom. Yet the Jew of Christendom, whose survival Augustine had considered effectively harmless and instructive, endures as the enemy in Gregorian doctrine. The demeaning but otherwise restrained Augustinian descriptions of the Jews as book-bearing slaves, desks, librarians, and "guardians of our books" (*capsarii, scriniaria, librarii, custodes librorum nostrorum*) simply do not appear in Gregory's writings. His Jews serve the interests of Antichrist and the devil. To perfect Christian unity, the church must work vigorously to convert them, albeit while observing the practical dictates of "Slay them not."

Augustine had constructed the Jew as a fossilized relic of antiquity, a Jew who, in fact, had never existed. Doctrinal and hermeneutical factors may have caused Pope Gregory the Great to retreat from the logic of these Augustinian constructions, but hardly in order to abandon the policy they had spawned. Ambivalence and contradiction continued to characterize constructions of Jews and Judaism in Christian theology; the constructions themselves, embedded in the dictates of Christian theology and hermeneutics, continued to enjoy a life of their own.

85. Cf. above, chapter 1, n. 118.
86. Gregory, *Moralia* 14.44.52, CCSL 143A:729. Other references to the carnality of the Jews include *Moralia* 7.8.8; *Expositiones in librum primum Regum* 3.41, 3.47, 3.63, 3.66, 5.99; and *Homiliae in Hiezechihelem* 2.9.2, 2.10.8.
87. Gregory, *Moralia* 34.4.8, CCSL 143B:1738–39.

CHAPTER 3

Isidore of Seville

*Anti-Judaism and the
Hermeneutics of Integration*

Like Gregory the Great, Isidore of Seville is often considered one of the last of the Latin church fathers. He, too, "was a true bridge-builder between early and late medieval times, a bridge-builder also between the Germanic and Roman nations";[1] and, much as Gregory did, Isidore contributed directly to the developing idea of the Jew in early medieval Christendom. Yet Isidore undertook this responsibility deliberately, with a determination that rendered anti-Jewish polemic more of a critical aspect of his scholarly opus than it had been for Gregory's or for Augustine's. Not since Tertullian had a Latin churchman compiled a treatise of *Adversus Iudaeos* doctrine as extensive as Isidore's *De fide catholica contra Iudaeos* (On the Catholic Faith against the Jews),[2] which proved popular and influential for generations to come, both within and beyond the confines of Christian Spain.

Isidore's writings echo numerous motifs of Augustine's anti-Jewish polemic—and his doctrine of Jewish witness—including the exegesis of Psalm 59:12 ("Slay them not"), the resistance of the Jews to religious assimilation in pagan (especially Roman) antiquity, and the Jews' func-

---

1. Walter Ullmann, *The Growth of Papal Government in the Middle Ages,* 2d ed. (New York, 1962), pp. 28–29.
2. PL 83:449–538. A critical edition of the first of the work's two books appears in Vernon Philip Laurentius Ziolkowski, ed., "The *De fide catholica* of Saint Isidorus, Bishop" (Ph.D. diss., St. Louis University, 1982).

tion as the desks (*scriniaria*) of Christians in a properly ordered Christian world.[3] A principal investigator of Isidore's anti-Judaism has rightly acknowledged his debt to Augustine, Jerome, and others, suggesting that "it is the great bishop of Hippo that was, indisputably, Isidore's model and inspiration" and that the *De fide* in particular demonstrates "this tendency of assimilation from the oeuvre of Augustine."[4]

Nonetheless, although Isidore may have relied heavily on the works of his predecessors, the zeal with which he attacked the Jews and Judaism exceeded that of all earlier Latin fathers. Castigating the Jews more harshly than did Augustine, Isidore challenged the disingenuousness of the error that caused ancient Jewry to crucify Jesus,[5] and that which led contemporary Jews to reject Christ and Christianity:

> Denying Christ, the son of God, with nefarious disbelief, the Jews—impious, hardhearted, incredulous toward the prophets of old, and impervious toward those of late—prefer to ignore the advent of Christ rather than to acknowledge it, to deny it rather than to believe it. Him whom they accept as yet to come, they wish not to have come. Him who they read will rise from the dead, they do not believe to have arisen. Yet thus they feign not

3. Isidore, *Quaestiones in Vetus Testamentum: In Genesin* 6.16–18 (ad Genesis 4:15), PL 83:226:

> Quicunque eos ita perdiderit, septem vindictas exsolvet, id est, auferet ab eis septem vindictas, quibus alligati sunt propter reatum occisi Christi, ut hoc toto tempore, quod septenario dierum numero volvitur, magis quia non interiit genus Judaeorum, satis appareat fidelibus Christianis, sed solam dispersionem meruerint, juxta quod ait Scriptura: "Ne occideris eos. . . ." Hoc revera mirabile est, quemadmodum omnes gentes quae a Romanis subjugatae sunt, in ritum Romanorum sacrorum transierint . . . ; gens autem Judaeorum sive sub paganis regibus, sive sub Christianis, non amiserit signum legis. . . . Sed et omnis imperator, vel rex, qui eos in suo regno invenit, cum ipso signo eos invenit, et non occidit; id est, non efficit ut non sint Judaei.

Unlike the mature Augustine, for whom the doctrine of Jewish witness went hand in hand with a literal—and deliberately not typological—reading of biblical history, Isidore has here interwoven the Augustinian interpretation of Psalm 59:12 with an allegorical/typological understanding of the story of Cain. See also ibid. 8.7, col. 236: "Quid est enim hodie aliud gens ipsa, nisi quaedam scriniaria Christianorum, bajulans legem et prophetas ad testimonium assertionis Ecclesiae, ut nos honoremus per sacramentum, quod nuntiat illa per litteram?"

4. Bat-Sheva Albert, "Études sur le *De fide catholica contra Judaeos* d'Isidore de Séville" (Ph.D. diss., Bar-Ilan University, 1977), 1:61–62; see also her "*De fide catholica contra Judaeos* d'Isidore de Séville: La Polémique anti-judaique dans l'Espagne du viie siècle," *REJ* 141 (1982), 289–316.

5. Isidore repeatedly rebuked the Jews for their guilt in the crucifixion; in *De fide*, for instance, see 1.5.9, 1.5.11, 1.19–28, 1.36.3. On Augustine, see above, chapter 1, n. 111. On Isidore, see also Bat-Sheva Albert, "Isidore of Seville: His Attitude toward Judaism and His Impact on Early Medieval Canon Law," *JQR*, n.s. 80 (1990), pp. 210–11; and Norman Roth, *Jews, Visigoths and Muslims in Medieval Spain: Cooperation and Conflict*, Medieval Iberian Peninsula Texts and Studies 10 (Leiden, Netherlands, 1994), p. 15.

to understand these things, for they know that they have been fulfilled through their own sacrilege.[6]

The Jews of Isidore's own day displayed malice toward Jesus "as if they emitted a fetid odor"; and, like the ignorance feigned by Cain concerning the whereabouts of his brother Abel, Isidore concluded that "the denial of the Jews is false."[7] Isidore considered the dispersion and subjugation of the Jews in exile not so much a means to facilitate their testimony on behalf of Christianity, but more a desideratum unto itself, at least until the Jews should convert to Christianity.[8] Affirming the allegiance of the Jews to Antichrist,[9] he joined Gregory the Great in applauding Christian efforts to expedite this conversion, and he expressed particular concern for the baptism and Christian upbringing of Jewish children. The conversion of the Jews, Isidore believed, would soon bring Christian history to its long-sought fulfillment.

We shall return in due course to these Isidorean deviations from Augustinian precedent, but I mention them at the outset to illustrate the complexity of Isidore's role in our story. Well ensconced in patristic tradition, on one hand, Isidore's anti-Jewish polemic contained little (if any) argumentation or biblical exegesis that was new; one can appreciate its logic and significance only by situating it within the Augustinian tradition. His aforecited allegations of Jewish duplicity notwithstanding, Isidore agreed in the final analysis that the Jews crucified Jesus because they failed to recognize him for what he really was. Referring to Jeremiah 14:7, Isidore wrote, "For when he says, 'we have sinned against you,' he represents the *persona* of the Jews, who sinned against God when they crucified him as he came in human form. . . . Thinking that this was just as it seemed, they killed the man, as if he could not save them."[10] On the other hand, the unusual extent of Isidore's anti-Jewish hostility demonstrates how widely applications of that Augustinian tradition might vary. An evaluation of the Isidorean phase in the career of Christianity's hermeneutically crafted Jew thus

6. Isidore, *De fide catholica* 1.1.1–2, ed. Ziolkowski, p. 4, PL 83:449–50.

7. Isidore, *Quaestiones in Vetus Testamentum: In Regum I* 17.5, PL 83:406; *In Genesin* 6.6, col. 224.

8. See, for example, Isidore, *Quaestiones in Vetus Testamentum: In Genesin* 6.16 (quoted above, n. 3), where the testimonial function of Jewish dispersion is deemphasized or entirely overlooked.

9. For instance, Isidore, *De fide catholica* 1.18.1, 2.6.2.

10. Ibid. 1.15.9, ed. Ziolkowski, pp. 89–90, PL 83:474. On Jewish blindness, cf. also 1.62.1, 2.5.4, etc.; on the Jewish inability to comprehend the true meaning of Scripture, cf. 1.62.1, 2.20.3, etc.

depends heavily on an overall estimation of Isidore himself, his cultural program and ecclesiastical leadership, and the Isidorean Renaissance that bears his name.

Seldom does scholarly understanding of a historical period depend so heavily on like or dislike for its leading personage as it does in the case of Isidore and the cultural climate of seventh-century Spain. Many scholars of early medieval history have criticized Isidore for his rampant plagiarism, for the crudeness of his attempts to assimilate the teachings of classical literature into a Christian curriculum, or for the naïveté with which he portrayed Visigothic Spain as the legitimate, more competent successor of imperial Rome. Theodore Mommsen, who edited Isidore's historiographical works for the Monumenta Germaniae Historica, lamented the negligence and inexperience that characterized Isidore's treatment of historical sources.[11] An early-twentieth-century biographer deemed Isidore's work as an encyclopedist "a mass of confusion and incoherence" and his scholarship a "pseudo-science" of subservience to religious authority.[12] A generation later, M. L. W. Laistner noted that Isidore "made no original contributions either to theological thought or to secular learning."[13]

More recent investigators, however, have evaluated Isidore's achievements with greater sympathy.[14] They have praised his efforts not simply to compile but also to integrate and to unify the numerous, typically fragmented, and often contradictory strands of classical learning that a long-decadent Roman civilization had bequeathed to barbarian Europe. They have highlighted the thoroughness of Isidore's search for diverse sources of knowledge, the relative open-mindedness of his attempt to preserve ancient culture in an avidly Christian environment, the conciseness of his style, the constancy of his concern to transmit and apply received knowledge within an educational framework. Laistner's summary judgment to the contrary, one can, in fact,

---

11. MGH, Auctores antiquissimi, 11:244.

12. Ernest Brehaut, *An Encyclopedist of the Dark Ages: Isidore of Seville* (New York, 1912), pp. 48, 76–77.

13. M. L. W. Laistner, *Thought and Letters in Western Europe, A.D. 500 to 900*, rev. ed. (Ithaca, N.Y., 1957), p. 120.

14. Among others, see Ernest Robert Curtius, *European Literature and the Latin Middle Ages*, trans. Willard R. Trask, Bollingen Series 36 (1953; reprint, Princeton, N.J., 1990), pp. 450–57; Pierre Riché, *Education and Culture in the Barbarian West from the Sixth through the Eighth Century*, trans. John J. Contreni (Columbia, S.C., 1976), pp. 255–303, passim; and, above all, the works of Jacques Fontaine, especially *Isidore de Séville et la culture classique dans l'Espagne wisigothique*, 2d ed., 3 vols. (Paris, 1983).

discern novelty and inspiration in Isidore's scholarly activity, especially
during the reign of King Sisebut (612–620), no doubt the most cultured
and perhaps the most capable of the Catholic Visigothic rulers. Consistent with his hope to free Catholic Spain from external and internal
enemies alike, Sisebut warred against Byzantines and other groups with
strongholds on the Iberian Peninsula; he maintained the battle of the
church against heresy; and, critical for our story, he ordered that all
Jews in his kingdom convert to Christianity.[15] Significantly, these years
of his rule brought Isidore's literary career to a climax.[16] They saw the
composition of his major encyclopedic works—the *Etymologiae* (Etymologies), *De natura rerum* (On the Nature of Things), and *Sententiae*
(Sentences)—which he dedicated to Sisebut and/or wrote at the
king's behest. These same years witnessed the initial completion (that
is, in their original versions) of his historical treatises, including the
Chronicon, a universal chronicle of world history, and the *Historia
Gothorum*, a history of the Goths, Vandals, and Suevi in Spain.[17] Such
correspondence between Isidore's literary creativity and the Hispano-
Catholic program of Sisebut's monarchy buttresses Judith Herrin's notably favorable appraisal of the "Isidorean inheritance":

> Isidore's immense productivity, which lay at the base of all later ecclesias-
> tical thought in Visigothic Spain, was prepared by a training in the Late
> Antique curriculum barely studied elsewhere in the West. It was then
> moulded by and directed towards local needs and conditions specific to
> seventh-century Spain. In particular, it was put at the service of a monarchy
> only recently converted to the Catholic faith after a fratricidal conflict. In
> these circumstances, his theories, both political and ecclesiastical, developed
> in a tight symbiotic relationship with Visigothic practice, both in state and

15. See the account of Isidore's own *Historia Gothorum*, in *Las historias de los
Godos, Vandalos y Suevos*, ed. Cristóbal Rodríguez Alonso, Fuentes y estudios de historia leonesa 13 (León, Spain, 1975), pp. 270–75. See also E. A. Thompson, *The Goths
in Spain* (Oxford, 1969), pp. 161–68; Juan Gil, "Judíos y cristianos en la Hispania del
siglo vii," *Hispania sacra* 30 (1977), 1–47; and Peter Linehan, *History and the Historians
of Medieval Spain* (Oxford, 1993), chap. 2.

16. Above all, see José A. de Aldama, "Indicaciones sobre cronología de las obras
de S. Isidoro," in *Miscellanea isidoriana: Homenaje a S. Isidoro de Sevilla en el xiii
centenario de su muerte* (Rome, 1936), pp. 57–89; Jocelyn N. Hillgarth, "The Position
of Isidorian Studies: A Critical Review of the Literature, 1936–1975," *Studi medievali*,
3d ser. 24 (1983), 817–905, passim.

17. Along with these two historical works one might list Isidore's *De viris illustribus*,
which also appeared first during the latter half of Sisebut's reign and likewise survives
in more than one version. See Isidore of Seville, *El "De viris illustribus"* . . . : *Estudio y
edición crítica*, ed. Carmen Codoñer Merino, Theses et studia philologica salamanticensia
12 (Salamanca, 1964), pp. 18ff. This work has little bearing on the present inquiry.

church. Yet from these thoroughly Iberian roots and focus, Isidore's works were to enjoy a most remarkable destiny *outside* Spain.[18]

Hardly by coincidence, Isidore's *De fide catholica contra Iudaeos*, itself a theological encyclopedia of sorts,[19] also appeared during the reign of Sisebut. Although the impact of Isidore's anti-Judaism, along with that of his other achievements, extended throughout Latin Christendom for centuries to come, it too demands interpretation against the particular cultural and historical background that spawned it.

ISIDORE ON JEWS AND JUDAISM

Granted that hostility toward the Jews pervades much of the Isidorean corpus, and its avowedly exegetical works in particular, where ought one to commence such an analysis? Discounting several works of doubtful authenticity,[20] and noting the highly derivative nature of most of Isidore's biblical commentary, we turn first to the *De fide catholica* and then to conciliar legislation in which he played a leading role.

"Perhaps the ablest and most logical of all the early attempts to present Christ to the Jews,"[21] Isidore's *De fide catholica* offers nearly

18. Judith Herrin, *The Formation of Christendom* (Princeton, N.J., 1987), p. 245 (emphasis Herrin's).

19. See Richard McKeon, "The Organization of Sciences and the Relations of Cultures in the Twelfth and Thirteenth Centuries," in *The Cultural Context of Medieval Learning*, ed. John Emery Murdoch and Edith Dudley Sylla, Boston Studies in the Philosophy of Science 26 (Dordrecht, Netherlands, 1975), p. 152.

20. Chief among these is *Liber de variis quaestionibus adversus Iudaeos seu ceteros infideles vel plerosque haereticos iudaizantes ex utroque testamento collectus*, ed. Angel Custodio Vega and A. E. Anspach, Scriptores ecclesiastici hispano-latini veteris et medii aevi 6–9 (El Escorial, Spain, 1940), whose editors have argued at length, pp. ix–lxxxii, for its Isidorean authorship. Cf. also Angel Custodio Vega, "Le 'Liber de variis quaestionibus' no es de Félix de Urgel," *Ciudad de Dios* 161 (1949), 217–68. This attribution has been accepted, with little further discussion, by numerous scholars, including Henri de Lubac, *Exégèse médiévale: Les Quatre Sens de l'écriture*, Théologie 41–42, 59 (Paris, 1959–64), 1,1:139–40, 158, etc.; and Bernhard Blumenkranz, *Les Auteurs chrétiens latins du Moyen Âge sur les Juifs et le Judaisme* (Paris, 1963), pp. 95–99. Yet other writers have cast sufficient doubt on the Isidorean authorship of this work to militate against its discussion here. See José Madoz, "Una obra de Félix de Urgel falsamente adjudicada a San Isidoro de Sevilla," *Estudios eclesiásticos* 23 (1949), 147–68, and "Contrastes y discrepancias entre el 'Liber de variis quaestionibus' y San Isidoro de Sevilla," ibid. 24 (1950), 435–58; R. E. McNally, "Isidoriana," *Theological Studies* 20 (1959), 437–38; L. García Iglesias, *Los judíos en la España antigua* (Madrid, 1978), p. 143; and Hillgarth, "Position," pp. 843–45. Hillgarth, p. 845, similarly rejects the Isidorean authorship of a work entitled *Isaiae testimonia de Christo domino*, ascribed to Isidore by Laureano Castán Lacoma, "Un opúsculo apologético de San Isidoro, inédito," *Revista española de teología* 20 (1960), 319–60, and García Iglesias, *Los judíos*.

21. A. Lukyn Williams, *Adversus Judaeos: A Bird's-Eye View of Christian Apologiae until the Renaissance* (Cambridge, England, 1935), p. 217.

two hundred quotations from the Hebrew Bible and Apocrypha in support of essential Christian beliefs. The work, dedicated to Isidore's sister Florentina, a prioress who had apparently requested her brother to instruct her in these matters, opens with a brief statement of purpose:

> As to those things which have been foretold on diverse occasions in the books of the Old Testament concerning the birth of our Lord and savior as regards his divinity; his incarnation, passion, and death; his resurrection, and his [ultimate] kingdom and judgment—I thought that a few of the innumerable things should be cited for the benefit of [Christian] men of knowledge, so that the authority of the prophets might strengthen the gift of faith and might demonstrate the ignorance of the unbelieving Jews.[22]

The first of the treatise's two books addresses matters of Christology: the divinity of Jesus, his incarnation, the Trinity, the milestones of Jesus' earthly career (from his virgin birth in Bethlehem into the house of David to his crucifixion, resurrection, and ascension), the authority of his apostles, and his still-awaited second coming. The second book treats the implementation of the divine plan for human salvation over the course of terrestrial history: God's respective calls to the Gentiles and to the Jews, his rejection of the latter and new covenant with the former, the commandments of the law versus the sacraments, and the New Testament's fulfillment of earlier biblical prophecy. As I noted above, Isidore drew extensively from the works of earlier church fathers. Yet the structure and progression of Isidore's anti-Jewish argument are distinctive, and they will presently prove essential to an appreciation of its underlying logic.[23]

As archbishop of Seville and chief prelate of the Spanish church, Isidore had ample opportunity to apply his doctrine concerning the Jews in formulating ecclesiastical policy and legislation. He presided over the Council of Seville in 624, which called for policing the Jews ordered by Sisebut to baptize their children, lest they substitute Christian children for their own.[24] More significantly, Isidore presided over the Fourth Council of Toledo in 633, ten canons of which concerned the Jews. Some of these decrees—forbidding Jewish ownership of

22. Isidore, De fide, praef., ed. Ziolkowski, p. 1, PL 83:449–50.
23. See the outline below.
24. Paulus Hinschius, ed., Decretales pseudo-isidorianae et capitula angilramni (1863; reprint, Aalen, Germany, 1963), pp. 396–97. See Paul Sejourné, Le Dernier Père de l'Église: Saint Isidore de Séville—Son rôle dans l'histoire du droit canonique (Paris, 1929), pp. 31f., who argues for the authenticity of this purportedly pseudo-Isidorean decretal.

Christian slaves, Jewish influence over Christians (whether through bribery or by holding public office), and Judaizing on the part of Jewish converts to Christianity[25]—echoed or reinforced the legislation of previous church councils and Visigothic rulers. Others, however, may well afford insight into Isidore's own attitudes toward the Jews and thus warrant particular attention. Adumbrating later Visigothic discrimination against "Jews, whether baptized or unbaptized,"[26] the council forbade Christians of Jewish origin to hold public office,[27] and it underscored the gravity of the issue of proselytizing by force in three separate decrees. Reflecting the reality of Jewish survival in Spain despite Sisebut's edict of conversion, Canon 57 banned the baptism of the Jews against their will, but with several important reservations, implied and explicit:

> Concerning the Jews, the holy synod has decreed henceforth to compel no one to accept the faith, because God has compassion for whom he wishes and renders obstinate whom he wishes; for not against their will should such people be saved, but with their consent, so that the semblance of justice be kept intact. Just as man, obeying the serpent of his own free will, was ruined, so a man is saved through believing—owing to the call of God's grace and the conversion of his own mind. Therefore, rather than be subdued they should be urged to convert, not under compulsion but through the power of their free will. Those, however, who were previously coerced to become Christian, as happened at the time of the most pious ruler Sisebut, for it is now a fact that they, having been admitted to the divine sacraments, have received the grace of baptism, have been anointed with chrism, and have partaken of the body and blood of the lord—they should appropriately be forced to retain the faith which they adopted, albeit through compulsion or out of necessity, lest the Lord's name be blasphemed, and the faith which they have adopted be deemed vile and contemptible.[28]

Principled objections to forced conversion notwithstanding, the decree does not follow Gregory the Great in prescribing penalties for those who baptized Jews against their will, and it emphatically upholds the

25. Canons 58–59, 61, 63–66, in José Vives, ed., *Concilios visigóticos e hispano-romanos*, España cristiana: Textos 1 (Barcelona, 1963), pp. 211–14.

26. *Leges Visogothorum* 12.2.10, 12.2.15, MGH, Leges 1:416–17, 423–24: "Judei seu baptizati, sive non extiterint baptizati."

27. Canon 65, in Vives, *Concilios visigóticos*, p. 213; cf. Jean Juster, "The Legal Condition of the Jews under the Visigothic Kings," ed. Alfred Mordechai Rabello, *Israel Law Review* 11 (1976), 583–85.

28. Vives, *Concilios visigóticos*, pp. 210–11; cf. Juster, "Legal Condition," pp. 261ff., 409ff.

validity of those forced conversions that resulted from King Sisebut's unprecedented edict. In Canon 60 the council ordered that Jewish children be removed from their parents and raised in a Christian environment: "Lest the sons and daughters of the Jews be further entangled in the error of their parents, we decree that they be separated from their company, having been assigned to monasteries or God-fearing Christian men and women, so that under their care they learn the practice of the faith and, thus better instructed, they may make progress in both their behavior and their belief."[29] And, reaffirming an earlier law of Sisebut,[30] Canon 63 demanded not only that children born of mixed marriages between Christians and Jews be raised as Christians but that Jewish husbands of Christian women must themselves convert to Christianity.[31]

Isidore's anti-Jewish pronouncements have evoked scholarly interest and discussion along various lines. Readers of the *De fide catholica* have questioned the extent of Isidore's interaction with Spanish Jewry, and they have sought to identify the intended applications of his polemical treatise. Did Isidore write this work for disputing directly with the Jews, keeping converted Jews within the church, providing catechetical instruction for the baptized children of Jews, preaching to the Christian laity, or for enlightening the Catholic clergy?[32] Additionally, historians have related Isidore's polemic and legislation to their interpretation of the Visigoths' anti-Jewish policy in general.[33] What suddenly triggered such extreme hostility toward the Jews during the last

---

29. Vives, *Concilios visigóticos*, p. 212. Although some versions of this canon refer to the baptized children of the Jews, Bat-Sheva Albert has argued, at length and persuasively, that such was not the understanding of Isidore's decree in seventh-century Spain. See her "Isidore of Seville," p. 216 n. 37.

30. *Leges Visigothorum* 12.2.14, MGH, Leges 1:422–23.

31. Vives, *Concilios visigóticos*, pp. 213; cf. Juster, "Legal Condition," pp. 568–69.

32. For example: James Parkes, *The Conflict of the Church and the Synagogue: A Study in the Origins of Antisemitism* (London, 1934), pp. 276, 357–58; Solomon Katz, *The Jews in the Visigothic and Frankish Kingdoms of Spain and Gaul*, Medieval Academy of America Monographs 12 (1937; reprint, New York, 1970), p. 35; Blumenkranz, *Les Auteurs*, pp. 90–91; and Albert, "*De fide catholica*," pp. 305ff.

33. A thorough historiographical review lies beyond the scope of this study. For a broad sampling of opinion, see Ramón Hernández, "La España visigoda frente al problema de los judíos," *La ciencia tomista* 94 (1967), 627–85; P. D. King, *Law and Society in the Visigothic Kingdom*, Cambridge Studies in Medieval Life and Thought 3, 5 (Cambridge, England, 1972), pp. 130ff.; Bernard S. Bachrach, "A Reassessment of Visigothic Jewish Policy, 589–711," *AHR* 78 (1973), 11–34, and *Early Medieval Jewish Policy in Western Europe* (Minneapolis, Minn., 1977), chap. 1; Bat-Sheva Albert, "Un Nouvel Examen de la politique anti-juive wisigothique," *REJ* 135 (1976), 3–29; García Iglesias, *Los judíos*, pp. 106ff.; and Roger Collins, *Early Medieval Spain: Unity in Diversity, 400–1000*, 2d ed. (New York, 1995), pp. 128–43.

125 years of Visigothic rule in Spain? Did it derive primarily from the kings' personal piety and commitment to the ideals of the church or more from considerations of political expediency? Did secular or ecclesiastical leaders take the initiative in formulating these policies? As in fifteenth-century Spain, might measures against the Jews have aimed primarily to eliminate Judaizing among recent converts to Christianity? Did Visigothic monarchs wish to comply with or to emulate the anti-Jewish policies of Byzantine emperors from Justinian to Heraclius, some of whom eventually called for the baptism or expulsion of all Jews in the empire? Acknowledging the correspondence between Isidore's greatest literary productivity and the reign of King Sisebut, investigators have also debated Isidore's stance on the royal decree that Spanish Jews must convert. For in addition to the conciliar canons discussed above, the archbishop addressed the issue of forced conversion in at least four of his own works. In the *Sententiae*, Isidore wrote that religious belief should not be imposed by force, although it is possible that this passage antedates Sisebut's decree.[34] The *Etymologiae* and *Chronicon* record the conversion of Spanish Jewry under Sisebut's rule and, albeit subtly, appear to approve of the royal action.[35] The *Historia Gothorum* first notes that Sisebut converted the Jews unwisely, "for he compelled with force those whom one was supposed to bring to the faith with reason." Yet the text proceeds immediately to mollify its indictment with reference to Philippians 1:18: "in every way, whether in pretense or in truth, Christ is proclaimed."[36] Weighing this evidence, some scholars have judged Isidore a supporter of Sisebut's decree;[37] others have stressed his opposition to the edict, at times even judging him, whether in a positive or negative sense, a humane advocate of the Jewish cause;[38] and still others have

---

34. Isidore, *Sententiae* 2.2.4, PL 83:601: "Fides nequaquam vi extorquetur, sed ratione atque exemplis suadetur. A quibus autem exigitur violenter, perseverare in eis non potest"; cf. 2.2.13, col. 602. On the date of this work, see Marc Reydellet, "Les Intentions idéologiques et politiques dans la *Chronique* d'Isidore de Séville," *Mélanges d'archéologie et d'histoire de l'École française de Rome* 82 (1970), 397 n. 2.

35. See below, at n. 54.

36. Isidore, *Las historias*, pp. 270–73.

37. Sejourné, *Le Dernier Père*, pp. 31f., 114, 253–55; Baron, *A Social and Religious History of the Jews*. 2d ed. (New York, 1952–83), 3:247 n. 47; Bernhard Blumenkranz, *Juifs et Chrétiens dans le monde occidental, 430–1096* (Paris, 1960), p. 108; Albert, "Un Nouvel Examen," p. 21; Alfredo Mordechai Rabello, *The Jews in Visigothic Spain in Light of the Legislation* [Hebrew] (Jerusalem, 1983), pp. 51ff.; and Roth, *Jews, Visigoths, and Muslims*, p. 13.

38. Williams, *Adversus Judaeos*, p. 215; de Lubac, *Exégèse médiévale*, 2,1:170 ("empreinte d'humanité"); Juster, "Legal Condition," pp. 263–64 nn. 13–14; Bachrach, *Early*

sought a middle ground, deeming him inconsistent and his misgivings the result of hindsight, or perhaps a reaction to the rampant Judaizing that ensued in the wake of insincere conversions.[39] Investigators likewise disagree concerning the significance of the anti-Jewish measures of the Fourth Council of Toledo: Although some have emphasized the harshness of this presumably Isidorean legislation, linking it to the program of Sisebut,[40] others have downplayed its anti-Jewish motivation, suggesting that the council's real antagonism pointed elsewhere.[41] Finally, students of Isidore have pondered the place of the archbishop, his *De fide catholica*, and the Toledan decrees in the evolution of Christian anti-Judaism. In retrospect, they have stressed his reliance on and transmission of earlier traditions, judging him a master of "patristic vulgarization."[42] Looking forward in time, they have considered the subsequent popularity of the *De fide catholica*—the earliest extant work in medieval German[43]—the impact of Isidorean legislation on medieval canon law,[44] and attitudes toward Isidore in Jewish historiography of the later Middle Ages.[45]

Medieval Jewish Policy, p. 10; Pierre Cazier, "De la coercition à la persuasion: L'Attitude d'Isidore de Séville face à la politique anti-juive des souverains visigotiques," in *De l'antijudaïsme antique à l'antisemitisme contemporain*, ed. Valentin Nikiprowetzky (Lille, France, 1979), pp. 125–46; Marc Reydellet, *La Royauté dans la littérature latine de Sidone Apollinaire à Isidore de Séville*, Bibliothèque des écoles françaises d'Athènes et de Rome 243 (Rome, 1981), pp. 544–45; and Herrin, *Formation*, p. 238.

39. For instance, José Luis Romero, "San Isidoro de Sevilla: Su pensamiento historicopolítico y sus relaciones con la historia visigoda," *Cuadernos de historia de España* 8 (1947), 68; and Jacques Fontaine, "Isidore de Séville et l'astrologie," *Revue des études latines* 31 (1954), 294 n. 4.

40. For example: Parkes, *Conflict*, pp. 356–57; Sejourné, *Le Dernier Père*, pp. 253–55; Blumenkranz, *Juifs et Chrétiens dans le monde occidental*, pp. 109–13; and Albert, "Isidore of Seville," pp. 212ff.

41. Cf. the various targets of the Toledan decrees proposed by José Madoz, "El primado romano en España en el ciclo isidoriano," *Revista española de teología* 2 (1942), 245f. (relapsed Jewish converts to Christianity); Hernández, "España visigoda," pp. 658–62 (Judaizing Christians); and Gil, "Judíos y cristianos," pp. 10ff. (Arian heretics).

42. Albert, "Études," 1:101; cf. Laureano Castán Lacoma, "San Isidoro de Sevilla, apologista antijudaico," in *Isidoriana: Estudios sobre San Isidoro de Sevilla en el xiv centenario de su nacimiento*, ed. Manuel C. Díaz y Díaz (León, 1961), p. 455, who praised Isidore for building a cathedral out of the ideas and traditions inherited from earlier fathers.

43. Karl Weinhold, ed., *Die altdeutschen Bruchstücke des Tractats des Bischofs Isidorus von Sevilla "De fide catholica contra Judaeos,"* Bibliothek der ältesten deutschen Literatur-Denkmäler 6 (Paderborn, Germany, 1874); and Hillgarth, "Position," p. 888.

44. Bat-Sheva Albert, "The 65th Canon of the IVth Council of Toledo (633) in Christian Legislation and Its Interpretation in the 'Converso' Polemics in XVth Century Spain," in *Proceedings of the Eighth World Congress of Jewish Studies* (Jerusalem, 1982), B:43–48, and "Isidore of Seville," pp. 213–20.

45. See Roth, *Jews, Visigoths, and Muslims*, pp. 16–18; and, especially, Ram Ben-Shalom, "The Image of Christian Culture in the Historical Consciousness of the Jews of

These scholarly discussions testify to Isidore's prominence in the history of Jewish-Christian polemic; viewed collectively, however, they also point to aspects of the *De fide* that recent scholarship has not adequately probed. All of these lines of inquiry relate Isidore and his anti-Judaism to strictly external referents—comparing them with earlier patristic writers and traditions, relating them to the contemporary concerns of Visigothic kingdom and church, and assessing their subsequent impact and dissemination. Neither have modern researchers explained the place of the *De fide catholica* in the entirety of the Isidorean corpus, nor have they subjected its contents to deliberate thematic and structural analysis. A few have reflected impressionistically on the nature of the treatise—perhaps an attempt at systematic theology, or a catechetical work structurally dependent on the Apostle's Creed, or a mystical meditation on Scripture[46]—while summary characterizations of its tone have ranged from hostility to "meekness."[47] Yet owing to Isidore's debt to his predecessors, most assessments discern no novelty in Isidore's polemic, nor do they allow for the possibility that its substance developed over time.[48] As a result of such estimations, much of the significance of the *De fide catholica* has remained unnoticed.

TERRESTRIAL HISTORY, CONVERSION OF THE JEWS, AND THE ISIDOREAN VISION

A more truly Isidorean reading of Isidore might proceed from three related observations. First, Isidore composed the *De fide catholica* pre-

Twelfth to Fifteenth-Century Spain and Provence" [Hebrew] (Ph.D. diss., Tel Aviv University, 1996), 1:371–77.

46. (Sister) Patrick Jerome Mullins, *The Spiritual Life According to Saint Isidore of Seville*, Catholic University of America Studies in Medieval and Renaissance Language and Literature 13 (Washington, D.C., 1940), pp. 145ff.; Ph. Delhaye, "Les Idées morales de Saint Isidore de Séville," *RTAM* 26 (1959), 19; and Cazier, "De la coercition," pp. 139–40.

47. Hernández, "España visigoda," p. 677: "mansedumbre." Cf. also José Madoz, *San Isidoro de Sevilla: Semblanza de su personalidad literaria*, ed. Carlos G. Goldaraz (León, Spain, 1960), p. 45: "Pero no es nada polémica, como del título pudiera sospecharse, sino plácidamente expositiva, y con ulteriores propósitos de edificación, según se desprende de la dedicatoria del autor a su hermana Florentina."

48. Bat-Sheva Albert, for instance, has concluded that "without a polemic against the Talmud, Isidore could hardly produce any new arguments" ("*De fide catholica*," p. 290). Castán Lacoma, "San Isidoro," p. 448, has surmised that rabbinic literature and Hebrew were not totally unknown to Isidore.

cisely at the time of Sisebut's decree that the Jews must convert to Christianity (614–615);[49] the interdependence between polemical treatise and royal edict might well extend beyond their chronological coincidence to the motivations and presuppositions underlying each. Second, and more generally, the inner logic of Isidore's literary and ecclesiastical career must be understood against the background of Sisebut's designs for the Visigothic monarchy; as in Judith Herrin's aforecited judgment, Isidore's "theories, both political and ecclesiastical, developed in a tight symbiotic relationship with Visigothic practice, both in state and church." Both men numbered among the most learned of their generation. Both blended their interests in classical science and literature with steadfast commitments to Catholic Christianity and Visigothic Spain. In their respective, even convergent, fashions, both leaders combated the various opponents of these mutual allegiances. Deeming them threats to Visigothic hegemony and to Catholic unity, Sisebut battled against all alien elements in Spain, including Byzantines, Arian heretics, and Jews; he also authored a work of Christian hagiography as well as an anti-Arian treatise.[50] In Jacques Fontaine's words, Sisebut "understood his mission in such a way that its moral, religious, and political elements were inextricably mingled. He was thus an active collaborator in the Isidorean renaissance, which had as its aim nothing less than the reconstruction of the civil and religious life of Visigothic Spain."[51] Isidore similarly struggled against heretics and Jews, usually maintaining the policies of Sisebut, even after the latter's death. In his various encyclopedic works, Isidore undertook to endow Visigothic Spain with a viable Christian synthesis of classical culture, one that would confirm Spain's legitimacy as successor to imperial Rome, just as Sisebut sought prestige for his throne by emulating the Eastern emperors of Byzantium, even as he fought their armies in battle. Simply put, both men strove to integrate the society and culture of Spain under Catholic Visigothic rule, and at the same time to accredit that rule as the fulfillment of classical Roman and Christian traditions. Third, Isi-

49. Aldama, "Indicaciones," esp. pp. 86–87; and Albert, "De fide catholica," pp. 304–5.

50. Riché, Education and Culture, p. 263; and Collins, Early Medieval Spain, pp. 60–68.

51. Jacques Fontaine, "King Sisebut's Vita Desiderii and the Political Function of Visigothic Hagiography," in Visigothic Spain: New Approaches, ed. Edward James (Oxford, 1980), p. 97; see also Jacques Fontaine, "Théorie et practique du style chez Isidore de Séville," Vigiliae christianae 14 (1960), 77 and n. 28.

dore gave clearest expression to these shared aspirations in his two major works of historiography, his universal *Chronicon* and his Hispano-centric *Historia Gothorum*. In its original version, each of these historical accounts climaxed and concluded in the reign of Sisebut.[52] One modern reader[53] has suggested that Isidore thus likened Sisebut to the biblical King Solomon, the monarch, conqueror, and sage of ancient Israel who secured its borders, united its twelve tribes, built its temple to God, and enjoyed well-deserved renown for his wisdom and eloquence. Most noteworthy, then, is the place accorded Sisebut's conversion of the Jews in Isidore's histories. The *Historia Gothorum* lists it first among Sisebut's accomplishments. The full text of the *Chronicon* mentions it along with but two other achievements of the king; in Isidore's abridgement of the work, it is the only achievement mentioned.[54] Without doubt the Jews assumed vital importance in Isidore's outlook on history and in his vision of the ideal Visigothic monarchy, and this significance warrants further elaboration.

If one may link Augustinian and Gregorian constructions of the Jew to considerations of exegesis, the philosophy of history, and anthropology, the key to Isidore's distinctive ideas on the Jews and Judaism lies chiefly in the second of these—that is, in his reading of terrestrial history. Recognizing Isidore's debt to his patristic predecessors, above all Augustine, one must therefore identify the singular features of his historiography with care. Isidore's *Chronicon* borrowed much from Augustinian accounts of human history, and from the *De civitate Dei* in particular: the cardinal importance of divine providence in human affairs, the division of history as we know it into six ages, and the parallel spiritual and political dimensions of God's plan for historical development. Nevertheless, nurturing the inclination of the Spanish

---

52. On the dating of these works, see Aldama, "Indicaciones," passim; and Madoz, *San Isidoro*, pp. 28ff. On the relationship between their different versions and on their "redaction history," see the comments of Theodor Mommsen in MGH, Auctores antiquissimi 11:252–56, 407–10; and, more recently, the arguments of Luis Vásquez de Parga, "Notas sobre la obra histórica de San Isidoro," in *Isidoriana: Estudios sobre San Isidoro de Sevilla en el xiv centenario de su nacimiento*, ed. Manuel C. Díaz y Díaz (León, Spain, 1961), pp. 99–105, Rodríguez Alonso in Isidore, *Las historias*, pp. 11–66, and Hillgarth, "Position," pp. 835–36.

53. Marc Reydellet, "La Conception du souverain chez Isidore de Séville," in *Isidoriana: Estudios sobre San Isidoro de Sevilla en el xiv centenario de su nacimiento*, ed. Manuel C. Díaz y Díaz (León, Spain, 1961), p. 465.

54. MGH, Auctores antiquissimi 11:479–80; the abridged version of the *Chronicon* appears in Isidore's *Etymologiarum sive originum libri xx* 5.39.42, ed. W. M. Lindsay, 2 vols. (Oxford, 1911), n.p.

Orosius two centuries before him, Isidore departed radically from Augustine by elaborating an essentially monistic construction of human experience. Here one finds instructive similarity between Gregory the Great and Isidore, but Isidore's temperament and his overtly historiographic interests yielded a view of human history more positivistic than that suggested in Gregorian biblical commentary.[55]

Precisely what distinguished these ideas of Isidore? Augustine had posited a fundamental distinction between the histories of heavenly and earthly cities, despite their temporary intersection in the saeculum. Gregory had excluded the saeculum from his reading of history, which, owing to his ascetic convictions, he "sketched only from a celestial perspective,"[56] drastically devaluing the experience of this world. Isidore, however, while upholding Gregory's assertion of a single and sole realm of historical development, portrayed the political events of this world as the critical manifestation of that development![57] Providential history in the *Chronicon* entails the identity of divine and mundane history, inasmuch as God actualizes his design for human salvation within a terrestrial context. Mundane historical developments correspond directly with progress toward the eschaton. More than in Gregorian doctrine, and in contrast with Augustinian teaching, these developments will eventually prove the time ripe for the final redemption, and they will figure directly in the process of Christian salvation.

Lacking both the neutral political sphere of the Augustinian saeculum and the Gregorian aversion for the worldly,[58] Isidore's history reverts to a relatively simplistic, tension-free understanding of Christian

55. Particularly helpful in identifying the underlying perspective of Isidorean historiography are Romero, "San Isidoro"; Antonio Truyol y Serra, "The Idea of Man and World History from Seneca to Orosius and Saint Isidore of Seville," *Cahiers d'histoire mondiale* 6 (1961), 698–713; Arno Borst, "Das Bild der Geschichte in Enzyklopädie Isidors von Sevilla," *Deutsches Archiv für Erforschung des Mittelalters* 22 (1961), 1–62; Reydellet, "Les Intentions"; and Paul Merritt Bassett, "The Use of History in the *Chronicon* of Isidore of Seville," *History and Theory* 15 (1976), 278–92. To contrast Isidore with Gregory in this regard, see above, chapter 2, at nn. 69–72.

56. Straw, *Gregory the Great: Perfection in Imperfection* (Berkeley, Calif., 1988), p. 11.

57. For instance, Isidore, *De fide* 1.58.1, ed. Ziolkowski, p. 171, PL 83:495: "regnum ejus in caelo, et in terra aeternum, ac perpetuum permanebit."

58. See, for instance, Jacques Fontaine, "La Vocation monastique selon Saint Isidore de Séville," in *Théologie de la vie monastique: Études sur la tradition patristique*, Théologie 49 (Paris, 1961), pp. 353–69; and "Grammaire sacrée et grammaire profane: Isidore de Séville devant l'exégèse biblique," in *Los visigodos: Historia y civilización*, Antigüedad y cristianismo 3 (Murcia, Spain, 1986), pp. 311–29.

empire or kingship (*imperium* or *regnum christianum*) that characterized Eusebius and other fourth-century writers, including the younger
Augustine.[59] This was the Christian optimism, the *do ut des* ("I give
so that you may give") mentality that discerned the fulfillment of God's
promise of salvation in the Christianization of Rome, against which
the older Augustine's *De civitate Dei* reacted so emphatically.[60] Yet
Isidore did not simply return to the outlook of fourth-century fathers.
He borrowed from the older Augustine too, and he composed a universal chronicle of world history that was distinctive, one whose structure and style bespoke his own, early medieval worldview. The *Chronicon*'s narration of its six historical epochs includes earthly and pagan
affairs alongside matters divine and spiritual. Commencing with creation and not with Adam (as they do in Augustine's works), they betray
no metaphoric correspondence to the proverbial ages in a single human's life and thus do not symbolize the spiritual growth of God's
chosen people from its youth to its adulthood. Rather, they serve to
depict the totality of human history as Isidore perceived it: Israel and
the nations, East and West, natural and supernatural, that recorded in
Scripture *and that related in classical mythology*—all in the same continuum. Isidore's chronology is more precise than Augustine's, his periods more carefully demarcated, and his division of political history
more rigorous. Isidore dealt directly with specific kings and kingdoms,
not the vast hegemonies of Assyria and Rome that one encounters in
the *De civitate Dei*; all of them had a role to play in the divinely
ordained progression of terrestrial history, from creation to the final,
seventh age of glory.

Augustine, we recall, afforded minimal attention to the political
highlights of the sixth age—like the *pax romana*—which extended
from the incarnation to the present. Yet Isidore deemed the sixth age
as all-important, and it, more than any other, exemplifies the special
character of his chronicle. Its annals are as long as those of the five
earlier ages combined, its scope entirely extrabiblical, and its history
predominantly political—again, in striking contrast with the Augustinian model. As if to underscore that contrast, Isidore's sixth age begins

59. See above, chapter 1, at nn. 89ff., and chapter 2, at nn. 69ff.

60. See Theodor E. Mommsen, "St. Augustine and the Christian Idea of Progress,"
Journal of the History of Ideas 12 (1951), 346–74; Herbert A. Deane, *The Political and
Social Ideas of St. Augustine* (New York, 1963), passim; and Robert A. Markus, *Saeculum: History and Society in the Theology of St Augustine* (1970; reprint, Cambridge,
England, 1988), esp. chaps. 2–3.

not in the middle of Jesus' ministry but only in the wake of the brief
mention of his life,[61] and following the replacement of the Old Testament by the New:

> Octavian Augustus reigned fifty-six years. During his reign, he celebrated
> three triumphs after his Sicilian [triumph]: a Dalmatian [triumph], an Asian
> [triumph], and, lastly, an Alexandrian [triumph for his victory] against An-
> tony; thereafter, [he gained control of] Spain. Then, with peace achieved
> throughout the whole world, on land and at sea, he closed and bolted the
> gates of Janus. Under his rule, the sixty-nine weeks noted in Daniel [9:24–
> 27] were completed; and, with the cessation of the kingship and priesthood
> of the Jews, the lord Jesus Christ was born of a virgin in the forty-second
> year of his reign. [Thereafter begins] the sixth age of terrestrial history [*sexta
> aetas saeculi*].[62]

Juxtaposing the fulfillment of biblical messianic prophecy and the birth
of Jesus with the Augustan apogee of Roman political achievement,
Isidore's record of the incarnation epitomizes his blend of spiritual and
worldly history: What better a demonstration than the physical embodiment of God on earth, coincident with the *pax romana*! Moreover,
with the triumph of Rome and the establishment of Christianity already
established fact, Isidore's sixth age epitomizes the identification of *Romanitas* and *Christianitas*, yielding an uninterrupted review of pagan
emperors, their Christian successors, and the Germanic rulers of Spain.
Neither the conversion of Constantine (who, eventually, at the end of
his life, received Arian baptism)[63] nor the end of the Western empire
marks the end of an era in this historical narrative. Rome lacks unique
soteriological import. Duly constituted kingship (*regnum*) survived the
empire in the West, so that its fall hardly undercut the basis for historical optimism; Spanish monarchs assumed no less significance than
did Roman or Byzantine emperors. Structurally, the sixth age links the
incarnation and the final judgment, the first and second comings of
Christ. It is Christian history, in which God's plan for the salvation of
his people draws progressively closer to its full and final realization.

61. Contra Augustine, *De Genesi contra Manichaeos* 1.23.40, and *De vera religione*
27.50.
62. Isidore, *Chronicon*, MGH, Auctores antiquissimi, 11:453–54; my thanks to Sarah
Johnston for her help in translating the confusing Latin original of this seemingly simple
text.
63. Ibid., p. 466: "heu pro dolor! bono usus principio et fine malo." On this tradition
concerning Constantine, see Samuel N. C. Lieu and Dominic Montserrat, eds., *From
Constantine to Julian: Pagan and Byzantine Views* (London, 1996), p. 100; and Timothy
D. Barnes, *Constantine and Eusebius* (Cambridge, Mass., 1981), pp. 204–5, 260.

As the *Chronicon* records the reigns of Eastern and Western monarchs in succession, it highlights their victories over Jews, heretics, and Byzantine invaders of the West, those who evidently impede the realization of a properly ordered Christendom. Presumably, when these problems have been overcome, the sixth age will give way to the seventh. History will culminate in a final age of glory.

When will this final redemption occur? During Sisebut's reign, when Isidore first wrote the *Chronicon,* he reported the king's conversion of the Jews and at once reflected that "the time remaining in the sixth age is known to God alone."[64] Isidore's chronicle thus concludes, it would seem, on a note of uncertainty. Yet the movement of the sixth of history from the *pax romana* to Catholic Visigothic kingship, and from the incarnation—entailing "the cessation of the kingship and priesthood of the Jews [*cessante regno ac sacerdotio Iudaeorum*]"—to the conversion of Iberian Jewry, is suggestive.[65] Marc Reydellet has elaborated: "Isidore lives in a world where all disparities seem to be conclusively reconciled: The Jews become Christians; all of Spain is reorganized around [the Visigothic capital of] Toledo. One does not mean to state that Isidore displayed a blind optimism—but simply that the great conflict of good and evil is played out within each individual. Yet in the order of collective history, the plan of God can seem to be on a course of total and definitive realization."[66] The conversion of the Jews at the end of the sixth age heralded that realization; and, Reydellet thus has concluded, Isidore's universal chronicle "was, in the history of its genre, the only one which had a conclusion."[67]

The concerns and structure of Isidore's other major historiographical treatise, the *Historia Gothorum,* echo this sense of the *Chronicon.* In its first version, it too dates from the reign of Sisebut, and it too served as "a declaration of independence on the part of Visigothic

64. Isidore, *Etymologiae* 5.39.42, ed. Lindsay, with critical nn.; see also Richard Landes, "Lest the Millennium Be Fulfilled: Apocalyptic Expectations and the Pattern of Western Chronography, 100–800 C.E.," in *The Use and Abuse of Eschatology in the Middle Ages,* ed. Werner Verbeke et al., Mediaevalia lovanensia 1, 15 (Louvain, Belgium, 1988), esp. pp. 165–66.

65. See Isidore, *Quaestiones in Vetus Testamentum: In Genesin* 6.16, PL 83:226, quoted above, n. 3, where the Jewish role in the sevenfold scheme of Christian history is clearly of eschatological significance.

66. Reydellet, "Les Intentions," p. 399.

67. Ibid., p. 398.

Spain and an affirmation of its worth against the ancient [Roman] mistress of the Mediterranean world."[68] But if the *Chronicon* legitimizes Visigothic kingship in a blending of *Romanitas* and *Christianitas* that followed upon the incarnation, the history of the Goths roots its patriotic vision in the glories of Spain and the Christian character of the Visigothic kingdom it spawned: "Of all lands from the West to India, you, Spain, holy and ever-fruitful mother of princes and of nations [*principum gentiumque mater*] are the most beautiful. You now are justly queen of all provinces, from whom not only the West but also the East receives its light. You are the splendor and jewel of the world, a very distinguished part of the earth, in which the glorious fertility of the Getic people takes much pleasure and flourishes greatly."[69] The panegyric of Isidore's well-known *Laus Spaniae* continues, but its ramifications for Isidore are already clear: Spain, mother of kings, is uniquely suited to the fulfillment of Christian historical-political aspirations. A geographical, spatial entity, Spain has nurtured the foremost Christian monarchy, much as the temporal progression of universal *Chronicon*'s sixth age culminates in the Visigothic kingdom. For the *Chronicon*'s emphasis on the incarnation, effecting the Christianization of human history through God's participation in it, the *Historia Gothorum* substitutes the conversion of Visigothic Spain and her rulers—to justify her claims to Rome's erstwhile primacy and her opposition to Byzantine imperialism. Not so much the historical Jesus of the *Chronicon* but Christ the king accords divine sanction to the Catholic rulers of the *Historia Gothorum*; his values pervade the totality of the Visigothic church—monarch and prelates, clergy and laity together—and render it the genuine kingdom of Christ (*regnum Christi*), the defense of the members of Christ (*tuitio membrorum Christi*).[70]

---

68. Jocelyn N. Hillgarth, "Historiography in Visigothic Spain," in *La storiografia altomedievale*, Settimane di Studio del Centro italiano di studi sull'alto medioevo 17 (Spoleto, Italy, 1970), 1:296.

69. Isidore, *Las historias*, pp. 168–71. On the authenticity of this passage, see the introductory essay of Alonso Rodríguez, pp. 57ff.; and Madoz, *San Isidoro*, pp. 29ff.

70. See the helpful treatments of Ullmann, *Growth of Papal Government*, pp. 29–31; Reydellet, *La Royauté*, chap. 10; and Suzanne Teillet, *Des Goths à la nation gothique: Les Origines de l'idée de nation en Occident du ve à viie siècle* (Paris, 1984), pt. 3. Cogent reservations concerning Teillet's perceptions of genuine Gothic nationalism in Isidorean historiography have been aired by Jocelyn N. Hillgarth, reviewing Teillet in the *Journal of Ecclesiastical History* 39 (1988), 578–81, and perhaps adumbrated by Madoz, "El primado romano." Yet Isidore's commitment to Spain as the locus for the

The earliest version of the *Historia Gothorum* reaches a natural conclusion in the career of King Sisebut:

> At the beginning of his reign, leading the Jews to the Christian faith, he was zealous indeed, but not wisely so; for he compelled with force those whom one was supposed to bring to the faith with reason. But, as it is written, whether in pretense or in truth, Christ is proclaimed. He was, moreover, refined in his eloquence, learned in his thought, and educated, to an extent, in the sciences.
>
> He was also renowned for his military accomplishments and victories. . . . Twice, in person, did he successfully defeat the Byzantines, and he conquered some of their cities for himself. He was so merciful following his victory, that he freed for ransom many from the opposing army who had been taken captive and led into slavery, and the price of the redemption of the captives became his treasure.[71]

Curiously, Isidore chose to praise Sisebut for three varieties of accomplishment. The king succeeded in battle. As already mentioned, he was himself learned. But before all else, he converted the Jews. Noting the transcendental value of history for Isidore—and its resulting utility as a grammar to understand the divine economies of creation and salvation—one can hardly overlook the moral of this story. Spain mothered the Visigoths' Christian kingdom, whose Catholic rulers cultivated the kingship of Christ. Not by happenstance did the same ruler who subdued Spanish territory to his Christian rule and who joined Isidore in integrating the cultural legacies of Athens and Jerusalem convert the Jews, the sole remaining threat to Hispano-Catholic unity.[72] In both

---

fulfillment of Christian *Heilsgeschichte* in the current, sixth age seems firmly established, and the presence or absence of Gothic nationalism in his worldview bears but minimally on the present argument.

71. Isidore, *Las historias*, pp. 270–75.

72. On the recalcitrance of the Jews, see Jacques Fontaine, "Conversion et culture chez les wisigoths d'Espagne," in *La conversione al Christianismo nell'Europa dell'alto medioevo*, Settimane di Studio del Centro italiano di studi sull'alto medioevo 14 (Spoleto, Italy, 1967), pp. 133–34: "Le problème politique de l'unité nationale, posé à Liuvigild par le catholicisme de la majorité de la population de son royaume, s'est déplacé sur une minorité beaucoup plus difficile à convertir et à intégrer que ne l'avait été sous Reccared celle de ses compatriotes ariens: le problème juif ne cessera plus d'apparaître insoluble, jusqu'à la chute du royaume wisigothique." See also Jeremy duQuesnay Adams, "Ideology and the Requirements of Citizenship in Visigothic Spain: The Case of the *Judaei*," *Societas* 2 (1972), 317–32; and José Orlandis, "Hacia una major comprensión del problema judío en el reino visigodo-católico de España," in *Gli Ebrei nell'alto medioevo*, Settimane di Studio del Centro italiano di studi sull'alto medioevo 26 (Spoleto, Italy, 1980), 1:114–96. Most telling is the declaration of Receswinth in *Leges Visigothorum* 12.2.3, MGH Leges 1,1:413: "Nam cum virtus Dei totum universaliter acie verbi sui radicitus heresum extirpaverit surculum, sola Iudeorum nequitia ingemiscimus regiminis nostri arva esse polluta."

these expressions of Isidore's distinctive reading of history, the present, Christian age derives its personality from Christ; it then approaches its final redemptive fulfillment in the conversion of Spanish Jewry.

REREADING THE *DE FIDE CATHOLICA*

This centrality of the Jews in Isidore's historiography provides a key to the meaning and the singularity of his seemingly unoriginal anthology of anti-Jewish arguments. Written in tandem with Sisebut's conversion decree, the *De fide catholica* also situates the Jews and their conversion between the appearance of Christ in human history and the future fulfillment of Christian historical aspirations.

The structure of the *De fide catholica* is outlined below.

The Thematic Structure of Isidore's
De fide catholica contra Iudaeos

BOOK I: CHRISTOLOGY

Christ, the son of God (chapters 1–4)
1. Christ was born of God the father
2. Christ was ineffably born of God the father before the beginning of time
3. Christ is God and Lord
4. On the significance of the Trinity

The divine incarnation
The birth of Jesus (chapters 5–13)
5. The son of God, God, was made a man
6. On the name of Jesus
7. Christ was of the seed of Abraham according to the flesh
8. Christ was born of the tribe of Judah
9. Christ was born of the line of David
10. Christ was born of a virgin, without the coition of a male
11. Christ was born in Bethlehem
12. The birth of Christ was indicated by a sign of the stars
13. The Magi brought gifts

Divinely ordained messiahship (chapters 14–17)
14. He was anointed by God the father
15. In his first coming he came poor and abject
16. He made signs and miracles
17. He was supposed to be seen in the flesh

Infidelity and opposition of the Jews: betrayal, arrest, trial, execution (chapters 18–28)
    18. The Jews would not acknowledge him
    19. Not acknowledging him, the Jews congregated against him
    20. He was put up for sale
    21. He was betrayed by his disciple
    22. He was delivered up by himself
    23. He was arrested
    24. He was put on trial
    25. In his passion he was deserted by his disciples
    26. He was accused by false witnesses
    27. The Jews cried out that he be crucified
    28. The Jews damned their own descendants

Flagellation; affliction and passion on the cross (chapters 29–48)
    29. He was whipped, and he was beaten with palms
    30. The head of Christ was struck with a rod
    31. He was crowned with thorns
    32. He was dressed in scarlet clothes
    33. While he suffered, he kept silent
    34. He carried the cross
    35. He was affixed to the cross
    36. His hands and feet were affixed with nails
    37. He was crucified between two robbers
    38. His clothes were divided up
    39. He was given gall and vinegar to drink
    40. They placed a sponge full of vinegar on a hyssop branch
    41. The inscription on his cross was not ruined
    42. While hanging on the cross, he prayed to the father on behalf of his enemies
    43. He was crucified for our sins
    44. He died
    45. During the passion it grew dark
    46. They did not break his legs
    47. He was struck with a lance
    48. Blood and water flowed from his side

Burial, resurrection, liberation of the damned, appointment of apostles (chapters 49–54)
    49. He was buried
    50. A rock was placed at the entry of the grave
    51. He descended to hell
    52. Upon his descent, he freed those whom he wished from death

53. The body of Christ did not decay in the grave
54. He arose from the dead

Ascension; rule through the church of the apostles (chapters 55–60)

55. The apostles were sent to preach
56. He ascended to heaven
57. He sits at the right of the father
58. The reign of Christ will be eternal
59. After his ascension, Christ dispatched the Holy Spirit among the apostles
60. The apostles spoke in different languages

The second coming and final judgment (chapter 61)

61. He will come in the future to judge

Epilogue (chapter 62)

BOOK 2: JEWS AND GENTILES, JUDAISM AND CHRISTIANITY

A single divine plan for human salvation: the divine calling of the Gentiles and the Jews (chapters 1–5)

1. On the calling of the nations
2. All nations were ordered to believe in Christ
3. Jews and Gentiles are called to Christ
4. On the calling of the Gentiles to the faith before the Hebrews
5. At the end of the world the Jews will believe in Christ

The disbelief and rejection of the Jews; the election of the Gentiles (chapters 6–13)

6. Many of the people of the Jews would not believe
7. Because of the Jews' disbelief Christ would pass over to the Gentiles
8. The Jews having been expelled, the Gentiles entered
9. Because of their sin against Christ the Jews were vanquished and dispersed
10. On the destruction of Jerusalem
11. On the rejected Jews and the reprobation of the synagogue
12. On the perpetual destruction of Jerusalem
13. On the irreparable ruin of Jerusalem

Replacement of the Old Testament with the New
Cessation of the old law (chapters 14–18)

14. The Old Testament having been canceled, there would be a New

15. On the cessation of the Sabbath
16. On the end of circumcision
17. On the sacrifices
18. On food

Christian sacraments and their efficacy; inadequacy of Jewish understanding (chapters 19–25)

19. On the sacraments of the Christian faith
20. Scripture should be understood not only historically but also mystically
21. The Jews do not understand the testament of the law
22. The Jews, unless they believe in Christ, will not understand the Scriptures
23. Two testaments have been given by God
24. The remission of sins would be through baptism
25. The Gentiles are supposed to be sanctified with unction

The salvific power of the sign of the cross and the body of Christ (chapters 26–27)

26. Believers may be saved through the sign of the cross
27. How the sacrament of the Eucharist was prefigured

Recapitulation (chapter 28)

The first book, containing sixty-two chapters, deals almost exclusively with the earthly career of Jesus; like his vision of human history and his political theory, Isidore grounded his anti-Jewish polemic in his Christology. Not before the sixty-first chapter (the final chapter before the epilogue) of book 1 does the *De fide catholica* shift its sights from the incarnation to the second coming and final judgment. Book 2 then delves into the essential processes of Christian salvation history, exploring the relationship between Old and New Testaments and that between their respective proponents. Chapters 1 through 13 integrate the annals of Jews and Gentiles into the same divine plan for salvation: Both peoples received the call of God; owing to their sin against Jesus, however, the Jews and Jerusalem were vanquished, and the church replaced the synagogue; only in the last days will God save the Jews and restore them to the community of his faithful. Chapters 14 through 25 compare the provisions of the old covenant and the new: the symbolic fulfillment of otherwise antiquated Mosaic law in the salvific sacraments of the church; the need to interpret Scripture mystically, through belief in Christ. A proper hermeneutic thus facilitates salvation, symbolized in chapter 26 by the sign of the cross, which represents both the crucifixion and the church established in its wake. As in Ezekiel's prefigurative vision of the two sticks of Judah and Israel, more than the cross of Calvary is symbolized, and the motif of integration rears its head once again; "it is [also] shown that Judah and Jerusalem should be transformed into one and should acknowledge the sign of the cross."[73] Concluding book 2 (again, prior to a brief recapitulation) and returning to the theme of the Incarnation, chapter 27 concerns the Eucharist, the sacramental expression of the body of Christ, to which Isidore likened the perfect unity of all Christian believers. Needless to say, in this unity and integrity as yet unbaptized Jews had no share: "For Israel is destroyed, and the people of the Gentiles succeeds. The Old Testament is taken from them [that is, the Jews], and the New is given to us. The gift of the bread of salvation, along with the cup of the blood of Christ, is granted to us, hunger and thirst to them. And a different name is given to the new people—that is, Christian; and all the events of the past resonate with the freshness of grace."[74]

If the first book of the De fide catholica defines the foundations and parameters of the Christian epoch in human history, the second book identifies the dynamics of its inauguration, its development, and its consummation: the replacement of the Jews by the Gentiles, the fulfillment of the Old Testament in the New, and, at last, the conversion of the Jews to Christianity. Book 2 of Isidore's polemic, in other words, bridges the gap between the first sixty chapters of book 1 and chapter 61. It elaborates the mechanisms of progress from the present age of Christian history, that deriving from the incarnation, to its culmination in the seventh age of glory. The De fide catholica suggests that human history will culminate in the resolution of conflict—in this case, that between Jew and Christian, old law and new—when all people will acknowledge the sign of the cross and receive the sacrament of the Eucharist. In practical terms, only with the conversion of the Jews will a fully integrated Christian society resemble the body of Christ born at the time of the divine incarnation long ago.[75] Only then can history

73. Isidore, De fide 2.26.6, PL 83:535.
74. Ibid. 2.27.5, PL 83:536.
75. On the formative impact of the notion of Christ's mystical body in Isidorean theology, see José F. Sagües, "La doctrina del cuerpo místico en San Isidoro de Sevilla," Estudios eclesiásticos 17 (1943), esp. 235–36, 524–46. One must carefully weigh the possibility that this concept, reflected in Isidore's threefold division of a properly ordered Christian society into classes of clerics, monks, and laypersons, itself nourished his determination to convert the Jews of Spain.

reach its proper climax, approach the end of its present age, and announce the final judgment and redemption.

Echoing the Isidorean vision of history which we have analyzed above, the *De fide catholica* constitutes a theological manifesto for King Sisebut's conversion of the Jews. Its distinctive Isidorean hermeneutic—its interpretation of standard *Adversus Iudaeos* texts in keeping with an integrated, positivistic, Christian interpretation of worldly events—bespeaks the mutual wish of king and prelate to blend the diverse strains in their polity, their society, and their culture into a single Spanish Catholic unity. Isidore here anticipated the importance that the *Chronicon* and *Historia Gothorum* attributed to the reign of Sisebut in particular and their view of the relationship among classical civilization, Christianity, and Spain in general. Anti-Jewish polemic thus sits well beside the other works—from dictionary to encyclopedia to chronicle—that Isidore composed at the request of King Sisebut and those that he dedicated to him. For the structure of the *De fide catholica* articulates the question: How can one actualize Christian hope for the future, fueling progress from the beginning of the sixth historical age to its end? And the works of the Isidorean corpus respond collectively: in the cultivation of a Christian Latin culture, in Visigothic Spain, under the rule of a king like Sisebut, and, finally, with the conversion of the Jews.

Such a reading of the *De fide catholica* allows for more straightforward responses to other questions that have engaged modern scholars for some time: the purpose of the treatise, its place in seventh-century Visigothic policy toward the Jews, Isidore's stance on Sisebut's decree of forced conversion, and Isidore's lasting contribution to Christian anti-Judaism. Rationalizing Sisebut's edict of conversion, the *De fide* and its message stand independent of any specific practical use that Isidore may have intended for his treatise. Wooing Jews to Christianity, instructing recently baptized Jewish children in the essentials of Christian faith, preaching to the Christian laity, or educating the clergy—any or all these applications were possible, some perhaps even likely, and hardly mutually exclusive. But one need not view an understanding—or the composition—of the *De fide* as dependent on any one of them in particular. The logic of Isidore's polemic further suggests that Visigothic policy toward the Jews in fact aimed at their conversion, for reasons that reflected the mutual interests of royal and ecclesiastical authorities. At least in the case of Sisebut and Isidore, considerations of politics and religious ideology evidently converged; prince and prelate shared in fostering the persecution of Judaism, and one might well use their example as a point of departure for evaluating the entirety of Visigothic royal and ecclesiastical legislation concerning the Jews in Visigothic Spain.[76] Interpreted as we have suggested, the De fide certainly clarifies Isidore's ostensive ambivalence toward Sisebut's policy of forced conversion. Conversion of the Jews ranked high on Isidore's list of priorities, and the magnitude of its importance did not hinge on the means for effecting it. As the ordinances of the Council of Seville (624) and the Fourth Council of Toledo (633) indicate, Isidore continued to affirm the validity of the royal edict, and his additional steps to reach the same goal of a fully Catholic Visigothic Spain—as in compelling the children of Jews to be raised as Christians—placed little value on the consent of the Jews to their conversion. Slight reservations concerning Sisebut's decree do not obviate such an appraisal of Isidore's outlook. Perhaps as a theoretical consideration, or perhaps in view of problems in its implementation, Isidore deemed Sisebut's tactics less than optimal. Yet as Isidore himself explained and as his conciliar legislation subsequently confirmed, the end in this case justified the means.

As for Isidore's place in the history of Christian anti-Judaism, this understanding of the De fide catholica yields a qualified response. On one hand, Isidore did not abandon Augustinian tradition, his focus on the conversion—rather than the preservation—of the Jews notwithstanding. Although they do not overtly dominate his anti-Jewish polemic, essential elements of the doctrine of Jewish witness do appear in Isidore's writings. More important, Isidore followed Augustine in construing the Jews from the perspective of his philosophy of history: The Jews perform a particular historical function in the divine economy of salvation. Their continued existence mirrors the present "incompleteness" of salvation history; and they serve didactically to demonstrate the route that this history must follow in order to arrive at its culmination. Much as Augustine's Jews exemplified vital characteristics of the saeculum, Jews and Judaism in the Isidorean corpus shed light on the Sevillian's overriding concern for the integration of the (presently fragmented) Christian state, society, and culture. As Isidore viewed Visigothic Spain on the threshold of the fulfillment of history,

76. See Orlandis, "Hacia una major comprensión," pp. 155ff., who has discerned the origin of Visigothic Spain's perception of its Jewish problem and its anti-Jewish policy in the reign of Sisebut.

the Jew of the present and his conversion in the future, respectively, demarcated the two endpoints of that final, critical historical progression. No less than did the doctrine of Augustine and its memorable exegesis of "Slay them not, lest my people forget," an Isidorean hermeneutic of integration had created a Jew with purpose and power in Christian history.

On the other hand, Isidore's anti-Jewish polemic in its Spanish-Visigothic context exemplifies how Christian constructions of Judaism, even when declaring their concurrence with the doctrine of Jewish witness, could develop so as to clash with Augustine's own original premises. Along with King Sisebut, Isidore worked more aggressively and systematically than had Gregory the Great to convert the Jews: "Slay them not" mandated the survival of Judaism in the sixth age of history, whereas Isidore hoped that the conversion of the Jews would precipitate the seventh. If Gregory had posited the affinity between Jew and Antichrist, Isidore highlighted the enmity between the Jews and Christ; no less than two dozen chapters in book of the *De fide* recount the sufferings of Jesus and the Jews' responsibility for them. Finally, Isidore gave clearer expression to the idea that the Jews detracted from Christian unity, that they did not belong in a properly integrated Christian kingdom. This idea proved most influential during centuries to come, and it seemed to underlie the anti-Judaism of Agobard of Lyons.

CHAPTER 4

Agobard of Lyons

Battling the Enemies of Christian Unity

> That people, which has fallen completely into evil ways and which has not recognized the goodness and wisdom of God—and has therefore remained in its hostile, errant condition of old—ought to be deemed worthless in the eyes of all believers and ought not to be honored by anyone on account of its riches or wealth. Rather, defiled with the leprosy of Naaman because of its yearning for such things, it must be detested as most sordid and impure by all of the faithful who have been purified with the baptismal waters of Elisha.[1]

The strident voice of Agobard, archbishop of Lyons during the reign of the Carolingian emperor Louis the Pious, rings loud in the annals of medieval Jewish-Christian relations. To be sure, Agobard was not a scholar of the order of Gregory the Great or Isidore of Seville. His well-known complaints regarding the Jews of his day hardly amounted to a systematic theological exposition. Still, Agobard's concern with the Jews and the extant correspondence that airs it are too significant to overlook, even in this study of theological tradition. His vehement protests against the Jewish policy of Louis the Pious testify to the continuing evolution of the image of the Jew in Latin Christendom, from Augustine to early medieval theologians like Gregory and Isidore, and beyond. Moreover, his reactions to the dissonance between such tradition and the realities of his day heralded many of the later develop-

---

1. Agobard of Lyons, *De iudaicis superstitionibus et erroribus* 23, CCCM 52:217.

ments to be studied in subsequent chapters of this book. Agobard has rightly been labeled as a precedent setter, as one "emblematic of the future."[2] Yet did he, as his rhetoric may readily tempt one to conclude, truly break away from the teachings of Augustine concerning the Jews to espouse an alternative, rival stance on their role in a properly ordered Christian society? Our rereading of Agobard would suggest otherwise: that his application of inherited patristic ideas within a distinctly medieval sociopolitical context manifested both commitment to and discomfort with Augustinian tradition. I believe that Agobard numbers among the developers of the Augustinian legacy we have studied, just as he foreshadowed many of the ways in which late medieval churchmen would effectively discard it.

AGOBARD'S CAMPAIGN AGAINST JEWS AND JUDAISM

Born on the Spanish side of the Pyrenees in 769,[3] Agobard arrived in Lyons in 792, joined the Catholic priesthood in 804, served under the direction and tutelage of the Visigothic Bishop Leidrad, and finally succeeded him in the see of Lyons in 816. Little time elapsed before Agobard began to clash with the Jews of Lyons. He insisted upon his right to proselytize among them, and especially among their slaves, while they, who enjoyed extensive privileges and protection from Louis the Pious, claimed that Agobard could not proceed without their consent. Agobard protested to Louis's court at Aachen against imperial favoritism toward the Jews but was personally rebuffed, and in 823 he directed the first of his anti-Jewish letters, De baptismo

2. Kenneth R. Stow, Alienated Minority: The Jews of Medieval Latin Europe (Cambridge, Mass., 1992), pp. 34–35; see also Manfred Kniewasser, "Bischof Agobard von Lyon und der Platz der Juden in einer sakral verfassten Einheitsgesellschaft," Kairos, n.s. 19 (1977), 203–27.

3. On Agobard's life and career, see, above all, Egon Boshof, Erzbischof Agobard von Lyon: Leben und Werke, Kölner historische Abhandlungen 17 (Cologne, 1969). Earlier biographical accounts include A. Bressolles, Saint Agobard: Evêque de Lyon (769–840), L'Église et l'état au Moyen-Âge 9 (Paris, 1949); and J. Allen Cabaniss, "Agobard of Lyons," Speculum 26 (1951), 50–76, and Agobard of Lyons: Churchman and Critic (Syracuse, N.Y., 1953). On Agobard's campaign against the Jews and Judaism, see also, among others, Bernhard Blumenkranz, Les Auteurs chrétiens latins du Moyen Âge sur les Juifs et le Judaisme (Paris, 1963), pp. 152–68; Arthur J. Zuckerman, "The Political Uses of Theology: The Conflict of Bishop Agobard and the Jews of Lyons," in Studies in Medieval Culture, ed. John R. Sommerfeldt (Kalamazoo, Mich., 1970), 3:23–51; Kenneth R. Stow, "Agobard of Lyons and the Medieval Concept of the Jew," Conservative Judaism 29 (1974), 58–65; and Kniewasser, "Bischof Agobard von Lyon."

mancipiorum Iudaeorum (On the Baptism of the Slaves of the Jews), to three clerical confidants at the emperor's court who had heard his case.[4] Ensuing events did little to resolve the dispute, and several years later tempers flared once more, this time over the conversion of a particular Jewish slave girl to Christianity. In 826 Agobard again sent his contacts in Aachen a written appeal, *Contra praeceptum impium de baptismo iudaicorum mancipiorum* (Against the Impious Edict Concerning the Baptism of the Slaves of the Jews),[5] and again Louis proceeded with his own, opposing policy. Shortly thereafter, Agobard and some of his episcopal colleagues drafted a lengthy treatise, *De iudaicis superstitionibus et erroribus* (On the Superstitions and Errors of the Jews),[6] which Agobard dispatched directly to the emperor, along with his own written plaint *De insolentia Iudaeorum* (On the Insolence of the Jews).[7] In 827 or 828 Agobard reviewed his concerns with Bishop Nibridius of Narbonne in *De cavendo convictu et societate iudaica* (On Avoiding the Table and Companionship of the Jews).[8] Some scholars have attributed to Agobard yet an additional episcopal letter concerning the Jews, in which the bishop solicited the help of the emperor in baptizing willing Jewish young people over the objections of their parents.[9]

The particular circumstances and the precise summaries of Agobard's letters concern us less than do the theoretical issues of public policy they raise and the considerations of theology underlying those

---

4. Agobard, *De baptismo mancipiorum Iudaeorum*, CCCM 52:115–17. For the chronology of Agobard's works, see the introduction of L. van Acker to CCCM 52. On the extent, both alleged and actual, of Jewish involvement in the early medieval slave trade, see the most recent discussion in the appendix to Michael Toch, "Wirtschaft und Verfolgung: Die Bedeutung der Ökonomie für die Kreuzzugspogrome des 11. und 12. Jahrhunderts, mit einem Anhang zum Sklavenhandel der Juden," in *Juden und Christen zur Zeit der Kreuzzüge*, ed. Alfred Haverkamp, Vorträge und Forschungen des Konstanzer Arbeitskreises für mittelalterliche Geschichte (Sigmaringen, Germany, 1999).

5. Agobard, *Contra praeceptum impium de baptismo iudaicorum mancipiorum*, CCCM 52:185–88.

6. Agobard, *De iudaicis superstitionibus et erroribus*, ibid., pp. 199–221.

7. Agobard, *De insolentia Iudaeorum*, ibid., pp. 191–95.

8. Agobard, *De cavendo convictu et societate iudaica*, ibid., pp. 231–34.

9. See Bernhard Blumenkranz, "Deux compilations canoniques de Florus de Lyon et l'action antijuive d'Agobard," *Revue historique de droit français et étranger*, 4th ser. 33 (1955), 243–54, 574–75. Blumenkranz's attribution of this letter to Agobard has been accepted by Stow, *Alienated Minority*, pp. 35–36, but rejected by Boshof, *Erzbischof Agobard*, pp. 135ff., and Van Acker, CCCM 52:xiv ff. Most recently, see Klaus Zechiel-Eckes, "Sur la tradition manuscrite des *Capitula . . . de coertione Iudeorum*," *RB* 107 (1997), 77–87.

issues. For the most part, Agobard objected to the privileged position that the Jews appeared to command in Frankish society, on at least four grounds.

First, Agobard resented the imperial directive that forbade him from baptizing the slaves of the Jews against their master's will. Although the rationale for his argument does not relate overtly to the Jews or to Judaism, a brief review should establish its relevance for us nonetheless. How, asked Agobard, could he refuse the wishes of any non-Christians who "desire to be made members of Christ in the body of the church"?[10] He asserted repeatedly that he intended not to deprive the Jews of their property, for which he would have them compensated, or to convert anyone by force. Rather, he beheld in his missionary work a fundamental responsibility, which outweighed protecting the Jews' economic rights in its importance. Even slaves are human beings, creatures of God, whose role in their constitution and spiritual welfare far exceeds that of any masters who purchased their bodies in the marketplace; slaves may owe physical service to their human master, but their spiritual debt remains God's alone. God himself desires the enlightenment and salvation of all persons, and his apostles of old never hesitated to admit anyone, whether enslaved or free, into the church. Anyone truly pious must recognize that "the one omnipotent God, creator of all and most just ruler, who formed the first man from the dust of the earth and made him a helpmate just like him from his rib, and who generated the entire human race from them—from a single source and a single root, as it were—fashioned all people in the same condition."[11] Slaves had no less of a right to be offered salvation in Christ, and Agobard accordingly found it utterly unbelievable that "a ruling so opposed to ecclesiastical regulations would be issued by the most Christian, most pious emperor,"[12] Louis.

Alongside Agobard's commitment to save the souls of the Jews' pagan slaves thus loomed a second concern, perhaps even more basic than the first: The imperial policies of Louis the Pious, including the issuance of charters and the appointment of special officials to protect the Jews and their economic interests,[13] violated the Christian character of the

10. Agobard, *De baptismo mancipiorum Iudaeorum*, CCCM 52:115.

11. Agobard, *Contra praeceptum impium de baptismo iudaicorum mancipiorum*, ibid., p. 187.

12. Ibid., p. 185.

13. On Louis's Jewish policies, see Solomon Katz, *The Jews in the Visigothic and Frankish Kingdoms of Spain and Gaul*, Medieval Academy of America Monographs 12

realm. Agobard wrote directly to Louis, stressing the urgency "that your most pious majesty know precisely how the Christian faith is harmed by the Jews in various ways." And he proceeded to ascribe the damage to Christianity deriving from the Jews' privileged status, for which the emperor bore the responsibility:

> Lying, they boast to simple Christians that they are dear to you on account of their ancestors; that they honorably come and go in your presence; that most esteemed [Christian] people seek their prayers and their blessings, admitting that they wished to have a lawgiver of the sort that the Jews had. They say that your advisers have been incited against us on their account, because we prohibit Christians from drinking their wine. As they haughtily proclaim this, they brag that they received large amounts of silver from them [that is, Louis's advisers] for the purchase of wine, and that, in reviewing the laws of the church, no reason can be found why Christians must abstain from their food and drink. They present edicts in your name, sealed with golden seals, whose contents we think are untrue. They show off women's clothing, as if it had been sent by your relatives or the ladies of the palace to their wives. They expound the glory of their ancestors. They are permitted to build new synagogues in violation of the law. It has reached the point that simple Christians say that Jews preach better to them than do our own elders. Worst of all, the aforementioned royal officials ordered that market days, which used to be on Saturdays, be changed, so that their Sabbath not be violated, and they gave them [that is, the Jews] the choice of days on which they should be held henceforth. The officials claim that it is to the convenience of Christians on account of the leisure of Sunday, when it would, in fact, prove more inconvenient to the Jews [that is, were market days on Saturdays]. For those [Christians] who live nearby, purchasing their required provisions on Saturday, have more free time to spend Sunday leisurely in the solemnities of the mass and at sermons. And those who come from afar on the occasion of the market, appearing at both [Saturday] evening and [Sunday] morning prayers, return uplifted to their own homes after the solemnity of the mass has been performed.[14]

Measuring the Jews' gain against such decreased religious devotion among Christians, Agobard reiterated his disbelief that Louis could have knowingly permitted these abuses, over which the Jews have rejoiced and Christians have mourned. Imperial Jewish policy has resulted in nothing less than the disgrace of Christianity, which numerous

---

(1937; reprint, New York, 1970), pp. 84–87; Zuckerman, "Political Uses," passim; and Bernard S. Bachrach, *Early Medieval Jewish Policy in Western Europe* (Minneapolis, Minn., 1977), chap. 5.

14. Agobard, *De insolentia Iudaeorum*, CCCM 52:194.

Christians aggravate when they persist in eating with the Jews and spending time in their company.

Imperial policy, however, was not the sole culprit. From the conversion of Jewish slaves and imperial favoritism on the Jews' behalf in general, Agobard turned his attention to a third issue: the noxious behavior and impudence of the Jews. Jews and Christians alike testify that when defects in the internal organs of ritually slaughtered animals render them nonkosher, the Jews sell them to Christians, offensively calling them "Christian cattle."[15] So too do they sell Christians wine unfit for their own use, even after it has fallen on to the ground and been soiled. Compounding the offense, they refuse to eat at a Christian's table, and Catholics, as a result, have come to feel inferior to Jews. Contemporary Jewry have inherited their forebears' animosity toward Jesus. "Just as our lord Jesus Christ, about to set all at rest with the blood of his cross, was sold at the time of his passion by a false disciple and was purchased by his real persecutors so that they might ridicule him and crucify him, so too he is now, in essence, acquired by the impious Jews for the purpose of even more unrestrained censure and blasphemy."[16] Daily do they revile Jesus and his faithful, and, among Christians, they insolently proclaim the superiority of their faith, wooing souls away from the church even as Agobard has had little success in converting Jews to Christianity.[17] Christian women employed by Jews are typically exploited sexually, and, in maintaining that Jews perpetrate "shocking acts too turpid to record" on the bodies of their Christian slaves, Agobard may have had castration or some other form of sexual mutilation in mind.[18] Children of the devil (filii diaboli), the Jews exert themselves with deceitful hatred; ultimately, they seek revenge for all they have lost to Christians.[19]

Fourth, and finally, Agobard did not rest with an indictment of Jewish behavior toward Christians. In rather exceptional fashion, he subjected the religious practices and writings of the Jews to scrutiny and

15. Ibid., p. 193.

16. Agobard, De iudaicis superstitionibus et erroribus 1, ibid., p. 199.

17. Agobard, De insolentia Iudaeorum, ibid., pp. 192–93, and De cavendo convictu et societate iudaica, ibid., pp. 231–34.

18. Agobard, De insolentia Iudaeorum, ibid., pp. 195; cf. the comments of Van Acker, ibid., p. v n. 5, and Blumenkranz, Les Auteurs, p. 163 n. 53.

19. Agobard, De insolentia Iudaeorum, CCCM 52:192, De iudaicis superstitionibus et erroribus 22, ibid., p. 216, and so forth.

to attack. For not only the Jews themselves but also their beliefs served as tools of the devil,[20] and, within the framework of his campaign to influence imperial policy—not merely as an academic exercise or an attempt to bolster the morale of his own congregants—Agobard ventured beyond the limits of traditional patristic *Adversus Iudaeos* polemic. This is not to say that he ignored or rejected patristic tradition. Citations of the apostles, the fathers, and the bishops of the Gallican church who spurned Jewish fellowship fill approximately half of Agobard's well-known *De iudaicis superstitionibus et erroribus*. But the treatise then castigates the Jews for beliefs and textual traditions which suggest that Agobard had more than a casual acquaintance with the Jews and Judaism of his day. Its length notwithstanding, the passage that follows is well worth quoting.

> [In addition to deriding Jesus,] they also say that their deity is corporeal and is distinguished by his limbs and his corporeal features and that, like us, he hears with one body part, sees with another, and speaks or does whatever else he does with yet another; and thus the human body was fashioned in the image of God, except that he has inflexible, rigid fingers, inasmuch as he does no work with his hands. He sits like some terrestrial king on a throne borne by four beasts, and he is housed in some sort of great palace. He even thinks many vain and pointless thoughts, which, because they all come to naught, turn into demons. As we have said, they relate countless abominations concerning their god, such that they worship an image which they have fashioned and erected for themselves in the folly of their hearts, not the true, completely unalterable God, of whom they are totally ignorant.
>
> They believe that the letters of their alphabet exist eternally and that before the beginning of the world they received different tasks, over which they were supposed to preside in this world. The law of Moses was written many eons before the world came into being. They further maintain that there are many terrestrial worlds, many hells, and many heavens. They assert that one of these, which they call "racha," that is the firmament, supports God's mill, in which manna is ground for food for the angels. They call another one "araboth," in which they contend that the Lord resides, and, according to them, this is what is written in the Psalm, "Make way for him who rides on the 'araboth.'"[21] God therefore has seven trumpets, one of which measures a thousand cubits.
>
> What more? There is not a page, not a sentence of the Old Testament concerning which lies have not been fabricated and recorded by their sages; or they themselves, even today, constantly contrive some new superstition,

20. Agobard, *De iudaicis superstitionibus et erroribus* 1, ibid., p. 199.
21. Psalm 68:5, following the Vulgate (67:5).

and, when asked about such, they dare to respond. In the teachings of their sages they read that Jesus was a respected young man among them and was educated in the teaching of John the Baptist, and that he had many disciples, to one of whom he gave the name Kepha, that is Peter, a rock, on account of the hardness and dullness of his intelligence. When he was expected by the people on a festival day, certain youths from his sect ran up to meet him, singing to him out of reverence and respect for their teacher, "Hosanna, son of David." At the end of his life, accused falsely on many counts, he was jailed upon the order of Tiberius, because his daughter, whom he had promised the virgin birth of a son, gave birth to a fetus of stone, whence he was hanged from gallows as a detestable magician and was hit by a rock in his head. Thus killed, he was buried next to a certain aqueduct and was entrusted to the care of a certain Judas. Yet at night the aqueduct was suddenly overcome by a flood, and though sought for twelve months on Pilate's order, he was never found. Then Pilate issued the following decree to them: "It is evident," he said, "that he who was slain by you out of jealousy and has been found neither in his grave nor in any other place has risen as he had promised, and for this reason I order you to worship him; he who does not do so should know that he is destined to hell." Their elders contrived all these things, and read them enthusiastically with a foolish obstinacy—so that owing to such tales the entire truth of Christ's virtue and power might be discarded and so that he should not be worshiped in truth as God as he should have been, because it was so ordained only by the law of Pilate. . . . Finally, they claim that Christians worship idols, and they are not ashamed of saying that those virtues obtained by us through the intercession of the saints are the work of the devil.[22]

Whatever the specific sources of Agobard's information, there is no question that his polemic against Judaism assumed a currency that sets him apart from Gregory, Isidore, and other churchmen who preceded him. Whether from Jews or from Jewish converts to Christianity, whether from Jewish traditions with roots in the land of Israel or in Babylonia, whether from access, however slight, to rabbinic literature or entirely by word of mouth, Agobard acquired knowledge of contemporary—that is, living—postbiblical Judaism, which he proceeded to attack with vehemence.[23] In Agobard's letters, *Adversus Iudaeos* polemic does not suffice with the standard contrast of Old Testament and

22. Agobard, *De iudaicis superstitionibus et erroribus* 10, CCCM 52:205-7.
23. See the most instructive analyses of Ch. Merchavia, *The Church versus Talmudic and Midrashic Literature, 500-1248* [Hebrew] (Jerusalem, 1970), pp. 71-84; and Robert Bonfil, "The Culture and Religious Traditions of French Jewry in the Ninth Century, as Reflected in the Writings of Agobard of Lyons" [Hebrew], in *Studies in Jewish Mysticism, Philosophy and Ethical Literature Presented to Isaiah Tishby on His Seventy-Fifth Birthday*, ed. Joseph Dan and Joseph Hacker (Jerusalem, 1986), pp. 327-48.

New, nor with the occasional condemnation of talmudic teaching (*deuterosis*) found in the writings of earlier authors like Jerome. To these Agobard added a pointed attack on the Judaism of his own day. Owing, perhaps, to the ongoing debate over iconoclasm and to Agobard's own iconoclastic leanings, his list of contemporary Jewish atrocities begins with charges of anthropomorphism: that rabbinic tradition and contemporary Jewish mysticism have effectively transformed God into a human being, thus replacing the genuine worship of the deity with idolatry. Beside the biblical Jew wallowing hopelessly in "useless antiquity" Agobard has depicted a Judaism that fabricates falsehoods concerning every aspect of ancient biblical—that is, Old Testament—teaching. Note well: Such fabrication did not occur simply at one particular time in the past; it continues in the present, as Jews persist in their contrivance of new superstitions, groundless absurdities concerning God and Scripture. Agobard's examination of contemporary Jewish religion led him to some (no longer extant) edition of *Toledot Yeshu*, an early medieval collection of derisive Jewish tales of Jesus and his disciples that circulated among numerous Jewish communities in a variety of forms.[24] Recent evidence has again confirmed for Agobard the continuing validity of Jerome's claim that the Jews actively engage in anti-Christian blasphemy.

These and other examples of Jewish error and hostility led Agobard to the conclusion that the Jews are the most hateful and detestable of peoples.[25] On the basis of the teachings of their sages, they flagrantly violate the books of the law and the prophets in their own Scriptures, even the sanctity of their Sabbath.[26] In short, they and their beliefs concerning God outstrip the error of all other unbelievers. Their sin exceeds that of the biblical Amalekites, the Midianites, and even the Saracens, because none of these nations received God's law and proph-

---

24. On the *Toledot Yeshu* see Samuel Krauss, *Das Leben Jesu nach jüdischen Quellen* (Berlin, 1902); William Horbury, "The Trial of Jesus in the Jewish Tradition," in *The Trial of Jesus: Cambridge Studies in Honor of C. F. D. Moule*, ed. Ernst Bammel, Studies in Biblical Theology 2, 13 (Naperville, Ill., 1970), pp. 103–21; Joel E. Rembaum, "The New Testament in Medieval Anti-Christian Polemics" (Ph.D. diss., University of California, Los Angeles, 1975), pt. 1, chap. 4; Günter Schlichting, *Ein jüdisches Leben Jesu: Die verschollene Toledot-Jeschu-Fassung Tam u-mu'ad*, Wissenschaftliche Untersuchungen zum Neuen Testament 24 (Tübingen, Germany, 1982); and Herbert Basser, "The Acts of Jesus," in *The Frank Talmage Memorial Volume I*, ed. Barry Walfish (Haifa, Israel, 1993), pp. 273–82.

25. Agobard, *De insolentia Iudaeorum*, CCCM 52:194.

26. Agobard, *De iudaicis superstitionibus et erroribus* 10, ibid., pp. 207–8.

ecies as did the Jews, who proceeded to kill their savior and God's son nonetheless.[27] Heretics may dissent over certain matters of Christian doctrine, but they still share essential truths with the church. "What distinguishes . . . the Jews, however, is that they lie concerning everything, blaspheming our divine lord Jesus Christ and his church in every respect, believing nothing about him to be true except the fact of his death."[28]

Many investigators have already considered Agobard's letters on the question of the Jews, some with an eye to reconstructing the historical circumstances that gave rise to them, others concerned with Agobard's feud with Louis the Pious and its impact on the status of early medieval Jewry. Although the letters assuredly contribute much to an understanding of these matters, our present interest lies elsewhere: What fundamental principles fueled Agobard's anti-Judaism? Unlike Augustine, Gregory, and Isidore, Agobard left little in the way of discursive theology or a theoretical statement of principles; neither do his extant writings reveal an interest in historiography, nor do they present a systematic picture of his Catholic, episcopal worldview. Instead, they address an array of specific, practical issues that confronted Agobard over the course of his episcopate. Rather than offer a blueprint for an ideally ordered Christian society, they tend to bemoan real problems and to advocate immediate, concrete means of dealing with them. Still, Agobard's prominence in the history of Jewish-Christian relations, the range of his efforts, and the extent of his correspondence concerning the Jews warrant an attempt to induce the general from the particular.

A PROPERLY ORDERED CHRISTIAN EMPIRE

How, then, did Agobard's complaints and demands derive from the logic of an early medieval Christian mentality? What place did the Jews fill in his view of Christian society? As has been noted, Agobard repeatedly identified the Jews and their religion as the archenemies of Christendom. They were the children and the tools of the devil. Inasmuch as they spurned all belief in Jesus, he wrote that "they assumed for themselves both the name and the discourse of the Antichrist," the period of whose deceptive rule was rapidly approaching.[29] All this cer-

27. Ibid. 21, pp. 215–16.
28. Ibid. 9, p. 205.
29. Ibid. 19, 27, pp. 214, 221.

tainly counted for much in the thought of a ninth-century bishop and would, perhaps, suffice to explain the virulence of Agobard's polemic. Nevertheless, the progression of four foci in that polemic—from imperial protection of the Jews' slaves from Christian missionizing, to more general favoritism for the Jews in imperial policy, to the abusive hostility of Jews toward Christians, to the intolerable errors of contemporary Judaism—does permit one to delve further. It establishes that Agobard's diatribes against imperial Jewish policy comport well with a fundamental conception of proper order in the Christian empire. This rudimentary concern fueled much of Agobard's public activity during his quarter-century as archbishop of Lyons—in his stance regarding Jews and Judaism, in his dealings with fellow Catholic clergymen, and in his posture vis-à-vis the office and policies of Emperor Louis the Pious.

Modern scholars have rightly noted the exceptional in Agobard's anti-Jewish writings: Compared by Heinrich Graetz to the villainous Haman, he seems to have been the first medieval churchman to devote an entire treatise to the proper treatment of the Jews in Christendom, the first to polemicize in deliberate, concerted fashion against the Jews' postbiblical traditions, and perhaps the first to make Jewish policy a critical bone of contention in the thorny relationship between clerical and secular authorities.[30] A careful reading of Agobard, however, yields a more balanced picture. On one hand, Agobard indeed departed from the norms of traditional *Adversus Iudaeos* polemic, and in so doing heralded transformations in the Christian idea of the Jew that would become more prevalent only in the twelfth and thirteenth centuries. He focused on contemporary Jews as killers of Christ; he classified Jews in relation to Muslims and heretics; he vehemently expressed his horror over indications that Jews enjoyed a social status superior to that of Christians, particularly as reflected in the Christian purchase and consumption of Jewish food; he emphatically linked the Jews to Antichrist and the devil; he indicted the Jews for abandoning biblical precepts in order to espouse newly contrived superstitions; he proselytized enthusiastically among the Jews, and his missionary tac-

30. Heinrich Graetz, *Geschichte der Juden*, 5, 4th ed. (Leipzig, 1909), pp. 234–41; Blumenkranz, *Les Auteurs*, pp. 152ff.; Merchavia, *Church*, chap. 2, passim; Stow, "Agobard of Lyons," and *Alienated Minority*, pp. 33ff.; Bat-Sheva Albert, "Jews and Judaism in Carolingian Literature and Exegesis" [Hebrew], in *Proceedings of the Tenth World Congress of Jewish Studies* (Jerusalem, 1990), B1:78ff.

tics may have included preaching to the Jews in their synagogue;[31] and he speculated that many Jews no longer had a role to play in the divine economy of salvation and would not be redeemed at the time of the final redemption. Adopting the terminology of one recent investigator, one can conclude that Agobard *politicized* the discourse of anti-Jewish polemic in ninth-century Frankland, intensifying its tone and demanding its more consistent application to the realia of Christian-Jewish interaction.[32]

On the other hand, Agobard had profound respect for his predecessors in the Catholic Church, and this respect receives expression throughout his correspondence. In effect, Agobard acknowledged and maintained the Augustinian principle of "Slay them not," particularly as translated into law and administrative policy by early medieval popes and church councils. He affirmed the property rights of the Jews, offering to compensate them for those of their slaves who would opt for Christian baptism.[33] The minimal sum he proposed to pay may well have been unfair, but one must evaluate Agobard's position by recalling that Gregory had forbidden Jewish slave owners any compensation whatsoever.[34] Agobard further avowed that he wished to convert no Jew against his or her will;[35] and he took care to find and to cite traditional support and legal precedent for his arguments. Again, a cursory glance at Agobard's *De iudaicis superstitionibus et erroribus* leaves an impression of intense hatred for Jews and Judaism, whereas a more deliberate review of the traditions amassed in this treatise yields a more nuanced assessment. For most of the precedents cited seem to call for Christians—and Christian clergy above all—to avoid Jewish company, not for secular princes to implement specific discriminatory measures against the Jews. Agobard and his coauthors praised Saints Hilary, Cyprian, and Atha-

---

31. Mentioned in the letter of questionable authorship; see above n. 9.

32. See David E. Timmer, "Biblical Exegesis and the Jewish-Christian Controversy in the Early Twelfth Century," *Church History* 58 (1989), 311ff., who argues that this phenomenon first appeared in the early-twelfth-century writings of Rupert of Deutz.

33. Agobard, *De baptismo mancipiorum Iudaeorum*, CCCM 52:116.

34. Gregory, *Epistulae* 4.9, CCSL 140:226 (Shlomo Simonsohn, *ASJD*, 492–1404, Pontifical Institute of Mediaeval Studies: Studies and Texts 94 [Toronto, 1988], p. 9). See also Walter Pakter, *Medieval Canon Law and the Jews*, Münchener Universitäts-schriften—Juristische Fakultät—Abhandlungen zur Rechtswissenschaftlichen Grundla-genforschung 68 (Ebelsbach, Germany, 1988), pp. 91ff.; and Shlomo Simonsohn, *The Apostolic See and the Jews: History*, Pontifical Institute of Mediaeval Studies: Studies and Texts 109 (Toronto, 1991), pp. 160–61.

35. Agobard, *Contra praeceptum impium de baptismo iudaicorum mancipiorum*, CCCM 52:188.

nasius for their abhorrence of the Jews and their avoidance of contact with them. They recounted how Ambrose of Milan defied the Roman emperor Theodosius the Great, who had ordered that a Syrian bishop compensate the Jews for his destruction of their synagogue; more than it reproves the emperor (Theodosius or, by extension, Louis the Pious), here this story lauds the prelate (Ambrose or Agobard) for risking serious punishment, as he prevented the reward of God's enemies at the expense of his faithful.[36] Of the eleven conciliar canons then cited by Agobard, six forbid Christians to have social, sexual, and/or religious intercourse with Jews.[37] Only five seek to impose restrictions upon the Jews directly; and, of these, the (three) decrees against Jewish ownership/ conversion of Christian slaves and Jews serving as judges or tax collectors have ample grounding in fourth- and fifth-century Roman law.[38] Only two conciliar canons, demanding that Jews not appear in public from Holy Thursday until after Easter Sunday, may bespeak a more extreme anti-Jewish policy on the part of the Gallican church.[39] Some evidence suggests, however, that such decrees may have aimed at protecting the Jews as well as "removing the infidel Jew from the sight of the faithful at a time when the Christian calendar focused on the antagonism between the two religions."[40] Most likely of Spanish origin, Agobard certainly had access to the harsher episcopal decrees of the Visigothic councils of Toledo—not to mention the examples of King Sisebut and his royal successors—upon which to base his appeals to the imperial

36. Agobard, *De iudaicis superstitionibus et erroribus* 2–3, ibid., pp. 199–201. On the confrontation between Ambrose and Theodosius over the synagogue that was destroyed at Callinicum, see Neil B. McLynn, *Ambrose of Milan: Church and Court in a Christian Capital* (Berkeley, Calif., 1994), pp. 298–315; and the literature cited in Jeremy Cohen, "Roman Imperial Policy toward the Jews from Constantine until the End of the Palestinian Patriarchate (ca. 429)," *Byzantine Studies* 3 (1976), 5 n. 26.

37. Council of Laodicea (380) 37–38, in J. D. Mansi et al., eds., *Sacrorum conciliorum nova et amplissima collectio* (Florence and Rome, 1757–1927), 2:580–81; Council of Agde (506) 40, CCSL 148:210; Council of Epaone (517) 15, CCSL 148A:27–28; Council of Clermont (535) 6, ibid., pp. 106–7; and Council of Macon (581–583) 15, ibid., p. 227.

38. Council of Macon 13, 16–17, CCSL 148A:226–27. Cf. Amnon Linder, *The Jews in Roman Imperial Legislation* (Detroit, Mich., 1987), pp. 307, 326, and s.v. Slavery.

39. Council of Orleans (538) 33, CCSL 148A:126; and Council of Macon 14, ibid., p. 226.

40. Simonsohn, *The Apostolic See and the Jews: History*, p. 131. See also James Parkes, *The Conflict of the Church and the Synagogue: A Study in the Origins of Antisemitism* (London, 1934), pp. 327, 330, 332; and Solomon Grayzel, *CJ*, rev. ed. (New York, 1966), p. 34. On traditions of anti-Jewish violence during Holy Week, see, most recently, David Nirenberg, *Communities of Violence: Persecution of Minorities in the Middle Ages* (Princeton, N.J., 1996), pp. 202ff.

court in Aachen. Yet the substance of Agobard's demands of Louis the Pious never venture far beyond the relatively tolerant Jewish policy of Gregory the Great or of the Theodosian Code[41] before him. Agobard assuredly clamored for a reversal in the imperial penchant for showing favoritism toward the Jews. Yet his demand for subordinating the Jews in Christian society and his vitriolic rhetoric notwithstanding, he never called for removing them, persecuting them physically, confiscating their property, or interfering with the basic practices of their religion: "Because they live among us and we ought not to be hostile toward them— nor destructive toward their lives, health, or property—let us follow the rule ordained by the church, hardly an obscure one but one set forth clearly, as to how we must be both cautious and humane with regard to them."[42]

In the matter of the Jews, then, Agobard lamented the gap between the sociopolitical realia of his day and his vision of proper order in Frankish society.[43] Such an overriding concern with order, in fact, appears to have dominated his career. In a number of his letters, Agobard lashed out against the veneration of icons, trial by ordeal, and other popular superstitions, all because they deviate from the logic and letter of Christian norms and because the proliferation of popular custom promotes disunity in Christian society. "We are one host, one body of Christ, indeed one Christ," he proclaimed to Louis the Pious, urging him to draft a single code of law for the entire empire.[44] He protested doctrinal and behavioral abuse among the Catholic clergy as similarly detracting from Christian unity. He insisted that powerful laypersons not undermine the spiritual vocation of the clergy by imposing their

41. Cohen, "Roman Imperial Policy"; Bernard S. Bachrach, "The Jewish Community in the Later Roman Empire as Seen in the *Codex Theodosianus*," in *To See Ourselves as Others See Us: Christians, Jews, "Others" in Late Antiquity*, ed. Jacob Neusner and Ernest S. Frerichs (Chico, Calif., 1985), pp. 391–421.

42. Agobard, *De insolentia Iudaeorum*, CCCM 52:193. Contra Albert, "Jews and Judaism," the evidence fails to establish that Agobard sought to import the extremely harsh policy of the Visigoths in the realm of the Franks.

43. My reading of Agobard thus shares much with that of Stow, *Alienated Minority*, pp. 32ff.; cf. also Gavin I. Langmuir, *Toward a Definition of Antisemitism* (Berkeley, Calif., 1990), pp. 85–86.

44. Agobard, *Adversus legem Gundobadi* 3, CCCM 52:20. Agobard thus identified with the position enunciated by Florus of Lyons—who himself collaborated in Agobard's efforts to restrain the Jews (see above, n. 8)—that is cited in Karl F. Morrison, *The Two Kingdoms: Ecclesiology in Carolingian Political Thought* (Princeton, N.J., 1964), p. 37: "The whole church is one sacrifice of God and one body of Christ. . . . In Christ we are one bread; in Christ we are incorporate and united."

own temporal agenda upon them, upsetting the proper relationship between holy and profane. He rebuked Alcuin's disciple Fridugis for questioning his noncritical exegesis of Scripture that valued a Catholic doctrinal consensus above grammatical accuracy.[45] And he vigorously opposed the innovative liturgical reforms of Bishop Amalarius of Metz as misguided and subversive.[46]

Yet more than all of these polemical campaigns waged by Agobard, his troubled relations with Louis the Pious prove most instructive for an appreciation of his stance on the Jewish question. In addition to the emperor's treatment of the Jews, two matters of public policy elicited impassioned emotional appeals from Agobard to Louis and his court: the usurpation of ecclesiastical properties by laypersons, and provisions for the succession to Louis's imperial throne. Either case surely bore on economic wealth and political power, but Agobard appealed primarily to the Christian unity of Frankish society and to the social and political priorities this basic value dictated. Thus in 823, in *De dispensatione ecclesiasticarum rerum* (On the Dispensation of Ecclesiastical Property), Agobard affirmed the unimpeachable authority of Gallican episcopal councils whose canons sought to limit the establishment of proprietary churches and the control of church property by the unordained. Even though the emperor or his representative may not have participated in those synods, they legislated on behalf of the better welfare of the church and Christendom, adhering faithfully to numerous biblical precedents, and the emperor must obey. Here was a basic issue of priorities. One must render unto God what is God's no less than what is Caesar's to Caesar, and "we especially ought to fear God and to honor God, his house, and all his members."[47] As Walter Ullmann has summarized the argument of Agobard and his colleagues, "every one of the councils was concerned with the unity of the whole Christian body—universality and unity based upon the corporateness of Christian society are the main tenets of these councils. . . . To Agobard it is axiomatic that a violation of 'canons' constitutes an action against God Himself and against the whole body of Christians; a transgression of 'canons' is also an action that endangers the faith itself. For

45. Agobard, *Contra obiectiones Fredegisi* 7–14, CCCM 52:287–94.
46. On the linkage between Agobard's concern for Christian unity and his stance with regard to biblical exegesis and Christian liturgy, see Henri de Lubac, *Exégèse médiévale: Les Quatre Sens de l'écriture*, Théologie 41–42, 59 (Paris, 1959–64), 1,2:37–38.
47. Agobard, *De dispensatione ecclesiasticarum rerum* 20–21, CCCM 52:134–35.

the canons were made 'Deo auctore' and there can be no excuse what-soever for their violation."[48]

Similar considerations underlay Agobard's ongoing struggle with Louis over the division of his empire among his sons.[49] Louis had suc-ceeded his father Charlemagne in 814 only because the latter had out-lived his other legitimate sons, and, from the outset of his reign, Louis seemed determined to plan more conscientiously for the disposition of his own estate. His particular approach to imperial governance soon found expression in the *Ordinatio imperii* (Imperial Ordinance) of 817, an edict promulgated with the assent of both the Gallican clergy and the lay aristocracy, asserting the unity of Louis's Christian empire and, contrary to Frankish custom, designating his eldest son Lothar as his coemperor and future heir.[50] Much more than inheritance was at stake here. Louis deliberately stressed the imperial, rather than royal, char-acter of his rule; his edicts typically refer to emperor and empire, not to king and kingdom. This empire, which claimed to include all of continental Latin Christendom, was declared one and united; although Louis granted Lothar's two brothers a subordinate royal status, Fran-çois Ganshof has concluded emphatically that "there is not the slightest suggestion of partition." Moreover, "what gave the unitary arrange-ment for the succession to the imperial throne its full significance was its religious basis." Louis and his episcopal advisers presented the *Or-dinatio* as an act of God's will, heralding the reconstitution of the em-pire on the basis of sacerdotal values.[51]

Although the interests of the Frankish church and those of the em-peror appeared to converge in the *Ordinatio* and its commitment to the Christian unity of the empire, recent scholarship has established that the

48. Walter Ullmann, *The Growth of Papal Government in the Middle Ages,* 2d ed. (New York, 1962), pp. 134–35. On the ecclesiology of Agobard's episcopal party, see ibid., pp. 180ff.; Karl F. Morrison, *Tradition and Authority in the Western Church, 300–1140* (Princeton, N.J., 1969), chap. 9, and *Two Kingdoms,* esp. chaps. 2–3; and Boshof, *Erzbischof Agobard,* chap. 4.

49. On the linkage between the two issues of contention, lay usurpation of church property and the division of the empire, see François L. Ganshof, "Am Vorabend der ersten Krise der Regierung Ludwigs des Frommen," *Frühmittelalterliche Studien* 6 (1972), 42.

50. MGH, Leges 2,1:270–73.

51. François L. Ganshof, "Some Observations on the *Ordinatio imperii* of 817," in his *The Carolingians and the Frankish Monarchy: Studies in Carolingian History,* trans. Janet Sondheimer (London, 1971), pp. 278–81. See also François L. Ganshof, "À propos de la politique de Louis le Pieux avant la crise de 830," *Revue belge d'archéologie et d'histoire de l'art* 37 (1968), 37–48; and Peter R. McKeon, "The Empire of Louis the Pious: Faith, Politics and Personality," *RB* 90 (1980), 54–59.

ideological ramifications of the *Ordinatio* gradually strengthened the hand of the clergy at the expense of the emperor himself. Admittedly, J. M. Wallace-Hadrill noted about the ideology of unification, "Louis was himself Christ's vicar and representative; the unity of the Church was inseparable from the unity of society."[52] But the identification of church and society extended the authority of the episcopate on multiple levels. In matters of state, the bishops naturally sought to harmonize public policy with the interests and values of the church; in matters religious, they unhesitatingly demanded the emperor's compliance and cooperation. An imperial capitulary issued between 823 and 825 avows that every subject of the realm has his proper respective part in Louis's ministry, and, labeling the bishops his true helpers (*veri adiutores*), commits the emperor's *potestas* to the service of episcopal *auctoritas*. The empire thus seemed dedicated to the "politics of conversion," and the hierocratically ordered unity that such a policy entailed. No wonder that various bishops, with Agobard most prominent among them, viewed the provisions of the *Ordinatio* as sacrosanct; when Louis began to renege on these arrangements, they reacted first with horror, then in outright revolt. Trouble began to loom on the horizon in June 823, when Louis's second wife Judith gave birth to the future Charles the Bald, who, obviously, had received nothing in the *Ordinatio* of 817. Within weeks, Louis compelled Lothar to adopt the young Charles as his godson and to grant him a share in the future division of the realm. As the decade wore on, Judith's increasing influence at court contributed to growing alienation between Louis, on one hand, and Lothar and his episcopal supporters, on the other. In a manifesto of 829, the bishops reaffirmed the priority of clerical authority in the empire and chastised Louis accordingly; open rebellion ensued in 830 and 833.[53]

---

52. J. M. Wallace-Hadrill, *The Frankish Church* (Oxford, 1983), p. 229.

53. In addition to the works cited in nn. 48, 50–51, see, above all, Olivier Guillot, "L'Exhortation au partage des responsabilités entre l'empereur, l'épiscopat et les autres sujets vers le milieu du règne de Louis le Pieux," in *Prédication et propagande au Moyen Âge: Islam, Byzance, Occident*, ed. George Makdisi et al., Penn–Paris–Dumbarton Oaks Colloquia 3 (Paris, 1983), pp. 87–110; and Egon Boshof, "Einheitsidee und Teilungsprinzip in der Regierungszeit Ludwigs des Frommen," in *Charlemagne's Heir: New Perspectives on the Reign of Louis the Pious (814–840)*, ed. Peter Godman and Roger Collins (Oxford, 1990), pp. 161–89. Also helpful are Thomas F. X. Noble, "The Monastic Ideal as a Model for Empire: The Case of Louis the Pious," *RB* 86 (1976), 235–50; Peter R. McKeon, "817: Une Année désastreuse et presque fatale pour les Carolingiens," *Le Moyen Âge* 84 (1978), 6–12; and, on the empress Judith in particular, Elizabeth Ward, "Caesar's Wife: The Career of the Empress Judith, 819–829," in *Charlemagne's Heir: New Perspectives on the Reign of Louis the Pious (814–840)*, ed. Peter Godman and Roger Collins (Oxford, 1990), pp. 205–27.

Ganshof, Wallace-Hadrill, and other scholars have recognized Agobard as the ideological spokesman for the opposition to Louis and Judith.[54] In 829, in his so-called mournful letter, *De divisione imperii* (On the Division of the Empire), Agobard hailed the *Ordinatio*, the majestic ceremony of its promulgation, its affirmation of the oneness of the realm (*ut unum regnum esset*), and its confirmation by the pope, and he grieved over its subsequent violation by the misguided Louis.[55] In 833, in the thick of the rebellion, Agobard called upon Louis to heed a papal appeal for reconciliation, acknowledging the supremacy of the spiritual sword and his foremost imperial responsibility to uphold the unity of the church—and to enforce the terms of the *Ordinatio*: "Let your sublime prudence deign to ponder piously what the Apostle says: 'Perilous times will come in the last days.' The blessed Pope Gregory already deplored these perils in his day, when the situation was much and incomparably better than now. . . . Alas, if the ship of the church was already rotten, and its planks were already putrefying, what is the situation now?"[56] Later that year, following (what would prove to be the short-lived) deposition of Louis and reinstatement of Lothar, Agobard wrote again on behalf of Louis's sons and against Judith, this time to justify the extreme measures just taken against emperor and empress. Louis had forsaken his duties as Christian monarch, proving incapable of controlling his own spouse and ineffective in his rule of the empire. Simply put, he had permitted the subversion of the proper order in Christian society. While the emperor should have been waging war against the external enemies of Christendom, he had sewn the seeds of injustice and discord within the boundaries of Christian society. "The house of God, which is the church of the living God, the pillar and bedrock of truth, prays that the barbarians be defeated by the most Christian emperor, not that his subjects be upset and barbarized. It is not the role of the most Christian emperor to confound his subjects and divide the united."[57]

54. Ganshof, "Some Observations," pp. 278ff.; Wallace-Hadrill, *Frankish Church*, pp. 232–33.

55. Agobard, *De divisione imperii*, CCCM 52:247–50.

56. Agobard, *De privilegio apostolicae sedis* 6, ibid., pp. 305–6. The letter of Pope Gregory IV to the Frankish bishops, affirming the superiority of ecclesiastical over secular/imperial power, appears in MGH, Epistulae 5:228–32. Following others before him, Louis Halphen, *Charlemagne and the Carolingian Empire*, Europe in the Middle Ages: Selected Studies 3 (Amsterdam, 1977), p. 196, suggests that Agobard might have composed this letter; yet Van Acker, CCCM 52:xxi–xxii, following Boshof, *Erzbischof Agobard*, pp. 225ff., believes that the papal attribution is genuine.

57. Agobard, *Liber apologeticus* 3, CCCM 52:310–11.

Times like these were ripe for opportunism, but Wallace-Hadrill has portrayed Agobard as a veritable man of principle. He sought not bloodshed but what he deemed a just peace. He believed that he rebelled not against the office of the emperor but against a man whose wife led him to forsake that office:

> Oaths had been broken, the moral fabric of the empire had collapsed and the heathen were attacking it from outside. Such was the judgement of God on sin. Everywhere there were Augustinian signs of Antichrist. On Agobard's correspondence the rebellious bishops based their case . . . against Louis: he had been negligent, unjust, cowardly and depraved; his court was a sink and his advisers evil. In brief, he was a self-declared tyrant and no king. . . . The moral drama of Louis's annihilation was thus very much Agobard's responsibility.

Notably, Agobard did not flee with Lothar when Louis regained the throne in 834 but accepted punishment and, ultimately, reinstatement from the emperor. According to Wallace-Hadrill, Agobard remained conservative and consistent to the end. "What mattered had been decided by the Bible, the Fathers and the canons of the councils. Similarly with the *Ordinatio*: everything had been decided with God's help and there was no going back and no room for argument."[58]

Though many might dispute such a sympathetic portrait of Agobard, I shall avoid taking sides in the conflict between Louis and Agobard, who have continued to find their respective supporters and detractors in twentieth-century historiography.[59] Nevertheless, I accept the view of Wallace-Hadrill, Egon Boshof, and others that Agobard's position on virtually every issue bespoke his belief in the sublime unity of all believers in the body of Christ.[60] Such bonding, like that between head and members of the body or between bridegroom and bride, assures for both the integrity and the proper hierarchical ordering of the relationship. Thus Agobard explained in a treatise, *De fidei veritate et*

---

58. Wallace-Hadrill, *Frankish Church*, pp. 232–33. Cf. the similar appraisal of Janet L. Nelson, "On the Limits of the Carolingian Renaissance," in *Renaissance and Renewal in Christian History*, ed. Derek Baker, SCH 14 (Oxford, 1977), p. 63.

59. Cf., for example, the favorable assessments of Agobard by A. Bressolles, "La Question juive au temps de Louis le Pieux," *Revue d'histoire de l'Église de France* 28 (1942), 51–64, and *Saint Agobard*, chap. 7, and Cabaniss, *Agobard of Lyons*, chap. 7, with the more critical comments of Bernhard Blumenkranz, in his review of A. Bressolles, *Saint Agobard: Evêque de Lyon (769–840)*, in *RMAL* 8 (1952), 59–61, and the works cited above, nn. 3, 9.

60. Boshof, *Erzbischof Agobard*, esp. chap. 2; and Wallace-Hadrill, *Frankish Church*, pp. 232–33.

totius boni institutione (On the Truth of the Faith and the Institution of the Total Good, ca. 830),

> This particular unity is that inestimable, ineffable good, which the eye has not seen, the ear has not heard of, and has not arisen in the human heart, and which God has prepared for those who love him, since that Lamb is the betrothed of his flock, the shepherd of his sheep. It is he who is a lamb in his passion, a lion in his resurrection, an eagle in his ascension, the cornerstone (of Ephesians 2:20), and the rock cut from the mountain without hands and made into a great mountain that filled the whole earth.[61]

Several years later he reiterated to the clergy of Lyons in a pastoral encyclical, *De modo regiminis ecclesiastici* (On the Manner of Ecclesiastical Governance): "The wondrous goodness of the creator is demonstrated when the head adheres to the body in such perfect unity and the head directs the body."[62] Since the fall of Adam from paradise, the devil has waged war against this sublime, holy alliance. He, his compatriot angels, and his human agents above all detract from the unity of the Catholic faith in manifold ways, persecuting and insidiously preying upon the faithful on a daily basis. These enemies of the church constitute a distinct body of the damned, with the devil or Antichrist as its head, doomed to a future punishment of eternal misery. For the time being, however, it threatens the steadfastness of individual Christians, luring them into a sinful life of vanity and worldliness; for their part, Christians must persist in the spiritual struggle, tolerantly and patiently bringing the weight of Scripture and rational argument to bear on their foes, asserting their cause with a regimen of prayer, pious works, and abstinence.[63] Christians must avail themselves of God's help in this struggle while it remains accessible; for the end fast approaches, and the final, eternal judgment will then be pronounced.[64]

Upon the birth of his son Charles to Empress Judith in 823, Louis the Pious first compromised his commitment to the *Ordinatio imperii*, precipitating the protracted conflict with Agobard over imperial unity and succession. Agobard composed his *De dispensatione ecclesiastica-*

---

61. Agobard, *De fidei veritate et totius boni institutione* 8, CCCM 52:260.

62. Agobard, *De modo regiminis ecclesiastici* 7, ibid., p. 330.

63. Agobard, *Adversus legem Gundobaldi* 5–6, ibid., pp. 21–23, and *De fidei veritate et totius boni institutione* 12, ibid., p. 264: "Contra quos pugnandum est, non armis corporalibus, sed spiritalibus, exemplis videlicet Scripturarum et auctoritate, ratiociniis fidei et veritatis. . . . Pugnandum est non sola oratione, sed et labore, abstinentia, continentia, vigiliis."

64. Agobard, *De privilegio et iure sacerdotii* 14, ibid., p. 64, and *De fide veritate et totius boni institutione* 28, ibid., pp. 278–79.

rum rerum in 823. And the same year saw the opening salvos fired in Agobard's conflict against the Jews and Louis's allegedly favorable policy toward them. This convergence appears more instructive than strictly fortuitous, and it may allow us to appreciate the significance of Agobard's anti-Judaism by relating it to other political and ideological issues that engaged him. Bernhard Blumenkranz has located the Jewish question at the top of Agobard's sociopolitical agenda, arguing that *Adversus Iudaeos* polemic motivated and thus explains most of his other chief concerns. Agobard's iconoclasm, contended Blumenkranz, stemmed from sensitivity to Jewish charges of Christian idolatry, his opposition to trial by ordeal (from which Jews were exempt) from fear that Christians might fare worse than Jews in Frankish courts, his feud with Amalarius of Metz from the latter's friendship with Jews, and his role in the rebellions against Louis the Pious from the emperor's beneficent Jewish policy.[65] These explanations, however, are largely speculative, and they yield an impression of Agobard as nothing short of a fanatic, totally obsessed by his hatred of the Jews. An alternative reading of Agobard suggests that such was not the case, his genuine hatred for Jews and Judaism notwithstanding. The substance of his anti-Jewish polemic—that is, the arguments he raised and the actions he advocated—appears more traditional than fanatical. Strikingly, the concordance to Agobard's extant works attests to no mention of the contemporary Jewish problem anywhere but in the five letters devoted specifically to the subject;[66] had the Jews fueled Agobard's other concerns, one would have expected otherwise. Rather, the issues of principle undergirding his attack on the Jews comport well with those of his other campaigns, more than these betray an anti-Jewish etiology.

What was the crux of Agobard's episcopal policy? Ensuring the unity and proper ordering of Christendom. Agobard manifested this preoccupation in addressing every issue on his agenda, from liturgy and popular superstition to biblical exegesis, proprietary churches, and the division of the empire. So too with regard to the Jews. Their station in Frankish society, measured against the nature of their religious belief and practice, endangered that essential unity and order. Repeatedly Agobard complained that the Jewish problem placed him on the horns

65. Blumenkranz, *Les Auteurs*, pp. 152–55. Bachrach, *Early Medieval Jewish Policy*, pp. 88, 101–2, accepts the linkage between the issue of imperial Jewish policy and Agobard's opposition to Amalarius.
66. See the microfiche concordance to CCCM 52, s.vv. Iudaei, iudaicus, and so forth.

of a dilemma: Either he would contravene the law of God and the church, or he would incur the wrath of the emperor, and this situation was simply intolerable in a properly ordered Christian society.[67] How can an emperor who piously fights against pagans and, as an act of piety, compels them to accept Christianity allow the Jews immunity from Agobard's more salutary forms of proselytization? If Agobard must obey those charged with implementing imperial Jewish policy, why do they show no respect for him and his episcopal office?[68] Scripture, the church fathers, and Gallican conciliar canons all resounded in their opposition to current practice in the empire, and Louis, wrote Agobard, had no choice: "Your piety emphatically commands that a solution be undertaken."[69] The present alternative was completely unacceptable: Catholics were becoming inferior to the Jews. "For what reason," thundered Agobard, "are the servants of sin preferable to the servants of God, the children of a handmaiden to those of a free woman, the disinherited to the heirs, the children of the devil to the children of God?"[70]

What, then, is Abogard's place in our story? Agobard shared in the monistic view of Christian society that characterized Gregory the Great and Isidore of Seville before him—and that typified many medieval prelates after him[71]—but he extended its applications to new limits. Likening a well-integrated Christian society to the body of Christ and regarding the Jew as exemplifying contamination and malaise in that Christian body, Agobard focused on the discrepancy between the theological construction of the Jews in Christianity and the present status of the Jews in Christendom much more than did any of his predecessors. In so doing, he scrutinized contemporary Judaism in a meticulous manner never mandated in Augustinian teaching and thus anticipated later developments that eventually subverted its doctrine of Jewish witness.

Did Agobard espouse a conception of the Jews fundamentally different from that of Augustine and Gregory? I think not. I believe not that Agobard intended to reject the doctrine of the fathers and councils

---

67. Agobard, *De baptismo mancipiorum Iudaeorum*, CCCM 52:117, and *Contra praeceptum impium de baptismo iudaicorum mancipiorum*, ibid., p. 188.
68. Agobard, *De baptismo mancipiorum Iudaeorum*, ibid., p. 116–17.
69. Agobard, *De iudaicis superstitionibus et erroribus* 1, ibid., p. 199.
70. Ibid. 22, p. 216.
71. See, for example, Steven Fanning, *Hubert of Angers, 1006–1047*, Transactions of the American Philosophical Society 78, 1 (Philadelphia, 1988), pp. 7, 87.

that preceded him but that he reflected the ambivalences, the internal inconsistencies, and the room for differing interpretations of their legacy—all of which his attempt to translate theology into public policy compounded. Agobard's anti-Jewish polemic may appear more extreme than that of Isidore, perhaps because he did not enjoy the cooperation of his king in the manner that Isidore did. Yet Agobard advocated much more limited measures to restrict the Jewish presence in his Christian society than Isidore had proposed. He emphatically reiterated the Jews' right to life, property, and the maintenance of their religion. He had greater familiarity with Jews and Judaism than had Western Christian writers before him, but his negative portrayal of them was as much stereotypical, drawn from the polemics of Jerome and others, as it derived from personal interaction with contemporary Jewish communities. Neither did Agobard succeed in altering Carolingian Jewish policy—Bernard Bachrach has called him an "ignominious failure" in this regard[72]—nor did Christian anti-Judaism undergo any major transformation during the two centuries that followed his episcopate. Directing his own anti-Jewish treatise to Charles the Bald, Agobard's Lyonnaise successor Amulo marshaled many of the same distinctive arguments,[73] but Christian Jewish polemic and policy generally maintained a more moderate tone until the Crusades.[74] No less than Agobard exemplified an alternative, harsher medieval Christian attitude toward the Jews and Judaism, his anti-Judaism testifies to the variety of expressions and contexts in which the Augustinian doctrine of Jewish witness continued to evolve—and to the growing incompatibility of that doctrine with the world and worldview of medieval Christendom, on one hand, and with its Jews, on the other hand.

72. Bachrach, *Early Medieval Jewish Policy*, p. 102.

73. Amulo, *Epistola seu liber contra Judaeos ad Carolum regem*, PL 116:141–84. See also A. Lukyn Williams, *Adversus Judaeos: A Bird's-Eye View of Christian Apologiae until the Renaissance* (Cambridge, England, 1935), pp. 358–65; Blumenkranz, *Les Auteurs*, pp. 195–200; and Merchavia, *Church*, pp. 85–92.

74. On the limited influence of the collection of anti-Jewish conciliar canons prepared by Agobard's secretary, Florus, see Blumenkranz, "Deux compilations," esp. pp. 568–70. For additional exceptions to the rule, see Bernhard Blumenkranz, "Die Entwicklung im Westen zwischen 200 und 1200," in *Kirche und Synagoge: Handbuch zur Geschichte von Christen und Juden*, ed. Karl Heinrich Rengstorf and Siegfried von Kurtzfleisch (Stuttgart, 1968–70), 1:109ff. Christian anti-Jewish polemic during the two centuries after Agobard is well exemplified in the writings of Fulbert of Chartres and Peter Damian; see Blumenkranz, *Les Auteurs*, pp. 237–43, 265–71, and David Berger, "St. Peter Damian: His Attitude toward the Jews and the Old Testament," *Yavneh Review* 4 (1965), 80–112.

Reconceptualizing Jewish Disbelief in the Twelfth Century

The twelfth century ushered the civilization of medieval Latin Christendom into maturity. The continuing Christian reconquest of Spain, the Crusades, and the ongoing conversion of central and northern Europe all contributed to its geographical expansion. Far-reaching economic development revitalized its commerce, reawakened its urban markets, and promoted a qualitative shift in its conceptualization of wealth—to one emphasizing the accumulation of financial profit over the mere ownership of land. Growth and consolidation characterized its ecclesiastical and political institutions. In the wake of Gregorian reform, popes, prelates, theologians, and canon lawyers expounded the theoretical and practical ramifications of a Catholic vision for an ideally ordered Christian society with unprecedented determination; at the same time, kings and emperors struggled to articulate and apply wellgrounded justifications for their own authority, defending it against subordination to the church, on one hand, and the encroachment of their feudal barons, on the other. Such inclination to change, expansion, and development found expression in the cultural and intellectual life of the period, in the acclaimed "renaissance" of the twelfth century. Urban schools broke the old monastic monopoly on literacy and learning. Access to hitherto inaccessible books and ideas evoked new modes of reading, contemplating, and interpreting traditional texts—transformations in epistemology and hermeneutics that sought to blend recognition of the Western world's changing visage with a compelling defense of established Christian doctrine. Respect swelled for the classics, for the sciences, for the arts, prompting experimentation and innovation in clerical and lay culture alike, from multifaceted reverence for the "goddess" Natura among churchmen to the veneration of courtly love among troubadours and their princely patrons.

New territories, markets, urban centers, schools, institutions of governance, libraries, varieties of cultural expression, and alternative patterns of Christian self-definition all fostered untold, unprecedented mobility in the society of the Latin West. In a word, the various components of that society scrambled to capitalize on the wealth of new opportunity. And yet, given the conservative nature of their mentality, which distrusted innovation as quintessentially sinful, the ideological spokesmen for high medieval Christianity found the spirit of their age discomfiting. For all that diversity increased, and for all that they themselves gave expression to it, they never abandoned the ideal of Christian unity or their program for fostering it in their society. Their commitment resulted in markedly increased sensitivity to the conformity—or nonconformity—of individuals and ideas to the orthodox formulations of the Catholic establishment.[1] And they gave rise to what one modern scholar has termed "a language of exclusion" and "a discourse of otherness" in twelfth-century Christendom, which, seeking to promulgate newly clarified norms of Christian identity, reacted to change and dissidence on a variety of levels.[2] At least three of these contributed directly to our story.

First, as they strove to expound and to realize their vision of Christian unity, churchmen displayed a penchant for classification in the face of sociocultural novelties: Where, precisely, did particular ideas, individuals, and practices "fit" into a Christian scheme of things?[3] Struggling to determine "how the authority of revelation within the church was related to other ways of knowing,"[4] scholars thus embarked upon a systematic reappraisal of the relationship between revealed knowl-

---

1. On the gradual—and painful—process whereby Christendom came to accommodate innovation and diversity during the High Middle Ages, see Jacques le Goff, *Medieval Civilization*, trans. Julia Barrow (Oxford, 1988), chap. 8, passim; and Beryl Smalley, "Ecclesiastical Attitudes to Novelty, c. 1100–c. 1250," in *Church, Society and Politics*, ed. Derek Baker, SCH 12 (Oxford, 1975), 1:113–31.

2. Miri Rubin, review of *The Formation of a Persecuting Society: Power and Deviance in Western Europe, 950–1250*, by R. I. Moore, *Speculum* 65 (1990), 1026.

3. See Jacques le Goff, *The Medieval Imagination*, trans. Arthur Goldhammer (Chicago, 1988), pp. 181ff.

4. Jaroslav Pelikan, *The Christian Tradition: A History of the Development of Doctrine* (Chicago, 1971–89), 3:255.

edge and scientific learning, along with their respective truths and methodologies. Or, as Caroline Bynum has demonstrated, individuals of the twelfth century typically sought to translate religious self-discovery into a process of affiliation and self-classification within a corporate, communal structure.[5] Second, as territorial expansion widened the geographical frontiers of Christendom and multiplied contacts between Christians and other religious communities, theologians felt impelled to analyze competing belief systems and to articulate arguments for confuting them. Inside and outside established institutions of learning, the twelfth century witnessed the development of missionary theology, hitherto an uncultivated field in the medieval Latin West. Third, heightened awareness of others outside the fold went hand in hand with growing sensitivity to difference, disagreement, and deviation from within. Having appeared but little in early medieval Europe, heresy first became a significant religious and social problem in the twelfth century, and historians have long pondered why. With interesting results, recent research has often focused on the orthodox adversaries of heresy more than on the heretics themselves, attributing the appearance of medieval heresy to processes endemic to Catholic Christendom: The discourse of Gregorian reform generated anti-ecclesiastical criticism among its most zealous advocates as well as its opponents. Movement and conflict proliferated in the ranks of medieval society, and these in turn provoked the more rigorous definition of social boundaries and the stigmatization of those whose tendencies threatened the establishment. The clerical establishment projected its own doubts and insecurities concerning traditional Christian doctrine onto an inverted, demonic, imagined other, who came to personify beliefs and practices catalogued by patristic heresiologists of many centuries earlier.[6] As one anthropologist has astutely observed, it is chiefly

---

5. Among many others, see especially Caroline Walker Bynum, *Jesus as Mother: Studies in the Spirituality of the High Middle Ages* (Berkeley, Calif., 1982), esp. chap. 3; and G. R. Evans, *Old Arts and New Theology: The Beginnings of Theology as an Academic Discipline* (Oxford, 1980).

6. Janet L. Nelson, "Society, Theodicy and the Origins of Medieval Heresy," in *Schism, Heresy and Religious Protest*, ed. Derek Baker, SCH 9 (Cambridge, England, 1972), pp. 65–77; Edward Peters, *The Magician, the Witch, and the Law* (Philadelphia, 1978), chap. 2; R. I. Moore, *The Origins of European Dissent*, corr. ed. (Oxford, 1985), and *The Formation of a Persecuting Society: Power and Deviance in Western Europe, 950–1250* (Oxford, 1987); Alexander Patschovsky, "Die Ketzer als Teufelsdiener," in *Papsttum, Kirche und Recht im Mittelalter: Festschrift für Horst Fuhrmann zum 65. Geburtstag*, ed. H. Mordek (Tübingen, Germany, 1991), pp. 317–34; the various essays collected in Scott L. Waugh and Peter D. Diehl, eds., *Christendom and Its Discontents: Exclusion, Persecution, and Rebellion, 1000–1500* (Cambridge, England, 1996); and others.

"in its attempt to extend and secure its authority that the Church comes to define and deal with heresy as a danger to Truth. The beliefs and practices of an incompletely Christianized population are not in themselves the subject of Church anxiety."[7]

How did these developments bear upon perceptions of Jews and Judaism? The impassioned pronouncements of Agobard did not circulate widely among churchmen of the following centuries, and Christian attitudes generally reverted to the more tolerant formulations of Augustine and Gregory the Great, which continued—though not without exception—to prevail throughout most of the eleventh century.[8] Yet even before the First Crusade and the anti-Jewish violence that accompanied it, portents of change loomed on the horizon. Apocalyptic generated by the turn of the millennium,[9] the rhetoric of papal reform, and the Investiture Controversy generated a polarized view of society, allowing the proponents of reform more readily to identify the allies and foes of the ideal Christian *respublica*. As the only religious minority officially present in Christendom, the Jews provided the most accessible examples of who or what such enemies might be like; from the first decade of the eleventh century, popular violence struck at Europe's Jews in conjunction with other dissidents, and, as early as 1062, Pope Alexander II found it necessary to intervene to prevent the slaughter of Jews in the holy war of the Spanish Reconquista.[10] The very idea of holy war against the enemies of Christ, to the extent that it had matured before the First Crusade, certainly endangered any positive role that the Jews had been preserved to fulfill in Christendom, as the

7. Talal Asad, "Medieval Heresy: An Anthropological View," *Social History* 11 (1986), 355.

8. See the summaries in Bernhard Blumenkranz, *Les Auteurs chrétiens latins du Moyen Âge sur les Juifs et le Judaisme* (Paris, 1963), pp. 168ff.; and Heinz Schreckenberg, *Die christlichen Adversus-Judaeos-Texte und ihr literarisches und historisches Umfeld (1.–11. Jh.)*, Europäische Hochschulschriften 23, 172, 2d ed. (Frankfurt am Main, 1990), pp. 500ff. On the very limited circulation of Agobard's written works, see Max Manitius, *Geschichte der lateinischen Literatur des Mittelalters*, Handbuch der Altertumswissenschaft 9, 2 (Munich, 1911–31), 1:389.

9. See Daniel F. Callahan, "Ademar of Chabannes, Millennial Fears and the Development of Western Anti-Judaism," *Journal of Ecclesiastical History* 46 (1995), 19–35; and Richard Landes, *Relics, Apocalypse, and the Deceits of History: Ademar of Chabannes, 989–1034* (Cambridge, Mass., 1995), pp. 40–46, and "The Massacres of 1010: On the Origins of Popular Anti-Jewish Violence in Western Europe," in *FWW*, pp. 79–112.

10. Shlomo Simonsohn, *ASJD, 492–1404*, Pontifical Institute of Mediaeval Studies: Studies and Texts 94 (Toronto, 1988), pp. 35–36.

slaughter of German Jews by crusaders in 1096 established. The calculation that the twelfth-century Jewish chronicler accurately attributed to these crusaders seems logical indeed: "Why should we concern ourselves with going to war against the Ishmaelites dwelling about Jerusalem when in our midst is a people who disrespect our God—indeed, their ancestors are those who crucified him. Why should we let them live and tolerate their dwelling among us? Let us use our swords against them first and then proceed upon our 'stray' path."[11] In certain Christian circles, Pope Alexander's admonitions that "it is impious to wish to annihilate those who are protected by the mercy of God" and that "the situation of the Jews is surely different from that of the Saracens"[12] had evidently fallen on deaf ears.

Albeit, perhaps, indirectly, the massacres of 1096 initiated a century of developments that would prove critical in the subsequent history of medieval European Jewry and in the development of the Christian idea of the Jew. One surely ought not to behold in the crusaders' anti-Jewish violence a conscious repudiation of the Augustinian doctrine of Jewish witness or a reversal in medieval Jewish policy that marked the "beginning of the end" for the Jews of the Middle Ages. In virtually every respect (demographic, economic, social, and cultural), the medieval civilization of western European Jews followed the lead of the majority, Christian experience, and it reached the peak of its achievement only during the twelfth and thirteenth centuries.[13] Nevertheless, attacks upon Jews during the Crusades, although not within the official mandate of the crusaders, undoubtedly awakened Christian society to the anomaly of the Jews' position: enemies/killers of Christ whose lives and errant religion God had protected for the greater good of Christendom. Against the background of the multifarious changes undergone by

11. A. Neubauer and M. Stern, eds., *Hebräische Berichte über die Judenverfolgungen während der Kreuzzüge*, Quellen der Geschichte der Juden in Deutschland 2 (Berlin, 1892), p. 4; trans. in Shlomo Eidelberg, ed., *The Jews and the Crusaders: The Hebrew Chronicles of the First and Second Crusades* (Madison, Wis., 1977), p. 26. For the confirmation of this description in Christian sources, see below, chapter 6, nn. 83, 85.

12. Above, n. 10; trans. in Robert Chazan, ed., *Church, State, and Jew in the Middle Ages* (New York, 1980), p. 100.

13. See the discussions in Robert Chazan, *European Jewry and the First Crusade* (Berkeley, Calif., 1987), pp. 197–210; Simon Schwarzfuchs, "The Place of the Crusades in Jewish History" [Hebrew], in *Culture and Society in Medieval Jewry: Studies Dedicated to the Memory of Haim Hillel Ben-Sasson*, ed. Menachem Ben-Sasson et al. (Jerusalem, 1989), pp. 251–69; and Jeremy Cohen, "Recent Historiography on the Medieval Church and the Decline of European Jewry," in *Popes, Teachers, and Canon Law in the Middle Ages: Essays in Honor of Brian Tierney*, ed. James Ross Sweeney and Stanley Chodorow (Ithaca, N.Y., 1989), pp. 251–62.

Christian civilization in the twelfth century, the new "discourse of otherness" understandably wrestled with the Jews and Judaism, scrutinizing and classifying them along with everything else in the Christian experience. The crusaders' disorderly departure from the norm of "Slay them not" only fueled the urgency to define the proper place of the Jews in the new Christian order of things. The age-old and "ineluctable demand that the church make sense of Judaism and clarify its relation to the ancient people of God"[14] assumed new importance during the twelfth century, as R. I. Moore has argued forcefully:

> Most obviously, the entire movement for the reinvigoration of the Church, the revival of learning, and the reassertion of royal authority, which goes under the amorphous but universal heading of "reform," was founded on the conviction that the laws, customs, and standards of antiquity must be restored, both in religious and in secular matters. Without implying special hostility or malice on the part of any group or individual, such a programme was bound to heighten awareness of the patristic account of the position of Jews in Christian society, to be preserved securely but miserably as a reminder to Christians of the death of their Saviour. No less ineluctably it entailed the recollection, and suggested the enforcement, of the long list of social and legal disadvantages and prohibitions imposed upon the Jews by the *Codex juris civilis*, mainly with the object of ensuring that they should never be in a position to exercise power over Christians.[15]

Not at all surprisingly, then, recent historical research has investigated various dimensions of the twelfth century's key, transitional significance in the history of Jewish-Christian relations. Some scholars have focused above all on the policies of the papacy and the burgeoning literature of canon law, assessing the impact of new styles of papal government, Gratian's *Decretum* and its glossators, and papal and conciliar legislation on the Jewish question.[16] Moore himself has highlighted the rise to power of a new urban ecclesiastical bureaucracy, which buttressed the social basis for its authority and prestige in the

14. Pelikan, *Christian Tradition*, 3:34.
15. R. I. Moore, "Anti-Semitism and the Birth of Europe," in *Christianity and Judaism*, ed. Diana Wood, SCH 29 (Oxford, 1992), p. 37.
16. Walter Pakter, *Medieval Canon Law and the Jews*, Münchener Universitätsschriften—Juristische Fakultät—Abhandlungen zur Rechtswissenschaftlichen Grundlagenforschung 68 (Ebelsbach, Germany, 1988); Shlomo Simonsohn, *The Apostolic See and the Jews: History*, Pontifical Institute of Mediaeval Studies: Studies and Texts 109 (Toronto, 1991); and Kenneth R. Stow, *The "1007 Anonymous" and Papal Sovereignty: Jewish Perceptions of the Papacy and Papal Policy in the High Middle Ages*, Hebrew Union College Annual Supplements 4 (Cincinnati, Ohio, 1984).

demonization and exclusion of numerous marginal groups, including lepers, heretics, and, most notably, Jews.[17] Still other historians have discerned the roots of medieval antisemitism in twelfth-century Christendom's guilt, fears, and doubts concerning the materialistic and irrational within itself and its resulting use of the Jew as scapegoat, now perceived as embodying all of Christendom's own sinful inadequacies.[18] Recently, Robert Chazan has explored the worsening popular perceptions of Jews in northern Europe of the twelfth century and the ominous antisemitic stereotypes to which they gave rise.[19] Most germane for our present inquiry are studies of the complex role of the Jews in the intellectual history of the period. On one hand, Jews contributed to the Christian renaissance of the twelfth century. Testifying, one might argue, to a certain degree of *convivencia* in the interaction of Christian and Jewish (and even Muslim) communities in Spain, Jews distinguished themselves as translators of scientific and philosophical works from Arabic into Latin, sometimes via Hebrew.[20] Moreover, the Jew and his tradition nourished the newly reinvigorated Christian study of the Old Testament; the Hebrew Bible contained the *hebraica veritas*, ostensibly the most ancient, most accurate text of Scripture, and rabbinic scholarship and religious practice offered invaluable insight into its ancient, presumably literal meaning. Many a Christian scholar, Beryl Smalley observed, assumed that in talking to a medieval rabbi "he was telephoning to the Old Testament."[21] For their part, not only

---

17. Moore, *Formation*, esp. pp. 27–45.

18. Gavin I. Langmuir, *History, Religion, and Antisemitism* (Berkeley, Calif., 1990), esp. chap. 14, and *Toward a Definition of Antisemitism* (Berkeley, Calif., 1990), passim; Lester K. Little, "The Function of the Jews in the Commercial Revolution," in *Povertà e richezza nella spiritualità dei secoli xi e xii*, Convegni del Centro di studi sulla spiritualità medievale 8 (Todi, Italy, 1969), pp. 271–87, and *Religious Poverty and the Profit Economy in Medieval Europe* (Ithaca, N.Y., 1978), pp. 42–57.

19. Robert Chazan, *Medieval Stereotypes and Modern Antisemitism* (Berkeley, Calif., 1997).

20. See Marie-Thérèse d'Alverny, "Translations and Translators," in *Renaissance and Renewal in the Twelfth Century*, ed. Robert L. Benson and Giles Constable (Cambridge, Mass., 1982), pp. 421–62 (with extensive notes and bibliography); David Romano, "Los hispanojudíos en el mundo científico y en la transmisión del saber," in *Luces y sombras de la judería europea (siglos xi–xvii)* (Navarre, Spain, 1996), pp. 17–57, along with his additional studies cited therein; I owe this latter reference to Eleazar Gutwirth. Though dated, Moritz Steinschneider, *Die hebräischen Übersetzungen des Mittelalters und die Juden als Dolmetscher* (1893; reprint, Graz, Austria., 1956), has not lost its value in this regard.

21. Beryl Smalley, *Hebrew Scholarship among Christians in XIIIth Century England as Illustrated by Some Hebrew-Latin Psalters*, Lectiones in Veteri Testamento et in rebus judaicis 6 (London, 1939), p. 1. On the Judaic enrichment of twelfth-century Christian

did twelfth-century Jews participate, eagerly or otherwise, in such intellectual exchange, but they also emulated various expressions of the Christian "renaissance" of their age in their own, distinctly Jewish media of cultural expression.[22] On the other hand, increased cultural contacts, including interreligious debate, intensified Christian sensitivity to contemporary Jews and Judaism, aggravating the perception of them as a threat to the integrity of Christendom. This century, as Jaroslav Pelikan has noted, produced more extant works of Christian anti-Jewish polemic than all previous centuries combined,[23] and numerous scholars have therefore studied the representation of Jews and Judaism in these and other theological texts of the period. To what extent do they continue in or depart from previous works in the tradition of *Adversus Iudaeos*? Do they employ new varieties of argumentation, drawing on new types of evidence? Do they persist in addressing a primarily Christian audience, or do they begin to dispute more directly with contemporary Jews, perhaps with an interest in proselytizing among them? Although genuine efforts to missionize appear to have been lacking in Christendom before the thirteenth century, Amos Funkenstein and Anna Sapir Abulafia have shown how the rationalism of the twelfth-century renaissance in fact added to the virulence of interreligious polemic. Some Christian writers may now have portrayed the Jew as subject to conversion on rational grounds, and others soon came to interpret his persistent refusal to convert first as a treacherous betrayal of reason, then as glaring proof of an utterly inhuman irrationality. Here, Funkenstein and Abulafia have argued, lay the source of

---

biblical exegesis, see also, among others, Herman Hailperin, *Rashi and the Christian Scholars* (Pittsburgh, Pa., 1963), esp. pt. 3; Aryeh Graboïs, "The *Hebraica veritas* and Jewish-Christian Intellectual Relations in the Twelfth Century," *Speculum* 50 (1975), 613–34; Beryl Smalley, *The Study of the Bible in the Middle Ages*, 3d ed. (Oxford, 1983), chaps. 3–5; and Gilbert Dahan, *Les Intellectuels chrétiens et les Juifs au Moyen Âge* (Paris, 1990), pt. 3.

22. For example, see Avraham Grossman, "The Jewish-Christian Polemic and Jewish Biblical Exegesis in Twelfth Century France (On the Attitude of R. Joseph Qara to Polemic)" [Hebrew], *Zion*, n.s. 51 (1985), 29–60; Ephraim E. Urbach, *The Tosaphists: Their History, Writings and Methods* [Hebrew], 4th ed. (Jerusalem, 1980), esp. 2:744ff.; Jeremy Cohen, "A 1096 Complex? Constructing the First Crusade in Jewish Historical Memory, Medieval and Modern," in *In the Shadow of the Millennium: Jews and Christians in Twelfth-Century Europe*, ed. Michael A. Signer and John H. van Engen (Notre Dame, Ind., 1999); and Ivan G. Marcus, "The Dynamics of Jewish Renaissance and Renewal in the Twelfth Century," in *In the Shadow of the Millennium: Jews and Christians in Twelfth-Century Europe*, ed. Michael A. Signer and John H. van Engen (Notre Dame, Ind., 1999).

23. Pelikan, *Christian Tradition*, 3:246.

the thought process that ultimately deprived the Jew of the valuable, testificatory role in Christian society that Augustine had allotted him.[24]

Neither will this book undertake a comprehensive review of these various investigations of Jewish-Christian interaction in the twelfth century, nor will it argue that any one factor in changing Christian attitudes toward Jews and Judaism outweighed all others in importance. At work here was clearly an intricate, enigmatic process, one that defies any simple, one-dimensional explanation. Rather, noting how many of the explanatory strategies cited above converge in attributing the new Christian outlook on the Jews to Christians' changing perceptions of themselves, we consider how selected twelfth-century Christian thinkers reconceptualized the hermeneutically crafted Jew: What happened to Augustine's doctrine of Jewish witness and its legacy? What new medieval issues and concerns, different in substance and character from the considerations of exegesis, philosophy of history, and anthropology undergirding the Augustinian doctrine, began to weigh heavily on European constructions of the Jew? How did the hermeneutical Jew and his function in Christendom change, and why? Again avoiding neat, all-purpose solutions, I do not merely rehash past

24. Amos Funkenstein, *Perceptions of Jewish History* (Berkeley, Calif., 1993), pp. 172–201; Anna Sapir Abulafia, "Jewish-Christian Disputations and the Twelfth-Century Renaissance," *JMH* 15 (1989), 105–25, "Christian Imagery of Jews in the Twelfth Century: A Look at Odo of Cambrai and Guibert of Nogent," *Theoretische Geschiedenis* 16 (1989), 383–91, "Jewish Carnality in Twelfth-Century Renaissance Thought," in *Christianity and Judaism*, ed. Diana Wood, SCH 29 (Oxford, 1992), pp. 59–75, "Twelfth-Century Humanism and the Jews," in *Contra Iudaeos: Ancient and Medieval Polemics between Christians and Jews*, ed. Ora Limor and Guy G. Stroumsa (Tübingen, Germany, 1996), pp. 161–75, "Twelfth-Century Renaissance Theology and the Jews," in *FWW*, pp. 125–39, and *Christians and Jews in the Twelfth-Century Renaissance* (London, 1995). See also Kurt Schubert, "Das christlich-jüdische Religionsgespräch im 12. und 13. Jahrhundert," *Kairos* n.s. 19 (1977), 161–86; Marianne Awerbuch, *Christlich-jüdische Begegnung im Zeitalter der Frühscholastik*, Abhandlungen zum christlich-jüdischen Dialog 8 (Munich, 1980); Jeremy Cohen, "Scholarship and Intolerance in the Medieval Academy: The Study and Evaluation of Judaism in European Christendom," *AHR* 91 (1986), 592–613; and Dahan, *Les Intellectuels*, esp. pt. 4. On the lack of twelfth-century Christian interest in missionizing among the Jews, see David Berger, "Mission to the Jews and Jewish-Christian Cultural Contacts in the Polemical Literature of the High Middle Ages," *AHR* 91 (1986), pp. 576–91; and Robert Chazan, *Daggers of Faith: Thirteenth-Century Christian Missionizing and Jewish Response* (Berkeley, Calif., 1989), chap. 1. The most recent studies of high medieval polemics between Christians and Jews also include Simon Schwarzfuchs, "Religion populaire et polémique savante: Le Tournant de la polémique judéo-chrétienne au 12ᵉ siècle," in *Medieval Studies in Honour of Avrom Saltman*, ed. Bat-Sheva Albert et al., Bar-Ilan Studies in History 4 (Ramat Gan, Israel, 1995), pp. 189–206; and Daniel J. Lasker, "Jewish-Christian Polemics at the Turning Point: Jewish Evidence from the Twelfth Century," *HTR* 89 (1996), 161–73.

arguments for the critical importance of the thirteenth century as opposed to the twelfth in accounting for the exclusion of the Jews from
late medieval Christian society. The remainder of this book will evaluate the evidence for the gradual dismantling of the Augustinian position on the Jews during both the twelfth and the thirteenth centuries.
Seeking to add more nuanced perspective to our understanding of this
history, I reflect more extensively concerning twelfth-century Christian
authors whom I have treated only briefly in the past. In so doing, I
modify some of the positions advanced in my earlier study of *The Friars
and the Jews*, at the same time as I hold fast to others.

If, in that book, I took issue with regard to Funkenstein's assessment
of the twelfth-century developments in Christian anti-Judaism, here I
return to his seminal research on a more assenting note. In his article
on "Changes in Christian Anti-Jewish Polemics in the Twelfth Century," first published in Hebrew thirty years ago, Funkenstein argued
that two new elements proved critical in the developing Christian attack on the Jews: the introduction of rational-philosophical argumentation into the literature of religious polemic, and increasing Christian
familiarity with postbiblical Jewish literature.[25] Recognizing the un-
questionable importance of these two developments, I propose the addition of a third—not because it overshadowed either or both of those
on Funkenstein's list but because it accompanied them, complemented
them, and, ultimately, served as a catalyst in facilitating their impact.
During the twelfth century, as Christian writers struggled to classify
the diverse components of the enlarging world around them, the array
of those who did not belong to the community of the truly faithful—
that is, those who did not adhere to the norms of Christian orthodoxy—expanded considerably. As a result of this "widening of the
field" of those who refused to accept Christianity, the Jew ceased to
function in Christian thought as the sole or even predominant
"other."[26] Instead of the sole active, readily visible non-Christians in
Christian experience, the Jews now became a subset of a larger class
of unbelievers, and this eventually upset their position in Christian
thought.

---

25. Funkenstein, *Perceptions*, pp. 172–201; the essay originally appeared as
"Changes in the Patterns of Christian Anti-Jewish Polemic in the Twelfth Century" [He-
brew], *Zion*, n.s. 33 (1968), 125–44. An abridged, slightly reoriented version of this
essay subsequently appeared in English as "Basic Types of Christian Anti-Jewish Polemics
in the Later Middle Ages," *Viator* 2 (1971), 373–82.
26. Cf. Pelikan, *Christian Tradition*, 3:215–67.

Such change came to manifest itself in a number of ways. Although Christianity's unceasing debate with Judaism may well have provided a basis for disputing other groups outside the fold, the generic nature of Christianity's opponents now demanded a more logically systematic and scientific defense of the faith. No longer could one rely on the assertion of Christianity primarily through the negation of Jewish belief. Considerations of *ratio* and dialectic began to govern the presentation of arguments based on biblical *auctoritas*: Neither biblical testament could successfully counter the objections of infidels who denied the divinely revealed character of Scripture altogether; even against those who did respect biblical authority, one could no longer assume that "a stereotyped enumeration of proofs taken from the Bible for the proof of Christianity,"[27] especially when adduced in the order of appearance in Scripture, would continue to suffice. No less important, and notwithstanding the old adage about "safety in numbers," the need for the Jew to share the brunt of Christian religious polemic with additional "others" paradoxically contributed to his gradual removal from a unique, privileged status in Christendom, marginalizing him and demoting him still further in the Christian mentality. If the terminology and orientation of the *Adversus Iudaeos* tradition formerly highlighted that which rendered the Jew unique in Christendom, twelfth-century clerical writers began to focus on that which he shared with other marginal types. This common ground included the postbiblical traditions of the Jews, which Christian polemicists now began to attack in the same vein as they impugned other infidels and dissidents for espousing absurd, noncanonical doctrines. Thus, as Moore has shown, leper, heretic, and Jew became virtually interchangeable designations in twelfth-century Christian taxonomies of society, exemplifying marginality and an impurity that threatened the essential fabric of Christian existence.[28] At the end of the century, one encountered in Alan of Lille's *De fide catholica contra haereticos* a new genre of polemical treatise, which debated systematically and in turn against heretics, Saracens,

---

27. Funkenstein, "Basic Types," p. 374.
28. Moore, *Formation*; see also Alexander Patschovsky, "Feindbilder der Kirche: Juden und Ketzer im Vergleich (11.–13. Jh.)," in *Juden und Christen zur Zeit der Kreuzzüge*, ed. Alfred Haverkamp, Vorträge und Forschungen des Konstanzer Arbeitskreises für mittelalterliche Geschichte (Sigmaringen, Germany, 1999); Sara Lipton, "Jews, Heretics, and the Sign of the Cat in the *Bible moralisée*," *Word and Image* 8 (1992), 362–77; and Elizabeth Carson Pastan, "*Tam haereticus quam Judaeos*: Shifting Symbols in the Glazing of Troyes Cathedral," *Word and Image* 10 (1994), 66–83. Cf. the reservations expressed by Chazan, *Medieval Stereotypes*, p. 91f.

and Jews.[29] Not long thereafter, the Dominican canonist Raymond of
Penyafort followed the lead of Gratian and other twelfth-century masters by grouping together all "those who dishonor God by worshipping
him vilely, namely Jews, Saracens, and heretics."[30]

Yet a further result of the classification of Jews within the same
genus as other nonconformists was the attribution of one's group's
qualities, whether real or imagined, to members of the others. Even as
Jews continued to personify that which Christian society deemed imperfect in itself, it could now be assumed that what they shared with
Muslims and heretics was not limited to the fact of their opposition to
Catholic Christianity. Inasmuch as Muslims and Jews shared ethnic,
linguistic, and, presumably, religious characteristics, one could logically
conclude that they harbored similar hostility toward Christendom, the
former from without, the latter from within. If the types, practices, and
beliefs of the heterodox were catalogued by Catholic heresiologists, so
did Honorius Augustudensis list eight "heresies" or sects in classical
Judaism.[31] Twelfth-century Christians' indiscriminate use of the term
"heresy" to characterize Judaism—and "heretics" when referring to
Jews—will warrant attention because, never having converted to Christianity, Jews had never strayed from it. Thus did an early-thirteenth-
century canonist reflect with hindsight on references to heretics and
other enemies of the church in Gratian's *Decretum*:

> Note that the term "heretic" is used sometimes in a narrow sense, some-
> times in a broad sense: in a narrow sense, meaning one who was initially
> within the Church and was later separated from it on account of heresy,
> and in this sense is in every case excommunicate . . . ; in a broad sense,
> meaning whoever holds differently from the Roman Church concerning the

29. PL 210:305–430; see also the partial edition and introduction of Marie-Thérèse
d'Alverny, "Alain de Lille et l'Islam: Le 'Contra Paganos,'" in *ICM*, pp. 301–50. For
similar tendencies in other contemporary polemical works, see Gilbert Dahan's edition
of William of Bourges, *Livre des guerres du Seigneur et deux homélies*, SC 288 (Paris,
1981); and Marie-Humbert Vicaire, " 'Contra Judaeos' meridionaux au début du xiii^e
siècle: Alain de Lille, Evrard de Béthune, Guillaume de Bourges," in *Juifs et judaïsme de
Languedoc*, Cahiers de Fanjeaux 12 (Toulouse, France, 1977), pp. 269–93. On the frequent and natural linkage between Judaism and Islam—and heretics—see also the comments of Norman Daniel, *Islam and the West: The Making of an Image*, rev. ed. (Oxford,
1993), pp. 213–18.
30. Raymond of Penyafort, *Summa de paenitentia* 1.4 init., ed. Xaverio Ochoa and
Aloisio Diez, Universa bibliotheca iuris 1A (Rome, 1976), p. 308; trans. in Chazan,
Church, State, and Jew, p. 38. In Gratian's *Decretum*, see, for instance, C. 2 q. 7 c. 24–
26, C. 28 q. 1, D.1 c. 67 de cons.
31. Honorius Augustudensis, *Liber de haeresibus*, PL 172:233.

articles of faith, and in this sense not every heretic is excommunicate—since, although they are heretics (inasmuch as both groups oppose the articles of faith), neither the Jews nor the Saracens could have been excommunicated, since they were never inside the Church.[32]

I believe that the reclassification of the Jews, together with other enemies of the church, within a broader category of infidels or heretics began during the twelfth century to disempower the hermeneutically crafted Jew of patristic theology, depriving him of that singularity which distinguished him and underlay his worth. At the same time, I hasten to stress the long, gradual nature of this process. The labeling of the Jews as heretics offers a good case in point. Some scholars have argued that such an identification signified a departure from Augustinian precedent, bespeaking the charge that contemporary medieval Judaism had forsaken its biblical heritage. One must, I agree, afford this terminological shift from infidel to heretic in some twelfth-century Christian designations of the Jews its due recognition; and yet, one ought not to overestimate its meaning. As the Decretist we have just quoted affirmed, one may brand the Jews "heretics" for contesting the essential beliefs of the church, not for abandoning—or having been banned from—any religious community, Christian or Jewish, as the technical sense of the term "heretic" implied. Eventually some churchmen perceived in medieval Judaism a heresy of this second, strictly defined sort as well, but this took time, and the distinction is profoundly important. In a similar vein, the Jews' loss of privileged status in the Christian theological mind-set proceeded slowly and in some quarters never appears to have transpired at all. However much the Jew had to make room, as it were, for other outsiders in the Christian scheme of things, he remained the most obvious and accessible, throughout the twelfth century and even beyond. For, unlike the Jews, most Muslims resided outside Christendom, and most heretics did not voluntarily confess their dissidence to the Catholic authorities. If the Jew was now but one member of a larger category, he still typified the dangerous in the eyes of his Christian beholders—a role he had already come to play in Byzantine Christianity, among Christian writers in the

---

32. Laurentius, *Glossa palatina* ad C. 24 q. 3 c. 26 (Biblioteca Apostolica Vaticana, ms. Pal. lat. 658, fol. 72rb), cited in Othmar Hageneder, "Der Häresiebegriff bei den Juristen des 12. und 13. Jahrhunderts," in *The Concept of Heresy in the Middle Ages (11th-13th C.)*, ed. W. Lourdaux and D. Verhelst, Mediaevalia lovaniensia 1, 4 (Louvain, Belgium, 1976), p. 50 n. 28.

Muslim world, and even in Sunni Islam—dominating their attention and concern to a noteworthy extent indeed.[33]

Latin Christendom's encounter with Islam provides the most instructive instance of how Christian theological discourse came to discern a qualitative parity between the Jews and other outsiders.[34] As with Judaism, early medieval churchmen took little interest in Islam, although not, as some historians have assumed, for lack of accessible information or of opportunity.[35] Then, just as the anti-Jewish violence of 1096 helped to awaken western Europe to the anomaly of its Jewish minority, so did events of the eleventh century—the reconquest of Spain and Sicily and, above all, the First Crusade—render the contacts between Christians and Muslims inevitable, more frequent, and increasingly intense. The existence of Islam, Richard Southern has noted, became "the most far-reaching problem in medieval Christendom; it was a problem at every level of experience."[36] Here was not merely a subjugated religious minority; the devotees of Islam endangered the Christian world above all militarily, confronting it with—as one modern Muslim scholar has put it—"a permanent divine scandal, insofar as God, in his impenetrable wisdom, had armed, trained, and assured the victory of evil and lies."[37] Interestingly, the correspondence between developing Christian attitudes toward Jews and Muslims continued well beyond the First Crusade. Just as they did for Judaism and Jews, the twelfth

33. Cf. the fascinating studies of Kathleen Corrigan, *Visual Polemics in the Ninth-Century Byzantine Psalters* (Cambridge, England, 1992), esp. chaps. 3, 5; David M. Olster, *Roman Defeat, Christian Response, and the Literary Construction of the Jew* (Philadelphia, 1994); Sidney H. Griffith, "Jews and Muslims in Christian Syriac and Arabic Texts of the Ninth Century," *Jewish History* 3 (1988), esp. 84ff.; and Steven M. Wasserstrom, *Between Muslim and Jew: The Problem of Symbiosis under Early Islam* (Princeton, N.J., 1995).

34. I do not subscribe to the theory—or the arguments in its behalf—advanced by Allan and Ellen Cutler, who have claimed that "medieval anti-Semitism . . . was primarily a function of medieval anti-Muslimism"; see their *The Jew as the Ally of the Muslim* (Notre Dame, Ind., 1986), and my review in *Judaism* 37 (1988), 240–42.

35. Benjamin Z. Kedar, *Crusade and Mission: European Approaches toward the Muslim* (Princeton, N.J., 1984), chap. 1.

36. Richard W. Southern, *Western Views of Islam in the Middle Ages* (Cambridge, Mass., 1962), p. 3.

37. Hichem Djaït, *Europe and Islam*, trans. Peter Heinegg (Berkeley, Calif., 1985), p. 13. See also Rosalind Hill, "The Christian View of the Muslim at the Time of the First Crusade," in *The European Mediterranean Lands in the Period of the Crusaders*, ed. P. M. Holt (Westminster, England, 1977), pp. 1–8; and Penny J. Cole, " 'O God, the Heathen Have Come into Your Inheritance' (Ps. 78.1): The Theme of Religious Pollution in Crusade Documents, 1095–1188," in *Crusaders and Muslims in Twelfth-Century Syria*, ed. Maya Shatzmiller, The Medieval Mediterranean: Peoples, Economies and Cultures 1 (Leiden, Netherlands, 1993), pp. 84–111.

and thirteenth centuries saw the appearance of well-informed polemics against Islam, of concerted efforts to missionize among Muslims both in Europe and overseas, of attempts to subject Muslim unbelievers to papal jurisdiction, and of a growing tendency to reclassify Muslims as heretics rather than simply as infidels.[38] Beginning in the fourteenth century, one historian has recently suggested, Muslims, too, had begun to lose their claim to the status of "privileged other" in the medieval Christian worldview.[39]

As the only religious minority the Latin West knew and tolerated during the early Middle Ages, the Jews invariably presented Christendom with a paradigm for the evaluation and classification of the Muslim "other," a springboard for formulating a deliberate response to him and his faith. As a result, there arose in Christendom an array of multidimensional associations between the two faiths and their followers. Like the Jews, Muslims were monotheists, who worshiped the God of the Bible, venerated sacred texts written (from right to left!) in an exotic, non-Western language, but refused to accept Christianity. Moreover, owing to their dispersion, the Jews served as natural intermediaries—merchants, diplomats, translators, and conveyors of ideas—between the two regnant medieval religious cultures, at times representing the one to the other. When circumstances demanded that Christians articulate their posture vis-à-vis Muslims and Islam, why should they not have drawn on their pronouncements concerning Jews and Judaism?

Despite the distinction between Muslims and Jews in Pope Alexander II's directive *Dispar nimirum est* (ca. 1065)—Christians may legitimately wage war upon the former but may not attack the latter[40]—canon law habitually treated Muslim and Jew in tandem, once Christendom came to incorporate a resident Muslim population. The church fathers of late antiquity had obviously not envisioned Muslims in a

38. Kedar, *Crusade and Mission*, chaps. 2–4. John Tolan, "Anti-Hagiography: Embrico of Mainz's *Vita Mahumeti*," *JMH* 22 (1996), 25–41, demonstrates that the evaluation of Islam—like that of Judaism—as heresy derived more from Christendom's contemporary concern with heretics than from any systematic evaluation of Muslim doctrine as truly heretical. On the progression of this tendency into the thirteenth century, see also Kurt Villads Jensen, "War against Muslims According to Benedict of Alignano, O.F.M.," *Archivum franciscanum historicum* 89 (1996), esp. 186ff.

39. Michel-Marie Dufeil, "Vision d'Islam depuis l'Europe au début du xive siècle," in *ICM*, pp. 235–58.

40. Gratian, *Decretum*, C. 23 q. 8 c. 11; see above, nn. 10, 12. Cf. also the discussion of Henri Gilles, "Législation et doctrine canoniques sur les Sarrasins," in *ICM*, pp. 195–213.

properly ordered Christian world; but, in practice, high medieval jurists related to them and the Jews as what James Powell has termed "coordinate communities."[41] Some found an instructive precedent in the section of Justinian's *Codex* (1.9) entitled *De Iudaeis et Caelicolis*, comparing Saracens with the latter, because both Jews and these particular pagans "revere and worship God in a half-baked, literal fashion [*semi plene*] and err less grievously than other heretics."[42] Gratian's *Decretum* and most subsequent compilations of medieval canon law typically legislated concerning Jews and pagans/Muslims under the same rubric.[43] The Third Lateran Council of 1179 decreed that neither Jews nor Saracens might own Christian slaves or keep Christian domestic servants in their employment. The Council of Montpellier in 1195 added Saracens to the traditional ban on Jews holding public office or exercising authority over Christians. Pope Innocent III admonished King Alfonso VIII of Castile, lest he "appear to restrict the freedom of the church and to elevate the synagogue and mosque"; and, under Innocent's leadership, the Fourth Lateran Council (1215) decreed that both Jews and Saracens under Christian rule wear distinguishing marks on their clothing, because "it sometimes happens that Christians mistakenly have sexual relations with Jewish or Saracen women, and Jews or Saracens with Christian women."[44]

Innocent's successors took further steps in the same direction. Honorius III and Gregory IX continued to issue edicts banning Jews and

41. James M. Powell, "The Papacy and the Muslim Frontier," in *Muslims under Latin Rule, 1100–1300*, ed. James M. Powell (Princeton, N.J., 1990), p. 186. See also James Muldoon, *Popes, Lawyers, and Infidels: The Church and the Non-Christian World, 1250–1550* (Philadelphia, 1979), esp. chaps. 1–3; and Kedar, *Crusade and Mission*, chap. 5.

42. Azo, *Summa* 1.9.3, quoted by Gilles, "Législation et doctrine canoniques," p. 196. On Azo's equation of Justinian's pagans with present-day Saracens, see also David Abulafia, "Monarchs and Minorities in the Christian Western Mediterranean around 1300: Lucera and Its Analogues," in *Christendom and Its Discontents: Exclusion, Persecution, and Rebellion, 1000–1500*, ed. Scott L. Waugh and Peter D. Diehl (Cambridge, England, 1996), p. 260 n. 118.

43. Peter Herde, "Christians and Saracens at the Time of the Crusades: Some Comments of Contemporary Canonists," *Studia gratiana* 12 (1967), 359–76; Gilles, "Législation et doctrine canoniques"; and Benjamin Z. Kedar, "*De Iudeis et Sarracenis*: On the Categorization of Muslims in Medieval Canon Law," in *Studia in honorem eminentissimi cardinalis Aplhonsi M. Stickler*, ed. Rosalio Joseph Castillo Lara, Pontificia studiorum universitas salesiana: Studia et textus historiae iuris canonici 7 (Rome, 1992), pp. 207–13. See also above, n. 41.

44. Solomon Grayzel, *CJ*, rev. ed. (New York, 1966), pp. 112–13 (Simonsohn, *ASJD*, 492–1404, pp. 85–86), 296–99, 308–9 (with slight variation from Grayzel's translation).

Muslims from public office in Christendom and insisting that they compensate the church for tithes on lands once owned by Christians. Innocent IV confirmed a royal statute of James I of Aragon commanding Jews and Muslims to listen to the missionary sermons of Dominican and Franciscan friars.[45] The same passage of his Decretalist commentary that justified the burning of the Talmud—during his pontificate and that of Pope Gregory IX before him—asserted the right of the Holy See to enforce natural law on Jews and Muslims, as well as the essential precepts of their religions, should their own prelates fail to do so.[46] In 1263 Urban IV instructed that guilt had condemned the Saracens as well as the Jews to perpetual servitude.[47] And, in the next century, the briefs of the Spanish canonist Oldradus de Ponte expanded upon such occasional associations of these two communities of infidels to elaborate strikingly similar legal theories toward them both. Oldradus adapted the apostle Paul's typological identification of the enslaved Hagar with the Jews to include the Saracens as well; they, too, have been excluded from the community of God's faithful (prefigured in the household of Abraham) by his free wife Sarah, who typifies the Catholic Church. Defending the legitimacy of war against the Muslims of Spain, Oldradus reasoned:

> So we are to understand the Church in Abraham's words to his wife Sarah, who was complaining about that accursed handmaiden who despised her: "Behold," he says, "your handmaiden is in your own hand; use her as you wish"; for Sarah signifies the Holy Catholic Church, the handmaiden Hagar the accursed sect of Muhammad which took its origin from her. Therefore, the Holy Church, symbolized by Sarah, may use that accursed handmaiden as the blessed Sarah had used her, by beating her. She may use her as the Lord commands, by driving her out and depriving her children of inheritance and possession, that they not share with the free children. For since they are the offspring of a slave woman, and are therefore themselves slaves

45. Simonsohn, *ASJD*, 492–1404, pp. 120, 130–32, 136–40, 147–49, 183–85; and Grayzel, *CJ*, pp. 172–73, 184–87, 192–95, 208–9, 254–57.

46. The correct reading of Innocent's *Apparatus super quinque libros Decretalium* ad X.3.34.8 has been established by Benjamin Z. Kedar, "Canon Law and the Burning of the Talmud," *Bulletin of Medieval Canon Law*, n.s. 9 (1979), 79–82. Instructive discussions of Innocent's position and its lasting impact appear in Muldoon, *Popes*, chaps. 2–3; and Kedar, *Crusade and Mission*, chap. 5.

47. Simonsohn, *ASJD*, 492–1404, p. 221: "non est conveniens vel honestum, ut eisdem Iudaeis et Saracenis, quos propria culpa submisit perpetuae servituti, exercendi vim potestatis in Christianis." Emperor Fredrick II also referred to Muslims as *servi camerae nostrae*, exactly what he had dubbed the Jews; see Abulafia, "Monarchs and Minorities," p. 237.

(for the children follow the womb)—indeed, slaves reproved by the Lord—they are not legally competent to hold rights of jurisdiction, lordship, or honor.[48]

The Jews, wrote Oldradus, have long been liable to similar treatment, particularly when they cause scandal or offense to the church. Conversely, Oldradus followed the Decretist Alanus and most thirteenth-century Decretalists in concluding that Muslims living peacefully and submissively under Christian rule should enjoy the same toleration extended to the Jews; in so doing, he effectively applied the Augustinian rationale for such a policy to the Saracens as well![49] As James Muldoon has concluded, all this amounted to "a blurring of the lines distinguishing Jews and Muslims. Christians saw them as joined by common opposition to the Christian faith and overlooked the religious and other differences between them. This blurring of distinctions between various non-Christians seems part of a general process of reducing the world to two classes of people, those within the Church and those outside it."[50] What Muldoon has termed "a blurring of distinctions between Jews and Muslims" was by no means limited to canon law. Much as with Judaism, Christian culture familiarized itself with Islam selectively, on an ideological "need-to-know" basis: It sufficed with that which was necessary for polemic; it concentrated on abusive stories about Muhammad and the carnal delights of paradise while ignoring serious theology; it distinguished between the condemnable Islamic creed and ideas and texts of value, like those of classical philosophy, worthy of importation from the Muslim world; it invented stereotypes that underscored the distance between Muslims and Christian culture; and, when Muslims departed from these norms and narrowed the gap between themselves and Western society, Christian policy grew more intolerant toward them.[51] In a word, like that of the Jew, much of the

48. Norman Zacour, *Jews and Saracens in the Consilia of Oldradus de Ponte*, Pontifical Institute of Medieval Studies: Studies and Texts 100 (Toronto, 1990), pp. 52 (trans.), 82.

49. Ibid., pp. 54–58, 83–84. For a summary of earlier opinions, see Herde, "Christians and Saracens," pp. 364ff.; cf. also Frederick H. Russell, *The Just War in the Middle Ages* (Cambridge, England, 1975), pp. 113–22, 196–210.

50. Muldoon, *Popes*, p. 52.

51. Daniel, *Islam and the West*, esp. chap. 8; cf. Norman Daniel, *The Arabs and Medieval Europe* (London, 1975), chaps. 1–5; Southern, *Western Views*, chaps. 1–2; Jennifer Bray, "The Mohammetan and Idolatry," in *Persecution and Toleration*, ed. W. J. Sheils, SCH 21 (Oxford, 1984), pp. 89–98; and Jean Flori, "La Caricature de l'Islam dans l'Occident médiévale: Origine et signification de quelques stéréotypes concernant l'Islam," *Aevum* 66 (1992), 245–56.

Christian image of the Muslim was contrived; it is hardly surprising that Christian society often accused both of the same heinous crimes against nature and humanity.[52] Moreover, the Christian linkage of Jew with Muslim induced many churchmen who directed their energies against the former to turn their sights upon the latter as well—from polemicists like Peter Alfonsi and Peter the Venerable of Cluny to mendicant missionaries like Raymond Martin and from a pope like Innocent IV to his cardinal-legate Odo of Châteauroux and his royal ally King Louis IX of France.[53]

As the aforecited Jewish chronicler of the persecutions of 1096 attested, however, the Christian association of Muslim with Jew—just like that of heretic and Jew—worked both ways: Not only did the Muslim share in the characteristics of the Jew, but the Jew came to assume the characteristics of the Muslim and thus to lose that unique quality that had assured his exceptional function—and concomitant right to remain—in Christendom. Perhaps we can already begin to sense the significance of the categorization of Jews with other outsiders, and the "Muslim connection" especially, for our renewed appreciation of Funkenstein's reading of changes in Christian anti-Judaism during the twelfth century.[54] The new emphasis on rationalist argumentation surely befitted the need to dispute in compelling terms with a more "generic" enemy, not simply with the Jew over the interpretation of biblical prophecy. The mounting awareness of postbiblical Jewish literature went hand in hand with polemic against the religion of Muhammad, which sanctified the teachings of recent, nonbiblical texts that had no standing in Christianity. Just as they did with the Talmud, many Christian polemicists moved to dismiss such Muslim writings as absurd, while others claimed to find validation of Christianity in these texts of their enemies.[55]

Part 3 illustrates these impressions with a discussion of selected twelfth-century Christian authors, and part 4, with reference to selected mendicant friars of the thirteenth century. Part 3 commences with the school of Anselm of Canterbury, who advanced a new brand of ra-

---

52. See, for instance, Malcolm Barber, "Lepers, Jews and Moslems: The Plot to Overthrow Christendom in 1321," *History* 66 (1981), 1–17.

53. On Odo and Louis, see Kedar, *Crusade and Mission*, pp. 149ff., 161ff.

54. Cf. the preliminary discussion in Jeremy Cohen, "The Muslim Connection: On the Changing Role of the Jew in High Medieval Theology," In *FWW*, pp. 141–62.

55. See Thomas E. Burman, *Religious Polemic and the Intellectual History of the Mozarabs, c. 1050–1200*, Brill's Studies in Intellectual History 52 (Leiden, Netherlands, 1994).

tionalist religious polemic against the Jews and other dissenters, a polemic appropriate to a generically reconceptualized opponent. The discussion then turns to the perceptions of Jews and Judaism expressed against the backdrop of holy war by two of the twelfth century's leading clerics: Peter the Venerable and Bernard of Clairvaux. Finally, we shall consider the works of several unusually colorful Christian theologians of the twelfth century and their dreams of perfection in a Christendom properly ordered. Throughout one should keep the following question in mind: If Jews were losing the distinctiveness that they had once "enjoyed" in Christian thought, how did twelfth-century thinkers relate to that which had once made the Jew exceptional?

CHAPTER 5

Reason in Defense
of the Faith

*From Anselm of Canterbury
to Peter Alfonsi*

I have suggested that the reorientation of Christian religious polemic
to confront a larger array of nonbelievers contributed to its greater
reliance on rational argumentation, which, in turn, altered the character of Jews and Judaism in medieval Catholic thought. This chapter
investigates the process in the writings of several early-twelfth-century
theologians, from the champion of "faith in search of understanding
[*fides quaerens intellectum*]," Anselm of Canterbury (1033–1109), to
one of the most popular, widely read apologists of the age, Peter Alfonsi.

ANSELM OF CANTERBURY

With Lanfranc [of Bec]'s great pupil Anselm we meet the highest
achievement of what may be called the medieval Augustinian use
of dialectic, the summit of early scholastic genius and the ripest
fruit of the monastic schools. . . . Among all the host of medieval
philosophers and theologians perhaps only Aquinas and Bonaventure are in his company as thinkers who have put into currency,
so to say, ideas which may again and again provoke controversy
and meet with contradiction, but which cannot with impunity
be despised, for they will again and again make their appeal to

another generation in the future. . . . Anselm's characteristic and
original trait lies in the strong and serene confidence with which
he explores the great mysteries of the faith—the nature of God,
the Trinity, the incarnation and Redemption, Predestination and
Freewill—with the aid of reason.[1]

After having spent more than three decades in the renowned monastery
of Bec, Anselm left the cloister to assume the archbishopric of Canterbury in 1093, precisely as medieval Latin Christendom, on the verge
of the First Crusade, prepared to enter the most creative, dynamic
phase of its history. Anselm's "coming out" into the real world, fraught
with danger and controversy for the religious, demanded that he address the question of infidels and their disbelief, just as the events of
the Crusade and its aftermath were leaving a permanent imprint on the
relationship between Christendom and the non-Christian world. In
view of David Knowles's lavish praise for Anselm and the latter's pioneering role in the development of medieval dialectic and scholasticism, a link between Anselm and changing Christian perceptions of
the Jew should not surprise us. How, whether directly or indirectly,
did the Anselmian reliance on reason in the exposition of Christian
doctrine affect the character of the Jew in the Christian mind-set? Specifically, did the rationalization of religious polemic nourished by Anselm's legacy undermine the notion of the Jew as witness in twelfth-
century Christian thought?

At first glance, Anselmian theological discourse may not appear receptive to the doctrine of Jewish witness, which respected the Jews for
their literal exposition of Scripture and their involvement in the terrestrial, secular events of God's plan for human history. Anselm displayed
minimal interest in the questions of biblical exegesis that weighed so
heavily in this Augustinian idea. Although biblical ideas and categories
resound throughout his corpus, "there is scarcely a single explicit quotation from the Bible in the whole of Anselm's works";[2] and where an
exegetical method is evident, it owes more to that of the younger Augustine, subduing signifier to signified, identifying the different senses
of Scripture with the various parts of the soul, devaluing the literal and

1. David Knowles, *The Evolution of Medieval Thought* (New York, 1962), pp. 98–
100. On Anselm's life and the development of his ideas, see, above all, Richard W.
Southern, *Saint Anselm: A Portrait in a Landscape* (Cambridge, England, 1990).
2. Southern, *Saint Anselm,* pp. 69–70.

historical—hardly the exegesis of the older Augustine that undergirded his doctrine of Jewish witness.[3] Furthermore, Anselm approached the issues of salvation history thematically, harping on the essential conditions of believer and infidel, redeemed and unredeemed. He seemed notably unconcerned with the particular events of history, with reading or writing their sequential narrative, with pilgrimage and crusading, or with any direct involvement in the world outside the church.[4]

Predilections like these seriously constricted the range of opportunity for confronting the Jews in particular, or infidels in general, within the Anselmian corpus. Yet the few instances scattered throughout Anselm's works proved not insignificant in the development of twelfth-century Christian anti-Judaism, so what he did have to say demands careful examination. Two letters urge clergymen to provide for the needs of one baptized Jew named Robert, "who has fled to us, as if from the hands of the devil to the servants of God and true Christians," so that he not suffer on account of his conversion to Christianity. "Let him rejoice that he has crossed over from perfidy to the true faith, and let him establish on the basis of our own piety that our faith is closer to God than the Jewish one (*fides nostra propinquior est deo quam iudaica*)."[5] In his *Epistula de sacrificio azimi et fermentati* (Letter on the Sacrifice of Unleavened and Leavened Bread), Anselm responded to Byzantine accusations that Roman Catholic insistence upon the use of unleavened bread for the Eucharist amounted to Judaizing. Latin Christians do not use unleavened bread in the mass, argued Anselm—nor did Jesus use it at the Last Supper—for the reasons that the Jews of old used it but for different, specifically Christological reasons. So too, more generally, "we do not Judaize when we now do something that

3. On Anselm's reliance on Scripture and his exegetical method, see Jean Châtillon, "Saint Anselme et l'Écriture," in *MSC*, pp. 431–42; Helen Lang, "Anselm's Theory of Signs and His Use of Scripture," in *MSC*, pp. 443–56; and Klaus Guth, "Zum Verhältnis von Exegese und Philosophie im Zeitalter der Frühscholastik (Anmerkungen zu Guibert von Nogent, *Vita* I, 17)," *RTAM* 38 (1971), 121–28.

4. Yves M.-J. Congar, "L'Église chez Saint Anselme," in *Congrès international du IXᵉ centenaire de l'arrivée d'Anselme à Bec*, Spicilegium becense 1 (Paris, 1959), pp. 371–99; H. E. J. Cowdrey, "Pope Urban II's Preaching of the First Crusade," *History* 55 (1970), 183–84; G. R. Evans, "St. Anselm and Sacred History," in *The Writing of History in the Middle Ages: Essays Presented to Richard William Southern*, ed. R. H. C. Davis and J. M. Wallace-Hadrill (Oxford, 1981), pp. 187–209; and Aryeh Graboïs, "Anselme, l'Ancien Testament et l'idée de croisade," in *MSC*, pp. 161–73.

5. Anselm of Canterbury, *Epistulae* 380, in *Opera omnia*, ed. Franciscus Salesius Schmitt (Edinburgh, 1946–61), 5:323–24; cf. also Anselm, *Epistulae* 381, p. 324, where Anselm again wrote of him "qui de perfidia ad verae fidei misericordiam et pietatem conversus est."

the Jews used to do in observance of Judaism, provided that we do it not for the sake of Judaism but for some other reason."[6]

Although modern scholars have understandably tried to mine Anselm's few statements concerning Jews and Judaism for all their worth, I believe that these first few references prove largely unexceptional.[7] Any noteworthy degree of tolerance one might seek to infer from Anselm's parallel use of the term *faith* to refer both to Christianity and to Judaism (*fides nostra . . . iudaica*) in his letters on Robert's behalf seems offset by his repeated mention of Jewish *perfidia* and his likening of the proselyte's Jewish origins to the hands of the devil (*de manibus diaboli*).[8] And although Anselm's defense of the Latin eucharistic rite ostensibly upholds the literal sense of the Old Testament commandment to offer the Passover sacrifice with unleavened bread, his distinction between Jewish and Christian rationales for common rituals would constitute the obvious means for defending numerous Catholic practices that had roots in ancient Judaism.

Other Anselmian passages, however, appear more significant. In his defense of Catholic trinitarian doctrine against the skeptical objections of Roscelin of Compiègne, Anselm quoted Roscelin as somehow equating Jews and pagans: "The pagans defend their law; the Jews defend their law. Therefore we Christians ought also to defend our faith."[9] Such generic equivalence between pagans and Jews finds confirmation in a colorful Anselmian parable:

For God himself displays his enmity towards the devil in the way that a certain king would against a certain prince who was his enemy. For in his kingdom this king has rather a large city [*villam*], in the city a particular castle, and above the castle a vault. In the city certain houses are soundly built; yet many are infirm. In the castle, however, the fortification is so great that if anyone took refuge there, he would not be harmed by anyone, unless that person could gain entrance himself. The safety of the vault is such that if anyone could ascend there, never would he want to return from there.

---

6. Anselm of Canterbury, *Epistula de sacrificio azimi et fermentati* 3, in *Opera omnia* 2:226.

7. Cf. the comments of Gilbert Dahan, "Saint Anselme, les Juifs, le Judaïsme," in *MSC*, pp. 521–22; and Anna Sapir Abulafia, "St Anselm and Those outside the Church," in *Faith and Identity: Christian Political Experience*, ed. David Loades and Katherine Walsh, SCH Subsidia 6 (Oxford, 1990), pp. 14–16.

8. Above, n. 5.

9. Anselm, *Epistula de incarnatione verbi* 2, in *Opera omnia*, 2:10: "Pagani defendunt legem suam, Iudaei defendunt legem suam. Ergo et nos Christiani debemus defendere fidem nostram."

The king has all these things within his domain. His enemy is so strong that he absconds totally unhindered with whatever he finds outside the city. He frequently even enters the city and damages those houses which he finds insecure, and those people who inhabit them he takes captive. Those houses which he finds secure, after he cannot destroy them, he reluctantly leaves them at last. He cannot ascend into the castle nor cause any harm to those who take refuge there, unless they return to the combat of the city. But if they return out of love for their parents, inasmuch as they hear that they are being killed and maltreated, or if they look back through an aperture or window, he can easily kill or wound them. Wherefore it is necessary that they never heed the cry of their parents nor return to combat nor look back, but always, just as they began, they must flee until they reach the height of the vault. For once they arrive there, they will be entirely secure.

And so that king is God, who wages war with the devil. Within his kingdom he has the community of Christians, within the community of Christians the society of monks [*monachatum*], and above the society of monks the fellowship of angels. Within the community of Christians certain people are firmly ensconced in virtue, though many are insecure. In the monastic world the security is such that if anyone taking refuge there shall be made a monk—unless, recanting, he departs—he cannot be injured by the devil. In the fellowship of angels there is the joy of such great security that if anyone ascends there he will never wish to return. The king—that is, God—has all this in his domain. Yet his enemy—that is, the devil—is so powerful that he carries off without resistance and submerges into hell all the Jews and pagans whom he finds outside the community of Christians. He often enters the community of Christians itself and harms through temptation all those whom he finds infirm, and he takes captive the souls inhabiting their bodies. Yet those whom he finds secure, after failing to conquer them, he at last releases, albeit with regret. He cannot break into the monastic world, nor can he cause any harm to those who have been made monks, unless they have returned to the secular world in body or in spirit.[10]

I quote this interesting simile in its entirety in order to demonstrate three aspects of Anselm's conceptualization of the Jews. First, Anselm juxtaposed Jews and pagan nonbelievers in this metaphoric picture of the world; in the grand scheme of things, they share the same status.

---

10. Richard W. Southern and Franciscus Salesius Schmitt, eds., *Memorials of St. Anselm*, Auctores britannici Medii Aevi 1 (Oxford, 1969), pp. 66–67. Anselm's parable of a ruler's castle within a city bears a marked resemblance to Moses Maimonides' parable in *Guide of the Perplexed* 3.51. Although I have found no evidence of—or scholarly comment on—the cross-cultural career of such a motif, I note with curiosity that the characters in Anselm's parable divide into seven classes and that Maimonides' parable describes seven ranks of men. See Steven Harvey, "Maimonides in the Sultan's Palace," in *Perspectives on Maimonides*, ed. Joel L. Kraemer (Oxford, 1991), pp. 60–66, where the importance of sevens in Maimonides' exemplum is underscored. I thank Joel Kraemer and Daniel Lasker for their suggestions in this regard.

Second, when situated amid the blatantly feudal signposts of Anselm's map,[11] Jews and pagans have a place in God's kingdom—outside the protective "city walls" of the church, to be sure, but a place nonetheless. No feudal king would have limited a survey of his domains to the community within the fortifications of his *villa*, forgoing the lands outside, which were, ultimately, the basis for his personal wealth. As far as this simile related to the Jews, perhaps one can discern an echo of Augustine's attribution of functional value to their continued existence and religious practice. And third, in his taxonomy of the constituents of this world, Anselm classified Jews and pagans according to the same criteria on which he appraised everyone else: their commitment to God and a spiritual life, expressed in their ability to withstand the attack of the devil. Significantly, the parable expresses no binary opposition between infidel and Christian; for the distinction between them—all infidels fall prey to the devil, whereas many (though not all) Christians do—seems no more glaring than does that between the community of Christians at large and the monastic world, where most monks escape the devil's harm, or than does that between the monastic world and the fellowship of angels, where the devil harms no one. For Anselm, then, the Jew was essentially a ranked *typos*, exemplifying the lack of faith that precludes one from salvation, leading him, ultimately, to hell—but a typos with a place on Anselm's map of the world.

These observations should assist in our appreciation of the *Cur Deus homo* (Why Did God Become Human?),[12] the treatise that offers the most insight into Anselm's estimation of Jewish unbelief. As a speculative work on divine nature, this book has been termed "breathtaking," "remarkable," "a virtuoso performance with few rivals in the history of Christian thought";[13] and numerous scholars have hailed Anselm's attempt to prove the truth of the doctrine of the incarnation rationally and *remoto Christo*[14]—without presupposing belief in Jesus or other specifically Christian beliefs. In the framework of a dialogue with his student Boso, Anselm here set out to expound rational answers

    11. Southern, *Saint Anselm*, pp. 221–27. See also the discussion of this text in Abulafia, "St Anselm," pp. 11ff.

    12. In Anselm, *Opera omnia*, 2:37–133.

    13. Evans, "St. Anselm," p. 204; G. R. Evans, "The *Cur Deus homo*: The Nature of St. Anselm's Appeal to Reason," *Studia theologica* 31 (1977), 38; and Jaroslav Pelikan, *The Christian Tradition: A History of the Development of Doctrine* (Chicago, 1971–89), 3:106–7.

    14. Anselm, *Cur Deus homo*, praef., in *Opera omnia*, 2:42.

to the challenge often raised by infidels: "For what reason and to meet what need did God become a man and, as we believe and confess, restore life to the world through his death, since he could have done this either through another being, whether angelic or human, or simply by willing it?"[15] To reach a compelling solution, Anselm proposed: "Let us stipulate that the incarnation of God and the things which we believe about that man never happened. And let us agree that the human being is created for the sake of a blessedness, which cannot be had in this life, that one cannot arrive at that state unless one's sins have been remitted, and that no person passes through this life without sin—and [let us agree on] the other things in which belief is necessary for eternal salvation."[16] In brief, Anselm then proceeded to argue that the need for proper order in God's created world demanded true satisfaction for the rebellious disorderliness of human sin. But because human beings owed God their service and total obedience even before they sinned, they could offer God nothing else to compensate sufficiently for their crime in its aftermath; and because they are the most perfect of God's earthly creatures, such satisfaction "cannot be made unless there be someone who, for the sin of humankind, repays God something greater than everything which exists besides God."[17] Only God himself, therefore, could render satisfaction for human sin. Still, justice and order stipulated that humankind render payment for its own obligations. Hence, only the gratuitous sacrifice of one truly both divine—and thus free of sin himself—and human could make amends for the sin of humankind and assure its salvation. Anselm argued at length that the need for the self-sacrifice of the incarnate God neither compromised the dignity or perfection of God nor subordinated God or his human incarnation to any external necessity. All proceeded from the beneficence of God—the justice and order with which he imbued his creation, his commitment to the salvation of his creatures, and the completely voluntary nature of his human offspring's self-sacrifice.

At whom did Anselm direct this defense of the doctrine of the incarnation; who were the targets of the *Cur Deus homo*, whom both Boso and Anselm called infidels (*infideles*) on several occasions during their conversation? Many have simply assumed that the *Cur Deus*

15. Ibid. 1.1, p. 48.
16. Ibid. 1.10, p. 67.
17. Ibid. 2.6, p. 101.

homo's prime targets had to have been Jews, Christendom's resident infidels, as it were, and Muslims, whom many European Christians commonly called pagans.[18] For medieval Christians, the Jews were the most familiar opponents of the doctrine of the incarnation; and, not long before the composition of the *Cur Deus homo*, Anselm spent the winter of 1092–93 together with Gilbert Crispin, abbot of Westminster, who was then at work on his own anti-Jewish treatise, *Disputatio Iudaei et Christiani* (The Disputation of a Christian and a Jew).[19] The *Cur Deus homo* does presuppose basic monotheistic faith in the God of the Bible on the part of its audience, and the objections to the doctrine of incarnation refuted by the work—namely, that incarnation would in various ways compromise the perfection of the deity—do echo those of Jewish and Muslim critics of Christianity. Early in the treatise Anselm singles out the Jews as the enemies of Jesus responsible for his crucifixion: "Why did the Jews persecute him all the way to the point of his death?" he inquires of Boso.[20] And subsequently, Anselm affirms that the saving power of the crucifixion extended even to those people responsible for it. Quoting 1 Corinthians 2:8 to reason that had they known the true nature of their deed, "they would not have crucified the Lord of glory," Anselm adapted Augustine's view of the ignorance of Jesus' crucifiers to his own, distinctly rationalist perspective: "For a sin committed knowingly and what is done in ignorance differ so much from each other, that the evil act, which, because of its severity, they could never have committed had they understood it, is venial, because it was committed in ignorance. For no person could ever desire, at least knowingly, to kill God."[21] This passage demonstrates the extent to which Anselm kept his book free of invective; as some have already observed, such commitment to level-headed, reasonable encounter between opposing viewpoints perhaps led Anselm

---

18. For example: René Roques, "Les *Pagani* dans le *Cur Deus homo* de Saint Anselme," in *Die Metaphysik im Mittelalter: Ihr Ursprung und ihre Bedeutung*, ed. Paul Wilpert, Miscellanea mediaevalia 2 (Berlin, 1963), pp. 192–206, and Roques's introduction to his edition of Anselm of Canterbury, *Pourquoi Dieu s'est fait homme*, SC 91 (Paris, 1963), pp. 65–74; Julia Gauss, "Anselm von Canterbury: Zur Begegnung und Auseinandersetzung der Religionen," *Saeculum* 17 (1966), 277–363, and "Die Auseinandersetzung mit Judentum und Islam bei Anselm," in *Die Wirkungsgeschichte Anselms von Canterbury*, ed. Helmut Kohlenberger, Analecta anselmiana 4 (Frankfurt am Main, 1975), 2:101–9.

19. See Richard W. Southern, "St. Anselm and Gilbert Crispin, Abbot of Westminster," *Medieval and Renaissance Studies* 3 (1954), 80–98, and *Saint Anselm*, pp. 198ff.

20. Anselm, *Cur Deus homo* 1.9, in *Opera omnia*, 2:61.

21. Ibid. 2.15, p. 115.

to moderate the traditional Christian view of Jewish guilt for deicide. Finally, at the conclusion of the *Cur Deus homo*, Boso compliments Anselm for succeeding in his endeavor: "For so well do you prove that God did, out of necessity, become a man, that even if the few things which you have taken from our books—such as what you have stated concerning the three persons of God and concerning Adam—were to be removed, you would satisfy not only the Jews but also the pagans with rational argument alone [*sola ratione*]."[22]

Despite these references to the Jews in the *Cur Deus homo* and elsewhere, however, a number of investigators have come to question the extent of Anselm's participation in and immediate contribution to the Jewish-Christian debate. Anselm's attempt to rationalize the discourse of religious apologetic, some have noted, influenced the tenets of Christian anti-Jewish polemic more in the works of his successors than in his own—and at times, as we shall see, in an unusually hostile vein far removed from the temperance of the *Cur Deus homo*. In addition, establishing the responsiveness of the *Cur Deus homo* to Jewish anti-Christian polemic has proven rather difficult. Those Jewish arguments ostensibly echoed and rebutted in Anselm's treatise are either from a later period or from a region far removed from Anselm's England.[23]

Most recently, Anna Sapir Abulafia has challenged the identification of *pagani* with Muslims in the *Cur Deus homo* and has sought virtually to eliminate the anti-Jewish dimension of the treatise.[24] According to Abulafia, "there is not one word in any of Anselm's writings that betrays any knowledge at all of Islamic teachings";[25] Anselm's *pagani* might denote Danes as easily as Muslims and ought best to be understood simply as non-Christian heathens. Neither Jews nor Muslims, Abulafia has maintained, could be Anselm's true adversaries in the *Cur Deus homo*, because he included the doctrine of original sin—"no man passes through this present life without sin"—among the presuppositions that he shared with these opponents. Abulafia has argued further

22. Ibid. 2.22, p. 133.

23. Amos Funkenstein, *Perceptions of Jewish History* (Berkeley, Calif., 1993), pp. 178–81; and Dahan, "Saint Anselme."

24. See especially Abulafia, "St Anselm," pp. 11–37. See also Anna Sapir Abulafia, "Theology and the Commercial Revolution: Guibert of Nogent, St Anselm and the Jews of Northern France," in *Church and City*, ed. David S. H. Abulafia (Cambridge, England, 1992), pp. 23–26, and "Christians Disputing Disbelief: St Anselm, Gilbert Crispin and Pseudo-Anselm," in *RIM*, pp. 131–35.

25. Abulafia, "St Anselm," p. 20.

that in Boso's concluding praise of Anselm, "you would satisfy not only the Jews but also the pagans with rational argument alone," the phrase "by reason alone [*sola ratione*]" refers exclusively to pagans, not to Jews. She even suggests that Anselm's deflection of guilt from Jesus' killers, inasmuch as Paul had considered them ignorant of their own wrongdoing, might refer to the Roman soldiers at the crucifixion, not the Jews. The *infideles* of the *Cur Deus homo* display the characteristics of no non-Christian religion; they can only be identified with skeptical, doubting Christians, like Roscelin, whose rationally grounded misgivings concerning the incarnation stood between them and authentic faith. As opposed to the polemical works of his disciples, Abulafia has concluded repeatedly, the writings of Anselm manifest no genuine polemical or missionary intentions vis-à-vis the Jews; only indirectly may they have contributed to the development of Christian anti-Jewish polemic in the High Middle Ages.

These questions warrant careful review. As Abulafia has stated, we have proof neither that Anselm knew—and thus responded—to the attacks of Jewish and Muslim thinkers upon the doctrine of the incarnation nor that Anselm composed the *Cur Deus homo* for polemical or missionary purposes (that is, for use in direct confrontation with Jewish disputants). One certainly ought to include skeptical and heretical Christians among the *infideles* confronted in this treatise, just as Abulafia has proposed. Nevertheless, I believe that the case for excluding the Jews from Anselm's concerns in the *Cur Deus homo* has been overstated. The suggestion that Anselm alluded only to Roman soldiers and not to Jews when downsizing the guilt of Jesus' executioners falls outside the range of currently accepted exegetical alternatives for the "powers that rule the world" that knew not the enormity of their crime in 1 Corinthians 2:8.[26] And nothing mandates the conclusion that in Boso's closing remark to Anselm, "you would satisfy not only the Jews but also the pagans by reason alone," the qualification of *sola ratione* applies solely to pagans and not to Jews;[27] to the

---

26. Ibid., p. 18: "technically speaking, the context of his words does not even exclude the possibility that he had the Roman soldiers in mind who actually crucified Jesus"; and n. 25: "Anselm is referring to the murderers of I Cor. 2.8, whose identity is not specified." Yet see Jeremy Cohen, "The Jews as the Killers of Christ in the Latin Tradition, from Augustine to the Friars," *Traditio* 39 (1983), esp. 8–16.

27. Anselm, *Cur Deus homo* 2.22, in *Opera omnia*, 2:133: "non solum Iudaeis sed etiam paganis sola ratione satisfacias"; and Abulafia, "St Anselm," p. 19 and n. 29.

contrary, one wonders how the theoretical arguments of the *Cur Deus homo* could have satisfied the Jews, if not "by reason alone"![28] Although Anselm clearly had the Catholic doctrine of original sin in mind—and referred to it frequently—throughout the treatise, its language does not make it perfectly clear that he stipulated a belief in original sin as a premise for his arguments to follow. In the case of Odo of Cambrai considered below, the observation that "no man passes through this present life without sin" may reflect empirical observation more than doctrinal presupposition: We simply know from experience that everybody sins.[29] Even had Anselm intended to postulate the Catholic notion of original sin, one need not determine that his targeted infidels shared that belief, as John McIntyre has explained; for Anselm may simply have used this premise to demonstrate just how compelling was the doctrine of incarnation, hoping that such a demonstration would render the infidel more amenable to other Christian beliefs as well.[30] In any event, the *Cur Deus homo* surely emphasizes the sorts of issues raised by medieval Jews and Muslims in their critique of the incarnation: its appropriateness in view of divine and human nature, its necessity versus the voluntary nature of Jesus' self-sacrifice, the availability of less cataclysmic means to make "satisfaction" for human sin, and the like.[31] We shall see that Abulafia perceives an avid commitment to anti-Jewish polemic among Anselm's disciples, who in some instances avoided mention of the Jews altogether; why, then, need

28. Abulafia herself, "St Anselm," p. 31, appears to agree: "If a couple of Christian presuppositions were removed, the *Cur Deus Homo* would satisfy even Jews and pagans. . . . Jews and pagans are brought in at this point, I believe, to illustrate the presumed universal acceptability of the rational argument of the *Cur Deus Homo*."

29. See above, at n. 16; and cf. Anselm's discussion of the slightest of sins (*unius tam parvi peccati*, in *Cur Deus homo* 1.21, in *Opera omnia*, 2:88), with that of Odo of Cambrai below, at n. 59.

30. John McIntyre, *St. Anselm and His Critics: A Re-Interpretation of the Cur Deus homo* (Edinburgh, 1954), pp. 54ff. In a similar vein, see the entreaty of Gilbert Crispin to his Gentile interlocutor in the *Disputatio Christiani cum gentili*, "Submit to faith for just a little while," below, at n. 45.

31. See the works cited above, n. 18; Daniel J. Lasker, *Jewish Philosophical Polemics against Christianity in the Middle Ages* (New York, 1977), chap. 5; and G. R. Evans, "A Theology of Change in the Writings of St. Anselm and His Contemporaries," *RTAM* 47 (1970), 53 and n. 1. Admittedly, we lack evidence that Anselm could have encountered such arguments personally among northern French or English Jews of his day. But if, when summarizing the contemporary "Jewish challenge" to the early-twelfth-century Christian theologians on whom her work concentrates, Anna Sapir Abulafia has freely drawn on Jewish texts from later in the century (*Christians and Jews in the Twelfth-Century Renaissance* [London, 1995], chap. 5), why need one emphatically disallow the extension of such a challenge to Anselm himself?

one labor to minimize such concern in Anselm, who did, albeit spar-
ingly, make direct reference to the Jews?[32]

In retrospect, Abulafia herself states that "Jewish rejection of Christianity may well have stimulated the composition of the *Cur Deus
Homo*"; yet Anselm's lack of interaction with contemporary Jews and
Judaism fuels her insistence that his "*infideles* are not specifically Jews
and pagans, and that the *Cur Deus Homo* was not, in the first instance,
addressed to them."[33] I would suggest that this distinction—that Anselm may have written the *Cur Deus homo* at least partly in response
to Jewish disbelief but that the work did not speak primarily of or to
the Jews—may be more confusing than helpful. Perhaps we can profit
by recognizing the role of a contrived, hermeneutically crafted Jew in
Anselm's thought, a Jew who bespeaks a different distinction: Anselm
may have had little knowledge of or concern with the Judaism and
Jews of his day. Yet this did not deter him from directing his arguments
to Jews as he conceived them; nor did the lack of a conversionist program and polemical intent per se preclude allotting the Jew specific
characteristics and functions. Anselm's thematic reformulation of historical categories, his monastic disdain for the specific events and realia
of history, and his preference for rational argument over biblical testimony—all these comported well with his near conflation of Jews
(who interpret Scripture literally) and pagans (who reject it outright)
within the broader, generic classification of infidels. Earlier works of
Adversus Iudaeos polemic had considered Judaism a particular chronological stage, now obsolete, in God's plan for human history; its Old
Testament had given way to the New. Anselm now reconstructed that
traditional idea in more abstract, epistemological terms: He construed
Judaism as exemplifying a primitive theological mind-set, representative of an inability to grasp the logic of Christianity, appropriately and

---

32. Abulafia, *Christians and Jews*, p. 86.
33. Abulafia, "St Anselm," p. 31. One senses similar uncertainty in Anna Sapir Abulafia, "Christian Imagery of Jews in the Twelfth Century: A Look at Odo of Cambrai
and Guibert of Nogent," *Theoretische Geschiedenis* 16 (1989), 384: "There is every
reason to suppose that Anselm knew that Jewish doubts about the incarnation overlap
with the rational questions being asked about it by Christians. At the close of the work
he actually states that his rational arguments will confute Jews as well as Pagans [but
cf. 'St. Anselm,' p. 19 and n. 29!]. But this does not mean that Anselm wrote his work
for those who stood completely outside the Christian community." And see also Abulafia,
"Christians Disputing Disbelief," p. 133: "It is true that the criticisms levelled against
the incarnation in the *Cur Deus Homo* concur with Jewish objections to it. However,
the fact that Anselm's *infideles* lack an alternative religion of their own cannot be ignored. . . . Anselm's unbelievers cannot be real non-Christians."

necessarily surpassed by faith in Christ. One can thus understand Anselm's failure to distinguish sharply between his Jews, his pagans, and his infidels; he really had no need to do so.

Where lies the importance of the Jews in Anselm's writings? Together, the passages reviewed here confirm that the Jews, now clumped together with other unbelievers, had lost some of their singularity in his Christian theological discourse—just as their crime of deicide had lost its exceptional, heinous character. As G. R. Evans has observed, "when Anselm refers to the *infideles* in the *Cur Deus homo* he means those who dispute the doctrine of the redemption: he gives no other details of their opinions, because he intends to meet the objections of every dissident on this point."[34] Regardless of whether Anselm intended as much, this too became part of his bequest to Christian polemical literature of the twelfth century. Not least significantly, his *Cur Deus homo* inaugurated an age in which the Jew shared the brunt of Christian religious polemic with the pagan, an age in which pagan usually meant Muslim.

APPLICATIONS OF ANSELMIAN TEACHING

Anselm's rationalization of his defense of Christianity, coupled with his inclusion of the Jews among theologically primitive infidels who refused to believe, helped to alter perceptions of the Jew's character and raison d'être in twelfth-century Christian thought. Without detracting from the overall significance of Anselmian rationalism in medieval intellectual history, however, one must note that such change developed over considerable time and often subtly. The pages that follow document both the essentials and the graduality of Anselm's influence, hoping to redress its neglect by some scholars and its overestimation by others. We shall turn first to Gilbert Crispin, who tried—with only minimal success—to accommodate Anselmian rationalism alongside his traditional anti-Jewish polemic; then to Odo of Cambrai (and Tournai), who reformulated Anselm's arguments against infidels within a specifically anti-Jewish framework; and then to Guibert of Nogent, who used ostensibly rationalist presuppositions to nourish bitter hostility toward the Jews of his day. Anselm made no effort to engage the Jews and Judaism in disputation; some of his disciples did,

34. G. R. Evans, *Old Arts and New Theology: The Beginnings of Theology as an Academic Discipline* (Oxford, 1980), p. 144.

whether in direct, personal confrontation or indirectly, in polemical treatises intended for Christian readers. Anselm verbalized no conviction that a rational justification of Christian faith should expedite the conversion of Jews; others, committed to more systematic scholastic defense of the faith, did. Not least important, Anselm, consistently moderate in his tone, never renounced the Augustinian notion that Jews do have a place on the Christian map of the world. Among his successors, though not his immediate ones, there were those who eventually did. But how did such new ideas gain expression, and at what pace did they result in a significant break with tradition?

GILBERT CRISPIN

Friend, confrere, and perhaps the most exemplary student of Anselm, Abbot Gilbert Crispin of Westminster (ca. 1045–1117) is familiar both to Anselmian scholars and to students of medieval Jewish-Christian relations. Anselm and Gilbert spent their formative years together as monks in the monastery of Bec, until Gilbert left for England around 1079 at the behest of their former abbot Lanfranc, now archbishop of Canterbury. In 1085 Gilbert rose to the abbacy of Westminster, where Anselm visited him in 1086 and again in the winter of 1092–93. Precisely during these years Anselm exerted himself in defending the Catholic doctrine of the incarnation, and his efforts bore fruit first in the *Epistula de incarnatione Verbi* (A Letter on the Incarnation of the Logos) and then in the *Cur Deus homo*, completed in 1098. For his part, Gilbert had turned to matters of religious polemic, and, as Richard Southern has argued, the renewed interaction between the two men evidently left its mark on each of them. Gilbert may well have sensitized Anselm to the issues of the Jewish-Christian debate and to Jewish skepticism concerning the incarnation above all. Anselm's commitment to reason in defense of the faith in turn found expression in Gilbert's well-known *Disputatio Iudaei et Christiani* (A Disputation of a Jew and a Christian, dedicated to Anselm by Crispin) and its companion volume, *Disputatio Christiani cum gentili* (A Disputation of a Christian with a Gentile), both of which antedated the completion of the *Cur Deus homo*.[35] Gilbert's polemical treatises manifest the earliest attempts to

---

35. Gilbert Crispin, *The Works of Gilbert Crispin, Abbot of Westminster*, ed. Anna Sapir Abulafia and G. R. Evans, Auctores britannici Medii Aevi 8 (London, 1986), pp. 1–87; cf. also his sermon for Palm Sunday, *Sermo in ramis palmarum*, pp. 171–75.

apply the dictates of Anselmian reason and dialectic to polemic against the Jews; they reveal just how tentative those attempts actually were and how they may have laid the groundwork for later developments to follow.[36]

The *Disputatio Iudaei et Christiani* left its mark on medieval and modern readers alike. The work survives in more than thirty manuscripts, twenty from the twelfth century alone, and served as a model and reference for other polemical treatises of the period.[37] Its modern editors have termed it "a final attempt" at friendly discussion between medieval Christian and Jew, the "apogee" of the traditional genre of *Adversus Iudaeos* polemic based primarily on the interpretation of passages from the Old Testament.[38] Where, exactly, did its transitional importance lie? On one hand, the substance of the polemic itself, though unusually lucid and spirited, remains largely old-fashioned. Gilbert composed his defense of Christianity in order to educate Christians, at their request. He expounded this defense in dialogue form in order to engage his readers, but the dialogue per se is fictional. It addresses several of the age-old issues of the Jewish-Christian debate—the authority of Mosaic law, its literal versus figurative interpretation, Jesus' fulfillment of messianic prophecies in the Old Testament, the incarnation, the virgin birth, the Trinity, and the reliability of the Septuagint and Vulgate translations of the Hebrew Bible—adducing scripturally grounded arguments exclusively, with the exception of one attempt at rational argumentation. Most important, Gilbert constructed

36. On Gilbert Crispin and his connection to Anselm, see G. R. Evans, "Gilbert Crispin, Abbot of Westminster: The Forming of a Monastic Scholar," *Studia monastica* 22 (1980), 63–81, and *Anselm and a New Generation* (Oxford, 1980), pp. 198–208; and the works of Southern cited above, n. 19.

37. See the introductory comments of Anna Sapir Abulafia in *Works of Gilbert Crispin*, pp. xxvii–xxx; and David Berger, "Gilbert Crispin, Alan of Lille, and Jacob ben Reuben: A Study in the Transmission of Medieval Polemic," *Speculum* 49 (1974), 34–47.

38. Bernhard Blumenkranz, "Die Entwicklung im Westen zwischen 200 und 1200," In *Kirche und Synagoge: Handbuch zur Geschichte von Christen und Juden*, ed. Karl Heinrich Rengstorf and Siegfried von Kurtzfleisch (Stuttgart, 1968–70), pp. 113–14; and Anna Sapir Abulafia, "An Attempt by Gilbert Crispin, Abbot of Westminster, at Rational Argument in the Jewish-Christian Debate," *Studia monastica* 26 (1984), 56. On the *Disputatio Iudaei*, see also Blumenkranz, "La *Disputatio Judei cum Christiano* de Gilbert Crispin, abbé de Westminster," *RMAL* 4 (1948), 237–52, and the preface to his edition of Gilbert Crispin, *Disputatio Iudei et Christiani*, Stromata 3 (Utrecht, Netherlands, 1956), pp. 5–20; R. J. Z. Werblowsky, "Crispin's Disputation," *JJS* 11 (1960), 69–77; and the additional essays by Anna Sapir Abulafia: "The *Ars disputandi* of Gilbert Crispin, Abbot of Westminster," in *Ad fontes: Opstellen aangeboden aan prof. dr. C. van de Kieft*, ed. C. M. Cappon et al. (Amsterdam, 1984), pp. 139–52, and "Gilbert Crispin's Disputations: An Exercise in Hermeneutics," in *MSC*, pp. 511–20.

his Jewish interlocutor to permit the exposition of Christian beliefs—rather than accurately to represent the traditions of Judaism—and this primarily through his inability to understand what his own books have to say about them. Gilbert's Jewish disputant bears little resemblance to contemporary medieval Jews;[39] he epitomizes the obsolete, the exclusively literal understanding of the Old Testament, that which existed when "there were not yet any Christians [*necdum etiam Christiani erant*],"[40] and that which is now, adopting Augustine's terminology, a fossil of useless antiquity.

On the other hand, Gilbert took pains to package his work of *Adversus Iudaeos* polemic more realistically than did many of his predecessors. His letter of dedication to Anselm suggests that disputation between Jews and Christians had begun to assume a dimension of contemporary relevance, that it now extended beyond a strictly literary domain. We read that Gilbert and a particular learned Jew of Mainz met and discussed matters biblical and theological on numerous occasions; although the Jewish discussant of the *Disputatio* does not faithfully represent a contemporary Jewish scholar, Gilbert's description of these meetings has a ring of credibility to it, and one need not hasten to dismiss them as fiction too. Some such genuine instances of debate evidently drew an audience, composed of local Jews and Christians alike. These Christians, Gilbert reported, prevailed upon him to commit his arguments to writing. One of the Jewish listeners converted to Christianity and became a monk in Gilbert's abbey, confirming further that religious disputation was no longer strictly an academic exercise. Finally, it appears that Gilbert drew from Anselm's work in progress when he proposed to submit rational proof of the incarnation for the consideration of the Jew, who, having heard such proof, may choose "to accept it on rational terms or to reject it on rational grounds." Yet Gilbert did not seriously entertain that latter possibility of rejection. "The text [*auctoritas*] of the Scriptures, to be sure, has not been understood in its exact sense, but you will consider it so evident, that you will be able to come up with nothing that may be argued against it." There follows in brief the distinctly Anselmian reasoning: Submerged in its inherited, original sin, humankind was powerless to make amends for the sin of its first parents, so that it might, appro-

39. On Gilbert's unrealistic formulation of the Jew's arguments, see Abulafia, "*Ars disputandi*," passim.

40. Gilbert, *Disputatio Iudaei* 126, in *Works of Gilbert Crispin*, p. 42.

priately, gain restitution to its former glorious state. In order to avoid any subsequent misdirection of human loyalties, only God—and not an angel—*could* pay the price of such restitution; but by rights only humankind *should* pay that price. The incarnation of the deity in the person of a human being provided the only solution.[41]

This recourse to rational argument in the *Disputatio Iudaei et Christiani* proved to be little more than a diversion, or perhaps an addition to Gilbert's original composition, for which Anselm was largely responsible. Nonetheless, soon after completing this work Gilbert composed his *Disputatio Christiani cum gentili*, in which he set out to offer a more systematic rational defense of Christianity.[42] Again Gilbert presented his arguments in the form of a dialogue with an artificially constructed interlocutor, this time a Gentile philosopher. Again each disputant makes seven statements in the course of the debate. And again the discussion explores the basic points of contention in the Jewish-Christian debate: the law, its proper interpretation, and the duration of its authority; the incarnation; and the Trinity. The *Disputatio Christiani cum gentili* was clearly a sequel to the *Disputatio Iudaei et Christiani*; whereas the earlier disputation against the Jew had argued almost entirely on the basis of biblical evidence (*auctoritas*), the disputation with the Gentile undertakes to defend the same fundamental beliefs with reason (*ratio*). "I do not accept your sacred writings, and I do not admit any prooftexts taken from them," Crispin's Gentile announces at the outset; "nor do you accept my scriptures, and I shall not offer any evidence from them." The Christian, in turn, concurs: "Let us therefore omit the textual evidence of our scriptures, until God gives us the skills necessary for dealing with it; let us follow reason as our judge."[43]

As such, the *Disputatio Christiani cum gentili* would appear to break new ground in the literature of medieval religious polemic. Yet this impression requires clarification on at least two different counts.

41. Ibid. 93, p. 31: "Scripturarum vero auctoritas non exactu sensu interpretata, sed tam evidens tibi apponetur, ut nil excogitare queas, quod contra opponatur"; the ensuing discussion continues through par. 105, pp. 32–35. Cf. the parallel argument in Anselm's *Cur Deus homo* 2.6, p. 101: "necesse est ut de hominibus perficiatur illa superna civitas, nec hoc esse valet, nisi fiat praedicta satisfacio, quam nec potest facere nisi deus nec debet nisi homo: necesse est ut eam faciat deus-homo." On the difference between Anselm and Gilbert concerning the devil's jurisdiction over human beings after the fall, see Abulafia, "Attempt," p. 68.

42. See Abulafia, "Attempt."

43. Gilbert, *Disputatio Christiani cum gentili* 8–9, in *Works of Gilbert Crispin*, pp. 63–64.

First, despite the protestations of the two discussants, the treatise does not meet its self-proclaimed goal, because most of the debate concerns the proper interpretation of biblical evidence, not an analysis of the dictates of reason. Immediately after the Christian's assent to the *ratio*-based ground rules for the disputation, the Gentile himself retreats from his earlier position, claiming that each of them knows—and perhaps attributes some worth or credibility to—the sacred texts of the other (*littere vestre sunt apud nos, sicut et nostre sunt aput [sic!] vos*).[44] The Christian then implores the Gentile in good Anselmian fashion, "submit to faith for just a little while, for, in yielding to faith, you may come to understanding."[45] The two proceed to consider the authority and proper interpretation of biblical law as evidenced in Scripture itself. When they come to discuss the incarnation, Gilbert's Christian offers essentially the same Anselmian argument we encountered in the *Disputatio Iudaei et Christiani* and, even more blatantly than Anselm would do in the *Cur Deus homo*, links it to the doctrine of original sin, which he simply assumes and never subjects to debate. Then, in the concluding section of the debate, the Christian discusses the Trinity only after the Gentile has left the room, in protest over his Christian colleague's failure to address this issue rationally; the Christian explains that analyzing such mysteries of the faith in front of nonbelievers endangers the beliefs of the faithful.[46] In all, the *Disputatio Christiani cum gentili* hardly provides the rational argument that it promises its readers at the start. Gilbert may have asserted the desideratum of rationalizing his polemical discourse, but he did not succeed in realizing that intention.

Second, in view of the substantive and structural correspondences between Gilbert's two polemical treatises, how ought we to understand the motivation underlying the composition of the second? The *Disputatio Iudaei et Christiani*, as noted, was well written, engaging, and popular; it may well have inspired Anselm in his own preparation of the *Cur Deus homo*. Why, then, did Gilbert feel impelled to compose the *Disputatio Christiani cum gentili*, which proved considerably less successful and considerably less popular?[47] Acknowledging the direct

---

44. Ibid. 11, p. 64.
45. Ibid. 15, p. 65: "Cede paulisper fidei, nam cedendo fidei, venies ad cognitionem tante rei."
46. Ibid. 84, p. 81.
47. The work survived in only one twelfth-century manuscript; Abulafia, "Attempt," p. 71.

influence of Anselm seems unavoidable, especially because his distinctive rationale for the incarnation finds expression in both of Gilbert's polemical treatises. If so, can the goals of the *Cur Deus homo* help us understand the orientation of Crispin's works, particularly the *Disputatio Christiani cum gentili*? Whom, specifically, does Crispin's Gentile represent? Just as I argued above that Anselm sought to respond to the challenges of Jews, perhaps Muslims, and other infidels in the *Cur Deus homo*, here I would concur wholeheartedly with Anna Abulafia's assessment that the *Disputatio Christiani cum gentili* is, in part, a work of anti-Jewish polemic. For "in many ways," Abulafia has concluded, the Gentile "can be characterized as a rational Jew asking what the Jew had asked in the *Disputatio Iudei*, but this time round in a rational setting."[48] Yet *Jew* and *Gentile* were hardly interchangeable terms in the medieval theologian's vocabulary.[49] One must therefore recognize that the polemic of the *Disputatio Christiani cum gentili* is not exclusively anti-Jewish but that Gilbert has conflated the Jews and other infidels in the personage of his Gentile. Perhaps, as Julia Gauss has suggested, this Gentile embodied the Muslim critique of Christianity; he may certainly have included classical pagan and Christian dimensions too, as Abulafia has maintained.[50] The Jews were still the most visible and accessible infidels in the eyes of European Christians. Their continued existence and their objections to Christianity were still emblematic of the doubts, insecurities, and challenges plaguing Latin Christendom. But they were no longer the only infidels; and Christian writers like Anselm and Gilbert Crispin now came to view them as one subset in a larger category. The widening scope of Christian religious polemic entailed the development of new, rational justifications for Christianity that targeted Jews and other others at the same time. Crispin followed the lead of Anselm, attempting to adapt his new rational apologetic to a specifically polemical medium. They contributed to a process that would eventually deprive Christianity's Jews of much more of their privileged status. Yet the first steps were tentative, very gradual, and not overly successful. Gilbert Crispin's Jews remained blind, thoroughly biblical, and constructed to serve as a catalyst in the exposition of the true, Christian faith.

48. Abulafia, "Christians Disputing Disbelief," p. 137.
49. See the instructive caution expressed by Yves M.-J. Congar, " 'Gentilis' et 'Iudaeus' au Moyen Âge," *RTAM* 36 (1969), 222–25.
50. Gauss, "Anselm von Canterbury," p. 296f.; and Abulafia, "Christians Disputing Disbelief," pp. 137ff.

ODO OF CAMBRAI

Although he may have had no direct contact with Anselm, Anselm's ideas may well have inspired Bishop Odo of Cambrai. At the very least, Odo exemplified an Anselmian "community of thought" at the turn of the twelfth century,[51] and he took the Anselmian initiative vis-à-vis the Jews one step farther than did Gilbert Crispin. Odo composed his *Disputatio contra Iudaeum Leonem nomine de adventu Christi filii Dei* (A Disputation against a Jew Named Leo Concerning the Advent of Christ, the Son of God)[52] in the middle of the first decade of the century, following Anselm's example, after he had left the cloister (of St. Martin of Tournai) to assume his episcopal see. As Gilbert had done in the *Disputatio Iudaei et Christiani*, Odo couched his anti-Jewish polemic in the form of a polite dialogue with a Jewish interlocutor, which did not result in the latter's conversion to Christianity. He too reported that he had previously debated with a Jew (named Leo) in Senlis and that he had used those actual exchanges as a basis for his current work; like Anselm and Gilbert before him, he now directed his anti-Jewish arguments to the instruction of Christian monks.

Odo's *Disputatio* addresses two Christian beliefs: that in the divine incarnation, and that in the virgin birth of Jesus. With but minimal reference to Scripture, the treatise offers an essentially Anselmian justification for the incarnation. God willed to create a heavenly city, populated by angels, but when some of those angels fell from heaven, he chose to repopulate his city with an even greater number of human beings. This plan, willed by God, must be brought to fruition; otherwise, unfulfilled desire would suggest imperfection in the deity, which cannot be. Yet the same divine perfection demands that human beings achieve their heavenly glory justly, that is, not without providing compensation—in Odo's terminology, satisfaction—to God for their sins, and this lies beyond human capabilities. Although the law provides for human penance that leads to the remission of sin, adequate satisfaction requires something more, that which only a sinless being, not already overwhelmed by the burdens of penance, can achieve. Who may ac-

---

51. Evans, *Anselm and a New Generation*, pp. 139–47.
52. PL 160:1103–12; trans. (with reference to extant mss.) in Odo of Tournai (Cambrai), *On Original Sin and A Disputation with the Jew, Leo, Concerning the Advent of Christ, the Son of God*, trans. Irven M. Resnick (Philadelphia, 1994), pp. 85–97.

complish this satisfaction, restoring sinful humans to God and making them blessed? Odo replied:

> No creature can remove that which in some other creature opposes God, lest God appear to need a creature to remove what is opposed to him [namely, sin] in a creature. . . . A creature that frees a creature from sin restores it to God and makes it blessed. But it is better to be blessed than merely to be. And so they would attribute to the creature what is greater and to the creator what is lesser, if the creator made that which exists and a creature made that which is blessed.

Moreover, because no created being is entirely free of sin, and because only a sinless being can provide satisfaction for sin, "no creature suffices to compensate for even the least sin."[53] Logic demonstrates that only God can render adequate satisfaction for human sin, even though he has no obligation to do so; justice dictates that humans ought to render this satisfaction, even though they lack the ability to do so. "It is therefore necessary for the two natures to converge and for God to become a man."[54] This necessity of the incarnation and of Christ's self-sacrificing death, Odo hastened to clarify, did not compromise the ultimate perfection of God, for it stemmed from within God, from his will and his grace, rather than from something external imposed upon him. "It is necessary to pay what it was not necessary to promise"; the promise had been made "with abundant grace [*magna gratia*]."[55]

Turning to the virgin birth, Odo confronted his Jew's objection that simply stating the notion of God's conception, gestation, and birth within his mother's reproductive organs entails the utmost disgrace (*sine magna tamen verecundia non dicimus*). Odo replied that God remains completely untainted, even by the most vile things he enters or sees. Then he explained that, from the perspective of reason, one should not consider the human body fashioned by God to be abhorrent or impure:

> Reason judges in one way and sense in another. For sense judges by usefulness, pleasure, desire, and their contraries. We prefer the usual to the unusual, the useful to the harmful, and that which pleases us agreeably to that which disagreeably offends. Reason investigates the nature of things more subtly. Reason prefers animated things to inanimate, sensible to in-

---

53. Odo, *Disputatio contra Iudaeum*, PL 160:1105–6, with several departures from the translation of Resnick, pp. 88–89.
54. Ibid., col. 1108.
55. Ibid., col. 1109, trans. Resnick, p. 94.

sensible, and heavenly to earthly. Too hastily does a peasant prefer that a snake disappear from the cleft of a rock than that the rock disappear from his wall, being mindful of desire and what is agreeable to look upon, because the sight of a serpent is horrible but the sight of a rock is not horrible. But reason truly prefers a serpent to a rock, however precious. Sense prefers the best house to a fruit-bearing tree, so that it prefers that a tree be cut down than that a house burn down. But truly reason prefers the live tree to the inanimate house. A peasant would rather have many beasts perish in the woods than lose one coin from his purse, although reason does not regard any coin as comparable in value to an animal. The peasant would prefer that many stars fall from heaven rather than one shrub perish in his field, although reason properly places heavenly things above earthly things. So too our sense despises our genitalia, viscera, and excrement, and judges them unclean. Reason, however, judges nothing unclean but sin, because God created all things good. . . . Reason is preferred to sense and judges the senses. Sense, however, cannot aspire to reason but often considers the subtle judgment of reason foolish and insane. We, however, having put off the sense of the flesh, think of the human body according to the direction of reason: that it is joined to a person's mind in unity and will dwell with it in eternal unity, forever a participant in honor or glory. . . . If our body is such as this, we who are sinners, what shall we say of the body of the virgin from whom the Lord was born? Clearly the holy angel Gabriel said that she is "full of grace."[56]

The Jew concedes the compelling reasonability of Odo's arguments on both of these doctrinal issues. In either case, however, he refuses to renounce his allegiance to Judaism and convert to Christianity—"lest, deceived by the subtlety and cunning of words, I might stray from the very firm ground of the holy law," and because "I do not dare to entrust the truth of our heritage to your words."[57]

Obvious similarities in substance and style notwithstanding, Odo's *Disputatio* parts company with the works of Anselm and Gilbert Crispin in interesting ways. Unlike Gilbert, Odo relied almost entirely on the power of reason; even when disputing with a Jew, he shied away from biblical *auctoritas*. In rationalizing his anti-Jewish polemic, Odo ventured even farther than did Anselm. For although Leo of the *Disputatio* may represent the objections of other nonbelievers to Christian doctrine, much like Gilbert Crispin's Gentile, Odo's interlocutor is first and foremost a Jew, whose allegiance lies with the letter—or *sensus*—of the law above all else. Odo's *Disputatio* does not even hint at a

56. Ibid., cols. 1110–1112, trans. Resnick, pp. 95–97.
57. Ibid., cols. 1109, 1112, trans. Resnick, pp. 93, 97.

belief in original sin, the subject of a much lengthier treatise by Odo,[58] despite its critical link to belief in the incarnation. Although Anselm may have presupposed original sin in his justification of why God had to become human, Odo astutely sidestepped the issue, thus eliminating such a priori grounds for Jewish objection. In the *Disputatio* he and Leo agree to analyze the nature of any sin, even "the very least sin we can—in order to see thereby how heavy sin is in all other cases."[59] Leo suggests a fleeting, vain thought as the least imaginable of sins, and Odo generalizes on the ponderous effects of sin from that example, effectively preempting the need for original sin in his demonstration. Who could deny the logic of Leo's conclusion? "If sin, as you say, is so weighty, we are in the greatest danger, because we sin daily."[60] Odo has verified that sin is a fact of daily human life; he thereby avoids having to prove that it adheres to the essence of postlapsarian human nature. Odo's *Disputatio* thus argues the necessity of the incarnation without postulating any belief that a Jew could not accept; it betrays the conviction that reason can, in fact, effect conversion, leading from understanding to faith. "I undertake to prove to you not only that man can, but even that it is necessary that man achieve the glory of angels. When I shall have done this with Christ's help I pray that, after having abandoned error, you will become a Christian."[61]

If rational argument can secure the conversion of the Jew, without recourse to his Scripture or his Judaism, then little differentiates the *infidelitas* of the Jew from that of any other infidel. Yet, at the same time as it confirms that the Jew had begun to lose his privileged distinctiveness in Christian thought, Odo's *Disputatio* also suggests that this distinctiveness was far from lost. Odo's Christianity entailed belief in more than just the necessity of the incarnation; and when Odo turned to his second point of contention with the Jews, Christian belief in Jesus' virgin birth, rational argument surely helped, but it did not prove sufficient. Medieval Jews commonly linked the incarnation to the virgin birth in their assessments of Christianity, terming this latter issue the crux of their inability to accept the faith of the European

58. Odo of Cambrai, *De peccato originali*, PL 160:1071–1102, trans. Resnick, pp. 39–82.

59. Odo, *Disputatio contra Iudaeum*, PL 160:1105, trans. Resnick, p. 88.

60. Ibid., col. 1106, trans. Resnick, p. 89.

61. Ibid., trans. Resnick, p. 90.

majority.[62] Odo recognized the importance of the matter and could not ignore it, not even in this treatise composed for monastic instruction. It is revealing that here, just as the nature of its argumentation began to change, so too did the dialogue lose some of its politeness and cordiality. We read first that the Jew became derisive: "In one thing especially we laugh at you and think that you are crazy. You say that God was conceived within his mother's womb, surrounded by a vile fluid, and suffered enclosure within this foul prison for nine months when finally, in the tenth month, he emerged from her private parts. Who can admit this notion without embarrassment?"[63] After responding with his homily on reason and sense, already quoted at length, Odo countered in kind: "Where is that which you called the uncleanness of woman, the obscene prison, the fetid womb? Confess, you wretch, your stupidity."[64] I would suggest that the virgin birth in Odo's *Disputatio* assumes a role analogous to that of the Trinity in the polemical works of Gilbert Crispin. Over this point, recall, Gilbert's Gentile left the debate in protest, because his Christian colleague could not adduce rational arguments to validate it; in both of his polemical treatises, Gilbert proclaimed that one could profitably discuss this matter in the presence of faithful Christians alone. In Odo's polemic, proving the doctrine of the virgin birth exceeds the limits of rational argument. Here calm, rational discussion breaks down; here intemperate hostility obfuscates the exchange of ideas.

A review of Odo's discourse on reason and sense will confirm this impression. For all that Odo developed his contrast with eloquence and passion, he does not even claim to prove the fact—or the necessity—of Jesus' birth, merely its logical possibility. Repeated references to reason may deflect attention from the unavoidable conclusion, but they cannot hide the fact that belief in the virgin birth is grounded not in *ratio* but in *auctoritas* and in the faith required to interpret it properly. In this instance, Odo found key biblical evidence in the statement of archangel Gabriel to Mary that she was "full of grace [*gratia plena*],"

---

62. See, for example, the famous outburst of Moses Nachmanides at the Disputation of Barcelona in 1263, in Moses ben Nachman, *Kitvei RaMBa''N*, ed. Charles B. Chavel (Jerusalem, 1963), 1:310–11. See also the various references cited by David Berger, ed., *The Jewish-Christian Debate in the High Middle Ages: A Critical Edition of the Niẓẓaḥon Vetus*, Judaica: Texts and Translations 4 (Philadelphia, 1979), pp. 274–77; and Lasker, *Jewish Philosophical Polemics*, chap. 7.

63. Odo, *Disputatio contra Iudaeum*, PL 160:1110, with slight departures from the translation of Resnick, p. 95.

64. Ibid., col. 1112, trans. Resnick, p. 97.

a text from the New Testament (Luke 1:28, Vulgate) whose authority no Jew would have admitted. As in Gilbert Crispin's treatment of the Trinity, in the absence of faith the Jewish-Christian debate devolves into a contest of hermeneutics: Who reads Scripture better—he who accepts its plain, literal meaning, its *sensus* in Odo's terms, or he who ferrets out its underlying, spiritual, value-laden meaning, for Odo its "reason"? More than they address the issue of the virgin birth, Odo's remarks are truly ad hominem; they contrast the plain, peasant's understanding of signs and value with those of one who is truly enlightened. The peasant—one can obviously read Jew[65]—prefers the spiritless sense of the inanimate rock, the lifeless wooden house, inherently vacuous money, and the desolate shrub; the rational—that is, Christian—reader chooses the animate serpent, the fruit-bearing tree of life, the divinely created animals of the forest, and the heavenly stars on high, respectively.

Where does all of this leave the Jew whom Odo fashioned for his *Disputatio*? On one hand, targeted by solely rational arguments for the incarnation, Odo's Jew now shares aspects of his disbelief with other infidels, who could not be convinced in any other way but who could be converted thus. On the other hand, Odo's Jew remained intensely biblical. His law and its literal sensus obviated his acceptance of Christianity. I agree with Anna Abulafia that Odo's *Disputatio* begins to stigmatize Judaism as inherently irrational and that this association definitely fanned the flames of Christian anti-Judaism as time wore on.[66] Nevertheless, the Jew still fulfilled an important function in Odo's theological perspective: His literal adherence to the law of the Bible still facilitated the instruction of Odo's Christian monks in Christianity; he still constituted the primary "other"; he remained the blind Jew in

65. One may well compare Odo's colorful description of the Jew's peasant-like nature with the comments appearing two centuries later in Raymond Lull's *Liber praedicationis contra Iudaeos* 50, CCCM 38:74: "Et cum praeceptum non portet meritum salvationis, in hoc apparet rusticitas et ruditas Iudaeorum, qui stant ad litteram et non ad sensum allegoricum et tropologicum et anagogicum, sicut faciunt Christiani."

66. Anna Sapir Abulafia, "Twelfth-Century Humanism and the Jews." in *Contra Iudaeos: Ancient and Medieval Polemics between Christians and Jews*, ed. Ora Limor and Guy G. Stroumsa (Tübingen, Germany, 1996), pp. 163–66, and "Christian Imagery," pp. 384ff. I have doubts, however, concerning Abulafia's proposed emendation ("Christian Imagery," p. 390 n. 21) of Odo's reproof of Leo for disparaging Christian belief in the virgin birth, following immediately on the passage cited above in n. 64 to read: "Nunquid tunc *eras* [replacing *erat* in PL 160:1112] sensualis, cum animalibus, sine ratione cum hominibus." Despite the manuscript variant discovered by Abulafia supporting such a reading, I have found no other instance in the *Disputatio* where Odo refers to Leo in the imperfect indicative.

front of the mirror, whose image had allowed Augustine to define himself as a Christian.

GUIBERT OF NOGENT

Although various other writers of the early twelfth century followed in
Anselm's footsteps,[67] our initial sampling of his school of thought concludes with Guibert of Nogent. Born probably in 1064,[68] Guibert entered the Benedictine monastery at Fly not long after his twelfth birthday, and he reported that there he came to know Anselm, before the
latter assumed his bishopric in England:

> While he was still prior at Bec, he admitted me to his acquaintance, and
> though I was a mere child of most tender age and knowledge, he readily
> offered to teach me to manage the inner self, how to consult the laws of
> reason in the government of the body. Both before he became abbot and
> as abbot, he was a familiar visitor at the abbey of Fly where I was, wel-
> comed for his piety and his teaching. He bestowed on me so assiduously
> the benefits of his learning and with such ardor labored at this that it seemed
> as if I alone were the unique and special reason for his frequent visits.[69]

Guibert also left us a *Tractatus de incarnatione contra Iudaeos* (A Treatise on the Incarnation against the Jews),[70] composed by 1111, which
contrasts instructively with the corresponding works of Anselm, Gilbert
Crispin, and Odo of Cambrai. In assessing Guibert's treatise, one
should situate his anti-Judaism within the overall context of his personality and worldview and thus make frequent reference to his *Monodiae*, or memoirs, written in 1115.

After a brief dedicatory epistle to Bernard, deacon of Soissons, Guibert opened his *Tractatus* by explaining that the real target of his po-

---

67. On Pseudo-Anselm, Pseudo-William of Champeaux, and Hildebert of Lavardin,
none of whom has been considered here, see the studies of Anna Sapir Abulafia: "Jewish-
Christian Disputations and the Twelfth-Century Renaissance," *JMH* 15 (1989), 105–25,
"Christians Disputing Disbelief," pp. 142–46, and "Twelfth-Century Humanism," pp.
169–73.
68. On the chronology of Guibert's life and writings, see the comments of John F.
Benton in his translation of Guibert's *Monodiae*, entitled *Self and Society in Medieval
France: The Memoirs of Abbot Guibert of Nogent* (1970; reprint, Toronto, 1984), pp.
7–33, 229–39; on the dating of Guibert's birth in particular, see also R. I. Moore, "Guibert of Nogent and His World," in *Studies in Medieval History Presented to R. H. C.
Davis*, ed. Henry Mayr-Harting and R. I. Moore (London, 1985), p. 114 n. 36.
69. Guibert of Nogent, *Monodiae* 1.17, in *Autobiographie*, ed. Edmond-René Labande, Les Classiques de l'histoire de France au Moyen Âge 34 (Paris, 1981), pp. 138–
41, trans. Benton, *Self and Society*, p. 89.
70. PL 156:489–528.

lemic was a Christian who inclined toward the ideas of the Jews; reprehensible though the Jews were, their disbelief is, in a certain sense, tolerable, whereas that of a lapsed Christian eludes comprehension entirely. Guibert referred specifically to Count John of Soissons, who had evidently expressed doubts concerning the incarnation and virgin birth that Guibert readily associated with the Jews:

> However tolerable it might be when our faith is disparaged by those who have in no way accepted its dogmas, when those who seem reconciled to Christ in grace attack it and malign it, the minds of all good people are piously consumed with enmity at such a report. The Jewish ignorance that grumbles somewhat concerning the Virgin's conception of the son of God is surely embedded in that people, and one ought to be duly ashamed that God, who had come to his ancestors as their savior, was betrayed by them. Yet a Christian, who does not disclaim the worth of this name, who enters churches though he is pitiful and fainthearted, who somehow respects the altars and the priests, who participates in the Eucharist of the faithful and in the confession of sinners, who reveres the memory of the Lord's passion and still undertakes to give alms—this sort, I say, why does he incline to the teachings of the Jews? Why does he adopt and fortify their arguments against us? Their murmurings, which they themselves dare not utter aloud, he raises up with his own power (which, with God as judge, will flourish but shortly). What they barely pronounce in their throats he proclaims and, hard to believe, argues it with the words of their own superstition. One hates the idea; one simply cannot endure that he declares himself a Christian. What madness is it, that one who refuses to be considered or labeled a Jew or a pagan upholds their ceremonies, defends their laws, displays hatred toward Christian laws—in fact hates what he adores!

Guibert had no classification for such an individual. He termed him a "neuter," one who belonged to no sect; this person acclaimed that which he did not follow, and vice versa. Yet he strayed from Christianity on matters "that derived from a most disgusting Jewish origin," and Guibert thus set out to silence these Jewish "whisperers of impure doctrine along with their advocate."[71]

In its first book, the *Tractatus* dwells primarily on the doctrine of the virgin birth. "No sane person doubts that that blessed woman was teeming with the holy spirit," but the Jews, who still perform the ancient, now meaningless rituals of Mosaic law, fail to distinguish between Mary and other mothers.[72] Having no understanding of the mys-

71. Guibert, *Tractatus de incarnatione contra Iudaeos* 1.1, PL 156:489–92; on the identification of John of Soissons, see Guibert's *Monodiae* 2.5, ed. Labande, p. 252.
72. Guibert, *Tractatus* 1.1, PL 156:491.

tery, they object that God would not and should not have assumed human form, that this defied natural law and compromised his dignity; they express horror at the idea that God would have entered the inner organs of a woman. In response, Guibert discussed the need to find a remedy for original sin, in atonement for which the sacrifices and circumcision of the Jews proved insufficient. Hebrew Scripture often attributes human characteristics to God in a fashion more unbecoming than in any Christian teaching. Human nature itself has no impurity or shamefulness that renders it unseemly for God; these originate in sin, which Jesus, born of a virgin, did not inherit. Accordingly, the human body, either that of the virgin or that of God incarnate himself, need not evoke horror or disgust—not even with regard to its reproductive organs—as the Jews wrongfully suggest. Of Mary's genitals Guibert argued that "those members, which then devoted themselves to that [divine] offspring, were more dignified than are those foulest of mouths, which fill themselves daily with deceit and luxury and deride the life-giving sacraments."[73]

The second book of Guibert's treatise continues in a similar vein, responding further to Judaic-heretical objections. In the absence of sin and the carnal desire it generates, the sexual organs remain blessed and venerable. As for the ostensive deviation from the laws of nature that a virginal birth entailed, both nature itself and human history allow for such a possibility: Adam and Eve were not born of any sexual union, and members of various other species, from cats to vultures to bees, have reproduced in a nonsexual manner. To these arguments from reason Guibert then added traditional biblical prooftexts for the virgin birth, primarily from Isaiah, and he adduced numerous examples of the divine spirit infusing persons far less worthy than Mary. The book concludes with another rhetorical appeal to the Jews, and to their heretical sympathizers:

Desist, you stubborn ones; let your verbosity come to an end, since every argument is of no avail. You who devote your hearts to theft or to usury,

73. Ibid. 1.6, col. 497; and on Jesus' need to defecate, cf. 2.1, col. 499. On the importance of psychoanalytic and sexual categories for an understanding of Guibert and his anti-Jewish polemic, see John F. Benton, "The Personality of Guibert of Nogent," *Psychoanalytic Review* 57 (1970–71), 563–86; Jonathan Kantor, "A Psycho-Historical Source: The *Memoirs* of Abbot Guibert of Nogent," *JMH* 2 (1976), 281–304; the rejoinder of M. D. Coupe, "The Personality of Guibert de Nogent Reconsidered," *JMH* 9 (1983), 317–29; and the insightful alternative offered by Seth Lerer, "*Transgressio studii*: Writing and Sexuality in Guibert of Nogent," *Stanford French Review* 14 (1990), 243–66.

how can you perceive the reasons for the sacraments of God and the mysteries of those reasons . . . ? Vainly do I contend with your obstinacy, since unless you believe in him whom we believe to be Christ, you will never be able to be free of this dispute with us, nor will you who abhor the son have the proper sentiments concerning his mother.[74]

The third and final book of the treatise opens with consideration of the earthly career of Christ, his passion and death, his truly messianic character, and his resurrection, offering mainly scriptural evidence in support of its arguments. Discussion next turns to the erroneous Jewish claim that divine teaching can undergo no ostensive change and to a critique of the Jews' literal, carnal understanding of the Old Testament in general; the Jews, argued Guibert, did not truly observe the law in any sense, and their literal interpretation of it focused entirely on worldly gain. The *Tractatus* responds to Jewish charges that Christians engage in idolatry when they revere the crucifix and other images of Jesus, and it briefly addresses the belief in the Trinity. In its last chapter,[75] the work relates the story—"which seems more powerful than any verbal argument"—of a certain Jew of Laon who refused conversion to Christianity even after witnessing a cleric take a burning log in his hand and, having invoked the name of Christ, remain completely unscathed. But Guibert's specification that the story (*cuiusdam . . . Iudaei relatio*) concerned the recalcitrant Jew more than the zealously faithful Christian cleric warrants reflection: How did this anecdote serve his polemical purposes better than any discursive argument? How was it a fitting conclusion to his entire polemical treatise, particularly when the miracle failed to convert the Jew? These questions point to the underlying motivations of Guibert's polemic and to the place of the Jew in his early-twelfth-century Christian world-view.

One surely cannot deny Guibert his place in the Anselmian community of thought. Guibert himself testified to his relationship with Anselm and to the latter's lasting influence upon him; we read in the *Monodiae* that Guibert's pious mother also sought Anselm's advice on more than one occasion.[76] In his ideas on the incarnation, in his teaching on atonement and the redemptive work of Christ, and in his Marian theology Guibert followed closely in Anselm's footsteps, espousing many of the

74. Guibert, *Tractatus* 2.5, PL 156:506.
75. Ibid. 3.11, col. 529.
76. Guibert, *Monodiae* 2.4, ed. Labande, p. 244.

ideas as well as the rationalist spirit of the *Cur Deus homo*.[77] As Anselm
had done in the *Cur Deus homo*, Guibert attacked the disbelief of the
Jews and that of heterodox Christians in similar contexts and with the
same arguments and reproof. He too affirmed the indispensable role of
faith in allaying Christian doubt and in achieving theological understanding. To be sure, Guibert did allude to certain misgivings or reluc-
tances of the Jews concerning their relationship with John of Soissons:
They dare not voice their objections to Christianity as openly as he does,
and they actually consider his Judaizing behavior insane, because "he
approved of their religion in word and publicly practiced ours."[78] Yet
Guibert has conflated the Jews and heretical Christians in the *Tractatus*,
at times beyond all distinction, so that one cannot ascertain the intended
recipient of many of his pejorative remarks. In the *Monodiae*, Guibert
repeatedly associated Jews with bad Christians, as well as with irrationality and vice. In one well-known anecdote, a Jew mediated between a
Christian cleric and the devil, to whom the cleric had to offer a libation
of his own semen in order to gain instruction in black magic; the magic
so gained facilitated the monk's regular fornication with a nun, which
remained unpunished until the eventual intervention of Anselm.[79] The
genuine faith of a young confrere at Fly, converted from Judaism following the Crusaders' massacre of Jews in Rouen in 1096, surprised Guibert, because the sincere conversion of Jews "in our day is unusual."[80]
The *Monodiae* report that a Jew assisted John of Soissons's mother in the
murder of her brother, and another Jew in the adulterous exploits of
John himself;[81] the work relates incidents of greed, theft, and usury

77. See especially Jaroslav Pelikan, "A First-Generation Anselmian, Guibert of Nogent," in *Continuity and Discontinuity in Church History: Essays Presented to George
Huntston Williams on the Occasion of His 65th Birthday*, ed. F. Forrester Church and
Timothy George, Studies in the History of Christian Thought 19 (Leiden, Netherlands,
1979), pp. 71–82; and Edmond-Réné Labande, "Guibert de Nogent: Disciple et témoin
de Saint Anselme au Bec," in *MSC*, pp. 229–36. Penny J. Cole, *The Preaching of the
Crusades to the Holy Land, 1095–1270* (Cambridge, Mass., 1991), p. 24, has suggested
that Guibert incorporated the Christology-free logic (*remoto Christo*) of Anselm's *Cur
Deus homo* in his rendition of Urban II's inauguration of the First Crusade at Clermont.
See Guibert's *Gesta Dei per Francos* 2.4, in *Recueil des historiens des croisades: Historiens occidentaux* (Paris, 1844–95), 4:138: "Ponamus modo in Iherusalem Christum
neque mortuum, nec sepultum, nec ibidem aliquando vixisse. Certe, si haec deessent
omnia, solum illud ad subveniendum terrae et civitati vos excitare debuerat, quia de
Syon exierit lex et verbum Domini de Iherusalem."
    78. Guibert *Tractatus* 1.1, PL 156:489; *Monodiae* 3.16, ed. Labande, p. 424, trans.
Benton, p. 210.
    79. Guibert, *Monodiae* 1.25, ed. Labande, pp. 200ff.
    80. Ibid. 2.5, p. 252, trans. Benton, p. 137.
    81. Ibid. 3.16, ed. Labande, pp. 422ff.

bringing Christians to their downfall,[82] shortcomings Guibert attributed to Jews in the *Tractatus*.

Much as he discerned the origins of Islam in a Christian heretic's manipulation of Muhammad,[83] Guibert followed Anselm in beholding a link between Jewish objections to Christianity, as he perceived them, and *infidelitas* among Christians of his own day. Like Anselm, he sensed among Jews—and Muslims—a category of disbelief they shared with Christians who had gone astray. Displaying relatively little interest in the literal meaning of Scripture, he too cared above all about its morally edifying senses and those of human history, a predilection that predominates not only in his theological works but also in his exegetical writings and even in his historical chronicle of the First Crusade.[84] In addition, Anna Abulafia has discerned yet another Anselmian dimension in Guibert's anti-Judaism.[85] Guibert, recall, avowed his debt to Anselm in recognizing the need to subject the conduct of one's body to the dictates of reason, which, as Guibert elaborated, reflected the victory of the spiritual over the carnal longings of the individual. "His teaching was to divide the mind in a threefold or fourfold way, to treat the operations of the whole interior mystery under the headings of appetite, will, reason, and intellect [*sub affectu, sub voluntate, sub ratione, sub intellectu*]."[86] For Anselm, these four aspects of the soul corresponded to the four senses of Scripture: literal, allegorical, tropological, and anagogical. For Guibert, who shared this hermeneutical perspective, the Jews' materialism and carnality entailed a rejection of the rational in matters of self-governance; they resulted in an inability to interpret the Bible any way but literally; and such refusal to understand Scripture in its figurative senses obviated the faith underlying belief in the virgin birth and in the essential purity of Mary's sexual body that such belief predicated. According to Abulafia, Guibert took

82. Ibid. 3.19, p. 450f.

83. Guibert, *Gesta Dei per Francos* 1.3–4, in *Recueil* 4:127–30; and see Penny J. Cole, "'O God, the Heathen Have Come into Your Inheritance Inheritance' (Ps. 78.1): The Theme of Religious Pollution in Crusade Documents, 1095–1188," in *Crusaders and Muslims in Twelfth-Century Syria*, ed. Maya Shatzmiller, The Medieval Mediterranean: Peoples, Economies and Cultures 1 (Leiden, Netherlands, 1993), pp. 97–100.

84. See Jacques Chaurand, "La Conception de l'histoire de Guibert de Nogent," *CCM* 8 (1965), 381–95; and Jonathan Riley-Smith, *The First Crusade and the Idea of Crusading* (London, 1986), chap. 6, passim.

85. See Abulafia's treatment of Guibert in "Christian Imagery," pp. 386–88, "Theology," pp. 26–40, and "Twelfth-Century Humanism," pp. 166–69.

86. Guibert, *Monodiae* 1.17, ed. Labande, p. 140, trans. Benton, p. 89; and see Guth, "Zum Verhältnis."

great interest in that which prevented the Jews from submitting to variegated proofs of the truth of Christianity,[87] and his conclusions extended far beyond the limits of traditional *Adversus Iudaeos* polemic.
In Guibert's thought,

> the supposed literalness of the Jews becomes actual carnal behaviour. This
> behaviour aligns Jews with animals and excludes them from any spiritual
> aspirations. The Pentateuch offers Jews nothing but material gain; thus to
> Guibert the Law of Moses exemplifies the usurious role of the Jews in the
> expanding northern French economy. In short, Jews are evil in mind and
> body. As such they are the natural accomplices of evil Christians. Guibert
> seems to associate all evil with the Devil; the Jews are no exception to the
> rule.[88]

Abulafia's reconstruction of the Anselmian "logic" for Guibert's
anti-Judaism is certainly plausible, but I have doubts as to the extent
of Guibert's interest in a true, systematic analysis or explanation of
Jewish disbelief. Genuine interest in such understanding might have
resulted in a different kind of anti-Jewish treatise, perhaps more akin
to the Christian-Jewish dialogues of Gilbert Crispin and Odo of Cambrai—or even to the restrained, moderately pitched *Cur Deus homo*—
which would have presented Jewish arguments more reliably and
would have sought to refute them more methodically and evenhandedly. Guibert's *Tractatus*, however, is poorly organized and written in
difficult, often confounding language. It makes no attempt to portray
the Jews or their ideas at all realistically. There is no dialogue here, no
credible intent to engage the Jew in conversation, no expression of
willingness to work with a Jew—even a contrived one—toward his
conversion. To the contrary, Guibert's language is unrestrained, acer-
bic, and offensive; his formulations of Jewish-heretical objections to
Christianity, though addressing the same themes (virgin birth, incarnation, Trinity, mutability of the law, messianic character of Jesus, and
so forth) as did Anselm, Gilbert, Odo, and others before him, have no
ring of authenticity, no echo of any personal encounters that might
have aroused his concerns; even his presentation of the arguments of
the *Cur Deus homo* is thoroughly unconvincing. Although Guibert
claimed that his formerly Jewish confrere at Fly found the *Tractatus*

---

87. Abulafia, "Twelfth-Century Humanism," p. 167: "Guibert's . . . predominant
concern is to ferret out precisely what prevents Jews from accepting this belief, even when
it has been explained to them ad nauseam by means of scriptural and rational arguments."
88. Abulafia, "Theology," p. 40.

edifying,[89] one cannot believe that it would have effectuated the conversion of anyone, *sola ratione* or otherwise.

Rather than to investigate the Jewish mentality, I would argue, Guibert undertook to caricature it. He had little concern for the logic of Jewish disbelief, but his caricature of that disbelief fueled his attack on John of Soissons and other heretics like him, whom Judaism had led astray from Christianity—or at least so Guibert wanted us to believe. In Guibert's eyes, the Jews represented everything that threatened the spiritual welfare of Christendom: black magic, allegiance to the devil, sexual depravity, material greed, brutish hostility, and doctrinal infidelity, all of which he associated with Christian heretics like John. It is telling that Guibert attacks Jewish error and evil only within the context of their impact on Christians, whether in the theological doubts of John of Soissons, in his adulterous liaisons "with a wrinkled old woman," in his mother's murder of her brother, or in a treacherous cleric's covenant with the devil; to this list we may add the parallel between Jewish usury and that of various heretics, whom Guibert dubbed "devourers of the poor [*pauperum corrosores*]."[90] Guibert, it would seem, cared less about Jews and Judaism per se and more about the spiritual health of his Christian world.

How did Guibert view his Christian world? Rife with magic, plagued by the devil, filled with incubi and good and evil spirits, the world portrayed in Guibert's *Monodiae* appears in many ways a throwback to the world of Gregory the Great five centuries earlier, a world described expressively by Carole Straw, where "visible and invisible, natural and supernatural, human and divine, carnal and spiritual are often directly and causally connected . . . , [where] invisible reality exists alongside the visible reality it sustains and determines."[91] Such a monistic worldview, we recall, had led Gregory to devalue the literal exegesis of the Old Testament that the Jews personified, to disparage the worth of postlapsarian human sexuality, and to attribute little significance to the terrestrial history in which, he believed, the Jews sought their ultimate salvation. The Jews stood out as the enemy par excellence in the Gregorian worldview, those in whom all the imperfections of Christendom seemed to converge and persist.

89. Guibert, *Monodiae* 2.5, ed. Labande, p. 252.
90. Ibid. 3.19, p. 452, trans. Benton, p. 222.
91. Carole Straw, *Gregory the Great: Perfection in Imperfection* (Berkeley, Calif., 1988), pp. 9–11; cf. above, chapter 2, n. 54.

Much the same can be said for the worldview of Guibert of Nogent, who did not ignore his debt to Gregory.[92] For Guibert, too, the Jews remained carnal, materialistic, "sons of the devil"[93]—in a word, the enemies of Christendom. Yet Christendom had changed considerably since Gregory's day, and the rate of change only increased with its entry into the twelfth century. Urban life was being revitalized. Money played a much larger role in the economy and society than it had during the preceding centuries, arousing fear and distrust in many religious quarters. Reason and dialectic were making their mark on the definition of Christian faith. The Investiture Controversy and the Crusade boosted the prestige and power of the Catholic clergy, underscoring the distinction between the church and its enemies. Greater ecclesiastical power generated more widespread anti-ecclesiastical dissent. Many sought new outlets for the expression of their religious commitments, typically defining their niche in medieval society within new communal, corporate frameworks. At the same time, many strove to preserve continuity between natural and supernatural worlds in the grand scheme of things and, on a microcosmic level, to promote the correspondence between appearance and interiority within the individual Christian.

As Evans has pointed out, Guibert of Nogent exemplified such concern for conversion specifically within the Christian community,[94] a concern, I would suggest, that dominated both the substance and the structure of his memoirs. In its first book, the *Monodiae* tell of the arduous nature of the conversion process and of the obstacles that impede it, especially as experienced by Guibert and his mother.[95] In a brief second book we read primarily of successful converts: Guibert, now abbot at Nogent-sous-Coucy; his mother, at last a nun; William,

92. Curiously, Gregory's appearances in Guibert's *Monodiae* are strikingly similar to those of Anselm, which perhaps suggests the recognition of an equally formative influence. Guibert reported that his mother felt special admiration for Gregory, even though she had never read his works; having heard that Gregory "had been eminent for his wonderful understanding and had abounded in extraordinary wisdom," she first put Guibert in school on the day of his festival (1.4, ed. Labande, p. 26, trans. Benton, pp. 44–45), and she eventually followed Gregory's counsel in preferring a cloistered life to one in the secular world (1.12, ed. Labande, p. 84). For his part, Guibert declared that in studying biblical exegesis at the "special encouragement" of Anselm—and the figurative exegesis of Scripture above all—he concentrated on the commentaries of Gregory, "in which are to be found the best keys of that art" (1.17, ed. Labande, p. 138, trans. Benton, p. 89).

93. Guibert, *Tractatus* 2.1, PL 156:499.

94. Evans, *Anselm and a New Generation*, pp. 59–62.

95. Guibert explicitly acknowledges this concern in *Monodiae* 1.8, ed. Labande, p. 48.

the baptized Jew in the monastery at Fly; and others. The third and final book, of almost the exact same length as the first, contrasts with it neatly, describing disorder and rebellion outside the monastery in the city, where usurious heretics run rampant, growing farther and farther removed from God. Worst of these was John of Soissons, in whom, as we know from Guibert's *Tractatus de incarnatione*, exterior and interior, like his behavior and belief, reeked of disparity.

Guibert used his caricature of the Jews to personify the substance and error of John's heresy. They blindly maintained their ancient forebears' enmity toward Christ. They persistently defied each of the many validations of Christian teaching presented to them, whether through rational argument, biblical testimony, or a miracle performed before their very eyes. Wedded to carnality in mind as well as body, they were inherently incapable of the faith that could ultimately arrive at understanding and, thereby, genuine conversion. Guibert lashed out virulently at the Jews, virtually without restraint, even as his underlying concern was with John of Soissons and the deviation from true Christian devotion that John and his anti-clerical lifestyle represented. In so doing, Guibert demonstrated yet another possible application of the Anselmian conflation of Jews and other infidels, whether Christian or not. Whereas Gilbert Crispin and Odo of Cambrai emulated the moderation and temperance of Anselm's appeal to the infidel, Guibert of Nogent demonstrated how conviction in the absolute harmony between faith and reason could lead to new levels of intolerance in the Jewish-Christian debate.[96] Not insignificantly, such conviction also led Guibert to polemicize condescendingly against Islam.[97] Other twelfth-century churchmen would soon follow his example.

PETER ALFONSI

Peter Alfonsi rounds out this discussion of the new rationalist tenor in Christian anti-Jewish polemic. Filling more than 130 columns in Migne's Patrologia, Peter's *Dialogi Petri et Moysi Iudaei* (Dialogues of Peter and Moses the Jew)[98] comprise the longest polemical tract con-

---

96. Again, see the studies of Abulafia cited above, n. 85.

97. See above, n. 83.

98. PL 157:535–672. A critical edition of the work appeared in Klaus-Peter Mieth, "Der Dialog des Petrus Alfonsi, Seine Überlieferung im Druck und in den Handschriften: Textedition" (Ph.D. diss., Free University of Berlin, 1982); it has subsequently reappeared in Peter Alfonsi, *Diálogo contra los Judíos*, ed. Klaus-Peter Mieth, trans. Esperanza Ducay (Huesca, Spain, 1996), which I have not yet seen.

sidered in this chapter, and, in view of the seventy-nine extant manuscripts containing all or part of the work,[99] evidently the most popular
as well. Yet our main interest in the *Dialogi* lies not in such statistics
but in the distinctive character of the work itself. Whereas Anselm's
Cur Deus homo and Guibert's *Tractatus de incarnatione* aimed their
arguments primarily at Christians, and whereas the Jews depicted in
the disputations of Gilbert Crispin and Odo of Cambrai did not accept
Christianity, Peter's *Dialogi* retrace the process whereby rational argument did in fact effect conversion, in this case the conversion of the
author himself.

Peter lived the first half of his life as a Spanish Jew named Moses,
perhaps of the Aragonese city of Huesca; his Sefardic-Hispanic heritage
no doubt rendered him more cosmopolitan than the other churchmen
discussed in this chapter. He converted to Christianity in Huesca in
1106, not long after the city had fallen to the armies of the Reconquista
and Moses had become the court physician of King Alfonso I. In the
wake of his conversion, Alfonsi composed both his *Dialogi* and his
widely translated anthology of Mediterranean folktales, the *Disciplina
clericalis*. The second decade of the twelfth century found him in England, where he instructed English scientists in astronomy, translated
Arabic scholarship in the field into Latin, and perhaps served as a physician to King Henry I. From England Alfonsi may have moved to
northern France, where he pursued his scientific career further; inconclusive archival evidence suggests that he may have returned to Argon
by 1121. One cannot help but wonder as to the extent of contact, if
any at all, Alfonsi may have had with the Anselmian circle while in
northern Europe.[100]

Although the facts of Peter's biography remain obscure, the *Dialogi*
offer us insight into the intellectual quest that resulted in his conversion—or at least into the constructions of Jews and Judaism with which
he justified it after the fact—inasmuch as they describe a debate between Peter, in the wake of his baptism, and Moses, his Jewish alter
ego from beforehand. As Peter explains at the outset,

---

99. John Tolan, *Petrus Alfonsi and His Medieval Readers* (Gainesville, Fla., 1993),
pp. 192–98.

100. On Peter's life and career see ibid., pp. 9ff.; Jeremy Cohen, "The Mentality of
the Medieval Jewish Apostate: Peter Alfonsi, Hermann of Cologne, and Pablo Christiani," in *Jewish Apostasy in the Modern World*, ed. Todd M. Endelman (New York,
1987), pp. 23–29, along with the additional sources cited therein; and María Jesús Lacarra, *Pedro Alfonso*, Colección "Los Aragoneses" 3 (Saragossa, Spain, 1991).

when it became known to the Jews—who had known me previously and had considered me to be well trained in the books of the prophets and teachings of the sages and to have some knowledge of all the liberal arts— that I had accepted the law and belief of the Christians and was one of them, some of them [the Jews] thought that I would never have done this unless I had forsaken all sense of shame and despised God and his law. Others asserted that I had done this because I had not understood the words of the prophets and the law properly. Still others assigned it to vainglory and falsely accused that I had acted for worldly gain, insofar as I believed that the Christian people dominated over all others. So that all may understand my intention and hear the rationale, I have thus composed this little book, in which I have set forth to overcome the credulity of all other peoples and have then concluded [by demonstrating] that the Christian religion is superior to all others. Finally, I have set down all the objections of any opponent of the Christian religion, and, after they have been stated, I have destroyed them with rational argument and scriptural proof to the best of my ability. I have fashioned the entire book as a dialogue, so that the mind of the reader might understand more readily. To defend the arguments of the Christians, I have used the name which I now have as a Christian; to present the arguments of the adversary, the name which I had before baptism.[101]

Elsewhere I have discussed the mentality that may have led Peter Alfonsi to baptism;[102] here I propose to focus on the logic of the arguments he presented by way of "apology" for his conversion. The preface from which we have quoted hints that this resulted from a process of disenchantment with Judaism, a comparative study of possible alternatives, and, finally, the determination that only Christianity accorded sufficiently with *ratio* and *auctoritas*. This process underlies the structure of the *Dialogi*, and it will prove instructive in the ensuing analysis.

Responding to Moses's query as to where the Jews have erred in their interpretation of God's law, Peter specifies three main reasons— drawn from the "many, many errors in which you venture insane explanations of the law"—for his dissatisfaction. First, the sages of the Jews in their "doctrine" (*doctrina*, by which Peter means the Talmud) attribute a human form and body to God and thus demean his ineffable majesty with utterly irrational teaching. Second, the Jews' hope for redemption from their present captivity, hope based on their literal interpretation of Scripture, has proven fruitless and misguided. Third, despite their literal observance of biblical law, Jews presently succeed

101. Peter, *Dialogi Petri et Moysi Iudaei*, PL 157:538.
102. Cohen, "Mentality."

in observing only a small percentage of the Mosaic commandments, indicating that God could not possibly find such observance pleasing or acceptable.[103] And thus the *Dialogi* proceed.

The first, longest, and most original of Alfonsi's twelve chapters indicts Jewish theology for its crude anthropomorphisms, primarily with explicit reference to talmudic homilies (*aggadot*) that violate both reason and any defensible interpretation of the Old Testament.[104] Peter cites the rabbinic dicta that God wears tefillin (phylacteries), that he rages and grieves over the present dispersion of the Jews, that he is located in the West—all of these beliefs that no sane mind could entertain: How can God reside in the West if "the West" does not have an absolute, independent existence but varies according to an individual's frame of reference? Unless we believe that God has need of food and drink, how can one maintain that he cries, for his shedding of tears would deplete his substance? Why would a truly omnipotent deity prefer to grieve over his people's captivity rather than to expedite their miraculous redemption? From here Peter moves on to explore several ramifications of such rabbinic instruction. He presents reasoned arguments for the existence of God and the mechanisms of his created world, which the Jews fail to understand properly. He adduces additional aggadot that resound, to his ears, with absurdity—stories of angels protesting God's revelation of the law to Moses, of the slaughter of Esau and his numerous followers with one stone, of Rabbi Joshua ben Levi's defiance of the angel of death, and so forth—in order to discredit rabbinic theology in general. And he devotes chapter 3 of the *Dialogi* to yet another expression of Judaism's preference for the material over the spiritual: the completely groundless belief in the physical resurrection of the dead during the messianic era.

In support of his second argument concerning the present dispersion of the Jews, Peter switches gears in chapter 2. Here he relies on talmudic evidence, which he now accepts as valid, to confirm his specific contentions: The Jews of the second temple period were particularly obedient and pious, and they enjoyed the leadership of venerable, righteous teachers like Yochanan ben Zakkai, Choni "the Circle-Drawer,"

---

103. Peter, *Dialogi*, PL 157:540.

104. Ch. Merchavia, *The Church versus Talmudic and Midrashic Literature, 500–1248* [Hebrew] (Jerusalem, 1970), chap. 3, offers a thorough treatment of Peter's rabbinic citations. On Alfonsi's anti-Jewish polemic, see also Manfred Kniewasser, "Die antijüdische Polemik des Petrus Alphonsi (getauft 1106) und des Abtes Petrus Venerabilis von Cluny († 1156)," *Kairos*, n.s. 22 (1980), 34–49.

Chanina ben Dosa, and Akiva ben Joseph; had but one of these sages lived at the end the first temple period, maintained Alfonsi, the Jews might have avoided its destruction and the ensuing Babylonian captivity.[105] Nevertheless, rabbinic homilies also document that the Jews have suffered inordinately since the Romans' destruction of their second commonwealth. What accounts for this discrepancy, explaining the magnitude of God's punishment of the Jews on the heels of such noteworthy piety? Only an exceptionally heinous crime could justify what the Jews have suffered, Peter declares to Moses—namely, "that you killed Christ the son of God, saying that he was a magician, born of a prostitute, and that he led the entire people into error. Your elders alleged these and similar charges, making the entire people a partner in their depraved intention; they unjustly brought a just man to a judgment blatantly unfair, and they crucified him and killed him. The magnitude of such a crime has been the cause of such prolonged captivity." The rabbis saw and comprehended the portents of God's impending punishment, which followed the crucifixion by forty years, although they concealed their meaning from the community at large. They deceptively explained that gratuitous hatred caused the destruction of the temple, whereas, in fact, greed and hatred on the part of the Jews caused the death of Jesus, and the death of Jesus was the cause of their exile.[106]

Peter's third argument, elaborated in chapter 4 of the *Dialogi*, follows neatly: Having lost their land, their independence, and their temple, the Jews can no longer observe most of the Mosaic commandments, as they foolishly claim they must do in order to merit salvation. Why, the talmudic rabbis themselves admitted that God remains deaf to Jewish prayer after the temple's destruction! Only one road, Peter entreats Moses, will lead to the Jews' salvation: "I give due thanks to him who liberated me from that very error of theirs, and devotedly I pray that he might liberate you too."[107]

At this point, Moses concedes that Peter has cogently demonstrated the rationale for his departure from Judaism, but he insists that Peter explain why he opted for Christianity:

> Thus far you have explained most clearly—and demonstrated with rational arguments—how inane and defective is the faith of the Jews in every respect,

105. Peter, *Dialogi*, PL 157:570.
106. Ibid., cols. 573–74.
107. Ibid., col. 597.

how illogical and displeasing to God is their prayer, and why you withdrew from their faith; and you have shown me in what grievous error I still remain. Yet I am astonished: When you left the faith of your ancestors, why did you choose the faith of the Christians and not that of the Saracens, among whom you grew up and with whom you were conversant?

Alfonsi knew Arabic; he was familiar with Arabic literature. Why did he not convert to Islam, a faith that seemed "founded on the basis of unshakable reason"?[108] Chapter 5 of the *Dialogi* thus contains the first overtly anti-Muslim polemical work composed in medieval Latin Christendom. Offering an exposition of Islam more serious than that of any previous writer,[109] it explains that Peter spurned Islam because Muhammad never purged it completely of pagan idolatry, because of its focus on the carnal in matters of doctrine and praxis, and because Muhammad was not a true prophet.

Then, at last, Peter arrives at his defense of Christianity, to which the last seven chapters of the *Dialogi* are devoted. Reconstructing the order in which a skeptical Jew might have struggled with difficult aspects of Christian doctrine, Moses and Peter address the Trinity, the virgin birth, the incarnation, Jesus' realization of biblical messianic prophecy, the voluntary nature of his crucifixion, his resurrection and ascension, and his New Testament's fulfillment of the Torah of Moses. In this second half of the *Dialogi* Peter again draws from rabbinic teaching, sometimes to corroborate the tenets of Christianity and sometimes to demonstrate the error of the Jews. On occasion he even ventures beyond the realm of legend and homily (*aggadah*) into that of rabbinic law (*halakhah*). He cites the ruling that Passover may not begin on Monday, Wednesday, or Friday, arguing that the first-century rabbinic patriarch Gamaliel, really a Christian, thus recognized the importance of those weekdays in the events leading up to Jesus' passion. In a different vein, he asserts that the rabbinic requirement of baptism for converts to Judaism originated in imitation of Christianity, the rabbis' deceptive attribution of the ordinance to Moses notwithstanding.[110]

When considering Alfonsi on previous occasions, I have usually had

108. Ibid.

109. On Peter's contribution to Christendom's knowledge of Islam, see Benjamin Z. Kedar, *Crusade and Mission: European Approaches toward the Muslim* (Princeton, N.J., 1984), p. 92; Norman Daniel, *Islam and the West: The Making of an Image*, rev. ed. (Oxford, 1993), p. 22f. and s.v. Pedro de Alfonso; and Guy Monnot, "Les Citations canoniques dans le 'Dialogus' de Pierre Alfonse," in *ICM*, pp. 261–77.

110. Peter, *Dialogi*, PL 157:660, 665.

to suffice with a rather hurried review, intended more to downplay his significance in the medieval history of the Jewish-Christian debate, especially when compared with Christian polemicists of the thirteenth century.[111] Here, however, lies an appropriate opportunity to appreciate Alfonsi and his *Dialogi* in their own right, within their own historical context, and to weigh more methodically the manner in which they contributed to the twelfth-century developments that now concern us. Whether or not Alfonsi ever met Anselm or any of his "school" considered above, one certainly encounters aspects of their approach to Jewish disbelief in the *Dialogi*. One cannot evade the underlying spirit of the *Cur Deus homo* in Alfonsi's treatise, the genuine desire to overcome doubt with rational argument and to bring the infidel to sincere Christian faith. Throughout the *Dialogi*, Peter moves at Moses's pace, ensuring his understanding and eliciting his consent before advancing, never losing control. The tone of the conversation is generally polite, even solicitous, with relatively few unrestrained exclamations of amazement at the irrationality of the Jews. Although the *Dialogi* do not offer a thoroughly Anselmian rationale for the incarnation,[112] their vehement opposition to divine anthropomorphisms in Jewish teaching, a telling reversal of Jewish objections to Christian doctrine,[113] confirms the central importance of the incarnation issue for apologists of the period. Alfonsi followed Anselm in recognizing that rational argument alone will not suffice to effect conversion, and he, too, endeavored to delineate precisely the necessary part that it did play in the process. Peter sets out from the "palace of great reason"[114] to establish the existence of God and the corollaries that derive therefrom; and he repeatedly demands that reason serve as a criterion for the admissibility of religious doctrine, both in the case of the interpretation of biblical prophecy and, even more so, in the case of extrabiblical teaching. When, for example, Moses adduces God's statement, "I deal death and

111. Jeremy Cohen, *The Friars and the Jews: The Evolution of Medieval Anti-Judaism* (Ithaca, N.Y., 1982), pp. 27–28, and "Scholarship and Intolerance in the Medieval Academy: The Study and Evaluation of Judaism in European Christendom," *AHR* 91 (1986), 598–99.

112. Yet Alfonsi does follow Anselm in his insistence on the appropriateness of the sacrifice/satisfaction offered in atonement for human sin; Peter, *Dialogi*, PL 157:645. Cf. Tolan, *Petrus Alfonsi*, p. 40.

113. Anna Sapir Abulafia, "Bodies in the Jewish-Christian Debate," in *Framing Medieval Bodies*, ed. Sarah Kay and Miri Rubin (Manchester, England, 1994), pp. 126ff., and *Christians and Jews*, p. 117.

114. Peter, *Dialogi*, PL 157:554.

give life" (Deuteronomy 32:39) to support Jewish belief in resurrection of the dead, Peter immediately responds, "That prooftext [*auctoritas*] deviates from the path of reason!"[115] By this he means not to reject the authority of the biblical verse but the sense—that is, the particular interpretation—in which Moses has offered the passage in evidence. Unless incontrovertible biblical testimony demands otherwise, Peter elaborates, one ought never to interpret a specific scriptural text so as to strain human sensibilities.[116] Or, in defending his own interpretation of a different verse, Peter outlines his ground rules more carefully:

> In explanation of that prophecy this sense can be accepted by a sane intellect, such that neither any biblical text nor any rational argument may seem opposed to these words. Indeed, anything in the obscure words of the prophets can be understood in different ways, so that anyone interpreting this prophecy should stray neither from biblical testimony nor from the path of reason; and it is not at all inappropriate if anyone expounds it in a different but legitimate manner. If, however, its exposition is such that it either is or seems contrary to Scripture or to reason, it should rightfully be considered lacking in virtue. Therefore, since your explanation is found to be opposed both to Scripture and to reason, it should, in all fairness, be rejected.[117]

At the same time, if Alfonsi could present Peter as discrediting the rationality of Jewish homily with relative ease, he understood that he could not establish the undeniability of Christianity without resorting to the Bible—and thus without reliance on faith in its divine origins. In the case of key Christian beliefs, like that in the incarnation, Moses admits that "the Deity *could* unite itself with a human being,"[118] but he presses Peter as to why we should believe that it was done. Similarly, Moses acknowledges the possibility of Jesus' ascension as reasonable, but he questions whether Peter "can demonstrate with any prophetic prooftext that he was supposed to be lifted up."[119] In either case, Peter responds with biblical testimonies that had long figured prominently in the Christian *Adversus Iudaeos* tradition; notably, such recourse to biblical evidence does not prevent Moses from admitting the compel-

---

115. Ibid., col. 582.
116. Ibid., cols. 582–83: "Quodigitur et a naturae usu dissentit, et ipsi prophetae contrarietatem ingerit, nequaquam secundum libitum uniuscujusque ad sensum naturae contrarium debet exponi, cum aliter sano sensu possit intelligi, nisi necessaria ratio ita coegerit accipi."
117. Ibid., col. 588.
118. Ibid., col. 618.
119. Ibid., col. 651; see also Tolan, *Petrus Alfonsi*, pp. 39–41.

ling rationality of Peter's arguments throughout their discussion. Echoing Anselm's counsel that faith must lead to understanding, the *Dialogi* close with Peter's statement that if Moses will accept on faith what Christians accept on faith (*si tu quod credimus, ipse etiam crederes*),[120] he too will receive the divine illumination that will perfect his intellectual grasp of religious truth.

Alfonsi's *Dialogi* reflect additional features of its Sefardic origins and twelfth-century context. As various investigators have shown, Peter drew on the Hispano-Jewish traditions in which he had grown up to support his denunciation of Islam; he borrowed extensively from the ideas of the tenth-century Jewish philosopher Saadya, who had profound influence on Andalusian Judaism; and the issues over which he criticized rabbinic aggadah, especially the matters of divine corporeality and the resurrection of the dead, engaged numerous Spanish and Provençal Jewish scholars of the High Middle Ages. Perhaps, as Amos Funkenstein has suggested, his work manifests a deeper understanding of Jewish thought than of Christian theology.[121] Alfonsi's love for scientific study may betray a proclivity for the Aristotelian ideas that had begun to gain a foothold and to circulate in Jewish, Muslim, and Christian philosophical circles.[122] Without a doubt, the *Dialogi*'s inclusion of anti-Muslim polemic within an essentially anti-Jewish theological treatise testifies to the new Christian perception of the Jews as one of several groups of infidels that challenged the integrity of the true faith. Granted that Alfonsi devoted much more attention to Judaism in this work—one would hardly expect otherwise from one who had converted to Christianity as a mature adult. Yet the structure of the *Dialogi* illustrates that both religions appeared to Alfonsi as parallel alterna-

---

120. Peter, *Dialogi*, PL 157:672.

121. On Alfonsi's grounding in Jewish tradition, see Funkenstein, *Perceptions*, pp. 183–89; Merchavia, *Church*, chap. 3; Bernard Septimus, "Petrus Alfonsi on the Cult of Mecca," *Speculum* 56 (1981), 517–33; Barbara Phyllis Hurwitz, "*Fidei causa et tui amore*: The Role of Petrus Alphonsi's Dialogues in the History of Jewish-Christian Debate" (Ph.D. diss., Yale University, 1983), esp. chaps. 3–4. On the complexities of medieval Christian ideas concerning bodily resurrection, see Caroline Walker Bynum, *The Resurrection of the Body in Western Christianity, 200–1336*, Lectures on the History of Religions, n.s. 15 (New York, 1995).

122. Cohen, "Mentality," pp. 26ff. and 43 n. 18, with particular reference to Alfonsi's letter to the *perypatetici*. Cf., however, the opposing view of John Tolan, "La *Epístola a los peripatéticos de Francia* de Pedro Alfonso," in *Estudios sobre Pedro Alfonso de Huesca*, ed. María Jesús Lacarra, Colección de estudios altoaragoneses 41 (Huesca, Spain, 1996), pp. 381–402, and *Petrus Alfonsi*, pp. 66–70. Tolan has also provided a critical edition and English translation of the letter, *Petrus Alfonsi*, pp. 163–81.

tives, of like status and worthy of similar polemical refutation. Significantly, Peter here attacks Muslims and Jews on strikingly comparable grounds: for the anthropomorphisms and poor logic allegedly characteristic of their doctrine as well as for their neglect of the true, spiritual interpretation of Scripture.

By all accounts, the most noteworthy attribute of the *Dialogi* remains its diatribe against the teachings of the talmudic rabbis. Alfonsi was the first medieval Christian writer to employ rabbinic texts in his anti-Jewish polemic in any extensive or systematic fashion. Agobard of Lyons, we recall, knew of and mentioned various postbiblical Jewish teachings, but he displayed neither any personal familiarity with postbiblical Jewish sources nor any sense of their importance for Jews and their religion. That Alfonsi had genuine knowledge of rabbinic books appears undeniable; whether he had firsthand access to them or consulted some anthology of excerpts from talmudic and midrashic literature, either in their original language or in translation, is unclear but of lesser importance at present.[123] Alfonsi's assessment of the rabbis (*vestri doctores*, as he speaks of them to Moses in the *Dialogi*) and their literature (*doctrina*) in his overall evaluation of the Jews and Judaism matters much more. In view of subsequent developments in Christian anti-Jewish polemic of the twelfth and thirteenth centuries, one needs to ascertain whether Alfonsi attacked rabbinic aggadot individually, to demonstrate their specific errors and thus to discredit Judaism, or viewed these homilies as exemplifying the singular and erroneous nature of rabbinic Judaism in general. Put more simply, did the specific homilies that Alfonsi attacked lead him to consider biblical and rabbinic Judaism as qualitatively different kinds of Jewish disbelief? Did the errors he perceived in rabbinic texts bear upon the character and function of the Jews in his Christian scheme of things?

The aggadah's ostensive attribution of human characteristics to God upset Alfonsi most; he condemned such homilies and their rabbinic authors for demeaning the divine majesty and perfection and for deviating from the teachings of reason and Scripture. Peter has no dearth of disparaging terms with which he characterizes such rabbinic error in the *Dialogi*: bad, evil, insane, indecent, ridiculous, worthy of derision, stupid, foolish, lewd—the list goes on. Beyond his intense dislike for this rabbinic lore, however, some recent investigators of Alfonsi and his writings have detected an indictment of the Jews for heresy.

123. Merchavia, *Church*, pp. 94, 122–23.

According to one recent monograph, "Alfonsi wishes to show that these texts contain doctrine heretical by the standards of classical Judaism, making Judaism as it was practiced by Alfonsi's contemporaries a heretical deviation from the Law."[124] And from here one can proceed to the conclusions that "the *Dialogi* present a radically new attack on Judaism, far more negative than the Latin works of the Augustinian tradition," that "Judaism for Alfonsi is a conspiratorial, anti-Christian sect," and that the thirteenth-century "vilification of the Talmud by the friars [as heretical] was anticipated by Peter Alfonsi (whose *Dialogi* were widely disseminated)."[125] From such a perspective—that is, if Alfonsi posited a rupture between biblical and rabbinic Judaism, such that contemporary Jews no longer provide the biblical testimony central to the Augustinian doctrine of Jewish witness but rather undermine the welfare of Christian society—he and his opus represent a major turning point in the history of Christian anti-Judaism.

Do the *Dialogi* in fact support such a reading of Alfonsi? Some evidence may suggest that they do. First, Peter repeatedly charges that the Jewish sages misinform concerning the meaning of Scripture: Not only do they misinterpret its text, they teach that which has no basis in the Bible or at times contradicts it outright. Regarding the aggadah that God wears phylacteries, for example, Peter questions Moses: "Whence was the mystery of so secret a matter revealed to your sages, when neither Moses himself left written record of it anywhere nor did any prophet after him report it?"[126] How could the rabbis call Balaam wicked when Moses himself labeled him a prophet; they must considered themselves wiser than Moses![127] Belief that God grieves over the Jews' exile implies that the deity has no power to rectify the situation, and this contradicts the numerous biblical stories of divine miracles; it is therefore abominable (*nefas*).[128] Second, Peter expresses his generalized opposition to the very idea of an

124. Tolan, *Petrus Alfonsi*, p. 22. See also the lengthier explication of this view in John Tolan, "Los *Diálogos contra los Judíos*," in *Estudios sobre Pedro Alfonso de Huesca*, ed. María Jesús Lacarra, Colección de estudios altoaragoneses 41 (Huesca, Spain, 1996), esp. pp. 181–93.

125. Tolan, *Petrus Alfonsi*, p. 19; Abulafia, *Christians and Jews*, p. 138. Tolan's ensuing quotation of Alfonsi, that Judaism "is faithful to the Old Law 'only in part, and that part is not pleasing to God,'" simply takes the title of the *Dialogi*'s chap. 4 (PL 157:593) out of its context; for the chapter intends to demonstrate that in their dispersion the Jews are unable to observe most of the commandments of the Old Testament, not that they have substituted new laws for them.

126. Peter, *Dialogi*, PL 157:542.

127. Ibid., col. 550. In Numbers 22:5, the Vulgate translates the Hebrew *Petor*, the place of Balaam's residence, as *ariolum* (seer), as if the Hebrew read *poter*.

128. Peter, *Dialogi*, PL 157:551.

oral law originating in the revelation at Sinai, a notion that constituted the cornerstone of rabbinic Jewish theology. To the question (just quoted) concerning the source of the homily on God's phylacteries, Moses responds that the tale was transmitted from ancient Jewish teachers to contemporary ones. To this Peter retorts: "When your argument strays to the shelter of so irrational a conclusion, you will feel free to affirm every falsehood as the tradition of the ancients."[129] Along similar lines, Peter implies on occasion that the career of Jesus signified a watershed in the history of Judaism, marking its transition from a divinely countenanced religion to a rabbinic distortion thereof. When Moses objects that Peter contradicts himself in the *Dialogi*, first lauding the rabbis of Jesus' day for their piety and understanding and then condemning their subsequent—and enduring—misunderstanding of God's law, Peter replies that his praise applied only to the sages who lived before the advent of Christ.[130] Understandably, then, the Jewish sages who lived after Jesus contrived the unconscionable belief in the resurrection of the dead during the messianic era; no one had mentioned it before.[131] Similarly, rabbis who followed Jesus introduced the requirement of baptism for converts to Judaism, and, falsely ascribing the rule to Moses, "they ushered the people into error."[132] Finally, Peter argues that the sages understood the gravity of Jewish guilt for the crucifixion and of the enduring punishment in which it has resulted, but they deliberately withheld the facts from the people, even altering the contents of the famous rabbinic story of the ten martyrs that would have revealed the truth.[133] Peter maintains further that the first-century leaders of the Jews moved to crucify Jesus because of their envy of him and their fear that he would deprive them of their privileged position. I have elsewhere demonstrated the link between the indictment of the Jews for intentional deicide and the notion that rabbinic Jews had deliberately deserted their biblical heritage: Simple disbelief (*infidelitas*) derived from blindness and ignorance, but deliberate rejection of the truth despite full awareness of it amounted to heresy. Did Peter make this critical connection, and, if so, was he mindful of its implications? Some students of Alfonsi have responded in the affirmative.[134]

129. Ibid., col. 543.
130. Ibid., cols. 595–96.
131. Ibid., col. 582.
132. Ibid., col. 660.
133. Ibid., cols. 573–76.
134. Tolan, *Petrus Alfonsi*, pp. 19ff., and "*Diálogos*," pp. 190ff.; and Abulafia, *Christians and Jews*, p. 120.

Nevertheless, further evidence casts considerable doubt on such a reading of Alfonsi. Although Alfonsi accused the rabbis of fomenting error among the Jews, the *Dialogi* pose the dispute between Jews and Christians as pertaining to hermeneutics above all else. "Make me understand," Moses charges Peter as their discussion opens, "how it seems to you that the Jews have erred in their interpretation of the law [that is, the Old Testament], and how you in fact understand it better." And Peter replies: "insofar as I see them attending only to the superficial meaning of the law, expounding the letter not spiritually but carnally, whence they have been deluded by the greatest error." When Moses asks for specific examples, Peter provides his aforementioned list of major plaints: anthropomorphism in the aggadah, the belief that observance of the law will result in redemption from captivity, and the belief that Jews still observe the law in a manner pleasing to God.[135] It appears, then, that Peter's condemnation of Judaism, developed at length in the first four chapters of the *Dialogi*, gives expression to his conviction that the Jews misinterpret Scripture, not that they have abandoned it. Even over the issue of divine corporeality, the linchpin in Peter's attack on talmudic aggadah, the debate focuses on methods of exegesis. Moses brings support from ostensive anthropomorphism in the Bible; "if it is explained literally, I do not know why you say that it is absurd." For his part, Peter argues otherwise:

> The sayings of the prophets are obscure, not sufficiently clear to everyone. For this reason, when we find things in the prophetic books in which, interpreting them literally, we would stray from the path of reason, we must interpret them allegorically, so that we may return to the path of rectitude. Necessity compels us to do this, since otherwise the meaning of the letter can make no sense [*non potest litterae ratio stare*]. Your doctors, however, have not recognized God as one should; explaining the words of the prophets superficially, they have fallen into error concerning him.[136]

Adherence to the letter of Scripture underlies the misunderstanding of the Jews and their rabbinic homilies. Even when Peter supplies convincing rational proof for his argument, Moses repeatedly requests that he furnish biblical evidence, for the Jew best understands and appreciates the text of the Bible. "Thereby at least authority might establish the faith for those whose minds the weight of profound argumentation will not illuminate."[137] One invariably recalls the Jew Leo in Odo of

135. Peter, *Dialogi*, PL 157:540.
136. Ibid., col. 553.
137. Ibid., col. 586; cf. also cols. 608, 651.

Cambrai's *Disputatio*, who admitted the validity of rational arguments for the incarnation and virgin birth but who refused to convert for fear of abandoning the law. Alfonsi viewed Judaism as so firmly grounded in the literal reading of Scripture that the rabbis would never interpret sacred texts otherwise. It was self-evident to him that Judaism's literalist hermeneutic extended to rabbinic aggadot as well—hence his Christian insistence on the figurative interpretation of biblical anthropomorphisms and his failure to consider that Jews might adopt a similar approach to rabbinic ones. Here lies the crux of the issue: From Peter's Christian perspective, any Jewish interpretation of the Old Testament was necessarily literal, as opposed to its true, allegorical, Christological meaning; such was the carnal nature of the Jews, and such was their role in the divine economy of salvation. Although his Hispano-Jewish upbringing and education should have enabled Peter to allow for the figurative interpretation of the aggadah—or at least to explain the postbiblical character of contemporary Judaism to his Christian readers more systematically—an essentially Augustinian theological perspective prevented him from doing so. The Jews represented the letter of the sacred text. At the beginning of their discussion, Moses thus contends and Peter agrees that the Jews are the guardians of the law (*legis cultores*).[138] Admittedly, Peter insists that their exposition of the law resembles the chatter of schoolboys and women.[139] But that hardly makes them heretics.

These considerations should assist in evaluating the remaining evidence for Alfonsi's alleged indictment of rabbinic Judaism as heretical. Peter's observation that the Jewish teachers and scribes killed Jesus out of envy and fear need not imply that they knew his real identity.[140]

---

138. Ibid., col. 540.

139. Ibid., cols. 540, 567.

140. Despite his inference (above, n. 134) that Alfonsi condemned the Jews for killing the son of God not out of ignorance but out of envy—and therefore intentionally—Tolan, *Petrus Alfonsi*, p. 217 n. 34, himself admits that "envy and blindness are not necessarily incompatible." Based on my study of "The Jews as the Killers of Christ," pp. 11–12, Tolan further recognizes that Bede articulated this conclusion several centuries before Alfonsi, albeit for exegetical rather than polemical considerations. I think it significant that although Bede had explicitly linked the Jews' envy to a lack of ignorance, drawing the conclusion that Tolan attributes to Alfonsi—"Iudaeorum principes non per ignorantiam sed per invidiam crucifixisse filium Dei" (*In Marci Evangelium expositio*, CCSL 120:585)—Peter did not. In fact, Peter considered first-century Jewish leaders ignorant of Jesus' salvific role and thus joined other twelfth-century churchmen in linking the Jews' ignorance with their envy. Cf. Rupert of Deutz, *In Iohannis Evangelium* 9 (ad 9:41), CCCM 9:510: "Nam vere caeci sunt per odium lucis et veritatis"; and Robert of

Alfonsi, recall, lavished praise on the talmudic sages at the time of Jesus, "righteous men, who ought to have been prophets, had it been a time of prophecy."[141] Such an appraisal would surely not comport with their condemnation for intentional deicide, but it would less likely preclude their succumbing to greed and opportunism, much like the biblical Jeroboam who, as Peter explains, seceded from the united Israelite kingdom after Solomon's death despite his wisdom. Peter can therefore include these guilty Jews in Jesus' acclaimed prayer from the cross (Luke 23:34): "Father, forgive them; they do not know what they are doing."[142] More revealing still, to Moses' query as to why Peter has condemned the Jews if Jesus freely willed to die for the salvation of humankind, Peter responds by drawing two analogies: to someone who burns the ship of his enemy, "ignorant of the latter's desire [*nescius voluntatis huius*]" to burn it in any event; and to one who plans to demolish his house in order to use the stones in a different building but finds it destroyed by his enemy, "not for the sake of fulfilling the owner's wishes of which he was ignorant [*nesciebat*] but out of hatred." Having secured Moses' admission that he who burned the ship and he who tore down the house are guilty and deserve punishment, Peter concludes: "For the same reason, those who killed Christ, not in order to fulfill his wishes but under the spell of hatred and envy, are guilty and deserving of judgment."[143] Like the destroyers of ship and house in Peter's analogies, and despite their condemnable hostility toward Jesus, they too must have been ignorant of Jesus' intentions and, therefore, of his identity.

What most closely approaches a condemnation of rabbinic Judaism as a heretical departure from the religion of the Old Testament is Al-

---

Melun, *De Epistula I ad Corinthios*, ad 2:8, in Robert of Melun, *Oeuvres*, ed. Raymond M. Martin and R. M. Gallet (Louvain, Belgium, 1932–52), 2:181: "Si sciebant eum esse Deum, sciebant eum esse inmortalem, quare nec mori posse. Quomodo ergo eius mortem querebant, si eum non posse mori sciebant . . . ? Invidia tamen concitati, persequi non desistebant. Huius enim nature est invidia, ut contra sua bona aliena incommoda querat." On Rupert's ascription of the Jews' exegetical blindness to their envy, see David E. Timmer, "Biblical Exegesis and the Jewish-Christian Controversy in the Early Twelfth Century," *Church History* 58 (1989), 317–18; and on a similar convergence of Jewish characteristics in the *Glossa ordinaria*, see Michael A. Signer, "The *Glossa ordinaria* and the Transmission of Medieval Anti-Judaism," in *A Distinct Voice: Medieval Studies in Honor of Leonard E. Boyle, O.P.*, ed. Jacqueline Brown and William P. Stoneman (Notre Dame, Ind., 1997), pp. 597–98.
141. Peter, *Dialogi*, PL 157:569–70.
142. Ibid., cols. 649–50.
143. Ibid., col. 646.

fonsi's distinction between the praiseworthy Jewish sages who preceded Jesus and the deceitful ones who followed him; here Alfonsi did anticipate the more concerted expressions of subsequent Christian polemicists. Nevertheless, although Alfonsi thereby suggested a potential rationale for the indictment of contemporary Judaism as heresy, he himself did not follow through to draw the conclusion, and one wonders whether he actually appreciated the possibility. Anyone conversant with talmudic literature should have realized that two or three of the five laudable sages chosen by Alfonsi to exemplify the righteousness of the late ancient Jewish community[144] not only lived after Jesus but outlived the destruction of the second temple; the Talmud portrayed Yochanan ben Zakkai, Chanina ben Dosa, and Akiva ben Joseph as standing at the forefront of the rabbinic enterprise that Alfonsi appeared to condemn. Peter further obscures the suggestive distinction between Judaism before and after Jesus by freely citing passages from the Talmud, the midrash,[145] and even a rabbinic text entitled *Secreta secretorum* (Secrets of Secrets)[146] in support of Christian doctrine, while making no effort to reconcile the inconsistency this entailed. Nowhere does he claim that all of these worthy rabbinic teachings preceded the career of Jesus or that all of the condemnable instruction came later. As opposed to the thirteenth-century friars who found proof for Christianity in rabbinic texts and simultaneously branded rabbinic Judaism a heresy, Alfonsi simply did not unravel the significance—or ensure the consistency—of his arguments. His attack on the rabbis notwithstanding, Peter explains to Moses in the *Dialogi* that God has permitted the Jewish people to live on, even after their deicide, so that they might serve all other peoples, so that, dispersed throughout the world, they might offer living witness to the magnitude of their crime, and so that they might ultimately convert to Christianity.[147] Although Peter does

---

144. See above, at n. 105.

145. Ibid., cols. 567–81 passim, 596 (God no longer hears the prayers of the Jews since the destruction of their temple), 650 (the righteous are resurrected to heaven immediately upon their death), and 665 (the first day of Passover may not fall on Monday, Wednesday, or Friday).

146. Ibid., col. 611; for the text's identification, see Merchavia, *Church*, pp. 123–24.

147. Peter, *Dialogi*, PL 157:574–75:

Quid putas causae est propter quod Deus gentem hanc ubique terrarum dispersam perpetuae servituti subjecit, et tot malorum multatione damnavit? Respondebitque alter: Ob tale peccatum, quod Dei Filium invidiae tantum causa occiderunt, ideo in haec mala devenerunt. Quod si in ipso tempore quo peccatum a vobis est

not cite Psalm 59:12 in this context, the key Pauline and Augustinian motifs of Jewish servitude and Jewish testimony still figured prominently in Alfonsi's estimations of the Jews and Judaism.

On balance, then, Peter Alfonsi certainly took a pioneering step in his citation of rabbinic sources, both to discredit Judaism and to validate Christianity. We can appropriately include him, along with Anselm and his northern European colleagues, among the proponents of a new rationalist approach to anti-Jewish polemic around the turn of the twelfth century. As these spokesmen for Christianity sought to present the truth of their faith as self-evident, they underscored those rational, universally acceptable arguments that they could muster in its behalf. Against the background of the changing map of twelfth-century Christendom, they directed their polemic at Jews and at other infidels, grouping the Jews together with Muslims, other pagans, and heterodox Christians. The Jew began to share Christian attention and concern with other unbelievers, at the same time as current events generated new ecclesiastical and scholarly interest in the Jews and Judaism. The polemical treatise of a relatively learned convert like Alfonsi exposed alleged absurdities of rabbinic literature to Christian scrutiny, and this too proved influential in various ways. Some would eventually grapple with the phenomenon of rabbinic Judaism per se and seek to define its place in Christendom's taxonomy of infidelitas. Others would soon extrapolate from their assessment of the idea to an ad hominem reappraisal of its Jewish exponents, which, as in the case of Guibert of Nogent, might be nothing short of vitriolic.

All of these developments had the potential for "hollowing out" the Augustinian doctrine of Jewish witness,[148] with its fundamental maxim of "Slay them not." Yet these seeds planted at the beginning of the twelfth century, at times haphazardly and unwittingly, germinated and bore fruit slowly. One cannot overemphasize the graduality of this pro-

---

commissum, totam Judaicam progeniem funditus delevisset, multis temporum circulis transactis, culpa oblivione deleta, a nullo mortalium sciretur, sicque et infamiae opprobrium, et malorum evitaretis periculum, sicut et de multis contigit gentibus et regibus, quorum gesta temporum sunt vetustate deleta. Est et alia causa, propter quam Deus Judaicam noluit perdere gentem. Videbat enim quosdam de semine vestro quandoque in se credituros, atque salvandos, et ideo propter eos noluit omnino vestram disperdere stirpem.

148. As in Abulafia, *Christians and Jews*, p. 134.

cess. While some seemed to move farther away from Augustinian teaching, others appeared to reaffirm it quite strenuously. But the rising and sharpening interest in the Jew proved irreversible, especially as contact between Christendom and the non-Christian world increased. Crusading and its ideology provided one such stimulus for rethinking the place of the Jew in a Christian scheme of things, with markedly mixed results.

CHAPTER 6

Against the Backdrop of Holy War

*Bernard of Clairvaux and
Peter the Venerable*

Writing just prior to, during, and in the wake of the First Crusade, the Christian authors considered in the preceding chapter could not avoid the influence of current events and the world around them. As I suggested, the anti-Jewish violence of 1096, though not a part of the official mandate of the crusaders, invariably roused many churchmen to come to grips with the problematic function of the Jew in Christian society. Concerns sharpened and perspectives matured. Concurrently, confrontation with the Muslim world induced many to associate Jews and Muslims, projecting the characteristics of one group onto the other and incorporating both groups into a larger genus of infidels who, by their existence and in their beliefs, challenged the supremacy of Christianity. No one, to be sure, posited complete equivalence between Jew and Muslim; Gratian canonized Pope Alexander II's ruling of *Dispar nimirum est*, "the situation of the Jews is surely different from that of the Saracens," in the statutes of his *Decretum*, completed in 1140.[1] Nonetheless, parallels between the two groups in matters of law and

Portions of my ensuing treatment of Bernard appeared in Jeremy Cohen, "'Witnesses of Our Redemption': The Jews in the Crusading Theology of Bernard of Clairvaux," in *Medieval Studies in Honour of Avrom Saltman*, ed. Bat-Sheva Albert et al., Bar-Ilan Studies in History 4 (Ramat Gan, Israel, 1995), pp. 67–81, copyright © Bar-Ilan University Press, Ramat Gan, and are included here with the kind permission of Bar-Ilan University Press.

    1. See above, introduction to part 3, n. 40.

ideology certainly made sense, and the tendency to classify them together proved irreversible.

The present chapter takes us forward into the 1140s and the writings
of two of the most influential churchmen of the High Middle Ages. By
midcentury the schism between Pope Innocent II and antipope Anacletus II, whose Jewish lineage probably contributed much to his defeat,[2]
and the anti-Jewish hostilities accompanying the Second Crusade had
only intensified the Jewish problem for Christian theologians. The issue
of the Jews' role in a properly ordered Christian society, particularly
one at war with the infidel to avenge the sufferings of the crucified
Jesus and his memory, assumed a new dimension of practical relevance.
Peter the Venerable, the Benedictine abbot of Cluny, and Bernard of
Clairvaux, leader of the recently founded Cistercian order, involved
themselves both in the papal schism and in the call for the Crusade.
Each supported Innocent over Anacletus, and each took a stance on
the proper station of the Jews in Christendom as he voiced his staunch
support of holy war. Not insignificantly, the two abbots found themselves involved—and at times at loggerheads with one another—in several other ecclesiastical causes célèbres of their day, from the rivalry
between old and new monastic orders to the expanding, controversial
place of dialectic in Christian theology. As a pair, Bernard and Peter
inherited, developed, and applied some of the noteworthy contributions
of Anselm and his disciples to the Christian perception of the Jew: the
conflation of Jews with other infidels, the concomitant construction of
Judaism as a category of *infidelitas* or disbelief, the linkage between
Jewish carnality and irrationality, and the encounter with the postbiblical literature of the Talmud. At the same time, the writings of
Bernard and Peter demonstrate the graduality and complexity of the
these developments. As the new ideas interacted with older, more established Christian traditions concerning Jews and Judaism, they
yielded ambivalence and inconsistency, and they produced variegated
mixtures of the Augustinian doctrine of Jewish witness with assumptions underlying a more exclusionary brand of late medieval anti-
Judaism.

2. See Aryeh Graboïs, "From 'Theological' to 'Racial' Antisemitism: The Controversy
of the Jewish Pope in the Twelfth Century" [Hebrew], *Zion*, n.s. 47 (1982), 1–16; and
Mary Stroll, *The Jewish Pope: Ideology and Politics in the Papal Schism of 1130*, Brill's
Studies in Intellectual History 8 (Leiden, Netherlands, 1987), esp. chap. 15.

BERNARD

Radulf . . . , the priest of idolatry, arose against the nation of God to destroy, slay, and annihilate them just as wicked Haman had attempted to do. He set forth from France and traveled across the entire land of Germany . . . to seek out and contaminate the Christians with the horizontal-vertical sign. . . . Wherever he went, he spoke evil of the Jews of the land and incited the snake and the dogs against us. . . . The lord heard our outcry, and he turned to us and had pity upon us. In his great mercy and grace, he sent a decent priest, one honored and respected by all the clergy in France, named Abbot Bernard, of Clairvaux in France, to deal with this evil person. Bernard . . . said to them: "It is good that you go against the Ishmaelites. But whosoever touches a Jew to take his life, is like one who harms Jesus himself . . . , for in the book of Psalms it is written of them, 'Slay them not, lest my people forget.'" All the Gentiles regarded this priest as one of their saints. . . . When our enemies heard his words, many of them ceased plotting to kill us. . . . Were it not for the mercy of our creator in sending the aforementioned abbot and his later epistles, no remnant or vestige would have remained of Israel. Blessed be the redeemer and savior, blessed be his name.[3]

The rabbinic leaders of medieval European Jewry did not lavish their praise upon many a Christian cleric; these words of Rabbi Efraim of Bonn's *Sefer Zekhirah* (Book of Remembrance), a narrative lament over the anti-Jewish violence that accompanied the Second Crusade, testify to a noteworthy phenomenon indeed. Their subject, Bernard of Clairvaux (1090–1153), numbered among the most powerful Catholic luminaries of the twelfth century. Guiding light of the Cistercian Order, consultant to popes, prelates, and princes, ideologue of the Second Crusade, and pioneering champion of monastic theology and mysticism, Bernard represented key aspects of the distinctive cultural creativity of Latin Christendom in the High Middle Ages.[4] His career, his person-

---

3. A. Neubauer and M. Stern, *Hebräische Berichte über die Judenverfolgungen während der Kreuzzüge*, Quellen der Geschichte der Juden in Deutschland 2 (Berlin, 1892), p. 59; I have departed slightly from the translation of Shlomo Eidelberg, *The Jews and the Crusaders: The Hebrew Chronicles of the First and Second Crusades* (Madison, Wis., 1977), pp. 121–22. See Kenneth R. Stow, *The "1007 Anonymous" and Papal Sovereignty: Jewish Perceptions of the Papacy and Papal Policy in the High Middle Ages,* Hebrew Union College Annual Supplements 4 (Cincinnati, Ohio, 1984), pp. 4ff., 21ff., who has located Efraim at the beginning of a series of medieval Jewish writers who recognized, applauded, and studied the protective policy of the church vis-à-vis the Jews, understanding that the survival of European Jewry depended heavily upon it.

4. Among many others, see Watkin Williams, *St. Bernard of Clairvaux* (Westminster, Md., 1952); E. Rozanne Elder and John R. Sommerfeldt, eds., *The Chimaera of His Age: Studies on Bernard of Clairvaux*, Cistercian Studies 63, 5 (Kalamazoo, Mich., 1980); G. R. Evans, *The Mind of St. Bernard of Clairvaux* (Oxford, 1983); and Jean Leclercq,

ality, and his scholarly opus embodied much of that special twelfth-
century ethos that began to undermine the established position of the
Jews and Judaism in a traditional Christian mentality. Still, as contemporary Jews hastened to acknowledge, Bernard displayed unusual concern for the safety of Jews during the Crusade that he himself helped
to inspire. Efraim did not overlook Bernard's championship of the Augustinian policy of "Slay them not," which called for preserving the
Jews on account of their embodiment of the church's biblical heritage.
The abbot of Clairvaux himself construed the Jews as "living letters"
of the law, and this book thus owes its title to him. How can one make
sense of his conformity to new patterns of twelfth-century thought, on
one hand, and his commitment to the Augustinian doctrine of Jewish
witness, on the other? Where, precisely, does he fit in our story?

A survey of references to the Jews and Judaism in Bernard's opus
places him squarely within long-standing traditions of *Adversus
Iudaeos* in Christian theology.[5] Bernard's writings echo many of the
standard anti-Jewish stereotypes that one finds strewn throughout the
works of his patristic and early medieval predecessors: The Jews have
always been cruel, jealous, and incredulous. Having hatefully expelled
and crucified its own child Jesus, the synagogue continued to spurn the
light of faith, heaping reproach and blasphemy upon its savior, and it
even sought, spitefully, to stand between the Gentiles and Christian
salvation. Hard of heart and superstitious, the Jews and their teachers
have concerned themselves with the carnal, exterior meaning of their
law, blindly shunning its true, interior, spiritual meaning; within the
divine economy of salvation, they have functioned as the agents of the
devil. And the list goes on.[6]

Without negating the significance of Bernard's traditional stance vis-
à-vis the Jews, a more deliberate rereading of his writings reveals sev-

---

Bernard de Clairvaux, Bibliothèque d'histoire du Christianisme 19 (Paris, 1989). On the
historical background of the Second Crusade, see also Steven Runciman, *A History of
the Crusades, Volume II: The Kingdom of Jerusalem and the Frankish East, 1100–1187*
(1952; reprint, New York, 1965), pp. 247–88; and Virginia G. Berry, "The Second Crusade," in *A History of the Crusades, Volume I: The First Hundred Years*, gen. ed. Kenneth M. Setton, ed. Marshall W. Baldwin (Madison, Wis., 1969), pp. 463–512.

    5. David Berger, "The Attitude of St. Bernard of Clairvaux toward the Jews," *Pro-
ceedings of the American Academy for Jewish Research* 40 (1972), 89–108.

    6. See, for example, the diverse comments in three of Bernard's *Sermones: In vigilia
nativitatis* 6.11, *In feria IV hebdomadae sanctae*, and *In resurrectione Domini* 1, in
Bernard of Clairvaux, *Opera*, ed. Jean Leclercq et al. (Rome, 1957–77), 4:243, 5:56–67,
73–94.

eral themes worthy of additional comment. First, one cannot avoid the pervasive ambivalence concerning the Jewish people, for which Bernard remained heavily indebted to Augustine. Jewish misunderstanding of divine revelation notwithstanding, the sacred texts and traditions of the Jews contain not heresy but the true word of God; for all of their hypocrisy and sin, the Jewish scribes and Pharisees surely did sit in the chair of Moses (Matthew 23:2). The Jews persecuted Jesus and his followers blindly, out of ignorance. Owing, perhaps, to their kinship with Jesus, God has preserved the Jews, albeit in a state of subjugation and servitude. "No servitude is more dishonorable or more burdensome than the servitude of the Jews," Bernard wrote Pope Eugenius III;[7] and yet, "present circumstances excuse you" from fighting the Jews in the militant manner that the church must now combat other infidels and heretics, inasmuch as the time mandated by God for Israel's forgiveness and redemption has not yet materialized.[8] In all this, Bernard's instruction innovated little. As David Berger and others have noted, however, the tone of moderation in his teaching extends still farther.[9] Although one rightly criticizes the Jews for their worldly orientation and materialism, they did receive God's promise of temporal reward and thus come upon their worldly gain by right.[10] And, though surely not as much as Christians do, Bernard was prepared to acknowledge that even the Jew can espouse a love for God.[11]

Second, Bernard followed Anselm, Guibert of Nogent, and others in highlighting Jewish carnality:

If [as in Isaiah 40:6–8] all mortal flesh is like grass, then that carnal people of the Jews was like grass. Has not the grass withered, just as that people, devoid of all fullness of the spirit, has adhered to the dry letter? Has not the flower died, while the vaunting which they used to derive from the law has remained? But if that flower has not died, where, then, is the kingdom,

7. Bernard of Clairvaux, *De consideratione* 1.3.4, in *Opera*, ed. Leclercq et al., 3: 398.
8. Ibid. 3.1.3, in *Opera*, ed. Leclercq et al., 3:433.
9. See Berger, "Attitude," and the authors cited below, n. 68.
10. Bernard of Clairvaux, *Sermones in festivitate omnium sanctorum* 1.7, in *Opera*, ed. Leclercq et al., 5:332: "Sic vos insensati filii Adam, divitias quaeretis, divitias desideratis usque adhuc, cum iam beatitudo pauperum divinitus commendata, praedicata mundo, credita sit ab hominibus? Quaerat eas paganus, qui sine Deo vivit; quaerat Iudaeus, qui terras promissiones accepit."
11. Bernard, *De diligendo* 3.7, in *Opera*, ed. Leclercq et al., 3:124: "Facile proinde plus diligunt, qui se amplius dilectos intelligunt; cui autem minus donatum est minus diligit. Iudaeus sane, sive paganus, nequaquam talibus aculeis incitatur amoris, quales Ecclesia experitur."

where is the priesthood, where are the prophets, where is the temple, and where are those wondrous things of which they were accustomed to boast?[12]

Bernard, too, associated Jewish carnality with a strictly literalist exegesis of Scripture, and Jewish exegesis, in turn, he linked with a singular, inhuman sort of intellectual deficiency. Like Anselm and Guibert, he had little interest in the literal, historical meaning of the Bible but focused on the allegorical and, even more, on the moral or tropological sense of the sacred text.

Third, Bernard followed Anselm in his construction of the Jews as a category of disbelief, a typos of misguided orientation in matters spiritual. His Jews, as one investigator has recognized with surprise, "remain in a peculiar way unreal"[13]—a perception that could militate both toward moderation and toward racial-ethnic stereotyping in Bernard's writings. Defending Bernard against allegations of antisemitism, numerous scholars have emphasized that Bernard included Christians in various condemnations of the Jews.[14] Bad Catholics, for whose salvation God's son sacrificed his blood, are worse than the Jews who slew him. Christians who do not follow Jesus as they should accordingly share in God's judgment of the Jews and in their unparalleled guilt for the crucifixion.[15] Self-righteous critics of established monastic rules are the "new Pharisees";[16] cells of unsupervised monks are "synagogues of Satan";[17] heretics exceed the archetypical blindness of the Jews, so that in their eyes "the churches are regarded as synagogues."[18] And, in one of Bernard's most oft-quoted comments concerning the Jews, Christian usurers "out-Jew" the Jews themselves: "Wherever there are no Jews, we lament that Christian moneylenders—if it is fitting for them to be called Christians and not more [appropriately] baptized Jews—behave Jewishly in a manner even worse [*peius iudai-*

12. Bernard, *Sermones in laudibus virginis matris* 1.4, in *Opera*, ed. Leclercq et al., 4:17.

13. Friedrich Lotter, "The Position of the Jews in Early Cistercian Exegesis and Preaching," in *FWW*, p. 174.

14. For instance, ibid., pp. 164–65, 173–74; and cf. Friedrich Lotter, "Das Prinzip der 'Hebraica veritas' und die heilsgeschichtliche Rolle Israels bei den frühen Zisterziensern," in *Bibel in jüdischer und christlicher Tradition: Festschrift für Johann Maier zum 60. Geburtstag*, ed. Helmut Merklein et al., Bonner biblische Beiträge 88 (Frankfurt am Main, 1993), pp. 480–81, 503.

15. Bernard of Clairvaux, *Sermo in feria IV hebdomadae sanctae* 11, in *Opera*, ed. Leclercq et al., 5:64; and *Sermones super Cantica canticorum* 11.2, 46.5, 75.10, in *Opera*, ed. Leclercq et al., 1:55–56, 2:58–59, 253.

16. Bernard, *Epistulae* 91.4, in *Opera*, ed. Leclercq et al., 7:240.

17. Ibid. 254.1, in *Opera*, ed. Leclercq et al., 8:156.

18. Ibid. 241.1, in *Opera*, ed. Leclercq et al., 8:125.

zare]."[19] Although some scholars have read this statement as a nondiscriminatory—that is, not specifically anti-Jewish—condemnation of usury, others have beheld a definition of the immoralities of usury as essentially Jewish in nature, attributing a new, quasi-racist variety of anti-Judaism to the Cistercian abbot. As Lester Little has suggested, "Bernard thereby gave new significance to a hitherto innocuous Latin verb, *iudaizare*, which meant merely to proselytize and to convert people to Judaism, a counterpart of the verb 'to Christianize.' The money trade, the crucial activity of the Commercial Revolution, was thus now considered to be exclusively the work of the Jews. Christian moneylenders were really Jews."[20] In a similar seemingly racist vein, as he ardently supported Innocent II over his rival Anacletus, Bernard denounced the latter as "that beast of the Apocalypse"[21] and as "the enemy of the cross,"[22] proclaiming that "it constitutes an injury to Christ for someone of Jewish lineage to have seized the throne of Peter."[23]

The foregoing allusions to the Jews in Bernard's writings suffice to demonstrate the complexity of his attitudes. Nevertheless, as stipulated throughout this book, one can best attempt to understand Christian perceptions of the Jew and Judaism by situating them within a broader matrix of their perceivers' ideas. In Bernard's case, the Jews had a place in his formulations on at least two central doctrinal concerns: the interpretation of the Song of Songs, and the call for the Second Crusade.

THE HERMENEUTICS OF SACRED LOVE

Bernard composed eighty-six sermons on the Song of Songs during the last eighteen years of his life; he completed his exposition of just two of the canticle's eight chapters by the time of his death.[24] Frequently

19. See below, at n. 57.
20. Lester K. Little, *Religious Poverty and the Profit Economy in Medieval Europe* (Ithaca, N.Y., 1978), pp. 56–57. Cf. also Stroll, *Jewish Pope*, pp. 125, 159ff.; and Graboïs, "From 'Theology' to 'Racial' Antisemitism," pp. 11ff.
21. Bernard, *Epistulae* 125.1, in *Opera*, ed. Leclercq et al., 7:308.
22. Ibid. 126.7, in *Opera*, ed. Leclercq et al., 7:314; additional objects of this characterization on Bernard's part included Peter Abelard (ibid. 331, 8:269) and the entire collective of Jewish *amatores saeculi* (*Sermones in resurrectione Domini* 1.16, in *Opera*, ed. Leclercq et al., 5:92).
23. Bernard, *Epistulae* 139.1, in *Opera*, ed. Leclercq et al., 7:335–36.
24. On the chronology of these sermons, see the introduction of Jean Leclercq to the fourth volume of Bernard of Clairvaux, *On the Song of Songs*, trans. Kilian Walsh and Irene M. Edmonds, Cistercian Fathers Series 4, 7, 31, 40 (Kalamazoo, Mich., 1971–80), 4:xi–xii. I regularly consulted these volumes in preparing my own translations.

acclaimed as the crowning expression of Bernard's monastic mysticism, these texts articulate the fundamental principles of his Christian world-view, in which the Jews figured instructively. Two clusters of sermons in particular warrant attention here. Sermons 13 through 18 expound the phrase in Song of Songs 1:2 (in the Vulgate), "Your name is oil poured out [*oleum effusum nomen tuum*]," which sermon 14 relates directly to the Jews and Judaism. But one must first take note of sermon 13, in which Bernard focused on the sin of ingratitude to God, committed most offensively by hypocrites—those feigning thanks to the deity for their advantages but actually attributing them to their own virtues or achievements—among whom the Pharisees numbered prominently:

> The Pharisee may offer thanks, and yet there is no divine praise for his justice; for that act of thanksgiving, if you remember the Gospel well, does not render him any more acceptable. For what reason? Because whatever word of devotion may sound in one's mouth does not suffice to excuse the vanity of the heart before him who discerns the depths of a person from afar. Do you not recognize that the Pharisee, in offering thanks, honors God with his lips but himself in the intention of his heart?[25]

Bernard hastened to explain that such hypocrisy afflicts even "extremely religious and spiritual men,"[26] and he vehemently enjoined his monks to guard against it. What has this to do with the bride's cry of affection for her groom, "Your name is oil poured out"? Ingratitude would certainly not become this affectionate bride of Christ, along the symbolic lines Bernard, like so many other medieval commentators, employed to interpret the Song of Songs, and he devoted his next homily, Sermon 14, to a lengthy illustration of his exegesis.

The oil of Song 1:2 signifies the knowledge of God, which the Jews of old refused to share with Gentiles who genuinely craved the light of salvation. "The synagogue protested, asserting that a church of the Gentiles would be impure and unworthy, taunting the baseness of their idolatry and the blindness of their ignorance, and said: 'What right have you? Do not seek to touch me!'"[27] On the model of the Pharisee, the synagogue thereby exemplifies the sin of ingratitude, because, "glorying in the law and congratulating itself for its justice,"[28] it ascribes

25. Bernard, *Sermones super Cantica canticorum* 13.2.2, in ed. Leclercq et al., 1:69.
26. Ibid. 13.3.3, in *Opera*, ed. Leclercq et al., 1:70.
27. Ibid. 14.1.1, in *Opera*, ed. Leclercq et al., 1:75.
28. Ibid., in *Opera*, ed. Leclercq et al., 1:76.

its possession of God's covenant to its merits and jealously refuses to heed the Gentiles' submission to divine grace. As a result, God rewards each group with its just deserts: "The Jew seeks judgment, and let him have it; let the Gentiles honor God for his mercy."[29] Having hoarded the knowledge of God for himself, the Jew forfeits God's favor, while the heavenly oils of divine grace descend upon the breasts (ubera) of the church mentioned in the Latin canticle's opening verse.[30] For its part, "the synagogue still carouses outside with its friends the demons . . . , for it deems itself pure and just from the observance of the law. But when the veil of the mortifying letter is rent upon the death of the crucified word, the church daringly breaks in to his [that is, the word's, Christ's] sanctuary with the spirit of liberty in the lead; she is acknowledged, she is welcome, she is allotted the place of her rival, and she is made his bride."[31] Unlike the synagogue, the church, in becoming the bride of Christ, does not prove ungrateful; for "whereas the synagogue, as we have said, grumbles and recalls its own merits . . . , the church remembers his kindness" and utters the ultimate expression of thanksgiving: "Your name is oil poured out."[32]

Various aspects of this sermon prove especially revealing. Suiting his message to the medium of a biblical commentary, Bernard explained the failure of the Jews as a result of their carnal, literal understanding of God's word, expressed in the message of this verse in particular. With reference to the inability of carnal Israel (Israel secundum carnem) to acknowledge God's love, he asked:

> On what basis could it say this? It is not that it has no oil, but that it has no poured oil. It has it, albeit concealed; it has it in its scriptures but not in people's hearts. In public it clings to the letter; it holds a full, closed jar in its hands, and it does not open it in order to be anointed. . . . Why have oil in jars, if you do not feel it on your limbs? What good does it do you to keep reading the pious name of the savior in your books and to have no piety in your way of life?[33]

29. Ibid.

30. 1:2 in the Masoretic Text, where ddyk is rendered dodekha, "your love," rather than dadekha, "your breasts." Cf. Ivan G. Marcus, Rituals of Childhood: Jewish Acculturation in Medieval Europe (New Haven, Conn., 1996), pp. 89–90.

31. Bernard, Sermones super Cantica canticorum 14.2.4, in ed. Leclercq et al., 1: 78.

32. Ibid. 14.5.7, in Opera, ed. Leclercq et al., 1:80–81.

33. Ibid. 14.5.8, in Opera, ed. Leclercq et al., 1:81. See also Ephraim E. Urbach, "The Homiletical Interpretations of the Sages and the Expositions of Origen on Canticles, and the Jewish-Christian Disputation." In Studies in Aggadah and Folk-Literature, ed. Joseph Heineman and Dov Noy, Scripta hierosolymitana 22 (Jerusalem, 1971), pp. 258–62.

So hermeneutics provides the key to releasing the salvific oil from its jar, or the word of God from the letter: The Jew "relies on the text [*pacto*] of a covenant, I on the accord [*placito*] of God's will."[34] Moreover, although their commitment to the written letter of this covenantal text has brought death and blindness upon them, God will ultimately restore Jews to life and vision. Thus will the Jews' blindness be "partial, for the Lord does not reject his people completely . . . ; he does not reject them for all eternity, for the remnants he will save."[35] This sermon and the ones that follow repeatedly voice the hope that the Jew will acknowledge his destiny and open himself to God: "Open, be anointed, and no longer will you be a rebellious house."[36] Finally, Bernard directed this entreaty and others like it not only to the Jews but also—and probably above all—to Christians. Although he built his exposition of "Your name is oil poured out" on the allegorical contrast between the ungrateful Pharisee and the disciple of Jesus, or that between synagogue and church, he found the truly consequential aspect of this biblical verse in its tropological or moral sense. The church that thus lavishes praise on God is the church of the perfect, outside whose doors rest Bernard and his monks, still not perfected but "reveling in hope" for the future.[37] They now resemble the female companions of the bride in Solomon's Song, who, for the time being, must suffice with "a mere subtle breath, not the rich sprinkling" that Bernard craved.[38] And yet, eschewing all forms of ingratitude, "if they undertake to follow more closely in the footsteps of the mistress, they will delight at least in the odor of the poured oil, and they will be moved by their perception of the odor to desire and seek more noble things."[39] They, too, may eventually address Christ as does his perfect consort.

Several years later, perhaps midway through the 1140s, Bernard again considered the Jews in sermon 60, which expounded the words of the bridegroom (Song 2:13), "The fig tree has brought forth its green

34. Bernard, *Sermones super Cantica canticorum* 14.2.4, in *Opera*, ed. Leclercq et al., 1:78.

35. Ibid. 14.2.2, in *Opera*, ed. Leclercq et al., 1:76.

36. Ibid. 14.5.8, in *Opera*, ed. Leclercq et al., 1:81; cf. also 15.5.8, 16.8.15, in *Opera*, ed. Leclercq et al., 1:87–88, 97–98.

37. Ibid. 14.3.5, in *Opera*, ed. Leclercq et al., 1:79. On the dialectic between perfection and imperfection in these sermons, see also E. Ann Matter, *The Voice of My Beloved: The Song of Songs in Western Medieval Christianity* (Philadelphia, 1990), pp. 123ff.

38. Bernard, *Sermones super Cantica canticorum* 14.4.6, in *Opera*, ed. Leclercq et al., 1:80.

39. Ibid. 14.3.5, in *Opera*, ed. Leclercq et al., 1:79.

figs." Again Bernard laid the groundwork for his discourse in the previous sermon, commenting on "the voice of the turtle-dove is heard in
our land" (Song 2:12), which suggested that the groom had tarried
before coming for his bride: "As long as people received only a terrestrial reward, the land, for their worship of God, even that land flowing
with milk and honey, they hardly recognized that they were wanderers
on earth, and they did not lament in the manner of the turtle-dove as
if they remembered their homeland. Rather, mistaking exile for homeland, they devoted themselves to consuming heavy foods and drinking
sweetened wine. Thus for a long time the voice of the turtledove has
not been heard in our land."[40] The allusion to people who sought exclusively material satisfaction in a land flowing with milk and honey,
such that they mistook that land of their terrestrial exile for the promised land of their supernal home, certainly befits Bernard's perception
of the Jews. Sermon 59 then confirms this inference with a concluding
reference to the green fruit produced by the fig tree, unripe and unfit
for consumption. "Perhaps denoting the hypocrites, they have the appearance of good figs, but only in their likeness, not their taste."[41]
Building on the sermons' earlier characterization of Pharisee and Jew,
the linkage of these figs with carnal Israel should come as no surprise.

Sermon 60 makes that identification definite. According to Bernard,
the Bible clearly intended to describe not an actual fig tree but "a people, weak in their flesh, meager in their perception, humble in their
intellect," as opposed to the fruit of the vine, mentioned next in the
same verse, which signifies the martyr's blood.[42] The unripe figs' pro-
pensity is not "first to seek the kingdom of God and his justice, but,
as the apostle says [1 Corinthians 7:33], to contemplate worldly matters, how they might please their wives or they their husbands."[43] These
people, Bernard argued, must be the Jews, who descended from the
noble, holy root of Hebrew patriarchs but failed to bring forth worthy
fruit. When the unworthiness of this unsavory fruit reached its full
maturity—in the malice of the Jews who killed Jesus—then the sweet
perfume of the fruit of the vine, the blood of Christ, could begin to
exercise its salvific power. Bernard again harped on the carnality and
misguided priorities of the Jewish people. "Whence these green figs?

40. Ibid. 59.2.4, in *Opera*, ed. Leclercq et al., 2:137.
41. Ibid. 59.4.10, in ed. Leclercq et al.,, 2:141.
42. Ibid. 60.1.2, 60.2.7, in *Opera*, ed. Leclercq et al., 2:142, 145–46.
43. Ibid. 60.1.2, in *Opera*, ed. Leclercq et al., 2:142.

And indeed, what about that people is not unripe? Certainly not its occupation, not its passion, not its understanding; and not the rite which it has for worshipping God. Its occupation was, on the whole, to wage war, its passion was for profit, its understanding was in the crassness of the letter, and its worship was with the blood of sheep and cattle."[44] This time, however, Bernard did more than to label the Jews' hermeneutic literalist and deficient and their materialism excessive; from their rejection of Jesus he drew far-reaching conclusions concerning the Jew's intellectual disposition, again with reference to figs. "Starting out with useless fruits, it ended up with pernicious and venomous ones. O crass and snake-like disposition, to hate the man who both cures people's bodies and redeems their souls! O intellect no less crass and certainly cow-like [*nihilominus intellectum grossum et certe bovinum*], which did not comprehend God even in God's works."[45] Bernard contended that in reaching this judgment he displayed more kindness to the Jews than did Isaiah, who proclaimed (1:3) that whereas the ox and the ass recognize their masters, Israel did not. "O Jew, see that I am more lenient toward you than your own prophet. I have likened you to beasts [*comparavi te iumentis*]; he places you beneath them."[46] Even the most wondrous of miracles did not suffice to bring the Jews to their senses:

> Not the flight of demons nor the obedience of the elements nor the life of the dead succeeded in dispelling this bestial and more than bestial dullness of the mind [*bestialem hanc, et plus quam bestialem, hebetudinem*] from them. On account of this blindness, no less amazing than wretched, it happened that they hastened into that horrendous and enormously crass misdeed of laying their sacrilegious hands on the majestic Lord. Henceforth it could be said that "the fig tree has brought forth its green figs"; for the precepts of that people's law began to be, as it were, on their way out, so that, in keeping with the old prophecy, as the new usages arrived the old ones would be discarded. In very much the same way, the green figs fall and make way for the good figs that follow.[47]

44. Ibid. 60.1.3, in *Opera*, ed. Leclercq et al., 2:143.
45. Ibid. 60.1.4, in *Opera*, ed. Leclercq et al., 2:144. For additional associations of Jews and figs in early-twelfth-century Christian exegesis, see Willis Johnson, "Before the Blood Libel: Jews in Christian Exegesis after the Massacres of 1096" (M.Phil. thesis, University of Cambridge, 1994), pp. 52ff.
46. Bernard, *Sermones super Cantica canticorum* 60.1.5, in *Opera*, ed. Leclercq et al., 2:144.
47. Ibid.

Once more, Bernard did not close his sermon without a return to the tropological, affirming "by the grace of God which is among us that we have both fig trees and vines. The fig trees are those more pleasant in their ways, the vines those more fervent in their spirit."[48] In Bernard's monastic community, too, monks must first sprout and shed their bitter fruit of sinfulness before savoring sweeter figs and relishing the spiritual fragrance of the Christ-like vine.

I believe that these sermons on the Song of Songs can enrich an appreciation of Bernard's significance in our story. They confirm his interest in the Jews as an archetype, embodying characteristics—above all a particular species of *infidelitas*—that other infidels or even Christians might share with them; and they demonstrate how such perceptions bore upon the most central of Bernard's theological concerns. Bernard's oft-quoted comparisons between Jews and wicked Christians may thus reflect a twelfth-century penchant for classifying like and unlike patterns of religious belief and behavior, more than they bespeak any exceptional tolerance for Jews in Christendom. Although Bernard would never have sought to argue the truth of Christianity *remoto Christo,* as Anselm had done a generation or two before him, his anti-Judaism still picked up where that of Anselm and his disciples had left off. No less than Odo of Cambrai, Guibert of Nogent, or Peter Alfonsi, Bernard considered the truth of Christianity self-evident to any rational intellect. And he went farther than his early-twelfth-century predecessors in clarifying the logical ramifications of such a conviction: If Jewish commitment to things material and carnal went hand in hand with a strictly literal interpretation of the Bible, the Jews' obstinate refusal to submit to self-evident, rational truth must reflect an intellect that is inhuman, bovine, and beastly.[49]

In Bernard's estimation, however, a bovine intellect did not impede the divinely ordained testimonial role of the Jews in Christendom, and the sermons on the Song of Songs illustrate a marked commitment to Pauline and Augustinian ideas of the Jews. Though bitter, one ought not to discard the unsavory green figs, because they will eventually prove useful; the Jews do have a function in Christendom, and God will eventually have mercy on Israel. The error of the Jews derives directly from their blindness; their commitment to a literal understand-

48. Ibid. 60.3.9, in *Opera,* ed. Leclercq et al., 2:147.
49. For earlier Christian intimations of the same idea, see below, n. 121.

ing of the Old Testament, though misguided, is genuine. "Judah," wrote Bernard in sermon 14, "has much of the oil of the knowledge of God but greedily keeps it enclosed in a jar, as it were, within himself."[50] Like Augustine's capsarius, or enslaved book bearer, the Jew thus preserves in closed jars that treasured "oil" which provides for the salvation of the church. The very context of commentary on the biblical canticle contributes to the profundity of this point. Relying on their own ability to observe the law, Jews cannot see beyond the literal, sexual meaning of Solomon's love poetry; unripe figs, they remain focused on "worldly matters, how they might please their wives or they their husbands." Christian allegory, which expounds the love between Christ the bridegroom and his ecclesiastical bride, thus seals the triumph of church over synagogue; for the Jew "relies on the text of a covenant, I on the accord of God's will." Yet the Jew and his sacred text still constitute the roots that nourish the fullness of the new covenant, which extends from allegorical to tropological and anagogical senses of Hebrew Scripture as well. Bernard's sermon shifts freely and repeatedly from this allegorical contrast between Judaism and Christianity to the moral imperatives of the biblical text for his Cistercian community; the allegory of the canticle sustains its tropology.[51] Nor does Bernard's exposition of the text ignore its fourth, anagogical, future-oriented sense, which also bears upon the Jews. Bernard acknowledged that he and his monks had not yet consummated their union with God, reaching the stage where they could echo the biblical bride in hailing their beloved, "Your name is oil poured out." The church that utters these words, Bernard explained, "reclines within, but it is a church that for the time being is only of the perfect [*Ecclesia interim perfectorum*]." Yet hope of entering this church remains for the faithful,[52] as it does even for the Jews. Echoing Paul, so Bernard elaborated in one of the later sermons:

50. Bernard, *Sermones super Cantica canticorum* 14.2.2, in *Opera*, ed. Leclercq et al., 1:77.

51. Helpful treatments of Bernard's distinction among the various senses of Scripture include Ann W. Astell, *The Song of Songs in the Middle Ages* (Ithaca, N.Y., 1990), pp. 92–104; Jean Leclercq, "Ecriture sainte et vie spirituelle: Saint Bernard et le 12ᵉ siècle monastique," *Dictionnaire de spiritualité ascétique et mystique*, 4,1 (Paris, 1960), 187–94; and Henri de Lubac, *Exégèse médiévale: Les Quatre Sens de l'écriture*, Théologie 41–42, 59 (Paris, 1959–64), 1, 2:586–99.

52. Bernard, *Sermones super Cantica canticorum* 14.3.5, in *Opera*, ed. Leclercq et al., 1:78.

The charity of the church, which does not begrudge her own delight even to her rival, the synagogue, is great. What is kinder than her being prepared to share with her enemy the very one whom her soul loves? Yet no wonder, because salvation is from the Jews. The savior will return to the place from which he had come, so that the remnants of Israel might be saved. Let not the branches be ungrateful to the root, nor sons to their mother; let not the branches begrudge the root what they took from it, and let not the sons begrudge their mother what they sucked from her breasts. Let the church hold firmly onto the salvation which the Jews lost; she holds it until the plenitude of the Gentiles may enter in, and thus all Israel may be saved.[53]

The implications of Bernard's biblical hermeneutic for the Jews extend further still. If Anselm and Guibert of Nogent identified the different senses of Scripture with various faculties of the human soul, Bernard beheld in them different types of individuals.[54] As some scholars have suggested, Bernard believed so strongly in the affective quality of biblical interpretation—in "a process of interiorization that changes the verbal contents of Scripture into personal and interior enlightenments"—that he viewed the sacred text as constitutive of an individual's character.[55] The difference between Old Testament and New, law and Christ, or "the veil of the mortifying letter" and the grace of "the crucified word"—which tears that veil apart and facilitates the church's displacement of the synagogue—thus becomes the difference between Jew and Christian. The Christian strives to unite, essentially, with Christ. The Jew, by contrast, is the letter of the law.

THE IDEOLOGY OF HOLY WAR

If Bernard's sermons on the Song of Songs hint at such a conclusion, his consideration of Jews and Judaism within the context of his support for the Second Crusade renders it definitive. The preceding discussion of Bernard commenced with reference to his exceptional concern for

53. Ibid. 79.2.5, in *Opera*, ed. Leclercq et al., 2:275.
54. See above, chapter 5, n. 3.
55. Denis Farkasfalvy, "The Role of the Bible in St. Bernard's Spirituality," *Analecta cisterciensia* 25 (1969), 9; and cf. Claude Bodard, "La Bible, expression d'une expérience religieuse chez S. Bernard," in *Saint Bernard, théologien*, Analecta sacri ordinis cisterciensis 9 (Rome, 1953), p. 44: "De cette expérience la Bible n'est pas seulement la norme, elle en est aussi un élément constitutif. C'est sur l'Ecriture que se fonde la foi, et c'est par l'Ecriture que Dieu s'approche de nos âmes. La Bible est, en effet, considérée par S. Bernard comme un livre vivant qui s'adresse à des vivants." See also P. Dumontier, *Saint Bernard et la Bible* (Paris, 1953), on Bernard's biblical hermeneutic and psychology, and esp. pp. 99ff., 132ff., with reference to the sermons on the Song of Songs.

the safety of the Jews during the Crusade and to the praise he therefore elicited from contemporary Jews. Yet although Bernard journeyed to the Rhineland in 1146 to prevent a repetition of the massacres that had transpired fifty years earlier, his protection of the Jews is remembered chiefly through his letters 363 and 365, the former an encyclical urging participation in the Second Crusade and the latter a reproof of the Cistercian monk Radulf mentioned by Efraim of Bonn. The second of these texts dwells primarily on the evils of Radulf and briefly explains—in traditional Pauline and Augustinian terminology—why the Jews must not be attacked:

> Is it not more fruitful if the Church defeats the Jews over time, convicting or converting them, than if it eliminates them all with the sword at one and the same time? Has that universal prayer of the Church, which is offered for the perfidious Jews from sunrise to sunset, that the Lord God take the veil from their hearts so that they may be led from their darkness to the light of truth, been instituted to no avail? If she did not hope that those who are incredulous will believe, it would seem useless and vain to pray for them. But with the eye of piety she considers that the Lord bestows grace upon him who renders good for evil and devotion for hatred.[56]

Owing to its more general and theological character, the first of Bernard's letters has understandably commanded more attention, and the ensuing analysis demands its quotation at length. After several lines of greeting, the missive beckons for its recipients to join the Crusade:

> (A)(1) My message to you is in the cause of Christ [de negotio Christi], in whom is our salvation. . . . (2) Behold that now is the acceptable time, now is the day of ample salvation. (3) The earth is shaken and trembles because the God of heaven has begun to lose his land. . . . (4) And now, owing to our sins [peccatis nostris exigentibus], the enemies of the cross have embarked sacrilegiously to devastate the blessed land, the land of promise, with the sword. If there be no one who can resist, they will soon invade the very city of the living God, overturn the workhouses of our redemption, and pollute the holy places. . . .
>
> (B)(1) What are you doing, you gallant men? What are you doing, you servants of the cross? Will you thus give a holy thing to the dogs or pearls to swine? (2) How many sinners here, confessing their sins, have obtained pardon after the filth of the pagan was eliminated by the swords of our ancestors? The evil one sees this and is jealous, he grinds his teeth and wastes away. (3) He arouses the vessels of his iniquity, lest any signs or traces of such piety should remain if, somehow, he should be able to obtain what God despises. (4) An irreparable loss, this would indeed be a source of insurmountable grief

---

56. Bernard, *Epistulae* 365.2, in *Opera*, ed. Leclercq et al., 8:321.

for all generations to come, but it would be a source of limitless confusion and endless shame especially for this most wretched generation.

(C)(1) What then do you think, brothers? Is the hand of the Lord shortened or has it been rendered impotent to work salvation, so that he calls upon petty worms to save and restore his heritage for him? Could he not send more than twelve legions of angels, or even just say the word, and the land would be liberated? By all means has he the power to do this whenever he wishes; but, I tell you, the Lord your God is testing you. . . . (2) For God has pity on his people and provides the means to save those who have grievously fallen away.

(D)(1) Consider with what great care he undertakes to save you, and be amazed. . . . He does not want your death but that you should turn to him and live, inasmuch as he seeks an opportunity to work not against you but for you. (2) For what is it if not a thoroughly exquisite occasion for salvation, conceivable only for God, that the Almighty deem murderers, thieves, adulterers, perjurers, and the like, worthy to assign to his service, like a people which acted righteously? Do not be bashful, you sinners. God is beneficent. If he wished to punish you he would not thus be asking for your service. . . . (3) Either he is putting himself in need or he is pretending to do so, so that he may render payment to those that fight on his behalf, pardon for sins and eternal glory. (4) I call blessed the generation which seizes the opportunity for such copious indulgence, which this year—one pleasing to God, a year of jubilee in fact—finds alive.

(E)(1) Your land is well reputed to be rich in its brave men and robust in its youth. . . . Gird yourselves bravely and undertake joyful combat with the zeal of the Christian name. (2) Let not that moral combat cease, but that blatant malice, with which you are accustomed to strike one another down, to slay one another, so that you are consumed by one another. Why such a base passion for depravity? . . . To consign oneself to such danger is insane, not virtuous—not courageous but indicative of madness. (3) But now, you mighty soldier, you man of war, you have a campaign in which you may fight without danger, in which to conquer is glorious and to die is profitable [*lucrum*]. (4) But if you are a wise merchant, a seeker of profit in this world, let me bring to your attention some wonderful options [*magnas quasdam . . . nundinas*]. Do not forgo them. Take up the sign of the Cross and you will simultaneously be pardoned for all those sins that you confess with a contrite heart. The outlay in materials costs little; if one ventures with devotion, he will undoubtedly gain the kingdom of God. (5) They who have already taken up this heavenly sign have therefore done well; and if others hurry and take up what is for them too the sign of salvation, they will do well and cause themselves no harm. . . .

(F)(1) We have heard and rejoiced that the zeal for God's glory burns among you; but wise moderation is still entirely appropriate. (2) The Jews are not to be persecuted, killed, or even put to flight. Ask those who know the Sacred Scriptures what they read foretold of the Jews in the psalm. "God," says the Church, "instructs me concerning my enemies, 'Slay them not, so that my people should not forget.'" (3) The Jews are indeed for us the living letters [*vivi . . . apices*] of Scripture, constantly representing the Lord's passion. They have been dispersed all over the world for this reason: so that in enduring just punishments for such a crime wherever they are, they may be the witnesses of our redemption. Hence the Church, speaking in the same psalm, adds, "only disperse them in thy power, and subjugate them, God my protector." And so it has been done: Dispersed and subjugated they are; under Christian princes they endure a harsh captivity. (4) But "they will be converted toward the end of time," and "it will be at the time of their redemption." (5) Finally, the Apostle states that at the time of the ingathering of all the nations, then all Israel shall be saved. But those who die in the interim will remain in death.

(G)(1) I do not mention that wherever there are no Jews, we lament that Christian moneylenders—if it is fitting for them to be called Christians and not more [appropriately] baptized Jews—behave Jewishly in a manner even worse [*peius iudaizare*]. (2) If the Jews are utterly wiped out, how can one hope for their promised salvation, their eventual conversion at the end of time? (3) So too the Gentiles: if they were similarly subjugated for all time, then clearly they should likewise be awaited in their state of judgment rather than sought out with swords. Yet since they have now begun to act violently against us, it is necessary for those who do not carry a sword without cause to repel force with force. It is an act of Christian piety both "to vanquish the arrogant" and also "to spare the subjected," especially those concerning whom there is legislation and a promise, and from among whose ancestors was Christ according to the flesh. . . . (4) Yet at least this much should be exacted from them in accordance with the spirit of the apostolic mandate: that all those who take up the sign of the cross they release completely from all payments of usury.

(H) [There follows a warning against participation in unauthorized, unofficial crusading ventures.][57]

Scholarly discussion of this text has proceeded from a number of perspectives; but beyond consideration of the document itself, the problematic order of its various versions, and its status as an encyclical calling Christians to holy war,[58] investigators have generally treated the

57. Ibid. 363, in *Opera*, ed. Leclercq et al., 8:311–17.

58. Above all, see the following studies of Jean Leclercq: "L'Encyclique de Saint Bernard en faveur de la croisade," *RB* 81 (1971), 282–308, "À propos de l'encyclique de Saint Bernard sur la croisade," *RB* 82 (1972), 312, and "Pour l'histoire de l'encyclique de Saint Bernard sur la croisade," in *Études de civilisation médiévale (ixe–xiie siècles): Mélanges E.-R. Labande* (Poitiers, France, 1974), pp. 479–90. The two longer of these studies were reprinted in Jean Leclercq, *Recueil d'études sur Saint Bernard et ses écrits*, Storia e letteratura 92, 104, 114, 167 (Rome, 1962–87), 4:227–63. See also the helpful essays of Giles Constable, "The Second Crusade as Seen by Contemporaries," *Traditio* 9 (1953), 276ff.; and Adriaan H. Bredero, "Studien zu den Kreuzzugsbriefen Bernhards von Clairvaux und seiner Reise nach Deutschland im Jahre 1146," *Mitteilungen des Instituts für österreichische Geschichtsforschung* 66 (1958), 331–43.

letter in two distinct contexts.[59] First, this letter explains Bernard's rationale for and perception of the Crusade. Along these lines, many have correctly emphasized Bernard's idealized or metahistorical view of human history and political interactions, and his resulting ambivalence with regard to crusading.[60] One should note that letter 363 does not insist that the holy war must be directed toward the Holy Land. To the contrary, Bernard deemed the haven of the monastery a spiritual Jerusalem preferable over the earthly one; and in one instance he actually counseled a would-be pilgrim to shun the pleasures of this world and enroll as a citizen—"not of that earthly Jerusalem to which Mount Sinai in Arabia is joined . . . but of that free Jerusalem which is above and the mother of us all".[61] His view of the infidels as threatening the

59. Curiously, this letter has recently been subjected to a flurry of scholarly analyses. They include Yvonne Friedman, "An Anatomy of Anti-Semitism: Peter the Venerable's Letter to Louis VII, King of France (1146)," in *Bar-Ilan Studies in History*, ed. Pinhas Artzi (Ramat Gan, Israel, 1978), pp. 88ff.; Gilbert Dahan, "Bernard de Clairvaux et les Juifs," *Archives juives* 23 (1987), 59–64; Lotter, "Das Prinzip," pp. 504ff.; Cohen, " 'Witnesses of Our Redemption' "; and no fewer than three discussions in *FWW*: Jeremy Cohen, "The Muslim Connection: On the Changing Role of the Jew in High Medieval Theology," in *FWW*, pp. 156–59, Lotter, "Position," pp. 174–81, and Robert Chazan, "Twelfth-Century Perceptions of the Jews: A Case Study of Bernard of Clairvaux and Peter the Venerable," in *FWW*, pp. 190–95.

60. On Bernard's ideological posture vis-à-vis the Crusades, see Eberhard Pfeiffer, "Die Stellung des hl. Bernhards zur Kreuzzugsbewegung nach seinen Schriften," *Cistercienser Chronik* 46 (1934), 273–83, 305–11; Paul Rousset, *Les Origines et les caractères de la première croisade*, Université de Genève, Faculté des lettres, Thèse 105 (Geneva, 1945), chap. 8; Etienne Delaruelle, "L'Idée de croisade chez Saint Bernard," in *Mélanges Saint Bernard: XXIVe congrès de l'Association bourguignonne des sociétés savantes, Dijon, 1953* (Dijon, France, 1954), pp. 53–67; Pierre Dérumaux, "Saint Bernard et les infidèles," in *Mélanges Saint Bernard: XXIVe congrès de l'Association bourguignonne des sociétés savantes, Dijon, 1953* (Dijon, France, 1954), pp. 68–79; and Evans, *Mind of St. Bernard*, pp. 24–36. By way of instructive contrast, see also Friedrich Lotter, *Die Konzeption des Wendenkreuzzugs: Ideengeschichtliche, kirchenrechtliche und historisch-politische Voraussetzungen der Missionierung von Elb- und Ostseeslawen um die Mitte des 12. Jahrhunderts*, Vorträge und Forschungen: Sonderband 23 (Sigmaringen, Germany, 1977), pt 1.

61. Bernard, *Epistulae* 64.1, in *Opera*, ed. Leclercq et al., 7:157 (cf. Galatians 4:25); and see also Bernard, *Epistulae* 459, in *Opera*, ed. Leclercq et al., 8:437, and *Sermones in vigilia nativitatis* 2, in *Opera*, ed. Leclercq et al., 4:203–11. On Bernard's conceptualization of Jerusalem and its idealized replication in the monastery, see also Thomas Renna, "Bernard of Clairvaux and the Temple of Solomon," in *Law, Custom, and the Social Fabric in Medieval Europe: Essays in Honor of Bryce Lyon*, ed. Bernard S. Bachrach and David Nicholas, Studies in Medieval Culture 28 (Kalamazoo, Mich., 1990), pp. 8off.; Peter Raedts, "St Bernard of Clairvaux and Jerusalem," in *Prophecy and Eschatology*, ed. Michael Wilks, SCH Subsidia 10 (Oxford, 1994), pp. 169–82; M. B. Pranger, *Bernard of Clairvaux and the Shape of Monastic Thought: Broken Dreams*, Brill's Studies in Intellectual History 56 (Leiden, Netherlands, 1994), pp. 32ff.; and Adriaan H. Bredero, "Jerusalem in the West," in his *Christendom and Christianity in the Middle Ages: The Relations between Religion, Church, and Society*, trans. Reinder Bruinsma (Grand Rapids, Mich., 1994), pp. 79–104.

frontiers of Christendom and embodying the antithesis of all its ideals stemmed largely from misinformation or preconceived stereotypes, which the abbot had little interest in abandoning. For Bernard the Crusade was a pilgrimage, whose process mattered considerably more than its geographical destination or military objectives. It was, in fact, a jubilee, a divine bequest whereby Christians could demonstrate their readiness to receive the gift of deliverance from sin. It provided those outside of religious orders a singular opportunity to undertake a spiritual vocation that would facilitate the redemption of Christendom. Of truly sacramental quality, explained Giles Constable, the "crusade had therefore a salvatory and penitential value far beyond the interests of the individual crusader; he who died on crusade was a martyr and a saint, who stored up merit in heaven for his brethren. It was the concern therefore not only of the participants themselves but of the entire Christian community."[62]

As such, one may profitably evaluate Bernard's outlook on holy war within the predominantly monastic efforts to define and express the theological significance of the First Crusade. The "idea of the crusade," Jonathan Riley-Smith and others have demonstrated, crystallized only after this Crusade had ended, primarily in the second round of Latin chronicles on the campaigns of 1096–99: not the eyewitness accounts of writers who participated in the Crusade (those of Fulcher of Chartres, Raymond of Aguilers, Peter Tudebode, and the *Gesta Francorum*), but the derivative, more carefully conceived and crafted texts of monastic authors (Robert the Monk, Baldric of Bourgueil, and Guibert of Nogent).[63] From their cloistered perspective, the crusading army constituted a virtual "monastery on the move";[64] in modern anthropological terms, the march to Jerusalem signified a religious "rite of passage."[65] Its true objective lay not in military victory or territorial conquest. Rather, it proffered a framework for expending one's phys-

---

62. Constable, "Second Crusade," p. 241.
63. Jonathan Riley-Smith, *The First Crusade and the Idea of Crusading* (London, 1986). The cultural processes whereby the Crusades assumed theological significance in high medieval Europe have also been discussed, among numerous others, by Rousset, *Les Origines*, chaps. 7–10; Bernard McGinn, "*Iter sancti sepulchri*: The Piety of the First Crusaders," in *Essays on Medieval Civilization*, ed. Bede Karl Lackner and Kenneth Roy Philp, Walter Prescott Webb Memorial Lectures 12 (Austin, Tex., 1978), pp. 33–71; H. E. J. Cowdrey, "Martyrdom and the First Crusade," in *Crusade and Settlement*, ed. P. W. Edbury (Cardiff, Wales, 1985), pp. 46–56; and I. S. Robinson, *The Papacy, 1073–1198* (Cambridge, England, 1990), pp. 324ff.
64. Riley-Smith, *First Crusade*, pp. 2, 150.
65. McGinn, *Iter sancti sepulchri*, pp. 43ff.

ical energies in order to realize God's plan for human history and salvation. Viewed in retrospect, the drama of the Crusade allowed its players to mollify the disparity between physical and the spiritual, to bridge the gap between worldly and heavenly. Ideals of Christian piety and eschatology infused new meaning into the realities of war; literary and theological archetypes, many of them derived from the narrative of Scripture, reidentified the participants. Casualties became martyrs, heroic warriors became saints, and, not least important, the armies of the Catholic Church marching on Palestine became the biblical children of Israel en route to conquer the promised land.[66]

This background of early-twelfth-century reflection on the First Crusade helps to explain the ambiguity in Bernard's attitude toward holy war. To the extent that it promised to hasten the redemption, as he believed the Second Crusade would, he advocated it staunchly. To the extent that it threatened to obscure the otherworldly objectives of Christian spirituality, he resisted—as in his refusal to allow the foundation of a Cistercian monastery in Jerusalem or in his stated preference for the more real Jerusalem in Clairvaux. Such concern also underlay his sponsorship of the Templars, a new, religious breed of knight and crusader who exemplified the priority of the means of holy war over its stated political ends.[67] I shall argue presently that the same crusading ideology explains much of the function of the Jews in letters 363 and 365.

Second, letter 363 has weighed heavily in scholarly evaluations of Bernard's attitudes toward the Jews and Judaism. Some have viewed Bernard's defense of the Jews in 1146 as evidence of a saintly piety, anachronistically transforming Bernard into a model of modern religious tolerance and pluralism.[68] Others have compared Bernard's en-

---

66. On the importance of Old Testament imagery in particular, see also Adolf Waas, "Volk Gottes und Militia Christi—Juden und Kreuzfahrer," in *JIM*, pp. 421–26; and Marie-Dominique Chenu, *Nature, Man, and Society in the Twelfth Century: Essays on New Theological Perspectives in the Latin West*, ed. Jerome Taylor and Lester K. Little (Chicago, 1968), pp. 146–61, esp. 158ff.

67. Bernard of Clairvaux, *De laude novae militiae*, in *Opera*, ed. Leclercq et al., 3: 205–39; see also the helpful study of Colin Morris, "*Equestris ordo*: Chivalry as a Vocation in the Twelfth Century," in *Religious Motivation: Biological and Sociological Problems for the Church Historian*, ed. Derek Baker, SCH 15 (Oxford 1978), pp. 87–96.

68. For example, Richard S. Storrs, *Bernard of Clairvaux: The Times, The Man, and His Work* (New York, 1893), pp. 177–81; Ailbee J. Luddy, *The Life and Teaching of St. Bernard* (Dublin, 1950), pp. 530ff.; and Williams, *St. Bernard*, p. 271f. As recently as fifteen years ago, Bernard was deemed "a pioneer in amical judeo-christian relations" by M. Conrad Greenia, prefacing his translation of *In Praise of the New Knighthood*

cyclical to Peter the Venerable's nearly simultaneous letter to King Louis VII of France, to be analyzed later in this chapter.[69] Still others have focused on the innovative elements in Bernard's anti-Judaism that manifest themselves in this letter despite its call for restraint—and specifically on Bernard's equation of essentially Jewish behavior with the immoralities of usury. Projecting the religious and moral guilt that plagued a maturing medieval Christian civilization onto an archetypical Jewish enemy, such animosity had emerged previously in Bernard's bitter opposition to antipope Anacletus II. According to these scholars, as Bernard highlighted the contrast between Judaism and Christianity by calling for participation in the Crusade, "in his own way he helped foster the mentality that was so receptive to the preaching of Ralph [i.e., Radulf]."[70]

These two lines of scholarly inquiry concerning Bernard's encyclical have almost always remained distinct; but curiously, it is their convergence that provides new insight into the underlying import of the letter regarding the Jews. Bernard's concerns with the Crusade lay not with matters military and political but with its salvific consequences, both for the individual soul and for Christendom at large. Although he himself stood at the head of an established monastic order, his idealized, symbolic view of terrestrial history reflects much of the "delirious messianism" that M.-D. Chenu has attributed to the "evangelical awakening" of the twelfth century:

(De laude novae militiae) in Bernard of Clairvaux, *Treatises III*, Cistercian Fathers Series 19 (Kalamazoo, Mich., 1977), p. 127. Even Gavin I. Langmuir, who has taken the lead in exposing twelfth-century Christendom's projection of its own insecurities onto the Jews (cf. above, introduction to part 3, n. 18), has stressed Bernard's virtuosity in this context; see his "The Faith of Christians and Hostility to Jews," in *Christianity and Judaism*, ed. Diana Wood, SCH 29 (Oxford, 1992), pp. 85–86. Most recently Lotter, "Position," p. 181, has argued strenuously that Bernard was the chief representative of an atypical medieval religious tolerance that characterized his Cistercian order: "The assessment of Bernard has to take as a basis not so much the ambivalent and stereotyped statements of his anti-Judaic theology but rather the awakening of conscience in the moment of crisis and imminent disaster. In that moment the human and religious background of Cistercian ethics of charity was activated and transformed into the decision to intervene energetically in favor of those in need of help."

69. Bernhard Blumenkranz, "Die Entwicklung im Westen zwischen 200 und 1200," in *Kirche und Synagoge: Handbuch zur Geschichte von Christen und Juden*, ed. Karl Heinrich Rengstorf and Siegfried von Kurtzfleisch (Stuttgart, 1968–70), 1:122, suggested that Bernard here reacted polemically against the more virulent statements of Peter, to be considered below.

70. Little, *Religious Poverty*, pp. 48–49; see the sources cited above, n. 60; and cf. Berger, "Attitude," pp. 103–8, who cites Salo Wittmayer Baron, *A Social and Religious History of the Jews*, 2d ed. (New York, 1952–83), 4:121, 301.

Here are the true people of Israel, decidedly liberated from terrestrial servitude. Here is the new Jerusalem, triumphing over the antichrists foretold by the apocalypses. And here, near at hand, is the coming of the spirit. In manifestoes, in programs, in pontifical approbations, in sermons, in polemical tracts, in chronicles, these scriptural themes of the messianic era were exploited to convey with unction the message of hope about to be realized. The allegorization of history, however customary, was not simply a literary device; it was a means of explaining the working out in time of the kingdom of God in successive stages.[71]

I would hesitate to term Bernard's messianism delirious. But his eschatological orientation does explain his outlook on the Crusades and his attitude toward the Jews, inasmuch as it dictated the significance of each. The geographical, military, and social parameters of the Crusade—even the infidels under attack—mattered for their contribution to the Crusade's sacramental efficacy. Their role in the process whereby God would save his people determined their essential qualities for Bernard, and these he conceived and expressed in accord with established paradigms of biblical, patristic, and monastic theology. Like the early-twelfth-century chronicles of the First Crusade, Bernard construed the participants and particulars in the drama of the Crusades as archetypes, players in the divinely ordained enactment of human salvation-history.[72]

Not by coincidence, then, did Bernard address the issue of the Jews within the same text and context.[73] As his allegations of Jewish avarice attest, the abbot of Clairvaux was no champion of religious tolerance; yet the massacres of Jews in the Rhineland in 1096 had demonstrated how anti-Jewish violence could divert the energies of the Crusade from its primary objectives. Moreover, the Jews also had their singular task in the salvific history of the world, and, invoking the Augustinian doctrine of Jewish witness, Bernard cited (F2) the admonition of Psalm 59: 12, "Slay them not, so that my people should not forget." He explained

---

71. Chenu, *Nature, Man, and Society*, pp. 268–69.

72. On the Crusade's eschatological dimension as appreciated by Bernard, see Bernard McGinn, "Saint Bernard and Eschatology," in *Bernard of Clairvaux: Studies Presented to Dom Jean Leclercq*, Cistercian Studies Series 23 (Washington, D.C., 1973), esp. pp. 182–83; and Hans-Dietrich Kahl, "Crusade Eschatology as Seen by St. Bernard in the Years 1146 to 1148," in *The Second Crusade and the Cistercians*, ed. Michael Gervers (New York, 1992), pp. 37–47.

73. Our findings stand diametrically opposed to Lotter's conclusion, "Position," p. 177, that in Bernard's thought "the crusade has nothing to do with the Jews, for their condition is different from that of the Saracens."

(F3) that "the Jews are indeed for us living letters [*vivi . . . apices*] of Scripture, constantly representing the Lord's passion. They have been dispersed all over the world for this reason: so that in enduring just punishments for such a crime wherever they are, they may be the witnesses of our redemption." Testimonial and eschatological considerations mandated their history, their survival, their status in a properly ordered Christian world, and their distinctive character.[74] Accordingly, the exigencies of the Second Crusade offered a doubly appropriate opportunity to address their situation.

Did Bernard expand upon the classic Pauline-Augustinian posture? Clarifying how the Jews perform their peculiar didactic function, especially within the framework of the "jubilee" of the Crusade, the conceptual structure of Bernard's letter 363 (in its fuller versions)[75] suggests that he did. Outlined schematically, with reference to the translation above, this conceptual structure unfolds as follows:

A.   The problem: The time of redemption is at hand (A2), but the Holy Land is under attack (A3); owing to sin in Christendom, the enemies of Christ threaten the very means whereby Christians may achieve salvation (A4, A5).

B.   The challenge: Unless Christians respond (B1), the forces of evil, aroused by the successes of the church (B2), will triumph over those of piety (B3), a shameful, grievous catastrophe (B4).

C.   The paradox: God needs no human assistance to defeat his enemies but could easily do so himself (C1); rather, he has engineered the present situation out of pity for his people (C2).

D.   The rationale: Devising a means to effect, not to thwart, the salvation of Christians (D1), the beneficent God prefers that sinners find righteousness in his service to punishing them (D2). He has assumed the appearance of obligation to those who join the Crusade, in order to be able to pardon them for their sins and save them (D3). Such is the rare blessing of the moment (D4).

E.   The method: Christendom must exploit its military prowess for a worthy cause (E1). The evil of internecine warfare must cease (E2), and energies must be directed against noble objectives, for whose sake

74. Cf. Dahan, "Bernard de Clairvaux."
75. See above, n. 58.

one ought well to conquer and to die (E3). Likewise, merchants must reorient their priorities, investing not for earthly gain but to attain God's kingdom (E4). Those who have joined and those who will join the Crusade will be saved (E5).

F. The warning: Commendable Christian zeal notwithstanding (F1), crusaders must take care not to harm or disturb the Jews and thus to contravene the divine command (F2). The Jews attest to Christian salvation in their dispersion (F3); at the (now imminent) end of time those who survive will convert (F4–5).

G. The consideration: Jewish behavior is not laudable, nor that of Christian usurers, who, in the absence of Jews, behave even more Jewishly than Jews themselves (G1); still, destruction of the Jews would prevent the realization of God's plan for them (G2). Were Gentiles similarly subjugated, their conversion might be awaited, but each enemy of God must be opposed appropriately (G3). Nonetheless, crusaders should be released from usurious debts owed to the Jews (G4).

Thus analyzed, Bernard's letter reveals its inner logic and symmetry: Sin threatens the desired goal of imminent salvation (A, B), and God's design for human history includes mechanisms for overcoming this obstacle. The Crusade and the infidels help to achieve this objective (C), because they allow Christians to redirect their otherwise sinful pugnacity and materialism in order to merit them pardon and reward (D). Within such an eschatological pattern, the Saracens who threaten the Holy Land are perceived—or, more precisely, are constituted conceptually—in relation to this belligerent dimension of Christian guilt. In attacking the Holy Land, they are the agents of sacrilegious violence par excellence (A4, G3); as such they assist the devil (B3) as the vessels of his iniquity (*vasa iniquitatis suae*). Archetypically exemplifying the "blatant malice" that now plagues Christendom, they function as its rightful targets, inviting the salvific sublimation of such Christian malice into "moral combat" (E1–3). Bernard's charge to the newly founded military order of the Templars, *In Praise of the New Knighthood*, confirms this impression; for it hails the Crusade as facilitating the rehabilitation of "the impious and the criminal, the sacrilegious and the plunderers, murderers, perjurers, and adulterers. . . . Thus has Christ seen fit to take revenge on his enemies, so that the more powerfully he might be wont to triumph, so too the more gloriously—not only over them, but through their very agency. It is surely delightful and appropriate that he now begin to have as his defenders those whom he endured for so long as his attackers, and that from his enemy he fashion his soldier."[76]

Bernard's posture toward the Jewish infidel mirrors this stance vis-à-vis the Saracen: Mercantile commitments to this world on the part of Christians obviate their acquisition of the next (E4–5), whose conquest is accordingly depicted in economic metaphors (*negotium, lucrum, nundinas*, and so forth) as well. Just as Bernard's "Gentiles" correspond to Christian sins of physical violence, his Jews represent typologically (as *vivi apices*, living letters) the worldly materialism of the temple's merchants whose tables Jesus overturned,[77] the inversion of the spiritual and the carnal—in life and in the sacred text—and the rejection of the rational for the proclivities of a "bovine intellect." The materialistic typology of the Jews accounts for their mention apropos of Bernard's crusading appeal to Christian merchants in letter 363, and it explains Bernard's estimation of that sinful Christian behavior which subverts the cultivation of authentic spirituality as Judaizing (*iudaizare*).[78] Yet this peculiar use for the Jews in the divine economy of salvation—to contrast dialectically and instructively with Christian spirituality in their lifestyle, their aspirations, and their understanding of Scripture—is best fostered by their dispersion, preservation, and subjugation in Christendom (F3–5, G2), no less than vanquishing the Muslim Gentile facilitates the sublimation of Christian malice into virtue (G3). In Bernard's worldview, I submit, each brand of infidel thus served the divine purpose, personifying the guilt of Christendom and, by succumbing to the forces of Christendom in its distinctive fashion, allowing for its expurgation. For precisely this reason "it is an act of Christian piety both 'to vanquish the arrogant' and also 'to spare the subjected'" (G3). Hence the urgency of Bernard's call for crusaders to refrain from anti-Jewish violence, to heed the biblical and Augustinian directive of "Slay them not" (F1–2), and still to prevent Jewish materialism from impeding the Crusade (G4).

In the eyes of the twelfth-century rabbinic chronicler, Bernard of Clairvaux may indeed have deserved the unusual classification as "a decent priest". One can similarly understand why modern historians

76. Bernard of Clairvaux, *De laude novae militiae* 5.10, in *Opera*, ed. Leclercq et al., 3:223.

77. Ibid. 5.9, p. 222.

78. On Bernard's original use of the term, see Berger, "Attitude," p. 104, n. 65; and Little, *Religious Poverty*, p. 56.

of anti-Judaism have indicted Bernard for adding a new, economic, even racist dimension to the hatred of Jews in Christendom. Yet the key to Bernard's letter on the Crusade and the Jews lies in the intersection of these two concerns, just as the appraisal of Jews and Judaism in his exposition of the Song of Songs both derives from and contributes to the hermeneutical outlook he strove to develop in those sermons. The Crusade worked to expedite Christian salvation by reorienting Christian behavior; Saracen and Jew served this common purpose equally well in their respective ways. Perhaps even more than the realia of Jewish-Christian relations in the twelfth century, the internal structures of Bernard's hermeneutic and philosophy of history dictated his idea of the Jews and their function in Christendom.

PETER

Any helpful discussion of Bernard's teachings regarding the Jews and Judaism begs a comparison with those of his illustrious contemporary, Abbot Peter the Venerable of Cluny (ca. 1094—1156). As Bernard left the imprint of his distinctive spirituality on the young order of Cîteaux, amply contributing to its developing character, Peter helped to guide the older, Benedictine variety of European monasticism through one of the more critical phases in its history.[79] Like Bernard, Peter sided with Pope Innocent II over his rival Anacletus II;[80] he, too, numbered among the outspoken supporters of the Second Crusade; and he also exemplifies Christendom's association of anti-Jewish polemic with its broader struggle against the Muslim infidel.

Although Peter's anti-Jewish formulations have earned him a measure of notoriety in the annals of Western antisemitism, his constructions of the Jews and Judaism owe much to Guibert of Nogent (and the Gregorian worldview that inspired him) and to Peter Alfonsi earlier in the century, and they even recall the emotional tirades of Agobard of Lyons. Contrasting Peter the Venerable's pronouncements with the

---

79. On Peter's life and monastic career, see, among others, Giles Constable's appendixes to his edition of Peter the Venerable, *Letters* (Cambridge, Mass., 1967), 2:233ff.; Giles Constable, "The Monastic Policy of Peter the Venerable," in *PAPV*, pp. 119–42; and Jean-Pierre Torrell and Denise Bouthillier, *Pierre le Vénérable et sa vision du monde: Sa vie—son oeuvre, l'homme et le démon*, Spicilegium sacrum lovaniense 42 (Louvain, Belgium, 1986), pt. 1.

80. See Stroll, *Jewish Pope*, pp. 162ff., and, regarding Peter's objection to Anacletus's Jewish background, n. 23.

exceptional efforts of Bernard of Clairvaux to protect the Jews during
the Second Crusade, some scholars have condemned Peter for his hatred and hostility.[81] Others have struggled to downplay the intensity of
his anti-Jewish sentiments, preferring to remember Peter as "the great
peacemaker of his age," a man of "remarkable intelligence and sympathy," or, when compared with the Cistercian Radulf, "more moderate" than he first appears.[82] As with Bernard, we shall study the dynamic, the inner logic, and the ramifications of Peter's ideas without
any design to indict or to apologize for him. These two most influential
churchmen shared a great deal more than one has frequently acknowledged; together they conveyed much of the depth and complexity in
the attitudes of twelfth-century Christianity toward the Jew.

IN SUPPORT OF THE CRUSADE

The comparison profitably begins with a letter that Peter dispatched to
King Louis VII of France on the eve of the Second Crusade, in the same
year that Bernard composed his encyclical calling for participation in
the Crusade.[83] To summarize:[84] (i) Peter's letter 130 opens with a declaration of unmitigated support for the Crusade and Louis's leading
role in it, despite the abbot's inability to participate personally in the
expedition. Who could not find words of praise and encouragement
for this noble endeavor? Christendom has witnessed a renewal of the
ancient miracles whereby Moses led the Israelites out of Egypt and
Joshua led them in to the promised land; surely the merits of a Christian king like Louis must outweigh those of the Jews, who themselves
enjoyed the providence of God in their conquests. (ii) The letter then
turns to the Jews of Peter's own day in light of the struggle against the
Saracens. Echoing the reasoning that impelled crusaders to attack the

---

81. For example: A. Lukyn Williams, *Adversus Judaeos: A Bird's-Eye View of Christian Apologiae until the Renaissance* (Cambridge, England, 1935), pp. 384–94; Blumenkranz, "Die Entwicklung," pp. 120ff.; Dahan, "Bernard de Clairvaux," p. 60; and
Gavin I. Langmuir, *Toward a Definition of Antisemitism* (Berkeley, Calif., 1990), pp.
197–208, and "Faith of Christians," pp. 83–85.
82. David Knowles, "Peter the Venerable," *Bulletin of the John Rylands Library* 39
(1956), 142; James Kritzeck, "Moslem-Christian Understanding in Medieval Times,"
Comparative Studies in Society and History 4 (1962), 397; Virginia G. Berry, "Peter the
Venerable and the Crusades," in *Petrus Venerabilis, 1156–1956: Studies and Texts Commemorating the Eighth Centenary of His Death*, ed. Giles Constable and James Kritzeck,
Studia anselmiana 40 (Rome, 1956), p. 149. See also the additional apologies for Peter's
anti-Judaism cited in Langmuir, *Toward a Definition*, p. 202.
83. Peter the Venerable, *Epistulae* 130, in *Letters*, ed. Constable, 1:327–30.
84. Cf. the differing schema proposed in Friedman, "Anatomy," pp. 91ff.

Jews of northern Europe in 1096, as understood by both Jewish and Christian chroniclers of the Crusade,[85] Peter wondered out loud, as it were, about the rationale underlying the call for the new Crusade:

> What good is it to pursue and persecute the enemies of the Christian faith in far and distant lands if the Jews, vile blasphemers and far worse than the Saracens, not far away from us but right in our midst, blaspheme, abuse, and trample on Christ and the Christian sacraments so freely and insolently and with impunity? How can zeal for God nourish God's children if the Jews, enemies of the supreme Christ and of the Christians, remain totally unpunished? Has that which a certain holy king of the Jews once said [Psalm 139:21] escaped the notice of the king of the Christians? "O Lord," he said, "shall I not hate those who hate you and be consumed with enmity for your enemies?"

Peter hastened to temper his outcry with the qualification that he did not wish for Christians to attack the Jews physically:

> I recall that written about them in the divine psalm, the prophet speaking thus in the spirit of God: "God," he said, "has shown me in the matter of my enemies, slay them not." For God does not wish them to be entirely killed and altogether wiped out, but to be preserved for greater torment and reproach, like the fratricide Cain, in a life worse than death. . . . So the fully just severity of God has dealt with the damned, damnable Jews from the very time of the passion and death of Christ—and will do so until the end of time. Those who shed the blood of Christ, their brother according to the flesh, are enslaved, wretched, fearful, mournful, and exiled on the face of the earth—until, as the prophet has taught, the remnants of this wretched people shall turn to God once the multitude of the Gentiles has already been called.

(iii) Practically speaking, then, how ought Christian society to enforce this servile status of Jews upon them? Exceeding the demands of Agobard, who, railing against Jewish carnality, had also applied Psalm 139: 21 to the Jews,[86] Peter called for depriving the Jews of much of their wealth, which they have acquired not honestly by working the land (*de simplici agri cultura*) but by deceiving Christians. The Jews traffic in stolen property and, most offensively, in relics, icons, and other rit-

---

85. Neubauer and Stern, *Hebräische Berichte*, pp. 1, 4, 47; and Guibert of Nogent, *Monodiae* 2.5, in *Autobiographie*, ed. Edmond-René Labande, Les Classiques de l'histoire de France au Moyen Âge 34 (Paris, 1981), p. 246. Cf. above, introduction to part 3, at n. 11.

86. Agobard, *De iudaicis superstitionibus et erroribus* 10, CCCM 52:207; and Friedman, "Anatomy," pp. 94–95. On the influence of Agobard and other earlier churchmen on Peter, see below, nn. 120–21, 140.

ual objects stolen from churches and then sold to the synagogues of Satan, where the thieves find refuge as well. The Jews thereby compound their blasphemy, inasmuch as these murderers of Christ—"who inflicted him with as much insult and injury as they could while he lived among mortals, and now, while he basks in the majesty of his eternal divinity, do not cease from attacking him orally with as many blasphemies as they so dare"—make such shameful, intolerable use of things so sacred. What old, satanic law wrongfully protects Jewish property from confiscation, even if it has been stolen from Christians? (iv) And finally, the letter returns to the pressing issue of the day, the Crusade: To the extent possible, one should level the financial cost of the holy war upon the Jews. "Let their lives be spared but their money taken away," rather than imposing the entire burden of the Crusade upon the Christian faithful.

At first blush, Peter's blatant hostility toward the Jews diverges sharply from the protective tone of Bernard's letter, and historians have invoked various explanations for the difference.[87] Some have called attention to the indebtedness of Peter's monastery of Cluny, and its obligations to Jewish moneylenders in particular, which aroused Peter's ire and jealousy.[88] Some have argued that the Jews' usury did not infuriate Peter as much as did their trade in Christian ritual objects, which struck Peter as a personal affront on the body of Christ. Perhaps Peter's essential concern lay with the financial support of the Crusade, as opposed to Bernard's wish to define the mandate of the crusaders themselves; perhaps the issue of the Jews functioned as one more context in which the two abbots gave expression to the debates and rivalries which divided them. No doubt differences in religious temperament and personality came into play here as well; polemic against Jews, Muslims, and Christian heretics dominates the corpus of Peter's extant writings, whereas it assumes much less obvious significance in the works of Bernard. Peter appeared driven to punish the Jews for their enmity toward Christ which, he argued, manifested itself in Christendom incessantly and most dangerously in the economic sphere. According to Yvonne Friedman, "the proposal to punish the

87. In addition to the studies cited above, nn. 81–82, see Friedman, "Anatomy"; Jean-Pierre Torrell, "Les Juifs dans l'oeuvre de Pierre le Vénérable," *CCM* 30 (1987), 331–46; and Chazan, "Twelfth-Century Perceptions," pp. 195–99.

88. Peter vehemently expressed his objection to monasteries incurring indebtedness to Jews in his *De miraculis* 2.15, CCCM 83:125, and in *Epistulae* 56, in *Letters*, ed. Constable, 1:177f.

Jews for the crime of the crucifixion by a financial imposition . . . is Peter's contribution to medieval anti-Semitism."[89]

Nevertheless, without discounting the obvious differences between the letters of Bernard and Peter or the possibilities advanced for explaining them, one can reread the two documents in such a way as to lessen the distance between their respective constructions of Jews and Judaism. To be sure, Bernard's letter seeks primarily to inspire Christians, Peter's to denigrate the Jews. Yet both letters speak out in support of the Crusade. In so doing, both present guidelines for combating the infidels who endanger the security of Christendom, and thus they come to address the nature of the Jews alongside that of the Muslims. As opposed to the Muslim threat, both define the Jewish threat to Christian society largely in economic terms; and both link the economic activity of the Jews to their allegedly characteristic carnality, on one hand, while comparing it to that of Christian sinners, on the other hand—in Bernard's case that of Christian usurers, in Peter's that of Christian thieves of ritual objects. Both letters sympathize with the zeal that has motivated crusaders to attack the Jews: Peter's, as we have seen, in echoing their rationale, Bernard's by noting (F1), "We have heard and rejoiced that the zeal for God's glory burns among you." Both letters then proceed to oppose violent attacks upon the Jews, citing the Augustinian prooftext of Psalm 59:12.[90] If Bernard's letter appears to advocate a tolerant attitude toward the Jews and Peter's a severe one, both strive essentially to redress perceived deviations from the norm which should characterize that attitude: Bernard's the anti-Jewish violence preached by Radulf, Peter's the economic exploitation of Christian society by the Jews. Both texts identify the Jews with the law of the Old Testament, Peter's with mention that the Jews "observe the divine commandments" and Bernard's by dubbing them "living letters." And both eventually conclude by advocating that the Jews somehow share in the financial burden of the Crusade, at least to the extent of forfeiting their profits from usury or other unlawful trade.

No less important, just as Bernard's encyclical addresses the matter of the Jews from the perspective of a distinctive idea of crusading, so

89. Friedman, "Anatomy," p. 100.

90. Curiously, Peter conflated the younger Augustine's typological comparison of the Jews to Cain with the older Augustine's novel exegesis of Psalm 59:12, concluding that one ought not kill the Jews precisely in order that they might suffer as Cain did. See above, chapter 1, at nn. 7–8, 94–96, and cf. the similar blend of Augustinian motifs in Innocent III's later decree *Ut esset Cain* cited below, chapter 8, n. 118.

can one better understand Peter's letter by considering his appraisal of
Christian campaigns to liberate the Holy Land from Muslim control;
the issues of holy war led both abbots to reflect on the role of the Jews
in Christendom of their day and in salvation history at large. Beyond
its endorsement of the Crusade, likening it to the divinely ordained
wars of the ancient Israelites, the letter to Louis VII affords little insight
into Peter's crusading ideology; but his sermon *De laude dominici sepulchri* (In Praise of the Lord's Grave), preached in the presence of the
pope in the same year or the next, offers considerably more.[91] There
Peter extolled the sanctity and symbolic importance of the Holy Sepulcher at length. Jesus' grave connotes the chief reason (*summa causa*)
for exulting in Christ, that which truly facilitates Christian victory over
the enemies of God. The death of Jesus, his resurrection, and his ascension to heaven outweigh his birth in importance, and the honor of
the sepulcher accordingly exceeds that of the manger in Bethlehem;
inasmuch as the grave received the body of Jesus after his life, its excellence approximates that of the virgin mother who carried his body
in her womb before his birth. Scripture appropriately attests to the
centrality of the Holy Land and of Jerusalem in a Christian view of
the world. Just as Jesus' grave at the heart of the earth (*cor terrae*)
contained his body, so ought the Christian to embody the eternal memory of Christ in his heart, centrally located among human organs. Old
Testament prophets envisioned the holiness of the sepulcher, alongside
the virgin birth, the passion of Christ, the rejection of the Jews, the
calling of the Gentiles, and other such mysteries of the faith. Today
the sepulcher embodies the Christian hope for final salvation, hope that
has now spread throughout the entire world, only a few remaining Jews
and the wicked sect of Muhammad excepted. God has confirmed this
status of the sepulcher and the hope that proceeds therefrom in numerous ways, above all in the miraculous fire that kindles the lamps
in the Holy Sepulcher every Easter—a miracle the virtues and veracity
of which the sermon painstakingly elaborates.[92] Here, then, lies the
route to salvation: Forsaking the pleasures of this world, a Christian

---

91. Peter the Venerable, "Sermones tres," ed. Giles Constable, *RB* 64 (1954), 232–
54. See also Berry, "Peter the Venerable"; Benjamin Z. Kedar, *Crusade and Mission:
European Approaches toward the Muslim* (Princeton, N.J., 1984), pp. 99ff.; and Penny
J. Cole, *The Preaching of the Crusades to the Holy Land, 1095–1270* (Cambridge, Mass.,
1991), pp. 49–52.

92. Pope Gregory IX denounced this miracle as fraudulent in 1238; on the "career"
of the miracle, see the sources cited by Langmuir, *Toward a Definition* pp. 206–7, 384
n. 37, and McGinn, "*Iter Sancti Sepulchri*," p. 56 nn. 2, 6.

must dedicate himself to the holiness, memories, and miracles enshrined in the grave of his savior, joining the universal convocation of faithful souls it has attracted, liberating it from the baseness of the infidels.

Peter's *De laude* allows us to pursue our comparison of the abbots of Cluny and Clairvaux. Whereas Bernard presented the Crusade in a more tropological vein, rationalizing it as a heavenly ruse for allowing Christians to overcome the sinfulness that plagued their souls, Peter elucidated its importance in much more Christological and historical terms. For him, as opposed to Bernard, the specific military goal of the Crusade—control of the Holy Land, Jerusalem, and the Holy Sepulcher—mattered greatly. These concrete, physical spaces truly embody the sanctity of Christ and the salvation he offers, much as the miracle of fire with which God still illuminates this sacred space is "true, physical, and substantive [*verum, corporale, ac solidum*]."[93] Peter's sermon anchors the Crusade in the historical wonders that have derived from the historical career of Jesus, both before and after the crucifixion. And yet, Bernard and Peter still held much in common with regard to crusading. Each viewed participation in the Crusade as an act of ultimate spiritual concern that advanced a Christian toward salvation; and, albeit in the account of a vision attributed to Peter only after his death, he too reportedly deemed it better for a Cistercian novice to remain in his European monastery than to set out for the earthly Jerusalem.[94] Like Bernard, Peter also used the language of marketing to emphasize the polar opposition between the crusader's quest for redemption and a life of worldly pursuits:

> Listen, you devotees of worldly glory; listen, you who tend to glory in fleeting shadows, in wilting flowers, in empty winds; listen, you who are accustomed to find your glory in fragile might, in perishable wealth, in transitory pride. See to it that all this glory of yours is transferred to the grave of the dead man, and that that is preferred to every human vanity or ostentation. Just as in human transactions can there be no profit from a purchase without the price of the sale, nor can there be remuneration without the cost of the labor, so in divine commerce, the reward of resurrection cannot follow unless the price of redemption has preceded it.[95]

Moreover, like Bernard, Peter construed the Jews and their lifestyle as exemplifying the antithesis of what the crusader should emulate. The

---

93. Peter, "Sermones tres," p. 249.

94. Giles Constable, "The Vision of Gunthelm and Other Visions Attributed to Peter the Venerable," *RB* 66 (1956), 105–6.

95. Peter, "Sermones tres," pp. 246, 251.

letter to Louis VII underscores his association of the Jews with the sinful, misguided pursuit of financial profit. And from its own perspective on salvation history, the De laude develops the opposition further: The Jews do not interpret Scripture properly, in order to fathom the grandeur of Jerusalem or its holy sites and discern the way toward eternal life.[96] The Jews murdered the body of Christ that gave the sepulcher its sanctity. The annual miracle of the fire in the Holy Sepulcher, recalling the flame with which God accepted Abel's sacrifice over Cain's and Elijah's over that of the prophets of Baal, carries yet an additional message of contemporary relevance:

> And so at the present time, O Lord, omnipotent creator, do you clearly distinguish between us and the Jews or pagans; thus do you spurn their vows, their prayers, and their offerings; thus do you show that these are repugnant to you. Now that their offerings have been rejected, you approve of ours. In this way do you proclaim that the sacrifices, prayers, and vows of your Christians are pleasing to you: You direct a fire to proceed from heaven to the grave of your son, which only they respect and revere; with that same fire you set their hearts on fire with love for you; with its splendor do you enlighten them, now and forever. And since the perfidious enemies of your Christ disparage his death more than his other acts of humility, in adorning the monument of his death with a miracle of such light do you demonstrate how great is the darkness of error in which they are confined. While they despise his death above all, you honor the monument of his death above all; what they consider particularly shameful you prove to be especially glorious by means of so wonderful a sign. You reject the Jews like the hateful Cain, the pagans like the worshippers of Baal, and you do not light a fire on their offerings. Yet you do desire the hosts of the Christian people, just like the offerings of Abel; you approve of its sacrifice, like the holocaust of Elijah, and thus with a fire sent from heaven do you irradiate the grave in which your son, offered as a sacrifice in our behalf, lay at rest.[97]

The miracle of fire at Jesus' grave attests to the rejection of the synagogue, on the model of Cain, and the Saracens, on the model of the idolatrous prophets of Baal. As they did for Bernard, Jews and Saracens in Peter's eyes together epitomized the threat of infidelitas that endangered Christendom and that therefore, paradoxically, held out the promise of salvation for those who would join the Crusade.

Peter's crusading ideology, as expressed in De laude, can lead us to an enhanced appreciation of his epistle to Louis VII. Curiously, this

96. Ibid., p. 239.
97. Ibid., p. 252. On the Christian monopoly on genuine sacrifice, see Peter the Venerable, Contra Petrobrusianos 162, CCCM 10:95.

letter displays a chiastic structure, which unfolds in a series of a fortiori arguments, corresponding to the four segments of the text in our outline above:

(i/a)   *The Jews of old versus the crusader king (Louis VII):* If God ensured the victories of the former, how much more should he assist the latter. For "the former observed the divine commandments, but, to a certain extent, they exerted themselves in combat out of hope for an earthly reward; yet the latter endangers and even sacrifices his kingdom, his wealth, and even his life . . . so that, after the disappearance of his mortal kingdom, he might be crowned with honor and glory by the king of kings."

(ii/b)   *Saracens versus Jews:* "If the Saracens are detestable because, although they acknowledge (as we do) that Christ was born of a virgin and they share many beliefs about him with us, they reject God and the son of God (which is more important) and they do not believe in his death and resurrection . . . , how much more must we curse and hate the Jews who, believing nothing concerning Christ or the Christian faith and denying the virgin birth and all the sacraments of human salvation, blaspheme and insult him?"

(iii/b')   *Christian thieves versus Jews:* Whereas the former suffer capital punishment for trading in stolen church property, the latter go unpunished, owing to that ancient, satanic law that protects them. "The Jew grows fat and revels in his pleasures, while the Christian hangs from a noose!" Surely, Peter implied, the opposite should hold true.

(iv/a')   *The Jews of old versus the crusaders:* "Just as once, when their [the Jews'] ancestors were still in God's favor, the riches of the Egyptians were consigned to their use according to divine command," how much the more so, one reasons, "should the wealth of the Jews, even against their will, serve the needs of Christian peoples."[98]

The outer poles of the chiasmus compare the victories of the ancient Israelites with those of King Louis and the crusaders: If God saved and rewarded the Jews when they still found favor in his eyes, even though a craving for earthly profit rendered their faith imperfect, he certainly should ensure the military success and financial feasibility of the Cru-

98. Peter's letter is cited above, n. 83.

sade. For their part, the inner vertices of the chiasmus contrast the Jews with both external and internal enemies of the church: Owing to their greed and their blasphemy, the Jews are more injurious than others; if Christendom justly inflicts punishment on Saracens and Christian thieves, surely the Jews ought to suffer too. The structure of Peter's letter evidently confirms the thrust of its contents. Throughout their history, ancient and modern, the Jews have embodied greed and *infidelitas*. Having inherited the spiritual election of the ancient synagogue (a), the church now receives God's help to crusade against the forces of blasphemy and carnality both outside Christendom (b) and within (b')—in either case exemplified by the Jew—and, on the model of ancient Israel, it may appropriate the assets of its enemies toward this end (a'). Peter, like Bernard, construed the Jews and Judaism from his particular mid-twelfth-century vantage point, at which crusading, fraught with ecclesiological and eschatological significance, helped to crystallize the worldview of a Christian theologian.

COMBATING JEWISH OBSTINACY

Peter the Venerable did not limit his anti-Jewish polemic to his pronouncements on crusading; the largest of his extant works is, in fact, his treatise *Adversus Iudaeorum inveteratam duritiem* (Against the Inveterate Obstinacy of the Jews), which proves even more noteworthy in the development of our story. Recent investigators have reached the conclusion that Peter composed this work in stages.[99] It originally contained four relatively brief chapters, probably written by 1144, which marshaled largely biblical evidence in support of its traditional Christian assertions: that the Christ foretold by the biblical prophets was the son of God, not in a figurative sense but born "a natural birth out of the essence of his father"; that this son of God was himself the deity; that this messiah was not an earthly king but an eternal, heavenly ruler; and that the advent of Christ has already occurred.[100] Between 1146 and 1147, Peter appended discussions of the Mosaic commandments and of Christian miracles to the fourth chapter of his book, and he added a longer, fifth chapter attacking the Talmud as the source of

---

99. See Yvonne Friedman's introduction to her edition of Peter's *Adversus Iudaeorum inveteratam duritiem*, CCCM 58:lvii–lxx; and Torrell and Bouthillier, *Pierre le Vénérable*, pp. 172–74.

100. Cf. Peter, *Adversus Iudaeorum . . . duritiem* 4, CCCM 58:82–83.

Jewish error. In a harsh, sometimes nearly uncontrolled tone, the treatise intersperses a wide assortment of insults throughout its anti-Jewish arguments. Among other things, and more than most prior works of *Adversus Iudaeos* polemic, Peter's book casts the Jew as a wretched enemy of God, a blasphemer, more reprehensible than a Philistine, an agent of the devil, and a fugitive from the light of salvation, and it describes his Judaism as perfidy, perversity, wickedness, and deception.[101]

Unlike the anti-Jewish writings of Gilbert Crispin and Peter Alfonsi (from whom Peter of Cluny borrowed extensively), the polemic of Peter the Venerable did not enjoy a wide dissemination, and it had relatively little influence on subsequent generations.[102] Still, the *Adversus Iudaeorum . . . duritiem* attests to continuing development in various distinctive patterns of high medieval Christendom's perceptions of the Jews. From the opening lines of the work, one cannot overlook the legacy of Anselm and his followers, especially that of Guibert of Nogent. The original four chapters of the *Adversus Iudaeorum . . . duritiem* concentrate almost exclusively on the doctrine of the incarnation and its corollaries, the cornerstone of Anselmian apologiae for Christianity. Peter repeatedly emphasized the blatant rationality of these Christian beliefs, so thoroughly grounded in both *ratio* and *auctoritas* that those who reject Christian truth demonstrate their own irrationality beyond the shadow of a doubt. And of all peoples in the world, the Jews alone hold out in rejecting Christ. "Open your eyes at last," Peter challenged the Jews; "open your ears, and be ashamed that you are clearly the only blind people in the world, the only deaf people to remain."[103] Peter characterized Jewish disbelief as stupidity and insanity, and he linked it directly to the carnality of the Jewish character, which infects their understanding of the Bible as well. Why, he asked rhetorically, did God grace ancient Israelites with the miracles recorded in Hebrew Scripture?

---

101. For an incomplete list of Peter's deprecations, see the citations amassed by Torrell, "Les Juifs," p. 338, and Alexander Patschovsky, "Feindbilder der Kirche: Juden und Ketzer im Vergleich (11.–13. Jh.)," in *Juden und Christen zur Zeit der Kreuzzüge*, ed. Alfred Haverkamp, Vorträge und Forschungen des Konstanzer Arbeitskreises für mittelalterliche Geschichte (Sigmaringen, Germany, 1998).

102. See the comments of Friedman, CCCM 58:xxviii ff.

103. Peter, *Adversus Iudaeorum . . . duritiem* 1, CCCM 58:10. Cf. Peter the Venerable, *Contra sectam Saracenorum* 1.87, in his *Schriften zum Islam*, ed. Reinhold Glei, Corpus islamo-christianum: Series latina 1 (Altenburg, Germany, 1985), p. 146, which emphasizes to the Muslims the "falsitatem qua exceptis Iudaeis prae cunctis mortalibus irretiti et obruti estis."

Were these things done simply so that you, O Jew, could fill your stomach with all kinds of foods and meats? Were these things done simply so that you might become intoxicated and snore like a drunk? Were these things done simply so that you could devote yourself to your desires and be abandoned to your passions? Were all these things done simply so that you might abound in wealth, so that you might fill your chests with gold, silver, and treasures galore, and so that with the haughty pride of an overlord you might raise yourself above your inferiors? [Hardly!][104]

The substance of these refrains in the *Adversus Iudaeorum . . . duritiem* departs but little from arguments advanced previously by Odo of Cambrai, Guibert of Nogent, and Peter Alfonsi, and I do not feel impelled to quote the treatise at length, simply to illustrate the extreme to which Peter took his rhetoric. Yet we would do well to consider those respects in which Peter departed from the example of his predecessors, blending the new rationalist spirit of anti-Jewish polemic with his own particular Christian outlook. First, as some scholars have noted, belligerence and a combative spirit typify Peter's opus in general; he approached the contest with the Jews as one visible dimension to the perpetual struggle between God's faithful and the forces of Satan, a struggle that ensues in the terrestrial realm, in real, concrete interactions between real people, over the course of human history.[105] Peter therefore attributed cosmic importance to the refutation of Judaism, but, as in his crusading ideology, he never allowed his monastic concern for personal spiritual perfection to obscure the historical reality undergirding any tropological lesson. As it was for Anselm and company, Judaism for Peter too was surely a category of disbelief; yet the struggle against the Jews demanded a concerted effort to fight within the combative arena of salvation history, among whose many battlegrounds numbered Eden, Calvary, the Holy Sepulcher in Jerusalem of Peter's day, and Armageddon.

Second, Peter's historical-Christological orientation bore upon the very substance of the rational argumentation in his adversarial discourse. Balancing the timeless universalism of Anselmian doctrine with a sense of historical urgency and with the particularism that stemmed from a traditional Christian reading of history, Peter rewove the osten-

---

104. Peter, *Adversus Iudaeorum . . . duritiem* 3, CCCM 58:63; cf. the citation and comments of Anna Sapir Abulafia, "Bodies in the Jewish-Christian Debate," in *Framing Medieval Bodies,* ed. Sarah Kay and Miri Rubin (Manchester, England, 1994), 127–28.

105. See especially Jean-Pierre Torrell and Denise Bouthillier, "Une Spiritualité de combat: Pierre le Vénérable et la lutte contre Satan," *RT* 84 (1984), 47–81, and *Pierre le Vénérable,* passim; and Langmuir, *Toward a Definition,* pp. 197–208.

sibly more rationalist strands of Anselm's apologia into polemic that relied heavily on the evidence of Scripture and miracle. Whereas many twelfth-century polemicists claimed to have formulated, or aspired to formulate, rational proof of the incarnation—proof that stipulated no prior belief in the authority of any revealed text—they achieved very mixed results. Anselm and Odo endeavored to argue *remoto Christo* with varying degrees of success. Gilbert Crispin set out in that direction but quickly reverted to the citation of biblical testimonies, even in his *Disputatio Christiani cum gentili*. Peter Alfonsi adduced scientific arguments to attack Judaism but still relied on biblical prooftexts in defense of Christianity. What of Peter of Cluny? He seemed to follow the example of Guibert of Nogent, posing the rational truth of Christianity as self-evident, resorting occasionally to authority-free argumentation, and castigating the Jewish mentality for refusing to recognize the truth. Yet Peter went one step farther. If Jews refuse to submit to the biblical authorities that Christians accept as compelling evidence for their beliefs, they must submit to the most compelling rational arguments of all: the miracles that have validated Christianity from the days of Jesus until the present. Here, as Jean-Pierre Torrell and Denise Bouthillier have shown, one must appreciate Peter's *Adversus Iudaeorum . . . duritiem* against the background of his *De miraculis* (On Miracles), the composition of which occupied him throughout much of the 1140s. Miracles played a critical role in Peter's worldview, signaling the active intervention of God in the ongoing terrestrial struggle between the faithful and the forces of the devil.[106] Around the same time as he wrote *De miraculis* for Christians, then, Peter explained in his *Adversus Iudaeorum . . . duritiem* "with what kind of rational proof [*qua ratione*] the Jew may be compelled, willingly or unwillingly, to submit. And by what greater rational proof can you be persuaded than those immense and innumerable divine miracles which I have already recorded?"[107] Contrasting sharply with illusory signs of Satan's power, these proofs could not have misled so great and universal a human consensus for so long a time (*tanto universorum consensu diu*).[108] "To all these people, O Jew, it appears that the miracles of Christ, on ac-

106. Denise Bouthillier and Jean-Pierre Torrell, " 'Miraculum': Une Catégorie fondamentale chez Pierre le Vénérable," *RT* 80 (1980), 357–86, 546–66; and Torrell and Bouthillier, *Pierre le Vénérable*, pt. 2, esp. pp. 172–80.

107. Peter, *Adversus Iudaeorum . . . duritiem* 4, CCCM 58:106; cf. Anna Sapir Abulafia, *Christians and Jews in the Twelfth-Century Renaissance* (London, 1995), p. 88.

108. Peter, *Adversus Iudaeorum . . . duritiem* 4, CCCM 58:116.

count of which the world has converted to the Christian faith, are not magical, fantastic, false, or inane, but divine, true, solid, and useful."[109] Biblical testimony, Peter admitted, presupposes acceptance of the authority of revelation; dialectic alone proves insufficient to effect conversion, as Anselm ultimately would have agreed; among the other means of drawing neophytes to the baptismal font, physical compulsion is unacceptable, the incentive of material profit unseemly. Documented miracles, however, could not be denied, and, concluding this supplement to chapter 4 of the *Adversus Iudaeorum . . . duritiem*, Peter turned once again to his putative opponent. "At the end of this work I propose to you, O Jew, just one heavenly and public work of Christ which, against the acclaim of the entire world, you cannot deny, so that your silence condemn you and you be compelled to confess" the faith.[110] The text proceeds to describe the miracle of the divine fire at the Holy Sepulcher, and it offers the same comparison to God's acceptance of the sacrifices of Abel and Elijah as does Peter's *De laude*.[111] The church's victory over the synagogue in the wake of the crucifixion and the holy war to liberate the Holy Land from the Saracen pertain to the same ongoing conflict between God and his diabolical enemies.

Third, Peter's peculiar brand of polemical rationalism betrays a measure of genuine—and atypical—conversionist intention. His interest in concrete physical proof for the truth of Christianity suggests that, more than those Christian writers studied in the preceding chapter, and certainly more than Bernard, he sought arguments that would succeed in persuading the Jews,[112] just as he hoped for his anti-Muslim polemic to result in conversion.[113] The *Adversus Iudaeorum . . . duritiem* repeatedly urges the Jews to repent and accept the truth. At one point it questions the very sanity of debating with the insane: How can one

109. Ibid., CCCM 58:118.

110. Ibid., CCCM 58:122.

111. Ibid., CCCM 58:122–24, and see above, n. 97.

112. See Evans, *Mind of St. Bernard*, pp. 224–30 ("Peter the Venerable's Missionary Zeal"); David Berger, "Mission to the Jews and Jewish-Christian Cultural Contacts in the Polemical Literature of the High Middle Ages," *AHR* 91 (1986), 584; and Robert Chazan, *Daggers of Faith: Thirteenth-Century Christian Missionizing and Jewish Response* (Berkeley, Calif., 1989), pp. 23–24—contra Langmuir, *Toward a Definition*, pp. 203–4.

113. Above all, see James Kritzeck, *Peter the Venerable and Islam*, Princeton Oriental Studies 23 (Princeton, N.J., 1964); Kedar, *Crusade and Mission*, pp. 99–104; and Jean Pierre Torrell, "La Notion de prophétie et la méthode apologétique dans le *Contra Saracenos* de Pierre le Vénérable," *Studia monastica* 18 (1975), 257–82.

avoid exposing oneself and one's principles to ridicule when trying to communicate with those so stupid? To which Peter replied: "If I shall not be able to benefit all the Jews with this disputation of mine, I still, perhaps, might be able to derive an advantage for some."[114]

Fourth, the refusal of most Jews to acquiesce before the overwhelmingly rational and compelling evidence—biblical prooftexts, logical propositions, and miracles—that Peter amassed in defense of Christianity led him to a more drastic deduction concerning their mind and their humanity. In a series of rhetorical outbursts, Peter not only followed Bernard in attributing a bovine, beastly intellect to the Jews but labeled them beasts as opposed to people. On the heels of the discussion of miracles, Peter opened the final chapter of his treatise as follows:

> It seems to me, O Jew, that with so many prooftexts and with rational argumentation so extensive I have satisfied any human being, I think, concerning those matters which had been called into question. And if any human being, then you too, if you are in fact human. Lest I lie, I dare not profess that you are human, because I understand that the rational faculty which distinguishes the human being from other animals and beasts and renders him superior to them has been obliterated or suppressed in you. . . . Why are you not called a brute animal, why not a beast, why not a beast of burden? Consider the cow or, if you prefer, the ass—no beast is more stupid—and together with it listen to whatever things those beasts can hear. What will the ass reply? What will distinguish between its hearing and yours? The ass hears but does not understand; the Jew hears but does not understand.[115]

Humanity, reasoned Peter, should invariably lead to Christianity; the Jews, who refuse Christianity, are therefore cattle, dogs, swine.[116] One can rightly wonder whether the abbot of Cluny thoroughly pondered the ramifications of his equation; he could not possibly have foreseen its ensuing historical career.

Beyond these aspects of its distinctive rationalist polemic against the Jews, we remember Peter's *Adversus Iudaeorum . . . duritiem* for its attack upon the Talmud, which filled its fifth, final, and longest chapter. Peter the Venerable was the first medieval churchman to cite the Talmud by name; his condemnation of the Talmud exceeded that of

114. Peter, *Adversus Iudaeorum . . . duritiem* 5, CCCM 58:127.
115. Ibid., CCCM 58:125.
116. Ibid., CCCM 58:151: "Si eos canes vel porcos vocavi, in nullo excessi."

Peter Alfonsi; and he seemed to cast much of the blame for Jewish irrationality and disbelief directly on "the most frivolous fables" of talmudic aggadot.[117] Following the example of Alfonsi's *Dialogi*, the *Adversus Iudaeorum . . . duritiem* berates the absurdities and blasphemies in an array of fourteen talmudic homilies, many of which Peter of Cluny seems to have drawn directly from Alfonsi's work. Nonetheless, the Talmud plays a markedly different role in the polemic of the *Adversus Iudaeorum . . . duritiem*. Most obviously, the tone has changed, from that of Alfonsi's generally even-tempered conversation to that of an outright harangue:

> I extend to you before the whole world, O beastly Jew, that book of yours—yes, your book, that Talmud of yours, that illustrious doctrine of yours, which must be preferred to prophetic books and all authentic teachings. . . . The Jewish Talmud cannot be that book of which it is said, "In your book all are recorded" [Psalm 139:16]. . . . Who besides Satan can teach such absurd things, and who besides the Jew can listen to, if not believe, them—that the reading of the Talmud can prejudice the power of God, that the incredible recitation of an infernal book can impede the will and mandate of God? For is that book of yours, O Jew, holier than the five books of Moses, holier than the books of the prophets, better or more worthy . . . ? You have fought for so long against divine books with diabolical ones, and you have striven to tinge and obscure heavenly doctrine with the smoke of the infernal pit.[118]

As these brief excerpts suggest, Peter of Cluny attacked the Talmud not so much for casting anthropomorphic aspersions on the perfection of the deity (as Alfonsi had done) but most of all for allocating importance to itself in God's covenant with the Jews. Peter adduced rabbinic homilies proclaiming that importance which Alfonsi did not discuss: God studies the Talmud; studying the Talmud and swearing by it saved Rabbi Joshua ben Levi from the angel of death, who explained that Christians are condemned to hell for rejecting the Torah and the Talmud; Rabba bar Nachmani (whom Peter called Rabbi Nehemiah) enabled God himself to triumph in a talmudic debate. Peter, some have charged, may even have distorted the wording of the talmudic sources at his disposal in order to aggravate his indictment of them.[119] The

---

117. Ibid. 3, CCCM 58:57–58. For a detailed discussion of Peter's talmudic citations, see Ch. Merchavia, *The Church versus Talmudic and Midrashic Literature, 500–1248* [Hebrew] (Jerusalem, 1970), chap. 4.

118. Peter, *Adversus Iudaeorum . . . duritiem* 5, CCCM 58:125–26, 128, 139, 186.

119. Esp. Amos Funkenstein, *Perceptions of Jewish History* (Berkeley, Calif., 1993), pp. 191–92.

Talmud added blasphemy to the insanity of the Jews that Peter had attacked in the preceding chapters of his treatise; their insanity, though divinely wrought punishment for their sin, is not sinful in itself, but their blasphemy certainly is.[120] In its esoteric traditions, the Talmud conceals the manifold influence of Satan on the Jews, which leads them to value his teachings over the biblical instruction of God.

Amos Funkenstein has argued strenuously that Peter the Venerable hereby introduced a qualitatively new element into the medieval Christian attack on the Jews and Judaism. Peter, he has concluded, repudiated the Augustinian view of the Jews as somehow embodying the literal sense of the law; for Peter, the medieval Jew was no longer the real Jew of the Bible, and the Talmud was nothing less than a perversion of real Judaism. One can, to be sure, trace back to earlier Christian writers many of the motifs in Peter's polemic that contribute to such a conclusion: the bovine character of the Jews, the absurd anthropomorphisms of their fables, the negative impact of these tales on Jewish intelligence, the charge that the Jews have traded their God-given books for the writings of human beings, and the understanding of the Jewish rejection of Christianity as the work of the devil.[121] Yet, according to

---

120. Peter, *Adversus Iudaeorum . . . duritiem* 5, CCCM 58:127. The sinfulness of talmudic blasphemy hardly prevents that blasphemy, too, from constituting part of God's punishment of the Jews; here Peter has followed Agobard, *De iudaicis superstitionibus et erroribus* 20, CCCM 52:215, who himself followed Jerome, *In Evangelium Matthaei* 2 (ad 12:43–45) CCSL 77:99–100.

121. As de Lubac, *Exégèse médiévale*, 2,1:99ff., has shown, Origen (*De principiis* 4.2, GCS 22:305ff.) already likened heretics to Jews for their acceptance of the literal sense of Scripture; and both Jerome (*In Esaiam* 1 [ad 1.3], CCSL 73:9) and Augustine (*Enarratio in Psalmos* 67.38–39, CCSL 39:896) likened heretics to beasts for perverting the interpretation of the Bible. Many (Origen, *In Leviticum homiliae* 3.3, GCS 29:306; Jerome, *Epistulae* 121.10, CSEL 56,1:48–49; Augustine, *Contra adversarium legis et prophetarum* 2.1.2, PL 42:637; Leo the Great, *Sermones* 29.2, PL 54:228; Alcuin, *Commentaria in Apocalypsin* 5 [ad 10:3], PL 100:1144; and Rabanus Maurus, *De laudibus sanctae crucis* 2.10, PL 107:275) had also condemned the Jews for their superstitions and fables, and some (e.g., Bernhard Blumenkranz, ed., "*Altercatio Aecclesie contra Synagogam*: Texte inédit du xᵉ siècle," *RMAL* 10 [1954], 73) had linked such Jewish perfidy to intellectual deficiency. Isidore of Seville, *Etymologiae* 8.1.7–8 had labeled the synagogue a meeting place for cattle; and we have already noted (above, nn. 86, 120, and below, n. 140) parallels between the anti-Jewish arguments of Peter and those of Agobard of Lyons. On Agobard's legacy in Peter's polemic, as well as on the influence of John Chrysostom and Quodvultdeus, see also Marianne Awerbuch, *Christlich-jüdische Begegnung im Zeitalter der Frühscholastik*, Abhandlungen zum christlich-jüdischen Dialog 8 (Munich, 1980), p. 195; Yvonne Friedman, "Armenkultur und Literatur: Zur Entwicklung eines Motivs in der antijüdischen Polemik des 12. Jahrhunderts," *Kairos*, n.s. 26 (1984), 80–88; and Torrell, "Les Juifs," p. 334 n. 13, who points out that the earliest attested manuscript of Agobard's works numbered among the holdings of the library at twelfth-century Cluny. In this last regard, see Max Manitius, *Geschichte der lateinischen Literatur des Mittelalters*, Handbuch der Altertumswissenschaft 9, 2 (Munich, 1911–31), 1:389.

Funkenstein, Peter surpassed earlier churchmen in drawing a qualitative distinction between the ancient Judaism of God's biblical covenant
with Moses and the new law (*nova lex*) of the Talmud and contemporary Judaism:

> His aim is to construct a conflict between the talmudic sages and the divine
> law. . . . Since the cessation of prophecy, the Jews are engaged in the pro-
> duction of new canonical writings utterly alien to the Old Testament. These
> writings are kept secret so that their satanic nature remains likewise hidden,
> but they are meant to compete with the Scriptures and to suppress them.
> . . . These were new accusations, never before raised by Jerome, Augustine,
> or even Agobard, and certainly not by Alfunsi. The Talmud is the satanic
> secret of the Jews: *Peter the Venerable took present Judaism out of the
> framework of the Church doctrine of conditional tolerance* because, as he
> thought, Jews did change and hold today to the Old Testament only out-
> wardly. Their purpose is throughout destructive.[122]

Such a reading of Peter the Venerable underscores the convergence
of older anti-Jewish motifs within a new, more deliberately conceived,
more far-reaching indictment of Judaism. The vigor and vitriol of Peter's diatribe amount to more than a mere difference in tone. The Talmud, as portrayed in the *Adversus Iudaeorum . . . duritiem,* has altered
the parameters of the traditional Christian appraisal of the Jews. The
Talmud's contrived stories contrast sharply with the truly divine miracles recorded in Scripture; these talmudic tales have degraded the contemporary Jew, holding his heart in their grip, incapacitating the exercise of his reason, and rendering him subhuman. The Talmud may
have induced Peter to question the applicability of the "Church doctrine of conditional tolerance"—in essence, the Augustinian doctrine
of Jewish witness—to contemporary Judaism. The Jewish players in
the Augustinian drama of terrestrial history are portrayed decisively as
human; Peter's talmudic Jews are not. In Peter's view, the Jews reject
Christianity not, as Bernard of Clairvaux summarized Augustine's
view, because they are "living letters" of the biblical text but because
the Talmud has distanced them from that very text. Recalling Augustine's belief that the dispersion of the Jews among all nations of the
world (*per omnes gentes etiam ipsos esse dispersos*) indicates their continuing contribution to the divine economy of salvation,[123] one hardly

---

122. Funkenstein, *Perceptions*, p. 192 (emphasis mine).
123. Augustine, *De civitate Dei* 18.46, CCSL 48:644; cf. above, chapter 1, n. 22.

leaves Peter's *Adversus Iudaeorum . . . duritiem* with a similar impression.[124] Rather than serving as *praeparatio evangelica*, as preparation for Christianity in the grand scheme of salvation history, the doctrines of rabbinic Judaism directed others far away from the truth, to heresy, as they did in the case of Muhammad. As the momentum of his attack on the Talmud increased, Peter even questioned the tenability of his aforecited rationale for appealing rationally to talmudic Jews despite their insanity:

> I therefore do not wish to despise the words of my Lord, so as to reveal godly treasures only to have them trampled by such beasts. For although I may seem to have done so in my remarks above, there was, in fact, cause for this, which I mentioned previously: that if not for everyone—and even if not for most—this treatise of mine might prove beneficial at least for those few whom we sometimes see have turned to God, who were or could have been infected with this disease. But since intolerable things follow upon the strange, it is not right that one engage those who say these things as if they were human beings using their reason.[125]

One wonders whether Peter's appraisal of the Talmud undermines the Pauline-Augustinian hope for Jewish conversion at the end of the present era. In Funkenstein's estimation, Peter "views the Talmud as a genuine heresy, containing human traditions which are not intended to interpret the Bible but to compete with it."[126] The *Adversus Iudaeorum . . . duritiem* thus anticipated the allegations that the church leveled formally against the Talmud in the thirteenth century, as well as the dangerous implications of those allegations in the dynamics of Christian-Jewish interaction. "The new polemical stand of Peter the Venerable carried a strong potential for the erosion of the hitherto existing *modus vivendi* between tolerating Christianity and tolerated Judaism. On a lower, more popular level of discourse, the new attitude found expression in the first blood libels—very close to Peter's time."[127]

---

124. To the contrary, Peter highlights the dispersion of Christianity throughout the entire world as proof positive of its validity; see the passages cited by Langmuir, *Toward a Definition*, pp. 198–200. Cf. also the valuable comments of David Berger, ed., *The Jewish-Christian Debate in the High Middle Ages: A Critical Edition of the Niẓẓaḥon Vetus*, Judaica: Texts and Translations 4 (Philadelphia, 1979), pp. 269–70.

125. Peter, *Adversus Iudaeorum . . . duritiem* 5, CCCM 58:152; cf. above, n. 114, for Peter's original statement of purpose over which this passage expresses misgivings.

126. Funkenstein, *Perceptions*, p. 189.

127. Ibid., p. 194. See also Manfred Kniewasser, "Die antijüdische Polemik des Petrus Alphonsi (getauft 1106) und des Abtes Petrus Venerabilis von Cluny († 1156)," *Kairos*, n.s. 22 (1980), 76; and Abulafia, *Christians and Jews*, p. 129.

On prior occasions I have taken issue with Funkenstein's appraisal of Peter the Venerable, arguing that a systematic indictment of talmudic Judaism as heresy came only in the 1230s and 1240s, nearly an entire century after the composition of the *Adversus Iudaeorum . . . duritiem*. As the preceding paragraphs should indicate, I have here attempted to present Funkenstein's position more sympathetically, because I now concur that in its constructions of Jews and Judaism, Peter's polemic bespeaks a departure from the Augustinian norm; in no uncertain terms, it reflects and contributes to the convergence of the categories of Jew and heretic that characterized the High Middle Ages.[128] But at the same time as Peter's work attests to novelties of the twelfth-century anti-Jewish polemic—Anselmian rationalism, concern with rabbinic Judaism, reclassification of the Jewish unbeliever—it also confirms just how indefinite many of our twelfth-century churchmen actually were in their new assessments of the Jews. I agree with Funkenstein that Peter construed the Talmud as intolerable, as sinister, insane, blasphemous, diabolical Jewish doctrine. Perhaps, one might speculate, Peter had imagined what Pope Gregory IX, the first to order the Talmud seized and burned, later proclaimed officially: that here was "the major factor that keeps the Jews unyielding in their perfidy."[129] The minimal extent of Peter's influence on subsequent polemicists aside, however, I do not agree that the abbot of Cluny deemed the Talmud heretical in comparison with "real" biblical Judaism, that is, a *nova lex,* liable to rightful persecution for its innovative departures from Mosaic law. Peter lacked direct access to the Talmud.[130] Although he quoted its aggadic homilies, he displayed no familiarity with its halakhah or legal material, even less than the little bit cited in Alfonsi's *Dialogi*. Though he sensed the threat of such a postbiblical work to the standard Chris-

128. This conclusion finds further confirmation in the meticulous tabulations of Patschovsky, "Feindbilder." Interestingly, it seems that Amos Funkenstein also mollified his posture since his study of twelfth-century polemic first appeared, in 1968. There, "Changes in the Patterns of Christian Anti-Jewish Polemic in the Twelfth Century" [Hebrew], *Zion*, n.s. 33 (1968), 137, Funkenstein claimed to have "proof" that Peter the Venerable anticipated the thirteenth-century condemnations of the Talmud by one hundred years; in the 1993 English revision of this study (*Perceptions of Jewish History* [Berkeley, Calif., 1993], p. 189), however, the same sentence begins more tentatively, "Should I be able to show. . . ."

129. Simonsohn, *ASJD, 492–1404*, Pontifical Institute of Mediaeval Studies: Studies and Texts 94 (Toronto, 1988), pp. 171ff.; Grayzel, *CJ*, p. 240. Cf. below, chapter 8, n. 43.

130. Saul Lieberman, *Shkiin: A Few Words on Some Jewish Legends, Customs, and Literary Sources Found in Karaite and Christian Works* [Hebrew], 2d ed. (Jerusalem, 1970), pp. 27–42; and Merchavia, *Church*, pp. 133, 149ff.

tian appraisal of Judaism, Peter never approached the awareness voiced in 1247—exactly one hundred years later—by Pope Innocent IV, who delayed taking action against the Talmud after receiving an appeal from the Jews of northern France:

> The Jewish masters . . . recently asserted in our presence . . . that without that book which is called "Talmut" in Hebrew they are incapable of understanding *the Bible and the other statutes of their law* in keeping with their religion. We who, in keeping with the divine injunction, are obligated to tolerate them in the observance of that law therefore considered it proper to respond to them thus: We do not want to deprive them of their books unjustly, if, in so doing, we should deprive them of the observance of their law.[131]

Innocent proceeded to appoint an investigatory commission, which described how the Talmud deviated perversely from Scripture, "not only from a spiritual understanding [of the law] but even from a literal understanding."[132]

Although he considered talmudic blasphemies worthy of condemnation to a figurative "eternal fire,"[133] Peter reiterated the Augustinian maxim of "Slay them not" in the *Adversus Iudaeorum . . . duritiem*,[134] just as he did in his letter to King Louis. Peter made repeated reference to the divinely ordained subjugation of the Jews by other nations.[135] He acknowledged that Christians and Jews cherish the same Old Testament books,[136] and he even praised the Jews for preserving the biblical text intact throughout the centuries.[137] Peter often called the Jews blind, deaf, hard-hearted, stupid, and bovine,[138] but never fully cognizant of their error. The Jews, then, were ignorant of the truth they rejected; they were not deliberate unbelievers. Like Peter Alfonsi before him, Peter of Cluny affirmed that the interpretation of sacred texts "in the Jewish manner [*iudaico more*]"[139] meant a literal interpretation,

---

131. Simonsohn, *ASJD*, 492–1404, p. 197 (emphasis mine); Grayzel, *CJ*, pp. 274–80. Cf. below, chapter 8, n. 17.

132. Grayzel, *CJ*, rev. ed. (New York, 1966), p. 276n. Cf. below, chapter 8, n. 14.

133. Peter, *Adversus Iudaeorum . . . duritiem* 5, CCCM 58:166.

134. Ibid., CCCM 58:141.

135. Ibid. 4, CCCM 58:96, 5, CCCM 58:141. Cf. also Peter's *Contra Petrobrusianos* 80, CCCM 10:49–50.

136. Peter, *Adversus Iudaeorum . . . duritiem* 4, CCCM 58:99.

137. Peter, *Contra sectam Saracenorum* 1.67–68, in *Schriften zum Islam*, pp. 120–24.

138. Peter, *Adversus Iudaeorum . . . duritiem*, CCCM 58:1, 6, 13, 17, 28–29, 32–33, 42–43, 46–47, 54, 57–58, 62–63, 70, 78, 89, 125–26, 134, 151, etc.

139. Peter, *Contra Petrobrusianos* 77, CCCM 10:47; cf. "Sermones tres," p. 239.

and he had no patience for the fabulous homilies of the Talmud because he never imagined that Jews would understand them in any way except literally. The Greeks and Romans had their myths, which they knew to interpret metaphorically, "whence there would be no great cause for alarm if you too, O Jews, would have fables and would interpret their meaning as pertaining to something true and useful."[140] Much of the Jews' error in upholding talmudic doctrine derived from a mentality that discerned only the letter, admitting "neither metaphor, nor allegory, nor any of the many customary modes of figurative speech, through which all these things may rightfully be interpreted as applying to God."[141]

The parallels between—and the nearly simultaneous composition of—Peter's letter 130 to Louis VII, his *De laude dominici sepulchri*, his *De miraculis*, and his *Adversus Iudaeorum . . . duritiem* show how his anti-Judaism "fits" within the corpus of his writings and his worldview. And I believe that the peculiar features of Peter's *Adversus Iudaeorum . . . duritiem* considered thus far—its emphasis on Jewish irrationality and its limited attack on the Talmud—assume still greater clarity when one turns to another: Just as Peter's letter to Louis VII concerning the Crusade posed Jews and Muslims together as endangering the welfare of Christendom, so must Peter's anti-Jewish polemic be appreciated within the more general context of his campaigns against all forms of opposition to the Catholic Church. Peter polemicized against the early-twelfth-century heresy of Peter of Bruys,[142] and we remember him even more for his unprecedented efforts to convert the Saracens—which led him to journey to Spain, to commission of a translation of the Quran, and to compose two anti-Muslim treatises, a *Summa totius haeresis ac diabolicae secta Saracenorum sive Ismaelitarum* (Summa on the Entire Heresy and Diabolical Sect of the Saracens or Ishmaelites) and a treatise *Contra sectam Saracenorum* (Against the Sect of the Saracens).[143] More than any of his predecessors, in stark

---

140. Peter, *Adversus Iudaeorum . . . duritiem* 5, CCCM 58:157–58. Here, too, Peter followed Agobard, *De iudaicis superstitionibus et erroribus* 11, CCCM 52:208, in referring the darkness of disbelief bewailed by Paul in 2 Corinthians 6:14–15 to the post-biblical traditions of the Jews, whereas Jerome, *Epistulae* 22.29, CSEL 54:188–89, had interpreted the passage as referring to classical pagan culture. See Friedman, "Anatomy," p. 94 n. 37.

141. Peter, *Adversus Iudaeorum . . . duritiem* 5, CCCM 58:153.

142. See Peter's *Contra Petrobrusianos*, CCCM 10; and Jean Châtillon, "Pierre le Vénérable et les Pétrobrusiens," in *PAPV*, pp. 165–79.

143. See the texts in Peter, *Schriften zum Islam*, and the studies of Marie-Thérèse d'Alverny, "Deux traductions latines du Coran au Moyen Âge," *AHDL* 16 (1948), 69–

contrast to Bernard of Clairvaux, and in keeping with his historically focused eschatology, Peter endeavored systematically to understand, to explicate, and to refute the tenets of Islam.

When comparing Peter's polemic against Islam with his attack on Judaism, one surely must note some obvious differences: On one hand, Peter appealed to the Muslims in a tone much more solicitous than that which typified his anti-Jewish writings, and he acknowledged that they accepted Jesus as a prophet and believed in his virgin birth. On the other hand, Peter suggested to the Muslims that they ought to emulate both the Jews' willingness to engage in calm, civilized religious debate and their consistent loyalty to the text of Holy Scripture.[144] Nevertheless, even in these differences, one cannot but sense a measure of equivalence in Peter's estimation of Jewish and Muslim infidels, an impression confirmed by numerous similarities and points of interdependence that he beheld in them. As the corpus of shared Old Testament texts may have given Peter hope of converting the Jews, respect for the Muslims' philosophical and scientific achievements impelled him to approach them as "people not only rational by nature but reasonable in their talent and art."[145] Peter felt obligated to polemicize against Islam and Judaism alike, and, recalling Augustine's preaching against the Jews, he taught that even if one does not thereby convert the Muslims, one still convicts them of their error.[146] The followers of Muhammad, too, have survived to make some definite (albeit, perhaps, unfathomable) contribution to salvation history,[147] and, as he did for the Jews, Peter preferred nonviolent means to secure their conversion. Yet just as the Jews of Peter's day stubbornly resisted the truth of biblical argument, so did the Muslims, persistently rejecting the compelling dictates of human reason, fail to meet his expectations of them.

131; Charles Julian Bishko, "Peter the Venerable's Journey to Spain," in *Petrus Venerabilis, 1156–1956: Studies and Texts Commemorating the Eighth Centenary of His Death*, ed. Giles Constable and James Kritzeck, Studia anselmiana 40 (Rome, 1956), pp. 163–75; James Kritzeck, "Peter the Venerable and the Toledan Collection," in *Petrus Venerabilis, 1156–1956: Studies and Texts Commemorating the Eighth Centenary of His Death*, ed. Giles Constable and James Kritzeck, Studia anselmiana 40 (Rome, 1956), pp. 176–201; Kritzeck, *Peter the Venerable and Islam*; and Torrell, "La Notion."

144. Peter, *Contra sectam Saracenorum* 1.50, 1.67–68, in *Schriften zum Islam*, pp. 96–98, 120–24.

145. Ibid. 1.29, in *Schriften zum Islam*, p. 66.

146. Peter the Venerable, *Epistula de translatione sua* 5, in *Schriften zum Islam*, pp. 26–28; and see above, chapter 1, at n. 49.

147. Peter, *Summa totius haeresis Saracenorum* 16, in *Schriften zum Islam*, p. 20: "Quod quare illi permissum sit, ille solus novit cui nemo potest dicere, 'Cur ita facis?' et qui 'de multis etiam vocatis paucos electos esse' dixit."

Peter, in other words, encountered disparity between both Jewish and Muslim infidels as he assumed they were supposed to be and as he now construed them. And, as in the case of the Jews, Peter associated the Muslims' denial of Christ with their belief in talmudic fables not recorded in Scripture: "In order that the entire plenitude of iniquity might converge in Muhammad, and that nothing necessary for his perdition and that of others should be lacking, Jews were drawn close to the heretic. And deviously taking care that he not become a true Christian, the Jews whispered to Muhammad (a man longing for novelties) not the truth of Scripture but their own fables in which they abound even now."[148] In the picture painted by Peter, the aberrant, nonscriptural tendencies of each group actually nourish those of the other: Talmudic legends fuel Muhammad's blasphemy; Muslim conquest of much of the world intensifies Jewish disbelief.[149] Just as the postbiblical traditions of the Jews may have begun to alter their status—from unbeliever to heretic—in Peter's eyes, so too did he wonder aloud (and indecisively) about the proper classification of the Muslims:

> I cannot satisfactorily determine if the Muslim error should be called a heresy and its advocates heretics or if its adherents should be called pagans. For, on one hand, I see that certain things from the Christian faith they uphold and certain things they reject, just as heretics do. On the other hand, in keeping with pagan usage, they both do and teach things which no heresy is ever recorded to have done. . . . Choose, therefore, what you prefer. Either call them heretics because of their heretical point of view and the extent to which they agree with the Church in part and disagree in part; or call them pagans because of their blatant impiety, by which they outdo the errors of all heresies in their impious belief.[150]

As he did the Jews, Peter labeled Muhammad a "cowlike" man (*vaccinus homo*);[151] he accused him of espousing intolerable beliefs at the

---

148. Ibid. 7, in *Schriften zum Islam*, p. 8; and see Peter's *Contra sectam Saracenorum* 2.138, in *Schriften zum Islam*, p. 208: "Nam claret orbi praeter vos et ipsos, quod tam vos quam ipsi . . . a veritate auditum avertistis et ad fabulas hunc convertistis, a veritate christiana vos ad fabulas Mahumeti, Iudaei ad fabulas Talmud." Cf. also the additional citations in Torrell, "La Notion," pp. 276–77.

149. Peter, *Adversus Iudaeorum . . . duritiem* 4, CCCM 58:108ff. On such interconnections between Judaism and Islam—as well as groupings of the two along with Christianity—see Norman Daniel, *Islam and the West: The Making of an Image*, rev. ed. (Oxford, 1993), pp. 213ff., and Sidney H. Griffith, "Jews and Muslims in Christian Syriac and Arabic Texts of the Ninth Century," *Jewish History* 3 (1988), 65–87.

150. Peter, *Contra sectam Saracenorum* 1.13, in *Schriften zum Islam*, pp. 48–50; and cf. Peter, *Summa totius haeresis Saracenorum*, 13, in *Schriften zum Islam*, p. 14. See also Kritzeck, *Peter the Venerable and Islam*, p. 144 n. 122; and Daniel, *Islam*, pp. 212–13.

151. Peter, *Summa totius haeresis Saracenorum*, 8, in *Schriften zum Islam*, p. 10.

behest of the devil (*diabolo imbuente*);[152] and he condemned Muhammad's preference for the carnal over the spiritual—in lifestyle and in hermeneutic:

> He depicted a paradise not of an angelic society nor of a divine vision . . . but truly in such a manner of flesh and blood—indeed, the basest sort of flesh and blood—as he longed and craved for it to be prepared for himself. At times he promises his followers the consumption of meats and fruits of all kinds, at times streams of milk and honey and splendid waters, at times the embrace and delight of the most beautiful women and virgins—to which things his entire paradise is limited. . . . Beyond all these things, he removed all limits on gluttony and lust, whereby he might better lure people's carnal minds to himself; and having at once eighteen wives of his own, in addition to the wives of many others, thus committing adultery as if by divine injunction, he attracted a greater number of damned ones to himself, as if he were following the example of a prophet.[153]

For Muslims as for Jews, failure to submit to the imperatives of Scripture as logic demanded underlies their infidelity; inasmuch as the Saracens revere the biblical teachings contained in the Quran, how can they justify spurning prophetic testimony to the validity of Christianity?[154] Like that of contemporary Judaism, the doctrine of Islam is blatantly irrational; and if the miracles attesting to Judaism rank below those that validate Christianity,[155] Islam boasts no miracles at all.[156] Both of these blasphemous faiths now stand out among the world's community of religions, Judaism in its denial of the incarnation, Islam in its rejection of the authority of the Bible.[157]

One could cite many analogous arguments in Peter's polemic against the Petrobrusian heretics.[158] But the foregoing review should suffice to demonstrate that one ought not to isolate Peter the Venerable's anti-

---

152. Ibid.; on Islam as a satanic scheme, see also Peter, *Epistula ad Petrum de Ioanne*, PL 189:489 (cited by Langmuir, *Toward a Definition*, p. 199); and Torrell, "La Notion," pp. 279–80.

153. Peter, *Summa totius haeresis Saracenorum*, 9–10, in *Schriften zum Islam*, pp. 10–12.

154. Peter, *Contra sectam Saracenorum* 1.55ff., *Schriften zum Islam*, pp. 104ff.

155. Peter, *Adversus Iudaeorum . . . duritiem* 4, CCCM 58:106ff., 119ff.; cf. *Contra Petrobrusianos* 177ff., CCCM 10:105ff.

156. Peter, *Adversus Iudaeorum . . . duritiem* 4, CCCM 58:109–10; and see Bouthillier and Torrell, "Miraculum," pp. 378–81, and Torrell and Bouthillier, *Pierre le Vénérable*, 180–95.

157. See above, n. 103.

158. See the numerous citations amassed in Patschovsky, "Feindbilder," esp. nn. 116ff.

Jewish polemic from the remainder of his writings and doctrinal concerns. One can truly appreciate the distinguishing characteristics of that polemic only with reference to his pronouncements on crusading, miracles, Islam, and contemporary heresy. As a group, the various protégés of Satan posed a constant menace to Christendom, endangering the faith of Christians, promoting the blasphemy of disbelief in various guises, and eliciting from Peter a mélange of polemical rejoinders grounded in rational argument, biblical prooftext, and miracle. One might differentiate the three species of argument and their various targets. Yet the traditionally circumscribed discourse of Christian religious polemic had unquestionably widened; the Jew was now part of a larger and more generalized problem, and the nuances of Peter's attack on him derived from the common, fundamental characteristics of this phenomenon.

Acknowledging the not insignificant differences between Bernard of Clairvaux and Peter of Cluny, one must surely contrast the acclaim and influence of the former with the minimal impact of the latter, especially with regard to their pronouncements concerning Jews. Even so, both abbots testified to the linkage between Jew and Saracen in the mentality of twelfth-century Christendom. In the shadow of holy war against the infidel, Christians grappled with the perplexing place and function of the Jews in their world in terms that did not always comport with the assumptions of Augustine's doctrine of Jewish witness. The results varied widely. Similar factors—the urgency of the Crusade, a developing missionary theology, the roles of Jews in the twelfth-century European economy, new interest in and familiarity with post-biblical Jewish culture, and, not least in importance, the encounter with Islam—led contemporary churchmen in markedly different directions. Bernard may have highlighted the submissiveness of the Jew in Christian society and Peter his enmity,[159] but both reaffirmed a basically Augustinian posture vis-à-vis the Jews at the same time as they paved the way for others to challenge it. The beginnings of the church's war on Jewish usury and its first condemnations of the Talmud were now only a century away. Yet the road between these abbots of the 1140s and these developments of the mid–thirteenth century had its twists and turns. Twelfth-century Christendom produced countless visions of personal religious fulfillment and the most expeditious route for achieving it; these too contributed to the evolving Christian idea of the Jew.

159. As stressed by Chazan, "Twelfth-Century Perceptions."

CHAPTER 7

Renaissance Men and Their Dreams

The two preceding chapters discussed the most noteworthy contributions of twelfth-century Europe to our story, from Anselm of Canterbury to Bernard of Clairvaux and Peter the Venerable of Cluny. Yet many more churchmen of that century addressed the question of the Jew, and, although this book makes no pretense of considering them all, it cannot move on to the thirteenth century without a slightly fuller picture of the twelfth. The present chapter will thus reflect upon selected Christian perceptions of Jews and Judaism from the last two thirds of the century, chosen both for their intrinsic interest and for their usefulness in illuminating the overall significance of the period.

Because any such sampling derives no less from the perspective of the selector than from the nature of the alternatives, I feel bound to make passing mention of noteworthy twelfth-century writers whom I have chosen not to include. These divide somewhat readily into several distinct groups. Some theologians of the period followed on in the direction of Anselm and his community of thought, condemning the Jews for their irrational, carnally oriented hermeneutic that raised doubts concerning their humanity.[1] Others, like Rupert of Deutz and Joachim of Fiore, weighed the function of the Jews in Christendom against new conceptions of Christian history and corresponding ideas concerning the character of the Catholic Church. In Rupert's case, this

---

1. See, for example, above, chapter 5, n. 67.

produced not only his *Anulus seu dialogus inter Christianum et Iudaeum* (The Ring, or the Dialogue between a Christian and a Jew) but markedly intense anti-Jewish exegeses throughout the corpus of his writings;[2] in Joachim's, it yielded a treatise of *Adversus Iudaeos* polemic that bespoke his singular trinitarian scheme of salvation history.[3] Under a third rubric, we group those churchmen who struggled with the relationship between the Jews, the literalist hermeneutic that Christianity habitually associated with Judaism, and the renewed Christian interest in the study of the Old Testament.[4] Jewish teachers assumed new value during the twelfth-century renaissance for the direct access that they provided to the original Hebrew text of Scripture and its presumably original, historical meaning; but Christian interest in the *Hebraica veritas* and its Jewish *sensus* posed serious questions and dangers. If rabbinic exegesis of the Bible were assumed to convey its literal meaning, positive Christian valuation of the *Hebraica veritas* and its historical sense might attribute a new legitimacy to Jewish traditions, and this might undermine the basic contrast between carnal Judaism and spiritual Christianity underlying *Adversus Iudaeos* theology. When a Christian commentator expounded the historical, "Jewish" sense of a biblical passage or when he approached a rabbi for help in interpreting it, his exegesis might be construed as subverting some of the very theological assumptions on which his Christian faith rested. Several clerical writers, like Ralph of Flaix in his commentary on Leviticus[5]

2. See Maria Lodovica Arduini, *Ruperto di Deutz e la controversia tra Cristiani ed Ebrei nel secolo xii*, Istituto storico italiano per il Medio Evo: Studi storici 119–121 (Rome, 1979), which includes Rhabanus Haacke's critical edition of Rupert's *Anulus*; David E. Timmer, "Biblical Exegesis and the Jewish-Christian Controversy in the Early Twelfth Century," *Church History* 58 (1989), 309–21; and Anna Sapir Abulafia, "The Ideology of Reform and Changing Ideas Concerning Jews in the Works of Rupert of Deutz and Hermannus Quondam Iudeus," *Jewish History* 7 (1993), 44–50. On Rupert's career, opus, ecclesiology, and historiosophy, see also John H. Van Engen, *Rupert of Deutz* (Berkeley, Calif., 1983); and Maria Lodovica Arduini, *Rupert von Deutz (1076–1129) und der "Status Christianitatis" seiner Zeit: Symbolisch-prophetisch Deutung der Geschichte*, Beihefte zum *Archiv für Kulturgeschichte* 25 (Cologne, 1987).

3. Joachim of Fiore, *Adversus Iudeos*, ed. Arsenio Frugoni, Istituto storico italiano per il Medio Evo: Fonti per la storia d'Italia 95 (Rome, 1957); and see Beatrice Hirsch-Reich, "Joachim von Fiore und das Judentum," in *JIM*, pp. 228–63; and Heinz Schreckenberg, *Die christlichen Adversus-Judaeos-Texte (11.–13. Jh.)*, Europäische Hochschulschriften 23, 335, 2d ed. (Frankfurt am Main, 1991), pp. 345–58.

4. Cf. the discussion in Jeremy Cohen, "Scholarship and Intolerance in the Medieval Academy: The Study and Evaluation of Judaism in European Christendom," *AHR* 91 (1986), 599–604, as well as the perspective offered by Valerie I. J. Flint, "Anti-Jewish Literature and Attitudes in the Twelfth Century," *JJS* 37 (1986), 39–57, 183–205.

5. See Beryl Smalley, "Ralph of Flaix on Leviticus," *RTAM* 35 (1968), 52–68; and John H. Van Engen, "A Twelfth-Century Christian on Leviticus," in *In the Shadow of*

and Richard of St. Victor in a refutation of his confrere Andrew's literalist reading of Isaiah 7:14,[6] decried the "Judaizing" tendencies of clerics overly dependent on the historical *sensus* of Scripture; at the same time, they protested that their own exegesis was no less scholarly or accurate. Perhaps one can discern in these works the earliest of designs to "liberate" the primary meaning of the Old Testament from the "control" of the Jews, a tendency that matured only in later generations, when Christian Hebraists became more numerous and more adept. But the twelfth century and early years of the thirteenth did witness occasional, preliminary attempts to use the original Hebrew of the Masoretic Text against the Jews, as in the *Ysagoge in theologiam* (Introduction to Theology) of a certain Odo[7] and the *Liber bellorum Domini* (The Book of Wars of the Lord) by William of Bourges.[8] Finally, many twelfth-century authors continued to produce the traditional sort of anti-Jewish polemic, collections of biblical testimonies supporting Christian doctrine, although their works acknowledge that such polemic had assumed a new contemporary relevance, that medieval Jews and Christians now debated one another more frequently, and that the stakes of such encounters had increased.[9]

the Millennium: Jews and Christians in Twelfth-Century Europe, ed. Michael A. Signer and John H. van Engen (Notre Dame, Ind., 1999).

6. Richard of St. Victor, De Emmanuele, PL 196:601–66. On Andrew of St. Victor and the alleged threat of his "Judaizing" exegesis, see Beryl Smalley, The Study of the Bible in the Middle Ages, 3d ed. (Oxford, 1983), chap. 4; William McKane, Selected Christian Hebraists (Cambridge, England, 1989), chap. 2; Rainer Berndt, André de Saint-Victor (+1175): Exégète et théologien, Bibliotheca victorina 2 (Paris, 1991); and Michael A. Signer, "Andrew of St.-Victor's Anti-Jewish Polemic" [Hebrew], in The Bible in the Light of Its Interpreters: Sarah Kamin Memorial Volume, ed. Sara Japhet (Jerusalem, 1993), pp. 412–20, and his introduction to his edition of Andrew's Expositio in Ezechielem, CCCM 53E.

7. The text of the Ysagoge has been edited by Arthur Landgraf, Ecrits théologiques de l'école d'Abélard: Textes inédits, Spicilegium sacrum lovaniense 14 (Louvain, Belgium, 1934), pp. 61–289. See also Avrom Saltman, "Odo's Ysagoge: A New Method of Anti-Jewish Polemic" [Hebrew], Criticism and Interpretation 13–14 (1979), 265–80, and "Gilbert Crispin as a Source of the Anti-Jewish Polemic of the Ysagoge in theologiam," in Confrontation and Coexistence, ed. Pinhas Artzi, Bar-Ilan Studies in History 2 (Ramat Gan, Israel, 1984), pp. 89–99; and Anna Sapir Abulafia, "Jewish Carnality in Twelfth-Century Renaissance Thought," in Christianity and Judaism, ed. Diana Wood, SCH 29 (Oxford, 1992), pp. 59–75.

8. William of Bourges, Livre des guerres du Seigneur et deux homélies, ed. Gilbert Dahan, SC 288 (Paris, 1981); and see Marie-Humbert Vicaire, "'Contra Judaeos' meridionaux au début du xiiie siècle: Alain de Lille, Evrard de Béthune, Guillaume de Bourges," in Juifs et judaïsme de Languedoc, Cahiers de Fanjeaux 12 (Toulouse, France, 1977), pp. 282ff.

9. Among others, Walter of Châtillon (ca. 1135–ca. 1200), Tractatus sive dialogus contra Iudaeos, PL 209:423–58; Peter of Blois (d. ca. 1204), Contra perfidiam Iudaeorum, PL 207:825–70; and Adam of Perseigne (d. ca. 1221), Epistola 21, PL 211:653–

From a long list of twelfth-century authors who wrote about the Jews, I have here chosen to discuss three of the most fascinating: Peter Abelard, Hermann of Cologne, and Alan of Lille. Although these men did not constitute a distinct group or school of thought, their writings add a measure of variety and even of spice to our story, demonstrating the complexity of how the Jew figured in the mentality of the twelfth-century renaissance. Exemplars of this renaissance, the "humanism" it displayed, and the scholasticism it began to cultivate struggled to construct Jews and Judaism in keeping with their views of their Christian world. Their image of the Jews had some role to play in their search for Christian self, both individual and collective, and their definitions of that role offer insight into their age's distinctive quest for a comprehensive cultural synthesis. For two of our three subjects, the Jews and Judaism assumed but low priority relative to other, more urgent theological issues; yet this, too, will enhance our picture of the period, as one considers how the Jews functioned in the outlooks of those who did not deem their presence a serious social problem.

Curiously, the perceptions of the Jew in the works of Abelard, Hermann, and Alan relate instructively to dreams that their writings recount, and we recall Jacques le Goff's judgment that "the twelfth century may be considered the age of the reconquest of the dream by medieval culture and mentality."[10] Dreaming is inherently self-reflexive; it testifies to a search for personal fulfillment and integration, and its prominence in twelfth-century texts comports well with the period's acclaimed "discovery of the individual."[11] Evoking issues of the Jewish-Christian debate, dreams and their interpretation raise critical questions of hermeneutics, from the understanding of specific symbolic texts to the manner and mind-set in which one construes reality generally. And, as one investigator has recently observed, "because dreams occur while man is in the body and yet seem to lead him to a knowledge that transcends bodily limitations, they have a special

---

59. See also R. W. Hunt, "The Disputation of Peter of Cornwall against Symon the Jew," in *Studies in Medieval History Presented to Frederick Maurice Powicke*, ed. R. W. Hunt et al. (Oxford, 1948), pp. 143–56; David Berger, "Mission to the Jews and Jewish-Christian Cultural Contacts in the Polemical Literature of the High Middle Ages," *AHR* 91 (1986), 576–91; and Schreckenberg, *Die christlichen Adversus-Judaeos-Texte*, pt. 1, passim.

10. Jacques le Goff, *Time, Work, & Culture in the Middle Ages*, trans. Arthur Goldhammer (Chicago, 1980), p. 203.

11. Colin Morris, *The Discovery of the Individual, 1050–1200* (New York, 1972).

relevance to the thinker who seeks to explore the threshold between body and spirit."[12] Albeit introspective, a dream also situates its viewer in relation to the world around him, and its written record therefore constitutes a cultural artifact of historical value. Not inappropriately, I hope, our account of the twelfth century and its renaissance concludes with a discussion of three renaissance men and their dreams.[13]

PETER ABELARD

Renowned lover, correspondent, dialectician, teacher, and monk, Peter Abelard (1079–1142) captures the singular spirit of the twelfth century more than do most of his European contemporaries; although his writings that demand our attention antedated those of Bernard of Clairvaux and Peter the Venerable by several years, I therefore have chosen to include him here. As with so many other issues of his day, Abelard defied convention on questions of the Jews and Judaism, and he fits neatly into none of the patterns of Christian thought discussed thus far.[14] Many have hastened to congratulate Abelard for extraordinary tolerance and sympathy toward medieval Jews. Gavin Langmuir, for one, has written: "His *Dialogue of a Philosopher with a Jew* betrays none of the hostility so obvious in Peter the Venerable's polemic. His *Ethics* or *Scito te ipsum*—which Bernard forcefully condemned— showed an understanding of Jewish attitudes that far exceeded Bernard's qualified toleration."[15] Still, an analysis of the pertinent texts in their proper context suggests that Peter might not have deserved or welcomed such an enthusiastic appraisal of his works.

Abelard was also a dreamer. The entirety of his *Dialogus inter phi-*

12. Kathryn L. Lynch, *The High Medieval Dream Vision: Poetry, Philosophy, and Literary Form* (Stanford, Calif., 1988), p. 64. See also Peter Dinzelbacher, *Vision und Visionsliteratur im Mittelalter*, Monographien zur Geschichte des Mittelalters 23 (Stuttgart, 1981).

13. Guibert of Nogent also made allusion to dreaming in the introduction to his *Tractatus de incarnatione*, PL 156:490; cf. also his *Monodiae* 1.17, in *Autobiographie*, ed. Edmond-René Labande, Les Classiques de l'histoire de France au Moyen Âge 34 (Paris, 1981), p. 136.

14. On Abelard's career and opus, see, most recently, Constant J. Mews, *Peter Abelard*, Authors of the Middle Ages 2, 5 (London, 1995), with an extensive bibliography.

15. Gavin I. Langmuir, "The Faith of Christians and Hostility to Jews," in *Christianity and Judaism*, ed. Diana Wood, SCH 29 (Oxford, 1992), p. 87. Cf. also below, n. 22.

losophum, Iudaeum et Christianum (Dialogue between a Philosopher, a Jew, and a Christian) recounts a nocturnal dream in which, the author explained, "I was looking about [*aspiciebam*]," when

> suddenly three men, coming by different paths, stood before me. While still dreaming, I asked them at once what their profession might be and why they had come to me. They said: "We are men belonging to different religious schools of thought. Of course we all equally profess ourselves to be worshippers of the one God; however, we each serve him with a different faith and a different way of life. In fact, one of us who is a pagan, from those they call philosophers, is content with the natural law. The other two possess sacred writings; one is called a Jew, the other a Christian. Now, for some time we have been discussing and arguing among ourselves about our different religious schools of thought, and we have finally agreed to submit to your judgment."[16]

Abelard's *Dialogus* numbers among a collection of medieval religious texts that inquire "about the supreme good and the supreme evil and about what makes a man blessed or miserable"[17] by imagining a debate between three or more representatives of different religious viewpoints. Nor is this the only instance in which a dream either initiates or facilitates the ostensibly pluralistic, open-minded exchange of ideas, although in virtually every case, Abelard's included, the discussion serves to vindicate the contentions of the author and invalidate those of his opponents.[18] Nonetheless, one need not completely discount the motif of interreligious dialogue in Peter's *Dialogus* as a literary, polemical, or apologetic ploy. One scholar has recently noted that the opening word of the treatise, *aspiciebam* ("I was looking about"), appears some half-dozen times in Daniel 7 in the relation of Daniel's visionary quest for divine illumination;[19] perhaps Abelard identified with the ancient Jewish seer, exiled from his homeland, torn between conflicting loyalties, yet inspired to ascertain and to promulgate the truth. As a number

16. Peter Abelard, *Dialogus inter Philosophum, Judaeum et Christianum*, ed. Rudolf Thomas (Stuttgart, 1970), p. 41, and *Dialogue of a Philosopher with a Jew and a Christian*, trans. Pierre J. Payer, Medieval Sources in Translation 20 (Toronto, 1979), p. 19 (with slight modification). Helpfully instructive studies of the *Dialogus* include the works of Hans Liebeschütz, Rudolf Thomas, Maurice de Gandillac, Aryeh Graboïs, Jean Jolivet, and Anna Abulafia, cited below, nn. 20, 22, 51.

17. Abelard, *Dialogus*, p. 41, trans. Payer, p. 20.

18. See the sources cited in Jeremy Cohen, *The Friars and the Jews: The Evolution of Medieval Anti-Judaism* (Ithaca, N.Y., 1982), pp. 207–8 n. 17, to which one may add Nicholas of Cusa, *De pace fidei*, ed. Raymond Klibansky and Hildebrand Bascour, Opera omnia 7 (Hamburg, 1959).

19. Abelard, *Dialogue*, trans. Payer, p. 19 n. 2.

of recent investigators have suggested, one may well group the *Dialogus* alongside Abelard's personal *Historia calamitatum* (The Story of My Misfortunes) and his *Ethica*, all of them works from the last decade of his life, in which he defended the nobility of his intentions and the worthiness of his career, the controversies that plagued it notwithstanding.[20] At the same time as it constitutes one of the more serious medieval Christian encounters with classical, pagan philosophy, Abelard's oneiric colloquium is also self-reflexive, and it thus militates against an overly simplistic identification of the author with one discussant as opposed to the others.

Early in the first part of the *Dialogus*, in which the philosopher debates the Jew, the latter offers a lengthy, impassioned defense of his people, who persevere in their religious convictions and observances under the most difficult of circumstances:

> Surely, no people is known or is even believed to have endured so much for God as we constantly put up with for him; and no one ought to claim that there can be any dross of sin which the furnace of this affliction has not burned away. Dispersed among all the nations, alone, without an earthly king or prince, are we not burdened with such great demands that

20. On the connections among these three works, see Hans Liebeschütz, "The Significance of Judaism in Peter Abaelard's *Dialogus*," *JJS* 12 (1961), 13–17; D. E. Luscombe, "The *Ethics* of Abelard: Some Further Considerations," in *Peter Abelard*, ed. Eligius M. Buytaert, Mediaevalia lovaniensia 1, 2 (Louvain, Belgium, 1974), esp. pp. 70–73; Maurice de Gandillac, "Intention et loi dans l'éthique d'Abélard," in *PAPV*, pp. 585–610; and Chris D. Ferguson, "Autobiography as Therapy: Guibert de Nogent, Peter Abelard, and the Making of Medieval Autobiography," *Journal of Medieval and Renaissance Studies* 13 (1983), 199–204. Scholars have debated the date of the *Dialogus* rather extensively. As opposed to the traditional view that this was one of Abelard's last works, composed at Cluny during his final years, see the earlier dating—of the middle to late 1130s, or perhaps even earlier—argued by Eligius M. Buytaert, "Abelard's *Collationes*," *Antonianum* 44 (1969), 33ff.; D. E. Luscombe's introduction to his edition of Peter Abelard, *Ethics* (Oxford, 1971), p. xxvii; Constant J. Mews, "On Dating the Works of Peter Abelard," *AHDL* 52 (1985), 112–29, and *Peter Abelard*, pp. 35–36; and Anna Sapir Abulafia, "*Intentio recta an erronea?* Peter Abelard's Views on Judaism and the Jews," in *Medieval Studies in Honour of Avrom Saltman*, ed. Bat-Sheva Albert et al., Bar-Ilan Studies in History 4 (Ramat Gan, Israel, 1995), pp. 23–26. The traditional, later dating of 1140–42 has been defended by Rudolf Thomas in *Der philosophisch-theologische Erkenntnisweg Peter Abaelards im Dialogus inter Philosophum, Judaeum et Christianum*, Untersuchungen zur allgemeinen Religionsgeschichte, n.s. 6 (Bonn, 1966), pp. 27–29, in his edition of Abelard, *Dialogus*, pp. 11–12, and in "Die Persönlichkeit Peter Abaelards im 'Dialogus inter Philosophum, Iudaeum et Christianum' und in den Epistulae des Petrus Venerabilis: Widerspruch oder Übereinstimmung," in *PAPV*, pp. 256ff.; Jacques Verger, "Abélard et les milieux sociaux de son temps," in *Abélard en son temps: Actes du colloque international organisé à l'occasion du 9ᵉ centenaire de la naissance de Pierre Abélard* (Paris, 1981), p. 127 and n. 1; and Maurice de Gandillac, "Juif et judéité dans le 'Dialogue' d'Abélard," in *Pour Léon Poliakov: Le Racisme, mythes et sciences*, ed. Maurice Olender (Brussels, 1981), p. 385.

almost every day of our miserable lives we pay the debt of an intolerable ransom? In fact, we are judged deserving of such great contempt and hatred by all that anyone who inflicts some injury on us believes it to be the greatest justice and the highest sacrifice offered to God.

Pagans (presumably Muslims) and Christians alike persecute the Jews, so that they have no recourse to earthly comfort and prosperity. "Sleep itself . . . disquiets us with such great worry that even while sleeping we can think of nothing but the danger that looms over our throats." Even the princes whom the Jews pay dearly for their protection seek to hasten their demise in order dispossess them of their assets:

> Confined and constricted in this way, as if the whole world had conspired against us alone, it is a wonder that we are allowed to live. We are allowed to possess neither fields nor vineyards nor any landed estates because there is no one who can protect them for us from open or occult attack. Consequently, the principal gain that is left for us is that we sustain our miserable lives here by lending money at interest to strangers; but this just makes us hateful to them who think they are being oppressed by it.

Manifold hardships entailed by the observance of the law, from the pain and shame of circumcision to the harsh limitations of the dietary laws, only intensify the plight of the Jew. "More than any tongue can do, our very situation is enough to speak more eloquently to all of the supreme misery of our lives." Only a most cruel deity could leave such dedication and self-sacrifice unrewarded; and so, reasons the Jew, he and his coreligionists must be the elect of God.[21]

One cannot avoid hearing the voice of the persecuted Abelard himself in these pitiful exclamations; nor can one escape the conclusion that to some extent, at least, Abelard felt genuine sympathy for his Jewish contemporaries. Some of his recent readers have transformed Abelard into a prototype of modern ecumenism, a veritable Lessing of the twelfth century.[22] In Abelard's eyes, however, despite the compassion that it evokes, the suffering of medieval Jews did not establish the

---

21. Abelard, *Dialogus*, pp. 50–52, trans. Payer, pp. 32–35.

22. N. A. Sidorova, "Abélard et son époque," *Cahiers d'histoire mondiale* 4 (1958), 549. Among others, see also Liebeschütz, "Significance of Judaism," pp. 17–18; Aryeh Graboïs, "Un Chapitre de tolérance intellectuelle dans la société occidentale au xiie siècle: Le 'Dialogus' de Pierre Abélard et le 'Kuzari' d'Yehudah Halévi," in *PAPV*, pp. 641–52, and "The Christian-Jewish-Islamic Dialogue in the Twelfth Century and Its Historical Significance," *Ecumenical Institute for Advanced Theological Studies Yearbook* 1975–76, pp. 76–77; Amos Funkenstein, *Perceptions of Jewish History* (Berkeley, Calif., 1993), p. 182; and de Gandillac, "Juif." Cf. also above, n. 15.

validity of their religious beliefs; aggravating the Jews even as they slept, it prevented them from dreaming rationally and productively, in the manner that Abelard envisioned these dialogues. The first part of the *Dialogus* pits the natural law of the philosopher against the Mosaic law of the Jew, who cannot successfully refute the attacks of his opponent.

The philosopher argues the superiority of natural law over biblical law, because natural law teaches moral lessons alone, whereas the precepts of Scripture add ritual observances, "precepts of external signs [*exteriorum signorum praecepta*],"[23] which ultimately have no value. Although he acknowledges the zealous observances of the Jews, the philosopher belabors Abelard's well-known principle that human intention, not human behavior, accounts for fault or merit in the eyes of God.[24] As for the provisions of Mosaic law, the philosopher asserts that they do not embody the most rational, correct intention, and this on two grounds. First, the law promises an exclusively terrestrial reward for its followers, earthly comforts that fall far short of the spiritual happiness that rational humans surely ought to pursue. "A reward consisting of earthly things would so little measure up to beatitude that the life you could expect would be no different for you than for beasts of burden."[25] Given the present suffering of the Jews, a true devotee of the carnal promises of the Old Testament must conclude either that the Jews have forsaken the law or that God has reneged on his commitments to them. Second, biblical law has proven itself unnecessary for salvation. Before the revelation at Sinai, Abel, Enoch, Noah, his son Shem, Abraham, Lot, Melchizedek, Isaac, Jacob, and others "fostered justice and were most acceptable to God" through their observance of natural law;[26] even after Sinai, the pagan Job lived commend-

---

23. Abelard, *Dialogus*, p. 44. A helpful discussion of the philosopher's critique of Jewish law appears in Ursula Niggli, "Abaelards Ideen über die jüdische Religion und seine Hermeneutik im *Dialogus*," in *Les philosophies morales et politiques au Moyen Âge*, ed. R. Carlos Bazán et al. (Ottawa, 1995), 2:1101–20.

24. Abelard, *Dialogus*, pp. 52–53: "Revera zelus hic, quem in Deum habere videmini, multa et magna quacumque intentione sustinet. Sed plurimum refert, utrum hec intentio recta sit an erronea. Nulla quippe est fidei secta, que se Deo famulari non credat, et ea propter ipsum non operetur, que ipsi placere arbitratur. Non tamen ideo sectas omnium approbatis, qui solam vestram defendere aut longe ceteris nitimini preferre. Quod tamen quantum a ratione sit dissonum volo te perpendere et ex ipso quoque scripto legis, quam sequeris, arguere."

25. Ibid., p. 56, trans. Payer, p. 39.

26. Ibid., p. 53, trans. Payer, p. 36.

ably in God's eyes, King Solomon acknowledged that God hears the prayers of pagans, and God sanctified the prophet Jeremiah before his birth and circumcision.[27] The teachings of nature, in fact—so the philosopher implies here and Abelard maintained specifically elsewhere[28]— approximate the doctrine of Christianity much more closely than does the law of Moses. And, "if these were sufficient for the salvation of some people before the law [of Moses] or even now, why was it necessary to add the yoke of the law and to increase transgressions through the multiplication of precepts?"[29] What, presses the philosopher, do they add "to the law which Job prescribes for us by his example, or to the discipline of morals which our philosophers left to posterity in what concerns the virtues, which are sufficient for beatitude?"[30]

The Jew of the *Dialogus* responds at length to the charges of the philosopher, and his arguments appear to serve divergent purposes. On one hand, the Jew's responses accentuate the deep, fundamental differences between his own theological outlook and that of the philosopher—and so, by extension, that of Abelard as well. We might fairly characterize the bulk of the Jewish argumentation in the *Dialogus* as argument by default. For instance, the Jew contends regarding the law that "even if we cannot convince you that it was given by God, you, for your part, cannot refute this."[31] Most of the world agrees that God commanded the Jews to keep his law. If he did so command and the Jews do not obey, they have sinned grievously; but if he did not so command and they observe the law anyhow, what fault have they incurred? Piety moves one to believe that the beneficent God provided law to restrain human malice through the fear of punishment; otherwise, one might come to deny divine providence and to conclude "that the state of the world is run by chance." But if one believes in the providence of God, "which [law] has greater claim to being this law than ours, which has received such great authority from its antiquity and the common opinion of men?"[32] Simply put, the Jew believes in the law for lack of anything better. His case lacks compelling logic;

27. Ibid., pp. 59–60.
28. Peter Abelard, *Theologia christiana* 2.44, CCCM 12:149; cf. *Dialogue*, trans. Payer, p. 36 n. 28.
29. Abelard, *Dialogus*, p. 60, trans. Payer, p. 44.
30. Ibid., p. 84, trans. Payer, p. 71.
31. Ibid., p. 48, trans. Payer, p. 29 (with slight modifications).
32. Ibid., p. 49, trans. Payer, p. 31.

nothing about the law per se warrants its observance. The arguments mustered by the Jew pertain to what people have habitually believed about the law and what they may accustom themselves to believe without it; they offer no rational explanation for the substance of the law. The Jew of the *Dialogus* thus emerges as pre-philosophical or, more precisely, as unphilosophical. He lacks the knowledge and the proper intention required for spiritual fulfillment, whereas the philosopher appears to have much more of both. The closest the Jew comes to arguing the inner sense of his law is to maintain that commandments like circumcision and the dietary laws kept the Jews from intercourse with idolatrous pagans.[33] But because, as we know from the opening of the *Dialogus*, the modern-day pagan philosopher professes belief in the same single deity as the Jew or Christian, such Jewish particularism has outlived its rationale; it sounds more chauvinistically unenlightened, especially from the perspective of a classical pagan thinker,[34] than beneficial. Abelard's portrayal of Judaism thus confirms the suspicion that the philosopher voices to his interlocutors at the outset: "Did some rational consideration induce you into your respective religious schools of thought, or do you here simply follow the opinion of men and the love of your own people?"[35] The Jew has demonstrated that the latter profile applies to him, and one understands why the remaining two-thirds of the *Dialogus* depicts the conversation between the philosopher and the Christian. These two have left the Jew behind.

On the other hand, if the carnally oriented Jew of the *Dialogus* who, however pitiful, ranks little higher than a beast of burden drops out of the rational inquiry, the last word on biblical law remains to be said. For in denying that Mosaic law served any positive purpose, the philosopher impugns the Old Testament more than any orthodox Christian knowingly could have done; and, albeit unknowingly, Abelard's Jew himself lays the groundwork for arguments that a Christian could use in defense of his faith. Abelard, for example, did characterize the practice of circumcision as a fitting and, given the need to curtail human lust, intrinsically logical prefiguration of the blood-sacrifice of

---

33. Ibid., p. 47.

34. See J. N. Sevenster, *The Roots of Pagan Anti-Semitism in the Ancient World*, Supplements to *Novum Testamentum* 41 (Leiden, Netherlands, 1975), esp. chap. 3. Niggli, "Abaelards Ideen," argues forcefully that the philosopher's view of the Torah also reflects the criticisms of Jesus and Paul as recorded in the New Testament.

35. Abelard, *Dialogus*, p. 44, trans. Payer, p. 24.

Christ on the cross, and he acknowledged the wisdom in the Israelites remaining separate from other ancient peoples.[36] Abelard further defended the carnal rewards and punishments of biblical law as a worthy means of leading crude people toward a recognition of God.[37] Moreover, although the philosopher will not concede as much, the Jew does protest forcefully that the law contains the promise of everlasting spiritual reward. He declares to the philosopher "that the law itself commands the perfect love of God and neighbor which you claim comprises the natural law."[38] And he cites numerous Pentateuchal passages exhorting the Jews to love God, to sanctify themselves, and thus to merit divine election and reward—passages that Christian doctrine typically understood as finding fulfillment in the New Testament.

The philosopher, as noted, remains unconvinced. To his mind, neither does the Old Testament add to that possibility of salvation available in the observance of natural law, nor does the promise of Mosaic law extend beyond the material and the terrestrial. In other words, although the philosopher surely outstrips the Jew in his mastery of logic and dialectic, he, too, fails to understand the Christian promise of the Old Testament; and although he draws much closer to salvation than does the Jew, he cannot arrive at the final goal because he depends entirely on his own achievements. In that he resembles the Jew, and his self-assuredness likewise finds expression in a shortsighted biblical hermeneutic, one that cannot see beyond the literal sense. Thus the Christian upbraids him for Judaizing: "If you knew how to read Scripture in a prophetic spirit rather than in a Judaizing manner [si prophetizare magis quam iudaizare], and if you knew how to understand what is said of God under corporeal forms, not literally and in a material sense but mystically through allegory, you would not accept what is said as an unlettered person does."[39] Additionally, an inability to penetrate the prophetic significance of the law distances one from the spiritual reward it proffers.

> In regard to the old law in which the Jews glory, you think you have successfully shown that this beatitude was not promised there as a reward, nor is any exhortation to it employed there. However, when the Lord Jesus was handing down the New Testament he established just such a foundation for

36. Peter Abelard, *Commentaria in Epistolam Pauli ad Romanos* ad 2:16–29, 4:9–11, CCCM 11:87–96, 126–43, and *Sermo in circumcisione Domini*, PL 178:398–409.

37. Peter Abelard, *Expositio in hexaemeron*, PL 178:731–32.

38. Abelard, *Dialogus*, p. 70, trans. Payer, p. 56.

39. Ibid., p. 146, trans. Payer, p. 143 (with slight variation).

his teaching right at the beginning where he encouraged contempt for the world and the desire for beatitude. . . . All his precepts or exhortations are employed to this end: that all prosperity is to be held in contempt or adversities tolerated out of hope for that highest and eternal life. I do not think that your teachers have touched on this matter or invited your spirits to this goal of the good in a similar way.[40]

Why does the philosopher, for all of his rational acumen, fail to grasp the allegorical sense of Scripture? I would suggest that he too, like the Jew, lacks the Christian faith and the love of Christ that undergird the Bible's spiritual sense. Although Abelard's Christian cannot explicitly formulate that conviction in the *Dialogus*, because the discussants have pledged that they would argue with the philosopher solely on the basis of reason, the treatise hints clearly at such a conclusion. When, during the course of their discussion, the philosopher attacks Christianity for its irrationality by quoting Gregory the Great's judgment that "faith for which human reason offers proof does not have merit," the Christian calmly points out the limitations of the human intellect.[41] The Christian in the *Dialogus* hastens to explain that "no one in his senses would forbid rational investigation and discussion of our faith,"[42] but philosophical inquiry does not become the source of that faith. Although his use of dialectic in the exposition of theology extended considerably farther than Anselm's, Abelard continued to espouse the basic Anselmian conviction that faith precedes—that is, it exists logically prior to and independent of—human understanding.[43] How, in turn, does this outlook bear on the interpretation of Scripture? It postulates that the Old Testament, no less than the New, derives from divine revelation and gives expression to divine wisdom. When the philosopher in the *Dialogus* emphasizes the imperfection of the old law and cites Hebrews 7:18 to the effect that it has been rejected because of its infirmity and uselessness (*reprobatio fit precedentis mandati propter infirmitatem eius et inutilitatem*), the Christian accordingly condemns him for the stubbornness of his disbelief (*infidelitatis obstinatio*) and affirms that the New Testament completes the Old.[44]

40. Ibid., pp. 104–5, trans. Payer, pp. 95–96 (with slight modification).
41. Ibid., pp. 93, 97–98. On Abelard's understanding of this seemingly problematic statement and its ramifications, see Buytaert, "Abelard's *Collationes*," p. 25, and Thomas, *Der philosophisch-theologische Erkenntnisweg*, pp. 71–87.
42. Abelard, *Dialogus*, p. 97, trans. Payer, p. 86.
43. See A. Victor Murray, *Abelard and St Bernard: A Study in Twelfth Century "Modernism"* (Manchester, England, 1967), pp. 72–74, 139–58, esp. 150 and n. 2.
44. Abelard, *Dialogus*, pp. 87–88.

Testifying to his high valuation of the spiritual sense of the Old Testament, Abelard periodically lavished praise upon Origen, the ancient champion of Christian allegory par excellence, and defended him against his patristic and medieval critics.[45] The *Dialogus* adduces numerous biblical—and even postbiblical—texts as authorities, and, as Maurice de Gandillac has observed, it often appears "that it is Abelard who, by means of his characters, is conversing with himself" concerning their proper exposition.[46] Yet one finds the most telling confirmation of Abelard's commitment to the spiritual sense of the old law's external, material signs in the very character of the *Dialogus* itself. The philosopher, recall, criticizes the Jew for his brutish mentality, which focused exclusively on things earthly and physical, and he returns to the Jewish dependence on signs when conversing with the Christian. "Surely, the Jews alone, since they are animals and sensual and are imbued with no philosophy whereby they are able to discuss reasoned arguments, are moved to faith only by the miracles of external deeds, as if it were the case that it belongs to God alone to effect these things and that no illusion could be produced in them by demons."[47] The philosopher has posed the contrast sharply: the reasoned conclusions of philosophy versus the signifiers of biblical revelation. But Abelard composed his *Dialogus*, it seems, precisely to reject such a dichotomy. For the entirety of the exchange between philosopher, Jew, and Christian appeared to the author in a dream—in an experience of revelation, an encoded, visualized text, replete with physical imagery, that begs a symbolic interpretation! Adapting Eliezer Schweid's analysis of the early-twelfth-century Judah ha-Levi's *Kuzari*, which similarly depicts a debate between a philosopher, a Christian, a Muslim, and a Jew in the aftermath of a dream,[48] one can infer from the *Dialogus* that scholarly inquiry must proceed in the wake of divine revelation in order to understand it but that it can never supersede it. Scripture bears no blame

---

45. See, for instance, Peter Abelard, *Historia calamitatum*, ed. J. Monfrin (Paris, 1967), pp. 82 ("summum Christianorum philosophorum Origenem"), 102 ("maximum illum Christianorum philosophum Origenem"), and *Commentaria in Epistolam Pauli ad Romanos* 2 (ad 4:11), CCCM 11:143 ("Origenem, tam litterarum virum"). One cannot help but observe that of these two references to Origen in the *Historia calamitatum*, the first occurs in the chapter on Abelard's castration, whereas the second occurs in tandem with a reference to Origen's castration. Cf. Henri de Lubac, *Exégèse médiévale: Les Quatre Sens de l'écriture*, Théologie 41–42, 59 (Paris, 1959–64), 1:241, 278–79.

46. De Gandillac, "Intention et loi," pp. 600ff.

47. Abelard, *Dialogus*, p. 90 (and cf. p. 95), trans. Payer, p. 78.

48. Eliezer Schweid, "The Literary Structure of the First Book of the Kuzari" [Hebrew], *Tarbiz* 30 (1961), 261–62.

for prophesying through external signs. The Jews—and, evidently, the philosopher too—are at fault for not interpreting them properly.

Such a reading of the *Dialogus* helps to place Abelard's perception of the Jews and Judaism in its proper twelfth-century context; true to the character of Abelard's career and his scholarly opus, his interest in the Jews reflects a singular blend of exemplar and nonconformist. Abelard did not engage in anti-Jewish polemic. The *Dialogus* depicts no direct confrontation between Christian and Jew; neither does it address the central issues of the Jewish-Christian debate—the advent of the messiah, the incarnation, the virgin birth, and the Trinity—nor does it advocate any particular status or treatment for the Jews of Christian society, avoiding all mention of Augustine's doctrine of Jewish witness. Nonetheless, in keeping with the spirit of the times, it does harp on the irrationality and carnality of the Jewish religion; it makes mention of postbiblical Jewish traditions with no basis in the written law of Moses;[49] and its characterization of Judaism as a particular attitude toward life and religiosity jibes with Abelard's denunciation of materialistic Christians as worse than Jews.[50] The *Dialogus* contrasts the laws of Moses, nature, and the Gospel as means for attaining the greatest good, and, just as it asserts the superiority of natural philosophy over Judaism, so does it liken Jew and pagan philosopher for a shared hermeneutical deficiency and a resulting inability to achieve the salvation of a Christian. As such, Abelard manifested the twelfth century's interest in classification and its tendency to group the Jews alongside other infidels on its map of dissidents and minorities in Christendom. The Jew's declaration to the philosopher concerning you "who, following the practice of your ancestor Ishmael, receive circumcision during the twelfth year" may even indicate that the philosopher of the *Dialogus* is a Muslim, albeit one who voices the doctrine of classical philosophy more than that of Islam.[51]

49. Abelard, *Dialogus*, p. 79.

50. Abelard, *Historia calamitatum*, p. 99; J. T. Muckle, "The Personal Letters between Abelard and Heloise: Introduction, Authenticity and Text," *Mediaeval Studies* 15 (1953), 85. And see Abulafia, "*Intentio recta*," pp. 29–30.

51. Abelard, *Dialogus*, p. 68. Among those investigators willing to admit the Muslim origins of the philosopher, see René Roques, "Les *Pagani* dans le *Cur Deus homo* de Saint Anselme," in *Die Metaphysik im Mittelalter: Ihr Ursprung und ihre Bedeutung*, ed. Paul Wilpert, Miscellanea mediaevalia 2 (Berlin, 1963), pp. 195ff.; Jean Jolivet, "Abélard et le philosophe (Occident et Islam au xiie siècle)," *Revue de l'histoire des religions* 164 (1963), 181–89; and de Gandillac, "Juif," pp. 388–89. Graboïs, "Un Chapitre," p. 648, and Abulafia, "*Intentio recta*," pp. 25ff., oppose such a conclusion. A Muslim identification of Abelard's philosopher depends somewhat, although not entirely, on the

Who, then, is the Jew of Abelard's *Dialogus?* This Jew's passionate description of medieval Jewish existence has led some investigators to argue that Abelard characterized him realistically, on the basis of his own personal observations. Aryeh Graboïs has contended that Abelard derived his portrayal of Jewish legalism from the new schools of Jewish talmudic scholars (the Tosafists), with whom he might have interacted in early-twelfth-century Paris, and that Abelard probably knew a fair amount of Hebrew.[52] My own impressions, however, dictate otherwise. Despite its allusion to postbiblical tradition, the *Dialogus* depicts the Jew as a has-been. He and his Judaism are thoroughly biblical in their outlook and bound to the letter of the law, such that they constitute living relics of an ancient phase in the history of salvation not only superseded by Christianity but surpassed by natural philosophy as well. To the extent that the Jew of the *Dialogus* deviates from this antiquated mold, he does so, as we have seen, to anticipate the teachings of Christianity, as in his linkage of circumcision to a notion of original sin that few medieval European Jews could have entertained.[53] The Jew of the *Dialogus* is thus a fossil of something long gone; disinherited by Christianity, he remains excluded from the discussion of the burning issue on Abelard's agenda: the encounter between natural philosophy and Christian theology.

I believe that one can discern in Abelard's *Dialogus* another example of twelfth-century Christian thought struggling with, but not yet discarding, the patristic caricature of the Jew. The philosopher of the *Dialogus*, not the Jew, dominates the encounter between infidel and believer; the Jew has much less of a role to play. Still, his presence persists,

---

dating of the *Dialogus*; for some have argued that if Abelard composed the treatise while at Cluny after 1140, he may have reacted to Peter the Venerable's commitment to polemicize against Islam; see the sources cited above, n. 20. Abelard's willingness to view Muslim intellectuals in a relatively favorable light is perhaps confirmed by his statement in *Historia calamitatum*, p. 97: "Sepe autem, Deus scit, in tantam lapsus sum desperationem, ut Christianorum finibus excessis ad gentes transire disponerem, atque ibi quiete sub quacunque tributi pactione inter inimicos Christi christiane vivere."

52. Aryeh Graboïs, "The *Hebraica veritas* and Jewish-Christian Intellectual Relations in the Twelfth Century," *Speculum* 50 (1975), 617 and n. 20; and "Un Chapitre," pp. 650ff.

53. Abelard, *Dialogus*, pp. 65–66: "Quod si etiam humane culpe in primis parentibus exordia revolvas et dominicam in mulierem sententiam pene prolatam, cum ei videlicet dicitur, 'In dolore paries filio,' videbis quoque virum participem peccati in genitali precipue membro recte fieri pene consortem, ut in illo videlicet membro recte patiatur, per quod vite presentis exilio filios generat morituros, de paradiso se et nos pariter propria transgressione in huius vite deiciens erumpnas."

both to demonstrate the inferiority of his point of view and to allow the Christian to respond to the philosopher most effectively. Abelard nowhere challenged the propriety of Jewish existence in Christendom; rather, he sympathized with its lamentable state. Furthermore, Abelard's writings hardly depict the Jew as a deliberate unbeliever, as one who knows the truth but spitefully rejects it anyway, or as a heretic. To the contrary, in his appraisal of the motives of those who crucified Jesus, Abelard surpassed all of his predecessors in what Langmuir termed his "understanding of Jewish attitudes." Although the *Dialogus* hints at this understanding, it receives its fullest expression in Abelard's *Ethica* or *Scito te ipsum* (Know Thyself).

With its radical insistence that neither human action nor the will to act but only the intention of the mind (or informed consent) constitutes the source of merit or sin, this work ensured Abelard a place in the history of moral philosophy. For if an evil intention, and only an evil intention, can render an action sinful, then one must reevaluate the most heinous of misdeeds committed in the absence of such intention— from adultery to murder, and even the most notorious murders of all:

> If one asks whether those persecutors of the martyrs or of Christ sinned in what they believed to be pleasing to God, or whether they could without sin have forsaken what they thought should definitely not be forsaken, assuredly, according to our earlier description of sin as contempt of God or consenting to what one believes should not be consented to, we cannot say that they have sinned in this, nor is anyone's ignorance—or even the unbelief with which no one can be saved—a sin. For those who do not know Christ and therefore reject the Christian faith because they believe it to be contrary to God, what contempt of God have they in what they do for God's sake and therefore think they do well?[54]

Abelard's language here bears paraphrasing. Sin resides in human intention. Those who crucified Jesus and persecuted him and his disciples did so in ignorance of the magnitude of their crime. Ignorance can never be sinful, not even the ignorance of or lack of that belief in God (*ignorare vero Deum vel non ei credere*)—Abelard appears to equate the two—required for salvation.[55] The infidelity of the Jews is therefore

---

54. Abelard, *Ethics*, pp. 54–57, departing slightly from Luscombe's translation.
55. Ibid., p. 64, we read of Cornelius before his conversion by Peter: "Qui quamvis antea lege naturali Deum recognosceret atque diligeret, ex quo meruit de oratione sua exaudiri et Deo acceptas elemosinas habere, tamen si eum ante fidem Christi de hac luce migrasse contingeret, nequaquam ei vitam promittere auderemus, quantumcunque bona

not sinful; nor was their responsibility for Jesus' death.[56] On the contrary, because they persecuted Jesus and his apostles out of a proper intention to serve God, "they would have sinned more gravely in fault if they had spared them against their own conscience."[57] Anselm, we recall, had minimized the guilt of the Jewish Christ-killers, concluding that a sin committed in ignorance could only be considered venial, not mortal. Picking up on Augustine's understanding that the Jews condemned Jesus because they truly believed him to be worthy of punishment, Abelard now went further still: Owing to their good intentions, not only did the Jews not sin, but they would have sinned had they acted otherwise! Abelard's detractors, with Bernard of Clairvaux in the lead, readily included his ostensive exoneration of Jesus' crucifiers among the propositions for which they condemned him at the Council of Sens in 1140.[58]

Again we encounter ambivalence—or the proverbial "mixed bag" of sentiments—in Abelard's evaluation of the Jews' deicide, which hardly rendered him a champion of toleration for ethnic or religious minorities. Although Abelard clearly had the Jews in mind when discussing the persecutors of Jesus,[59] he did not explicitly identify them as such, and one senses that his concern here lay mostly with the applications of his own doctrine of intentionality, not with Christian-Jewish relations. In any event, the Jews to whom he imputed noble intentions for rejecting Jesus were the Jews of first-century Jerusalem, not his contemporaries in twelfth-century Europe; and if, on the basis of the twelfth century's invocation of rationalism in the Jewish-Christian debate, Abelard did not promulgate a harsher Christian attitude toward the Jews, so too did he refrain from openly advocating their toleration. Moreover, if the absence of evil intention or the absence of belief in God could render one guiltless, the lack of righteous intention—or the lack of the requisite knowledge of God—left one eternally damned.

---

opera eius viderentur, nec eum fidelibus sed magis infidelibus connumeraremus, quantocunque studio salutis esset occupatus."

56. On Abelard's identification of the Jews as Jesus' crucifiers, see ibid., p. 58, and his *Dialogus*, p. 51.

57. Abelard, *Ethics*, trans. Luscombe, pp. 66–67.

58. See Eligius M. Buytaert, "The Anonymous *Capitula haeresum Petri Abaelardi* and the Synod of Sens, 1140," *Antonianum* 43 (1968), 427, 437–38; and Constant J. Mews, "The Lists of Heresies Attributed to Peter Abelard," *RB* 95 (1985), 109. Cf. Peter Abelard, *Apologia, seu confessio fidei,* in *Opera,* ed. Victor Cousin (1849–59; reprint, New York, 1970), 2:721: "Crucifixores Christi in ipsa crucifixione gravissimum peccatum fateor commisisse." Cf. also Murray, *Abelard,* pp. 117–39.

59. Cf. Abulafia, "*Intentio recta,*" p. 14; and see above, at n. 54.

Exonerating the Jews from guilt, in other words, did not entail positing their admissibility into the kingdom of heaven. "It is sufficient for damnation not to believe in the Gospel, to be ignorant of Christ, not to receive the sacraments of the Church, even though this occurs not so much through wickedness as through ignorance."[60] Here, we should add, Abelard has condemned the Jews to damnation not specifically qua Jews but as infidels, for failing to believe as they should. Still, the *Ethica* does use its discussion of intentionality to denigrate Judaism specifically, reiterating that in compliance with arbitrary precepts of Mosaic law one hardly finds the route to salvation of the soul.[61] For Abelard, the Jews and Judaism did not merely fail to comprehend the truth of Christianity. They contravened the dictates of reason and thereby situated themselves outside the bounds of natural law and philosophy.

HERMANN OF COLOGNE

Judah ben David ha-Levi of Cologne became Hermannus quondam Iudaeus, Hermann the erstwhile Jew, when he approached the baptismal font in 1128 or 1129 at the age of twenty. In the wake of his conversion he soon became a Premonstratensian canon, received ordination as a priest, and rose to the abbacy of the Premonstratensian cloister in Scheda. Several decades after his baptism, probably some time after 1150, Hermann authored his *Opusculum de conversione sua* (A Little Work Concerning His Own Conversion), which provides a captivating, retrospective account of the journey that led him from Judaism to Christianity.[62]

This journey, relates the *Opusculum*, commenced at the age of thirteen, when Hermann dreamed that the emperor took him into his palace, welcomed him to his table, and bedecked him with magnificent gifts; a learned Jewish relative thereupon offered the youth an unsatisfying interpretation of his vision in terms of pleasures of the flesh (*secundum carnis felicitatem*). Seven years later, while engaged in his family's moneylending business in Mainz, Hermann extended a loan to Ekbert, bishop of Münster, without taking collateral. Apprised

60. Abelard, *Ethics*, trans. Luscombe, pp. 62–63.
61. Ibid., p. 18; cf. Abulafia, "*Intentio recta*," pp. 28–30.
62. Hermann of Cologne, *Opusculum de conversione sua*, ed. Gerlinde Niemeyer, MGH Quellen zur Geistesgeschichte des Mittelalters 4 (Weimar, Germany, 1963). For scholarly discussion of the authenticity of this work, see below, n. 66.

of the transaction, Hermann's family compelled him to travel to Münster, accompanied by a guardian named Baruch, and to remain with
the bishop for twenty weeks until Ekbert paid his debt. At Münster
the inner turmoil that led him to baptism began to surface. Inspired by
the rationality of Christian scholarship, Hermann grew fond of the
spiritual, allegorical reading of Scripture. He regularly joined Ekbert
on his pastoral rounds throughout the diocese, and he encountered the
proselytizing gestures of numerous Christians, who called upon him to
emulate the conversion of Paul. He borrowed Latin books, entered a
church out of curiosity, and, upset by the sight of the icons, challenged
Rupert of Deutz to a debate, in which the abbot ably replied to his
questions. Hermann's hosts at the court and residence of the bishop
extended themselves to him graciously; one servant, Richmar, wished
to undergo an ordeal by fire for the sake of Hermann's soul and was
restrained only by the bishop himself. Accompanying Ekbert to the
Premonstratensian cloister at Cappenberg, Hermann realized that its
self-sacrificing canons did not merit divine rejection and damnation; he
wondered whether the Jews, rather than the Christians, deserved the
punishment of God—witness their present dispersion and captivity.

Ekbert finally repaid what he had borrowed, and Hermann returned home for Passover distraught and perplexed, searching, both
inwardly and in frequent conversation with clergymen, for the right
path to follow. His guardian Baruch denounced him for fraternizing
excessively with Christians in Münster but then succumbed to a fatal
fever within days of making his accusations. Hermann entreated God
for a vision, vainly fasting for three days in the hope of meriting one.
Threatened with excommunication by the now alarmed Jewish community, he agreed to demands that he marry a young Jewess of Cologne, but once the honeymoon ended his doubts returned. He soon
was convinced of the validity of Christianity, but he found intellectual
understanding alone, without the requisite emotional commitment, insufficient to facilitate a total conversion. He began to cross himself, especially as the devil persisted in undermining his attraction to the
church. Finally, the piety of two nuns in Cologne who prayed on his
behalf induced him to undergo baptism. He fled Cologne, by chance
intercepted letters from its Jewish community to the Jews of Mainz
calling for his punishment, stopped off in the synagogue of Worms to
preach on the shortcomings of Judaism, kidnapped his younger half-
brother from his home in Mainz, took refuge in various cloisters, and
finally received the sacrament in Cologne. Several days before his bap-

tism, Hermann dreamed of himself in the heavenly company of the en-
throned Jesus; he dreamed also of his two Jewish cousins who,
damned to hell for their rejection of Christianity, could not share in
his rapture. Only after his conversion did Hermann truly appreciate
the significance of his earlier adolescent dream, which, he now recognized, foretold his entry into the kingdom of heaven and his feasting
at the table of Christ.

Hermann and his *Opusculum* have intrigued modern scholars, and
for good reason. Historians of autobiography may debate whether Hermann's treatise—or any other twelfth-century text—gives expression
to what we now consider a genuine autobiographical impulse, but there
can be no question that the *Opusculum* captures much of the distinctive spirit of its own age. The book recounts one twelfth-century individual's search for himself, and, as what some have deemed the most
compelling autobiographical account of conversion since Augustine's
Confessiones, its story relates to some of the chief religious and social
concerns of the day: the importance of the individual and his impulses,
the nature of religious community, biblical hermeneutics, the use of
ratio and *auctoritas* in theological argument, religious disputation, and
the dynamics of the conversion process itself. The literary artifice of
the *Opusculum* similarly testifies to the cultural climate in which it
appeared. Karl Morrison has instructively compared the structure of
Hermann's treatise with the basic unit of contemporary scholastic discourse: "The planned movement of the reader from the dream that
opened his hermeneutic gap to the one that closed it, from question to
correct answer, resembles the dialectical passage in scholastic exposition from the *quaestio* (the first dream), to contrary arguments (the
carnal interpretation), to positive arguments (the spiritual interpretation), and, finally, to the scholar's own conclusion (Herman-Judah's
concluding apostrophe on the eucharistic feast)."[63] Indeed, the bracketing of Hermann's memoirs between dreams and their interpretations
suggests that the issue of hermeneutics, as a means for unlocking and
assimilating the significance of revelation, lies at the heart of his little
book. As one recent study of dreaming in the Middle Ages concludes,

---

63. Karl F. Morrison, *Conversion and Text: The Cases of Augustine of Hippo, Herman-Judah, and Constantine Tsatsos* (Charlottesville, Va., 1992), p. 48. The fourteenth-
century Jewish apostate Abner of Burgos, who became Alfonso of Valladolid, also considered his dreams an important factor in his conversion to Christianity; see the Castilian
text published by Isidore Loeb, "Polémistes chrétiens et juifs en France et en Espagne,"
REJ 18 (1889), 54–57.

"susceptible to either a mundane, literal reading, or a divine, allegorical one, Hermann's enigmatic dream provides a ground upon which two radically different approaches to the world are explored. Hermann the proselyte, of course, finally embraces the 'higher' reading of his dream, using it and its interpretation to justify in part the radical religious change he has undergone."[64]

Understandably, most of the plentiful previous studies of Hermann and his *Opusculum*, my own included, have either focused on the thought and behavioral processes that culminated in his baptism[65] or debated the reliability of the autobiography.[66] In the present context, however, I wish to mine the *Opusculum* for its perceptions of Jews and Judaism. Granted, here is no work of anti-Jewish polemic; just as one found no discussion of key polemical issues, the past advent of the messiah, the incarnation, the virgin birth, and the Trinity, in Abelard's *Dialogus*, so too have they no place in Hermann's *Opusculum*. Yet the work, written decades after the events it claims to have reconstructed, sometimes in minute detail, is not simply a memoir of its author's youth. Rather, it uses the story of Hermann's conversion as a device for contrasting—and, possibly, for reconciling—two opposing dimensions in his identity. Who, Hermann's modern readers have wondered, constituted his intended audience? Was he preaching, quite literally, to the converted—that is, to Christians—perhaps in order to eliminate any lingering suspicion of himself in their eyes? Or did he seek to address "semi-Christians" as well, those still living within the Jewish com-

64. Steven F. Kruger, *Dreaming in the Middle Ages*, Cambridge Studies in Medieval Literature 14 (Cambridge, England, 1992), p. 165.

65. Bernhard Blumenkranz, "Jüdische und christliche Konvertiten im jüdisch-christlichen Religionsgespräch des Mittelalters," in *JIM*, pp. 275ff.; Arduini, *Ruperto di Deutz*, pp. 50–57; Sander L. Gilman, *Jewish Self-Hatred: Anti-Semitism and the Hidden Language of the Jews* (Baltimore, Md., 1986), pp. 29–31; Jeremy Cohen, "The Mentality of the Medieval Jewish Apostate: Peter Alfonsi, Hermann of Cologne, and Pablo Christiani," in *Jewish Apostasy in the Modern World*, ed. Todd M. Endelman (New York, 1987), pp. 29–35, and the earlier studies cited at p. 44 n. 25; Morrison, *Conversion and Text*, pp. 39–75; Kruger, *Dreaming*, pp. 154–65; and Abulafia, "Ideology of Reform," pp. 50–56.

66. Avrom Saltman, "Hermann's *Opusculum de conversione sua*: Truth or Fiction?" *REJ* 147 (1988), 31–56; Aviad M. Kleinberg, "Hermannus Judaeus's *Opusculum*: In Defense of Its Authenticity," *REJ* 151 (1992), 337–53; Friedrich Lotter, "Ist Hermann von Scheda's *Opusculum de conversione sua* eine Fälschung?" *Aschkenas* 2 (1992), 207–18; and, with reference to subsequent hagiographical tradition, Jean-Claude Schmitt, "La Memoire des Prémontrés: À propos de l'‘Autobiographie' du Prémontré Hermann le Juif," in *La vie quotidienne des moines et chanoines réguliers au Moyen Age et temps modernes*, ed. Marek Derwich (Wroclaw, Poland, 1995), pp. 439–52.

munity who, like the adolescent Judah, had begun to see the light of Christian truth?[67] While allowing for either or both of these possibilities, we shall consider the *Opusculum* above all for the reflexivity underscored by its dreams, for its constructions of Jews that empowered Hermann to make sense of himself in his own eyes. Though not in a systematic, learned dialogue, Hermann's treatise contributes to our story much as Peter Alfonsi's *Dialogi* did, by enriching our picture of twelfth-century Christendom's perceptions of Judaism. It illustrates how a newcomer to the medieval church imagined and understood his former Jewish self.

Hermann's portrayal of the Jews echoes many of the motifs in the writings of other twelfth-century churchmen. Most emphatically does the *Opusculum* stress the materialism and carnality of the Jewish community in which Hermann grew up, and these contrast sharply with the priorities of the surrounding Christian society. Hermann first met Bishop Ekbert in Mainz when he had traveled there on business, for "all Jews are enserfed to commerce [*negotiationi inserviunt*]."[68] When he loaned Ekbert money without taking collateral, his friends and relatives rebuked him, because, "by the custom of the Jews, which I knew very well, I ought to have exacted a pawn twice the amount of the loan."[69] This overriding concern for money mandated that Hermann remain with the bishop for as long as he did, such that Jewish avarice may have not only disenchanted the young Judah regarding his Judaism but also allowed for the development of his attraction to Christianity. Whereas Jews wished to extend only secured loans of money at interest, Hermann's Christian hosts in Münster gladly lent him books that increased his religious knowledge, presumably interest free. Not surprisingly, the Jewish commitment to earthly pleasures extended from material wealth to carnal delights,[70] and the *Opusculum* posits a revealing triangular connection among the synagogue, Satan, and sex. Aware of his attraction to the church, the Jews urged Judah to marry; and the devil, envious of his spiritual growth and intent upon his ruin, "coupled a woman to me in marriage." Hermann sought to postpone his be-

67. Of his Jewish acquaintances Hermann wrote, *Opusculum*, pp. 113–14: "Illi me Christianis tam pertinaci studio favere videntes, semi-christianum vocare ceperunt." Cf. below, at n. 97.

68. Ibid., p. 72, trans. Morrison, *Conversion and Text*, p. 78.

69. Ibid., p. 73, trans. Morrison, p. 78.

70. Cf. the comments of Bernard of Clairvaux, chapter 6, at nn. 43, 51.

trothal to the maiden selected for him, but, convinced that marriage
would root him in their community more firmly, the Jews stood firm
in their resolve. "They proposed that I choose one of two alternatives:
to wit, either, without any excuse, to agree to consummate the marriage, according to the precepts of the law, or, if some other course
of action took my fancy, to leave their synagogue"—that is, to suffer
excommunication. Hermann acquiesced and married. "I gave perfect
joy to the devil, who was raging against me, and gave myself over
entirely to destruction. . . . The Jews, indeed, delighted in my false
happiness," but his Christian friends despaired, they explained, because "contrary to our hope, you have chosen instead to follow your
lusts."[71]

Such a polar opposition between Jewish and Christian values had
other ramifications, too. Whereas all of the Christians depicted in the
Opusculum treated Hermann graciously and hospitably, the Jews appear belligerent, suspicious, and conspiratorial. Recalling the charges
of Bernard of Clairvaux that the synagogue selfishly sought to exclude
the Gentiles from its covenant with God, the Jews remembered by Hermann displayed the utmost hostility toward Christians, to be sure.[72]
Yet they also showed their hatred for Judah, causing him to suffer
infamia among his peers, plotting against him, and soliciting the help
of their coreligionists in Mainz in engineering his demise.[73] "Their zeal
flared up against me so fiercely that, if they had had a chance to do
the crime, they would not have shrunk from stoning me with their own
hands."[74] Virtually all of the Jews with whom Judah interacted in the
narrative—and especially those whom one would expect to protect his
interests—led him astray from his ultimate happiness. A relative, Isaac,
"a man then of great authority among the Jews," misguided him in
wrestling with his adolescent dream.[75] His father-in-law, Alexander,
sought his downfall in marriage; when Hermann resisted, "he turned

71. Hermann, *Opusculum*, pp. 98–101, trans. Morrison, pp. 94–96.

72. Of the devil, Hermann wrote, ibid., p. 105: "Mandata quippe legis ad memoriam
mihi cepit reducere, inter que et hoc Iudeis preceptum fuerat, ut in nullo penitus im-
mundos ac Deo execrabiles gentium ritus imitarentur, ne, quos sibi Deus ex omnibus
nationibus in populum peculiarem elegerat, illarum superstitionum in aliquo participes
aut consimiles viderentur." See also the statements of the young, still Jewish Judah recounted on p. 77; and cf. above, chapter 6, n. 27.

73. Ibid., pp. 95, 111–12.

74. Ibid., p. 110, trans. Morrison, p. 102.

75. Ibid., pp. 71–72, trans. Morrison, pp. 77–78.

from prayers and blandishments to threats and terrors in the fashion of a scorpion, brandishing its tail."[76] His wife served the purposes of the devil, much as Eve caused Adam to fall and Job's wife strove to subvert him.[77] And his tutor Baruch "cunningly [*callide*]" discerned his initial interest in Christianity and betrayed him to his family, revealing that inwardly he had already apostasized.[78] One compares these Jews to Bishop Ekbert and his man Richmar, who never abhorred proponents "of the Jewish or any other human error" but truly emulated Jesus in his prayer for the salvation of his crucifiers.[79] Or one contrasts them with Bertha and Glismut, two nuns of Cologne, who prayed for Hermann's soul; "with bowels full of piety and compassion, they gushed forth abundant tears over my great miseries, and they promised they would pour untiring supplications out to God for me, as long as it took for me to be worthy to receive the hoped-for consolation of heavenly grace."[80]

Distinguished by men like Isaac, Alexander, and Baruch, the Jews of the *Opusculum* suffer from impaired vision and spiritual blindness. They behold only the external, literal significance of sacred texts, dreams, icons, and even the crucifix itself, unable to grasp "the mystical understanding of the law of Moses" without "the interposed shadows of some kind of carnal figures."[81] They cannot but offer a carnal interpretation of Hermann's first dream. They cannot appreciate, as Rupert of Deutz explained to Hermann during their conversation in Münster, that written texts and visual images alike serve to educate by triggering symbolic associations and deeper understanding. Seeking visible, tangible proof for their beliefs, they cannot realize that "faith which is won over by miracles has either no or very little merit," as Ekbert instructed Hermann and Richmar—and as the philosopher of Abelard's *Dialogus* had criticized the Jew.[82] Like other twelfth-century texts, the *Opusculum* rebukes the Jews for their postbiblical traditions, but it never doubts that these traditions kept the Jews firmly ensconced in a superficial understanding of the Old Testament, such that their

76. Ibid., p. 99, trans. Morrison, p. 95.
77. Ibid., p. 98.
78. Ibid., pp. 76, 93.
79. Ibid., p. 87, trans. Morrison, p. 87.
80. Ibid., p. 108, trans. Morrison, p. 101.
81. Ibid., p. 104, trans. Morrison, p. 98.
82. Ibid., pp. 85–86, trans. Morrison, p. 86. See above, at n. 47.

error lay in their literalist exegesis. Early in his narrative, during his first visit to a church, "the Pharisaic doctrine that was once mine" limited Judah's appreciation of Christian icons—like sacred texts—to their external likeness and physical characteristics.[83] Subsequently, when debating with clerics over the meaning of Christological prophecies in the Bible, "most stubbornly supporting myself on the letter alone . . . I perverted them with some sinister interpretation."[84] And if rabbinic tradition undergirded Hermann's commitment to the literal *sensus* of Scripture before his conversion, so did talmudic lore contrast with the figurative *sensus* of his exegesis once he had committed himself to the church. When he preached to the Jews in the synagogue of Worms, against the stupid old wives' tales (*contra stultas et aniles . . . fabulas*) which their sage Gamaliel had pieced together from written texts, "I uttered for them the honey-sweetness of spiritual allegories."[85] Perhaps most tragically of all from Hermann's point of view, his Jewish friends and relatives misread the transformation within himself. "The Jews, who have the zeal of the law but not according to knowledge, inconsolably bewailed me, with a most bitter sorrow, as one perfidious and lost."[86]

As we have seen in the preceding chapters, the attribution of materialism, carnality, literalism, and intellectual blindness to the Jew led twelfth-century churchmen to doubt his very humanity. Hermann followed suit. The *Opusculum* recounts that Bishop Ekbert "adverted to the example of the Jews, like some beasts of burden, content with the letter of the precepts alone, as with chaff, and Christians, like men using reason, refreshing themselves with spiritual understanding, as with the sweetest pith of straw." Taking Ekbert's lesson to heart, Hermann felt obliged to internalize the metaphor and thereby experience the transition from carnal to spiritual. "Knowing also that animals that do not chew the cud [*animalia non ruminantia*] are numbered by the law among the unclean, I transferred to the stomach of memory for frequent rumination with myself [*in ventrem memorie sepius mecum ruminanda transmisi*] whatever things I had heard in his preaching that pleased me."[87] As he did his relatives in his second dream, Hermann

83. Ibid., p. 75, trans. Morrison, p. 80.

84. Ibid., p. 97, trans. Morrison, p. 93.

85. Ibid., p. 113, trans. Morrison, p. 104. Cf. the similarly derisive remarks of Peter Alfonsi, above, chapter 5, n. 139.

86. Hermann, *Opusculum*, p. 120, trans. Morrison, p. 109. Cf. Romans 10:2.

87. Hermann, *Opusculum*, p. 74, trans. Morrison, p. 79.

believed the Jews worthy of damnation. Their exile and dispersion confirmed that their observances no longer pleased God.[88] The *Opusculum*
identifies Hermann's struggle against Judaism with a struggle against
the devil,[89] evoking the spirit of Peter the Venerable's polemical opus.
And, as Peter did, Hermann deemed the Jewish community worthy of
despoliation, like the ancient Egyptians despoiled by the Israelites on
the eve of their exodus. Whereas they departed with the material treasures of Egypt in hand, Hermann took "rational booty [*rationalem pre-
dam*]" when he left his life of bondage behind: nothing less than the
person of his half-brother, "which would not only adorn the temple of
the supreme being but would also be worthy to be his temple."[90]

For all of its conformity to constructions of earlier twelfth-century authors, however, the portrait of Jews and Judaism in the *Opusculum* still
reflects a singular, distinguishing perspective. Hermann related the battle
between Judaism and Christianity that had raged within him as a youth
from a distance of some twenty years at least. His story reveals no traces
of any subsequent interaction with the Jewish communities of the Rhineland. As I noted above, his treatise deals but negligibly with the substantive issues of *Adversus Iudaeos* polemic, and, notwithstanding his assertions of his own formidable scholarship, it displays little sophistication
in matters theological, either Jewish or Christian. The sole instance in
which the *Opusculum* treats standard themes of the Jewish-Christian debate at all seriously occurs in its recollection of the exchange that reportedly transpired between Rupert of Deutz and Judah ben David of Cologne during the latter's extended visit in Münster.[91] The question of
whether such a disputation actually occurred does not concern us at
present. What does warrant our attention is Hermann's reconstruction
of the Jewish, anti-Christian arguments that he supposedly made in Rupert's presence:[92] Christians bear great hostility toward the Jews; they

88. Ibid., p. 92: "Titubare intra me cepi et cogitare, ne forte Iudeis errantibus per
viam mandatorum Dei currerent Christiani, si inquiens, legalium illi adhuc rituum ob-
servantia placeret, non adeo eorundem observatores Iudeos gratie sue destituisset auxilio,
ut eos bonis omnibus patriaque proscriptos per omnes terre nationes longe lateque dis-
pergeret. Quo contra si sectam christiane religionis execraretur, non eos per orbem terrarum in tantum dilatari et confortari pateretur."

89. See ibid., pp. 69, 70, 97, 98, 100, 105, 114, 115, 118, 119, 121.

90. Ibid., p. 109, trans. Morrison, p. 102. Cf. above, chapter 6, at n. 98; and see the
comments of Morrison, *Conversion and Text*, pp. 61–62.

91. For an alternative dating of the debate, see Abulafia, "Ideology of Reform," p.
52; on the correspondence between the arguments of Rupert as recorded by Hermann
and those that characterize Rupert's own treatises, see Arduini, *Ruperto di Deutz*, pp.
59–66.

92. Hermann, *Opusculum*, pp. 77–79, trans. Morrison, pp. 80–81.

regularly spit upon the Jews with curses; blinded with envy of the benefits conferred by God on the Jews, they deny the Jews' lasting covenant
with God and despise them; Jews suffer Christian mockery with equanimity, persisting in their fulfillment of the divine will; Christians, however, proudly boast that they, not the Jews, observe God's law properly;
Christians glory in the veneration of icons, "the madness of this superstition of yours [*superstitionis vestre dementiam*]," which borders on
idolatry; and Christians distort the divine law with their own absurd
traditions, so that they do not practice what they preach:

> You are not doers of the law, as you say, but plainly judges of it. Laughable
> as it is to say, you correct it just as you want. You accept some things but
> reject others. Among the latter, you decide some are superstitious and oth-
> ers, said in a mystic fashion, are to be accepted, not in the way in which
> they actually were said, but according to whatever stupid, asinine, and de-
> praved fictions anyone pleases. Plainly, it is stupid temerity and madness
> worthy of unrestrained derision for human beings to wish to correct what
> God established and, under a terrible curse, commanded them to observe.
> You Christians are particularly liable to the curse, since while you presume
> to be judges of the law, you are also condemned as its prevaricators.

At first blush, Judah's denunciation of Christians may seem credible;
but upon further reflection, it appears more like a Christian indictment
of Judaism than a Jewish tirade against Christianity! Virtually all of
the charges—hostility and vulgarity toward the beliefs of the other,
envy of divine favor toward the other, selfish refusal to entertain the
possibility of divine election of the other, abandonment of the genuine
observance of divine law, irrationality, hypocrisy, substitution of absurd fictions for the authentic word of God, and the idolatry that results therefrom[93]—echo Christian condemnations of Jews that we have
already encountered in this book, from patristic literature to the polemics of the twelfth century.

One wonders if Hermann, writing in the cloister decades later, simply lacked familiarity with the current issues and literature of the Jewish-Christian debate. Or perhaps this confusion of Jewish and Christian
arguments in the *Opusculum*, whether deliberate or not, somehow derives from a lack of interest on the part of its author, or from his desire
to focus on other dimensions of the opposition between the two religions. However edifying the young Hermann may have found the in-

---

93. Cf. the comments of Peter Alfonsi on rabbinic anthropomorphisms, above, chapter 5, at nn. 104, 126–28.

struction of his Christian teachers, it did not determine the outcome of his personal quest. Feelings and impulses play a much more decisive role than doctrine in this narrative, and the feelings and impulses of the author himself above all. His fear of retaliation from his Jewish coreligionists, his fear of the devil, his gratitude for the kindness of his Christian benefactors, his lust for his wife, his inability to endure detraction in the Jewish community, his initial pity and his eventual envy of Christian monasticism—all these determine the progress and, ultimately, the outcome of the contest raging within Hermann. The *Opusculum* offers explicit corroboration. Regarding the Augustinian canons regular, Hermann reported that "I was sorry for them from my inmost being because of human feelings" and that this constituted a critical juncture in his development, precipitating his acknowledgment to God that "you desire the life of sinners, you invite them to conversion, so that they can live."[94] And in the wake of his moving encounter with the two nuns of Cologne, Hermann reflected: "Look at me. Neither the explanation [*ratio*] given by many concerning the faith of Christ nor the disputation of great clerics could convert me . . . but the devout prayer of simple women did."[95]

"Look at me [*ecce enim me*]." The author's demand of his reader resounds and intrigues. Throughout the *Opusculum*, Hermann's conflicting emotions overshadow all the standard issues of the Jewish-Christian debate with the exception of one: hermeneutics, the tension between different modes of interpretation. But it is not a particular biblical text the exegesis of which will decide the outcome of Hermann's story. Rather, as Hermann's dreams and the interpretations of them bracketing the narrative of the *Opusculum* suggest, it is the interpretive self-understanding of the author. As Sander Gilman has observed, Hermann "becomes his own text, and his allegorical reading of his conversion becomes the proof for his abandonment of the blindness of his former self, his perception of the world and its signs as transparent, revealing the glory of Christ, and his ability to see in his present state the pattern for the future."[96] Such an approach to Hermann and his treatise helps to make sense of the confusion, the ironies, the reversals, and the contradictions in the opposition between Judaism and Christianity with which the *Opusculum* is replete. Morrison has suggested that the author thereby

94. Hermann, *Opusculum*, pp. 90–91, trans. Morrison, pp. 89–90.
95. Ibid., p. 108, trans. Morrison, p. 101.
96. Gilman, *Jewish Self-Hatred*, p. 31.

engaged in "an exercise in cryptography," deliberately transmitting encoded messages to select readers who might themselves identify with the conflicts that he had experienced and was still experiencing. "Writing within a hostile Christian society and addressing a Jewish audience of some ambivalence, he deployed a Hebraic scholasticism," a markedly Jewish hermeneutical strategy that represented Hermann's "ambivalent disengagement from the old life"[97] to other semi-Christians similarly tormented by the Jewish hatred of apostates, on one hand, and the Christian suspicion of converts, on the other.

Without discounting Morrison's opinion concerning Hermann's lasting predilection for the Judaic in the *Opusculum*, I would prefer to focus on its rampant confusion of ideas and behavioral patterns traditionally associated with Jews and Christians. For Hermann did not simply employ Jewish hermeneutical devices in accounting for his conversion to Christianity, techniques that may well have manifested his various ambivalences. His narrative also blurs the distinction between Judaism and Christianity, in a provocative, self-contradictory manner that demands reflection. On several occasions, for example, the *Opusculum* beclouds the contrast between Jewish literalism and Christian symbolism that it has endeavored so artfully to underscore. The first Christian preacher whom Hermann heard in Münster declared that certain Mosaic laws must be observed "only according to the surface of the letter [*ad solam littere superficiem*]," including commandments—to honor one's parents and not to commit adultery—that Jesus himself had interpreted figuratively.[98] The books that Hermann borrowed from his Christian friends in Münster taught him to link "letters to syllables and syllables to words," so that he soon "mastered the science of reading the Scriptures,"[99] but the "science" so described hardly exceeds a straightforward, literal reading of sacred text. Though admonished by Ekbert that "you are never to ask or, above all, to yearn for some sign from God"[100] to effect conversion to Christianity, Hermann continued to do precisely that, begging God "to reveal to me 'the way of truth' by a night vision, as he once revealed mysteries of dreams to the holy Daniel."[101] Eventually, he expe-

97. Ibid., pp. 48, 60ff.

98. Hermann, *Opusculum*, p. 74, trans. Morrison, p. 79. Cf. Matthew 5:27ff., 12:46ff.

99. Ibid., p. 76 (translation mine).

100. Ibid., p. 85. trans. Morrison, p. 86.

101. Ibid., p. 94, departing from the translation of Morrison, p. 92; on the association to Daniel, cf. above, n. 19, and see Morrison, *Conversion and Text*, pp. 65–68.

rienced the heavenly vision that he had craved, not unlike the heavenly visions of Daniel, which similarly confirmed the salvation of the pious and the eternal punishment of the wicked. "And so, awakened, I recalled with what great prayers and tears and frequency of fasts I had sometimes striven to obtain such a vision from heaven for my enlightenment"[102]— in express contradiction of Ekbert's instruction. Ironically, and unlike his pupil, Hermann's Jewish tutor, Baruch, could see beyond the external and the superficial to perceive the spiritual truth; before anyone else, related the author, he recognized that "I could now be thought not a Jew but a Christian."[103]

Confusion in exegetical perspective readily extended to reversal in typical patterns of thought and behavior. Although the *Opusculum* repeatedly casts Jewish and Christian religious practices as opposites,[104] when it came to fasting in the hope of receiving his vision, Hermann naively decided to follow both "without distinction [*indifferenter*]."[105] Soon after praising Ekbert and Richmar for not bearing hostility toward the Jews and reflecting upon God's approval of the Christian mission to the Jews, Hermann rejoiced over the fatal illness of his tutor, who had revealed his Christian inclinations to his family. "I trusted in God's piety all the more because I had experienced it in this vengeance upon my accuser."[106] When Hermann kidnapped his half-brother to join him in his new, regenerative covenant with God, "the mother of the boy, most deeply troubled and terrified, had me searched for high and low."[107] Have we here an echo of the same popular folk motif, albeit with the roles of Jews and Christians reversed, underlying the tale of Chaucer's Prioress—a motif that may have originated in medieval Germany?[108] Although conversion should have freed Hermann from the yoke of the law, Hermann struggled hard to comply precisely with the letter of ecclesiastical regulation while undergoing the rite of baptism; although he had trouble at first, at last "I did what had to be done for salvation."[109] Perhaps still more revealing is the final, Christian interpretation of Her-

102. Hermann, *Opusculum*, pp. 117–18, trans. Morrison, p. 107.
103. Ibid., p. 93, trans. Morrison, p. 91.
104. Ibid., pp. 92, 96, 98.
105. Ibid., p. 94, trans. Morrison, p. 92.
106. Ibid., p. 94, trans. Morrison, p. 91.
107. Ibid., p. 115, trans. Morrison, p. 106.
108. On the medieval history of the motif, see Carleton Brown, *A Study of the Miracle of Our Lady Told by Chaucer's Prioress* (London, 1906), and "The Prioress's Tale," in *Sources and Analogues of Chaucer's Canterbury Tales*, ed. W. F. Bryan and Germaine Dempster (1941; reprint, New York, 1958), pp. 447–85.
109. Hermann, *Opusculum*, p. 119, trans. Morrison, p. 108.

mann's initial adolescent dream. At the age of thirteen, recall, Judah ben David dreamed of his welcome at the royal palace, where he dined with the king himself.[110] "There, as he splendidly feasted with his friends, I reclined next to him, as the dearest of friends. From the same vessel as he I ate a salad made up of many kinds of herbs and roots."[111] In good allegorical fashion, the closing pages of the *Opusculum* explain: "Thus, one may be fattened at the table on the flesh-meats of the immaculate lamb, Jesus Christ, and be inebriated with the cup of his sacrosanct blood. Continuing with the allegory, I think [*arbitror*] that the salad that I seemed [*visus sum*] to myself to eat at the royal table designates the gospel of Christ."[112] Hermann's Christian allegory works, but the author posed it tentatively ("I think . . . I seemed"), and one wonders at the possibility of another, simultaneous if discordant, reading of the dream: The interpretation's mention of the flesh-meats of an immaculate lamb (as in Exodus 12:5) and a sacrificial bloodlike beverage in inebriating quantities, consumed together with herbs (as in Exodus 12:8) while reclining at the table, clearly evokes images of a Passover seder. Precisely when Hermann celebrated his exodus out of the Jewish community and entry into the church, he fulfilled his childhood dreams in the unmistakable imagery of Jewish ritual.

Confusion abounds in the narrative of the *Opusculum*. Hermann evidently had trouble deciding what, exactly, would allow for passage from Judaism to Christianity. Having returned from Münster to Cologne, he disputed regularly with Christian clerics and thought: "If they could show me the authority [*auctoritatem*] of their sect from manifest testimonies of the law and prophets and affirm in a probable fashion that entrance to the kingdom of heaven was open to their sect alone (as they said), I would yield to reason [*rationi*]."[113] Has he here mistaken *ratio* for *auctoritas*, or vice versa? As noted above,[114] Hermann avowed that *ratio* did not effect his conversion. Why, then, while fleeing from his Jewish pursuers, did he risk his life to preach in the synagogue of Worms? And the opening lines of the *Opusculum* depict Hermann's conversion as a long, arduous process;[115] but later the au-

---

110. On Hermann's allusions to the biblical courtier Mordecai, see Morrison, *Conversion and Text*, pp. 66–68.

111. Hermann, *Opusculum*, p. 71, trans. Morrison, p. 77.

112. Ibid., p. 125, trans. Morrison, p. 112.

113. Ibid., p. 96, trans. Morrison, p. 93.

114. See above, n. 95.

115. Hermann, *Opusculum*, pp. 69–70.

thor reported, "Abruptly [*tota mox*], I converted to God with all contrition."[116]

The contradiction and confusion pervading the *Opusculum*, I believe, add novelty and color to the more standard perceptions of Jews and Judaism to which Hermann's treatise also gives expression. Despite the manifold polar oppositions between Judaism and Christianity that characterize the writings of twelfth-century churchmen, Hermann the erstwhile Jew of the Rhineland, even decades after his baptism, depicted two religious communities that had very much in common. Perhaps the dissonance between standard anti-Jewish motifs and Hermann's departure from them that one finds in the *Opusculum* provides unusual testimony to the twelfth-century's growing awareness of disparity between the hermeneutically crafted Jew of Christian theology and contemporary Jewry itself. At the very least, Hermann's *Opusculum* offers an impression of proximity between the Jewish and Christian cultures of twelfth-century Germany that finds confirmation in Jewish sources as well. Like their Christian neighbors, Ashkenazic Jews of this period experimented with new forms of communal association; to the extent that rabbinic law permitted, German-Jewish pietists sought to achieve a life of religious perfection by adopting mild ascetic practices; and, in the wake of the First and Second Crusades and the anti-Jewish violence they sparked, Jews too nurtured new ideals of martyrdom.[117] Holy war afforded Christian warriors an opportunity to sacrifice their bodies to God in emulation of the suffering of Jesus and thus provide for the salvation of their souls, much as the ascetic life of

116. Ibid., p. 92, trans. Morrison, p. 91.

117. On Ashkenazic pietism as an experiment in religious community, see, above all, Ivan G. Marcus, *Piety and Society: The Jewish Pietists of Medieval Germany*, Études sur le Judaïsme médiéval 10 (Leiden, Netherlands, 1981). On Jewish pietism and Jewish martyrdom, see also the classic introductory discussion of Jacob Katz, *Exclusiveness and Tolerance: Studies in Jewish-Gentile Relations in Medieval and Modern Times* (1961; reprint, New York, 1962), chaps. 7–8; and on martyrdom in particular, see Robert Chazan, *European Jewry and the First Crusade* (Berkeley, Calif., 1987), pp. 99–168, and Ivan G. Marcus, "From 'Deus vult' to 'the Will of the Creator': Extremist Religious Ideologies and Historical Reality in 1096 and Hasidei Ashkenaz" [Hebrew], in *Facing the Cross: The Persecution of Ashkenazic Jews in 1096*, ed. Yom Tov Assis et al. (Jerusalem, 1999). See also Jeremy Cohen, "The Hebrew Crusade Chronicles in Their Christian Cultural Context," in *Juden und Christen zur Zeit der Kreuzzüge*, ed. Alfred Haverkamp, Vorträge und Forschungen des Konstanzer Arbeitskreises für mittelalterliche Geschichte (Sigmaringen, Germany, 1999), and "The 'Persecutions of 1096'— From Martyrdom to Martyrology: The Sociocultural Context of the Hebrew Crusade Chronicles" [Hebrew], *Zion*, n.s. 59 (1994), 195–205, together with the many studies cited therein.

the monastery did for regular clergy;[118] and so did many Jews respond to the choice between death and conversion that the crusaders put before them by cultivating a new ethos of *Qiddush ha-Shem*, an unhesitating willingness to die a martyr's death in the sanctification of God's name.

Karl Morrison has rightly observed that Hermann's *Opusculum* resonates with the impact the violence of 1096 and 1146 exerted on Jewish communities of Ashkenaz. Hermann sought to assert his new identity with the sign of the cross, the very sign that epitomized the horror and threat of crusading for the Jews of the Rhineland. Hermann offered his young Jewish half-brother in baptism to the Christian God, recalling how numerous German Jews, in order to avoid conversion, sacrificed their children to their God in sanctification of his name. And Hermann's preoccupation with "guilt and revenge . . . abasement and vindication" echoes a similar preoccupation of the twelfth-century Hebrew chronicles that struggled, somehow, to make sense of the tragedies that had befallen the Jewish communities and inscribe their message in Jewish historical memory.[119] Yet I believe that the most important connection between the *Opusculum* and the crisis with which the crusades confronted Ashkenazic Jewry remains unnoticed. I have elsewhere sought to demonstrate how those Jews who survived the massacres of the First Crusade in order to reconstruct their communities during the twelfth century were primarily those who had converted, temporarily, to Christianity, and the children of such survivors; accordingly, the Hebrew chronicles they composed to memorialize the Jewish martyrs served no less to air the conflicts, guilt, and self-understanding of those who sought refuge in the church and later returned to Judaism.[120] Most illuminating is the expression of this "social logic"[121] in symbolic codes that betrayed considerable affinity to the Christian ideology of the crusade, suggesting that Jews participated in the cultural milieu of the Gentile majority at the same time as they portrayed themselves, as opposed to the crusaders, as the genuine martyrs and warriors of God. The critical choice between death as a Jewish martyr and baptism as a Christian proselyte obsessed the collective

118. See Jonathan Riley-Smith, *The First Crusade and the Idea of Crusading* (London, 1986), esp. pp. 2, 150–52.

119. Morrison, *Conversion and Text*, pp. 44, 51, 70.

120. Cohen, "'Persecutions of 1096,'" and "Hebrew Crusade Chronicles."

121. Cf. Gabrielle Spiegel, "History, Historicism, and the Social Logic of the Text in the Middle Ages," *Speculum* 65 (1990), 59–86.

consciousness of twelfth-century Ashkenazic Jewry, and it numbered among the concerns of one Judah ben David of Cologne, alias Hermann. Remembering the symbolic equivalence among crusader, martyr, and monk, he contemplates the monastic life at Cappenberg, where, at least according to the chapter headings in two manuscripts of the *Opusculum*, he eventually converted:

> While, groaning within myself, I considered these things and (if it is pious to express it this way) after a certain fashion wrestled with God for judgment in favor of these monks, straightway a heavy scruple of doubtfulness arose in my heart concerning the mutually contrary and diverse laws established by Jews and Christians. For since God's nature is good and his judgment mercy, I saw that it would be most appropriate for him to show the way of truth to his servants who truly "slay themselves all the day long" for him, according to the word of the Psalm [44:23]. I began to waver within myself and to think along these lines.[122]

Judah's Jewish coreligionists invoked the same words of the psalmist to glorify the Jews who suffered at the hands of the crusaders,[123] much as Christian texts had applied them to martyrs of the church ever since Paul's Epistle to the Romans (8:35–36). Wavering between Jewish and Christian religious communities, torn between "the mutually contrary and diverse laws" of synagogue and church, and weighing various alternatives of martyrdom and conversion, Hermann has here focused on the burning issue of Jewish-Christian relations in twelfth-century Germany and on a critical point of convergence between Jewish and Christian cultural history.

ALAN OF LILLE

By way of conclusion, both to this chapter and to this book's discussion of the twelfth century, we turn briefly to the writings of Alan of Lille (d. ca. 1203).[124] Alan died in his late eighties, such that his life spanned most of the twelfth century. His career linked study and instruction at

122. Hermann, *Opusculum*, pp. 91–92, trans. Morrison, p. 90. Note that the text of the *Opusculum*, at pp. 115, 118, places Hermann's conversion not at Cappenberg but at the monastery at Welanheim or at the church of St. Peter in Cologne itself.

123. A. Neubauer and M. Stern, *Hebräische Berichte über die Judenverfolgungen während der Kreuzzüge*, Quellen der Geschichte der Juden in Deutschland 2 (Berlin, 1892), pp. 16, 21.

124. On Alan's life, career, and writings, see Marie-Thérèse d'Alverny's introduction to Alan of Lille, *Textes inédits*, Études de philosophie médiévale 52 (Paris, 1965); and G. R. Evans, *Alan of Lille: The Frontiers of Theology in the Late Twelfth Century* (Cambridge, England, 1983).

the schools of Chartres and Paris with teaching and preaching in the culturally tempestuous south of France; there, after earning "an enduring reputation as a scourge of heretics," he retired to the Cistercian monastery of Cîteaux at the very end of his life.[125] Alan thus interacted directly or indirectly with many of the luminaries and key trends of the twelfth-century renaissance, to whose humanistic and scholastic creativity he himself made extensive contributions. The bibliography of his writings ranges from speculative and moral theology to biblical commentary, homiletics, religious polemic, rhetoric, and poetry; recognizing the breadth of his learning, his contemporaries dubbed him *doctor universalis*. His opus is distinguished by the systematic exposition of Christian theology in clear, convincing fashion; by a staunch, Chartrian commitment to the synthesis of natural reason and the revealed truths of Christianity, of the study of the seven liberal arts and theology; and by a highly individualistic poetic imagination. Alan also numbered among the noteworthy dreamers of the High Middle Ages. His *De planctu naturae* (On the Plaint of Nature) recounts the oneiric vision of a poet who laments the fallen state of the human nature, exemplified in sexual perversity, and visualizes the restoration of the natural realm through its subordination to the will and grace of God. Suggesting a Chartrian view of "*continuité ontologique* between creation and redemption,"[126] Alan's dream is utterly monistic in its idealistic aspirations. Seeking to reintegrate the realms of nature and grace, its poetic allegory bespeaks Alan's wish to envision "no contradiction between the formal autonomy of his allegorized natural order and the radical dependency of man on divine Grace. His harking back to the primal harmony of man and Nature is actually an imaginative view of the effect of such Grace, the psychic process involved in the *opus restaurationis*."[127]

Peter Abelard revealed how a twelfth-century renaissance commitment to nature, its laws, and its reason refashioned traditional Christian

---

125. See John M. Trout, "The Monastic Vocation of Alan of Lille," *Analecta cisterciensia* 30 (1974), 46–53, and "Alan the Missionary," *Cîteaux* 26 (1975), 146–54 (quotation on p. 148).

126. Winthrop Wetherbee, "The Function of Poetry in the 'De planctu naturae' of Alain de Lille," *Traditio* 25 (1969), 125.

127. Winthrop Wetherbee, "The Literal and the Allegorical: Jean de Meun and the *De planctu Naturae*," *Mediaeval Studies* 33 (1971), 266. See also the instructive discussions of Lynch, *High Medieval Dream Vision*, chap. 3; and P. G. Walsh, "Alan of Lille as a Renaissance Figure," in *Renaissance and Renewal in Christian History*, ed. Derek Baker, SCH 14 (Oxford, 1977), pp. 117–35.

perceptions of Jews and Judaism; in the case of Hermann of Cologne, it
was that renaissance's interest in self-discovery that precipitated his contribution to our story. In Alan's case, a dream of a totally integrated
Christian world order, free of dualism in all its forms—a vision no less
characteristic of the age—underlies his work of religious polemic. Alan
composed his *De fide catholica* (On the Catholic Faith), also called *Contra haereticos, Valdenses, Iudaeos et paganos* (Against Heretics, Waldensians, Jews, and Pagans), during the last fifteen years of the twelfth
century.[128] Alan aimed chiefly to defend Catholic Christianity against the
dualistic heresy of the Cathars, whom he encountered personally in
southern France; yet his systematic penchant for synthesis and integration led him to include the Waldensians, who rejected the authority of
the church, and, to a lesser extent, the Jews and the Muslims among the
objects of his polemic. Ultimately, Alan's work targeted "the failure of
all 'unbelievers' to belong to the *fidelis populus*," inasmuch as "unbelievers are foreigners, non-citizens of the City of God."[129] The *De fide* thus
raises the objections to Catholicism characteristic of each of these four
enemies of the church and then seeks to answer them methodically, resorting to arguments based on reason and authority, as appropriate. Primarily in the *De fide* did Alan address the Jews and Judaism, but one
ought not to lose sight of its place within the overall context of his career
and the corpus of his writings.

As opposed to Abelard's *Dialogus* and Hermann's *Opusculum*,
Alan's *De fide* returns us to the more straightforward variety of religious polemic that, owing to the concerns, the pursuits, and the temperament of its author, helps to provide some closure to this survey of
twelfth-century Christian perceptions of the Jew. One cannot help noting the downsized consideration that the Jews receive in this work,
which turns to them "almost as an afterthought," relegating them to
a "hurried appendix," as it were, of but secondary importance.[130]
Times had changed. Other enemies of Christian theology and ecclesiology now threatened the church no less than did the Jews, at times
much more. But equally significant is Alan's choice to integrate the

---

128. Alan's *De fide catholica* appears in PL 210:305–430; Marie-Thérèse d'Alverny's
critical edition of its fourth book against the Muslims appears as an appendix to her
"Alain de Lille et l'Islam: Le 'Contra Paganos,'" in *ICM*, pp. 331–50. On the connection
between this treatise and Alan's poetic works, see Cesare Vasoli, "Il 'Contra haereticos'
di Alano di Lilla," *Bollettino dell' Istituto storico italiano per il Medio Evo* 75 (1963),
135ff.

129. Evans, *Alan*, p. 128.

130. Ibid., p. 124; Vasoli, "Il 'Contra haereticos,'" p. 171.

Jews into this polemical-apologetic work. Alongside heretics and Muslims, they take their place within a larger genus of those who do not belong to the people of the faithful, and the *De fide* betrays a sensitivity to what these various subsets did and did not share. Among the four subsets, Jews and Muslims had much in common,[131] and some investigators[132] have therefore included Alan in a series of Christian apologists—Anselm, Gilbert Crispin, Peter Alfonsi, Abelard, Peter the Venerable, and Thomas Aquinas—who polemicized simultaneously against Jewish and pagan (or Muslim) infidels.

Organized systematically around objections and responses on key issues, the *De fide* testifies to Christendom's growing sensitivity to the other and its new interest in polemic and in missionary theology. Alan's resort to analogies (*similitudines*) to bolster his trinitarian arguments through reason and authority reflected current practice among various Jewish and Christian apologists alike.[133] Alan drew many of his anti-Jewish arguments in the *De fide* from Gilbert Crispin's *Disputatio Iudei et Christiani* and from a particular version that the twelfth-century Jewish polemicist Jacob ben Reuben used in his anti-Christian *Milḥamot ha-Shem* (Wars of the Lord) as well.[134] Like many other polemicists of the time, Alan defined the error of the Jews primarily as the carnal observance of the Mosaic commandments.[135] He too denounced simoniacal and otherwise avaricious Christian priests as Judaizers, guilty of selling Jesus to his enemies no less than Judas himself.[136] And, according to some historians,[137] Alan's *De fide* marks a new stage in

131. See the comparisons drawn by Alan in *De fide* 4.1, 4.11, PL 210:421, 427 (d'Alverny, "Alain de Lille et l'Islam," pp. 332, 343ff.).

132. For instance, Julia Gauss, "Die Auseinandersetzung mit Judentum und Islam bei Anselm," in *Die Wirkungsgeschichte Anselms von Canterbury,* ed. Helmut Kohlenberger, Analecta anselmiana 4 (Frankfurt am Main, 1975), pp. 105–6; and Roques, "Les Pagani," pp. 195–201.

133. Alan, *De fide* 3.5, PL 210:406–7. On these various analogies see Daniel J. Lasker, *Jewish Philosophical Polemics against Christianity in the Middle Ages* (New York, 1977), pp. 100–103; and Ch. Merchavia, *The Church versus Talmudic and Midrashic Literature, 500–1248* [Hebrew] (Jerusalem, 1970), pp. 214ff.

134. David Berger, "Gilbert Crispin, Alan of Lille, and Jacob ben Reuben: A Study in the Transmission of Medieval Polemic," *Speculum* 49 (1974), 34–47.

135. Alan, *De fide,* conclusio, PL 210:430: "Erubescant ergo haeretici de falso errore, Waldenses de excogitato dogmate, Judaei de legis Mosaicae observatione, pagani de abominabile errore. Convertantur haeretici ad catholicam unitatem abrenuntiantes pravis dogmatibus; Waldenses pravis persuasionibus, Judaei observantiis carnalibus, pagani superstitiosis opinionibus, ut sic ad veram unitatem perveniant, et a vera unitate fidei, ad veram aeternae beatitudinis unitatem ascendant."

136. See Alan's *Sermo ad sacerdotes in synodo* in *Textes inédits,* pp. 284–85.

137. Especially Funkenstein, *Perceptions,* pp. 196–98.

the role played by postbiblical, talmudic literature in Christian anti-Jewish polemic; for whereas Peter Alfonsi and Peter the Venerable condemned Judaism for its allegedly absurd rabbinic lore, the *De fide* cites a well-known talmudic homily in support of its claim that the messiah has already come:

> In its greatest part the law has been abolished; it seems therefore that the law has no validity. Indeed in *Sehale* Elias says that the world will endure six thousand years—two thousand shall have been of vanity, which refers to the time before Mosaic Law, two thousand under Mosaic Law, and the following two thousand of the messianic age. But it is obvious that more than four thousand have passed; thus it is apparent that the law has passed and the messiah has come.[138]

Nevertheless, Alan's writings contain no evidence of any personal familiarity with rabbinic literature. Making his sole reference to a passage in talmudic lore that he claimed bespoke the truth of Christianity, Alan hardly betrayed an awareness of the groundbreaking significance that Amos Funkenstein and others have attributed to his citation; Peter Alfonsi had already cited the Talmud in support of Christian doctrine several generations earlier.[139] The issues raised in the *contra Iudaeos* section of the *De fide* are thoroughly traditional: the Trinity, the validity of Mosaic Law, the incarnation, the virgin birth, the resurrection, and the ascension. The objections to Christianity refuted in the *De fide* may well reflect some knowledge of contemporary Jewish polemics, but the *De fide* adduces—and refutes—them in a highly theoretical, non-confrontational mode of discourse. And although the *De fide* makes no reference whatsoever to the Augustinian doctrine of Jewish witness, it makes no suggestion that the Jews have outlived their distinctive function in Christendom. Whether or not Alan believed that the Jews served a purpose in a properly integrated Christian society, he certainly deemed them worthy of inclusion in his virtual summa on disbelief within that society.

Alan, then, blended traditional themes and arguments of *Adversus Iudaeos* polemic with some of the twelfth century's distinctive contributions to the history of the Christian idea of the Jew. Alan's construction of the Jew, in fact, returns us to the Anselmian parable of the king in his fortified city at the beginning of our review of twelfth-century authors. In a sermon for Palm Sunday delivered around 1180, not long

---

138. Alan, *De fide* 3.10, PL 210:410; cf. Babylonian Talmud, *Sanhedrin* 97a.
139. See above, chapter 5, at nn. 105, 110.

before the composition of the *De fide*, Alan compared the world of God's creation to a city:

> In the higher part of the city he placed the upper heaven as if it were a castle, in which he collected the army of the angels, who, like a court in the service of God, would provide for the governance of lower creatures. But, proudly opposing their king and not maintaining their loyalty to their prince, certain members of the angelic army wished to usurp control of this castle for themselves, and therefore they were driven out into the lower depths of this atmosphere. This is a castle which cannot be taken with physical armaments, it cannot be overcome by the attack of its enemies, it is not upheld by the power of princes, nor is it purchased with the fortunes of the rich; but only the poor in spirit [as in Matthew 5:3] enter therein, only the humble pass muster. . . .
>
> The demons, however, seeing themselves shut out of the heavenly castle in the lower part of the world, devised a fearful rampart from which they could attack the supernal castle and keep anyone from entering it. By means of his wicked plan, the devil thus fortified a position for himself in the first woman, through which he forced the entire human race to be of his household; and so he craftily attacked the heavenly castle, such that all were of his household, and the way to the heavenly kingdom lay open to no one.
>
> But when the heavenly king saw that his enemy had established his rampart on earth, he himself wished to situate another [fortress] on earth, from which he could break into the fortress of the devil and subject those taken captive by the devil to his own jurisdiction. . . . A fortification was thus prepared for the son of God in the glorious virgin, whom he reinforced with multiple endowments of virtue. . . . Into this stronghold thus fortified went the son of God, who would wage war on the devil. . . . In this fortress the Holy Spirit made weaponry for him, when he endowed him with a plenitude of virtues. Thus armed he went forth from the castle, when he was born out of the virginal womb. In that very venture he began to attack the fortress of the devil and to release some of his household to his own custody. For from the time that he was born, he was sought for the Gentiles through the faith of the Magi, and he gradually destroyed the weapons of his formidably armed enemy, establishing a new fortress for himself: the Church. For through his preaching and the working of his virtue he converted those of the camp of the devil to his own camp—that is, he included them within the unity of the church. Yet when the devil saw his power weakened and the army of his camp diminished, he devised the death of the eternal king through the agency of his accomplices [*complices*], the unbelieving Jews [*per infideles Iudaeos*]. . . . Ascending into heaven, he [Christ] left his multiple fortifications on earth—that is, the faithful who are the rampart of God, who, endowed with various virtues, resist the effronteries of the devil.
>
> Each and every one of us, dearest brethren, should establish himself as a fortress for God, so that, finding suitable dwelling therein, he might thereby shut out the affront of diabolic temptation. Let everyone be aware of the means through which the devil tends to assault the fortifications of

the soul: the crossbow of pride which, ascending even up to the heavens, wounded Lucifer. Let one take care lest the arrows of the demons enter through the windows of the senses, lest luxury enters through sight, greed through the ear, gluttony through taste.[140]

Alan's sermon brings this survey of twelfth-century Christian constructions of Jews and Judaism full circle. Echoing the Anselmian parable that we encountered at the outset, Alan, writing nearly a full century later, retained the comparison of God's kingdom to a city dominated by a castle, which the devil seeks to attack and overcome; Alan, too, gave the Jew a place on his metaphoric map of the world. Yet the Jews did not fare quite so well on Alan's map as they had on Anselm's, though neither the corpus of Alan's writings nor his career suggests any singular anti-Judaism or anti-Jewish agenda. Precisely for that reason, perhaps, Alan's perceptions allow for some, admittedly limited, generalizing conclusions concerning the twelfth century in our story. Where Anselm had situated the Jews within the city of God's kingdom, Alan depicted him outside. Where Anselm had identified Jews and infidels as the first to fall victim to the onslaughts of the devil, Alan portrayed them as the devil's accomplices, the key players in his plot to murder the son of God. And where Anselm had interpreted his parable solely on a macrocosmic level, Alan's explanation of his metaphors focused on the microcosmic, likening every Christian individual to a fortress of God beset by diabolical enemies, whose armaments include the vices of pride, luxury, greed, and gluttony.

The analogy between macrocosmic and microcosmic at the heart of Alan's homily bespeaks a parallel between the Jewish-infidel accomplices of the devil who crucified Jesus and the arrows of the diabolical crossbow, the vices, that tempt the individual Christian. Alan's parable thus recalls not only Anselm's but also the constructions of Jews as vice personified, which we encountered in the works of Anselm's disciples, of Bernard of Clairvaux, and of Peter the Venerable. Twelfth-century Christian intellectuals had indeed reevaluated and redefined the significance of the Jew. The cultural renaissance of the period yielded new standards of human rationality against which to evaluate his disbelief. Occasional references to the Talmud and its lore added a new dimension to the Christian scrutiny of contemporary Jews against the background of earlier *Adversus Iudaeos* polemic and its underlying

---

140. Alan, *Sermo in dominica palmarum*, in *Textes inédits*, pp. 246–49. Cf. Anselm's parable above, chapter 5, at n. 10.

assumptions. The traditional linkage between synagogue and Satan took on new relevance in the Christian mind-set. Christian biblical scholarship reawakened sensitivity to the thorny issue of the literal sensus of Scripture and Jewish "control" over it. Changing circumstances led to a reclassification of the Jews along with other infidels, especially Muslims, and with heretics; they gave rise to a sense that Judaism constituted but one aspect of the disbelief that threatened the integrity of Christendom. In a word, a process of displacement had begun in Christian thought. But from its repeated mention by Rupert of Deutz[141] at the beginning of the century to its thorough exposition by Peter the Chanter at the end,[142] the Augustinian doctrine of Jewish witness still proved influential.

In sum, this investigation of the twelfth century yields mixed results. Despite occasional remarks susceptible to interpretation to the contrary, Christian theologians of the twelfth century did not yet articulate a construction of contemporary, rabbinic Judaism per se as a post-biblical Jewish heresy. Nevertheless, some of their pronouncements gravitated in that direction, and they certainly laid the groundwork for subsequent churchmen who did make that formulation explicit. The place accorded the Jews on Anselm of Canterbury's map of the world had surely been called into question and at times circumscribed, even if the poetic imagination of Alan of Lille had not yet eliminated it entirely. Perhaps more aptly than she originally imagined, one recent student of Alan's opus has observed that had Alan lived just a little later, he undoubtedly would have been a mendicant friar.[143]

---

141. For example, Rupert of Deutz, *In Amos* 4.9, PL 168:369: "quia propter hoc quod reliquiae salvandae sunt, etiam memoriae et honori Christi prodest vita et dispersio illorum, quemadmodum ipse dicit in psalmo, 'Deus ostendit mihi . . . in virtute tua.' Multum enim Christum colentibus confert hoc quod Christi inimici Judaei inter eos vivunt. Secum namque libros bajulant, in quibus inveniuntur cuncta, de quibus confirmamus fidem Christianam, nec dicere potest quis, quod nova doctrina sit, dum antiquam proferimus auctoritatem ex libris quos habent illi." See also Rupert's *De sancta Trinitate et operibus eius* 9.4, CCCM 21:536; 18.15, CCCM 22:1034; 38.15, CCCM 24:1994–95; and elsewhere.

142. Gilbert Dahan, "L'Article *Iudei* de la *Summa Abel* de Pierre le Chantre," *REA* 27 (1981), 105–26.

143. Evans, *Alan*, p. 12.

PART FOUR

The Friars Reconsidered

Our story ends in the thirteenth century, where, in certain respects, it actually began. Some fifteen years ago I advanced the thesis that Dominican and Franciscan friars of the thirteenth and early fourteenth centuries developed a new anti-Jewish ideology in Latin Christendom.[1] I argued that this outlook condemned medieval Jews for having deserted the biblical religion which, in Augustinian terms, justified a Jewish presence in Christian society; that, seeking to diminish such a presence, the mendicant orders thereby contributed to the decline and virtual disappearance of European Jewry during the later Middle Ages; and that the new, "mendicant" anti-Judaism derived from the "evolving self-consciousness" of medieval Christian civilization—from the critical place of the thirteenth century in its development and, ultimately, from factors having little to do with the Jews themselves.

My book on *The Friars and the Jews* has evoked criticism and has prompted debate in various quarters during a period in which scholarly interest in medieval Jewish-Christian relations in general has flour-

---

1. Jeremy Cohen, *The Friars and the Jews: The Evolution of Medieval Anti-Judaism* (Ithaca, N.Y., 1982). See also Jeremy Cohen, "The Jews as the Killers of Christ in the Latin Tradition, from Augustine to the Friars," *Traditio* 39 (1983), 1–27, and "Scholarship and Intolerance in the Medieval Academy: The Study and Evaluation of Judaism in European Christendom," *AHR* 91 (1986), 592–613.

ished.[2] Proposing both earlier and later alternatives, some have taken issue with my appraisal of the thirteenth century as the critical turning point in the history of medieval Christian attitudes toward Jews; others have questioned the extent to which the anti-Judaism of the friars marked any significant departure from existing ecclesiastical norms. Some have objected to generalizations concerning either or both of the new mendicant orders; others have challenged my reading of individual friars. Gratified by the breadth of this discussion, I have generally not offered rejoinders to my critics, although the observant reader has certainly noticed how they have enriched my rereading of medieval churchmen who antedated the friars. Indeed, reactions to my thesis on the significance of the friars, alongside the independent investigations of other historians, quickly convinced me that a fair assessment of later medieval Christian ideas of the Jew demanded a more conscientious investigation of their antecedents. The present study constitutes my attempt to move backward, as it were, in order better to appreciate Christian perceptions of Jews and Judaism as the Middle Ages unfolded.

The final part of this book, returns of necessity to events, writers, documents, and ideas discussed previously in *The Friars and the Jews*. Nevertheless, here I seek neither to rehash the analyses of that study nor to defend its conclusions in any kind of systematic fashion. The perspective of the present inquiry differs considerably. My concern here lies not with the mendicant orders as such nor with the influence of Christian ideas on events of medieval Jewish history. Rather, I return to thirteenth-century friars for the novelty in their perceptions and constructions of the Jew: If the power of the medieval church and the creativity of medieval Christian civilization peaked during the thirteenth century, and if they both found expression in the establishment and achievements of the mendicant orders, how did the medieval Jew, his books, and his religion continue to fare in the eyes of Christian theologians? If their twelfth-century predecessors had undermined the traditionally privileged placement of Jews on Christianity's map of the

2. Among the more instructive critical reviews, see Anna Sapir Abulafia, "The Evolution of Medieval Anti-Judaism," *Theoretische Geschiedenis* 11 (1984), 77–81; Robert I. Burns, "Anti-Semitism and Anti-Judaism in Christian History: A Revisionist Thesis," *Catholic Historical Review* 70 (1984), 90–93; Carlo Delcorno, "I mendicanti e gli Ebrei: A proposito di un recente libro," *Cristianesimo nella storia* 6 (1985), 263–73; Gordon Leff, review in the *Times Literary Supplement*, 5 November 1982, p. 1208; and Ora Limor, review essay [in Hebrew] in *Zion*, n.s. 51 (1986), 113–18. I consider the criticisms of Robert Chazan at some length in the next chapter.

world—grouping them with Muslims and heretics, doubting their rationality, and awakening to their postbiblical, rabbinic traditions—did thirteenth-century Christian thinkers proceed farther in a similar direction? If so, what bearing did their ideas have on the Augustinian doctrine of Jewish witness and the hermeneutically crafted Jew at its foundation?

Treatment of these questions will be selective, consciously emphasizing change rather than continuity. We turn first to thirteenth-century Christian attitudes toward the Talmud and rabbinic Judaism, exploiting the new and recent publication of pertinent documentary sources as an appropriate opportunity for their reevaluation. Bringing this study to its conclusion, we then consider the construction of Judaism in the works of the greatest thirteenth-century theologian of all, the Dominican friar Thomas Aquinas.

CHAPTER 8

Judaism as Heresy

Thirteenth-Century Churchmen
and the Talmud

No historian should deny that the condemnation and persecution of rabbinic literature by the late medieval church marked an important milestone in the history of Christian-Jewish relations. In a fashion entirely unprecedented, popes, inquisitors, and secular princes who cooperated with them attacked those books that constituted the mainstay of contemporary Jewish life, books that united most of Diaspora Jewry in allegiance to a constantly evolving corpus of postbiblical law, biblical interpretation, and rabbinic lore. Medieval Jews were now hard-pressed not only to defend against the lures and challenges of Christianity and to endure increasingly harsh forms of legal discrimination but also to ensure for the very survival of their Judaism, whose toleration Christian authorities had generally advocated hitherto. In a poetic dirge that has since found a permanent place in the traditional Jewish liturgy, the prominent thirteenth-century Ashkenazic rabbi, Meir ben Baruch of Rothenburg, thus lamented the burning of thousands of talmudic manuscripts in 1242.

> Did our redeemer give you to us in a pillar of fire,
> So that ultimately your pages would be consigned to the flames?
> Was it for this, Sinai, that God chose you,
> Rejecting greater mountains and shining forth upon you?
> Was it to serve as a beacon for a failing faith, one whose glory declines?
> I must offer a fitting parable:
> You are, Sinai, like a king crying at his son's banquet,

Knowing that the lad is to die—thus do you weep over the Torah.
Instead of your normal covering, O Sinai, you must don sackcloth,
You must put on the garb of widows, you must exchange your raiments.
I shall pour forth my tears until they become a stream,
Until they reach the graves of your two great ministers,
Moses and Aaron, buried there in the hill.
Then shall I ask—Is there a new Torah,
Thus permitting the burning of your pages?[1]

The details of the medieval Christian campaign against the Talmud, calling for the confiscation, censorship, and/or burning of rabbinic texts, require no comprehensive review; their story is well known and rather well documented.[2] Instead, attention here focuses on the Christian perceptions of Jews and Judaism underlying this direct impingement upon medieval Jewish life: What happened to the ecclesiastical traditions that mandated the toleration of the Jew and his religious rites in Christian society? If, in the day-to-day practice of their religion, the Jews embodied and preserved books that testified to the truth of Christianity, what justified this evidently sudden about-face in ecclesiastical policy?

Before examining the Christian sources that bear upon these questions, let us look briefly at the passage quoted from Meir of Rothenburg's elegy, *Sha'ali Serufah ba-'Esh* (Inquire, O Thou Consumed by Fire). Beyond the boundless grief of the poet, two related ideas appear to dominate these lines. First, addressing the Talmud (a masculine Hebrew noun) in the feminine (*Sha'ali Serufah*), Meir equated the Talmud with the Torah, the Mosaic law of the Jews and a feminine noun in Hebrew; and he then strengthened this association by identifying his

1. D. S. Goldschmidt, ed., *Seder ha-Qinnot le-Tish'a be-'Av* (Jerusalem, 1968), p. 136, trans. in Robert Chazan, ed., *Church, State, and Jew in the Middle Ages* (New York, 1980), pp. 229–30.

2. See Jeremy Cohen, *The Friars and the Jews: The Evolution of Medieval Anti-Judaism* (Ithaca, N.Y., 1982), pp. 51–99; Ch. Merchavia, *The Church versus Talmudic and Midrashic Literature, 500–1248* [Hebrew] (Jerusalem, 1970), pts. 2–3; Solomon Grayzel, "The Talmud and the Medieval Papacy," in *Essays in Honor of Solomon B. Freehof*, ed. Walter Jacob et al. (Pittsburgh, Pa., 1964), pp. 220–45; Kenneth R. Stow, "The Burning of the Talmud in 1553, in Light of Sixteenth-Century Catholic Attitudes toward the Talmud," *Bibliothèque d'Humanisme et Renaissance* 34 (1972), 435–59; Joel E. Rembaum, "The Talmud and the Popes: Reflections on the Talmud Trials of the 1240s," *Viator* 13 (1982), 203–23; Robert Chazan, "The Condemnation of the Talmud Reconsidered (1239–1248)," *Proceedings of the American Academy for Jewish Research* 55 (1988), 11–30; William Chester Jordan, "Marian Devotion and the Talmud Trial of 1240," in *RIM*, pp. 61–76; and Shlomo Simonsohn, *The Apostolic See and the Jews: History*, Pontifical Institute of Mediaeval Studies: Studies and Texts 109 (Toronto, 1991), pp. 300–342—and the additional bibliography cited therein.

addressee as Sinai, the locus of the biblical God's revelation to Moses. He thereby affirmed the foundational belief of rabbinic Judaism that the Torah revealed by God to Moses included not only the commandments inscribed in the Pentateuch but also an oral law, which the Talmud, together with other rabbinic treatises, recorded many centuries later. The tragic events that Meir lamented impelled him to insist that the Talmud indeed belonged to the original—and the sole—covenant of God with his chosen people. "Is there a new Torah, thus permitting the burning of your pages?!" From Meir's rabbinic perspective, such a sarcastic question did not even merit an answer, but his words suggest that those Christians who consigned the Talmud to the flames believed otherwise. Second, Meir's analogy to the king crying over his son's imminent death at the son's final banquet aggressively co-opts the overtly Christological metaphor of the last supper in support of his Jewish message: The Torah of the Jews, not Jesus, is the genuine offspring of the heavenly king. The Talmud, not the "new Torah" of Christianity, embodies the full and final interpretation of the Mosaic commandments. Moses and Aaron—not Jesus, not the fathers of the church, and not its popes—were the "great ministers" of divine instruction, its exemplary teacher and priest; their graves, not the Holy Sepulcher in Jerusalem or the relics of Christian saints, represent the ultimate monuments to God's elect.

The intense tone of Meir's defense of the oral law suggests that the thirteenth-century attack on the Talmud struck at the heart of contemporary rabbinic Judaism. Several new collections of thirteenth-century sources published during the 1980s and 1990s prod one to reconsider precisely how. Did the Christian condemnation of rabbinic books bespeak the conviction that talmudic Judaism was a heresy, a relatively recent distortion of Old Testament religion the only valid continuation or fulfillment of which lay in the gospel of Jesus?

PAPAL POLICY AND ITS RATIONALE

The ensuing discussion of the condemnation and burning of the Talmud during the late 1230s and the 1240s requires a brief recapitulation of its key events.[3] Pope Gregory IX heard the Talmud denounced by Nicholas Donin, an embittered Jewish apostate, in 1236. Three years later Pope Gregory issued a series of condemnatory bulls, ordering rulers and prel-

---

3. See the studies cited in the preceding note.

ates of Christian Europe to impound the Talmud and other Jewish writings on the first Sabbath during Lent in 1240 and to submit the books to ecclesiastical authorities for inspection. For whatever reason, Gregory's decrees were implemented only in the royal domains of France; there King Louis IX confiscated rabbinic texts, summoned leading French rabbis to his court in 1240 to defend the Talmud against Donin's charges, and, in the wake of the judgment of an ecclesiastical commission, proceeded to burn the Talmud in Paris in 1242. Soon after ascending the papal throne, Pope Innocent IV renewed Gregory's decrees in 1244. Yet this time the Jews protested directly to the papal curia, and in 1247 Innocent ordered King Louis to refrain from moving against the Talmud until a new investigation conducted by the papal legate Odo of Châteauroux should render a verdict. Odo convened several dozen prominent churchmen who reaffirmed the earlier condemnations and urged not to return confiscated talmudic texts to their Jewish owners. A series of subsequent popes followed suit in condemning the Talmud, which was burned under ecclesiastical direction on several additional occasions between the thirteenth and sixteenth centuries. The recent appearance of new editions of medieval papal correspondence pertaining to the Jews—Shlomo Simonsohn's multivolume *The Apostolic See and the Jews* and the second volume of Solomon Grayzel's *The Church and the Jews in the XIIIth Century*—offers a most appropriate opportunity for a reexamination of the question.

Some historians have challenged my earlier conclusion that ecclesiastical attacks on the Talmud derived from its indictment as a heretical departure from the teachings of the Bible. It has been argued, for example, that the notion of the Talmud as heresy originated with the former Jew Donin, such that "this position was not developed out of Christian theology, but rather reflected a strand in internal Jewish criticism." Pope Gregory IX and Pope Innocent IV merely echoed Donin's "loose set of allegations . . . , not however as carefully considered conclusions but rather as guidelines for broad investigation." That investigation, which, in this view, found its principal expression in Donin's disputation with Rabbi Yechiel ben Joseph of Paris in 1240, formally condemned the Talmud "in terms only of specific abuses and errors contained therein," not because it was heretical. When later popes took action against the Talmud, "the same specific allegations always formed the foundation for renewed condemnation."[4]

4. Chazan, "Condemnation of the Talmud," esp. pp. 29–30.

In my opinion, however, a methodical review of the evidence will not allow for such hasty dismissal of the heresy charges against the Talmud, and I propose to organize such a review around three stages in the development and expression of papal policy: from Nicholas Donin's denunciation of the Talmud before Pope Gregory IX until the Paris burning of 1242; the pontificate of Pope Innocent IV (1243–1254); and the actions of Pope Innocent's successors.

NICHOLAS DONIN, POPE GREGORY IX, AND THE CONDEMNATIONS OF PARIS

Nicholas Donin presented Gregory IX with thirty-five accusations against the Talmud and its Jewish exponents.[5] The first nine of these, along with one lower down on the list, concern the Jews' allegiance to rabbinic doctrine and their neglect of biblical precepts:

> The Jews assert that the Lord gave the law which is called Talmud.
> They say that [this law] was given orally,
> And they lie to the effect that it was implanted in their minds.
> They say that it was preserved for a long time without being written down, until there arrived those whom they call sages and scribes, who reduced it to writing so that it not be forgotten from people's minds. Its written version exceeds the text of the Bible in size.
> Among other absurdities, in it is contained [the belief] that the said sages and scribes are greater than the prophets.
> They [these sages] could do away with the words of the written law.
> One must believe them [the sages] if they should call the left the right or, on the contrary, they should turn the right into the left.
> One who does not observe what they teach deserves to die.
> They prohibit children from using the Bible because, as they say, it is not fit for instruction, but, preferring the doctrine of the Talmud, they have given various commandments of their own accord. . . .
> Whoever studies the aforementioned [talmudic] doctrine in the present will be secure in the future life.[6]

At least a dozen more of the thirty-five articles condemned the Talmud for its absurd homilies, much as Peter Alfonsi and Peter the Venerable had done a century earlier; most of the allegations of anti-Christian teaching in the Talmud appeared only toward the end of Donin's listing.

5. Isidore Loeb, *La Controverse sur le Talmud sous Saint Louis* (Paris, 1881), pp. 21–54. See also Judah M. Rosenthal, "The Talmud on Trial," *JQR*, n.s. 47 (1956), 58–76, 145–69; and Merchavia, *Church*, chap. 12.

6. Loeb, *La Controverse*, pp. 22–32, 53.

Little is known concerning Donin's Jewish background and the factors that propelled him to campaign against the Talmud, but his charges that contemporary Judaism esteemed the Talmud at the expense of its allegiance to the Bible seem to dominate the subsequent concern—and actions—of Pope Gregory IX. Perhaps "this set of allegations reflects internal Jewish dissatisfaction with rabbinic law" and was originally "proffered to a Christian audience as evidence of Jewish malfeasance, without defining carefully in terms of Christian theory the precise nature of this malfeasance."[7] But this should not obscure the fact that Pope Gregory, not at all impulsively, but having waited three years after Donin appeared before him, now saw fit to focus on the postbiblical development of Judaism in his anti-talmudic decrees. He wrote of the Jews of France and of other lands that,

> not content with the Old Law which God gave in writing through Moses, and even ignoring it completely, they affirm that God gave them another Law which is called the Talmud, that is teaching. They lie to the effect that it was handed down to Moses orally and implanted in their minds, and was preserved unwritten for a long time until there arrived those whom they call sages and scribes, who reduced it to writing so that it not be forgotten from people's minds. Its written version exceeds the text of the Bible in size. In it are contained so many abusive and wicked things that they are an embarrassment for those who mention them and a horror for those who hear them.[8]

Comparing Gregory's letter with the charges excerpted from Donin's indictment, one finds the latter's influence unmistakable, but this hardly deprives the pope of responsibility for the contents of his own decree. A marked sensitivity to doctrinal irregularity comports well with the overriding concerns and interests of Gregory IX. This same pope sought to oversee the curriculum at the University of Paris, to prohibit the study of the unexpurgated works of Aristotle, to promote legislative uniformity in Christendom through the promulgation of his *Decretales* (Decretals), and to intensify the campaign of his church against heresy. One ought hardly to assume that Gregory blindly parroted the accusations of a vindictive Jewish apostate; Gregory in fact exceeded Donin's thirty-five accusations in claiming explicitly that the Jews had substituted another law (*legem aliam*) for that of the Bible.[9]

7. Chazan, "Condemnation of the Talmud," pp. 17–18.

8. Shlomo Simonsohn, ed., *ASJD, 492–1404*, Pontifical Institute of Mediaeval Studies: Studies and Texts 94 (Toronto, 1988), p. 172; I have drawn from the translation in Grayzel, *CJ*, rev. ed. (New York, 1966), p. 241.

9. Cf. Rembaum, "Talmud and the Popes," pp. 205–15.

My reading of the evidence similarly fails to corroborate the claim
that the ensuing ecclesiastical investigation overlooked the matter of
heresy and condemned the Talmud for specific errors and abuses instead. Although the later Hebrew account of the disputation of Paris
involving Donin and several French rabbis attests to discussion of such
controversial, allegedly blasphemous talmudic passages, it opens with
a lengthy defense of the Talmud's antiquity and inextricable ties to the
divinely revealed law of Moses, and it closes on a similar note: "The
Talmud is an explanation [of Scripture], and were it not for the Talmud
a person could not understand the commandments thoroughly."[10]
More important, one errs in viewing the exchange between Donin and
the rabbis as the official ecclesiastical investigation in question. Rather,
as Chen Merchavia's careful analysis of Latin manuscript 16558 in the
Bibliothèque Nationale of Paris has established, the proceedings in
Paris in 1240 divided into two stages: the disputation between Donin
and the French rabbis, principally Yechiel ben Joseph; and the more
formal ecclesiastical inquiry.[11] This official proceeding seems not to
have included Donin and is not recorded in any Hebrew source; it
involved a number of distinguished prelates and theologians, who reviewed the evidence of the confiscated Jewish books and interrogated
both Yechiel and his rabbinic colleague Judah ben David of Melun.
Albeit not systematically, the extant texts of the "confessions" reportedly elicited from these rabbis echo the main themes of Donin's original
accusations, including talmudic Judaism's alleged abandonment of Old
Testament religion.[12] Yet the most decisive appraisal of the reasons for
the clerical ruling that the Talmud should burn derives from the pen
of one of the leading ecclesiastical investigators: Odo of Châteauroux,
who then served as chancellor of the University of Paris. Odo, we recall, was later enlisted by Pope Innocent IV to head another formal
inspection of the Talmud, and, upon receipt of that commission in
1247, he wrote to Innocent to summarize the ecclesiastical actions undertaken thus far. After reproducing the texts of Pope Gregory's de-

---

10. Samuel Grünbaum, ed., *Wikkuaḥ Rabbenu Yeḥiel mi-Paris* (Toruń, Poland,
1873), pp. 2, 15–16.
11. Merchavia, *Church*, pp. 240ff.
12. The texts of the confessions appear ibid., pp. 453–55, and in Loeb, *La Controverse*, pp. 55–57. I believe Chazan to have exaggerated in his statements, in "Condemnation of the Talmud," pp. 19–20, that these confessions "seem to represent merely a
tendentious depiction of the examination of the two scholars" and that "they certainly
contribute nothing of substance to our understanding of the proceedings in Paris."

crees, he recounted the findings of the original Parisian board of inquiry in no uncertain terms:

> All books that had been intercepted were put under stamp and seal, and many more things were found in the said books in the presence of Walter, Archbishop of Sens of happy memory, and of the venerable fathers, the bishops of Paris and Senlis, and of your chaplain Friar Godfried de Blevel, then regent of Paris, and of other masters of theology,[13] and even of the Jewish masters who confessed in the presence of these men that the above-named things [that is, what Donin and Pope Gregory had condemned] were contained in their books. A careful examination having afterwards been made, it was discovered that the said books were full of errors, and that a veil has been placed over the heart of these people to such an extent that they [the books] turn the Jews away from not only from a spiritual under-standing [of the law] but even from a literal understanding, and they incline them to fantasies and lies. . . . After the said examination had been made, and the advice of all the teachers of theology and canon law, and of many others, had been taken, all the said books which could be secured were incinerated by fire in accordance with the apostolic decree.[14]

13. Although Odo has not included himself here, perhaps out of modesty, he was definitely present at the Parisian inquiry. See the introduction to the Latin confessions of Rabbis Yechiel and Judah, in Merchavia, *Church*, p. 453, which identifies the leading churchmen present as "the archbishop of Sens, the bishop of Senlis, and the chancellor of Paris, now bishop of Tusculum and legate of the Apostolic See in the Holy Land"— that is, Odo. In his decree of 1244 against the Talmud (Simonsohn, *ASJD*, 492–1404, p. 181), Innocent IV similarly identified the chancellor of Paris as having presided over the investigation.

14. Grayzel, *CJ*, pp. 276–78 n. 3 (with various departures from Grayzel's transla-tion). Without mention of the key passage adduced here, Chazan, "Condemnation of the Talmud," pp. 24–25, has quoted only the continuation of Odo's letter:

> Dicit enim beatus Hieronymus loquens de leprosis, quos dominus curavit, quod nulla est adeo perversa doctrina que aliqua vera non contineat; similiter non inveniuntur heretici qui de aliquo symboli articuli bene non sentiant. Quia tamen libri aliqui insertos errores habebant, quamvis multa bona et vera continerent, auctoritate tamen conciliorum sunt damnati, similiter diversi heretici sunt damnati licet in omnibus non errarent. Sic quamvis predicti libri aliqua bona contineant, licet rara, nihilominus sunt dam-nandi. Hec doctrina est illa deuterosis, de qua facit beatus Hieronymus super evan-gelium Matthei mentionem, que irritum facit mandatum Dei, ipso domino attestante.

Moreover, I believe that Chazan has erred in understanding "quia tamen libri aliqui insertos errores habebant" to mean that "these books [of the Talmud] contain errors" but are not "intrinsically heretical." For in this sentence Odo referred not to the Talmud but to heretical works in general: not *these* books, but "various books [*libri aliqui*]" of heretics containing errors, which, as a matter of course, "although they contained many good and true statements, were still condemned by the authority of the councils." Sim-ilarly, reasoned the legate, "various heretics are condemned even though they do not err in everything." Only then does Odo's letter return to the matter of the Talmud on an emphatic note: "So, although the aforesaid books [*predicti libri*] contain some good, albeit rare, they nevertheless should be condemned." The analogy between heresy and heretical books, on one hand, and the oral law denounced by Jerome (identified by Odo as *deuterosis*) and the Talmud, on the other hand, is unmistakable. The Talmud, con-

Heading the ecclesiastical investigators' verdict that ordered the Talmud burned stood the charge that not only did it deter the Jews from Christianity, but it steered them away from the literal observance of Mosaic law. Talmudic Judaism did not hold true to the biblical faith and observance the toleration of which Augustine had repeatedly preached; by implication, the talmudic Jew did not serve the purpose that justified the Jewish presence in Christendom.

THE PONTIFICATE OF POPE INNOCENT IV

Sinibaldo Fieschi became Pope Innocent IV in 1243. In the spring of the following year, he renewed Gregory IX's decree of condemnation and confiscation against the Talmud, reiterating his predecessor's accusations against the Jews' oral law with the addition that in the Talmud "there are flagrant blasphemies against God and his Christ and the blessed virgin, and clearly entangled fantasies, contemptuous errors, and untold stupidities."[15] Yet this does not establish, as has been argued, that "the letter points to blasphemy and abuse as the core of the anti-Talmud proceedings."[16] Rather, Innocent's addition comes as a subordinate clause expanding upon the principal charge that the Jews have forsaken the Bible for the Talmud: Not only has the Talmud led them to ignore biblical law, runs Innocent's argument, but it also contains these abusive, anti-Christian teachings. Confirming that the matter of allegiance to the Old Testament remained the pope's chief concern, the appeal of French Jewry to Pope Innocent made no mention of blasphemies; if blasphemy were at issue, how could the Jews have sidestepped it completely? Instead, the Jewish appeal related exclusively to the compatibility of the Talmud with biblical law. Thus Innocent related to King Louis IX in 1247:

> The Jewish masters . . . recently asserted in our presence . . . that without that book which is called "Talmut" in Hebrew they are incapable of understanding *the Bible and the other statutes of their law* in keeping with their religion. We who, in keeping with the divine injunction, are obligated to tolerate them in the observance of that law therefore considered it proper to respond to them thus: We do not want to deprive them of their books

cluded Odo, was condemned and must be condemned for its heretical contents and character.

15. Simonsohn, *ASJD*, 492–1404, pp. 180–81; cf. Grayzel, *CJ*, p. 251.
16. Chazan, "Condemnation of the Talmud," p. 23.

unjustly, if, in so doing, we should deprive them of the observance of their law.[17]

For this reason did Innocent appoint Odo of Châteauroux to head yet another commission of inquiry: to determine whether the Talmud was a necessary tool, actually required to explain the genuine—that is, divinely revealed, albeit now obsolete—law of Moses, as the Jews themselves claimed, or if it comprised a different law unto itself (*alia lex*), as Popes Gregory and Innocent had originally alleged. Odo, as indicated, hastened to reaffirm the definitive judgment of his prior investigation, that the Talmud perverted the letter of law, not just its spiritual, Christological import. In the very passage of his letter quoted above,[18] he immediately added: "Whence it is apparent that the masters of the Jews of the kingdom of France recently lied to your holiness and to the venerable fathers, the lords cardinals, saying that without those books, which are called the Talmud in Hebrew, they cannot understand the Bible and the other provisions of their law in keeping with their faith."[19] In May 1248, as noted, Odo's commission ruled the Talmud worthy of condemnation and unfit for toleration—by the church— among the Jews of Christendom.

Joel Rembaum has argued vigorously that Pope Innocent, in fact, retreated from Pope Gregory's condemnation of the Talmud as heretical Judaism and espoused a more conciliatory posture.[20] Innocent's initial decree of 1244, in this view, was not issued enthusiastically. Given at the prompting of Odo and his Parisian colleagues, not on the pope's personal initiative, and sent exclusively to King Louis of France, the renewed condemnation of the Talmud for heresy was wholly incompatible with other decrees, in which Innocent protected the Jews and their religious practice. When the Jews protested that Christian toleration of Judaism should include the Talmud, perhaps

17. Simonsohn, *ASJD*, 492–1404, p. 197 (emphasis mine); cf. Grayzel, *CJ*, p. 275. On the Jewish appeal and its underlying confidence in the pope, see Kenneth R. Stow, *The "1007 Anonymous" and Papal Sovereignty: Jewish Perceptions of the Papacy and Papal Policy in the High Middle Ages,* Hebrew Union College Annual Supplements 4 (Cincinnati, Ohio, 1984).

18. At n. 14, precisely at the point of the ellipsis in that quotation.

19. Grayzel, *CJ*, pp. 276–78 n. 3, departing from Grayzel's translation.

20. Rembaum, "Talmud," pp. 215ff. Among those who have concurred, see Robert I. Burns, "Anti-Semitism and Anti-Judaism in Christian History: A Revisionist Thesis," *Catholic Historical Review* 70 (1984), 92–93; Simonsohn, *The Apostolic See and the Jews: History,* pp. 304–5; and, with more nuance, Kenneth R. Stow, *Alienated Minority: The Jews of Medieval Latin Europe* (Cambridge, Mass., 1992), pp. 256ff., and "*1007 Anonymous,*" pp. 37–42.

even invoking patristic precedent in their own behalf, Innocent accepted their position. His earlier allusion to anti-Christian blasphemy, after first condemning the Talmud, opened the door to a revised policy of "limited toleration" for rabbinic literature, and he instructed Odo to restore to the Jews those books that the church could tolerate "without injury to the Christian faith."[21] True to his more extreme position, Odo ruled rabbinic books intolerable, though not, as is claimed, on his preferred grounds of heresy; acceding to Innocent's point of view, he proclaimed: "We found them to contain innumerable errors, abuses, blasphemies, and evils which are an embarrassment for those who mention them and a horror for those who hear them, to such an extent that the said books cannot, by God, be tolerated without injury to the Christian faith."[22]

Each of these points is open to question. The attribution of the initiative for Innocent IV's decree of 1244 to Odo rests entirely on the speculation of Solomon Grayzel.[23] As for Innocent's alleged misgivings, Gregory IX may also have had reservations when issuing his decrees of 1239 to the princes and prelates of European Christendom. For he dispatched all of his letters to William of Auvergne, Bishop of Paris—perhaps, it has been suggested, with the hope that they would go no further;[24] Gregory, too, protected Jews on other occasions.[25] And yet, if one acknowledges the genuineness of Gregory's conviction that the Talmud derived from postbiblical Jewish heresy, why not that of Innocent as well? Nowhere do the texts reviewed here allow for a "compromise position" of limited tolerance for the Talmud, somewhere between depriving the Jews of their books after their inspection and allowing for their return. Such were the only options during the pontificate of Gregory IX; Innocent IV posed these same options to Odo in commissioning a further investigation; Odo acted accordingly in Innocent's behalf and decided between them.[26] I accept Rembaum's in-

21. Simonsohn, *ASJD, 492–1404*, p. 197; Grayzel, *CJ*, p. 279.

22. Grayzel, *CJ*, pp. 278–79 n. 3 (with departures from Grayzel's translation).

23. Rembaum, "Talmud," p. 215 n. 76; and Grayzel, *CJ*, p. 252 n. 3.

24. Cf. the suggestions of Stow, *Alienated Minority*, p. 256; and Lesley Smith, "William of Auvergne and the Jews," in *Christianity and Judaism*, ed. Diana Wood, SCH 29 (Oxford, 1992), pp. 115–17.

25. Simonsohn, *ASJD, 492–1404*, pp. 154–55, 163–65.

26. Thus has the most recent study of Innocent's Catholic worldview concluded that his anti-Jewish position only intensified as the 1240s reached their end; see Alberto Melloni, *Innocenzo IV: La concezione e l'esperienza della cristianità come regimen unius personae* (Genoa, 1990), esp. pp. 187–96, who also places Innocent's outlook on Jews and Judaism within the broader context of his stance on unbelievers and dissidents in general.

sightful proposal that, in his letter of 1247, Odo's appeal to Jerome's condemnation of Jewish *deuterosis* (a second law) may well have countered the Jews' citation of that church father's tolerance for the Talmud, both at the Paris disputation of 1240 and, perhaps, in their eventual appeal to Innocent.[27] This too confirms that the crux of the issue remained the orthodoxy—or the heterodoxy—of the oral law.

Jerome notwithstanding, the notion that contemporary rabbinic Judaism may no longer have been the Judaism of the Bible was virtually unprecedented in early-thirteenth-century Christian thought. Perhaps the popes themselves did not fully appreciate its significance; they certainly could not be expected to act upon it, or to define it, entirely systematically; they may well have had apprehensions; perhaps their own contributions to the growing corpus of medieval canon law (Gregory IX's codification of the *Decretales* and Innocent IV's lengthy commentary on it), coupled with the budding dispute between mendicant and secular clergy over progressive revelation, moved them to avoid overly sweeping denunciations of postbiblical tradition.[28] To expect that the popes should distinguish consistently between the charge that the Talmud "*contains* heretical teachings" and that it "is *eo ipso* heretical"[29] strikes me as unrealistic. Moreover, as a matter of course, the heresy of a text or an individual was established in ecclesiastical proceedings with specific examples of heretical propositions or beliefs. Thus had Nicholas Donin proceeded in 1236, and, when Odo's commission condemned the Talmud in 1248 for its "innumerable errors, abuses, blasphemies, and evils" which cannot "be tolerated . . . without injury to the Christian faith," I see no reason to doubt that it included the Talmud's postbiblical, innovative character among the errors in question. Pope Innocent's own commentary on the *Decretales*, completed only after Odo's second condemnation of the Talmud,[30] supports this conclusion; reedited from manuscript by Benjamin Kedar,

27. Rembaum, "Talmud," pp. 218–19; Grünbaum, ed., *Wikkuaḥ Rabbenu Yeḥiel*, p. 2; and see above, n. 14.

28. Cohen, *Friars*, pp. 257ff.; and Stow, *Alienated Minority*, pp. 255–57.

29. Chazan, "Condemnation of the Talmud," pp. 25, 27.

30. See Joannes A. Cantini and Ch. Lefebvre, "Sinibalde dei Fieschi (Innocent IV)," in *Dictionnaire de droit canonique*, ed. R. Naz (Paris, 1965), 7:1031; Jean Gaudemet, *Les Sources du droit canonique, viii*^{e}*-xx*^{e} *siècle* (Paris, 1993), p. 142; and James A. Brundage, *Medieval Canon Law* (London, 1995), p. 57. Cf. also Melloni, *Innocenzo IV*, p. 194 n. 22, who reasons that the condemnation of the Talmud in 1247–48 must have preceded these canonistic reflections of the pope, because it actually contributed to his formulation of such sweeping claims to jurisdiction over infidels.

the relevant passage reads: "The pope can judge the Jews if they violate
the moral precepts of their law and their own prelates do not punish
them, and likewise if they invent heresies against their own law. Impelled by this latter reason [*hac ratione*], Pope Gregory and Pope Innocent ordered the books of the Talmud, in which many heresies are
contained, to be burned, and they ordered those who follow or teach
the aforesaid heresies to be punished." Kedar has paraphrased with
precision: "In other words, the basic reason for the burning of the
Talmud is not that it contains attacks on Christianity or that it impedes
Jewish conversion to Christianity, but that it comprises deviations from
the true teachings of Mosaic law as understood by the Church."[31]

Still, I do find Rembaum's rejoinder to my earlier reading of these
documents from the pontificate of Innocent IV instructive. Innocent
may have had doubts when he first renewed Pope Gregory's condemnation of the Talmud; for whatever reason, theological or more practical, he certainly had them in the wake of the Jews' appeal. Although
the conception of talmudic Judaism as heretical had made its way into
canon law and papal policy by the middle of the thirteenth century,
the extent of its impact on day-to-day ecclesiastical policy varied considerably. Numerous factors, including relations with the Jewish community, bore upon the directives of any particular pope, Innocent included.[32] At times the actions and convictions of a papal legate,
whether zealous (like Odo) or lenient, might not comport fully with
the thinking of the pope who ultimately took responsibility for them.
One can continue to debate whether these possibilities held true for the
policy of Innocent IV concerning the Talmud. As Rembaum has noted,

31. Benjamin Z. Kedar, "Canon Law and the Burning of the Talmud," *Bulletin of
Medieval Canon Law*, n.s. 9 (1979), 80–81; and cf. Amos Funkenstein, *Perceptions of
Jewish History* (Berkeley, Calif., 1993), p. 195: "The collection of materials for the trial,
as well as the letters of Gregory IX and Innocent IV, show clearly that the 'authority'
of the Talmud, replacing that of the Bible, as well as its function as a 'new law' (*nova
lex*) were the primary concerns then." See also Walter Pakter, *Medieval Canon Law and
the Jews,* Münchener Universitätsschriften—Juristische Fakultät—Abhandlungen zur
Rechtswissenschaftlichen Grundlagenforschung 68 (Ebelsbach, Germany, 1988), pp. 73–
78; curiously, although Pakter (nn. 113, 129) acknowledges the validity of Kedar's corrections of the printed edition of Innocent's commentaries, he seems to ignore the significance of those corrections in his analysis of the text.

32. Joannes A. Cantini, "De autonomia judicii saecularis et de romani pontificis plenitudine potestatis in temporalibus secundum Innocentium IV," *Salesianum* 23 (1961),
464–74, has shown how one must distinguish in general between Innocent's broad definition of the plenitude of papal power de jure and his more limited application of the
concept de facto.

however, when limited toleration of the Talmud became a real option during subsequent decades, the ecclesiastical attitude toward the Talmud grew more complex.

POPE INNOCENT'S SUCCESSORS

Various scholars have observed that, as the Middle Ages wore on, the censure of the Talmud for anti-Christian blasphemies eclipsed its outright condemnation as postbiblical heresy. When Pope Alexander IV ordered the confiscation of the Talmud in France in 1258, he made no explicit mention of its deviation from biblical teaching.[33] When Christian authorities burned the Talmud on several occasions early in the fourteenth century, popes and inquisitors alike focused primarily on "blasphemies, errors, curses, and lies."[34] And when Pope Julius III issued his famous condemnation of the Talmud to the flames in 1553, he too attacked its blasphemies, although he did include "blasphemies against Mosaic law" in his list of accusations.[35] Moreover, although no evidence suggests that Innocent IV had such a policy in mind, some historians contend that his successors soon developed a third, intermediate course of action against the Talmud, short of indiscriminate burning but unwilling to let the allegedly noxious Jewish doctrine remain unchecked. The Jews would submit their books for inspection, and, once cleansed of offensive passages—if such were possible—these books might be restored to the Jews. At the behest of the Dominicans in his kingdom, James I of Aragon instituted such a policy in 1263, soon after the famous disputation of Barcelona between Friar Paul Christian and Rabbi Moses Nachmanides.[36] In Kenneth Stow's words, "the charge that the Talmud was an 'other law,' first made in 1239 by Gregory IX and curiously repeated one last time in 1267 by Clement

---

33. Simonsohn, *ASJD*, 492–1404, pp. 215–16.

34. See the decree of Pope John XXII against the Talmud ibid., p. 322, and in Solomon Grayzel, "References to the Jews in the Correspondence of John XXII," *Hebrew Union College Annual* 23 (1950–51), 54–58; and the pronouncements of the Dominican inquisitor Bernard Gui in his *Practica inquisitionis heretice pravitatis* 2.48–53, 3.47, ed. Celestin Douais (Paris, 1886), pp. 67–71, 170–71.

35. Shlomo Simonsohn, ed., *ASJD*, 1546–1555, Pontifical Institute of Medieval Studies: Studies and Texts 106 (Toronto, 1990), p. 2889.

36. Solomon Grayzel, "Popes, Jews, and the Inquisition from 'Sicut' to 'Turbato,'" in *Essays on the Occasion of the Seventieth Anniversary of The Dropsie University (1909–1979)*, ed. Abraham I. Katsch and Leon Nemoy (Philadelphia, 1979), pp. 163ff.

IV . . . was no longer heard. Almost without exception, the question of false, extrascriptural traditions was being astutely swept aside."[37]

Nonetheless, I believe that several caveats are in order. First, the idea that the papacy had consigned the Talmud to the flames as embodying heretical deviations from biblical Judaism, confirmed by Pope Innocent IV himself in his commentary on the *Decretales*, found confirmation among canon lawyers of the later Middle Ages.[38] Even if later popes and prelates may have retreated from the extreme actions of Popes Gregory and Innocent, the condemnation of the Talmud as heretical in principle was duly acknowledged in the legal traditions of the late medieval church. Second, although various papal pronouncements against the Talmud may have called not for its burning but only for its confiscation, one ought not simply to assume that the popes thereby advocated the censorship of selected passages and the return of expurgated volumes to the Jews; without explicit provision for censorship, confiscation and burning could have virtually the same immediate effect. And third, even popes who called for the confiscation and inspection of the Talmud (perhaps even with an implied expectation of censorship) and not its burning, so that books free of error might be restored to the Jews, continued to express the concern for postbiblical heresy. In 1267, Pope Clement IV ordered King James I of Aragon to have

> the entire Talmud, together with its commentaries and additions, and all their [other] books presented freely to you and your subordinates by the Jews. Once the books have been presented, they can restore to the said Jews

37. Stow, *Alienated Minority*, pp. 258–59, and his comment in Solomon Grayzel, *CJ, Volume II: 1254–1314*, ed. Kenneth R. Stow (New York, 1989), p. 102 n. 9, concerning the decrees of Pope Clement IV against the Talmud in 1267: "It should be noted that the discussion had shifted from the burning of books to censorship alone." See also Rembaum, "Talmud," pp. 221–23; Chazan, "Condemnation of the Talmud," pp. 27–29; David Berger, "Christians, Gentiles, and the Talmud: A Fourteenth-Century Jewish Response to the Attack on Rabbinic Judaism," in *RIM*, pp. 115–30, and *From Crusades to Blood Libels to Expulsions: Some New Approaches to Medieval Antisemitism*, Touro College Graduate School of Jewish Studies: Annual Lecture of the Victor J. Selmanowitz Chair of Jewish History 2 (New York, 1997), p. 10; Alexander Patschovsky, "Der 'Talmudjude': Vom mittelalterlichen Ursprung eines neuzeitlichen Themas," in *Juden in der christlichen Umwelt während des späten Mittelalters*, ed. Alfred Haverkampf and Franz-Josef Ziwes, Beihefte der *Zeitschrift für historische Forschung* 13 (Berlin, 1992), pp. 22–23; Simonsohn, *The Apostolic See and the Jews: History*, p. 311; and Anna Foa, "The Witch and the Jew: Two Alikes That Were Not the Same," in *FWW*, esp. pp. 364–74.

38. See the Decretalist comments of Hostiensis, reedited in Pakter, *Medieval Canon Law*, p. 81 n. 140; of Joannes Andreae, *Commentaria in Decretales* (1581; reprint, Turin, 1963), 3:172; and of Franciscus Zabarella, *In tertium Decretalium* (London, 1557), p. 181. And cf. Kedar, "Canon Law," p. 81 n. 6.

those which shall accord with the text of the Bible, as well as those concerning which there is no suspicion that they contain blasphemies and errors, or any falsity whatsoever. They should faithfully deposit the others, under seal as is appropriate, for safekeeping in places that they shall consider secure—until such time in the future as the Apostolic See, under advisement, ordains what should properly be done to them. We desire that the examination of the books, the restitution of some, and the consignment and deposition of the others take place in the presence and with the guidance of Dominican and Franciscan friars, as well as other persons who are prudent and educated.

In articulating the criteria for judging the books of the Jews, the papal decree first mentions their conformity to biblical teaching. So too, in the same bull, did Clement echo Pope Innocent IV almost verbatim in bemoaning the "damnable perfidy of the Jews":

We have heard with sorrow and now relate that the Jews of the Kingdom of Aragon, having neglected the Old Testament which the majesty of his creator conferred through his servant Moses, falsely pretend that the Lord handed down a certain other law or tradition which they call the Talmud. In its huge volume, which is said to be larger than the text of the Old and New Testaments, are contained innumerable abuses and blasphemies against the Lord Jesus Christ and his most blessed mother.[39]

In 1286 Pope Honorius IV wrote of the Talmud to the Franciscan archbishop of Canterbury, perhaps at the latter's request: "To its deadly doctrine they assign their own children from their early years, so that they might consume its malignant nourishment; and they do not fear to teach and inform them that one is more obliged to believe the contents of that book than those things stated expressly in the law of Moses."[40] In the early years of the fifteenth century, Benedict XIII decried the perverse, satanic doctrine of the Talmud, which, he specified, was fabricated "after the coming of the savior Jesus Christ" and contained heresies "not only against the text of the New Testament but also against that of the Old Testament."[41] Similarly, when sixteenth-

39. Simonsohn, ASJD, 492–1404, pp. 233–36; and Grayzel, CJ, Volume II, pp. 99–102, with nn. Cf. the admission of Rembaum, "Talmud," p. 222: "It has been suggested that Clement adhered to Gregory IX's policy in condemning the Talmud as having replaced the Bible. This is true regarding Clement's *theoretical* definition of the problem. However, the steps he prescribed to resolve the matter follow along the lines of Innocent IV's 1247 edict" (emphasis Rembaum's). Disagreement over Innocent IV aside, my present concern lies precisely with the theoretical definition of the problem, which has remained one of postbiblical heresy.
40. Simonsohn, ASJD, 492–1404, p. 262; and Grayzel, CJ, Volume II, pp. 157–62, 238–39.
41. Shlomo Simonsohn, ed., ASJD, 1394–1464, Pontifical Institute of Medieval Studies: Studies and Texts 95 (Toronto, 1989), p. 594. See also Antonius Domingues de Sousa

century Italian inquisitors set out to implement Pope Julius III's decree that the Talmud burn once again, their writ of condemnation opened with a denunciation of the Jews' abandonment of Scripture: "We have considered that nothing would be more conducive to their illumination than if we were able to lead them away from their impious and inane doctrines to the scrutiny of sacred letters (which they falsely assert they study)."[42]

In all, the stance of the late medieval papacy vis-à-vis the Talmud defies tidy generalization. After the middle of the thirteenth century, most medieval popes displayed little or no interest in rabbinic Judaism and its postbiblical literature; no doubt Jews of the time deemed that alternative the best of all. Those who did take a concerted stance undoubtedly proceeded from a variety of motivations. They determined the particulars of their policies out of consideration for conflicting interest groups, including the Jews themselves, for the better welfare of the church and the papacy in its numerous dimensions, and for the mandates of Christian doctrine. One ought not to assume that theological considerations necessarily took precedence in such formulation of papal policy; indeed, one should be quite surprised if they always did. Yet the realia of ecclesiastical policymaking and its implementation pertain but tangentially to this book's agenda. We are here concerned specifically with the Christian perception of the Jew and his Judaism that allowed for the condemnation of the Talmud in the first place, in spite of ecclesiastical doctrine that specifically called for preserving the Jews and their books. The thirteenth-century proceedings against the Talmud enunciated and implied the notion that contemporary Judaism had betrayed its biblical heritage and that the books of contemporary Judaism no longer qualified for that preservation. As Christendom had come to scrutinize the Jews alongside other infidels and Christian heretics, churchmen in the thirteenth century voiced the conviction that the Jewish behavior no longer comported with the construction of the Jew whom Augustine had intended to preserve. Belief in the oral Torah was a Jewish heresy. The talmudic literature of the Jews could make no claim to Jewish authenticity; this was the initial and primary reason for its ecclesiastical condemnation.

But what of the talmudic Jews? Echoed by popes who followed him,

---

Costa, "Canonistarum doctrina de Judaeis et Saracenis tempore concilii constantientis," *Antonianum* 40 (1965), 55–70.

42. Stow, "Burning of the Talmud," p. 437.

Gregory IX contended that the Talmud bears primary responsibility for the Jewish refusal to accept Christianity; he termed it "the major factor that keeps the Jews unyielding in their perfidy."[43] As several historians have noted, Pope Innocent IV moved readily from voicing his rationale for policing the doctrinal beliefs of infidels to advocating aggressive missionizing among them.[44] Why should one doubt that such a linkage appeared in ecclesiastical attitudes toward the Jews? The attack on rabbinic Judaism facilitated and then accompanied unprecedented efforts to convert the Jews of Latin Christendom, an undertaking that likewise strayed from the legacy of Augustine. Ironically, the pursuit of such missionary efforts could mollify the attack on the Talmud, even as it derived from the same theoretical underpinnings.

FRIAR PAUL CHRISTIAN AND THE SECOND DISPUTATION OF PARIS

If, in the eyes of some thirteenth-century churchmen, allegiance to the Talmud had rendered contemporary Judaism unacceptable in a properly ordered Christian society, how better to eradicate the problem than to convert those Jews to Christianity? The leading Dominican friar, Raymond of Penyafort (d. 1275), numbered among the chief confidants of Pope Gregory IX during the last decade of his pontificate. Raymond compiled Gregory's code of canon law, the *Decretales*; he served as Gregory's personal confessor, perhaps even until Nicholas Donin brought his indictment of the Talmud to the curia; no doubt with Gregory's blessing, he served a term as master-general of the Dominican order soon thereafter. Raymond, evidently, sensed an implicit connection between Gregory's concern with the Talmud and the logic for proselytizing among the Jews, and his efforts to attract Jewish and Muslim infidels into the church dominated the last decades of his life.[45] One of his better-known proselytes, the Jew Saul of Montpellier, had

43. Simonsohn, *ASJD*, 492–1404, p. 172.

44. James Muldoon, *Popes, Lawyers, and Infidels: The Church and the Non-Christian World, 1250–1550* (Philadelphia, 1979), pp. 11ff.; and Benjamin Z. Kedar, *Crusade and Mission: European Approaches toward the Muslim* (Princeton, N.J., 1984), pp. 159ff.

45. See the "Chronologia biographica s. Raimundi" in the introduction to Raymond of Penyafort, *Summa de paenitenia*, ed. Xaverio Ochoa and Aloisio Diez, Universa bibliotheca iuris 1A. (Rome, 1976), pp. lxiv–lxxiii; and the literature cited in Cohen, *Friars*, pp. 104–8.

left the Jewish community in the wake of controversy over various rabbinic texts; and, having converted to Christianity and joined Raymond's team of mendicant missionaries, he soon concluded that ostensibly Christological homilies in rabbinic literature might help in drawing other Jews to the baptismal font.

Saul of Montpellier became the Dominican friar Paul Christian and a leading proponent of the thirteenth-century church's mission to the Jews; his fame derives above all from his disputation against Moses Nachmanides in 1263, conducted under the supervision of Friar Raymond. This Disputation of Barcelona has received exhaustive treatment by numerous scholars over the last twenty years, and I propose no further contribution to its analysis at present.[46] Yet the recent publication of additional documentary evidence on the career of Friar Paul sheds new light on the significance of his approach to the Talmud, both during and after the disputation with Nachmanides. As is well known, Paul then cited an array of rabbinic homilies in support of basic Christian doctrine, hoping thereby to impeach the authority of Rabbi Moses and win the souls of Catalonian Jews for the church. How did such reliance on talmudic evidence in missionizing among the Jews jibe with the condemnatory stance of Pope Gregory IX, which Paul's Dominican master and patron Raymond of Penyafort may have helped to formulate? Did such "positive" use of the Talmud entail a retreat from its earlier condemnation as postbiblical heresy?

I argued previously that Friar Paul's endeavor to find proof for Christianity in rabbinic texts marked not a retreat from the theoretical rationale for the Talmud's condemnation but only a change in tactics; indeed, both the confiscation/destruction of Jewish books and the urgency for a Christian mission to the Jews suggested that contemporary Judaism no longer qualified for toleration in Augustinian terms. In Paul Christian's case, I sought to ground this assessment not only in an

---

46. Most recently, see Robert Chazan, *Barcelona and Beyond: The Disputation of 1263 and Its Aftermath* (Berkeley, Calif., 1992), with its extensive bibliography. On the life and career of Friar Paul Christian, see the sources cited in Jeremy Cohen, "The Mentality of the Medieval Jewish Apostate: Peter Alfonsi, Hermann of Cologne, and Pablo Christiani," In *Jewish Apostasy in the Modern World,* ed. Todd M. Endelman (New York, 1987), pp. 35–41; Robert Chazan, *Daggers of Faith: Thirteenth-Century Christian Missionizing and Jewish Response* (Berkeley, Calif., 1989), pp. 43ff., 70ff.; and Joseph Shatzmiller, ed., *La Deuxième Controverse de Paris: Un Chapitre dans la polémique entre Chrétiens et Juifs au Moyen Âge,* Collection de la *REJ* 15 (Paris, 1994), pp. 15–31.

analysis of the events and records of the Barcelona disputation but also in whatever else was then known of the friar's elusive but colorful career.[47] Several years ago, after the collapse of the Iron Curtain, Joseph Shatzmiller discovered in Moscow and eventually published a Hebrew report of another disputation in which Friar Paul played a principal role.[48] Soon after Pope Clement IV had recommended Paul to King James of Aragon in 1267 as one who was qualified to direct the campaign against Jewish books—mandated by the pope, recall, because the Jews "falsely pretend that the Lord handed down a certain other law"—the friar made his way north to Paris. A Latin document reports that, having arrived in the spring of 1269, "he preached to the Jews— who came by royal order—showing them that their law was null and worthless, that they had in fact not observed it for a long time, that indeed they deviated daily from all its precepts."[49]

Shatzmiller has demonstrated convincingly that this Latin report and his newly edited Hebrew text refer to the same encounter—or series of encounters—between Friar Paul and the Jews of Paris. The Hebrew account begins as follows:

> The following are the responses to the apostate who rose against us in the year 32 of the millennium [5032 *anno mundi* = 1271–72]; he came from Spain to destroy the remnant of Israel, and his name was Paul the destroyer. . . .[50]
>
> Thus began the words of Paul the apostate who came from Spain to destroy the remnant of the holy people in all the lands of the king of France; he sought to destroy and exterminate even women and children. He adopted some of the designs of the first heretic from the days of Rabbi Yechiel who was much like him. More and more was he the cause of wickedness and

47. Cohen, *Friars*, chap. 5.
48. Shatzmiller, *La Deuxième Controverse*, pp. 44–57. It is likely that this disputation of ca. 1270 provides the context for the composition of yet another known Hebrew polemical manuscript. See ibid., pp. 36–39; and Judah M. Rosenthal, ed., "A Religious Disputation between a Jew Called Menaḥem and the Convert Pablo Christiani" [Hebrew], in *Hagut Ivrit ba'Amerika: Studies in Jewish Themes by Contemporary American Scholars*, ed. Menaham Zohori et al. (Tel Aviv, 1974), 3:61–74, and "Polemical Tractates" [Hebrew], in *Salo Wittmayer Baron Jubilee Volume* (Tel Aviv, 1974), Heb. section, pp. 352–95. Also valuable are the observations of Joel E. Rembaum, "A Reevaluation of a Medieval Polemical Manuscript," *AJSR* 5 (1980), 81–99. I consider the debate of 1270 at greater length in a Hebrew essay on "The Second Disputation of Paris and Its Place in Thirteenth-Century Jewish-Christian Polemic," forthcoming in *Tarbiz*.
49. Leopold Delisle, "Notes sur quelques manuscrits du Musée Britannique," *Mémoires de la Société de l'histoire de Paris et de l'Île de France* 4 (1877), 189, trans. in Robert Chazan, "Confrontation in the Synagogue of Narbonne: A Christian Sermon and a Jewish Reply," *HTR* 67 (1974), 455. Cf. Shatzmiller, *La Deuxième Controverse*, p. 16 n. 18.
50. See below, n. 53.

sin; for until his dying day he had no repose, no quiet, no rest from transgression.

In the year 33 of the sixth millennium [5033 = 1272–73] the heretic
Paul came and summoned all the rabbis, and thus did he address them
before the masses of Paris [he-hamon mi-Paris, perhaps to be read as the
bishop of Paris, ha-hegmon mi-Paris] and the chief clerics assembled there:
"Hear me, house of Jacob and all the families of the house of Israel. Know
that if you do not obey and repent and leave your faith for superior beliefs
that I shall demonstrate to you, I will not desist until I demonstrate my
vengeance upon you, and I will exact the very blood of your lives. For I
wish to prove to you that you are without a faith, a people called Bougres,
heretics, worthy of being burned. I will pronounce the questions—on the
basis of each of which you deserve to be put to death. Now, take counsel
and summon all of your great sages and respond to me without delay; for
so have I been commanded by the king to bring you to redemption and to
perfection."[51]

The description of this second disputation of Paris quickly evokes
memories of Paul Christian's debate with Nachmanides in Barcelona:
an encounter between the friar and the leading rabbinic authorities,
forced upon the Jews against their will by the decree of the king, conducted before a large audience of Jews and Christians, supervised by
leading churchmen. As he had done in 1263, Friar Paul once again
adduced both biblical testimonies and rabbinic aggadot that, he
claimed, established the validity of Christianity beyond the shadow of
a doubt. The sages of the Talmud, claimed Paul, acknowledged that
the messiah and the messianic age had arrived; they admitted the divinity of the messiah; and they knew that the 'almah of Isaiah 7:14
should be understood as a virgin. The very questions that Friar Paul
put to the rabbis of Paris include all of the agenda for his debate with
Rabbi Moses in Barcelona:

The first concerns what you assert, on the basis of the prophets, that the
messiah has not come; on the basis of your books I shall prove to you that
he has already come and departed. Second, I shall prove to you that that
messiah of whom the prophets spoke was born, fatherless, of a virgin whom
no man had known carnally. Third, I shall make known to you that that
messiah was divine and assumed human flesh within that virgin. Fourth,
that messiah of whom the prophets had once spoken was destined to suffer
a death which they call passion, in order to free his people from hell. Fifth,
that the said messiah, who was divine, annulled all of the law of Moses
and despised anyone who observed it.[52]

51. Shatzmiller, La Deuxième Controverse, p. 44.
52. Ibid.

Shatzmiller has argued persuasively that the correspondence between the issues debated at Barcelona and then at Paris, viewed together with the other evidence of Paul Christian's activity in Paris around 1270, removes all reasonable doubt that this same Paul was in fact the Christian representative at this "second disputation of Paris."[53] By the same token, the account of the Parisian debate enhances understanding of Paul and his anti-Jewish polemic. This Hebrew text, to be sure, fails to match Rabbi Moses Nachmanides' report of his Barcelona debate in the coherence of its organization or the refinement of its style; and the Moscow manuscript Shatzmiller edited is not even complete. Nevertheless, the document does testify to several key aspects of the manner in which Parisian Jewry perceived Friar Paul and the challenge he had put to them.

First, the Hebrew report indicates that Paul Christian threatened the Jewish community in a manner very similar to that of Nicholas Donin, master of ceremonies at the "first" disputation of Paris thirty years earlier. The text first presents Friar Paul as having followed in the footsteps "of the first heretic from the days of Rabbi Yechiel who was much like him."[54] After listing the five questions on Friar Paul's agenda, the document records the initial response of the spokesman for Parisian Jews, Rabbi Abraham ben Samuel, who set out to defend the oral law against the friar's attack: "Is it not more than twelve centuries old? And no one has ever cast doubt upon it, except for one heretic in the days of Rabbi Yechiel."[55] According to the Hebrew account of Donin's debate with Yechiel in 1240, that rabbi had defended the antiquity of the Talmud in strikingly similar terms.[56] Friar Paul must have confronted the Jews with essentially the same hostile, disqualifying appraisal of their rabbinic tradition, an impression confirmed later in the debate when Paul adduced a midrash to establish that Jesus knew all of Scripture, the Mishnah, the Talmud, rabbinic law (*halakhot*), and rabbinic lore (*haggadot*)—to which Rabbi Abraham quickly retorted

---

53. Although the Hebrew epithet *ḥovel* (above, at n. 50) may well denote a Cordelier or Franciscan, as understood by Adolph Neubauer, "Another Convert Named Paulus," *JQR*, o.s. 5 (1893), 714, see Shatzmiller's defense of this translation of "destroyer," which allows for the identification of Paul Christian, in *La Deuxième Controverse,* pp. 15–22. Cf. also the alternative suggestion of Robert Chazan, "Chapter Thirteen of the *Mahazik Emunah*: Further Light on Friar Paul Christian and the New Christian Missionizing," *Michael* 12 (1991), 18 n. 18.

54. Shatzmiller, *La Deuxième Controverse,* p. 44.

55. Ibid., p. 45.

56. See above, n. 10.

sarcastically, "And until now you have said that they were books of sorcerers!"[57]

Second, the Hebrew narrative reveals that, from the perspective of the Jews, the debate took a turn for the worse when Friar Paul raised the matter of Jewish guilt in the crucifixion of Jesus:

> On one occasion, all the communities of Paris assembled in the building of the Dominicans' residence, and all of Israel gathered there, men, women, and children. All the uncircumcised of Paris also assembled there and all of the Parisian clergy—a vast number, many more than twenty thousand people; for the heretic, planning to destroy them in one fell swoop and to excite the teeth of lions against them, wished to speak of the torture and execution of Jesus. The heretic inquired of them, stating: "Listen, all you peoples, to the shame and the disgrace which these Jews committed on our savior Jesus, in that, for no crime of his, they afflicted him and killed him and hanged him and tortured him in grave and exotic ways, one worse than the next. All his wonders are certain, but they still do not confess their sin. They deserve to be killed, just as they killed him; and woe to those creatures that tolerate them. . . ."[58] The sage [Rabbi Abraham] was very much afraid to speak of the slaying of Jesus, because this revealed his [Friar Paul's] intention to exterminate all of the Jews.[59]

The Christian charge that all Jews everywhere shared in the guilt for the crucifixion of Jesus was commonplace, and Friar Paul had seen no need to raise the matter when debating Nachmanides in Barcelona. But I have shown elsewhere that Christian understanding of this collective Jewish guilt changed significantly during the thirteenth century, that the view of the postbiblical Jew as a heretic who had deliberately forsaken the truth—rather than the infidel who was ignorant of it—yielded a new interpretation of the Jews' deicide.[60] Anselm, recall, had considered it venial sin, because the Jews had killed Jesus in ignorance of his true identity; Abelard had minimized the Jewish guilt further still. Yet thirteenth-century Christian theologians began to argue that the Jewish leadership knew exactly who Jesus was and killed him nonetheless—or, more precisely, for that very reason! Foremost among these churchmen was the Dominican master Thomas Aquinas, considered at length in the next chapter. Suffice it to note here that Thomas gave his

---

57. Shatzmiller, *La Deuxième Controverse*, p. 54.

58. Paul cited Deuteronomy 32:18 and an otherwise unknown rabbinic midrash which allegedly implied that the Jews had killed their God; see Shatzmiller's comment ibid., n. 186.

59. Ibid., p. 56.

60. Jeremy Cohen, "The Jews as the Killers of Christ in the Latin Tradition, from Augustine to the Friars," *Traditio* 39 (1983), 1–27.

position its fullest expression only after having resided in Paris between
1269 and 1272,[61] at the same time that Friar Paul was active in the
same city. Rabbi Abraham ben Samuel evidently sensed that the new
evaluation of Jewish involvement in Jesus' boded ill for his community,
threatening the bedrock of its security as a small religious minority in
medieval Christendom.

And third, the Hebrew account of Friar Paul in Paris makes explicit
what one rightly infers but does not find spelled out clearly when reading the reports of the 1263 disputation in Barcelona: that the stakes of
the Jewish-Christian debate had increased. In the aforecited passages
and elsewhere, the text emphasizes repeatedly that the Jewish community considered its survival at risk. Literary artifice may account for
the likening of Friar Paul to the wicked Haman with blatant allusion
to biblical verses, but Parisian Jews could not dismiss as mere rhetoric
his message to the Christian mob of Paris: "They deserve to be killed,
just as they killed him; and woe to those creatures that tolerate them."[62]
Friar Paul discerned no redeeming social—or theological—value in a
Jewish presence in his Christian community. From the perspective of
our Hebrew narrator, his attack on the Talmud underlay his hope to
convert some Jews and somehow to eliminate the presence of the others. From Friar Paul's perspective, the Jews were "without a faith, a
people called Bougres, heretics, worthy of being burned."[63]

These conclusions find additional support in a Latin text reedited
by Shatzmiller alongside the Hebrew account of Friar Paul's Paris disputation, a text entitled *Sentencia lata per illustrem regem Ffrancorum
contra Judeos habitantes in dominacione sua* (A Judgment Given by
the Illustrious King of the French against the Jews Residing in His
Domain).[64] This document reads not like a formal decree of condemnation but more like a working draft of a position paper, perhaps
prepared in order to advocate the issuance of a formal decree. The
Sentencia includes various *Adversus Iudaeos* arguments that the king,

61. See John Y. B. Hood, *Aquinas and the Jews* (Philadelphia, 1995), pp. 107, 129
n. 36.

62. Shatzmiller, *La Deuxième Controverse*, p. 56.

63. Above, n. 51. Cf. the instructive observations of Joseph Shatzmiller, "The Albigensian Heresy as Reflected in the Eyes of Contemporary Jewry" [Hebrew], in *Culture
and Society in Medieval Jewry: Studies Dedicated to the Memory of Haim Hillel Ben-
Sasson*, ed. Menachem Ben-Sasson et al. (Jerusalem, 1989), p. 346.

64. Shatzmiller, *La Deuxième Controverse*, pp. 76–91; this text was originally published in Ch. Merchavia, "Un documento desconocido sobre la historia de los Judios en
la Francia medieval," *Sefarad* 26 (1966), 53–78, where the events in question are dated
between 1270 and 1306.

it reports, certified as true; it makes reference to the responses of Jews to these charges; and it repeatedly condemns the Jews for their blasphemy. Albeit tentatively, and despite discrepancies between this text and the Hebrew account of Friar Paul's disputation, Shatzmiller has inclined toward the likelihood that this Latin document offers additional testimony for Paul's campaign against French Jewry. After all, one ought not necessarily to expect exact correspondence between different reports of Paul's activity. Here are a Jewish text and a Christian one; one focusing on the exchanges between Friar Paul and the Jews and one reflecting a policymaking process in the royal chancery; one (the Hebrew report) evidently composed in the immediate aftermath of the disputation and one written, perhaps, as much as several decades later.[65]

Beyond mention of debate with the Jews, the *Sentencia* castigates the Jews for the malicious—that is, intentional—ignorance fueling their denial of Christianity; this notion undergirded Thomas Aquinas's understanding of their intentional deicide, discussed below. The Jew, concludes the *Sentencia*, "wills not to know or to understand."[66] What, then, mandates his special tolerated status in Christendom? "There is not a heathen or a Saracen in the whole world" who, when confronted with biblical evidence of Christianity, will not admit what the Jews persistently deny![67] The Jews protested to the king that they are neither idolaters or evildoers and, accordingly, the king ought not to expel them. Yet the king ordered them to convert or to forfeit any grounds for inclusion in his kingdom; in the judgment of God their impiety exceeds that of idolatry.[68] The *Sentencia* clearly deems the Jews of contemporary France intolerable. And its concluding paragraph links this intolerability to King Louis IX's decision to burn the Talmud, "since nothing is taught there that does not deviate from the truth, or [whose truth value] is greatly reduced and which is full of ambiguities." It condemns the Jews' hatred, "which deprives them not only of the fruit of Holy Scripture but also of the fruit of those traditions which they have put to writing."[69]

It is certainly possible that Friar Paul Christian's ideas concerning Jews and Judaism developed between his debate in 1263 with Moses

65. Merchavia, "Un documento desconocido."
66. Shatzmiller, *La Deuxième Controverse*, p. 90.
67. Ibid., p. 89.
68. Ibid., pp. 79–80.
69. Ibid., p. 91.

Nachmanides and his subsequent activity in Paris around 1270. But it is unlikely that they underwent a total reversal, and one can safely assume that if the *Sentencia* derives from Friar Paul's activity, it conveys a fair impression of his stance vis-à-vis talmudic Judaism. Rabbinic texts do contain some traditions that can steer the Jews toward the Christian truth. Nonetheless, the Jews' belief in the oral law, their allegiance to the teachings of the Talmud, deviates from biblical religion. It has no place in a properly ordered Christian society. Along with anti-Christian blasphemy, it renders rabbinic literature worthy of condemnation and contemporary Jews worthy targets of Christian missionizing—and perhaps, at least in the rhetorical hyperbole of the document, deserving of expulsion, or even death. The development of Friar Paul's thought in this direction finds instructive parallels in the ideas of two other Dominicans writing around the same time as Paul's sojourn in Paris: Raymond Martin and Thomas Aquinas.

THE POLEMICS OF FRIAR RAYMOND MARTIN

The most formidable expression of thirteenth-century Christendom's campaign to convert the Jews and discredit Judaism appears in the polemical opus of the Dominican friar Raymond Martin. Protégé of Raymond of Penyafort and confrere of Paul Christian, Raymond Martin shared their conviction that European Judaism warranted not the balance of maintenance and restriction advocated by Augustine, Gregory the Great, and even Abelard but a new, more aggressive missionary campaign to attract it to the church.[70] His polemical treatises attacked both Judaism and Islam, exemplifying the high medieval tendency to view Jews alongside Muslims as two facets of the same infidel challenge to Christendom.[71] Just as with Peter Alfonsi and Peter the Venerable,

---

70. The little that is known concerning Raymond Martin's life is reviewed in André Berthier, "Un Maître orientaliste du xiiie siècle: Raymond Martin O.P.," *Archivum fratrum praedicatorum* 6 (1936), 267–311; Peter Marc's introduction to Thomas Aquinas, *Liber de veritate catholice fidei contra errores infidelium*, ed. Peter Marc et al. (Turin, 1961–67), 1:53–57, 243, 369–71, 609–12; Jeremy Cohen, "The Polemical Adversary of Solomon ibn Adret," *JQR*, n.s. 71 (1980), 48–55, and *Friars*, pp. 129–30 n. 2; Ina Willi-Plein and Thomas Willi, *Glaubensdolch und Messiasbeweis: Die Begegnung von Judentum, Christentum und Islam im 13. Jahrhundert in Spanien*, Forschungen zum jüdisch-christlichen Dialog 2 (Neukirchen, Germany, 1980), pp. 16–18; and the introduction to Raymond Martin, *Capistrum Iudaeorum*, ed. Adolfo Robles Sierra, Corpus Islamo-Christianum: Series Latina 3/1, 5 (Würzburg, Germany, 1990–93), 1:7ff.—all with extensive bibliography.

71. Cf. Raymond Martin's anti-Muslim treatise, "*De seta Machometi o De origine, progressu et fine Machometi et quadruplici reprobatione prophetiae eius*," ed. Josep Her-

involvement in anti-Muslim polemic and the study of earlier Christian diatribes against Islam may have led Raymond Martin to conclude that the key to effective proselytizing among any infidels lay in the exploitation of their own sources against them.[72] Perhaps more than any other Christian of the thirteenth century, he devoted himself to the study of the Hebrew language, the Hebrew Bible, and rabbinic literature. His monumental *Pugio fidei adversus Mauros et Iudaeos* (Dagger of the Faith against the Muslims and the Jews), whose lion's share polemicizes against Jews and Judaism, adduces scores of Jewish sources from the Bible, from the Talmud, and from medieval rabbinic books, in order to validate the essential tenets of Christian belief. The work cites its sources first in their original Hebrew (or Aramaic), then translates them into Latin, and then elaborates their significance and utility in the Jewish-Christian debate. Completed after 1278, the *Pugio* proved popular during the later Middle Ages and again during the Catholic Reformation; perhaps the first genuine Christian Hebraist of medieval times, Raymond Martin may well have contributed to philo-Semitism in the long term, no matter how hostile the intent that motivated his efforts. The friar and his work have been the subject of several scholarly investigations over the last several decades.[73]

My previous treatments of Raymond Martin contended that he shared and refined the view of the Talmud that characterized his colleague Paul Christian: Outside the bounds of normative, biblical Judaism, rabbinic religion and its literature nonetheless contain proof of

nando i Delgado, *Acta historica et archaeologica mediaevalia* 4 (1983), 9–63. For discussion of Friar Raymond's attack on Islam, see the fairly recent essays in *ICM*: Angel Cortabarria, "La Connaissance des textes arabes chez Raymond Martin O.P. et sa position en face de l'Islam," pp. 279–300, and Josep Hernando i Delgado, "Le 'De seta Machometi' du Cod. 46 d'Osma, oeuvre de Raymond Martin (Ramón Martí)," pp. 351–71, both with extensive bibliographies of earlier investigations.

72. See Thomas E. Burman, *Religious Polemic and the Intellectual History of the Mozarabs, c. 1050–1200,* Brill's Studies in Intellectual History 52 (Leiden, Netherlands, 1994), pp. 204ff.

73. On the *Pugio fidei* and its influence, see Robert Bonfil, "The Nature of Judaism in Raymundus Martini's *Pugio fidei*" [Hebrew], *Tarbiz* 40 (1971), 360–75; Willi-Plein and Willi, *Glaubensdolch,* pp. 21–83; Jeremy Cohen, "Profiat Duran's *The Reproach of the Gentiles* and the Development of Jewish Anti-Christian Polemic," in *Shlomo Simonsohn Jubilee Volume: Studies on the History of the Jews in the Middle Ages and Renaissance Period,* ed. Daniel Carpi et al. (Tel Aviv, 1993), pp. 71–84, and *Friars,* chap. 6; Pier Francesco Fumagalli, "I trattati medievali 'Adversus Judaeos', il 'Pugio fidei' ed il suo influsso sulla concezione cristiana dell'Ebraismo," *La scuola cattolica* 113 (1985), 522–45; and Chazan, *Daggers,* chap. 7. On the Hebrew texts in the *Pugio* in particular, see Ch. Merchavia, "The Hebrew Versions of 'Pugio fidei' in the Saint-Geneviève Manuscript" [Hebrew], *Kiryat Sefer* 51 (1976), 283–88. See also above, nn. 70–71.

Christianity that can aid in winning the souls of the Jews. The *Pugio fidei*, in fact, cites virtually all of the Jewish texts cited by Friar Paul at the disputations of Barcelona (1263) and Paris (ca. 1270), as it improves upon his forensic strategy and develops the rationale for his anti-Judaism. I argued further that the *Pugio* bespoke a novel, three-tiered Christian view of Jewish history that underlay his approach to the Talmud. First, the *Pugio* identifies the law and prophecies of the Old Testament, which, along with their correct interpretations, establish the truth of Christianity. Second, maintains the *Pugio*, the Jewish rabbis compiled their Talmud and collections of midrash in the wake of the crucifixion of Jesus, validating them with their ridiculous assertion that God revealed rabbinic doctrine to Moses at Mount Sinai but that it had been transmitted orally from one generation to the text until their own day. Although most of talmudic teaching derives from rabbinic fabrication and is therefore invalid, the correct, Christological understanding of the Old Testament so thoroughly permeated their biblical heritage that the talmudic rabbis could not expunge it from their writings entirely. And third, the *Pugio* demonizes the "modern"—that is, the medieval—Jews of its own day, condemning them for maliciously following in the error of their talmudic forbears, as they continue to deviate from the norms of authentic Jewish belief and praxis.

Some scholars have objected to this reading of the *Pugio fidei*, and, once again, the appearance of previously unpublished documentary evidence—in this case another polemical treatise of Raymond Martin himself—facilitates a more nuanced review of the question. Friar Raymond's earlier anti-Jewish treatise, the *Capistrum Iudaeorum* (The Muzzle of the Jews), edited only recently by Adolfo Robles Sierra, sets out to "curb the malice and confound the perfidy" of the Jews by responding directly to the stratagems employed by them in debate with Christians. "In two ways do the Jews impugn or evade the truth concerning the [biblical] text: either by saying that it is not so in the Hebrew . . . , or, if perchance they admit the text to be so, by saying that it should not be understood or interpreted in such a fashion."[74] The author has therefore undertaken to translate Scripture literally, with reference to the consensus of Jewish exegesis, and to offer evidence for the Christian interpretation of the Old Testament in quotations from the Talmud and other works authoritative among the Jews. He has

---

74. Raymond Martin, *Capistrum Iudaeorum*, 1:54.

sought to equip his Christian reader with sufficient material to deal successfully with a variety of evasive Jewish tactics: outright denial of the truth, changing the subject, and filibustering with long speeches on the virtues of the Hebrew patriarchs. Although the assertion of Christian doctrine and the negation of Jewish teaching both pervade the entire *Capistrum*, the book divides neatly into two parts. The first presents seven biblical passages as evidence (*rationes*) that the messiah has already come; the second responds to seven common Jewish arguments (*nequitiae*) that the messiah has yet to arrive.

Although a thorough summary of these fourteen arguments and the evidence brought by Friar Raymond pro and con is not feasible here, a review of a brief section by way of example—the first of the seven messianic testimonies[75]—may enhance one's appreciation of the *Capistrum Iudaeorum*, its methods, and its messages. In support of its first Christological contention, that "the messiah [Jesus] was born *before* the destruction of the temple" (in 70 C.E.), the *Capistrum* quotes Isaiah 66:7–8: "Before she labored, she was delivered; before her pangs came, she bore a son. Who ever heard the like? Who ever witnessed such events?" The *Capistrum* then quotes two rabbinic homilies to elucidate the prophet's intent. The first midrash explains that "at the hour when the temple was destroyed the Israelites cried out like a woman in labor, as Scripture states [Jeremiah 4:31], 'I have heard a voice as of one in labor, anguish as of a woman bearing a child [and the verse continues: *the voice of the daughter of Zion panting, extending her hands*].'" The second midrash questions: "On what basis do you maintain that on the very day that the messiah was born the temple was destroyed? For Scripture [in this same passage from Isaiah 66] states, 'Before she labored, she was delivered; before her pangs came, she bore a son.'"[76]

---

75. Ibid., 1:68–71. I consider this polemical treatise at greater length in a Hebrew essay, "Raimundus Martini's *Capistrum Iudaeorum*," in *Isadore Twersky Memorial Volume*, ed. Carmi Horowitz and Michael Schnidman (Jerusalem, forthcoming).

76. Friar Raymond eventually realized that this second midrash did not quite substantiate his point but, rather, argued for the simultaneous birth of the messiah and destruction of the temple; see below, at n. 82. The lack of correspondence between attested versions of rabbinic sources and citations in the works of Raymond Martin does not constitute prima facie evidence of forgery on the friar's part; for scholarly debate over the question of his alleged forgeries, see the citations in Cohen, *Friars*, pp. 135–36 nn. 12–13. Even the difference between the *Capistrum*'s two quotations of Isaiah 66:7–8 in this passage speaks to the author's reliability: When he quoted the biblical text alone, he referred to the Vulgate ("in antequam parturiret peperit; in antequam veniret partus ei, et protulit masculum"), but when quoting the unattested rabbinic midrash, he translated its quotation from the Masoretic Text ("in dum parturiret peperit; in dum veniret dolor sibi, et emisit masculum") quite literally.

These rabbinic sermons lead Friar Raymond to make explicit that which he wished to deduce from his prooftext (his *reductio in rationem*): "From the aforesaid one deduces clearly that the prophet Isaiah called the Jewish people a woman in childbirth, and its anguish and grief over the destruction of the temple and devastation of the people her labor. In testifying to the time of that birth, he called the messiah a male child on account of his singular perfection [that is, having been born before the pangs of his mother's labor]." As my bracketed annotation to this passage suggests, the key to Friar Raymond's argument is the twice-repeated word in Isaiah's prophecy, *be-ṭerem*, which, he claims, one must translate as *before*. The Jews will try to explain the term otherwise, as meaning *until* (in this case *not until*—that the birth did *not* occur *until* the destruction of the temple), but one can show on several grounds that their translation "is blatantly false in this passage." The *Capistrum* adduces three other Old Testament texts in which *be-ṭerem* unmistakably means *before*. It cites the lexicon *Sefer ha-Shorashim* (The Book of Roots) of the Provençal rabbi David Kimchi (d. 1235) that confirms its translation of the term for this passage in Isaiah in particular.[77] And it reasons that if *be-ṭerem* meant *(not) until*, the sequel to Isaiah's prophecy would be most foolhardy (*stultissima*). All women deliver their children only after their labor pains commence. Why then should the prophet have exclaimed, "Who ever heard the like? Who ever witnessed such events?" Rejecting the rabbinic legend that the messiah was born simultaneously with the temple's destruction, too late to have been Jesus, Friar Raymond has employed his knowledge of Hebrew, of the Bible's Masoretic Text, and of rabbinic literature ancient and modern to persuade Jews of the chronology of Christian salvation history.

Even so small a sampling of the contents of the *Capistrum Iudaeorum* suffices to demonstrate its character as a handbook for Christian disputants and missionaries. Largely complete by 1267,[78] the *Capistrum* seems to reflect the aftermath of the 1263 Barcelona Disputation between Paul Christian and Moses Nachmanides. Whether or not Raymond Martin himself was present at that event,[79] in March 1264 he joined the commission established by King James I of Aragon at Friar

---

77. David Kimchi, *Radicum liber* [Hebrew], ed. J. H. R. Biesenthal and F. Lebrecht (1847; reprint, Jerusalem, 1967), col. 260.

78. Raymond Martin, *Capistrum Iudaeorum*, 1:276: "est hodie ab Incarnatione Domini annus M.CC.LX.VII."

79. See Cohen, *Friars*, p. 130 n. 2.

Paul's behest to censor Jewish books, and the agenda and general strategy of the *Capistrum* echo those of Paul's debate against Rabbi Moses:
proving to the Jews, with the aid of rabbinic midrash, that the advent
of the biblical messiah has already occurred. The *Capistrum* confirms
the impression, gleaned by Robert Chazan from the *Pugio fidei*,[80] that
Friar Raymond sought to improve upon the anti-Jewish argumentation
of his confrere Paul. The *Capistrum* organizes its arguments more systematically. It selects and analyzes its biblical and rabbinic sources with
greater care. It anticipates and refutes possible Jewish arguments more
thoughtfully. And it generally avoids the hot-tempered, excessively
emotional sort of argumentation in which both sides reportedly engaged at Barcelona.

Still, the *Capistrum Iudaeorum* constituted Raymond Martin's initial anti-Jewish effort, not his final one. The friar soon saw fit to begin
work on the considerably longer, more comprehensive *Pugio fidei*,
whose composition probably extended throughout the 1270s and perhaps even beyond. Some have assumed that the obstinacy of Friar Raymond's Jewish opponents, who refused to consider the rabbinic sources
cited in the *Capistrum* in Latin translation, induced him to compile his
larger work, which quoted extensively in the original.[81] Yet I believe
that the progression from *Capistrum* to *Pugio* in Raymond Martin's
polemical opus derived from more significant factors, which underscore
the differences between the earlier treatise, a handbook for missionaries
replete with specific instructions and cross-references, and the later
work, a veritable summa of anti-Jewish polemic. On one hand, the
Pugio attests to a broader, more sophisticated mastery of rabbinic literature. For example, Friar Raymond came to realize that the second
of the two rabbinic homilies cited in the *Capistrum* in support of his
interpretation of Isaiah 66:7–8 (that Israel gave birth to the messiah
before the temple was destroyed) actually served to undermine that
interpretation; and in the *Pugio* Raymond dismissed the midrash as
manifesting "the insanity of the Jews who say that the messiah was
born on the day of the temple's destruction."[82] Contrasted with the
Pugio in this and other such instances, the earlier *Capistrum* thus en-

80. Robert Chazan, "From Friar Paul to Friar Raymond: The Development of Innovative Missionizing Argumentation," *HTR* 76 (1983), 289–306, and *Daggers*, esp. pp.
118–36.

81. For example, Berthier, "Un Maître orientaliste," p. 309.

82. Raymond Martin, *Pugio fidei adversus Mauros et Iudaeos* 2.6.1–2 (1687; reprint,
Farnborough, England, 1967), pp. 348–49.

riches one's sense of the processes whereby the new mendicant missionary strategies of the thirteenth century matured gradually. On the other hand, a comparison between the *Capistrum Iudaeorum* and the *Pugio fidei* also reveals development in its author's Christian perspective on the Jews and Judaism of his day. The *Capistrum* testifies to an earlier stage in the crystallization of Raymond Martin's anti-Judaism, and it thus brings the novelties of the *Pugio* into a helpfully sharper focus.

Specifically, the *Capistrum Iudaeorum* gives expression to several of those ideas in which scholars have discerned the singularity of the *Pugio fidei*, but it does so in more rudimentary fashion. First, already in the *Capistrum* did Friar Raymond make noteworthy reference to the devil and to the direct ties between the devil and the Jews. Alluding to a Jewish interpretation of Genesis 49:10, that the messiah will not come until the commandments of the Sabbath and circumcision have been revoked, the *Capistrum* quotes a talmudic legend that when Rome had twice outlawed these divinely ordained observances during the Hadrianic persecutions,[83] the Jews had them reinstituted only with the assistance of the devil Ben Tamalyon:

> From these things which we have adduced from the Talmud it is clear that the messiah must have come for all those whom sin or stupidity or malice does not blind. And thus, by the grace of God, the perfidy of the Jews is struck by its own arrows and strangled by its own noose. We therefore ought not to replace in its worn out bag [that is, we ought not to overlook] the fact that, after the Sabbath and circumcision had been lost, the Jews regained them—not from God or his miracle, not from some prophet, not from an angel, but from the devil, that is Ben Tamalyon.[84]

More than other enemies of Christendom, the Jews continue to function as the foremost agents of the devil:

> If Muhammad, for instance, who at the outset was all alone, entirely uneducated, utterly impoverished, hated by his own kinsmen and foreigners alike, so far removed from our borders, and so obvious in his falsehood, could introduce so much corruption into the world on behalf of the devil— what do you think the devil can accomplish through the Jews, who are so numerous, almost all educated and most adept at trickery, so well endowed from the good life and the usuries allowed them by Christians, so loved by

---

83. A full century after the crucifixion—but this seems not to disturb the author of the *Capistrum*, who otherwise displayed a most detailed interest in the chronology of late ancient Jewish history.

84. Raymond Martin, *Capistrum Iudaeorum*, 1:88; see also 2:258–61.

our princes on account of the services they provide and the flatteries they spew forth, so scattered and dispersed throughout the world, so secretive in their deceptions that they display a remarkable appearance of being truthful?![85]

One can safely infer that the *Capistrum* includes the Jews among the apocalyptic allies of Gog and Magog, through which metaphor the prophet "foresaw and foretold . . . the persecution of the righteous which occurs daily, implemented by the heretics and other oppressors of the truth and holy faith, who are the habitation of demons and the abode [literally, roof] of the devil."[86]

Second, if, in a handful of passages, the *Capistrum* portrays Judaism as having degenerated into a diabolical perversion of biblical law after the lifetime of Jesus, it hints at Friar Raymond's maturing assessment of the postbiblical religion of the rabbis. The *Capistrum* decries rabbinic homilies on the deity for their anthropomorphisms.[87] It repeatedly condemns the rabbis of the Talmud for their insanity, for falsifying the calculation of the messianic era,[88] for lying profusely concerning Jesus and his crucifixion,[89] for corrupting the genuine text of Scripture in their practice of scribal emendation (*tiqqun soferim*),[90] and for their little book (no doubt the Hebrew *Toledot Yeshu* [The Story of Jesus]), which recounts the miracles of Jesus in terms most blasphemous.[91] None of these accusations against rabbinic Judaism, however, obviates Friar Raymond's persistent recourse to rabbinic texts to validate his Christological and anti-Jewish arguments or his satisfaction in wounding the Jews with their own arrows:

> As often as the Talmud offers us some prophetic prooftext, interpreting it concerning the messiah or concerning those things known to relate to the

85. Ibid., 2:24–27.
86. Ibid., 2:226; for prior instances of the connection drawn between the Hebrew *Gog* and *gag*, meaning roof, and, through synecdoche, perhaps habitation or abode, see Richard Kenneth Emmerson, *Antichrist in the Middle Ages: A Study of Medieval Apocalypticism, Art, and Literature* (Seattle, Wash., 1981), p. 85.
87. For example, Raymond Martin, *Capistrum Iudaeorum*, 2:58.
88. For example, ibid., 2:84.
89. Ibid., 2:116.
90. Ibid., 1:264, 2:156–59. This accusation contrasts instructively with an earlier statement of Friar Raymond praising Jews—as well as Christians—for preserving uncorrupted texts of their sacred scriptures. See Raymond Martin, "De seta Machometi," p. 60: "Item emulatio est inter Christianos et Iudeos specialiter de scripturis et ideo nec corruptinem [*sic*] Iudeorum simulassent Christiani, nec corruptionem Christianorum occultarent Iudei." Curiously, a manuscript variant omits "Christianorum occultarent Iudei."
91. Ibid., 1:282, 286.

messiah, if it has expounded the text well, it should be admitted in argument. For honey, as the wise man knows, is consumed eagerly, even though, if it is examined carefully, it proves to be the spittle of bees. If, however, as occurs more frequently, it [the Talmud] has expounded the text in a ridiculous or evil fashion, its interpretation should be rejected but the [admittedly messianic] prooftext retained. For thus the Jews could not reasonably say that we should not interpret it regarding the messiah or some related matter, since their ancestors interpreted it with reference to him. Yet in no way should we wish to accept that [interpretation] which, albeit false, they might have received from the prophets; we have no idea whence it came to be added to the [biblical] text.[92]

Selective citation of the Talmud, explains the *Capistrum*, should in no way imply any general acceptance of its authority; though the Jews may accept its doctrine in its entirety, they may have no such expectation of Christians. For, like a camel, which appears to split its hoof but in truth makes no such division—and is therefore unclean according to Mosaic dietary laws—the Jews

consume whole, without any discretion, whatever ridiculous stories and insanities of their sages they find mixed with the words of Holy Scripture and with certain true and worthwhile traditions in the fields of the Talmud. They accept it all and chew it all, since day and night they read and reread it all and do not stop committing it to memory; but entirely without discretion—without which even virtue degenerates into vice—do they believe and accept the false with the true, the profane and the impious with the sacred. . . . As often as we might adduce something true from the Talmud against them, to overcome some wickedness or to refute some objection of theirs, or even to establish a certain truth in earnest, they argue extensively that we ought not to, nor can we fairly adduce something from the Talmud on our behalf against them, unless we were to believe in the entire Talmud and accept it all. Yet the Talmud itself demolishes their stupidity, inasmuch as it teaches that one should do with Scripture and with the words of the sages as one does with pomegranates and with dates. He who eats dates wisely consumes the fruit outside and spits out the seed inside. And so too a man who eats a pomegranate wisely eats the seeds within and spits out the rind.[93]

Although Friar Raymond here admitted to eclecticism in no uncertain terms, the methodological assumptions of his *Capistrum* remain half-

92. Ibid., 2:30.
93. Ibid., 2:280–2. In *Ḥagigah* 15b, the Babylonian Talmud compares this advice on the wise consumption of dates to the process whereby Rabbi Meir profitably discriminated between the worthwhile and the reprehensible in the instruction of his heretical teacher, Elisha ben Abuya. My thanks to Dalia Ḥoshen for her helpful assistance in this regard.

baked, offering no historical or theoretical rationale to resolve its seemingly contradictory tendencies. As for the falsehood with which the
Talmud explains the words of Scripture, wrote the author, "we have
no idea whence it came to be added to the text."

Third, the *Capistrum*'s implied association of Jews with heretics who
wage the offensive of Gog and Magog against God's faithful on a daily
basis (*cotidie*) hints at a particular message concerning the Jews of Friar
Raymond's own day and age as well. As opposed to the rabbis of the
Talmud, who occasionally did acknowledge the messianic import of
Christological testimonies in Scripture, "modern" Jews, led by the great
medieval Jewish exegete "Rabbi Solomon [ben Isaac of Troyes, or Ra-
shi] and all of his successors,"[94] have deliberately obscured and perverted their correct interpretation.[95] This have they done "more out of
wickedness than out of ignorance."[96] Now that the victories of the
church have confirmed the truth of Jesus' miracles, modern Jews have
no excuse whatsoever to deny the truth of Christianity. Their malice
thus exceeds that of their talmudic ancestors.[97] They habitually refuse
to admit truths concerning Jesus that even the Saracens affirm;[98] they
continue actively to falsify the text of the Old Testament; and, as Friar
Raymond has heard of a specific Jew in Montpellier, they will not
shrink from altering the biblical text during the course of a debate in
order to mislead their listeners.[99] Raymond viewed contemporary Jewish observance as having little relation to the ancient precepts of Moses,
and thus did he bring his *Capistrum Iudaeorum* to a close on a note
of sheer horror and disgust:

> On these grounds it is sufficiently clear, I believe, that in a spiritual sense
> the Jews imitate and eat the camel. If it would not take too long, so too

94. Ibid., 1:184; see also 1:206, 2:134.
95. Ibid., 1:208: "Cum autem antiqui rabini, qui fuerunt prophetis et ceteris patribus
sanctis magis propinqui, et ideo plus de veritate et minus de versutia et falsitate habentes
quam moderni, exposuerint hoc et multa alia valde bene et congrue de Messia, quis sani
capitis, obsecro, fabulationes iniquorum, falsas insanias huiusmodi modernorum est ad-
missurus?"
96. Ibid., 1:144; see also 1:142, 206.
97. Ibid., 1:286: "Si autem consideretur quanto conatu Iudaei repellebant ea, vide-
bitur quanta fuerunt obdurati perfidia, et caecati malitia. Non minor comprobatur esse
duritia et malitia modernorum, cum eis ablata sit omnis causa et occasio suspicandi.
Nam et si suspicari potuit Dominum Iesum per artem aliquam, ut ipsi in libello supra-
dicto [see above, n. 91] mentiti sunt, fecisse miracula, per quam artem. antequam esset,
tam congrua tempori suo, necnon factis suis, et dictis, tam mortui quam viventis, statui
quoque ipsorum usque nunc dicta reddidit prophetarum?" See also 1:206, 2:142.
98. For example, ibid., 1:108, 254, 294, 2:86.
99. Ibid., 2:156–58.

would I demonstrate from the blindness of their hearts how, figuratively, they consume the owl and the bat, from their cunning [how they consume] the fox, from their strength the ass, from their ignorance the ox, from the filth of their mouths the pig and all the impure reptiles and birds. Let me be silent concerning the others. But do not the Jews, who take the sexual organ of everyone who is circumcised, adult or child, into their most defiled of mouths, with which they blaspheme Christ, and suck for as long as the blood flows—do they not eat just like the pig who soils his snout with abundant filth? Abraham did not do this; Moses did not order it; God did not command it. But the aforementioned demon, namely Ben Tamalyon, who restored to them the circumcision which God had taken away, consigned them to a reprobate moral sense.[100]

With relation to older arguments and stratagems of Christian *Adversus Iudaeos* polemic, much in these propositions of the *Capistrum Iudaeorum* is novel and distinctive. But one senses that the author has yet to spell out, perhaps even fully to comprehend, their ramifications, and they appear to fall short of enunciating a coherent theoretical position. By contrast, when the *Pugio fidei* treats the same three issues— the association between the devil and the Jews, the status of the oral law, and the distinctive character of contemporary Jewry—they give expression to a more coherently formulated view of contemporary rabbinic Judaism as demonic and deviant. Curiously, there are indications that Friar Raymond may have visited Paris in 1269–70[101]—at the same time as Friar Paul Christian appeared there, giving more explicit expression to similar ideas than he had in Barcelona, and, as noted, just as Thomas Aquinas was preparing to toughen his condemnation of the Jews' act of deicide. Might not all three of these Dominicans have responded to similar influences, whether in an exchange of ideas among themselves or in reaction to some specific event? One can only speculate along such lines, but it is known that Friar Raymond produced the bulk of the *Pugio fidei* in the years that followed immediately, during which time he systematized the ideas posed tentatively and less methodically in the *Capistrum Iudaeorum*.

   The *Pugio* reiterates the *Capistrum*'s claim that Satan restored the observance of the Sabbath and ritual circumcision to the Jews after divinely countenanced Roman decrees had outlawed them; but it now

   100. Ibid., 2:286–88.
   101. See the arguments of Marc in Thomas Aquinas, *Liber de veritate*, 1:53–72 (esp. 57), 612. Among others, Fumagalli, "I trattati medievali," p. 529, has accepted them outright; and Shatzmiller, *La Deuxième Controverse*, p. 31, has entertained their possibility.

argues more consistently that contemporary Jewish ritual reflects not the law of God but "the cult of the devil" and that no other demonstration will strike more effectively at the self-confidence of the Jews.[102] Alliance with the devil lies at the root of both the sin and the punishment of the Jews: Akiva and other talmudic rabbis were the devil's martyrs, not God's, killed not because they remained loyal to Old Testament precepts but because they forsook them, espousing the cause of false messiahs even after the career of Jesus.[103] Consequently, God has afflicted the Jews with a diabolically induced insanity, which has assured the quintessentially evil character of their beliefs and actions ever since: "The intention, the inclination, and the purpose of the devil with regard to human beings are never anything but evil—wherefore it is sufficiently evident how immense is the stupidity, how great the madness, how enormous the folly of the Jews, who do not cease to practice circumcision, the Sabbath, and the other rituals which God took away from them and the devil restored."[104] Christian writers, to be sure, had associated Jews and Judaism with Satan and with the Antichrist from the earliest days in the history of the church; yet, as modern historians have consistently observed, that association reached unprecedented intensity and assumed new and dangerous relevance in the mentality of late medieval Christendom. In the extent of its Judaic learning, the graphic nature of its accusations, and its focus precisely on those Jewish rituals that loomed most obvious in contemporary Christian perceptions, the *Pugio fidei* provided ample scholastic support for inhuman, satanic constructions of Judaism.[105]

The *Pugio*'s demonization of the Jews did not stop with general denunciation of their observance of the law. It focused particularly on their postbiblical literature and practice, and here, too, it organized occasional remarks of the *Capistrum Iudaeorum* into a more succinct

---

102. Raymond Martin, *Pugio fidei* 2.14.24, p. 461.
103. Ibid. 2.4.27, p. 329, and elsewhere.
104. Ibid. 3–3.11.25, p. 791.
105. On the *Pugio*'s qualitative advancement over earlier Christian writers in this regard, see especially Bonfil, "Nature of Judaism," pp. 365ff. On the connection between the devil and the Jews in late medieval thought, see also, among many others, Robert Bonfil, "The Devil and the Jews in the Christian Consciousness of the Middle Ages," in *Antisemitism through the Ages*, ed. Shmuel Almog, trans. Nathan H. Reisner (Oxford, 1988), pp. 91–98; Cecil Roth, "The Medieval Conception of the Jew: A New Interpretation," reprinted in *Essential Papers on Judaism and Christianity in Conflict: From Late Antiquity to the Reformation*, ed. Jeremy Cohen (New York, 1991), pp. 298–309; Joshua Trachtenberg, *The Devil and the Jews* (New Haven, Conn., 1943); Jeffrey Burton Russell, *Lucifer: The Devil in the Middle Ages* (Ithaca, N.Y., 1984), p. 192 n. 67; and, most recently, Foa, "Witch and the Jew."

ideological position. In so doing Friar Raymond followed Peter the Venerable in his denigration of diabolical absurdities in talmudic aggadah,[106] but he went considerably farther in scrutinizing and condemning the halakhah. Much like Nicholas Donin and his ecclesiastical supporters, Friar Raymond accused the Talmud of licensing heinous Jewish crimes against Christians;[107] he too branded the oral law as an unconscionable departure from biblical religion. And so, as it follows the *Capistrum Iudaeorum* in advocating an eclectic approach to the Talmud, rejecting its authority in general but prescribing its limited use in disputation against the Jews, the *Pugio fidei* at last enunciates a theoretical rationale for such selectivity. At the very beginning of the work one reads of its proposed reliance on the rabbinic texts of the Jews:

> The substance of this *Pugio*, especially inasmuch as it pertains to the Jews, is twofold: first and foremost, the authority of the law, of the prophets, and of the entire Old Testament; second, certain traditions, which I found in the Talmud and midrashim—that is, glosses—and traditions of the ancient Jews which I gladly raised up like pearls out of an enormous dung heap. . . .
>
> These traditions, which they call "the oral law [*torah shebbe-'al peh*]," they believe and state that God gave to Moses along with the law on Mount Sinai. Then Moses, they say, transmitted them to his disciple Joshua, Joshua to his successors, and so on, until they were committed to writing by the ancient rabbis. Yet it seems that to believe this, that God gave Moses all that is in the Talmud, should be deemed—on account of the absurdities which it contains—nothing other than the insanity of a ruined mind.
>
> Certain [traditions], however, which know the truth and in every way reveal the doctrine of the prophets and holy fathers, wondrously and incredibly bespeak the Christian faith too, as will become obvious in this book. They destroy and confound the perfidy of modern Jews [*modernorum . . . Judaeorum perfidiam*], and I do not think that one should doubt that they managed to make their way successively from Moses and the prophets and the other holy fathers to those who recorded them. For in no other way than from the prophets and fathers do we think that such things descended, since traditions of this sort are entirely contrary to those regarding the messiah and so many other matters which the Jews have believed from the time of Christ even until now.
>
> Some [traditions] of this sort were thus not meant to be rejected, since nobody sane would reject what he finds in places like the law and the prophets, even though both these are rejected among those [Jews] so perfidious. For a wise man never despises a precious stone, even if it might be

106. Raymond Martin, *Pugio fidei* 2.15.15, 2–3.5.16–17, 3–3.22.9–18, 3–3. 22.24–27, pp. 472ff., 573ff., 928ff., 936ff.

107. See below, n. 113.

found in the head of a dragon or a toad. Honey is the spittle of bees, and how could there be anything less worthy of those having a poisonous sting! Indeed he is not to be deemed foolish who knows how to render it fit for his own beneficial uses, as long as he knows how to avoid the harm of the sting.

We therefore do not reject such traditions but embrace them both for those reasons already mentioned and because there is nothing so capable of confuting the impudence of the Jews; there is found nothing so effective for overcoming their evil.[108]

This approach to rabbinic Judaism is obviously more complex and qualified than the blanket condemnation of papal decrees calling for the Talmud's confiscation—even though there, too, a disqualification of postbiblical, rabbinic Judaism in theory may result in different practical measures in the formulation of policy. But, how, precisely, ought one to understand the nuance of Raymond Martin's approach? How does the *Pugio fidei* justify its limited expropriation of rabbinic traditions on behalf of Christianity? I believe that the crux of Friar Raymond's position here lies not in according a partial legitimacy to the oral Torah of the rabbis—or in advocating something less than its total disqualification as a legitimate expression of Judaism—such that its literature intrinsically deserves to be tolerated in Christendom, even after the removal of its offensive passages. On the contrary, the Jews' very belief in the divine origin of their rabbinic traditions is, simply put, erroneous, "nothing other than the insanity of a ruined mind," a mind that has willfully opted for the false over the true. Nevertheless, two considerations provide the rationale for adducing certain talmudic traditions as evidence of Christianity. The first can be termed historical or analytical: These select traditions originate in Scripture, not in the

---

108. Raymond Martin, *Pugio fidei*, prooemium 5–9, pp. 2–4. In addition, see also the methodological explanation given by the *Pugio*, 2.14.8, p. 450:

Credere quippe quod quicquid magistri eorum deliraverunt olim, et ea quae nunc usque delirant cum discipulis suis; et quicquid sunt etiam deliraturi in posterum; omnia fuerint Moysi data in monte Sinai, nihil mihi videtur aliud quam praecipitatae mentis credulitas. De quibusdam vero sentire istud non est multum a ratione semotum; siquidem verisimile est, atque credibile quod Moyses, ac caeteri prophetae multas sententias Scripturarum, multaque mysteria fidei suis successoribus tradiderunt, et illi aliis successive usque ad istos qui Talmud, et alios Judaeorum libros scripserunt; ubi nos hujusmodi sententias, atque mysteria non sine modernorum maxima displicentia Judaeorum reperimus, et eis per haec veritatem fidei Christianae ita vehementer concludimus, quod oportet eos conscientia reluctante vel contemnere dicta suorum magistrorum ob praesentiam Christianorum; vel ea in dubium pro viribus vertere; cum nullum aliud adsit eis refugium, contra quos optima tunc est ista Glossa, sive traditio ad falsitatem, et impudentiam ipsorum hujuscemodi confutandam.

so-called oral law of the Talmud; one cannot conclude otherwise in view of their blatant Christological truth—and in view of the essential falsity of rabbinic doctrine. Of these exceptional traditions Friar Raymond wrote, "I do not think that one should doubt that they managed to make their way successively from Moses and the prophets ... to those who recorded them." A Christian may therefore resort to them as authoritative, because they do not convey the doctrine characteristic of the rabbis and "since nobody sane would reject what he finds in places like the law and the prophets." The second consideration is simply tactical: These Christological traditions will work to discredit and, hopefully, to convert the Jew of the present. Owing to their inclusion in the Talmud and midrash, "there is nothing so capable of confuting the impudence of the Jews" when debating with them.[109] On balance, then, one senses that the *Pugio fidei* distinguishes between the doctrines of the oral Torah recorded in the Talmud and midrash, and the actual compendia of textual traditions that the Talmud and midrash constitute. These compendia contain certain authentic interpretative traditions the substance of which antedates the talmudic rabbis and validates the Christian understanding of biblical prophecy. The Christian preacher ought certainly to exploit these traditions, for the Jews uphold the authority of everything in the Talmud. But that hardly obliges the Christian to do the same or to accord any legitimacy to rabbinic Judaism. When all is said and done, the aggregate of rabbinic doctrine remains "an enormous dung heap."

Finally, and especially in view of its stance concerning the oral law, the *Pugio fidei* buttresses the impression of contemporary Jewry gleaned in the review of the *Capistrum Iudaeorum*. Here I return to my earlier argument for a novel, three-tiered scheme of Jewish history operative in Friar Raymond's polemic, and I admittedly cannot vouch that Raymond Martin would himself have adopted or assented to the threefold division of Jewish history attributed to him here. The "tripartite scheme" derived from my own reading of his ideas and the semantics of its formulation matter relatively little. Yet differentiating repeatedly between modern Jews (*Iudaei moderni, Iudaei nostri temporis*) and ancient Jews (*Iudaei antiqui* or *antiquissimi*),[110] the *Pugio*

---

109. See also ibid. 2.6.4, 2.8.8, 2.14.4, 3–3.1.8, 3–3.2.13, 3–3.6.2, 3–3.15.5, pp. 351, 364, 44, 633, 655–56, 728, 838, and so forth.

110. For example, Raymond Martin, *Pugio fidei*, prooemium 6–7, p. 3 (*Rabini antiqui* versus *moderni Judaei*); 2.14.8, p. 450 (*magistri eorum ... olim* versus *nunc usque ... discipuli sui; isti qui Talmud ... scripserunt* versus *moderni ... Judaei*); 2.15.11, p.

leaves no room for doubt that Friar Raymond did afford special attention to contemporary Jewry, apart from his consideration of the talmudic sages, just as he distinguished the Judaism of the Bible from that
of the Talmud.[111] Throughout Friar Raymond's magnum opus, these
modern Jews do not emerge as a relic of the past, a vestige of an
antique religion now obsolete. Rather, they constitute a genuine,
threatening presence; in large measure, they are Friar Raymond's par-
tisan construction of the "real Jews" whom he has met, against whom
he has debated, and whose books he has studied. These *Iudaei moderni*
continue, actively and ingeniously, to subvert the teachings of their God
and to detract from the welfare of Christendom. Not only do they
maintain the postbiblical heresy of their talmudic forebears, they reject
the truth of the few talmudic traditions that do validate the teachings
of Christianity. Led by Rashi, they maliciously deny the messianic import of biblical prophecies that even the talmudic rabbis acknowledged.
They persist in the brazen corruption of Scripture, both in its pointing
(that is, the vocalization of its Hebrew consonants) and in key readings
of the text itself. Their willingness to lie knows no limits; "in disputing
against us, the Jews are borne by such great hatred for the truth, that,
without any measure of shame, they deny the meaning even of individual words."[112] Instructed by their Talmud to deceive Christians in
legal proceedings and even to kill innocent Christians, young boys in
particular, modern Jews constitute a most noxious threat to contem-

---

471 (*Patres Judaeorum* versus *nostri temporis Judaei patrum suorum nequitias imitan-
tes*); 3.2.1.3, p. 551 (*moderni vero Judaei . . . ad horum igitur perfidiam confutandam
dictum . . . quod habetur in Midrasch Tillim*); 2–3.8.3, p. 605 ([modern] *Judaei . . . quos
per subjectas traditiones majorum suorum ostendemus esse falsiloquos*); 3–3.6.13, p. 733
(*antiquissimorum suorum magistrorum traditiones*); 3–3.7.4, p. 740 (*falsitas Judaeorum
modernorum*); 3–3.7.6, p. 743 (a passage from the ancient Targum [considered by the
author, 3.3.5.5, p. 718, to be *expositio antiquissimorum Judaeorum*] is adduced to show
that *moderni Judaei falso punctant et falso legunt* a biblical verse); 3–3.16.24, p. 855
(*veritas hujus* [talmudic] *traditionis* versus *aliquorum modernorum Judaeorum perfidia*);
3–3.21.16, p. 912 (*dicunt Judaei nostri temporis . . . contrarium autem probatur in Seder
Olam* [an ancient rabbinic work]); and so forth.

111. Although acknowledging the distinction between the authentic teachings of
Scripture and the falsities of rabbinic Judaism underlying the introduction to the *Pugio*,
Chazan, *Daggers*, p. 174, has vehemently protested my identification of a third category,
that of contemporary Jews and Judaism, in the friar's thought. "Cohen's third category,
however, does not exist. To put the matter a bit more sharply, the purported third set
of beliefs is simply the sum total of the first two, with the scales weighted heavily in
favor of the second. . . . The tripartite scheme means nothing. There are really only two
groups for Friar Raymond (and all mainstream Christian theologians): pre-Christian Jews
and post-Christian Jews."

112. Ibid. 2–3.8.3, p. 605.

porary Christian society.[113] "According to the opinion of Seneca, no adversary is more prone to inflict harm than the familiar enemy; yet no enemy is more familiar or more unavoidable to the Christian faith and to us than the Jew."[114]

One can readily admit that the *Pugio fidei*'s distinction between the rabbis of the Talmud and the Jewish sages of Friar Raymond's own day does not match that between biblical Judaism and talmudic Judaism, either in its nature or in its depth. Leaving the formalities of the "tripartite scheme" in abeyance, one might better express the necessary point more discursively: The rabbis of the Talmud forsook the biblical religion of the patriarchs and prophets of the Old Testament for the diabolical fabrications of the oral law. Though they could not completely expunge all evidence of the Bible's Christological truth from their literature, their religion after the coming of Jesus ceased to be what God had intended Judaism to be before Jesus. In a word, they defied the hermeneutically crafted, patristic construction of the Jew. For their part, contemporary Jews maintain the heretical error and satanic loyalties of the classical rabbis, and they compound them. With deliberate malice, they falsely deny or deceptively remove all vestiges of Christian truth from their literature, and their current religious observances have no value for the church. Rather, they pose a clear and present danger to Christians and Christendom, and Friar Raymond Martin accordingly devoted his life to the scrutiny of Jewish rituals and sacred texts, to discrediting Judaism in his polemic, and to converting Jews to Christianity.

THE DOCTRINE OF JEWISH WITNESS AND ITS LIMITS

Did the approach to rabbinic Judaism underlying the papal decrees against the Talmud and the anti-Jewish efforts of Paul Christian and Raymond Martin embody a new Christian perception of the Jew in Christendom? Or did these notions of pre-Christian and post-Christian Jews merely echo the Augustinian views of all previous "mainstream" Christian theologians? Robert Chazan's criticism of my reading of these sources airs a basic challenge to the findings of my previous

---

113. Ibid. 3-3.22.21-22, pp. 935-36: "Ita agendum est de Christianis: Occidendi adhuc Christianos, et praecipitandi pueros ipsorum in foveas, et puteos, et etiam trucidandi, quando occulte possunt."

114. Ibid., prooemium 2, p. 2.

studies, and the scope of this criticism mandates a sizable quotation from it:

> All the negative activities of the friars (negative from the Jewish perspective) can be readily understood within the context of this earlier ecclesiastical view. For the prior Augustinian stance in no sense afforded the Jews carte blanche with regard to religious and social behaviors. The clear understanding always was that the Jews must behave in ways that would entail no harm to the Christian society that had extended hospitality to them. To cite the most famous formulation of this theory, "Just as the Jews ought not enjoy license to presume to do in their synagogues more than permitted by law, so too in those [privileges] conceded to them they should not suffer curtailment." What this traditional formulation does is to emphasize equally Jewish rights and responsibilities. The major responsibility was always understood as the duty to live in a manner that would entail no harm to the Christian majority. . . . The mendicant assault on the Talmud requires for its understanding no appeal to a new ideological stance on the part of the Church. The old ideology made ample provision for an attack on any teachings that could be construed as a breach of conduct on the part of the Jewish minority.
>
> There was a second elastic clause in the traditional view of the Jewish place in Christian society. That clause involved the issue of conversion. While forcible conversion was eschewed . . . and total conversion of the Jews was pushed off to the time of the Second Coming . . . , Christian responsibility to convert individual Jews was never denied or abandoned in theory. . . . Again, no new theory is called for; the old Augustinian view made ample provision for such proselytizing efforts.[115]

I have emphasized in this study how early medieval churchmen adapted the "old Augustinian view" to a variety of contexts and purposes, such that well before the thirteenth century Augustine's doctrine concerning the Jews had proven its elasticity. Moreover, I have here endeavored to underscore how thirteenth-century perceptions of the Jews built upon developments of earlier centuries; they were not quite as novel or unanticipated as I may have depicted them previously. And yet, our review of the condemnation of rabbinic Judaism in the thirteenth century confirms that it broke with age-old convention, defying some of the basic principles of the Augustinian doctrine of witness. My present purpose is not to show that the thirteenth-century church, or even the mendicant orders in particular, replaced the old view with the new. Rather, I wish to establish the appearance and significance of the new perception: that late medieval churchmen began to recognize

115. Chazan, *Daggers*, p. 176.

the Jew as something other than what Augustine had seen in him. Such recognition, as the condemnations of the Talmud and the new mendicant mission attest, worked to close up the Jews' "niche in the Christian cosmic structure";[116] it hardly remained a moot point in the dynamic of Christian-Jewish relations, even if it never became the sole— or primary—factor in the determination of the church's official Jewish policy.

Chazan has stressed correctly that ecclesiastical doctrine had always called for the restriction of Jewish behavior in keeping with the needs and better welfare of Christian society; indeed, the subordination of the Jew to the historical purpose of the church lay at the heart of Augustinian teaching. But the church's scrutiny of the Jews to ensure that they not undermine the fulfillment of that purpose—or, in simpler terms, to ensure that they cause no injury to the Christian community that tolerated them—typically extended to the interaction of Jews with Christians, not to the beliefs and practice of Judaism maintained within the Jewish community itself. Pope Gregory the Great's principle of *Sicut Iudaeis*,[117] quoted here to exemplify the early medieval Christian curtailment of Jewish freedom, offers a valuable case in point. For, as demonstrated in chapter 2, when Gregory protested stridently against Jewish enjoyment of privileges not rightfully theirs, he referred specifically to their ownership of Christian slaves, to their trafficking in Christian holy objects, and to any form of their proselytizing among Christians. All of these entailed Jewish encroachment upon Christians, their property, and their practice of Christianity. At the same time, however, Gregory included the day-to-day practice of the Jewish religion by the Jews, in accordance with their ancestral custom, among the rights expressly guaranteed to the Jewish community by the church. He never suggested that Christians ought to police the doctrines and rituals of contemporary Judaism. Even when Agobard of Lyons or Peter the Venerable of Cluny attacked various rabbinic teachings of the Jews that they deemed absurd, neither one of them suggested that the

---

116. I have borrowed the term from Stow, *Alienated Minority*, p. 270. See also Brenda Boulton, "Tradition and Temerity: Papal Attitudes to Deviants, 1159–1216," in *Schism, Heresy and Religious Protest*, ed. Derek Baker, SCH 9 (Cambridge, England, 1972), pp. 79–81, who argues persuasively that the Fourth Lateran Council of 1215 marked a watershed in the development of such attitudes: Beforehand, the papacy worked creatively to include spontaneous, nonnormative religious movements within the folds of the church; thereafter, papal policies toward deviants turned more conservative and inflexible, seeking their exclusion from Christian society.

117. See above, chapter 2, n. 11.

Jews' allegiance to their postbiblical traditions contravened the logic of their inclusion in Christendom. As angrily as Pope Innocent III decried alleged Jewish violations of the *Sicut Iudaeis* formula, advocating more oppressive forms of discrimination against the Jews, he invoked Augustine in declaring that they "ought not to be killed, so that the Christian people should not forget the divine law."[118]

"Slay them not, lest at any time they forget your law." Psalm 59:12 constituted the scriptural foundation for the Augustinian doctrine of Jewish witness, and Augustine explicitly understood the psalmist's injunction to mean not interfering with the practice of Jewish life. Augustinian doctrine postulates the equation of Judaism with the observance of Mosaic law: The Jews bear the books; the Jews preserve the books; the Jews embody the teachings of the books; and, in Bernard of Clairvaux's terms, the Jews are the living texts of those books. From the Augustinian perspective all this is axiomatic, not even subject to question. Augustine's doctrine of Jewish witness mandates the servitude of the Jews,[119] and it was this servile status that churchmen of the early medieval period sought to police. Not until the High Middle Ages did their scrutiny extend to the substance of contemporary Judaism.

Proceeding against the Talmud during the 1240s, Pope Innocent IV and his legate Odo of Châteauroux came to appreciate the ramifications of their actions. When French Jews appealed to the pope in the wake of his decree of 1244, they claimed that without the Talmud they could not observe the law of Moses. Innocent sought to investigate: If that were true, wrote the pope to King Louis IX of France, the Jews deserved to have their books returned to them. But, concluded the papal legate, the Jews of France had lied to Innocent; for the tomes of their Talmud "turn the Jews away from an understanding not only from a spiritual understanding [of the law] *but even from a literal understanding.*" Nothing less than the fundamental premise of Augustinian teaching was at stake; for the condemnation of the Talmud bespoke the conviction that rabbinic Judaism was not biblical Judaism. Friar Paul Christian preached in Paris that the Jews no longer deserved

---

118. Simonsohn, *ASJD*, 492–1404, p. 92; and Grayzel, *CJ*, pp. 126–27. Innocent's seemingly radical understanding of Psalm 59:12 ("that *the Christian people* should not forget *your law* [*ne divine legis obliviscatur populus christianus*]") evidently signifies an attempt to reconcile Augustine's rendition of the text ("lest at any time they forget your law [*legem tuam*]") with that of the Vulgate ("lest my people [*populi mei*] forget"). On the various readings of this verse, see above, chapter 1, n. 23.

119. See above, chapter 1, n. 11.

the toleration and protection of their Christian ruler, and his efforts
against the Talmud exemplified the same rationale, expressed succinctly
by Benzion Dinur: "The argument that the Talmud is the creation of
human beings and that its exclusive religious authority among the Jews
removes Judaism from the family of religions grounded in divine revelation entailed a practical conclusion: Church and state must relate to
the Jews as people, lacking a faith, who have no place whatsoever in
a Christian polity."[120] Friar Raymond Martin voiced the conclusion
that modern Jews willfully deviated from the biblical religion of ancient
Jews; because their Judaism perverted the Christian cosmic structure,
he too undertook to convert them to Christianity. Friars Paul and Raymond, to be sure, were not the first medieval clerics to advocate proselytizing among the Jews; Pope Gregory the Great himself had done so
many centuries earlier. For Gregory, however, converting the Jews
would signify the second coming of Christ, and, as such, it would confirm the historic function of the Jew as defined by Augustine and the
apostle Paul before him. In the missionary ideology of Friar Raymond,
the conversion of the Jews would redress their abandonment of that
historic role. Significantly, neither Paul Christian nor Raymond Martin
alluded to the doctrine of Jewish witness in any of the sources we have
reviewed. In the written records of the disputations of Paris and that
of Barcelona, as in all the hundreds of pages of the *Capistrum Iudaeorum* and the *Pugio fidei*, Psalm 59:12, with its imperative of "Slay them
not," receives no mention whatsoever.

To recapitulate: The Christian attack on the Talmud in the thirteenth century derived from the conviction that rabbinic Judaism was
not the Judaism of the Old Testament. Because the Jews' preservation
of that biblical Judaism underlay the injunction of "Slay them not, lest
at any time they forget your law," rabbinic Judaism undermined Christianity's theological rationale for Jewish survival in Christendom; contemporary Jews did not perform the testificatory function that underlay
their toleration and privilege. And if Judaism no longer rendered the
Jew worthy of protection in Christendom, the Christian mission to the
Jews now assumed unprecedented urgency and desirability. In none of
its early medieval permutations did the Augustinian doctrine of Jewish
witness allow for these developments. Rather, churchmen of the thirteenth century grew conscious of the disparity between the Jew of their
own day and the hermeneutically crafted Jew at the heart of the Au-

---

120. Benzion Dinur, *Israel in the Diaspora* [Hebrew] (Tel Aviv, 1958–72), 2, 2:507.

gustinian outlook. Their ideas contributed to new constructions of the Jew and Judaism in late medieval Christianity: not the Jew of the old law but the Jew of the Talmud—heretic, deliberate unbeliever, agent of Satan, and enemy of God, his revelation, and his church.

This talmudic Jew or *Talmudjude*, as avowed antisemites later came to dub him, has survived in Christian thought alongside the wandering, exiled Jew of the older Augustinian tradition.[121] The subsequent history of the interaction between these constructions, though deserving of extensive investigation, lies outside the purview of this book. Yet we move on to consider one more thirteenth-century churchman, who adds nuance and complexity to our story. His opus demonstrates the impact of the new perception of the Jews even on one who refused to swallow it whole, and as such it suggests that the lasting influence of that perception, albeit subtle and elusive, may in fact have been more profound than one has noticed.

121. See Patschovsky, "Der 'Talmudjude.'"

CHAPTER 9

Ambiguities of Thomistic Synthesis

Our story concludes with the most renowned medieval theologian of all, the Dominican Thomas Aquinas (1225–74). Because he, like most of the great scholastic masters of theology in his day, evidenced little interest in interreligious polemic, he did not number among the vociferously anti-Jewish mendicant friars of the thirteenth century.[1] Nevertheless, his constructions of the Jew and of Judaism remain interesting and noteworthy, so I return to them here. These Thomistic ideas exemplify yet another type of thirteenth-century churchman's perspective on the Jews, betraying additional evidence of the new appraisal of post-

---

1. Even so, some have objected sharply to the brief, passing mention of Aquinas in Jeremy Cohen, *The Friars and the Jews: The Evolution of Medieval Anti-Judaism* (Ithaca, N.Y., 1982); these include Dieter Berg, "Servitus Judaeorum: Zum Verhältnis des Thomas von Aquin und seines Ordens zu den Juden in Europa im 13. Jahrhundert," in *Thomas von Aquin: Werk und Wirkung im Licht neuerer Forschungen*, ed. Albert Zimmermann, Miscellanea mediaevalia 19 (Berlin, 1988), pp. 439–58; Jean-Pierre Torrell, "*Ecclesia Iudaeorum*—Quelques jugements positifs de Saint Thomas d'Aquin à l'égard des Juifs et du Judaïsme," in *Les Philosophies morales et politiques au Moyen Âge*, ed. R. Carlos Bazán et al. (Ottawa, 1995), 3:1734, 1739 n. 7; and John Y. B. Hood, *Aquinas and the Jews* (Philadelphia, 1995), esp. pp. x–xii. On the treatment of the Jews and Judaism by thirteenth-century scholastic theologians, see, among others, Jacob Guttmann, *Die Scholastik des dreizehnten Jahrhunderts in ihren Beziehungen zum Judenthum* (1902; reprint, Hildesheim, Germany, 1970); Gilbert Dahan, "Saint Bonaventure et les Juifs," *Archivum franciscanum historicum* 77 (1984), 369–405, and "Juifs et Judaïsme dans la littérature quodlibétique," in *FWW*, pp. 221–45; and Jeremy Cohen, "Scholarship and Intolerance in the Medieval Academy: The Study and Evaluation of Judaism in European Christendom," *AHR* 91 (1986), 604–13.

biblical, rabbinic Judaism considered in the previous chapter. Additionally, they bring this book to a close in keeping with the general tenor of its findings—not on a note of patent resolution but in a tone of guarded suggestion and qualification.

As this study was in progress, John Hood published the most comprehensive review of Thomistic teaching on the Jews and Judaism to date, and his welcome contribution allows one to focus more selectively on matters of particular concern. From the outset, however, I must take issue with Hood's concluding judgment that "in the medieval context, Aquinas's attitude toward Jews was pedestrian, even banal."[2] In articulating his ecclesiastical policy toward the Jews of contemporary Christendom, Thomas admittedly adopted a largely traditional, conservative posture; but in casting Jews and Judaism on grounds more theoretical, to fit his own theology of Christianity, he gave new expression to some of the innovative tendencies of his day. Not only do these distinctly Thomistic ideas demand our attention, but the very dissonance between policy ordinance and theological abstraction warrants recognition. Even as the Angelic Doctor of Paris reaffirmed the canonistic tradition of *Sicut Iudaeis*, closely linked to the Augustinian doctrine of Jewish witness, philosophical and hermeneutical considerations led him to construct a Jew who did not jibe with those traditions. As Friar Thomas took up the matter of the Jews and their religion in diverse contexts throughout his writings, he may not have polemicized directly against them, but that, too, speaks to their role and characterization in his theological system. I would hardly term that role and characterization banal.

TRADITIONAL GUIDELINES

In a letter to the recently widowed duchess of Brabant, often dubbed *De regimine Iudaeorum* (On the Governance of the Jews), Thomas responded to a series of eight questions of public policy that the duchess had posed to him.[3] Five of these queries concern the Jews. Of these, four address the extent to which a ruler may receive money from the

---

2. Hood, *Aquinas and the Jews*, p. 111.
3. Thomas Aquinas, *Epistola ad ducissam Brabantiae*, in *Opera omnia*, ed. Roberto Busa (Stuttgart, 1980), 3:594–95. Earlier studies of this letter include Henri Pirenne, "La Duchesse Aleyde du Brabant et le 'De regimine Judaeorum' de Saint Thomas d'Aquin," *Bulletin de la classe de lettres et des sciences morales et politiques de l'Academie royale de Belgique*, 5th ser., 14 (1928), 43–55, and the works cited below, n. 12.

Jews—as tribute, a gift, or a fine—especially because they derive their
wealth from usury; the final item questions whether the Jews must wear
a distinguishing sign on their clothing. In response, Thomas appeared to
proceed from several guiding principles: the immorality of usury; respect
for prevailing law and custom in the treatment of the Jews; and the conviction that "Jews, as a result of their guilt, are or were consigned to perpetual servitude [*perpetue servituti addicti*], and princes can thus treat
their property as if it were their own, save for this restriction—that the
subsistence necessary for life is not taken away from them."[4] Thomas
therefore ruled that rulers should strive to return the usurious profits of
the Jews to their original Christian owners, and perhaps to induce the
Jews to support themselves in a more commendable fashion. The doctrine of Jewish servitude notwithstanding, the Christian prince would do
well to forego even what the law might allow him so as to deter the Jews
from blaspheming Christ's name, exacting from them only that which
established precedent permitted. In the matter of distinctive Jewish dress,
however, Thomas deemed the issue an easy one (*plana est responsio*); the
recent decision of the Fourth Lateran Council that the Jews wear an
identifying sign must be observed, especially because biblical law itself
commands them to place distinctive fringes on their cloaks.[5]

Although in instructing the duchess of Brabant Thomas did not hesitate to invoke recent ecclesiastical strictures against Jewish usury and
fraternization with Christians (namely, the demand for distinctive
dress), the provisions of the *De regimine Iudaeorum* proceed directly
from the two basic premises of Augustinian doctrine and its applications in canon law: First, the sin of the Jews has resulted in their consignment to perpetual servitude in Christendom; second, no Christian
ruler may deprive them of that which they require to live as Jews under
his rule. The spirit of the doctrine of Jewish witness weighs no less than
the letter of legal statute in this equation, and, in suggesting that the
duchess willingly forgo levies rightfully hers in order to avoid Jewish
blasphemy, Thomas acknowledged the need to maintain a measure of
peaceful coexistence between Christians and Jews. Surprisingly, the Augustinian perception of the Jews as biblical may even have contributed
to the *De regimine*'s affirmation of the Lateran decree on Jewish dress;
for "this is also mandated in their own law."[6]

4. Thomas, *Epistola ad ducissam Brabantiae*, p. 594.
5. Ibid., p. 595.
6. Ibid.

In the second half of the second part of his *Summa theologiae*, Thomas formulated the essentials of proper Christian policy toward the Jews in more general terms.[7] Infidels should not assume dominion over Christians, for it would endanger the religious belief of the faithful. A slave of a Jew who converts to Christianity should immediately receive his or her freedom; "since the Jews themselves are the slaves [*servi*] of the Church, it can dispose of their property."[8] And, though the church exercises no spiritual jurisdiction over the Jews, it may at times, as a temporal penalty, restrict Christians from any communion with them. Still, Jews who have never converted to Christianity may not be compelled to accept the faith. The Christian population may engage in commerce with them. The church may not remove their children from their custody and baptize them, for this would violate natural law.[9] Above all, the church must permit the Jews to observe the rites and practices of their religion:

> Human government derives from divine government and should emulate it. Though God is omnipotent and supremely good, he permits certain bad things, which he could prevent, to transpire in the universe, lest, without them, greater goods might be forfeited or worse evils ensue. So, too, in human government, those in power rightly tolerate certain evils lest certain goods be impeded or greater evils be incurred. . . . So, then, although infidels may sin in their rites, they may be sustained on account of some good that proceeds from them or on account of some evil that is avoided. From the fact that the Jews observe their rituals, in which the truth of the faith we now hold was once prefigured, there proceeds the good that our enemies bear witness to our faith, and that which we believe is represented in a figure.[10]

In this formulation of policy, Thomas could not have subscribed to the logic of Augustinian doctrine more wholeheartedly: The continued ob-

---

7. Thomas Aquinas, *ST* 2–2.10.7–12 (Cambridge, England, 1964–76), 32:57–79. I have regularly consulted the translation in this Blackfriars edition.

8. Ibid. 2–2.10.10, 32:70.

9. On this precedent-setting Thomistic instruction in the history of canon law, see Aviad M. Kleinberg, "A Thirteenth-Century Struggle over Custody: The Case of Catherine of Parc-aux-Dames," *Bulletin of Medieval Canon Law* 20 (1990), 51–67; Walter Pakter, *Medieval Canon Law and the Jews*, Münchener Universitätsschriften—Juristiche Fakultät—Abhandlungen zur Rechtswissenschaftlichen Grundlagenforschung 68 (Ebelsbach, Germany, 1988), pp. 314–30; and Gilbert Dahan, *Les Intellectuels chrétiens et les Juifs au Moyen Âge* (Paris, 1990), pp. 149ff.

10. Thomas Aquinas, *ST* 2–2.10.11, 32:72–73 (drawing considerably from the Blackfriars translation).

servance of Jewish law by contemporary Jews offers figurative testimony to the truth of Christianity.[11]

BETWEEN INFIDELITY AND HERESY

Such marked conservatism in Thomas's Jewish policy, which Hood and others have considered at length,[12] contrasts sharply with notably nontraditional and still underappreciated aspects of his characterization of the Jews in contexts more theoretical. Curiously, the *Summa theologiae* offers its guidelines for dealing with the Jews of Christendom immediately after—and under the same rubric as—a more abstract discussion of the nature of Judaism. This section [*quaestio*] of the *Summa*, entitled *De infidelitate in communi* (On Disbelief in General)[13] first establishes the essential features of disbelief and then proceeds in good scholastic fashion to differentiate its principal varieties:

> If disbelief [*infidelitas*] be considered in comparison to faith, there are different sorts of disbelief, limited in number. For inasmuch as the sin of disbelief consists of resisting the faith, this can happen in two ways: Either one resists the Christian faith before it has been accepted, and the disbelief of the pagans or heathens is of this sort; or one resists the Christian faith after it has been accepted—whether in figurative terms, and such is the disbelief of the Jews, or in the very revelation of the truth, and such is the disbelief of heretics.[14]

Having distinguished the disbelief of pagans from that of Jews and heretics, the *Summa* turns next to the obvious question: Which sort of disbelief is the worst?

> With regard to disbelief, as has been noted, two things can be considered. One of these is its comparison to faith; in this regard, someone who resists the faith after accepting it sins against the faith more gravely than one who resists the faith before accepting it. . . . Accordingly, the disbelief of the

---

11. Additional Thomistic allusions to the Augustinian doctrine of Jewish witness are cited in Torrell, "*Ecclesia Iudaeorum*," pp. 1736, 1740 n. 18.

12. Among others, see Hans Liebeschütz, "Judaism and Jewry in the Social Doctrine of Thomas Aquinas," *JJS* 13 (1962), 63ff.; Bernhard Blumenkranz, "Le *De regimine Judaeorum*: Ses modèles, son exemple," in *Aquinas and the Problems of His Time*, ed. G. Verbeke and D. Verhelst, Mediaevalia lovaniensia 1, 5 (Louvain, Belgium, 1976), pp. 101–17; Alexander Broadie, "Medieval Jewry through the Eyes of Aquinas," in *Aquinas and the Problems of His Time*, ed. G. Verbeke and D. Verhelst, Mediaevalia lovaniensia 1, 5 (Louvain, Belgium, 1976), esp. pp. 62ff.; Berg, "Servitus Judaeorum," pp. 452ff.; and Hood, *Aquinas and the Jews*, pp. 87–105.

13. Thomas Aquinas, *ST* 2–2.10.1–6, 32:38–57.

14. Ibid. 2–2.10.5, 32:52.

heretics, who profess the faith of the Gospel and resist it by corrupting it [*ei renituntur eam corrumpentes*] is graver than that of the Jews, who have never accepted the faith of the Gospel [*fidem Evangelii nunquam susceperunt*]. Yet since they have accepted its figure [*susceperunt eius figuram*] in the old law, which they corrupt by interpreting it falsely [*quam male interpretantes corrumpunt*], their disbelief is a graver sin than the disbelief of the heathens who have in no way accepted the faith of the Gospel [*nullo modo fidem Evangelii susceperunt*]. The other thing to be considered with regard to infidelity is the corruption of matters that pertain to the faith. In this regard, since the heathens err in more matters than Jews, and Jews on more counts than heretics, the disbelief of the heathens is worse than that of Jews, and that of Jews worse than that of heretics. . . . Yet the first of these two injuries outweighs the second with respect to guilt . . . , wherefore, simply put, the disbelief of the heretics is the worst of all.[15]

Albeit subtly, these ostensibly dry academic passages betray several noteworthy departures from the theoretical foundations of the patristic doctrine that had long ago distinguished pagans from Jews and Christian heretics and that now undergirded Thomas's Jewish policy. First, in this formalized categorization of disbelief, Thomas outdid most of his high medieval predecessors in classifying the Jews as but one subset, alongside pagans/Muslims and heretics, within a larger species of nonbelievers and dissidents. As suggested throughout part 3 of this book, in ceasing to perceive the Jew as the sole or exemplary unbeliever and in detracting from the nearly exclusive *Adversus Iudaeos* focus of earlier Christian religious polemic, this tendency among high medieval theologians paradoxically deprived the Jew of privilege as well as distinction in the Christian mind-set. The *Summa theologiae*'s taxonomy of infidelity suggests that the earlier Christian notion of the uniqueness of the Jew had weakened, and with it the distinctive position that he commanded in a thoroughly Christian worldview. Second, Thomas's ordering of the three categories of disbelief may adumbrate an underlying linkage between Jew and heretic.[16] To be sure, each of his two rankings situates the Jews midway between heretics and pagans, who share the dubious distinction of the most sinful class of unbeliever. Yet Thomas noted explicitly that the ranking of heretic and Jew as worse than pagan outweighs that of pagan and Jew as worse than heretic in

15. Ibid. 2–2.10.6, 32:56.

16. Once again, cf. Alexander Patschovsky, "Feindbilder der Kirche: Juden und Ketzer im Vergleich (11.–13. Jh.)," in *Juden und Christen zur Zeit der Kreuzzüge*, ed. Alfred Haverkamp, Vorträge und Forschungen des Konstanzer Arbeitskreises für mittelalterliche Geschichte (Sigmaringen, Germany, 1999).

its importance, and the language of the comparisons corroborates that
the author has not struck an even balance. For although neither Jews
nor pagans have embraced Christianity (*nunquam/nullo modo fidem
Evangelii susceperunt*), the Jews have, in fact, embraced its prefiguration in the Old Testament (*susceperunt eius figuram*); and, if heretics
corrupt (*corrumpentes*) the teaching of the Gospel, the same verb denotes the Jews' corruption of their biblical law, which they interpret
falsely (*male interpretantes corrumpunt*).

Third, and most interesting of all, the *Summa*'s systematic linkage
between the sin of *infidelitas* and human intentionality parts company
with the logic underlying Augustine's attribution of the Jews' error to
genuine blindness; in Augustine's view, the Jews' rejection of Christian
salvation was thoroughly unintentional. The entire Thomistic discussion "On Disbelief in General" opens by distinguishing between two
senses of the term: "One sense is completely negative, so that one is
termed an infidel solely on the grounds that he does not have faith. In
the other sense disbelief can be understood according to opposition to
faith, as when someone resists hearing the faith or even denounces it.
. . . In this the nature of disbelief is fully realized, and in this sense is
disbelief a sin."[17] The disbelief of primary interest to the *Summa* constitutes deliberate opposition to the true faith, or dissent from it, and
this proceeds from a person's intention. "To dissent, which is the distinctive act of disbelief, is an act of the mind, but motivated by the
will. . . . Disbelief, like faith, is certainly in the mind as its proximate
subject, but in the will as in its first moving force."[18] Owing to the
correspondence between faith (or disbelief) and intention, then, just as
"there can be no good which does not derive from a rightful intention,"
so "among infidels can no act be good." In other words, infidels clearly
do not sin in everything they do, but "whenever they act by reason of
their disbelief, then do they sin."[19] Only on this basis does the *Summa*
proceed with its taxonomy of disbelief. One wonders whether Thomas
hereby intimated a notion of Jewish infidelity as a willful rejection of
the truth, devoid of redeeming social value—similar to that notion encountered among some of his Dominican confreres in the previous
chapter.

All of these inferences from Thomas's discussion of disbelief find

17. Thomas Aquinas, *ST* 2–2.10.1, 32:40.
18. Ibid. 2–2.10.2, 32:44.
19. Ibid. 2–2.10.4, 32:48–51.

confirmation elsewhere in his theological opus. The classification of Judaism as but one variety of *infidelitas* helps to account, perhaps, for the lack of any works of *Adversus Iudaeos* polemic in the Thomistic corpus. One surely may argue that Thomas's scholastic vocation insulated him from the direct contacts with Jews that typically evoked expressions of anti-Jewish hostility among Christian disputants, missionaries, and inquisitors;[20] but from patristic times to the thirteenth century, numerous churchmen had polemicized against the Jews without any direct external stimulus. For his part, Aquinas dedicated no work to a refutation of Judaism. Rather, he composed his magisterial *Summa contra gentiles* to overcome the challenge posed to Christianity by disbelief in general. This work includes both Muslims and the heterodox Christian devotees of Averroes among its targets, such that modern scholars have debated extensively concerning its precise and primary intent—polemical, missionary, didactic, deliberative, or even inspirational. Resolution of the question need hardly concern us at the moment, and several brief observations suffice. Thomas grouped the teachings of the Jews alongside those of ancient pagans, Saracens, and others in his analysis and critique of infidels' beliefs; he espoused the same nonviolent conversionist policy toward them all,[21] and, from his perspective, there apparently remained little need to single out the Jews for specific *Adversus Iudaeos* arguments. Within its more general context, however, the *Contra gentiles* does attack "the fables of the Jews and the Saracens,"[22] and, on one occasion, in arguing that "God cannot will evil," it refers specifically to rabbinic literature: "Thus the error of the Jews, who say in the Talmud that God sometimes sins and is purged of sin, is refuted."[23] Writing not long after rabbinic texts had been burned in Paris during the 1240s, Thomas clearly knew of the Talmud,[24] and Marcel Dubois has suggested that as Aquinas wrote the *Contra gentiles*, he actually had the *Extractiones de Talmut*, the col-

---

20. On the exceptional instance of Thomas's reported disputation with—and conversion of—two Jews during a Christmas holiday in the 1260s, see Torrell, "*Ecclesia Iudaeorum*," pp. 1732, 1738 n. 1.

21. See Marie-Thérèse d'Alverny, "La Connaissance de l'Islam au temps de Saint Louis," in *Septième centenaire de la mort de Saint Louis* (Paris, 1976), pp. 243–44; and Frederick H. Russell, *The Just War in the Middle Ages* (Cambridge, England, 1975), chap. 7.

22. Thomas Aquinas, *Summa contra gentiles* 3.27.11, in *Opera omnia*, 2:69.

23. Ibid. 1.95.8, 2:24.

24. Cf. the additional disparaging references to the Talmud in Thomas Aquinas, *Super Ad Timotheum* 1 1.2, 4.2, in *Opera omnia* 6:489, 495. and *Super Ad Titum* 1.4, *Opera omnia*, p. 509.

lection of incriminating talmudic passages compiled by the church in
the wake of the papal condemnations, in front of him.[25] If one lends
credence to the admittedly questionable tradition that Raymond of
Penyafort solicited the composition of the *Contra gentiles* to buttress
his missionary campaigns among Muslims and Jews,[26] the work perhaps embodies Thomas's concurrence with his confrere's conviction
that the presence of the Jew and the Saracen in Christendom served no
positive purpose.

DISBELIEF, INTENTIONALITY, AND DEICIDE

The brief criticisms of Jewish fables and of the Talmud in the *Contra
gentiles* underscore the absence of any outright condemnation of postbiblical Judaism or of belief in the oral Torah in the corpus of Thomistic writings. Nonetheless, as noted in previous chapters, hand in
hand with the view of rabbinic Judaism as a heretical deviation from
the religion of the Old Testament went the notion that the rabbis knew
the truth of Christianity and rejected it deliberately; worst of all, the
Jewish sages of the first century crucified Jesus even though they understood his role as messiah and son of God. Thomas Aquinas took
the lead in developing the case for this conclusion on the basis of key
New Testament passages, in striking contrast with their earlier Augustinian interpretation—reaffirmed by Anselm of Canterbury, Peter Abelard, and many others—that Jesus' murderers had acted in ignorance
of his true character.[27] In the final part of the *Summa theologiae*, Tho-

25. Marcel Dubois, "Thomas Aquinas on the Place of the Jews in the Divine Plan,"
trans. David Maisel, *Immanuel* 24/25 (1990), 253. Cf. Willehad Paul Eckert, "Thomas
von Aquino—Seine Stellung zu Juden und zum Judentum," *Freiburger Rundbrief* 20
(1968), 31.

26. This question has been hotly disputed. The arguments and sources in its favor
have been amassed in Peter Marc's introduction to Thomas Aquinas, *Liber de veritate
catholice fidei contra errores infidelium*, ed. Peter Marc et al. (Turin, 1961–67), esp. 1:
52–79, and have been helpfully reviewed in Laureano Robles, "En torno a una vieja
polémica: El 'Pugio fidei' y Tomás de Aquino," *Revista española de teología* 34 (1974)
321–50, 35 (1975), 21–41. The most resounding refutation is that of A. Gauthier's introduction to Thomas Aquinas, *Contra gentiles: Livre premier*, trans. R. Bernier and M.
Corvez (Besançon, France, 1961); Gauthier's arguments have been accepted by many,
including Torrell, *"Ecclesia Iudaeorum,"* p. 1739 n. 7, and Dubois, "Thomas Aquinas,"
pp. 242–53 (with additional bibliography). Nevertheless, Marc's theory has found additional support in various quarters, including Robert I. Burns, "Christian-Islamic Confrontation in the West: The Thirteenth-Century Dream of Conversion," *AHR* 76 (1971),
1408–9; and Anthony Bonner's introduction to his translation of Raymond Lull, *Selected
Works* (Princeton, N.J., 1995), 1:95–96.

27. Cf. Jeremy Cohen, "The Jews as Killers of Christ in the Latin Tradition, from
Augustine to the Friars," *Traditio* 39 (1983), 1–27.

mas questioned "whether the persecutors of Christ recognized him," and he arrived at the following conclusion:

> Among the Jews some were elders [*maiores*] and some were uneducated [*minores*]. The elders, who were called their princes, knew . . . that he [Jesus] was the messiah promised in the law; for they beheld in him those things which the prophets had predicted for the future. Yet they were ignorant of the mystery of his divinity. . . . Even so, one must understand that their ignorance did not excuse them from their crime, since it was, in a sense, voluntary ignorance [*ignorantia affectata*]. For they beheld the blatant signs of his divinity, but they corrupted them out of hatred and jealousy of Christ; and they wished not to believe his words, by which he proclaimed himself to be the son of God.[28]

The Jewish sages recognized Jesus as their savior, and although they may not have recognized Jesus' divinity in a literal sense, Thomas hastened to argue that this in no way lessened their guilt. He noted that their voluntary, "affected" variety of ignorance—much like their willful resistance to the true faith—"does not excuse from guilt but seems rather to increase guilt. For it shows that a person is so bent on sinning that he wishes to bring ignorance upon himself, lest he avoid sinning. And thus the Jews sinned—the crucifiers not only of Christ the man but also as God."[29]

Simply put, the ancient Jewish sages engineered the crucifixion of their messiah intentionally. To the extent that ignorance impeded their vision of his divinity, such self-wrought ignorance itself derived from their sinful intentions and thus only compounded their culpability. Recalling the *Summa theologiae*'s taxonomy of disbelief, which ascribes the sin of *infidelitas* to the human will, one notes also how close the Thomistic understanding of the crucifixion comes to identifying the educated Jews of Jesus' day as heretics: The heretic has received the truth but acts contrary to its dictates; he has had the truth revealed to him but proceeds, cognizant of his intention, to reject it. How different were the Jewish scholars who had the truth concerning salvation in Christ revealed to them, who recognized the truth of Jesus' messiahship and intended not to understand the mystery of his divinity, and who killed him?

Two important premises would appear to lie at the heart of this Thomistic reasoning: the bifurcation of educated and uneducated Jews,

28. Thomas Aquinas, *ST* 3.47.5, 54:68.
29. Ibid. ad 3, p. 70.

and an emphasis on intention in appraising the value of human behavior. Distinguishing between the scholarly and the simple in ancient Jewry, Thomas adopted an interpretative strategy employed by many exegetes before him to reconcile scriptural evidence that the Jews killed their savior intentionally with that implying that they acted in ignorance. Thomas applied such a hierarchical classification of ancient Jews more extensively than did many of his predecessors; as we shall see, it appears elsewhere in the *Summa theologiae*, where it strengthens the impression that Aquinas perceived postbiblical Judaism as smacking of heterodoxy.

As for his concern with intentionality, Thomas did retreat somewhat from the extreme Abelardian position that culpability for a sinful act depends entirely on the intention of its agent. Yet he still maintained adamantly that the sinfulness of a deed not intrinsically evil does so depend on intention,[30] and this principle sheds light on the nature and magnitude of the guilt of Jesus' Jewish crucifiers. One should note that Thomas did not apply his category of voluntary ignorance (*ignorantia affectata*) solely to the Jewish deicides of old, but he derived its particular application here from more general ideas about the relationship between ignorance and guilt. In his earlier discourse *De malo* (On Evil), Thomas had already maintained that "when someone expressly desires to be ignorant, in order that he not be restrained from sin by reason of his knowledge, such ignorance excuses sin neither completely nor partially, but rather increases it."[31] In keeping with his primary attribution of sin to intention, Thomas could therefore argue that "when someone willfully ignorant falls as a result into a certain sin, the cause of that sin seems to be the will to be ignorant more than ignorance itself."[32] Thomas reasoned further in a different context that, when the Jews rejected the truth of Christ's miracles, they sinned directly against

---

30. For example, ibid. 1–2.20.3, 18:92: "quando actus exterior est bonus vel malus solum ex ordine ad finem, tunc est omnino eadem bonitas et malitia actus voluntatis, quae per se respicit finem, et actus exterioris, qui respicit finem mediante actu voluntatis." On intentionality in Thomistic ethics in general, see the recent analyses of Bonnie Kent, *Virtues of the Will: The Transformation of Ethics in the Late Thirteenth Century* (Washington, D.C., 1995), esp. pp. 155–75; and William J. Hoye, "The Erroneous Conscience and Truth According to Thomas Aquinas," in *Les Philosophies morales et politiques au Moyen Âge*, ed. R. Carlos Bazán et al. (Ottawa, 1995), 2:1049–58. I am grateful to Tamar Rudavsky for calling these studies to my attention. See also Odon Lottin, "Le Problème de la moralité intrinsique d'Abélard à Saint Thomas d'Aquin," *RT* 39 (1934), 477–515, which, though dated, retains its basic importance and value.

31. Thomas Aquinas, *De malo* 3.8, in *Opera omnia*, 3:290.

32. Ibid. 3.6.5, 3:288.

the Holy Spirit; that sin against the Holy Spirit derives from willful malice (*ex certa malitia*), whereas sin against the Father derives from weakness and sin against the Son from ignorance; and that such "malice does not excuse sin but increases it, and sin against the Holy Spirit is therefore forgiven neither in its entirety nor in part."[33] Blending the results of these like-minded Thomistic discussions, one can conclude the following: Although, on the face of it, willful malice (*certa malitia*) may appear incompatible with all forms of ignorance, Thomas observed that it goes hand in hand with voluntary ignorance (*ignorantia affectata*). Entirely unforgivable, playing essentially the same role in human behavior, both augment sin rather than excuse it.[34] Jewish sin against Jesus exemplified both voluntary ignorance and willful malice, resulting in the ultimate culpability. Inasmuch as guilt derives from the human will, the Jews acted toward Jesus out of the worst of intentions. Just as a sin of willful malice contrasts sharply with a sin of simple ignorance, so does the deicide of the Jews; a sin of voluntary ignorance, it was caused more by "the will to be ignorant than ignorance itself." In all but the most limited, technical sense, then, the deicide and the disbelief of the Jewish sages of Jesus' day were deliberate.

CONTEMPORARY JEWS AND THE LETTER OF THE LAW

Thomas's differentiation between educated and uneducated in ancient Jewry, coupled with his emphasis on intention in defining the good and

33. Thomas Aquinas, *Quaestiones de quodlibet* 2.8.1, in *Opera omnia*, 3:448; see also Thomas Aquinas, *ST* 2–2.14.1, 32:116–21.

34. On *certa malitia* in general, see the four articles of *ST* 1–2.78, 25:188–203. Although various translators have rendered *certa malitia* as set, fixed, deliberate, or resolute malice, I have followed the simplest sense of *ST* 1–2.78.1.1, 25:188, which stipulates: "Ignorantia enim opponitur industriae, seu certae malitiae." Yet, as Thomas made clear in his response to that argument, ibid. ad 1, p. 190, this does not rule out the convergence of willful malice and voluntary ignorance: "Quandoque autem [ignorantia] excludit scientiam qua aliquis scit hoc malum non sustinendum esse propter consecutionem illius boni, scit tamen simpliciter hoc esse malum: et *sic dicitur ignorare qui ex certa malitia peccat*." Cf. also *ST*'s description of voluntary ignorance, 1–2.76.4, 25:154: "Talis ignorantia directe et per se est voluntaria: sicut cum aliquis sua sponte nescit aliquid ut liberius peccet. Et talis ignorantia videtur augere voluntarium et peccatum: ex intensione enim voluntatis ad peccandum provenit quod aliquis vult subire ignorantiae damnum, propter libertatem peccandi." Concluding the discussion of willful malice, 1–2.78.4 in turn establishes that it, too, augments culpability, owing to the sinful intention that underlies it. The article closes, ad 4, p. 202, by noting that "ille qui peccat ex certa malitia, secundum se eligit malum. . . . Et ideo electio in ipso est principium peccati; ex propter hoc dicitur ex electione peccare."

the sinful in human behavior, leads to additional evidence that he construed postbiblical, contemporary Judaism as a heterodox distortion of biblical teaching. Along with several other scholastic masters of his century, Aquinas helped to rehabilitate the literal sense of the Old Testament in the study of Christian theology; not only among students of biblical exegesis but also among historians of Christian-Jewish relations has his treatise on the old law in the *Summa theologiae* won him praise and admiration.[35] Committed to their rationality and positive value, Thomas analyzed the commandments of Mosaic law with equanimity and insight. He highlighted the convergence between the law of nature and the law of Moses. He openly drew from the writings of the twelfth-century Jewish philosopher Moses Maimonides in elaborating the rationale of biblical precepts. Thomas thereby contributed roundly to medieval Christian understanding of biblical religion in its pre-Christian context. Modern readers may expect that his positive, naturalistic, Aristotelian exposition of Israelite law in its plentiful detail should have helped to lift the veil of ignorance, misunderstanding, and even fear from the eyes of many a Christian student of the Old Testament. Yet the logic of Thomistic exegesis drove a hermeneutical wedge between the literal observance of biblical Judaism and the religion of postbiblical Jews, not unlike the conviction in their disparity that nourished thirteenth-century condemnations of the Talmud. This line of reasoning, too, attests to the extent to which the construction of contemporary Judaism as a distortion of its ancient heritage had penetrated Christian thought.

In order to understand these ramifications of the Thomistic exegesis so often lauded for its favorable attitude toward Hebrew Scripture, one must consider its interpretation of Mosaic law at some length. The *Summa* classifies the commandments of the Jews' Torah under three rubrics: moral precepts (*moralia*), eternally binding ordinances that embody the provisions of natural law; ceremonial precepts (*caeremoni-*

35. See the important essays of Yves M.-J. Congar, "Le Sens de l'économie salutaire dans la 'théologie' de S. Thomas d'Aquin (*Somme théologique*)," in *Festgabe Joseph Lortz*, ed. Erwin Iserloh and Peter Manns (Baden-Baden, Germany, 1958), 2:73–122; Marie-Dominique Chenu, "La Théologie de la loi ancienne selon Saint Thomas," *RT* 61 (1961), 485–97; Amos Funkenstein, "Gesetz und Geschichte: Zur historisierenden Hermeneutik bei Moses Maimonides und Thomas von Aquin," *Viator* 1 (1970), 163ff.; Marvin Fox, "Maimonides and Aquinas on Natural Law," *Diné Israel* 3 (1972), V–XXXVI; and Beryl Smalley, "William of Auvergne, John of LaRochelle and St. Thomas Aquinas on the Old Law," in *St. Thomas Aquinas, 1274–1974: Commemorative Studies*, (Toronto, 1974), 1:52ff.

alia), or detailed applications of the moral laws in the realm of divine-human relations, laws whose validity ceased with the institution of Christianity; and judicial precepts (*iudicialia*), or applications of the moralia in relations between human beings, which may or may not remain valid after the founding of Christianity. Of these three categories, the conflict between Christianity and Judaism pertained chiefly to the ceremonial laws. The Jews claimed to understand and observe these commandments in their historical, literal sense, whereas Christians typically understood them as prefigurations of the new covenant between Christ and his church. Early medieval Christian exegesis generally viewed the literal sense of these ceremonial laws as devoid of positive value, but thirteenth-century theologians began to argue otherwise. The Dominican Thomas Aquinas followed William of Auvergne, bishop of Paris when the Talmud was first condemned, and the Franciscan John of La Rochelle in voicing confidence in the goodness and right reason of the ceremonial precepts' literal significance; and, of these writers, the ideas of Aquinas had the most lasting impact of all.

At the beginning of the *Summa theologiae* Thomas explained what he meant by the literal and spiritual senses of Holy Scripture: "Words serve to signify in all the sciences, but this science [of theology, grounded in Holy Scripture] has this distinctive characteristic: that the things signified by the words themselves serve to signify. That first meaning whereby the words signify things belongs to the first sense, which is the historical or literal sense. That meaning whereby the things signified by the words in turn signify other things is called the spiritual sense; it is based on and presupposes the literal sense." Thomas held that "the literal sense is that [sense] which the [human] author intends." The spiritual sense resides in that second tier of signification, whereby that which the words literally mean itself means something else; often hidden from the human author of the biblical text, it reveals the intention of the divine author of Scripture. Notably, Thomas deemphasized the traditional Pauline dichotomy between the deadly letter and life-giving spirit of the law, and he affirmed the primacy of the literal sense in no uncertain terms: "Nothing necessary for faith is contained within the spiritual sense that Scripture does not teach openly through the literal sense somewhere else."[36]

---

36. Thomas Aquinas, *ST* 1.1.10 and ad 1, 1:36–39 (drawing from the Blackfriars translation); see also Thomas Aquinas, *Quaestiones de quodlibet* 7.6.2–3, in *Opera omnia*, 3:479–80. And cf. the earlier comments of Augustine, chapter 1, nn. 76–77.

Much of Christianity's claim to validity, however, hinged on the cessation of the ceremonial laws of Moses and their replacement by— or, more precisely, their symbolic fulfillment in—the provisions of the New Testament. As scholars of Christian exegesis of the Bible have generally agreed, the standard medieval attitude toward the Jewish Torah traced its origins back to Origen. He, as Beryl Smalley has summarized,

> approached the Old Law as an apologist for the faith against both pagan philosophers and Jews and as a preacher to Christians. To the Jews, who continue to observe their Law, he exposed and derided the irrationality and seeming futility of many precepts: he sought and found biblical texts where precepts contradicted one another; other texts commanded practices which were "absurd" and even impossible to act upon; they made sense only if interpreted as figures of the Christian revelation to come. To pagan philosophers he argued that the Old Testament should be read in its spiritual sense. . . . Some precepts had no literal sense at all; most of them demanded a spiritual interpretation of the "letter."[37]

The ceremonial precepts of the old law thus put Thomistic exegesis to a formidable test. On one hand, they required that Thomas uphold the superiority and the victory of the law's Christological sense. On the other hand, they demanded that he establish the intrinsic worth of their literal sense. Compounding the difficulty, they also obligated him somehow to demonstrate the rational connection between spirit and letter, to clarify how the ultimately triumphant Christological sense proceeds logically from the meaning inherent in the literal sense. How did Aquinas confront this challenge? Where did his efforts lead?

Commenting on the old law in general, the *Summa* takes a first step toward defining the spiritual and literal meanings—or purposes—of the Mosaic commandments: "The old law was given by the good God, who is the father of our lord Jesus Christ. For the old law directed men toward Christ in two ways. In the first way by bearing witness to Christ. . . . In the second way by means of a certain predisposition: While restraining people from idolatry, it enclosed them within the worship of one God, by whom the human race would be saved through Christ."[38] The message is plain enough: The law derives from God and is consequently expressive of his goodness. In its spiritual sense, the law testifies concerning Christ with its figurative language. The literal

---

37. Smalley, "William of Auvergne," 1:12.
38. Thomas Aquinas, *ST* 1–2.98.2, 29:8–11, departing slightly from the Blackfriars translation.

sense of that very language prepared the recipients of the law to receive Christ both by banning idolatry and by enforcing the worship of the one God upon them. But this straightforward formula proves problematic in the case of the ceremonial precepts. When understood literally, how did seemingly senseless commandments, like the little-known ban on mixing wool and linen in the same garment (Deuteronomy 22:11) or the famed commandment to circumcise the male foreskin, unite the Israelites in monotheism and prepare them for their eventual salvation? As Thomas himself conceded, such "observances of the old law can be said to have no reason in their very nature."[39] Rather, "the ceremonial precepts of the old law had a reason in their orientation toward something else";[40] and, if so, what literal value did they retain?

We seem to have fallen upon a contradiction. Thomas maintained staunchly that the ceremonial laws had a rational purpose within their literal meaning, while he then acknowledged that that purpose resides beyond their literal meaning. The *Summa* encounters this difficulty with a more nuanced definition of the letter of Old Testament commandments and the relationship between their literal and spiritual senses:

> The reasons for the ceremonial precepts of the old law can be understood in two fashions. In one sense, by reason of the divine worship meant to be observed at that time [*pro tempore illo*]. These reasons are literal, whether they pertain to shunning the worship of idols, or to the recollection of certain gifts of God, or to the comprehension of the divine excellence, or else to the indication of the mind-set then required of those who worshiped God. In another sense, their reasons can be designated according to what they ordain for prefiguring Christ. In this sense do they have figurative and mystical reasons, whether they are understood regarding Christ and the Church (which concerns the allegorical sense), or the mores of Christian people (which concerns the moral sense), or the state of future glory insofar as we are led in to it through Christ (which concerns the anagogical sense).[41]

The symmetry of Thomas's argument clarifies that just as the spiritual meaning of Scripture includes its allegorical, moral, and anagogical senses, so does its literal meaning include more than one aspect of its signification. And although much of that literal meaning—commemoration of benefits received from God, comprehension of his excellence, and designation of the mentality required for his worship—may not

---

39. Ibid. 1–2.102.1 ad 1, 29:132–33, adopting the Blackfriars translation.
40. Ibid. ad 2.
41. Ibid. 1–2.102.2, 29:134.

infuse the simplest understanding of the ceremonial laws, Thomas still classified it as literal. The *Summa* proceeds immediately to explain:

> Just as the meaning of metaphoric language in Scripture is literal, since the words are used for the purpose of signifying such a meaning, so too do the meanings of the law's ceremonial precepts, which commemorate divine gifts (on whose account the precepts were established) or other such things that pertained to that period, not exceed the bounds of literal causes. Whence the reason specified for the celebration of the Passover, that it is a sign of the liberation from Egypt, or for circumcision, a sign of the covenant which God struck with Abraham, pertains to the literal purpose.[42]

The literal significance of Mosaic law surely includes its plain and simple meaning; it is *literal* in the first instance because it is not *symbolic* of anything else. Yet the same literal meaning extends also to that which the ceremonial precepts *symbolized* in the religion of ancient Israel, though still retaining its *literal* character because it is not *spiritual,* or directly significative of Christ and his church.

Seeking to overcome the dilemma between his positive evaluation of the literal sense of the old law and its negative appraisal so endemic to traditional Christian theology, Aquinas attempted to straddle the proverbial fence. In their nonsymbolic literal meaning the ceremonial precepts lacked inherent value; they simply militated against behavior that, in the ancient Near East, might have smacked of idolatry. Much of their symbolic significance, however, still belonged to their "nonspiritual" literal sense, inasmuch as it did not pertain to the prefiguration of Christianity. When Thomas set out to explain the ceremonial laws, then, he often distinguished three layers of meaning: (a) the simplest, literal meaning, as we—and many of his early medieval predecessors—may have construed the term, on one hand; (c) the spiritual or Christological meaning, on the other hand; and, somewhere in between, (b) the symbolic meaning that pertained to the right worship of God in ancient Israel, which Thomas included within the literal meaning. One may consider several ceremonial commandments by way of example. Just as the law of Moses forbade the interweaving of wool and linen in clothing, so did it prohibit planting mixed species of seeds (Leviticus 19:19, Deuteronomy 22:9) and plowing with an ox and a donkey together (Deuteronomy 22:10). The *Summa* airs a putative challenge to these laws' rationality; and, in quoting its reply, I designate the various layers of signification as specified just above:

42. Ibid. ad 1, 29:134–37.

(a) All these agricultural mixtures were prohibited in their literal sense, out of an aversion for idolatry; since the Egyptians, in their worship of the stars, made various blends of seeds, animals and clothing, signifying various conjunctions of stars. (b) Or, all the different mixtures of this sort were forbidden out of an aversion for unnatural coition. (c) Nevertheless, they do have a figurative reason. For the statement, "You shall not sow your vineyard with different seeds," should be understood spiritually to the effect that the Church, which is a spiritual vineyard, may not be sown with different doctrines. So, too, the field, that is the Church, must not be sown with different seeds, that is with doctrine both Catholic and heretical. Nor might one plow with an ox and an ass at the same time; for a fool should not be paired with a wise man in preaching, since one would impede the other.[43]

The *Summa* similarly considers numerous regulations of the Israelites' sacrificial cult, and it questions why God limited animal sacrifice to oxen, sheep, goats, and doves, when he could have insisted on many better species. Again Thomas offered a tripartite explanation:

(a) First, to prevent idolatry, since idolaters offered all the other animals to their gods, or they used them for sorcery. Among the Egyptians, however, with whom the people used to dwell, it was considered abominable to kill these animals, for which reason they did not sacrifice them to their gods. . . . (b) Second, this was appropriate for the aforementioned orientation of the mind of man toward God, and this in two ways. First because animals of this sort above all are those through which human life is sustained, and because they are the cleanest and have the cleanest food. . . . Second because the purity of the mind was signified by the sacrifice of these animals. . . . It is obvious that charity and simplicity of the mind are symbolized in the dove. (c) Third, it was appropriate that these animals be offered as a figure of Christ. For, as is stated in the same gloss [just quoted by Aquinas], Christ is offered in the calf on account of the power of the cross, in the lamb on account of his innocence, in the ram on account of his dominion, in the goat on account of his appearance of sinful flesh. The union of his two natures was demonstrated by the turtledove and pigeon.[44]

The third level of significance of the commandments, their (c) spiritual or figurative (or Christological) sense, should be clear, and it requires no further comment here. But let us briefly reconsider these passages with an eye on the two dimensions of what Thomas construed as the literal sense. In the first instance, the regulations governing the sacrifices and other ceremonial commandments (a) served to deter the ancient Israelites from idolatry, because they forbade practices char-

43. Ibid. 1–2.102.6 ad 9, 29:226.
44. Ibid. 1–2.102.3 ad 2, 29:142–45 (drawing on the Blackfriars translation).

acteristic of the surrounding pagans and purposefully ordained that which the pagans deemed repugnant. Here Aquinas relied heavily both on the Aristotelian logic and on the specific historical arguments of Moses Maimonides' magnum opus, *The Guide of the Perplexed*, which had probably appeared in Latin translation by 1220.[45] Like Rabbi Moses, Friar Thomas rationalized cultic precepts, whose details otherwise appeared arbitrary and philosophically valueless, in terms of a specific sociohistorical context: the idolatrous ancient Near East at the time of the biblical Moses. In so doing, Thomas infused the simple, detailed, nonsymbolic literal sense of the ceremonial commandments with rational purpose that still derived from external historical contingencies and not from the essence of the precepts themselves. Yet although such a Maimonidean interpretation of particular ceremonial precepts contributed extensively to the *Summa*'s analysis, it did not suffice. For Thomas had also to establish a logical connection between literal and spiritual senses of Scripture, demonstrating that the precepts themselves had intrinsic worth; in the case of these commandments, he had to incorporate the primary intention of their ancient Jewish legislator—the basic definition of the literal sense, as we recall—into a specifically Christian scheme of salvation history. Accordingly, he discerned (b) another dimension of meaning in the literal sense of the ceremonial laws, a symbolic one but not an overtly "spiritual" or Christological one, and one he could reasonably ascribe to the worldview of Hebrew Scripture's Israelite author. Describing the literal sense of Mosaic law, in a passage quoted above, Thomas specified that "(a) while restraining people from idolatry, (b) it enclosed them within the worship of one God, by whom the human race would be saved through Christ." One notes with curiosity, perhaps even with a measure of amusement, how different investigators of medieval theology have appreciated this Thomistic innovation. One modern Jewish scholar has argued that Aquinas hereby transposed Maimonides' propaedeutic interpretation of specific ceremonial commandments to the whole of the ceremonial law of Moses, insofar as it intended to predispose the Jews to some other, greater good located beyond itself.[46] For their part,

---

45. On the Latin translation of the *Guide* see Smalley, "William of Auvergne," 1: 25–26.

46. Funkenstein, "Gesetz und Geschichte," pp. 167ff. Funkenstein's analysis sheds valuable light on the logic underlying the intermediate sense (b) in the Thomistic understanding of the ceremonial precepts.

Christian scholars have recently contended that Aquinas endowed the law's literal purpose with a symbolic dimension totally lacking in Maimonidean hermeneutic, symbolism designed to refute the Maimonidean challenge that the commandments "could be understood as rational without positing Christ as their end."[47] Whatever the case, this additional dimension to the literal meaning of Mosaic law, a symbolic meaning within the intention of its human author and not hidden within the purpose of its divine author, allowed Thomas to inject Aristotelian realism into his reading of the Bible without compromising that most essential principle of Christian theology: that the Old Testament had given way to the New.

We have come quite a distance, and one may reasonably wonder why, perhaps even joining company with scholars[48] who have discerned problems or inconsistencies in the Thomistic schema outlined here: How do the three levels on which Thomas interpreted the ceremonial precepts relate to one another? Exactly where do the boundaries between them lie? What inner logic combines them within a coherent Christian view of salvation history? Although my purpose is not to defend Aquinas against such criticism, I believe that some additional reflection on these questions will, at last, reveal the importance of Thomistic exegesis of the Old Testament in our story.

Facilitating the reconciliation of the law's historical validity with its present invalidity, Thomas grounded his understanding of the literal and figurative senses of the ceremonial precepts in a notion of historical appropriateness.[49] To testify to the future redemption, to induce people in the direction of monotheism, to provide for the observance of natural law, and to underscore its own inadequacies, the revelation of the old law was appropriate. In view of its relative imperfection, God appropriately revealed it through the mediation of angels. Owing to their monotheism and the birth of the savior among them, the Jewish people

47. Hood, *Aquinas and the Jews*, p. 41; Adrian Schenker, "Die Rolle der Religion bei Maimonides und Thomas von Aquin," in *Ordo sapientiae et amoris: Image et message de Saint Thomas d'Aquin . . . Hommage au Professeur Jean-Pierre Torrell*, ed. Carlos-Josaphat Pinto de Oliveira, Studia friburgensia n.s. 78 (Fribourg, Switzerland, 1993), pp. 186ff.

48. For instance, Smalley, "William of Auvergne," 1:55–56.

49. On the Jewish and Christian background to this Thomistic notion, see Stephen D. Benin, "Jews and Christian History: Hugh of St. Victor, Anselm of Havelberg and William of Auvergne," in *FWW*, pp. 203–19, and *The Footprints of God: Divine Accommodation in Jewish and Christian Thought* (Albany, N.Y., 1993).

appropriately received it. The appearance of a Jewish nation in the
wake of the exodus, coupled with increasing disregard for natural law
among all peoples, made the time appropriate for the law.[50] Individual
precepts responded appropriately to specific characteristics of the Jews,
carnal, stubborn, and greedy as they were. Among all these considerations, the temporal or time-bound appropriateness of the Mosaic precepts stands out as critical. Given the state of human nature in the
wake of the fall from Eden, on one hand, and the goal of future salvation through Christ, on the other, "it was fitting for the old law to
be given midway between the law of nature and the law of grace."[51]
The various purposes of the ceremonial commandments—to prevent
idolatry, to inculcate the values of monotheism, and to prefigure Christianity—all befitted the particular historical context of ancient Israel.
In a word, these precepts "were established for the worship of God *at
that time [pro tempore illo]*."[52] And here lies the root of their enigmatic
character, imperfect and perfect. For just as "nothing prevents something from being essentially imperfect even though it is perfect for its
time *[perfectum secundum tempus]*,"[53] so did the ceremonial laws,
though not intrinsically good, derive their limited value from their appropriateness to a particular time. Once that temporal context passed,
so did that limited perfection. "The literal reasons for the ceremonial
precepts designated above are related to divine worship, which was
grounded in faith in him who would come. Therefore, with the coming
of the one who was to come, that worship terminated, along with all
the reasons ordained for that worship."[54]

Thomas had defined the literal sense of Scripture, recall, as the
meaning intended by the human author of the biblical text, whereas
the spiritual sense conveyed the purpose of God, which the human
author frequently could not fathom. In the case of the ceremonial precepts, however, the integrity of the literal sense depended so heavily on
its limited, provisional validity, that one can hardly conceive of the
law's human legislator as ignorant of those limitations. If one realized

---

50. Thomas Aquinas, *ST* 1–2.98.3–6, 29:12–29.
51. Ibid. 1–2.98.6, 29:28.
52. Ibid. 1–2.102.5, 29:182 (emphasis mine); cf. above, nn. 41–42.
53. Ibid. 1–2.98.2 ad 1, 29:10.
54. Ibid. 1–2.103.3 ad 3, 29:242. Cf. also 1–2.98.2 ad 2, 29:10: "Dicendum quod
opera Dei perseverant in aeternum, quae sic Deus fecit ut in aeternum perseverent: et
haec sunt ea quae sunt perfecta. Lex autem vetus reprobatur tempore perfectionis gratiae,
non tanquam mala, sed tanquam infirma et inutilis pro isto tempore."

that the validity of the law's literal sense would cease, shouldn't one have necessarily recognized the preeminence of the spiritual sense that would supersede it? How could Moses and other learned Israelites have failed to discern the limited appropriateness of their law's literal meaning and its eventual nullification by the New Testament, prefigured in the spiritual sense of Hebrew Scripture?

Aquinas's differentiation between the literal sense (in its two dimensions) and the spiritual sense of Mosaic law therefore corresponds with his distinction between educated and uneducated in ancient Jewry, mentioned above in connection with Jewish responsibility for the crucifixion. In his commentary on Romans, Thomas actually classified biblical Jews into three groups, which neatly matched the three purposes of the ceremonial laws (two literal, one spiritual): (a) the "stubborn [*duri*], that is, the sinners and rebels," whom these laws sought to deter from idolatry; (b) the proficient (*proficientes*), for whom the ceremonial law was a teaching tool, instructing them in the worship of God; and (c) the perfect (*perfecti*), for whom the biblical cult signified salvation in Christ.[55] So too does the *Summa theologiae* link the various reasons for the commandments to (a) the stubborn (*duri*), the proud (*superbi*), and those prone to evil (*proni ad malum*) as opposed to (b) the good (*boni*),[56] and then to the people at large as opposed to (c) the priests, who explicitly grasped much of the Christological significance of the cultic rituals they performed.[57] The best of the ancient Israel, among whom Moses the prophetic legislator unquestionably numbered, understood both the literal purpose of the ceremonial law, linked to its specific historical time and circumstances, and its signification of a future spiritual fulfillment in the church. The Hebrew patriarchs and prophets had explicit faith in Christ, and this faith served to justify them despite the imperfection of their law: "Although the old law did not suffice for the salvation of humankind, additional help was made available to humans by God along with the law, through which they might be saved: namely, faith in the mediator, through which the ancient fathers were justified *just as we ourselves are justified*."[58] Although their "observance of the ceremonial precepts" did not justify

55. Thomas Aquinas, *Super Epistolam ad Romanos* 5.6, in *Opera omnia*, 5:462; see Hood, *Aquinas and the Jews*, p. 42.
56. Thomas Aquinas, *ST* 1–2.98.6, 29:26; 1–2.101.3, 29:122.
57. Ibid. 1–2.102.4 ad 4, 29:162.
58. Ibid. 1–2.98.2 ad 4, 29:12.

the Israelite fathers, it "was a sort of declaration of faith, insofar as these rites were figures of Christ."[59]

All this changed drastically with the incarnation, when the temporal appropriateness of the ceremonial precepts came to an end. The same observance that once had constituted a profession of faith now entailed mortal sin:

> All the ceremonial precepts are declarations of faith, which constitutes the interior worship of God. Now a person may declare his inner faith through his deeds, just as in his speech; and in either kind of declaration, if a person declares something false, he sins mortally. Although the faith in Christ which we have is the same as that which the ancient fathers had, still, since they preceded Christ and we follow, this very faith is represented by us and by them in different words. For it used to be stated by them, "Behold a virgin shall conceive and bear a son," which are words relating to a time in the future; yet we convey the same thing with words relating to the past, saying that she conceived and bore. So too the ceremonial precepts of the Old Law used to signify Christ as yet to be born and yet to suffer; our sacraments, however, signify him as having already been born and having already suffered. So, just as one who, in declaring his faith, would say that Christ was yet to be born—which the ancients used to say piously and truthfully—would now sin mortally, so too would one who now observed the ceremonial precepts, which the ancients used to observe piously and faithfully, commit mortal sin.[60]

This Thomistic condemnation of Jewish ritual after the life and death of Jesus resonates with a message that must be elaborated with care. In comparing the observance of the ceremonial commandments to a profession of faith, the *Summa* portrays the mortal sin of such observance after Jesus as an intentional sin of the will. Neither faith nor sin, believed Thomas, can be unintentional. In the case of faith, "the mind of a believer comes to be set on a specific belief not through reason but through the will";[61] as for sin, "that which is the proper and inherent cause of sin is the very will to sin," and "if an act is altogether involuntary, it is has no measure of sin."[62] The successful function of Mosaic rituals as a profession of explicit faith, especially in view of their intrinsic worthlessness, required that the performer of these rites understand their Christological significance—or, at the very least, their time-bound appropriateness—and observe them intentionally for that

59. Ibid. 1–2.103.2, 29:236–39.
60. Ibid. 1–2.103.4, 29:246.
61. Ibid. 2–2.2.2 ad 3, 31:64.
62. Ibid. 1–2.73.6, 25:76.

reason. Only thus could Thomas write that "the faith in Christ which we have is the same as that which the ancient fathers had." Logically, the same measure of intentionality that characterizes the profession of faith, whether in deed or in word, before the life of Jesus underlies its profession after his death. Therefore, "just as one who, in declaring his faith, would say that Christ was yet to be born—which the ancients used to say piously and truthfully—would now sin mortally, so too would one who now observed the ceremonial precepts, which the ancients used to observe piously and faithfully, commit mortal sin."

The reasoning of this Thomistic comparison dictates that just as the ancient fathers understood and intended the Christological implications of their observance of the law, so does the knowledgeable person who remains committed to the ceremonial law after Jesus intend the falsehood inherent in such action. Intention provides the key to an appraisal of such religious behavior. If the early Christian apostles continued to observe Jewish law after the crucifixion, they did so not out of obedience to the law per se but in order not to scandalize potential Jewish converts; owing to their intention, they did not commit mortal sin.[63] Thomas concluded similarly in the case of the judicial precepts: Although "the intention to observe them out of obedience to the law would subvert the truth of the faith, since it would thus be signified that the prior state of the people still prevailed and that Christ had not yet come,"[64] one who observed them for their social or political value

---

63. Ibid. 1–2.103.4 ad 1, 29:246–49. I find no support for Martin D. Yaffe's contention that the discussion of mortal sin in this article of the *Summa* applied exclusively to Jewish or Judaizing Christians, and not to Jews in general; see Yaffe's review of *Aquinas and the Jews*, by John Y. B. Hood, *AJSR* 22 (1997), 123–24. Although the sinfulness of Jewish practice after Calvary immediately raised the thorny matter of Jesus' Jewish apostles, both for Aquinas and for church fathers like Jerome and Augustine before him, the essential issue remained that of the observance of the law per se and the intention underlying such observance. Cf. the commentary in Thomas Aquinas, *Summa cum commentariis . . . Thomae de Via Caietani* (Venice, 1588), 2, 1:234: "Ceremonialia absolute et simpliciter non potuerunt post Christum immediate observari absque mendacio pernicioso, et propterea hodie servari non possunt, nec tunc servari absolute, quoniam absolute servata servantur ut viva, et necessaria ad salutem ex lege veteri, quod post Christum nunquam licuit. . . . Propter quod nunc nec ut viva propter mendacium nec ut mortua propter sepulturam [synagogae matris] iam servari possunt cremonialia illa absque peccato mortali." For Jews and Christians alike, then, observing the ritual laws of the Old Testament now invariably entails mortal sin. For the key patristic texts, see Jerome, *Epistulae* 112, CSEL 55:367–93; and Augustine, *Epistulae* 82, CSEL 34,2: 351–87. See also François Dolbeau, ed., "Sermons inédits de Saint Augustin prêchés en 397 (2ᵉᵐᵉ série)," *RB* 102 (1992), 44–63; and Carolinne White, ed., *The Correspondence between Jerome and Augustine of Hippo*, Studies in Bible and Early Christianity 23 (Lewiston, N.Y., 1990).

64. Thomas Aquinas, *ST* 1–2.104.3, 29:260.

did not commit mortal sin. Yet educated Jews who continued to observe their ceremonial law for its own sake did sin mortally; cognizant of the invalidity of the Mosaic commandments' literal sense, they had unquestionably sinful intentions.

The Thomistic analysis of Mosaic law manifests a perception of postbiblical Jews far different from the constructions of Jews underlying the Augustinian doctrine of Jewish witness. The postbiblical Jew of Augustinian theology differed little from the biblical Jew of Augustinian theology, one who rejected Christian salvation out of blind ignorance and lived on in Christendom as an instructive relic of the past. For Augustine, the Jew served that instructive purpose because he continued to observe and to embody the literal sense of the Old Testament; thus could Bernard of Clairvaux dub the Jews "living letters of the law." For Aquinas, however, Jewish observance of the Mosaic commandments now amounts to nothing less than a repudiation of their literal sense, which limited their appropriateness to a particular period in the past. Although Thomas's Jewish policy stood squarely within Augustinian tradition, the Jew who emerged from his biblical hermeneutic and his theology challenged the very rationale for that policy. Every time a Jew now observes a commandment from his law, he violates God's ancient covenant with Israel in its literal as well as its Christological sense. Moreover, just as the Jewish leaders crucified Jesus intentionally, knowing that he was their savior and choosing not to know that he was their God, so have learned Jews abandoned the letter of their law willfully. They have chosen to profess falsehood, and in that they resemble heretics, deliberate unbelievers. Thus freeing the literal sense of Scripture from the Jews and incorporating it into his Aristotelian philosophy of nature and Christian philosophy of history, Thomas proceeded to characterize Judaism as a variety of *infidelitas*, not as sui generis. One need not be Jewish to function as a Jew in the divine economy of salvation; merely "to do something with the intention that the precepts of the law be upheld is to Judaize."[65]

Not only in his interpretation of the crucifixion but also in his masterful analysis of biblical law did Thomas blur the distinction between contemporary Judaism and heresy. Like other thirteenth-century churchmen who condemned rabbinic literature, he too suggested that postbiblical Jews had consciously forsaken the divinely ordained reli-

---

65. Thomas Aquinas, *In 4 Sententiarum* 11.2.2.3 ad 7, in *Opera omnia*, 1:480.

gion of their Israelite ancestors. Regardless of whether he met and co-operated with Paul Christian and Raymond Martin in the late 1260s or early 1270s in Paris, Friar Thomas Aquinas echoed the ideological basis for their newly aggressive program of anti-Judaism, even as he opposed its implementation in practice.

Afterword

> I am a Jew. Hath not a Jew eyes? Hath not a Jew hands,
> organs, dimensions, senses, affections, passions? fed with the
> same food, hurt with the same weapons, subject to the same
> diseases, healed by the same means, warmed and cooled by
> the same winter and summer, as a Christian is? If you prick
> us, do we not bleed? if you tickle us, do we not laugh? if
> you poison us, do we not die? and if you wrong us, shall
> we not revenge?
>
> *William Shakespeare,* The Merchant of Venice

Shylock's thirst for revenge notwithstanding, his impassioned words in
the third act of Shakespeare's *Merchant of Venice* reverberate with a
double truth. As much as the rhetoric of this speech demands affirmative answers for Shylock's questions, both he and Shakespeare well
understood that European Christendom construed the Jew irrespective
of these basic human attributes. So, too, did a thirteenth-century Jewish
writer observe: "Behold how many Gentiles there are who ask if Jews
have a mouth or an eye or a nose!"[1] Christian culture had crafted a
Jew in keeping with the needs of its doctrine, as a foil for its interpretation of the Bible, and as an instructive antithesis of its own self-image.
This Jew served a purpose that has empowered him in Christendom;
his alterity has rendered him a vital character on that stage to which
the greatest of Western playwrights aptly likened "all the world."[2]

  This book has studied several key stages in the medieval career of

---

1. Moses ben Solomon of Salerno, *Ṭa'anot*, cited in David Berger, *The Jewish-
Christian Debate in the High Middle Ages: A Critical Edition of the Niẓẓaḥon Vetus,*
Judaica: Texts and Translations 4 (Philadelphia, 1979), p. 340. See the similar observation in Abraham ibn Ezra, *Commentary . . . on Isaiah* 52:14, ed. M. Friedlaender
(London, 1877), Hebrew p. 91: "There are those peoples in the world that think that
the form of the Jew differs from all other forms, and they ask: Does a Jew have a mouth
or an eye? So have I heard regarding the lands of Ishmael and Edom."
2. William Shakespeare, *As You Like It* 2.7. On the role of the Judaic hermeneutical
alternative in Western literary tradition from Paul to Levinas, see Jill Robbins, *Prodigal
Son / Elder Brother: Interpretation and Alterity in Augustine, Petrarch, Kafka, and Levinas* (Chicago, 1991).

Christianity's theologically and hermeneutically crafted Jew. The idea or image of the Jew wielded cultural significance no less than the living Jews of the time, and, in this, medieval European Christianity numbers among a diverse array of cultures and ideologies that have identified their most feared and dangerous enemies with Jews and Judaism—from the Christianity of early medieval Byzantium, oppressed by Islam from without and iconoclasm from within, to Sunni Islam in its opposition to Shi'ism, and from antifeminism in nineteenth-century Germany to xenophobic nationalism in twentieth-century Japan.[3] Yet I hazard the judgment that the Jew hardly played as critical a role in the self-consciousness of the world of medieval Islam, in modern Japan, or even in nineteenth-century Germany as he did in patristic and medieval Christianity. The selected images of Jews and Judaism in Christian theology from late antiquity to the High Middle Ages that we have considered underscore the complexity and extent of that role, one that defies any simple summary or generalization. Neither did the voices assembled here construct the Jew and his religious praxis, the *forma Iudaeorum*, in a single, clear-cut fashion, nor did they fall neatly into a univocal pattern of development. With his roots at the very core of its received doctrine and its worldview, medieval Christianity's hermeneutically crafted Jew could assume a variety of appearances; relative measures of harshness and moderation in these representations fluctuated widely over time; not even in the works of an individual theologian can one always expect to find a perfect logic and consistency. Sifting through the results of these analyses, I can venture several concluding observations nonetheless.

The teaching of Paul, as it translated the historical reality of Christianity's Jewish origins into a theology of salvation history, defined the basic parameters for subsequent Christian reflection on the Jews; setting limits which no orthodox theologian could readily traverse, Paul contributed a degree of constancy to the history of ideas we have followed. On one hand, Paul affirmed the veracity of Hebrew Scripture

---

3. Among others, see the illuminating studies of Sheila Briggs, "Images of Women and Jews in Nineteenth- and Twentieth-Century German Theology," in *Immaculate and Powerful: The Female in Sacred Image and Social Reality*, ed. Clarissa Atkinson et al. (Boston, 1985), pp. 226–59; Kathleen Corrigan, *Visual Polemics in the Ninth-Century Byzantine Psalters* (Cambridge, England, 1992); David M. Olster, *Roman Defeat, Christian Response, and the Literary Construction of the Jew* (Philadelphia, 1994); Steven M. Wasserstrom, *Between Muslim and Jew: The Problem of Symbiosis under Early Islam* (Princeton, N.J., 1995); and David G. Goodman and Masanori Miyazawa, *The Jews in the Japanese Mind: The History and Uses of a Cultural Stereotype* (New York, 1995).

and the importance of its revelation to Israel in God's plan for the redemption of humankind. Jesus' earthly career and his gospel made sense only within the basic structures of Jewish tradition: In the wake of the fall from Eden, original sin crippled the human potential for finding eternal life, and the demanding precepts of Mosaic law, revealed by God to Israel at Mount Sinai, demonstrated the powerlessness of men and women to merit divine reward. The Jews, observing the Old Testament in order to establish its inadequacies, had thus facilitated the salvation of all humanity in the New Testament, and the savior had appropriately been born in their midst. They had performed a vital function in the divine blueprint for human history, which no doubt bore upon the Pauline conviction that God would ultimately save them when this historical drama reached its end. Their salvation would cement the reconciliation—and bear witness to the perfect equivalence—of old and new covenants, both of them the word of the beneficent, all-powerful deity. On the other hand, Paul construed the continued observance of the law of the Torah as an exercise in futility: It could not earn a person redemption; it served, rather, to accentuate the sinful depths into which postlapsarian human nature had fallen; and, as the hallmark of Jewish identity, it distinguished Paul's enemies within the early church, Christians committed to remaining in the Jewish community, from his uncircumcised Gentile converts. In practice, a life of Torah constituted the antithesis of the rebirth in Christ's saving grace that Paul sought to promote. "For the written code kills, but the spirit gives life" (2 Corinthians 3:6). Ambivalence toward the Jew, based on a Christian hermeneutic for interpreting Scripture and history, thus began with Christianity's first great theologian.

What impact did this ambivalence have upon our story? Church fathers and medieval Catholic theologians generally proceeded from the premise that the Jews had, in fact, been God's chosen people. God had legislated the laws of their Old Testament in order to lay the groundwork for their fulfillment in the New. Not by happenstance was Jesus born a Jew. Moreover, God's favor for the Jews would again find renewed expression at the end of days. Then "will these natural branches be grafted back into their own olive tree," and "all Israel will be saved" (Romans 11:24–26). Although subsequent Christian thinkers may have subjected Paul's ideas to endless debate and a broad spectrum of interpretation, few could deny that at least in some basic, minimal sense, a Pauline scheme of salvation history guaranteed respectability to the Judaism of the past and to the Jews (who would convert) in the future.

But what of the Jew of the present, who lived in Christendom, here and now? Did his role as connecting link between the Jewish past and future entitle him to share in their positive valuation? Or, epitomizing the carnality, sinfulness, and hopelessness of the old covenant, should he properly evoke the rejection of all those who upheld the spirituality, atonement, and promise of the new? Maintaining the Pauline tradition, medieval Christianity ordinarily recognized the Jews as a textually defined community that still had a role to play in Christian history and therefore had to survive. On a theoretical level, popes, jurists, and theologians customarily acknowledged the need for that survival, and few ventured to advocate the general expulsion of all Jews from a properly ordered Christendom. With that as a given, however, perceptions could still—and did—vary extensively: How did the Jew of the present "fit" in Christian society? What purpose did he and his Judaism serve in their presence?

Against the background of Paul and the intervening fathers of the church, Augustine set the tone for much medieval Christian representation of the Jew with his doctrine of Jewish witness. Even as he echoed the *Adversus Iudaeos* formulations of his patristic predecessors, considerations of exegesis, the philosophy of history, and anthropology led Augustine to ascribe importance not only to the Jews of the past and future but also to those of the sixth, penultimate age of human history—at least as he perceived them. Just as the Jew had had a critical role to play in salvation history between Sinai and Calvary and would again function indispensably at Armageddon, so did his continued residence in Christendom serve a vital purpose; his Scripture, its expression through his practice of Judaism, and his subjugated status all testified to Christianity's fulfillment of God's biblical covenant with Israel. Augustine added a new dimension to the identification of Israel with its sacred texts. "Slay them not," he instructed Christians, precisely because they embody their scriptures; as Augustine imagined the Jews, they are no less than the living letters of their law.

Grounded in Pauline teaching, the Augustinian doctrine of witness thus provided medieval Christianity with a point of departure for crafting a Jew to suit its reading of history and its view of the world: From Augustine's perspective, the Jew belonged in Christendom, in much the same way as the Old Testament belonged in the Bible. During the centuries that followed Augustine medieval theologians received, resisted, modified, adapted, challenged, and undermined—but never rejected outright—his injunction of "Slay them not." By the thirteenth century, prominent churchmen perceived the European Jew as one who no longer fulfilled the role that Augustine had given him, as one who had deviated from the letter and life of the biblical text that it was his purpose to maintain. Again, I reiterate that there were numerous exceptions to this course of development; and, as I have endeavored to show, a particular thinker's constructions of the Jews and Judaism in the first instance demand appreciation as a product of his entire theological system. Nevertheless, our findings corroborate a trend away from the Augustinian model, coupled with a progressive rise in Christian estimations of the culpability of the Jew.

We have observed how at least three clusters of factors contributed to this pattern of change. First, Augustine's distinctive construction of the Jew derived from a worldview that found positive value in the literal sense of Scripture, in human sexuality, and, above all, in the saeculum of terrestrial history. As early medieval churchmen ceased to share in those convictions, the place of the Jew in the new Christian order that they strove to forge proved more difficult to define. Even as powerful prelates acknowledged legal and doctrinal precedents for the protection of Jews in their communities, they directed their interests and energies toward minimizing the influence of the Jew in Christian society and toward inducing his conversion. Second, as Latin Christendom entered the age of the Crusades, its encounter with the non-Christian world and the burgeoning of its cultural renaissance heightened sensitivity to nonbelief and dissidence in their many forms. Profound change in all aspects of European life generated a penchant for reevaluation and reclassification in Christian civilization, which in turn caused the singularity and privilege of the Jew in Christian eyes to diminish. Whereas the doctrine of witness had depicted a Jew who was unique, twelfth-century churchmen assessed the Jews in tandem with other infidels and with heretics, emphasizing that which the Jew shared with other "others," casting him as but a subset in a larger genus of dissenters. To be sure, the twelfth century's revival of biblical studies, with its new concern for Scripture's literal sense, underscored the nexus between the Jew and the Old Testament. At the same time, however, the scholastic scrutiny of Judaism led some Christian thinkers to question exactly how Jews met the criteria for inclusion in the new cultural synthesis. For in their literalist reading of the Bible and in their talmudic homilies, the Jews displayed no commitment to reason; and this image intensified when Christians projected their own irrational beliefs and doubts onto the Jews. Imputed reverence for the irrational certainly undermined the Jew's ability to contribute to the Christian order of things by representing—or embodying—the revealed word of God's law; if the Jew no longer contributed to a properly ordered Christian society, why reserve for him a place of distinction on its map? And third, as Christian interest in postbiblical Jewish literature deepened, concern moved beyond the reputed absurdities of talmudic aggadot to the very essence of contemporary Judaism: its belief in the authority of the oral Torah and its rabbinic mediators. Talmudic Judaism had not remained stationary in useless antiquity. Its adherents did not uphold and represent an obsolete biblical law of old whose only acceptable development lay in the new covenant of the church. By the thirteenth century, popes and mendicant friars reacted to such perceived heresy in contemporary Judaism and the culpability of its proponents: Even beyond their rejection of Christianity, they had consciously distorted the biblical testimony and the testimonial function that God had allotted to their ancestors.

In all, the movement away from Augustinian doctrine was typically gradual, often incomplete, and notably erratic. Officially, the medieval Catholic Church never advocated the expulsion of all Jews from Christendom or repudiated the doctrine of Jewish witness;[4] where it had effectively ceased to be operative, as in the polemic of Raymond Martin, at least an acknowledgment of Paul's eschatological vision for the Jews remained.[5] Still, late medieval Christendom frequently ignored the mandates implied in "Slay them not, lest at any time they forget your law." The expulsion, harassment, and persecution of its Jews by prince, cleric, and layperson alike all bespoke opposing constructions of the Jew and his Judaism—to the effect that they had no proper place in Christendom—regardless of whether such ideas directly caused any particular act of hostility.

The actual treatment of the Jews in late medieval Christendom lies beyond the scope of this inquiry, and I conclude with some final, somewhat speculative thoughts on the doctrine of witness itself. At the heart of this teaching, both in its original Augustinian context and its ensuing medieval career, lies the bond between the Jew and the text of Scrip-

---

4. See Kenneth R. Stow, "Expulsion Italian Style: The Case of Lucio Ferraris," *Jewish History* 3 (1988), 51–63; and Gilbert Dahan, "Juifs et Judaïsme dans la littérature quodlibétique," in *FWW*, pp. 226ff.

5. See Raymond Martin's *Pugio fidei adversus Mauros et Iudaeos* (1687; reprint, Farnborough, England, 1967), 3.3.23, which addresses the future conversion of the remnants of the Jews (*de conversione reliquiarum suarum*).

ture. The Jew testifies to the law revealed by God; he preserves the books that contain this law; but, even more important, he lives the law in his everyday life. At first sight, this may appear astounding: Medieval Christianity related to the Jew certain that his Judaism, his Jewish life, constituted a text of the revealed word of God. Put more bluntly, the word of God was incarnate in the Jew!

Upon further reflection, however, this deduction should astound somewhat less. Rather, owing to the foundational importance of the doctrine of divine incarnation in Christian theology, it should demonstrate the corresponding centrality of the role played by Judaism—and the negation of Judaism—in patristic and medieval Christianity. Few contrasts express the self-consciousness of that early Christianity better than the one between *Synagoga* and *Ecclesia.* The synagogue represents the old covenant of the law, the life of the Jew; the church represents the new covenant of grace, the life of the Christian. The synagogue embodies the Old Testament, the church the New. In medieval iconography, both figures regularly stand under the outstretched arms of the crucified Jesus, while his passion facilitates the rejection of the one, often portrayed holding the tablets of the covenant, and the election of the other.[6] What might it mean, then, to construe the Jews as the living letters of the old law? Mutatis mutandis, its meaning may well approximate Christianity's understanding of the incarnation of the divine Word in the person of Jesus. As one New Testament scholar has recently explained: "The idea of incarnation seems to have been simply the articulation of a growing sense that Jesus shows what God is like more clearly than anyone or anything else, that it is Jesus who above all reveals God to humankind."[7] The doctrine of Jewish witness affirms that, subjugated and dispersed, the Jew likewise reveals God to humankind; until the incarnation of God in Jesus (the Jew par excellence), he did so more clearly than anyone or anything else. Yet now Jesus' new covenant, having fulfilled and canceled God's old covenant with Israel, has forever altered—but not expunged—the value of Judaism;

6. Among others, see Bernhard Blumenkranz, *Le Juif médiéval au miroir de l'art chrétien* (Paris, 1966); Wolfgang S. Seiferth, *Synagogue and Church in the Middle Ages: Two Symbols in Art and Literature,* trans. Lee Chadeayne and Paul Gottwald (New York, 1970); and Michael Camille, *The Gothic Idol: Ideology and Image-making in Medieval Art* (Cambridge, England, 1989), chap. 4.

7. James J. G. Dunn, "Why 'Incarnation'? A Review of Recent New Testament Scholarship," in *Crossing the Boundaries: Essays in Biblical Interpretation in Honour of Michael D. Goulder,* ed. Stanley E. Porter et al., Biblical Interpretation Series 8 (Leiden, Netherlands, 1994), p. 256.

Christianity must assert and negate that value at one and the same time.[8]

More than anything else, our story has featured the ambivalence in which medieval Christianity construed the Jew and Judaism. At the root of this ambivalence, of course, lie the origins of Christianity within Judaism and the ongoing interaction among adherents of the two faiths ever since. As is generally agreed, the Christian doctrine of divine incarnation itself grew out of the wisdom tradition in Judaism of the second temple period.[9] But it is not commonly recalled that subsequent rabbinic tradition produced a notion of the Jew as encasing or embodying God's law remarkably similar to that implicit in the doctrine of Jewish witness. In a letter of congratulations upon his marriage, wellwishers of the famed Sefardic rabbi Moses Maimonides (1138–1204) addressed him as "the ark of our covenant."[10] And, explaining the religious self-confidence of Ashkenazic Jewry in the twelfth century, Haym Soloveitchik has concluded that it "saw the word of God as being, as it were, incarnated in two forms: first, in the canonized literature (i.e., the Talmud); second, in the life of its people."[11] At the very time when Bernard of Clairvaux dubbed the Jews "living letters" of their law, medieval Jews may have developed a remarkably similar image of themselves and their rabbis! This self-perception may in turn constitute their adaptation of an idea of incarnation in talmudic sources, which similarly identify Jewish sages with the ark of the covenant and with the Torah itself, the actual substance of divine revela-

8. Miri Rubin has demonstrated insightfully how the special association of the Jew with the word of God incarnate in Jesus contributed to anti-Jewish charges of host desecration during the later Middle Ages, even after the Augustinian injunction of "Slay them not" had begun to fall on deaf ears. See her "Imagining the Jew: The Late Medieval Eucharistic Discourse," in *In and Out of the Ghetto: Jewish-Gentile Relations in Late Medieval and Early Modern Germany*, ed. R. Po-Chia Hsia and Hartmut Lehmann (Washington, D.C., 1995), pp. 177–208.

9. Cf. Dunn, "Why 'Incarnation'?" pp. 247ff.; and Jacobus Schoneveld, "Torah in the Flesh: A New Reading of the Prologue of the Gospel of John as a Contribution to Christology without Anti-Judaism," in *Remembering for the Future*, ed. Yehuda Bauer et al. (Oxford, 1989), 1:867–78.

10. The letter appears in Mordechai Akiva Friedman, "Two Maimonidean Letters" [Hebrew], in *Isadore Twersky Memorial Volume,* ed. Carmi Horowitz and Michael Schnidman (Jerusalem, forthcoming). I am grateful to Professor Friedman for his suggestions in this regard.

11. Haym Soloveitchik, "Religious Law and Change: The Medieval Ashkenazic Example," *AJSR* 12 (1987), 212. On the confidence of medieval Ashkenazic Jews in the collective piety of their communities, see also Ivan G. Marcus, "Un Communauté pieuse et le doute: Mourir pour la Sanctification du Nom (Qiddouch ha-Chem) en Achkenaz (Europe du Nord) et l'histoire de Rabbi Amnon de Mayence," *Annales: Histoire, sciences sociales* 49 (1994) 1031–47.

tion. In Jacob Neusner's view, "the reason that the Torah was made flesh was that the Torah was the source of salvation. When the sage was transformed into a salvific figure through his mastery of the Torah, it was an easy step to regard the sage as the living Torah."[12] The sage had the power to effect salvation, through the piety of his behavior and in the authority of his instruction, because he was the incarnate word of God. Thus did the Palestinian Talmud liken the tragedy of the death of a rabbinic scholar to the burning of a Torah scroll[13]—both of them, as it were, the textual repository of God's law.

Yet the Talmud drew closer to the nearly contemporary Augustinian doctrine of Jewish witness and its symbolic language by paying additional tribute to the sanctity of the Torah scholar. "One accords an elder who has forgotten his knowledge of the Torah through no fault of his own [mahmat onso] the same degree of sanctity due an ark [containing the Torah scroll]."[14] What justified this homiletic connection between the sage of lapsed memory and the ark? The proof lay in Deuteronomy 10:2, the language of whose divine injunction to Moses the rabbis understood as all-inclusive. "I will inscribe on the tablets the commandments that were on the first tablets which you smashed, and you shall deposit them in the ark"—them meaning that both the remnants of the first tablets and the second, replacement set of tablets belonged in the ark of the covenant. And so the Talmud could conclude concerning the erstwhile scholar: "Be careful with an elder who has forgotten his knowledge of the Torah through no fault of his own; for as they say, the tablets and the fragments of the tablets lie in the holy ark."[15]

Naturally, the rabbis would have hastened to point out that the very biblical prooftext underlying this prescription specified that the second set of "tablets of the covenant" contained the exact same commandments as the first set. There was here no hint of one covenant replacing another; rather, rabbinic midrash sought to underscore the permanent sanctity of the text of God's law, even after such a text—or its human analogue—had perished or suffered irreparable damage. Still, one must

---

12. Jacob Neusner, The Incarnation of God: The Character of Divinity in Formative Judaism, South Florida Studies in the History of Judaism 63 (1988; reprint, Atlanta, Ga., 1992), pp. 202ff., and "Is the God of Judaism Incarnate?" Religious Studies 24 (1988), 213–38.

13. Palestinian Talmud, Mo'ed Qatan 3.7, 83b. For additional examples, see Friedman, "Two Maimonidean Letters," appendix 2.

14. Ibid. 3.1, 81d.

15. Babylonian Talmud, Berakhot 8b.

take note: Both the Talmud and Augustine compared the Jew well schooled in the law to the sacred text of that law; like the sacred text, such a Jew embodied the word of God. Giving expression to this correspondence, both the Talmud and Augustine depicted a Jew schooled in the Torah as a has-been, the remnant of the smashed tablets of the covenant, scattered and trodden upon. Even so, both the Talmud and Augustine agreed that such a Jew, deprived of his knowledge and authority, retains his right to respect; he merits a legitimate place in the ark of the covenant, albeit in his fragmented state, beside the permanent text of the testament that has replaced him. Curiously, both the Talmud and Augustine deemed the Jew's loss of his authority unintentional (*maḥmat onso*), an event over which he had no conscious control.

Did Augustine derive his doctrine of Jewish witness directly from the Talmud? Although I would consider this possibility most unlikely, he may have encountered Origen's identification of the first tablets broken by Moses with the literal interpretation of the law and the second, replacement set of tablets with the law's spiritual fulfillment.[16] However this understanding of Deuteronomy 10:2 may have originated and been transmitted in Christian exegesis, I believe that in the living letters of the law one finds an instructive instance of a symbolic motif shared by classical Jews and Christians. Its parallel usage in their various traditions illuminates characteristics common to their respective mentalities. It highlights how thoroughly the tenets of Christianity remained intertwined with those of the Judaism that had spawned it. Perhaps it adds yet additional nuance to the language of ambivalence with which Christians constructed their hermeneutical Jew in late ancient and medieval times.

16. Origen, *In Genesim homiliae* 9.1 (in Rufinus's Latin translation), GCS 29:88: "Primas tabulas legis in littera confregit Moyses et abiecit; secundam legem in spiritu suscepit et sunt firmiora secunda quam prima." Mordechai Akiva Friedman has suggested to me that Origen's interpretation may have found a polemical rejoinder in the rabbinic claim that Moses, not God, wrote the second set of tablets; see his "The Phrase *Kir Yad* and the Signing of the Second Tablets of the Decalogue in Tosefta and Midrash" [Hebrew], *Te'udah* 7 (1991), 161–89. On Origen's familiarity with rabbinic interpretation of the Bible, see, among others, N. R. M. de Lange, *Origen and the Jews: Studies in Jewish-Christian Relations in Third-Century Palestine* (Cambridge, England, 1976), chaps. 9–10; and Marc Hirshman, *A Rivalry of Genius: Jewish and Christian Biblical Interpretation in Late Antiquity*, trans. Batya Stein (Albany, N.Y., 1996), chaps. 7–8. Interestingly, the tablets of the law served as a symbol of Judaism in Christian art long before they did so in Jewish art; see Gad B. Sarfatti, "The Tablets of the Law as a Symbol of Judaism," in *The Ten Commandments in History and Tradition*, ed. Ben-Zion Segal and Gershon Levi (Jerusalem, 1990), esp. pp. 390–402.

References

PRIMARY SOURCES

Abraham ibn Ezra. *Commentary . . . on Isaiah*. Ed. M. Friedlaender. 3 vols. London, 1877.

Alan of Lille. *Textes inédits*. Ed. Marie-Thérèse d'Alverny. Études de philosophie médiévale 52. Paris, 1965.

Anselm of Canterbury. *Opera omnia*. Ed. Franciscus Salesius Schmitt. 6 vols. Edinburgh, 1946–61.

―――. *Pourquoi Dieu s'est fait homme*. Ed. René Roques. SC 91. Paris, 1963.

Augustine. *De doctrina christiana*. Ed. R. P. H. Green. Oxford, 1995.

―――. *La Genèse au sens littéral*. Ed. P. Agaësse and A. Solignac. 2 vols. Oeuvres de Saint Augustin 48–49. Paris, 1972.

―――. *The Literal Meaning of Genesis*. Trans. John Hammond Taylor. 2 vols. Ancient Christian Writers 41–42. New York, 1982.

Benton, John F., ed. *Self and Society in Medieval France: The Memoirs of Abbot Guibert of Nogent*. 1970; reprint, Toronto, 1984.

Berger, David, ed. *The Jewish-Christian Debate in the High Middle Ages: A Critical Edition of the Niẓẓaḥon Vetus*. Judaica: Texts and Translations 4. Philadelphia, 1979.

Bernard Gui. *Practica inquisitionis heretice pravitatis*. Ed. Celestin Douais. Paris, 1886.

Bernard of Clairvaux. *On the Song of Songs*. Trans. Kilian Walsh and Irene M. Edmonds. 4 vols. Cistercian Fathers Series 4, 7, 31, 40. Kalamazoo, Mich., 1971–80.

―――. *Opera*. Ed. Jean Leclercq et al. 8 vols. Rome, 1957–77.

―――. *Treatises III*. Trans. M. Conrad Greenia. Cistercian Fathers Series 19. Kalamazoo, 1977.

Biblia sacra cum glossis, interlineari, et ordinaria, Nicolai Lyrani postilla, ac moralitatibus, Burgensis additionibus, et Thoringi replicis. 6 vols. Venice, 1588.

Blumenkranz, Bernhard, ed. "*Altercatio Aecclesie contra Synagogam*: Texte inédit du xe siècle." *RMAL* 10 (1954), 5–159.

Chazan, Robert, ed. *Church, State, and Jew in the Middle Ages.* New York, 1980.

Cross, Wilbur L., and Tucker Brook, eds. *The Yale Shakespeare.* New York, 1993.

David Kimchi. *Radicum liber* [Hebrew]. Ed. J. H. R. Biesenthal and F. Lebrecht. 1847; reprint, Jerusalem, 1967.

Dinur, Benzion. *Israel in the Diaspora* [Hebrew]. 2 vols. in 10 pts. Tel Aviv, 1958–72.

Dolbeau, François, ed. "Sermons inédits de Saint Augustin prêchés en 397 (2ème série)." *RB* 102 (1992), 44–74.

Eidelberg, Shlomo, ed. *The Jews and the Crusaders: The Hebrew Chronicles of the First and Second Crusades.* Madison, Wis., 1977.

Franciscus Zabarella. *In tertium Decretalium.* London, 1557.

Gilbert Crispin. *Disputatio Iudei et Christiani.* Ed. Bernhard Blumenkranz. Stromata 3. Utrecht, Netherlands, 1956.

———. *The Works of Gilbert Crispin, Abbot of Westminster.* Ed. Anna Sapir Abulafia and G. R. Evans. Auctores britannici Medii Aevi 8. London, 1986.

Goldschmidt, D. S., ed. *Seder ha-Qinnot le-Tish'a be-Av.* Jerusalem, 1968.

Goodspeed, Edgar J., ed. *Die ältesten Apologeten.* Göttingen, Germany, 1914.

Grayzel, Solomon. *CJ.* Rev. ed. New York, 1966.

———. *CJ, Volume II: 1254–1314.* Ed. Kenneth R. Stow. New York, 1989.

Grünbaum, Samuel, ed. *Wikkuaḥ Rabbenu Yeḥiel mi-Paris.* Toruń, Poland, 1873.

Guibert of Nogent. *Autobiographie.* Ed. Edmond-René Labande. Les Classiques de l'histoire de France au Moyen Âge 34. Paris, 1981.

Hermann of Cologne. *Opusculum de conversione sua.* Ed. Gerlinde Niemeyer. MGH Quellen zur Geistesgeschichte des Mittelalters 4. Weimar, Germany, 1963.

Hinschius, Paulus, ed. *Decretales pseudo-isidorianae et capitula angilramni.* 1863; reprint, Aalen, Germany, 1963.

Isidore of Seville. *El "De viris illustribus"* . . . : *Estudio y edición crítica.* Ed. Carmen Codoñer Merino. Theses et studia philologica salamanticensia 12. Salamanca, 1964.

———. *Etymologiarum sive originum libri xx.* Ed. W. M. Lindsay. 2 vols. Oxford, 1911.

———. *Las historias de los Godos, Vandalos y Suevos.* Ed. Cristóbal Rodríguez Alonso. Fuentes y estudios de historia leonesa 13. León, Spain, 1975.

———(?). *Liber de variis quaestionibus adversus Iudaeos seu ceteros infideles vel plerosque haereticos iudaizantes ex utroque testamento collectus.* Ed. Angel Custodio Vega and A. E. Anspach. Scriptores ecclesiastici hispano-latini veteris et medii aevi 6–9. El Escorial, Spain, 1940.

Joachim of Fiore. *Adversus Iudeos.* Ed. Arsenio Frugoni. Istituto storico itali-
ano per il Medio Evo: Fonti per la storia d'Italia 95. Rome, 1957.
Joannes Andreae. *Commentaria in Decretales.* 5 vols. 1581; reprint, Turin,
1963.
Justin Martyr. *The Dialogue with Trypho.* Trans. A. Lukyn Williams. London,
1930.
Landgraf, Arthur, ed. *Ecrits théologiques de l'école d'Abélard: Textes inédits.*
Spicilegium sacrum lovaniense 14. Louvain, Belgium, 1934.
Lieu, Samuel N. C., and Dominic Montserrat, eds. *From Constantine to Julian:
Pagan and Byzantine Views.* London, 1996.
Linder, Amnon, ed. *The Jews in Roman Imperial Legislation.* Detroit, Mich.,
1987.
Mansi, J. D., et al., eds. *Sacrorum conciliorum nova et amplissima collectio.*
53 vols. Florence and Rome, 1757–1927.
Melito of Sardis. *On Pascha and Fragments.* Ed. and trans. Stuart George Hall.
Oxford, 1979.
Mieth, Klaus-Peter. "Der Dialog des Petrus Alfonsi, Seine Überlieferung im
Druck und in den Handschriften: Textedition." Ph.D. diss., Free University
of Berlin, 1982.
Moses ben Nachman. *Kitvei RaMBa"N.* Ed. Charles B. Chavel. 2 vols. Jeru-
salem, 1963.
Neubauer, A., and M. Stern, eds. *Hebräische Berichte über die Judenverfol-
gungen während der Kreuzzüge.* Quellen der Geschichte der Juden in
Deutschland 2. Berlin, 1892.
Nicholas of Cusa. *De pace fidei.* Ed. Raymond Klibansky and Hildebrand Bas-
cour. Opera omnia 7. Hamburg, 1959.
Odo of Tournai (Cambrai). *On Original Sin and A Disputation with the Jew,
Leo, Concerning the Advent of Christ, the Son of God.* Trans. Irven M.
Resnick. Philadelphia, 1994.
Origen. *Hexapla.* Ed. Fridericus Field. 2 vols. 1875; reprint, Hildesheim, Ger-
many, 1964.
Peter Abelard. *Dialogue of a Philosopher with a Jew and a Christian.* Trans.
Pierre J. Payer. Medieval Sources in Translation 20. Toronto, 1979.
———. *Dialogus inter Philosophum, Judaeum et Christianum.* Ed. Rudolf
Thomas. Stuttgart, 1970.
———. *Ethics.* Ed. D. E. Luscombe. Oxford, 1971.
———. *Opera.* Ed. Victor Cousin. 2 vols. 1849–59; reprint, New York,
1970.
Peter Alfonsi. *Diálogo contra los Judíos.* Ed. Klaus-Peter Mieth. Trans. Espe-
ranza Ducay. Huesca, Spain, 1996.
Peter the Venerable. *Letters.* Ed. Giles Constable. 2 vols. Cambridge, Mass.,
1967.
———. *Schriften zum Islam.* Ed. Reinhold Glei. Corpus islamo-christianum:
Series latina 1. Altenburg, Germany, 1985.
———. "Sermones tres." Ed. Giles Constable. *RB* 64 (1954), 224–72.
Raymond Lull. *Selected Works.* Trans. Anthony Bonner. 2 vols. Princeton,
N.J., 1995.

Raymond Martin. *Capistrum Iudaeorum*. Ed. Adolfo Robles Sierra. Corpus Islamo-Christianum: Series Latina 3/1, 5. 2 vols. Würzburg, Germany, 1990–93.

————. *"De seta Machometi o De origine, progressu et fine Machometi et quadruplici reprobatione prophetiae eius."* Ed. Josep Hernando i Delgado. *Acta historica et archaeologica mediaevalia* 4 (1983), 9–63.

————. *Pugio fidei adversus Mauros et Iudaeos.* 1687; reprint, Farnborough, England, 1967.

Raymond of Penyafort. *Summa de paenitentia.* Ed. Xaverio Ochoa and Aloisio Diez. Universa bibliotheca iuris 1A. Rome, 1976.

Recueil des historiens des croisades: Historiens occidentaux. 5 vols. Paris, 1844–95.

Robert of Melun. *Oeuvres.* Ed. Raymond M. Martin and R. M. Gallet. 3 vols. Louvain, Belgium, 1932–52.

Rosenthal, Judah M., ed. "Polemical Tractates" [Hebrew]. In *Salo Wittmayer Baron Jubilee Volume*, Heb. section, pp. 352–95. Tel Aviv, 1974.

————. "A Religious Disputation between a Jew Called Menaḥem and the Convert Pablo Christiani" [Hebrew]. In *Hagut Ivrit ba'Amerika: Studies in Jewish Themes by Contemporary American Scholars*, 3:61–74. Ed. Menahem Zohori et al. Tel Aviv, 1974.

Shatzmiller, Joseph, ed. *La Deuxième Controverse de Paris: Un Chapitre dans la polémique entre Chrétiens et Juifs au Moyen Âge.* Collection de la *REJ* 15. Paris, 1994.

Simonsohn, Shlomo, ed. *ASJD, 492–1404.* Pontifical Institute of Mediaeval Studies: Studies and Texts 94. Toronto, 1988.

————. *ASJD, 1394–1464.* Pontifical Institute of Mediaeval Studies: Studies and Texts 95. Toronto, 1989.

————. *ASJD, 1546–1555.* Pontifical Institute of Mediaeval Studies: Studies and Texts 106. Toronto, 1990.

Southern, Richard W., and Franciscus Salesius Schmitt, eds. *Memorials of St. Anselm.* Auctores britannici Medii Aevi 1. Oxford, 1969.

Tertullian. *Adversus Marcionem.* Ed. and trans. Ernest Evans. 2 vols. Oxford, 1972.

Thesaurus Sancti Gregorii Magni, series A (formae). Corpus Christianorum— Thesaurus Patrum Latinorum. Comp. Justin Mossay and Bernard Coulie. Turnhout, Belgium, 1986.

Thomas Aquinas. *Contra gentiles: Livre premier.* Trans. R. Bernier and M. Corvez. Besançon, France, 1961.

————. *Liber de veritate catholice fidei contra errores infidelium.* Ed. Peter Marc et al. 3 vols. Turin, 1961–67.

————. *Opera omnia.* Ed. Roberto Busa. 7 vols. Stuttgart, 1980.

————. *Summa cum commentariis . . . Thomae de Via Caietani.* 4 vols. Venice, 1588.

————. *ST.* 60 vols. Cambridge, England, 1964–76.

Vives, José, ed. *Concilios visigóticos e hispano-romanos.* España cristiana: Textos 1. Barcelona, 1963.

Weinhold, Karl, ed. *Die altdeutschen Bruchstücke des Tractats des Bischofs*

Isidorus von Sevilla "De fide catholica contra Judaeos." Bibliothek der äl-testen deutschen Literatur-Denkmäler 6. Paderborn, Germany, 1874.

White, Carolinne, ed. *The Correspondence between Jerome and Augustine of Hippo.* Studies in Bible and Early Christianity 23. Lewiston, N.Y., 1990.

William of Bourges. *Livre des guerres du Seigneur et deux homélies.* Ed. Gilbert Dahan. SC 288. Paris, 1981.

Ziolkowski, Vernon Philip Laurentius, ed. "The *De fide catholica* of Saint Isidorus, Bishop." Ph.D. diss., St. Louis University, 1982.

SECONDARY SOURCES

Abulafia, Anna Sapir. "The *Ars disputandi* of Gilbert Crispin, Abbot of West-minster." In *Ad fontes: Opstellen aangeboden aan prof. dr. C. van de Kieft,* pp. 139–52. Ed. C. M. Cappon et al. Amsterdam, 1984.

———. "An Attempt by Gilbert Crispin, Abbot of Westminster, at Rational Argument in the Jewish-Christian Debate." *Studia monastica* 26 (1984), 55–74.

———. "Bodies in the Jewish-Christian Debate." In *Framing Medieval Bodies,* pp. 123–37. Ed. Sarah Kay and Miri Rubin. Manchester, England, 1994.

———. "Christian Imagery of Jews in the Twelfth Century: A Look at Odo of Cambrai and Guibert of Nogent." *Theoretische Geschiedenis* 16 (1989), 383–91.

———. *Christians and Jews in the Twelfth-Century Renaissance.* London, 1995.

———. "Christians Disputing Disbelief: St Anselm, Gilbert Crispin and Pseudo-Anselm." In *RIM,* pp. 131–48.

———. "The Evolution of Medieval Anti-Judaism." *Theoretische Geschiedenis* 11 (1984), 77–81.

———. "Gilbert Crispin's Disputations: An Exercise in Hermeneutics." In *MSC,* pp. 511–20.

———. "The Ideology of Reform and Changing Ideas Concerning Jews in the Works of Rupert of Deutz and Hermannus Quondam Iudeus." *Jewish History* 7 (1993), 43–63.

———. "*Intentio recta an erronea?* Peter Abelard's Views on Judaism and the Jews." In *Medieval Studies in Honour of Avrom Saltman,* pp. 13–30. Ed. Bat-Sheva Albert et al. Bar-Ilan Studies in History 4. Ramat Gan, Israel, 1995.

———. "Jewish Carnality in Twelfth-Century Renaissance Thought." In *Christianity and Judaism,* pp. 59–75. Ed. Diana Wood. SCH 29. Oxford, 1992.

———. "Jewish-Christian Disputations and the Twelfth-Century Renais-sance." *JMH* 15 (1989), 105–25.

———. "St Anselm and Those outside the Church." In *Faith and Identity: Christian Political Experience,* pp. 11–37. Ed. David Loades and Katherine Walsh. SCH Subsidia 6. Oxford, 1990.

———. "Theology and the Commercial Revolution: Guibert of Nogent, St Anselm and the Jews of Northern France." In *Church and City,* pp. 23–40. Ed. David S. H. Abulafia. Cambridge, England, 1992.

————. "Twelfth-Century Humanism and the Jews." In *Contra Iudaeos: Ancient and Medieval Polemics between Christians and Jews*, pp. 161–75. Ed. Ora Limor and Guy G. Stroumsa. Tübingen, Germany, 1996.

————. "Twelfth-Century Renaissance Theology and the Jews." In *FWW*, pp. 125–39.

Abulafia, David. "Monarchs and Minorities in the Christian Western Mediterranean around 1300: Lucera and Its Analogues." In *Christendom and Its Discontents: Exclusion, Persecution, and Rebellion, 1000–1500*, pp. 234–63. Ed. Scott L. Waugh and Peter D. Diehl. Cambridge, England, 1996.

Adams, Jeremy duQuesnay. "Ideology and the Requirements of Citizenship in Visigothic Spain: The Case of the *Judaei*." *Societas* 2 (1972), 317–32.

Adler, William. "The Jews as Falsifiers: Charges of Tendentious Emendation in Anti-Jewish Christian Polemic." In *Translation of Scripture*, pp. 1–27. Philadelphia, 1990.

Albert, Bat-Sheva. "*De fide catholica contra Judaeos* d'Isidore de Séville: La Polémique anti-judaique dans l'Espagne du viie siècle." *REJ* 141 (1982), 289–316.

————. "Études sur le *De fide catholica contra Judaeos* d'Isidore de Séville." 2 vols. Ph.D. diss., Bar-Ilan University, 1977.

————. "Isidore of Seville: His Attitude toward Judaism and His Impact on Early Medieval Canon Law." *JQR*, n.s. 80 (1990), 207–20.

————. "Jews and Judaism in Carolingian Literature and Exegesis" [Hebrew]. In *Proceedings of the Tenth World Congress of Jewish Studies*, B1:77–84. Jerusalem, 1990.

————. "Un Nouvel Examen de la politique anti-juive wisigothique." *REJ* 135 (1976), 3–29.

————. "The 65th Canon of the IVth Council of Toledo (633) in Christian Legislation and Its Interpretation in the 'Converso' Polemics in XVth Century Spain." In *Proceedings of the Eighth World Congress of Jewish Studies*, B:43–48. Jerusalem, 1982.

Alvarez, Jesús. *Teología del pueblo judío*. Madrid, 1970.

Archambault, Paul. "Ages of Man and Ages of the World." *REA* 12 (1966), 193–228.

Arduini, Maria Lodovica. *Rupert von Deutz (1076–1129) und der "Status Christianitatis" seiner Zeit: Symbolisch-prophetisch Deutung der Geschichte*. Beihefte zum *Archiv für Kulturgeschichte* 25. Cologne, 1987.

————. *Ruperto di Deutz e la controversia tra Cristiani ed Ebrei nel secolo xii*. Istituto storico italiano per il Medio Evo: Studi storici 119–121. Rome, 1979.

Asad, Talal. "Medieval Heresy: An Anthropological View." *Social History* 11 (1986), 345–62.

Astell, Ann W. *The Song of Songs in the Middle Ages*. Ithaca, N.Y., 1990.

Awerbuch, Marianne. *Christlich-jüdische Begegnung im Zeitalter der Frühscholastik*. Abhandlungen zum christlich-jüdischen Dialog 8. Munich, 1980.

Baasten, Matthew. *Pride According to Gregory the Great: A Study of the Moralia.* Studies in the Bible and Early Christianity 7. Lewiston, N.Y., 1986.

Bachrach, Bernard S. *Early Medieval Jewish Policy in Western Europe.* Minneapolis, Minn., 1977.

———. "The Jewish Community in the Later Roman Empire as Seen in the *Codex Theodosianus.*" In *To See Ourselves as Others See Us: Christians, Jews, "Others" in Late Antiquity,* pp. 391–421. Ed. Jacob Neusner and Ernest S. Frerichs. Chico, Calif., 1985.

———. "A Reassessment of Visigothic Jewish Policy, 589–711." *AHR* 78 (1973), 11–34.

Baltrusch, Ernst. "Gregor der Grosse und sein Verhältnis zum römischen Recht am Beispiel seiner Politik gegenüber den Juden." *Historische Zeitschrift* 259 (1994), 39–58.

Barber, Malcolm. "Lepers, Jews and Moslems: The Plot to Overthrow Christendom in 1321." *History* 66 (1981), 1–17.

Barnes, Timothy D. *Constantine and Eusebius.* Cambridge, Mass., 1981.

Baron, Salo Wittmayer. *A Social and Religious History of the Jews.* 2d ed. 18 vols. New York, 1952–83.

Basser, Herbert. "The Acts of Jesus." In *The Frank Talmage Memorial Volume I,* pp. 273–82. Ed. Barry Walfish. Haifa, Israel, 1993.

Bassett, Paul Merritt. "The Use of History in the *Chronicon* of Isidore of Seville." *History and Theory* 15 (1976), 278–92.

Benin, Stephen D. *The Footprints of God: Divine Accommodation in Jewish and Christian Thought.* Albany, N.Y., 1993.

———. "Jews and Christian History: Hugh of St. Victor, Anselm of Havelberg and William of Auvergne." In *FWW,* pp. 203–19.

Ben-Shalom, Ram. "The Image of Christian Culture in the Historical Consciousness of the Jews of Twelfth to Fifteenth-Century Spain and Provence" [Hebrew]. 2 vols. Ph.D. diss., Tel Aviv University, 1996.

Benton, John F. "The Personality of Guibert of Nogent." *Psychoanalytic Review* 57 (1970–71), 563–86.

Berg, Dieter. "Servitus Judaeorum: Zum Verhältnis des Thomas von Aquin und seines Ordens zu den Juden in Europa im 13. Jahrhundert." In *Thomas von Aquin: Werk und Wirkung im Licht neuerer Forschungen,* pp. 439–58. Ed. Albert Zimmermann. Miscellanea mediaevalia 19. Berlin, 1988.

Berger, David. "The Attitude of St. Bernard of Clairvaux toward the Jews." *Proceedings of the American Academy for Jewish Research* 40 (1972), 89–108.

———. "Christians, Gentiles, and the Talmud: A Fourteenth-Century Jewish Response to the Attack on Rabbinic Judaism." In *RIM,* pp. 115–30.

———. *From Crusades to Blood Libels to Expulsions: Some New Approaches to Medieval Antisemitism.* Touro College Graduate School of Jewish Studies: Annual Lecture of the Victor J. Selmanowitz Chair of Jewish History 2. New York, 1997.

———. "Gilbert Crispin, Alan of Lille, and Jacob ben Reuben: A Study in the Transmission of Medieval Polemic." *Speculum* 49 (1974), 34–47.

―――. "Mission to the Jews and Jewish-Christian Cultural Contacts in the Polemical Literature of the High Middle Ages." *AHR* 91 (1986), 576–91.

―――. "St. Peter Damian: His Attitude toward the Jews and the Old Testament." *Yavneh Review* 4 (1965), 80–112.

Bernard, Robert W. "The Rhetoric of God in the Figurative Exegesis of Augustine." In *Biblical Hermeneutics in Historical Perspective: Studies in Honor of Karlfried Froelich on His Sixtieth Birthday*, pp. 88–99. Ed. Mark S. Burrows and Paul Rorem. Grand Rapids, Mich., 1991.

Berndt, Rainer. *André de Saint-Victor (1175): Exégète et théologien*. Bibliotheca victorina 2. Paris, 1991.

Berry, Virginia G. "Peter the Venerable and the Crusades." In *Petrus Venerabilis, 1156–1956: Studies and Texts Commemorating the Eighth Centenary of His Death*, pp. 141–62. Ed. Giles Constable and James Kritzeck. Studia anselmiana 40. Rome, 1956.

―――. "The Second Crusade." In *A History of the Crusades, Volume I: The First Hundred Years*, pp. 463–512. Gen. ed. Kenneth M. Setton. Ed. Marshall W. Baldwin. Madison, Wis., 1969.

Berthier, André. "Un Maître orientaliste du xiiie siècle: Raymond Martin O.P." *Archivum fratrum praedicatorum* 6 (1936), 267–311.

Bishko, Charles Julian. "Peter the Venerable's Journey to Spain." In *Petrus Venerablis, 1156–1956: Studies and Texts Commemorating the Eighth Centenary of His Death*, pp. 163–75. Ed. Giles Constable and James Kritzeck. Studia anselmiana 40. Rome, 1956.

Blumenkranz, Bernhard. "Augustin et les Juifs, Augustin et le Judaïsme." *Recherches augustiniennes* 1 (1958), 225–41.

―――. *Les Auteurs chrétiens latins du Moyen Âge sur les Juifs et le Judaisme*. Paris, 1963.

―――. "Le *De regimine Judaeorum*: Ses modèles, son exemple." In *Aquinas and the Problems of His Time*, pp. 101–17. Ed. G. Verbeke and D. Verhelst. Mediaevalia lovaniensia 1, 5. Louvain, Belgium, 1976.

―――. "Deux compilations canoniques de Florus de Lyon et l'action antijuive d'Agobard." *Revue historique de droit français et étranger*, 4th ser. 33 (1955), 227–54, 560–82.

―――. "La *Disputatio Judei cum Christiano* de Gilbert Crispin, abbé de Westminster." *RMAL* 4 (1948), 237–52.

―――. "Die Entwicklung im Westen zwischen 200 und 1200." In *Kirche und Synagoge: Handbuch zur Geschichte von Christen und Juden*, 1:84–135. Ed. Karl Heinrich Rengstorf and Siegfried von Kurtzfleisch. 2 vols. Stuttgart, 1968–70.

―――. *Die Judenpredigt Augustins*. Basel, 1946.

―――. "Jüdische und christliche Konvertiten im jüdisch-christlichen Religionsgespräch des Mittelalters." In *JIM*, pp. 264–82.

―――. *Le Juif médiéval au miroir de l'art chrétien*. Paris, 1966.

―――. *Juifs et Chrétiens dans le monde occidental, 430–1096*. Paris, 1960.

―――. *Juifs et Chrétiens: Patristique et Moyen Âge*. London, 1977.

―――. Review of *Saint Agobard: Evêque de Lyon (769–840)*, by A. Bressolles. *RMAL* 8 (1952), 59–61.

Bodard, Claude. "La Bible, expression d'une expérience religieuse chez S. Bernard." In *Saint Bernard, théologien*, pp. 24–45. Analecta sacri ordinis cisterciensis 9. Rome, 1953.

Bonfil, Robert. "The Culture and Religious Traditions of French Jewry in the Ninth Century, as Reflected in the Writings of Agobard of Lyons" [Hebrew]. In *Studies in Jewish Mysticism, Philosophy and Ethical Literature Presented to Isaiah Tishby on His Seventy-Fifth Birthday*, pp. 327–48. Ed. Joseph Dan and Joseph Hacker. Jerusalem, 1986.

——. "The Devil and the Jews in the Christian Consciousness of the Middle Ages." In *Antisemitism through the Ages*, pp. 91–98. Ed. Shmuel Almog. Trans. Nathan H. Reisner. Oxford, 1988.

——. "The Nature of Judaism in Raymundus Martini's *Pugio fidei*" [Hebrew]. *Tarbiz* 40 (1971), 360–75.

Borst, Arno. "Das Bild der Geschichte in Enzyklopädie Isidors von Sevilla." *Deutsches Archiv für Erforschung des Mittelalters* 22 (1961), 1–62.

Boshof, Egon. "Einheitsidee und Teilungsprinzip in der Regierungszeit Ludwigs des Frommen." In *Charlemagne's Heir: New Perspectives on the Reign of Louis the Pious (814–840)*, pp. 161–89. Ed. Peter Godman and Roger Collins. Oxford, 1990.

——. *Erzbischof Agobard von Lyon: Leben und Werke*. Kölner historische Abhandlungen 17. Cologne, 1969.

Boulton, Brenda. "Tradition and Temerity: Papal Attitudes to Deviants, 1159–1216." In *Schism, Heresy and Religious Protest*, pp. 79–81. Ed. Derek Baker. SCH 9. Cambridge, England, 1972.

Bouthillier, Denise, and Jean-Pierre Torrell. "'Miraculum': Une Catégorie fondamentale chez Pierre le Vénérable." *RT* 80 (1980), 357–86, 546–66.

Boyarin, Daniel. *Carnal Israel: Reading Sex in Talmudic Culture*. Berkeley, Calif., 1993.

Boyle, Marjorie O'Rourke. "Augustine in the Garden of Zeus: Lust, Love, and Language." *HTR* 83 (1990), 117–39.

Bray, Jennifer. "The Mohammetan and Idolatry." In *Persecution and Toleration*, pp. 89–98. Ed. W. J. Sheils. SCH 21. Oxford, 1984.

Bredero, Adriaan H. "Jerusalem in the West." In *Christendom and Christianity in the Middle Ages: The Relations between Religion, Church, and Society*, pp. 79–104. By Adriaan H. Bredero. Trans. Reinder Bruinsma. Grand Rapids, Mich., 1994.

——. "Studien zu den Kreuzzugsbriefen Bernhards von Clairvaux und seiner Reise nach Deutschland im Jahre 1146." *Mitteilungen des Instituts für osterreichische Geschichtsforschung* 66 (1958), 331–43.

Brehaut, Ernest. *An Encyclopedist of the Dark Ages: Isidore of Seville*. New York, 1912.

Bressolles, A. "La Question juive au temps de Louis le Pieux." *Revue d'histoire de l'Église de France* 28 (1942), 51–64.

——. *Saint Agobard: Evêque de Lyon (769–840)*. L'Église et l'état au Moyen-Âge 9. Paris, 1949.

Briggs, Sheila. "Images of Women and Jews in Nineteenth- and Twentieth-Century German Theology." In *Immaculate and Powerful: The Female in*

Sacred Image and Social Reality, pp. 226–59. Ed. Clarissa Atkinson et al. Boston, 1985.

Broadie, Alexander. "Medieval Jewry through the Eyes of Aquinas." In *Aquinas and the Problems of His Time*, pp. 57–68. Ed. G. Verbeke and D. Verhelst. Mediaevalia lovaniensia 1, 5. Louvain, Belgium, 1976.

Brown, Carleton. "The Prioress's Tale." In *Sources and Analogues of Chaucer's Canterbury Tales*, pp. 447–85. Ed. W. F. Bryan and Germaine Dempster. 1941; reprint, New York, 1958.

———. *A Study of the Miracle of Our Lady Told by Chaucer's Prioress.* London, 1906.

Brown, Peter. *Augustine of Hippo: A Biography.* London, 1967.

———. *The Body and Society: Men, Women and Sexual Renunciation in Early Christianity.* New York, 1988.

———. "Late Antiquity." In *A History of Private Life, 1: From Pagan Rome to Byzantium*, pp. 235–311. Ed. Paul Veyne. Cambridge, Mass., 1987.

———. "St. Augustine's Attitude to Religious Coercion." *Journal of Roman Studies* 54 (1964), 107–16.

Brundage, James A. *Medieval Canon Law.* London, 1995.

Buddensieg, Tilmann. "Gregory the Great, the Destroyer of Pagan Idols: The History of a Medieval Legend Concerning the Decline of Ancient Art and Architecture." *Journal of the Warburg and Courtauld Institutes* 28 (1965), 44–65.

Burman, Thomas E. *Religious Polemic and the Intellectual History of the Mozarabs, c. 1050–1200.* Brill's Studies in Intellectual History 52. Leiden, Netherlands, 1994.

Burns, Robert I. "Anti-Semitism and Anti-Judaism in Christian History: A Revisionist Thesis." *Catholic Historical Review* 70 (1984), 90–93.

———. "Christian-Islamic Confrontation in the West: The Thirteenth-Century Dream of Conversion." *AHR* 76 (1971), 1386–1434.

Buytaert, Eligius M. "Abelard's *Collationes.*" *Antonianum* 44 (1969), 18–39.

———. "The Anonymous *Capitula haeresum Petri Abaelardi* and the Synod of Sens, 1140." *Antonianum* 43 (1968), 419–60.

Bynum, Caroline Walker. *Jesus as Mother: Studies in the Spirituality of the High Middle Ages.* Berkeley, Calif., 1982.

———. *The Resurrection of the Body in Western Christianity, 200–1336.* Lectures on the History of Religions, n.s. 15. New York, 1995.

Cabaniss, J. Allen. "Agobard of Lyons." *Speculum* 26 (1951), 50–76.

———. *Agobard of Lyons: Churchman and Critic.* Syracuse, N.Y., 1953.

Callahan, Daniel F. "Ademar of Chabannes, Millennial Fears and the Development of Western Anti-Judaism." *Journal of Ecclesiastical History* 46 (1995), 19–35.

Camille, Michael. *The Gothic Idol: Ideology and Image-making in Medieval Art.* Cambridge, England, 1989.

Cantini, Joannes A. "De autonomia judicii saecularis et de romani pontificis plenitudine potestatis in temporalibus secundum Innocentium IV." *Salesianum* 23 (1961), 407–80.

Cantini, Joannes A., and Ch. Lefebvre. "Sinibalde dei Fieschi (Innocent

IV)." In *Dictionnaire de droit canonique*, 7:1029–62. Ed. R. Naz. Paris, 1965.

Caspary, Gerard E. *Politics and Exegesis: Origen and the Two Swords*. Berkeley, Calif., 1979.

Castán Lacoma, Laureano. "Un opúsculo apologético de San Isidoro, inédito." *Revista española de teología* 20 (1960), 319–60.

———. "San Isidoro de Sevilla, apologista antijudaico." In *Isidoriana: Estudios sobre San Isidoro de Sevilla en el xiv centenario de su nacimiento*, pp. 445–56. Ed. Manuel C. Díaz y Díaz. León, 1961.

Castritius, Helmut. "*Seid weder den Juden noch den Heiden noch der Gemeinde Gottes ein Ärgernis* (1. Kor. 10,32): Zur sozialen und rechtlichen Stellen der Juden im spätrömischen Nordafrika." In *Antisemitismus und jüdischen Geschichte: Studien zu Ehren von Herbert A. Strauss*, pp. 47–67. Ed. Rainer Erb et al. Berlin, 1987.

Cazier, Pierre. "De la coercition à la persuasion: L'Attitude d'Isidore de Séville face à la politique anti-juive des souverains visigotiques." In *De l'antijudaïsme antique à l'antisemitisme contemporain*, pp. 125–46. Ed. Valentin Nikiprowetzky. Lille, France, 1979.

Châtillon, Jean. "Pierre le Vénérable et les Pétrobrusiens." In *PAPV*, pp. 165–79.

———. "Saint Anselme et l'Écriture." In *MSC*, pp. 431–42.

Chaurand, Jacques. "La Conception de l'histoire de Guibert de Nogent." *CCM* 8 (1965), 381–95.

Chazan, Robert. *Barcelona and Beyond: The Disputation of 1263 and Its Aftermath*. Berkeley, Calif., 1992.

———. "Chapter Thirteen of the *Mahazik Emunah*: Further Light on Friar Paul Christian and the New Christian Missionizing." *Michael* 12 (1991), 9–26.

———. "The Condemnation of the Talmud Reconsidered (1239–1248)." *Proceedings of the American Academy for Jewish Research* 55 (1988), 11–30.

———. "Confrontation in the Synagogue of Narbonne: A Christian Sermon and a Jewish Reply." *HTR* 67 (1974), 433–57.

———. *Daggers of Faith: Thirteenth-Century Christian Missionizing and Jewish Response*. Berkeley, Calif., 1989.

———. *European Jewry and the First Crusade*. Berkeley, Calif., 1987.

———. "From Friar Paul to Friar Raymond: The Development of Innovative Missionizing Argumentation." *HTR* 76 (1983), 289–306.

———. *Medieval Stereotypes and Modern Antisemitism*. Berkeley, Calif., 1997.

———. "Twelfth-Century Perceptions of the Jews: A Case Study of Bernard of Clairvaux and Peter the Venerable." In *FWW*, pp. 187–201.

Chenu, Marie-Dominique. *Nature, Man, and Society in the Twelfth Century: Essays on New Theological Perspectives in the Latin West*. Ed. Jerome Taylor and Lester K. Little. Chicago, 1968.

———. "La Théologie de la loi ancienne selon Saint Thomas." *RT* 61 (1961), 485–97.

Clark, Elizabeth A. "Heresy, Asceticism, Adam, and Eve: Interpretations of

Genesis 1–3 in the Later Latin Fathers." In *Ascetic Piety and Women's Faith: Essays on Late Ancient Christianity*, pp. 353–73. By Elizabeth A. Clark. Studies in Women and Religion 20. Lewiston, N.Y., 1986.

———. *The Origenist Controversy: The Cultural Construction of an Early Christian Debate*. Princeton, N.J., 1992.

Cohen, Jeremy. *"Be Fertile and Increase, Fill the Earth and Master It": The Ancient and Medieval Career of a Biblical Text*. Ithaca, N.Y., 1989.

———. *The Friars and the Jews: The Evolution of Medieval Anti-Judaism*. Ithaca, N.Y., 1982.

———. "The Hebrew Crusade Chronicles in Their Christian Cultural Context." In *Juden und Christen zur Zeit der Kreuzzüge*. Ed. Alfred Haverkamp. Vorträge und Forschungen des Konstanzer Arbeitskreises für mittelalterliche Geschichte. Sigmaringen, Germany, 1999.

———. "The Jews as the Killers of Christ in the Latin Tradition, from Augustine to the Friars." *Traditio* 39 (1983), 1–27.

———. "The Mentality of the Medieval Jewish Apostate: Peter Alfonsi, Hermann of Cologne, and Pablo Christiani." In *Jewish Apostasy in the Modern World*, pp. 20–47. Ed. Todd M. Endelman. New York, 1987.

———. "The Muslim Connection: On the Changing Role of the Jew in High Medieval Theology." In *FWW*, pp. 141–62.

———. "The 'Persecutions of 1096'—From Martyrdom to Martyrology: The Sociocultural Context of the Hebrew Crusade Chronicles" [Hebrew]. *Zion*, n.s. 59 (1994), 195–205.

———. "The Polemical Adversary of Solomon ibn Adret." *JQR*, n.s. 71 (1980), 48–55.

———. "Profiat Duran's *The Reproach of the Gentiles* and the Development of Jewish Anti-Christian Polemic." In *Shlomo Simonsohn Jubilee Volume: Studies on the History of the Jews in the Middle Ages and Renaissance Period*, pp. 71–84. Ed. Daniel Carpi et al. Tel Aviv, 1993.

———. "Raimundus Martini's Capistrum Iudaeorum" [Hebrew]. In *Isadore Twersky Memorial Volume*. Ed. Carmi Horowitz and Michael Schnidman. Jerusalem, forthcoming.

———. "Recent Historiography on the Medieval Church and the Decline of European Jewry." In *Popes, Teachers, and Canon Law in the Middle Ages: Essays in Honor of Brian Tierney*, pp. 251–62. Ed. James Ross Sweeney and Stanley Chodorow. Ithaca, N.Y., 1989.

———. Review of *The Jew as the Ally of the Muslim*, by Allan and Ellen Cutler. *Judaism* 37 (1988), 240–42.

———. "Roman Imperial Policy toward the Jews from Constantine until the End of the Palestinian Patriarchate (ca. 429)." *Byzantine Studies* 3 (1976), 1–29.

———. "Scholarship and Intolerance in the Medieval Academy: The Study and Evaluation of Judaism in European Christendom." *AHR* 91 (1986), 592–613.

———. "The Second Disputation of Paris and Its Place in Thirteenth-Century Jewish-Christian Polemic" [Hebrew]. *Tarbiz*, forthcoming.

———. "'Slay Them Not': Augustine and the Jews in Modern Scholarship." *Medieval Encounters* 4 (1998), 78–92.

———. "A 1096 Complex? Constructing the First Crusade in Jewish Historical Memory, Medieval and Modern." In *In the Shadow of the Millennium: Jews and Christians in Twelfth-Century Europe*. Ed. Michael A. Signer and John H. van Engen. Notre Dame, Ind., 1999.

———. "'Witnesses of Our Redemption': The Jews in the Crusading Theology of Bernard of Clairvaux." In *Medieval Studies in Honour of Avrom Saltman*, pp. 67–81. Ed. Bat-Sheva Albert et al. Bar-Ilan Studies in History 4. Ramat Gan, Israel, 1995.

Cohen, Shaye J. D. "Was Judaism in Antiquity a Missionary Religion?" In *Jewish Assimilation, Acculturation, and Accommodation: Past Traditions, Current Issues, and Future Prospects*, pp. 14–23. Ed. Menachem Mor. Creighton University Studies in Jewish Civilization 2. Lanham, Md., 1992.

Cole, Penny J. "'O God, the Heathen Have Come into Your Inheritance' (Ps. 78.1): The Theme of Religious Pollution in Crusade Documents, 1095–1188." In *Crusaders and Muslims in Twelfth-Century Syria*, pp. 84–111. Ed. Maya Shatzmiller. The Medieval Mediterranean: Peoples, Economies and Cultures 1. Leiden, Netherlands, 1993.

———. *The Preaching of the Crusades to the Holy Land, 1095–1270*. Cambridge, Mass., 1991.

Collins, Roger. *Early Medieval Spain: Unity in Diversity, 400–1000*. 2d ed. New York, 1995.

Congar, Yves M.-J. "L'Église chez Saint Anselme." In *Congrès international du IXe centenaire de l'arrivée d'Anselme à Bec*, pp. 371–99. Spicilegium becense 1. Paris, 1959.

———. "'Gentilis' et 'Iudaeus' au Moyen Âge." *RTAM* 36 (1969), 222–25.

———. "Le Sens de l'économie salutaire dans la 'théologie' de S. Thomas d'Aquin (*Somme théologique*)." In *Festgabe Joseph Lortz*, 2:73–122. Ed. Erwin Iserloh and Peter Manns. 2 vols. Baden-Baden, Germany, 1958.

Constable, Giles. "The Monastic Policy of Peter the Venerable." In *PAPV*, pp. 119–42.

———. "The Second Crusade as Seen by Contemporaries." *Traditio* 9 (1953), 213–79.

———. "The Vision of Gunthelm and Other Visions Attributed to Peter the Venerable." *RB* 66 (1956), 92–114.

Corrigan, Kathleen. *Visual Polemics in the Ninth-Century Byzantine Psalters*. Cambridge, England, 1992.

Cortabarria, Angel. "La Connaissance des textes arabes chez Raymond Martin O.P. et sa position en face de l'Islam." In *ICM*, pp. 279–300.

Coupe, M. D. "The Personality of Guibert de Nogent Reconsidered." *JMH* 9 (1983), 317–29.

Cowdrey, H. E. J. "Martyrdom and the First Crusade." In *Crusade and Settlement*, pp. 46–56. Ed. P. W. Edbury. Cardiff, Wales, 1985.

———. "Pope Urban II's Preaching of the First Crusade." *History* 55 (1970), 177–88.

Cranz, F. Edward. "*De civitate Dei*, XV,2, and Augustine's Idea of the Christian Society." *Speculum* 25 (1950), 215–25.

———. "The Development of Augustine's Ideas on Society before the Donatist Controversy." *HTR* 47 (1954), 255–316.

Curtius, Ernest Robert. *European Literature and the Latin Middle Ages*. Trans. Willard R. Trask. Bollingen Series 36. 1953; reprint, Princeton, N.J., 1990.

Cutler, Allan and Ellen. *The Jew as the Ally of the Muslim*. Notre Dame, Ind., 1986.

Dagens, Claude. *Saint Grégoire le Grand: Culture et expérience chrétiennes*. Paris, 1977.

Dahan, Gilbert. "L'Article *Iudei* de la *Summa Abel* de Pierre le Chantre." *REA* 27 (1981), 105–26.

———. "Bernard de Clairvaux et les Juifs." *Archives juives* 23 (1987), 59–64.

———. "L'Exégèse de l'histoire de Caïn et Abel du xiiᵉ au xivᵉ siècle en Occident." *RTAM* 49 (1982), 21–89, 50 (1983), 5–68.

———. *Les Intellectuels chrétiens et les Juifs au Moyen Âge*. Paris, 1990.

———. "Juifs et Judaïsme dans la littérature quodlibétique." In *FWW*, pp. 221–45.

———. "Saint Anselme, les Juifs, le Judaïsme." In *MSC*, pp. 521–34.

———. "Saint Bonaventure et les Juifs." *Archivum franciscanum historicum* 77 (1984), 369–405.

D'Alverny, Marie-Thérèse. "Alain de Lille et l'Islam: Le 'Contra Paganos.'" In *ICM*, pp. 301–50.

———. "La Connaissance de l'Islam au temps de Saint Louis." In *Septième centenaire de la mort de Saint Louis*, pp. 235–46. Paris, 1976.

———. "Deux traductions latines du Coran au Moyen Âge." *AHDL* 16 (1948), 69–131.

———. "Translations and Translators." In *Renaissance and Renewal in the Twelfth Century*, pp. 421–62. Ed. Robert L. Benson and Giles Constable. Cambridge, Mass., 1982.

Daniel, Norman. *The Arabs and Medieval Europe*. London, 1975.

———. *Islam and the West: The Making of an Image*. Rev. ed. Oxford, 1993.

Daubercies, Pierre. *La Condition charnelle: Recherches positives pour la théologie d'une réalité terrestre*. Paris, 1958.

———. "La Théologie de la condition charnelle chez les maîtres de haut Moyen Âge." *RTAM* 30 (1963), 5–54.

De Aldama, José A. "Indicaciones sobre cronología de las obras de S. Isidoro." In *Miscellanea isidoriana: Homenaje a S. Isidoro de Sevilla en el xiii centenario de su muerte*, pp. 57–89. Rome, 1936.

Deane, Herbert A. *The Political and Social Ideas of St. Augustine*. New York, 1963.

De Gandillac, Maurice. "Intention et loi dans l'éthique d'Abélard." In *PAPV*, pp. 585–610.

———. "Juif et judéité dans le 'Dialogue' d'Abélard." In *Pour Léon Poliakov: Le Racisme, mythes et sciences*, pp. 385–401. Ed. Maurice Olender. Brussels, 1981.

De Lange, N. R. M. *Origen and the Jews: Studies in Jewish-Christian Relations in Third-Century Palestine*. Cambridge, England, 1976.

Delaruelle, Etienne. "L'Idée de croisade chez Saint Bernard." In *Mélanges Saint Bernard: XXIVᵉ congrès de l'Association bourguignonne des sociétés savantes, Dijon, 1953*, pp. 53–67. Dijon, France, 1954.

Delcorno, Carlo. "I mendicanti e gli Ebrei: A proposito di un recente libro." *Cristianesimo nella storia* 6 (1985), 263–73.

Delhaye, Ph. "Les Idées morales de Saint Isidore de Séville." *RTAM* 26 (1959), 17–49.

Delisle, Leopold. "Notes sur quelques manuscrits du Musée Britannique." *Memoires de la Société de l'histoire de Paris et de l'Île de France* 4 (1877), 183–238.

Delling, Gerhard. "The 'One Who Sees God' in Philo." In *Nourished with Peace: Studies in Hellenistic Judaism in Memory of Samuel Sandmel*, pp. 27–41. Ed. Frederick E. Greenspahn et al. Scholars Press Homage Series 9. Chico, Calif., 1984.

De Lubac, Henri. *Exégèse médiévale: Les Quatre Sens de l'écriture*. 2 vols. in 4 pts. Théologie 41–42, 59. Paris, 1959–64.

De Margerie, Bertrand. *Introduction à l'histoire de l'exégèse, 3: Saint Augustin*. Paris, 1983.

Dérumaux, Pierre. "Saint Bernard et les infidèles." In *Mélanges Saint Bernard: XXIVᵉ congrès de l'Association bourguignonne des sociétés savantes, Dijon, 1953*, pp. 68–79. Dijon, France, 1954.

Dinzelbacher, Peter. *Vision und Visionsliteratur im Mittelalter*. Monographien zur Geschichte des Mittelalters 23. Stuttgart, 1981.

Djaït, Hichem. *Europe and Islam*. Trans. Peter Heinegg. Berkeley, Calif., 1985.

Domingues de Sousa Costa, Antonius. "Canonistarum doctrina de Judaeis et Saracenis tempore concilii constantientis." *Antonianum* 40 (1965), 3–70.

Dubois, Marcel. "Jews, Judaism and Israel in the Theology of Saint Augustine: How He Links the Jewish People and the Land of Zion." *Immanuel* 22/23 (1989), 162–214.

———. "Thomas Aquinas on the Place of the Jews in the Divine Plan." Trans. David Maisel. *Immanuel* 24/25 (1990), 241–66.

Dufeil, Michel-Marie. "Vision d'Islam depuis l'Europe au début du xivᵉ siècle." In *ICM*, pp. 235–58.

Dumontier, P. *Saint Bernard et la Bible*. Paris, 1953.

Dunn, James J. G. "Why 'Incarnation'? A Review of Recent New Testament Scholarship." In *Crossing the Boundaries: Essays in Biblical Interpretation in Honour of Michael D. Goulder*, pp. 235–56. Ed. Stanley E. Porter et al. Biblical Interpretation Series 8. Leiden, Netherlands, 1994.

Eckert, Willehad Paul. "Thomas von Aquino—Seine Stellung zu Juden und zum Judentum." *Freiburger Rundbrief* 20 (1968), 30–38.

Elder, E. Rozanne, and John R. Sommerfeldt, eds. *The Chimaera of His Age: Studies on Bernard of Clairvaux*. Cistercian Studies 63, 5. Kalamazoo, Mich., 1980.

Emerson, Oliver F. "Legends of Cain, Especially in Old and Middle English." *Publications of the Modern Language Association* 21 (1906), 831–929.

Emmerson, Richard Kenneth. *Antichrist in the Middle Ages: A Study of Medieval Apocalypticism, Art, and Literature.* Seattle, Wash., 1981.

Evans, G. R. *Alan of Lille: The Frontiers of Theology in the Late Twelfth Century.* Cambridge, England, 1983.

———. *Anselm and a New Generation.* Oxford, 1980.

———. "The *Cur Deus homo*: The Nature of St. Anselm's Appeal to Reason." *Studia theologica* 31 (1977), 33–50.

———. "Gilbert Crispin, Abbot of Westminster: The Forming of a Monastic Scholar." *Studia monastica* 22 (1980), 63–81.

———. *The Mind of St. Bernard of Clairvaux.* Oxford, 1983.

———. *Old Arts and New Theology: The Beginnings of Theology as an Academic Discipline.* Oxford, 1980.

———. "St. Anselm and Sacred History." In *The Writing of History in the Middle Ages: Essays Presented to Richard William Southern,* pp. 187–209. Ed. R. H. C. Davis and J. M. Wallace-Hadrill. Oxford, 1981.

———. "A Theology of Change in the Writings of St. Anselm and His Contemporaries." *RTAM* 47 (1970), 53–76.

Fanning, Steven. *Hubert of Angers, 1006–1047.* Transactions of the American Philosophical Society 78, 1. Philadelphia, 1988.

Farkasfalvy, Denis. "The Role of the Bible in St. Bernard's Spirituality." *Analecta cisterciensia* 25 (1969), 3–13.

Feldman, Louis H. *Jew and Gentile in the Ancient World.* Princeton, N.J., 1993.

Ferguson, Chris D. "Autobiography as Therapy: Guibert de Nogent, Peter Abelard, and the Making of Medieval Autobiography." *Journal of Medieval and Renaissance Studies* 13 (1983), 187–212.

Flint, Valerie I. J. "Anti-Jewish Literature and Attitudes in the Twelfth Century." *JJS* 37 (1986), 39–57, 183–205.

Flori, Jean. "La Caricature de l'Islam dans l'Occident médiévale: Origine et signification de quelques stéréotypes concernant l'Islam." *Aevum* 66 (1992), 245–56.

Foa, Anna. "The Witch and the Jew: Two Alikes That Were Not the Same." In *FWW,* pp. 361–74.

Folliet, G. "La Typologie du *Sabbat* chez Saint Augustin: Son interprétation millénariste entre 389 et 400." *REA* 2 (1956), 371–90.

Fontaine, Jacques. "Conversion et culture chez les wisigoths d'Espagne." In *La conversione al Christianismo nell'Europa dell'alto medioevo,* pp. 87–147. Settimane di Studio del Centro italiano di studi sull'alto medioevo 14. Spoleto, Italy, 1967.

———. "Grammaire sacrée et grammaire profane: Isidore de Séville devant l'exégèse biblique." In *Los visigodos: Historia y civilización,* pp. 311–29. Antigüedad y cristianismo 3. Murcia, Spain, 1986.

———. *Isidore de Séville et la culture classique dans l'Espagne wisigothique.* 2d ed. 3 vols. Paris, 1983.

———. "Isidore de Séville et l'astrologie." *Revue des études latines* 31 (1954) 271–300.

———. "King Sisebut's *Vita Desiderii* and the Political Function of Visigothic

Hagiography." In *Visigothic Spain: New Approaches*, pp. 93–129. Ed. Edward James. Oxford, 1980.

———. "Théorie et practique du style chez Isidore de Séville." *Vigiliae christianae* 14 (1960), 65–101.

———. "La Vocation monastique selon Saint Isidore de Séville." In *Théologie de la vie monastique: Études sur la tradition patristique*, pp. 353–69. Théologie 49. Paris, 1961.

Fox, Marvin. "Maimonides and Aquinas on Natural Law." *Diné Israel* 3 (1972), V–XXXVI.

Fredriksen, Paula. "Divine Justice and Human Freedom: Augustine on Jews and Judaism, 392–398." In *FWW*, pp. 29–54.

———. "*Excaecati occulta justitia Dei*: Augustine on Jews and Judaism." *Journal of Early Christian Studies* 3 (1995), 299–324.

Friedman, Mordechai Akiva. "The Phrase *Kir Yad* and the Signing of the Second Tablets of the Decalogue in Tosefta and Midrash" [Hebrew]. *Te'udah* 7 (1991), 161–89.

———. "Two Maimonidean Letters" [Hebrew]. In *Isadore Twersky Memorial Volume*. Ed. Carmi Horowitz and Michael Schnidman. Jerusalem, forthcoming.

Friedman, Yvonne. "An Anatomy of Anti-Semitism: Peter the Venerable's Letter to Louis VII, King of France (1146)." In *Bar-Ilan Studies in History*, pp. 87–102. Ed. Pinhas Artzi. Ramat Gan, Israel, 1978.

———. "Armenkultur und Literatur: Zur Entwicklung eines Motivs in der antijüdischen Polemik des 12. Jahrhunderts." *Kairos*, n.s. 26 (1984), 80–88.

Fumagalli, Pier Francesco. "I trattati medievali 'Adversus Judaeos', il 'Pugio fidei' ed il suo influsso sulla concezione cristiana dell'Ebraismo." *La scuola cattolica* 113 (1985), 522–45.

Funkenstein, Amos. "Basic Types of Christian Anti-Jewish Polemics in the Later Middle Ages." *Viator* 2 (1971), 373–82.

———. "Changes in the Patterns of Christian Anti-Jewish Polemic in the Twelfth Century" [Hebrew]. *Zion*, n.s. 33 (1968), 125–44.

———. "Gesetz und Geschichte: Zur historisierenden Hermeneutik bei Moses Maimonides und Thomas von Aquin." *Viator* 1 (1970), 147–78.

———. *Perceptions of Jewish History*. Berkeley, Calif., 1993.

Gager, John G. *The Origins of Anti-Semitism: Attitudes toward Judaism in Pagan and Christian Antiquity*. New York, 1983.

Ganshof, François L. "À propos de la politique de Louis le Pieux avant la crise de 830." *Revue belge d'archéologie et d'histoire de l'art* 37 (1968), 37–48.

———. "Am Vorabend der ersten Krise der Regierung Ludwigs des Frommen." *Frühmittelalterliche Studien* 6 (1972), 39–54.

———. "Some Observations on the *Ordinatio imperii* of 817." In *The Carolingians and the Frankish Monarchy: Studies in Carolingian History*, pp. 273–88. By François L. Ganshof. Trans. Janet Sondheimer. London, 1971.

García Iglesias, L. *Los judíos en la España antigua*. Madrid, 1978.

Gaston, Lloyd. *Paul and the Torah*. Vancouver, B.C., 1987.

Gaudemet, Jean. *Les Sources du droit canonique, viiie–xxe siècle*. Paris, 1993.

Gauss, Julia. "Anselm von Canterbury: Zur Begegnung und Auseinandersetzung der Religionen." *Saeculum* 17 (1966), 277–363.

———. "Die Auseinandersetzung mit Judentum und Islam bei Anselm." In *Die Wirkungsgeschichte Anselms von Canterbury*, 2:101–9. Ed. Helmut Kohlenberger. 2 vols. Analecta anselmiana 4. Frankfurt am Main, 1975.

Gil, Juan. "Judíos y cristianos en la Hispania del siglo vii." *Hispania sacra* 30 (1977), 1–102.

Gilles, Henri. "Législation et doctrine canoniques sur les Sarrasins." In *ICM*, pp. 195–213.

Gillet, Robert. "Spiritualité et place du moine dans l'Église selon Saint Grégoire le Grand." In *Théologie de la vie monastique*, pp. 323–51. Théologie 49. Paris, 1961.

Gilman, Sander L. *Jewish Self-Hatred: Anti-Semitism and the Hidden Language of the Jews*. Baltimore, Md., 1986.

Ginzberg, Louis. "Augustine." *The Jewish Encyclopedia*, 2:314. New York, 1902.

Goodman, David G., and Masanori Miyazawa. *The Jews in the Japanese Mind: The History and Uses of a Cultural Stereotype*. New York, 1995.

Goodman, Martin. *Mission and Conversion: Proselytizing in the Religious History of the Roman Empire*. Oxford, 1994.

Graboïs, Aryeh. "Anselme, l'Ancien Testament et l'idée de croisade." In *MSC*, pp. 161–73.

———. "Un Chapitre de tolérance intellectuelle dans la société occidentale au xiie siècle: Le 'Dialogus' de Pierre Abélard et le 'Kuzari' d'Yehudah Halévi." In *PAPV*, pp. 641–52.

———. "The Christian-Jewish-Islamic Dialogue in the Twelfth Century and Its Historical Significance." *Ecumenical Institute for Advanced Theological Studies Yearbook* 1975–76, pp. 69–83.

———. "From 'Theological' to 'Racial' Antisemitism: The Controversy of the Jewish Pope in the Twelfth Century" [Hebrew]. *Zion*, n.s. 47 (1982), 1–16.

———. "The *Hebraica veritas* and Jewish-Christian Intellectual Relations in the Twelfth Century." *Speculum* 50 (1975), 613–34.

Graetz, Heinrich. *Geschichte der Juden*, 5. 4th ed. Leipzig, 1909.

Grayzel, Solomon. "The Papal Bull *Sicut Judaeis*." In *Studies and Essays in Honor of Abraham A. Neuman*, pp. 243–80. Ed. Meir Ben-Horin et al. Leiden, Netherlands, 1962.

———. "Popes, Jews, and the Inquisition from 'Sicut' to 'Turbato.' " In *Essays on the Occasion of the Seventieth Anniversary of The Dropsie University (1909–1979)*, pp. 151–88. Ed. Abraham I. Katsch and Leon Nemoy. Philadelphia, 1979.

———. "References to the Jews in the Correspondence of John XXII." *Hebrew Union College Annual* 23 (1950–51), 37–80.

———. "The Talmud and the Medieval Papacy." In *Essays in Honor of Solomon B. Freehof*, pp. 220–45. Ed. Walter Jacob et al. Pittsburgh, Pa., 1964.

Griffith, Sidney H. "Jews and Muslims in Christian Syriac and Arabic Texts of the Ninth Century." *Jewish History* 3 (1988), 65–87.

Grossman, Avraham. "The Jewish-Christian Polemic and Jewish Biblical Exegesis in Twelfth Century France (On the Attitude of R. Joseph Qara to Polemic)" [Hebrew]. *Zion*, n.s. 51 (1985), 29–60.

Guillot, Olivier. "L'Exhortation au partage des responsabilités entre l'empereur, l'épiscopat et les autres sujets vers le milieu du règne de Louis le Pieux." In *Prédication et propagande au Moyen Âge: Islam, Byzance, Occident*, pp. 87–110. Ed. George Makdisi et al. Penn–Paris–Dumbarton Oaks Colloquia 3. Paris, 1983.

Guth, Klaus. "Zum Verhältnis von Exegese und Philosophie im Zeitalter der Frühscholastik (Anmerkungen zu Guibert von Nogent, *Vita* I, 17)." *RTAM* 38 (1971), 121–36.

Guttmann, Jacob. *Die Scholastik des dreizehnten Jahrhunderts in ihren Beziehungen zum Judenthum*. 1902; reprint, Hildesheim, Germany, 1970.

Hageneder, Othmar. "Der Häresiebegriff bei den Juristen des 12. und 13. Jahrhunderts." In *The Concept of Heresy in the Middle Ages (11th–13th C.)*, pp. 42–103. Ed. W. Lourdaux and D. Verhelst. Mediaevalia lovaniensia 1, 4. Louvain, Belgium, 1976.

Hailperin, Herman. *Rashi and the Christian Scholars*. Pittsburgh, Pa., 1963.

Halphen, Louis. *Charlemagne and the Carolingian Empire*. Europe in the Middle Ages: Selected Studies 3. Amsterdam, 1977.

Harrison, Verna F. "Allegory and Asceticism in Gregory of Nyssa." *Semeia* 57 (1992), 113–30.

Harvey, Steven. "Maimonides in the Sultan's Palace." In *Perspectives on Maimonides*, pp. 47–75. Ed. Joel L. Kraemer. Oxford, 1991.

Herde, Peter. "Christians and Saracens at the Time of the Crusades: Some Comments of Contemporary Canonists." *Studia gratiana* 12 (1967), 359–76.

Hernández, Ramón. "La España visigoda frente al problema de los judíos." *La ciencia tomista* 94 (1967), 627–85.

Hernando i Delgado, Josep. "Le 'De seta Machometi' du Cod. 46 d'Osma, ouevre de Raymond Martin (Ramón Martí)." In *ICM*, pp. 351–71.

Herrin, Judith. *The Formation of Christendom*. Princeton, N.J., 1987.

Hill, Rosalind. "The Christian View of the Muslim at the Time of the First Crusade." In *The European Mediterranean Lands in the Period of the Crusaders*, pp. 1–8. Ed. P. M. Holt. Westminster, England, 1977.

Hillgarth, Jocelyn N. "Historiography in Visigothic Spain." In *La storiografia altomedievale*, 1:261–311. Settimane di Studio del Centro Italiano di studi sull'alto medioevo 17. Spoleto, Italy, 1970.

———. "The Position of Isidorian Studies: A Critical Review of the Literature, 1936–1975." *Studi medievali*, 3d ser. 24 (1983), 817–905.

———. Review of *Des Goths à la nation gothique*, by Suzanne Teillet. *Journal of Ecclesiastical History* 39 (1988), 578–81.

Hirschberg, H. Z. *A History of the Jews in North Africa: From Antiquity to Our Time* [Hebrew]. 2 vols. Jerusalem, 1965.

Hirsch-Reich, Beatrice. "Joachim von Fiore und das Judentum." In *JIM*, pp. 228–63.

Hirshman, Marc. *A Rivalry of Genius: Jewish and Christian Biblical Interpretation in Late Antiquity.* Trans. Batya Stein. Albany, N.Y., 1996.

Hood, John Y. B. *Aquinas and the Jews.* Philadelphia, 1995.

Horbury, William. "The Trial of Jesus in the Jewish Tradition." In *The Trial of Jesus: Cambridge Studies in Honor of C. F. D. Moule,* pp. 103–21. Ed. Ernst Bammel. Studies in Biblical Theology 2, 13. Naperville, Ill., 1970.

Hoye, William J. "The Erroneous Conscience and Truth According to Thomas Aquinas." In *Les Philosophies morales et politiques au Moyen Âge,* 2: 1049–58. Ed. R. Carlos Bazán et al. 3 vols. Ottawa, 1995.

Hunt, R. W. "The Disputation of Peter of Cornwall against Symon the Jew." In *Studies in Medieval History Presented to Frederick Maurice Powicke,* pp. 143–56. Ed. R. W. Hunt et al. Oxford, 1948.

Hunter, David G. "Resistance to the Virginal Ideal in Late-Fourth-Century Rome: The Case of Jovinian." *Theological Studies* 48 (1987), 45–64.

Hurwitz, Barbara Phyllis. *"Fidei causa et tui amore:* The Role of Petrus Alphonsi's Dialogues in the History of Jewish-Christian Debate." Ph.D. diss., Yale University, 1983.

Jensen, Kurt Villads. "War against Muslims According to Benedict of Alignano, O.F.M." *Archivum franciscanum historicum* 89 (1996), 181–95.

Johnson, Willis. "Before the Blood Libel: Jews in Christian Exegesis after the Massacres of 1096." M.Phil. thesis, University of Cambridge, 1994.

Jolivet, Jean. "Abélard et le philosophe (Occident et Islam au xiiᵉ siècle)." *Revue de l'histoire des religions* 164 (1963), 181–89.

Jordan, William Chester. "Marian Devotion and the Talmud Trial of 1240." In *RIM,* pp. 61–76.

Juster, Jean. *Les Juifs dans l'Empire romain: Leur condition juridique, économique et sociale.* 2 vols. Paris, 1914.

———. "The Legal Condition of the Jews under the Visigothic Kings." Ed. Alfred Mordechai Rabello. *Israel Law Review* 11 (1976), 259–87, 391–414, 563–90.

Kahl, Hans-Dietrich. "Crusade Eschatology as Seen by St. Bernard in the Years 1146 to 1148." In *The Second Crusade and the Cistercians,* pp. 37–47. Ed. Michael Gervers. New York, 1992.

Kantor, Jonathan. "A Psycho-Historical Source: The *Memoirs* of Abbot Guibert of Nogent." *JMH* 2 (1976), 281–304.

Katz, Jacob. *Exclusiveness and Tolerance: Studies in Jewish-Gentile Relations in Medieval and Modern Times.* 1961; reprint, New York, 1962.

Katz, Solomon. *The Jews in the Visigothic and Frankish Kingdoms of Spain and Gaul.* Medieval Academy of America Monographs 12. 1937; reprint, New York, 1970.

———. "Pope Gregory the Great and the Jews." *JQR,* n.s. 24 (1933–34), 111–36.

Kedar, Benjamin Z. "Canon Law and the Burning of the Talmud." *Bulletin of Medieval Canon Law,* n.s. 9 (1979), 79–82.

———. *Crusade and Mission: European Approaches toward the Muslim.* Princeton, N.J., 1984.

———. *"De Iudeis et Sarracenis*: On the Categorization of Muslims in Medieval Canon Law." In *Studia in honorem eminentissimi cardinalis Aplhonsi M. Stickler*, pp. 207–13. Ed. Rosalio Joseph Castillo Lara. Pontificia studiorum universitas salesiana: Studia et textus historiae iuris canonici 7. Rome, 1992.

Kelly, J. N. D. *Golden Mouth: The Story of John Chrysostom—Ascetic, Preacher, Bishop*. Ithaca, N.Y., 1995.

Kent, Bonnie. *Virtues of the Will: The Transformation of Ethics in the Late Thirteenth Century*. Washington, D.C., 1995.

Kevane, Eugene. "Augustine's *De doctrina christiana*: A Treatise on Christian Education." *Recherches augustiniennes* 4 (1966), 97–133.

King, P. D. *Law and Society in the Visigothic Kingdom*. Cambridge Studies in Medieval Life and Thought 3, 5. Cambridge, England, 1972.

Kleinberg, Aviad M. "Hermannus Judaeus's *Opusculum*: In Defense of Its Authenticity." *REJ* 151 (1992), 337–53.

———. "A Thirteenth-Century Struggle over Custody: The Case of Catherine of Parc-aux-Dames." *Bulletin of Medieval Canon Law* 20 (1990), 51–67.

Kniewasser, Manfred. "Die antijüdische Polemik des Petrus Alphonsi (getauft 1106) und des Abtes Petrus Venerabilis von Cluny († 1156)." *Kairos*, n.s. 22 (1980), 34–76.

———. "Bischof Agobard von Lyon und der Platz der Juden in einer sakral verfassten Einheitsgesellschaft." *Kairos*, n.s. 19 (1977), 203–27.

Knowles, David. *The Evolution of Medieval Thought*. New York, 1962.

———. "Peter the Venerable." *Bulletin of the John Rylands Library* 39 (1956), 132–45.

Krauss, Samuel. *The Jewish-Christian Controversy from the Earliest Times to 1798, Volume I: History*. Ed. and rev. William Horbury. Texte und Studien zum antiken Judentum 56. Tübingen, Germany, 1995.

———. *Das Leben Jesu nach jüdischen Quellen*. Berlin, 1902.

Kritzeck, James. "Moslem-Christian Understanding in Medieval Times." *Comparative Studies in Society and History* 4 (1962), 388–401.

———. *Peter the Venerable and Islam*. Princeton Oriental Studies 23. Princeton, N.J., 1964.

———. "Peter the Venerable and the Toledan Collection." In *Petrus Venerabilis, 1156–1956: Studies and Texts Commemorating the Eighth Centenary of His Death*, pp. 176–201. Ed. Giles Constable and James Kritzeck. Studia anselmiana 40. Rome, 1956.

Kruger, Steven F. *Dreaming in the Middle Ages*. Cambridge Studies in Medieval Literature 14. Cambridge, England, 1992.

Kunzelmann, A. "Die Chronologie der Sermones des hl. Augustinus." In *Miscellanea agostiniana*, 2:417–520. 2 vols. Rome, 1930–31.

Labande, Edmond-Réné. "Guibert de Nogent: Disciple et témoin de Saint Anselme au Bec." In *MSC*, pp. 229–36.

La Bonnardière, Anne-Marie. "Bible et polémiques." In *Saint Augustin et la Bible*, pp. 329–52. Ed. Anne-Marie la Bonnardière. Bible de tous les temps 3. Paris, 1986.

Lacarra, María Jesús. *Pedro Alfonso*. Colección "Los Aragoneses" 3. Saragossa, Spain, 1991.

Laistner, M. L. W. *Thought and Letters in Western Europe, A.D. 500 to 900.* Rev. ed. Ithaca, N.Y., 1957.

Landes, Richard. "Lest the Millennium Be Fulfilled: Apocalyptic Expectations and the Pattern of Western Chronography, 100–800 C.E." In *The Use and Abuse of Eschatology in the Middle Ages,* pp. 137–211. Ed. Werner Verbeke et al. Mediaevalia lovanensia 1, 15. Louvain, Belgium, 1988.

———. "The Massacres of 1010: On the Origins of Popular Anti-Jewish Violence in Western Europe." In *FWW,* pp. 79–112.

———. *Relics, Apocalypse, and the Deceits of History: Ademar of Chabannes, 989–1034.* Cambridge, Mass., 1995.

Lang, Helen. "Anselm's Theory of Signs and His Use of Scripture." In *MSC,* pp. 443–56.

Langmuir, Gavin I. "The Faith of Christians and Hostility to Jews." In *Christianity and Judaism,* pp. 77–92. Ed. Diana Wood. SCH 29. Oxford, 1992.

———. *History, Religion, and Antisemitism.* Berkeley, Calif., 1990.

———. *Toward a Definition of Antisemitism.* Berkeley, Calif., 1990.

Laporte, Jean. "Une Théologie systématique chez Grégoire." In *Grégoire le Grand,* pp. 235–43. Ed. Jacques Fontaine et al. Colloques internationaux du C.N.R.S. Paris, 1986.

Lasker, Daniel J. "Jewish-Christian Polemics at the Turning Point: Jewish Evidence from the Twelfth Century." *HTR* 89 (1996), 161–73.

———. *Jewish Philosophical Polemics against Christianity in the Middle Ages.* New York, 1977.

Lauras, A., and Henri Rondet. "Le Thème des deux cités dans l'oeuvre de Saint Augustin." In *Études augustiniennes,* pp. 99–160. Théologie 28. Paris, 1953.

Le Bohec, Yann. "Inscriptions juives et judaïsantes de l'Afrique romaine." *Antiquités africaines* 17 (1981), 165–207.

———. "Juifs et judaïsants dans l'Afrique romaine: Remarques onomastiques." *Antiquités africaines* 17 (1981), 209–29.

Leclercq, Jean. "À propos de l'encyclique de Saint Bernard sur la croisade." *RB* 82 (1972), 312.

———. *Bernard de Clairvaux.* Bibliothèque d'histoire du Christianisme 19. Paris, 1989.

———. "Ecriture sainte et vie spirituelle: Saint Bernard et le 12ᵉ siècle monastique." *Dictionnaire de spiritualité ascétique et mystique,* 4, 1:187–94. Paris, 1960.

———. "L'Encyclique de Saint Bernard en faveur de la croisade." *RB* 81 (1971), 282–308.

———. *The Love of Learning and Desire for God: A Study of Monastic Culture.* 3d ed. Trans. Catharine Misrahi. New York, 1982.

———. "Pour l'histoire de l'encyclique de Saint Bernard sur la croisade." In *Études de civilisation médiévale (ixᵉ–xiiᵉ siècles): Mélanges E.-R. Labande,* pp. 479–90. Poitiers, France, 1974.

———. *Recueil d'études sur Saint Bernard et ses écrits.* 4 vols. Storia e letteratura 92, 104, 114, 167. Rome, 1962–87.

Leff, Gordon. Review of *The Friars and the Jews: The Evolution of Medieval Anti-Judaism*, by Jeremy Cohen. *Times Literary Supplement*, 5 November 1982, p. 1208.

Le Goff, Jacques. *Medieval Civilization*. Trans. Julia Barrow. Oxford, 1988.

———. *The Medieval Imagination*. Trans. Arthur Goldhammer. Chicago, 1988.

———. *Time, Work, & Culture in the Middle Ages*. Trans. Arthur Goldhammer. Chicago, 1980.

Lerer, Seth. "*Transgressio studii*: Writing and Sexuality in Guibert of Nogent." *Stanford French Review* 14 (1990), 243–66.

Lieberman, Saul. *Shkiin: A Few Words on Some Jewish Legends, Customs, and Literary Sources Found in Karaite and Christian Works* [Hebrew]. 2d ed. Jerusalem, 1970.

Liebeschütz, Hans. "Judaism and Jewry in the Social Doctrine of Thomas Aquinas." *JJS* 13 (1962), 57–81.

———. "The Significance of Judaism in Peter Abaelard's *Dialogus*." *JJS* 12 (1961), 1–18.

Limor, Ora. Review essay [in Hebrew] on *The Friars and the Jews: The Evolution of Medieval Anti-Judaism*, by Jeremy Cohen. *Zion*, n.s. 51 (1986), 113–18.

Linder, Amnon. Review [in Hebrew] of *Ha-Kes ha-Qadosh veha-Yehudim*, by Shlomo Simonsohn. *Zion*, n.s. 61 (1996), 481–87.

Linehan, Peter. *History and the Historians of Medieval Spain*. Oxford, 1993.

Lipton, Sara. "Jews, Heretics, and the Sign of the Cat in the *Bible moralisée*." *Word and Image* 8 (1992), 362–77.

Little, Lester K. "The Function of the Jews in the Commercial Revolution." In *Povertà e richezza nella spiritualità dei secoli xi e xii*, pp. 271–87. Convegni del Centro di studi sulla spiritualità medievale 8. Todi, Italy, 1969.

———. *Religious Poverty and the Profit Economy in Medieval Europe*. Ithaca, N.Y., 1978.

Loeb, Isidore. *La Controverse sur le Talmud sous Saint Louis*. Paris, 1881.

———. "Polémistes chrétiens et juifs en France et en Espagne." *REJ* 18 (1889), 43–70, 219–42.

Lotter, Friedrich. "Ist Hermann von Scheda's *Opusculum de conversione sua* eine Fälschung?" *Aschkenas* 2 (1992), 207–18.

———. *Die Konzeption des Wendenkreuzzugs: Ideengeschichtliche, kirchenrechtliche und historisch-politische Voraussetzungen der Missionierung von Elb- und Ostseeslawen um die Mitte des 12. Jahrhunderts*. Vorträge und Forschungen: Sonderband 23. Sigmaringen, Germany, 1977.

———. "The Position of the Jews in Early Cistercian Exegesis and Preaching." In *FWW*, pp. 163–85.

———. "Das Prinzip der 'Hebraica veritas' und die heilsgeschichtliche Rolle Israels bei den frühen Zisterziensern." In *Bibel in jüdischer und christlicher Tradition: Festschrift für Johann Maier zum 60. Geburtstag*, pp. 479–517. Ed. Helmut Merklein et al. Bonner biblische Beiträge 88. Frankfurt am Main, 1993.

Lottin, Odon. "Le Problème de la moralité intrinsique d'Abélard à Saint Thomas d'Aquin." *RT* 39 (1934), 477–515.

Luddy, Ailbee J. *The Life and Teaching of St. Bernard*. Dublin, 1950.

Luneau, Auguste. *L'Histoire du salut chez les pères de l'Église: La Doctrine des âges du monde*. Théologie historique 2. Paris, 1964.

Luscombe, D. E. "The *Ethics* of Abelard: Some Further Considerations." In *Peter Abelard*, pp. 65–84. Ed. Eligius M. Buytaert. Mediaevalia lovaniensia 1, 2. Louvain, Belgium, 1974.

Lynch, Kathryn L. *The High Medieval Dream Vision: Poetry, Philosophy, and Literary Form*. Stanford, Calif., 1988.

Madoz, José. "Contrastes y discrepancias entre el 'Liber de variis quaestionibus' y San Isidoro de Sevilla." *Estudios eclesiásticos* 24 (1950), 435–58.

———. "Una obra de Félix de Urgel falsamente adjudicada a San Isidoro de Sevilla." *Estudios eclesiásticos* 23 (1949), 147–68.

———. "El primado romano en España en el ciclo isidoriano." *Revista española de teología* 2 (1942), 229–55.

———. *San Isidoro de Sevilla: Semblanza de su personalidad literaria*. Ed. Carlos G. Goldaraz. León, Spain, 1960.

Manitius, Max. *Geschichte der lateinischen Literatur des Mittelalters*. Handbuch der Altertumswissenschaft 9, 2. 3 vols. Munich, 1911–31.

Manuel, Frank E. *The Broken Staff: Judaism through Christian Eyes*. Cambridge, Mass., 1992.

Marcus, Ivan G. "Un Communauté pieuse et le doute: Mourir pour la Sanctification du Nom (Qiddouch ha-Chem) en Achkenaz (Europe du Nord) et l'histoire de Rabbi Amnon de Mayence." *Annales: Histoire, sciences sociales* 49 (1994) 1031–47.

———. "The Dynamics of Jewish Renaissance and Renewal in the Twelfth Century." In *In the Shadow of the Millennium: Jews and Christians in Twelfth-Century Europe*. Ed. Michael A. Signer and John H. van Engen. Notre Dame, Ind., 1999.

———. "From 'Deus vult' to 'the Will of the Creator': Extremist Religious Ideologies and Historical Reality in 1096 and Hasidei Ashkenaz" [Hebrew]. In *Facing the Cross: The Persecution of Ashkenazic Jews in 1096*. Ed. Yom Tov Assis et al. Jerusalem, 1999.

———. *Piety and Society: The Jewish Pietists of Medieval Germany*. Études sur le Judaïsme médiéval 10. Leiden, Netherlands, 1981.

———. *Rituals of Childhood: Jewish Acculturation in Medieval Europe*. New Haven, Conn., 1996.

Markus, Robert A. *The End of Ancient Christianity*. Cambridge, England, 1990.

———. "Gregory the Great and a Papal Missionary Strategy." In *The Mission of the Church and the Propagation of the Faith*, pp. 29–38. Ed. G. J. Cuming. SCH 6. Cambridge, England, 1970.

———. "The Jew as a Hermeneutic Device: The Inner Life of a Gregorian *Topos*." In *Gregory the Great: A Symposium*, pp. 1–15. Ed. John C. Cavadini. Notre Dame, Ind., 1995.

———. "The Sacred and the Secular: From Augustine to Gregory the Great." *Journal of Theological Studies*, n.s. 36 (1985), 84–96.

———. *Saeculum: History and Society in the Theology of St Augustine.* 1970; reprint, Cambridge, England, 1988.

Matter, E. Ann. *The Voice of My Beloved: The Song of Songs in Western Medieval Christianity.* Philadelphia, 1990.

McGinn, Bernard. "*Iter sancti sepulchri*: The Piety of the First Crusaders." In *Essays on Medieval Civilization*, pp. 33–71. Ed. Bede Karl Lackner and Kenneth Roy Philp. Walter Prescott Webb Memorial Lectures 12. Austin, Tex., 1978.

———. "Saint Bernard and Eschatology." In *Bernard of Clairvaux: Studies Presented to Dom Jean Leclercq*, pp. 161–85. Cistercian Studies Series 23. Washington, D.C., 1973.

McIntyre, John. *St. Anselm and His Critics: A Re-Interpretation of the Cur Deus homo.* Edinburgh, 1954.

McKane, William. *Selected Christian Hebraists.* Cambridge, England, 1989.

McKeon, Peter R. "817: Une Année désastreuse et presque fatale pour les Carolingiens." *Le Moyen Âge* 84 (1978), 6–12.

———. "The Empire of Louis the Pious: Faith, Politics and Personality." *RB* 90 (1980), 50–62.

McKeon, Richard. "The Organization of Sciences and the Relations of Cultures in the Twelfth and Thirteenth Centuries." In *The Cultural Context of Medieval Learning*, pp. 151–92. Ed. John Emery Murdoch and Edith Dudley Sylla. Boston Studies in the Philosophy of Science 26. Dordrecht, Netherlands, 1975.

McLynn, Neil B. *Ambrose of Milan: Church and Court in a Christian Capital.* Berkeley, Calif., 1994.

McNally, R. E. "Isidoriana." *Theological Studies* 20 (1959), 432–42.

McReady, William D. *Signs of Sanctity: Miracles in the Thought of Gregory the Great.* Pontifical Institute of Medieval Studies—Studies and Texts 91. Toronto, 1989.

McWilliam, Joanne. "Weaving the Strands Together: A Decade in Augustine's Eucharistic Theology." In *Collectanea augustiniana: Mélanges T. J. van Bavel*, 2:497–506. Ed. Bernard Brunig et al. Bibliotheca Ephemeridum theologiarum lovaniensium 92. 2 vols. Louvain, Belgium, 1990.

Meeks, Wayne A., and Robert L. Wilken. *Jews and Christians in Antioch in the First Four Centuries of the Common Era.* Society for Biblical Literature, Sources for Biblical Study 13. Missoula, Mont., 1978.

Mellinkoff, Ruth. *The Mark of Cain.* Berkeley, Calif., 1981.

Melloni, Alberto. *Innocenzo IV: La concezione e l'esperienza della cristianità come regimen unius personae.* Genoa, 1990.

Merchavia, Ch. *The Church versus Talmudic and Midrashic Literature, 500–1248* [Hebrew]. Jerusalem, 1970.

———. "Un documento desconocido sobre la historia de los Judios en la Francia medieval." *Sefarad* 26 (1966), 53–78.

———. "The Hebrew Versions of 'Pugio fidei' in the Saint-Geneviève Manuscript" [Hebrew]. *Kiryat Sefer* 51 (1976), 283–88.

Mews, Constant J. "The Lists of Heresies Attributed to Peter Abelard." *RB* 95 (1985), 73–110.

———. "On Dating the Works of Peter Abelard." *AHDL* 52 (1985), 73–134.

———. *Peter Abelard*. Authors of the Middle Ages 2, 5. London, 1995.

Meyvaert, Paul. "Gregory the Great and the Theme of Authority." *Spode House Review* 3 (December 1966), 1–12.

Miles, Margaret Ruth. *Augustine on the Body*. American Academy of Religion Dissertation Series 31. Missoula, Mont., 1979.

Mommsen, Theodor E. "St. Augustine and the Christian Idea of Progress." *Journal of the History of Ideas* 12 (1951), 346–74.

Monceaux, Paul. "Les Colonies juives dans l'Afrique romaine." *REJ* 44 (1902), 1–28.

Monnot, Guy. "Les Citations canoniques dans le 'Dialogus' de Pierre Alfonse." In *ICM*, pp. 261–77.

Moore, R. I. "Anti-Semitism and the Birth of Europe." In *Christianity and Judaism*, pp. 33–57. Ed. Diana Wood. SCH 29. Oxford, 1992.

———. *The Formation of a Persecuting Society: Power and Deviance in Western Europe, 950–1250*. Oxford, 1987.

———. "Guibert of Nogent and His World." In *Studies in Medieval History Presented to R. H. C. Davis*, pp. 107–17. Ed. Henry Mayr-Harting and R. I. Moore. London, 1985.

———. *The Origins of European Dissent*. Corr. ed. Oxford, 1985.

Morris, Colin. *The Discovery of the Individual, 1050–1200*. New York, 1972.

———. "*Equestris ordo*: Chivalry as a Vocation in the Twelfth Century." In *Religious Motivation: Biological and Sociological Problems for the Church Historian*, pp. 87–96. Ed. Derek Baker. SCH 15. Oxford 1978.

Morrison, Karl F. *Conversion and Text: The Cases of Augustine of Hippo, Herman-Judah, and Constantine Tsatsos*. Charlottesville, Va., 1992.

———. "'From Form into Form': Mimesis and Personality in Augustine's Historical Thought." *Proceedings of the American Philosophical Society* 124 (1980), 276–94.

———. "*I Am You*": The Hermeneutics of Empathy in Western Literature, Theology, and Art. Princeton, N.J., 1988.

———. *Tradition and Authority in the Western Church, 300–1140*. Princeton, N.J., 1969.

———. *The Two Kingdoms: Ecclesiology in Carolingian Political Thought*. Princeton, N.J., 1964.

Muckle, J. T. "The Personal Letters between Abelard and Heloise: Introduction, Authenticity and Text." *Mediaeval Studies* 15 (1953), 47–94.

Muldoon, James. *Popes, Lawyers, and Infidels: The Church and the Non-Christian World, 1250–1550*. Philadelphia, 1979.

Mullins, (Sister) Patrick Jerome. *The Spiritual Life According to Saint Isidore of Seville*. Catholic University of America Studies in Medieval and Renaissance Language and Literature 13. Washington, D.C., 1940.

Murray, A. Victor. *Abelard and St Bernard: A Study in Twelfth Century "Modernism."* Manchester, England, 1967.

Nelson, Janet L. "On the Limits of the Carolingian Renaissance." In *Renais-*

sance and Renewal in Christian History, pp. 51–69. Ed. Derek Baker. SCH 14. Oxford, 1977.

———. "Society, Theodicy and the Origins of Medieval Heresy." In *Schism, Heresy and Religious Protest*, pp. 65–77. Ed. Derek Baker. SCH 9. Cambridge, England, 1972.

Neubauer, Adolph. "Another Convert Named Paulus." *JQR*, o.s. 5 (1893), 713–14.

Neusner, Jacob. *The Incarnation of God: The Character of Divinity in Formative Judaism*. South Florida Studies in the History of Judaism 63. 1988; reprint, Atlanta, Ga., 1992.

———. "Is the God of Judaism Incarnate?" *Religious Studies* 24 (1988), 213–38.

Niggli, Ursula. "Abaelards Ideen über die jüdische Religion und seine Hermeneutik im *Dialogus*." In *Les philosophies morales et politiques au Moyen Âge*, 2:1101–20. Ed. R. Carlos Bazán et al. 3 vols. Ottawa, 1995.

Nirenberg, David. *Communities of Violence: Persecution of Minorities in the Middle Ages*. Princeton, N.J., 1996.

Nisbet, Robert. *History of the Idea of Progress*. New York, 1980.

Noble, Thomas F. X. "The Monastic Ideal as a Model for Empire: The Case of Louis the Pious." *RB* 86 (1976), 235–50.

O'Donnell, James J. *Augustine*. Boston, 1985.

Olster, David M. *Roman Defeat, Christian Response, and the Literary Construction of the Jew*. Philadelphia, 1994.

Orlandis, José. "Hacia una major comprensión del problema judío en el reino visigodo-católico de España." In *Gli Ebrei nell'alto medioevo*, 1:114–96. 2 vols. Settimane di Studio del Centro Italiano di studi sull'alto medioevo 26. Spoleto, Italy, 1980.

Pakter, Walter. *Medieval Canon Law and the Jews*. Münchener Universitätsschriften—Juristische Fakultät—Abhandlungen zur Rechtswissenschaftlichen Grundlagenforschung 68. Ebelsbach, Germany, 1988.

Parkes, James. *The Conflict of the Church and the Synagogue: A Study in the Origins of Antisemitism*. London, 1934.

Pastan, Elizabeth Carson. "*Tam haereticus quam Judaeos*: Shifting Symbols in the Glazing of Troyes Cathedral." *Word and Image* 10 (1994), 66–83.

Patschovsky, Alexander. "Feindbilder der Kirche: Juden und Ketzer im Vergleich (11.–13. Jh.)." In *Juden und Christen zur Zeit der Kreuzzüge*. Ed. Alfred Haverkamp. Vorträge und Forschungen des Konstanzer Arbeitskreises für mittelalterliche Geschichte. Sigmaringen, Germany, 1999.

———. "Die Ketzer als Teufelsdiener." In *Papsttum, Kirche und Recht im Mittelalter: Festschrift für Horst Fuhrmann zum 65. Geburtstag*, pp. 317–34. Ed. H. Mordek. Tübingen, Germany, 1991.

———. "Der 'Talmudjude': Vom mittelalterlichen Ursprung eines neuzeitlichen Themas." In *Juden in der christlichen Umwelt während des späten Mittelalters*, pp. 13–27. Ed. Alfred Haverkampf and Franz-Josef Ziwes. Beihefte der *Zeitschrift für historische Forschung* 13. Berlin, 1992.

Payer, Pierre J. *Sex and the Penitentials: The Development of a Sexual Code, 550–1150*. Toronto, 1984.

Pelikan, Jaroslav. *The Christian Tradition: A History of the Development of Doctrine.* 5 vols. Chicago, 1971–89.

———. "A First-Generation Anselmian, Guibert of Nogent." In *Continuity and Discontinuity in Church History: Essays Presented to George Huntston Williams on the Occasion of His 65th Birthday*, pp. 71–82. Ed. F. Forrester Church and Timothy George. Studies in the History of Christian Thought 19. Leiden, Netherlands, 1979.

Peters, Edward. *The Magician, the Witch, and the Law.* Philadelphia, 1978.

Pfeiffer, Eberhard. "Die Stellung des hl. Bernhards zur Kreuzzugsbewegung nach seinen Schriften." *Cistercienser Chronik* 46 (1934), 273–83, 305–11.

Pirenne, Henri. "La Duchesse Aleyde du Brabant et le 'De regimine Judaeorum' de Saint Thomas d'Aquin." *Bulletin de la classe de lettres et des sciences morales et politiques de l'Academie royale de Belgique*, 5th ser., 14 (1928), 43–55.

Powell, James M. "The Papacy and the Muslim Frontier," in *Muslims under Latin Rule, 1100–1300*, pp. 175–203. Ed. James M. Powell. Princeton, N.J., 1990.

Pranger, M. B. *Bernard of Clairvaux and the Shape of Monastic Thought: Broken Dreams.* Brill's Studies in Intellectual History 56. Leiden, Netherlands, 1994.

Quasten, Johannes, et al. *Patrology.* 4 vols. Westminster, Md., 1986.

Rabello, Alfredo Mordechai. *The Jews in Visigothic Spain in Light of the Legislation* [Hebrew]. Jerusalem, 1983.

Raedts, Peter. "St Bernard of Clairvaux and Jerusalem." In *Prophecy and Eschatology*, pp. 169–82. Ed. Michael Wilks. SCH Subsidia 10. Oxford, 1994.

Räisänen, Heikki. "Paul, God, and Israel: Romans 9–11 in Recent Research." In *The Social World of Formative Christianity and Judaism: Essays in Tribute to Howard Clark Lee*, pp. 178–206. Ed. Jacob Neusner et al. Philadelphia, 1988.

Rembaum, Joel E. "The New Testament in Medieval Anti-Christian Polemics." Ph.D. diss., University of California, Los Angeles, 1975.

———. "A Reevaluation of a Medieval Polemical Manuscript." *AJSR* 5 (1980), 81–99.

———. "The Talmud and the Popes: Reflections on the Talmud Trials of the 1240s." *Viator* 13 (1982), 203–23.

Renna, Thomas. "Bernard of Clairvaux and the Temple of Solomon." In *Law, Custom, and the Social Fabric in Medieval Europe: Essays in Honor of Bryce Lyon*, pp. 73–88. Ed. Bernard S. Bachrach and David Nicholas. Studies in Medieval Culture 28. Kalamazoo, Mich., 1990.

Reydellet, Marc. "La Conception du souverain chez Isidore de Séville." In *Isidoriana: Estudios sobre San Isidoro de Sevilla en el xiv centenario de su nacimiento*, pp. 457–66. Ed. Manuel C. Díaz y Díaz. León, Spain, 1961.

———. "Les Intentions idéologiques et politiques dans la *Chronique* d'Isidore de Séville." *Mélanges d'archéologie et d'histoire de l'École française de Rome* 82 (1970), 363–400.

———. *La Royauté dans la littérature latine de Sidone Apollinaire à Isidore de Séville*. Bibliothèque des écoles françaises d'Athènes et de Rome 243. Rome, 1981.

Richards, Jeffrey. *Consul of God: The Life and Times of Gregory the Great*. London, 1980.

Riché, Pierre. *Education and Culture in the Barbarian West from the Sixth through the Eighth Century*. Trans. John J. Contreni. Columbia, S.C., 1976.

Riley-Smith, Jonathan. *The First Crusade and the Idea of Crusading*. London, 1986.

Rist, John M. *Augustine: Ancient Thought Baptized*. Cambridge, England, 1994.

Robbins, Jill. *Prodigal Son / Elder Brother: Interpretation and Alterity in Augustine, Petrarch, Kafka, and Levinas*. Chicago, 1991.

Robinson, I. S. *The Papacy, 1073–1198*. Cambridge, England, 1990.

Robles, Laureano. "En torno a una vieja polémica: El 'Pugio fidei' y Tomás de Aquino." *Revista española de teología* 34 (1974) 321–50, 35 (1975), 21–41.

Rokeaḥ, David. "The Church Fathers and the Jews in Writings Designed for Internal and External Use." In *Antisemitism through the Ages*, pp. 39–69. Ed. Shmuel Almog. Trans. Nathan H. Reisner. Oxford, 1988.

Romano, David. "Los hispanojudíos en el mundo científico y en la transmisión del saber." In *Luces y sombras de la judería europea (siglos xi–xvii)*, pp. 17–57. Navarre, Spain, 1996.

Romero, José Luis. "San Isidoro de Sevilla: Su pensamiento historicopolítico y sus relaciones con la historia visigoda." *Cuadernos de historia de España* 8 (1947), 5–71.

Rondet, Henri. "Essais sur la chronologie des 'Enarrationes in Psalmos' de Saint Augustin." *Bulletin de littérature ecclésiastique* 61 (1960), 111–27; 65 (1964), 120–36; 68 (1967), 180–202; 71 (1970), 174–200; 77 (1976), 99–118.

Roques, René. "Les *Pagani* dans le *Cur Deus homo* de Saint Anselme." In *Die Metaphysik im Mittelalter: Ihr Ursprung und ihre Bedeutung*, pp. 192–206. Ed. Paul Wilpert. Miscellanea mediaevalia 2. Berlin, 1963.

Rosenthal, Judah M. "The Talmud on Trial." *JQR*, n.s. 47 (1956), 58–76, 145–69.

Roth, Cecil. "The Medieval Conception of the Jew: A New Interpretation." Reprinted in *Essential Papers on Judaism and Christianity in Conflict: From Late Antiquity to the Reformation*, pp. 298–309. Ed. Jeremy Cohen. New York, 1991.

Roth, Norman. *Jews, Visigoths and Muslims in Medieval Spain: Cooperation and Conflict*. Medieval Iberian Peninsula Texts and Studies 10. Leiden, Netherlands, 1994.

Rousset, Paul. *Les Origines et les caractères de la première croisade*. Université de Genève, Faculté des lettres, Thèse 105. Geneva, 1945.

Rubin, Miri. "Imagining the Jew: The Late Medieval Eucharistic Discourse." In *In and Out of the Ghetto: Jewish-Gentile Relations in Late Medieval and Early Modern Germany,* pp. 177–208. Ed. R. Po-Chia Hsia and Hart-mut Lehmann. Washington, D.C., 1995.

————. Review of *The Formation of a Persecuting Society: Power and Deviance in Western Europe, 950–1250,* by R. I. Moore. *Speculum* 65 (1990), 1025–27.

Ruether, Rosemary R. *Faith and Fratricide: The Theological Roots of Anti-Semitism.* New York, 1974.

Runciman, Steven. *A History of the Crusades, Volume II: The Kingdom of Jerusalem and the Frankish East, 1100–1187.* 1952; reprint, New York, 1965.

Russell, Frederick H. *The Just War in the Middle Ages.* Cambridge, England, 1975.

Russell, Jeffrey Burton. *Lucifer: The Devil in the Middle Ages.* Ithaca, N.Y., 1984,

Sagües, José F. "La doctrina del cuerpo místico en San Isidoro de Sevilla." *Estudios eclesiásticos* 17 (1943), 227–57, 329–60, 517–46.

Saltman, Avrom. "Gilbert Crispin as a Source of the Anti-Jewish Polemic of the *Ysagoge in theologiam.*" In *Confrontation and Coexistence,* pp. 89–99. Ed. Pinhas Artzi. Bar-Ilan Studies in History 2. Ramat Gan, Israel, 1984.

————. "Hermann's *Opusculum de conversione sua*: Truth or Fiction?" *REJ* 147 (1988), 31–56.

————. "Odo's *Ysagoge*: A New Method of Anti-Jewish Polemic" [Hebrew]. *Criticism and Interpretation* 13–14 (1979), 265–80.

Sarfatti, Gad B. "The Tablets of the Law as a Symbol of Judaism." In *The Ten Commandments in History and Tradition,* pp. 383–418. Ed. Ben-Zion Segal and Gershon Levi. Jerusalem, 1990.

Schenker, Adrian. "Die Rolle der Religion bei Maimonides und Thomas von Aquin." In *Ordo sapientiae et amoris: Image et message de Saint Thomas d'Aquin . . . Hommage au Professeur Jean-Pierre Torrell,* pp. 169–93. Ed. Carlos-Josaphat Pinto de Oliveira. Studia friburgensia n.s. 78. Fribourg, Switzerland, 1993.

Schlichting, Günter. *Ein jüdisches Leben Jesu: Die verschollene Toledot-Jeschu-Fassung Tam u-mu'ad.* Wissenschaftliche Untersuchungen zum Neuen Testament 24. Tübingen, Germany, 1982.

Schmitt, Jean-Claude. "La Memoire des Prémontrés: À propos de l'"Autobiographie' du Prémontré Hermann le Juif." In *La vie quotidienne des moines et chanoines réguliers au Moyen Âge et temps modernes,* pp. 439–52. Ed. Marek Derwich. Wroclaw, Poland, 1995.

Schoneveld, Jacobus. "Torah in the Flesh: A New Reading of the Prologue of the Gospel of John as a Contribution to Christology without Anti-Judaism." In *Remembering for the Future,* 1:867–78. Ed. Yehuda Bauer et al. 3 vols. Oxford, 1989.

Schreckenberg, Heinz. *Die christlichen Adversus-Judaeos-Texte und ihr literarisches und historisches Umfeld (1.–11. Jh.).* Europäische Hochschulschriften 23, 172. 2d ed. Frankfurt am Main, 1990.

————. *Die christlichen Adversus-Judaeos-Texte (11.–13. Jh.).* Europäische Hochschulschriften 23, 275. 2d ed. Frankfurt am Main, 1991.

Schubert, Kurt. "Das christlich-jüdische Religionsgespräch im 12. und 13. Jahrhundert." *Kairos* n.s. 19 (1977), 161–86.

Schwarzfuchs, Simon. "The Place of the Crusades in Jewish History" [Hebrew]. In *Culture and Society in Medieval Jewry: Studies Dedicated to the Memory of Haim Hillel Ben-Sasson*, pp. 251–69. Ed. Menachem Ben-Sasson et al. Jerusalem, 1989.

———. "Religion populaire et polémique savante: Le Tournant de la polémique judéo-chrétienne au 12ᵉ siècle." In *Medieval Studies in Honour of Avrom Saltman*, pp. 189–206. Ed. Bat-Sheva Albert et al. Bar-Ilan Studies in History 4. Ramat Gan, Israel, 1995.

Schweid, Eliezer. "The Literary Structure of the First Book of the Kuzari" [Hebrew]. *Tarbiz* 30 (1961), 257–72.

Seiferth, Wolfgang S. *Synagogue and Church in the Middle Ages: Two Symbols in Art and Literature.* Trans. Lee Chadeayne and Paul Gottwald. New York, 1970.

Sejourné, Paul. *Le Dernier Père de l'Église: Saint Isidore de Séville—Son rôle dans l'histoire du droit canonique.* Paris, 1929.

Septimus, Bernard. "Petrus Alfonsi on the Cult of Mecca." *Speculum* 56 (1981), 517–33.

Sevenster, J. N. *The Roots of Pagan Anti-Semitism in the Ancient World.* Supplements to *Novum Testamentum* 41. Leiden, Netherlands, 1975.

Shatzmiller, Joseph. "The Albigensian Heresy as Reflected in the Eyes of Contemporary Jewry" [Hebrew]. In *Culture and Society in Medieval Jewry: Studies Dedicated to the Memory of Haim Hillel Ben-Sasson*, pp. 333–52. Ed. Menachem Ben-Sasson et al. Jerusalem, 1989.

Sidorova, N. A. "Abélard et son époque." *Cahiers d'histoire mondiale* 4 (1958), 541–52.

Signer, Michael A. "Andrew of St.-Victor's Anti-Jewish Polemic" [Hebrew]. In *The Bible in the Light of Its Interpreters: Sarah Kamin Memorial Volume*, pp. 412–20. Ed. Sara Japhet. Jerusalem, 1993.

———. "From Theory to Practice: The *De doctrina christiana* and the Exegesis of Andrew of St. Victor." In *Reading and Wisdom: The De doctrina christiana of Augustine in the Middle Ages*, pp. 84–98. Ed. Edward D. English. Notre Dame, Ind., 1995.

———. "The *Glossa ordinaria* and the Transmission of Medieval Anti-Judaism." In *A Distinct Voice: Medieval Studies in Honor of Leonard E. Boyle, O.P.*, pp. 591–605. Ed. Jacqueline Brown and William P. Stoneman. Notre Dame, Ind., 1997.

Simon, Marcel. *Verus Israel: A Study of the Relations between Christians and Jews in the Roman Empire (135–425).* Trans. H. McKeating. New York, 1986.

Simonsohn, Shlomo. *The Apostolic See and the Jews: History.* Pontifical Institute of Mediaeval Studies: Studies and Texts 109. Toronto, 1991.

Smalley, Beryl. "Ecclesiastical Attitudes to Novelty, c. 1100–c. 1250." In *Church, Society and Politics*, 1:113–31. Ed. Derek Baker. SCH 12. 2 vols. Oxford, 1975.

———. *Hebrew Scholarship among Christians in XIIIth Century England as*

Illustrated by Some Hebrew-Latin Psalters. Lectiones in Veteri Testamento et in rebus judaicis 6. London, 1939.

———. "Ralph of Flaix on Leviticus." *RTAM* 35 (1968), 52–68.

———. *The Study of the Bible in the Middle Ages*. 3d ed. Oxford, 1983.

———. "William of Auvergne, John of LaRochelle and St. Thomas Aquinas on the Old Law." In *St. Thomas Aquinas, 1274–1974: Commemorative Studies*, 1:10–71. 2 vols. Toronto, 1974.

Smith, Jonathan Z. "The Prayer of Joseph." In *Religions in Antiquity: Essays in Memory of Erwin Ramsdell Goodenough*, pp. 253–94. Ed. Jacob Neusner. Studies in the History of Religions (Supplements to *Numen*) 20. Leiden, Netherlands, 1968.

Smith, Lesley. "William of Auvergne and the Jews." In *Christianity and Judaism*, pp. 107–17. Ed. Diana Wood. SCH 29. Oxford, 1992.

Soloveitchik, Haym. "Religious Law and Change: The Medieval Ashkenazic Example." *AJSR* 12 (1987), 205–21.

Southern, Richard W. *Saint Anselm: A Portrait in a Landscape*. Cambridge, England, 1990.

———. "St. Anselm and Gilbert Crispin, Abbot of Westminster." *Medieval and Renaissance Studies* 3 (1954), 78–115.

———. *Western Views of Islam in the Middle Ages*. Cambridge, Mass., 1962.

Spiegel, Gabrielle. "History, Historicism, and the Social Logic of the Text in the Middle Ages." *Speculum* 65 (1990), 59–86.

Steinschneider, Moritz. *Die hebräischen Übersetzungen des Mittelalters und die Juden als Dolmetscher*. 1893; reprint, Graz, Austria, 1956.

Storrs, Richard S. *Bernard of Clairvaux: The Times, The Man, and His Work*. New York, 1893.

Stow, Kenneth R. "Agobard of Lyons and the Medieval Concept of the Jew." *Conservative Judaism* 29 (1974), 58–65.

———. *Alienated Minority: The Jews of Medieval Latin Europe*. Cambridge, Mass., 1992.

———. "The Burning of the Talmud in 1553, in Light of Sixteenth-Century Catholic Attitudes toward the Talmud." *Bibliothèque d'Humanisme et Renaissance* 34 (1972), 435–59.

———. *Catholic Thought and Papal Jewry Policy, 1555–1593*. Moreshet: Studies in Jewish History, Literature and Thought 5. New York, 1976.

———. "Expulsion Italian Style: The Case of Lucio Ferraris." *Jewish History* 3 (1988), 51–63.

———. "Hatred of the Jews or Love of the Church: Papal Policy toward the Jews in the Middle Ages." In *Antisemitism through the Ages*, pp. 71–89. Ed. Shmuel Almog. Trans. Nathan H. Reisner. Oxford, 1988.

———. *The "1007 Anonymous" and Papal Sovereignty: Jewish Perceptions of the Papacy and Papal Policy in the High Middle Ages*. Hebrew Union College Annual Supplements 4. Cincinnati, Ohio, 1984.

Straw, Carole. *Gregory the Great: Perfection in Imperfection*. Berkeley, Calif., 1988.

Stroll, Mary. *The Jewish Pope: Ideology and Politics in the Papal Schism of 1130*. Brill's Studies in Intellectual History 8. Leiden, Netherlands, 1987.

Stroumsa, Guy G. "From Anti-Judaism to Antisemitism in Early Christianity?" In *Contra Iudaeos: Ancient and Medieval Polemics between Christians and Jews*, pp. 1–26. Ed. Ora Limor and Guy G. Stroumsa. Texts and Studies in Medieval and Early Modern Judaism 10. Tübingen, Germany, 1996.

Synan, Edward A. *The Popes and the Jews in the Middle Ages*. New York, 1965.

Taylor, Miriam S. *Anti-Judaism and Early Christian Identity: A Critique of the Scholarly Consensus*. Studia Post-biblica 46. Leiden, Netherlands, 1995.

Teillet, Suzanne. *Des Goths à la nation gothique: Les Origines de l'idée de nation en Occident du vᵉ à viiᵉ siècle*. Paris, 1984.

Thomas, Rudolf. "Die Persönlichkeit Peter Abaelards im 'Dialogus inter Philosophum, Iudaeum et Christianum' und in den Epistulae des Petrus Venerabilis: Widerspruch oder Übereinstimmung?" In *PAPV*, pp. 255–69.

———. *Der philosophisch-theologische Erkenntnisweg Peter Abaelards im Dialogus inter Philosophum, Judaeum et Christianum*. Untersuchungen zur allgemeinen Religionsgeschichte, n.s. 6. Bonn, 1966.

Thompson, E. A. *The Goths in Spain*. Oxford, 1969.

Timmer, David E. "Biblical Exegesis and the Jewish-Christian Controversy in the Early Twelfth Century." *Church History* 58 (1989), 309–21.

Toch, Michael. "Wirtschaft und Verfolgung: Die Bedeutung der Ökonomie für die Kreuzzugspogrome des 11. und 12. Jahrhunderts, mit einem Anhang zum Sklavenhandel der Juden." In *Juden und Christen zur Zeit der Kreuzzüge*. Ed. Alfred Haverkamp. Vorträge und Forschungen des Konstanzer Arbeitskreises für mittelalterliche Geschichte. Sigmaringen, Germany, 1999.

Tolan, John. "Anti-Hagiography: Embrico of Mainz's *Vita Mahumeti*." *JMH* 22 (1996), 25–41.

———. "Los *Diálogos contra los Judíos*." In *Estudios sobre Pedro Alfonso de Huesca*, pp. 181–230. Ed. María Jesús Lacarra. Colección de estudios altoaragoneses 41. Huesca, Spain, 1996.

———. "La *Epístola a los peripatéticos de Francia* de Pedro Alfonso." In *Estudios sobre Pedro Alfonso de Huesca*, pp. 381–402. Ed. María Jesús Lacarra. Colección de estudios altoaragoneses 41. Huesca, Spain, 1996.

———. *Petrus Alfonsi and His Medieval Readers*. Gainesville, Fla., 1993.

Torrell, Jean-Pierre. "*Ecclesia Iudaeorum*—Quelques jugements positifs de Saint Thomas d'Aquin à l'égard des Juifs et du Judaïsme." In *Les Philosophies morales et politiques au Moyen Âge*, 3:1732–41. Ed. R. Carlos Bazán et al. 3 vols. Ottawa, 1995.

———. "Les Juifs dans l'oeuvre de Pierre le Vénérable." *CCM* 30 (1987), 331–46.

———. "La Notion de prophétie et la méthode apologétique dans le *Contra Saracenos* de Pierre le Vénérable." *Studia monastica* 18 (1975), 257–82.

Torrell, Jean-Pierre, and Denise Bouthillier. *Pierre le Vénérable et sa vision du monde: Sa vie—son oeuvre, l'homme et le démon*. Spicilegium sacrum lovaniense 42. Louvain, Belgium, 1986.

———. "Une Spiritualité de combat: Pierre le Vénérable et la lutte contre Satan." *RT* 84 (1984), 47–81.

Trachtenberg, Joshua. *The Devil and the Jews*. New Haven, Conn., 1943.

Trout, John M. "Alan the Missionary." *Cîteaux* 26 (1975), 146–54.

———. "The Monastic Vocation of Alan of Lille." *Analecta cisterciensia* 30 (1974), 46–53.

Truyol y Serra, Antonio. "The Idea of Man and World History from Seneca to Orosius and Saint Isidore of Seville." *Cahiers d'histoire mondiale* 6 (1961), 698–713.

Ullmann, Walter. *The Growth of Papal Government in the Middle Ages.* 2d ed. New York, 1962.

Urbach, Ephraim E. "The Homiletical Interpretations of the Sages and the Expositions of Origen on Canticles, and the Jewish-Christian Disputation." In *Studies in Aggadah and Folk-Literature,* pp. 246–75. Ed. Joseph Heinemann and Dov Noy. Scripta hierosolymitana 22. Jerusalem, 1971.

———. *The Tosaphists: Their History, Writings and Methods* [Hebrew]. 4th ed. 2 vols. Jerusalem, 1980.

Vance, Eugene. "Augustine's Confessions and the Poetics of the Law." *Modern Language Notes* 93 (1978), 618–34.

———. "Saint Augustine: Language as Temporality." In *Mimesis: From Mirror to Method, Augustine to Descartes,* pp. 20–35, 251–52. Ed. John D. Lyons and Stephen G. Nichols Jr. Hanover, N.H., 1982.

Van Engen, John H. *Rupert of Deutz.* Berkeley, Calif., 1983.

———. "A Twelfth-Century Christian on Leviticus." In *In the Shadow of the Millennium: Jews and Christians in Twelfth-Century Europe.* Ed. Michael A. Signer and John H. van Engen. Notre Dame, Ind., 1999.

Van Oort, Johannes. *Jerusalem and Babylon: A Study into Augustine's City of God and the Sources of His Doctrine of the Two Cities.* Supplements to *Vigiliae christianae* 14. Leiden, Netherlands, 1991.

Vasoli, Cesare. "Il 'Contra haereticos' di Alano di Lilla." *Bollettino dell'Istituto storico italiano per il Medio Evo* 75 (1963), 123–72.

Vásquez de Parga, Luis. "Notas sobre la obra histórica de San Isidoro." In *Isidoriana: Estudios sobre San Isidoro de Sevilla en el xiv centenario de su nacimiento,* pp. 99–105. Ed. Manuel C. Díaz y Díaz. León, 1961.

Vega, Angel Custodio. "Le 'Liber de variis quaestionibus' no es de Félix de Urgel." *Ciudad de Dios* 161 (1949), 217–68.

Verger, Jacques. "Abélard et les milieux sociaux de son temps." In *Abélard en son temps: Actes du colloque international organisé à l'occasion du 9ᵉ centenaire de la naissance de Pierre Abélard,* pp. 107–31. Paris, 1981.

Vicaire, Marie-Humbert. "'Contra Judaeos' meridionaux au début du xiiiᵉ siècle: Alain de Lille, Evrard de Béthune, Guillaume de Bourges." In *Juifs et judaïsme de Languedoc,* pp. 269–93. Cahiers de Fanjeaux 12. Toulouse, France, 1977.

Waas, Adolf. "Volk Gottes und Militia Christi—Juden und Kreuzfahrer." In *JIM,* pp. 410–34.

Wallace-Hadrill, J. M. *The Frankish Church.* Oxford, 1983.

Walsh, P. G. "Alan of Lille as a Renaissance Figure." In *Renaissance and Renewal in Christian History,* pp. 117–35. Ed. Derek Baker. SCH 14. Oxford, 1977.

Ward, Elizabeth. "Caesar's Wife: The Career of the Empress Judith, 819–829."

In *Charlemagne's Heir: New Perspectives on the Reign of Louis the Pious (814–840)*, pp. 205–27. Ed. Peter Godman and Roger Collins. Oxford, 1990.

Wasselynck, René. "L'Influence de l'exégèse de S. Grégoire le Grand sur les commentaires bibliques médiévaux (vii^c–xii^c s)." *RTAM* 32 (1965), 157–204.

Wasserstrom, Steven M. *Between Muslim and Jew: The Problem of Symbiosis under Early Islam*. Princeton, N.J., 1995.

Waugh, Scott L., and Peter D. Diehl, eds. *Christendom and Its Discontents: Exclusion, Persecution, and Rebellion, 1000–1500*. Cambridge, England, 1996.

Werblowsky, R. J. Z. "Crispin's Disputation." *JJS* 11 (1960), 69–77.

Wetherbee, Winthrop. "The Function of Poetry in the 'De planctu naturae' of Alain de Lille." *Traditio* 25 (1969), 87–125.

———. "The Literal and the Allegorical: Jean de Meun and the *De planctu Naturae*." *Mediaeval Studies* 33 (1971), 264–91.

Wilken, Robert. *John Chrysostom and the Jews: Rhetoric and Reality in the Late 4th Century*. Berkeley, Calif., 1983.

———. *Judaism and the Early Christian Mind: A Study of Cyril of Alexandria's Exegesis and Theology*. New Haven, Conn., 1971.

Williams, A. Lukyn. *Adversus Judaeos: A Bird's-Eye View of Christian Apologiae until the Renaissance*. Cambridge, England, 1935.

Williams, Watkin. *St. Bernard of Clairvaux*. Westminster, Md., 1952.

Willi-Plein, Ina, and Thomas Willi. *Glaubensdolch und Messiasbeweis: Die Begegnung von Judentum, Christentum und Islam im 13. Jahrhundert in Spanien*. Forschungen zum jüdisch-christlichen Dialog 2. Neukirchen, Germany, 1980.

Wolfson, Elliot R. *Through a Speculum That Shines: Vision and Imagination in Medieval Jewish Mysticism*. Princeton, N.J., 1994.

Yaffe, Martin D. Review of *Aquinas and the Jews*, by John Y. B. Hood. *AJSR* 22 (1997), 122–25.

Zacour, Norman. *Jews and Saracens in the Consilia of Oldradus de Ponte*. Pontifical Institute of Medieval Studies: Studies and Texts 100. Toronto, 1990.

Zechiel-Eckes, Klaus. "Sur la tradition manuscrite des *Capitula . . . de coertione Iudeorum*." *RB* 107 (1997), 77–87.

Zimdars-Swartz, Sandra. "A Confluence of Imagery: Exegesis and Christology According to Gregory the Great." In *Grégoire le Grand*, pp. 327–35. Ed. Jacques Fontaine et al. Colloques internationaux du C.N.R.S. Paris, 1986.

Zuckerman, Arthur J. "The Political Uses of Theology: The Conflict of Bishop Agobard and the Jews of Lyons." In *Studies in Medieval Culture*, 3:23–51. Ed. John R. Sommerfeldt. Kalamazoo, Mich., 1970.

Index

Abel, 28, 55
Abner of Burgos (Alfonso of Valladolid), 291n.63
Abraham ben Samuel, 338–39, 340
Abraham ibn Ezra, 391n.1
Abulafia, Anna Sapir, 154–55
  on Anselm, 175–76, 176n.26, 177–78, 177n.28, 177n.31, 178n.33
  on Gilbert Crispin, 185
  on Guibert of Nogent, 197–98, 198n.87
  on Odo of Cambrai, 191, 191n.66
  on Peter Abelard, 277n.20, 285n.51
Adam and Eve, 57
Adversus Iudaeorum inveteratam duritiem. See Peter the Venerable
Agaësse, P., 57n.102
ages of man
  Augustine on, 24–26, 52, 53n.91, 110
  Isidore of Seville on, 110–12, 112n.65, 113n.70, 119–20, 122
Agobard of Lyons, 15–16, 67, 123–45, 360–61
  on Antichrist and Jews, 128–29, 132–33
  anti-Judaism of, as exceptional, 133–34, 143–45
  and Augustine, 124
  on Christian order/unity, 136–42, 136n.44, 143–44
  on conversion of Jews, 125–26, 134
  on crucifixion, 131–32, 133
  familiarity with Jews/Judaism, 129–30
  on imperial favoritism toward Jews, 126–28, 133, 136, 143–44

  on Jewish error/hostility, 128, 131–32, 133
  on Jewish redundancy, 70, 134
  life/career of, 124
  and Louis the Pious, 123, 124–25, 126–27, 133, 137
  missionizing/proselytizing among Jews, 124, 133–34
  on *Ordinatio imperii*, 138, 139, 140, 141
  and Peter the Venerable, 245, 261n.121
  policy toward Jews by, 68, 71, 134–36, 136n.42, 145
  on salvation/redemption, 134
  on slaves' right to salvation, 126
  —works:
  Contra praeceptum impium de baptismo iudaicorum mancipiorum, 125
  De baptismo mancipiorum Iudaeorum, 124–25
  De cavendo convictu et societate iudaica, 125
  De dispensatione ecclesiasticarum rerum, 137, 142–43
  De divisione imperii, 140
  De fidei veritate et totius boni institutione, 141–42
  De insolentia Iudaerum, 125
  De iudaicis superstitionibus et erroribus, 125, 129–30, 134–35, 247, 261n.120, 266n.140
  De modo regiminis ecclesiastici, 142

437

Bible, Old Testament
accuracy/authority of, 27–28, 31, 392–93
allegorical interpretation of, 88–89, 93, 96n.3
Bernard on, 249
carnality of Jews and, 223–24, 227–28, 229–30, 231–32
divine authorship of, 12
Jewish misunderstanding of, 29–30
Jews as embodying, 2, 3
literal vs. allegorical/spiritual interpretation of: Augustine on, 46–47, 46n.66, 48–51, 48n.74, 49n.81, 60; Hermann on, 295–96, 299–300; Peter Abelard on, 282–83; Peter Alfonsi on, 213–14; Thomas Aquinas on, 376–80, 382, 384–85
New Testament as completing/fulfilling, 283, 393
Paul on, 392–93
Peter the Venerable on, 249
preserving texts of, 349n.90
Romans on, 30
and Talmud, 354, 358; see also Talmud, condemnation of
—books:
Daniel, 276
Deuteronomy, 399, 400
Genesis, 24–25, 44, 47–48, 56–57; see also De Genesi ad litteram liber imperfectus; De Genesi ad litteram; De Genesi contra Manichaeos
Job, 88–89
Psalms: and conversion of Jews, 39–40; "for the things that shall be changed," 34, 34n.27; "Slay them not" (59:12), 33–41, 55, 64, 67, 83–84, 94, 95, 122, 134, 152, 217, 221, 222, 235–36, 241–42, 244, 247, 265, 361, 362, 394, 396 (see also witness, Jewish, doctrine of)
Bible, New Testament
anti-Jewish passages in, 6
Old Testament's fulfillment in, 393
—books:
Acts of the Apostles, 6
1 Corinthians, 29–30, 174
2 Corinthians, 266n.140
Galatians, 6–7
Gospels, 6
Hebrews, 6
Romans: on God's rejection of Jews, 7–8; on Jewish contribution to salvation, 7–8, 393; on Jewish conversion, 8, 393; on Jewish understanding of Old Testament, 30; and martyrdom, 305; on sexuality, 63

biblical pairs, concentric structures in, 60, 60n.114
blindness of Jews. See rejection of Christianity by Jews
Blumenkranz, Bernhard, 20, 64n.124, 100n.20, 125n.9, 143, 240n.69
Boshof, Egon, 125n.9, 141
Boso, 172–73
Boulton, Brenda, 360n.116
Boyle, Marjorie O'Rourke, 57n.105
Brown, Peter, 47, 55, 58
Buytaert, Eligius M., 277n.20
Bynum, Caroline, 149

Cain, 28–29, 35, 55, 249n.90
Cantini, Joannes A., 329n.31
Capistrum Iudaeorum. See Raymond Martin
carnality/materialism of Jews
Alan of Lille on, 308
Bernard of Clairvaux on, 223–24, 227–28, 229–30, 231–32, 244
Guibert of Nogent on, 197–98, 200
Hermann of Cologne on, 293, 295, 296–97
Peter Abelard on, 285
Peter Alfonsi on, 204
Peter the Venerable on, 255–56, 265–66, 266n.140
Caspary, Gerard, 60
Castán Lacoma, Laureano, 100n.20, 105n.42, 106n.48
castle within city, parable of, 170–71, 171n.10, 309–11
Cathars, 307
Chanina ben Dosa, 204–5, 216
Charlemagne, 73–74, 138
Charles the Bald, 139, 142
Chaucer, 301
Chazan, Robert, 153, 323n.12, 324n.14, 347, 357n.111, 358–60
Chenu, M.-D., 240–41
Choni ("the Circle-Drawer"), 204–5
church property, control of, 137
circumcision, 6–7, 12, 379
Peter Abelard on, 281–82, 285, 286
Raymond Martin on, 348, 352–53
Clement IV, pope, 330–32, 331n.37, 332n.39, 336
Codex (Justinian), 162
Codex theodosianus. See Theodosian Code
Commercial Revolution, 225
Constable, Giles, 238
Constantine, 13, 24, 111
Contra Faustum. See Augustine of Hippo

Composition: Binghamton Valley Composition
Text: 10/13 Sabon
Display: Sabon
Printing and binding: Maple-Vail Book Manufacturing Group